The Editor

NADIA URBINATI is Kyriakos Tsakopoulos Professor of Political Theory at Columbia University. She is a member of the Executive Committee of the Foundation Reset Dialogues on Civilization and the Feltrinelli Foundation. She is the author of *Mill on Democracy: From the Athenian Polis to Representative Government*, *Me the People: How Populism Transforms Democracy*, *The Tyranny of the Moderns*, *Democracy Disfigured: Opinion, Truth and the People*, and *Representative Democracy: Principles and Genealogy*. She has coedited numerous volumes, including *The Constructivist Turn in Political Representation*, Hans Kelsen's *On the Worth and Values of Democracy*, and *Condorcet's Political Writing*.

A NORTON CRITICAL EDITION

John Stuart Mill

ON LIBERTY AND OTHER WRITINGS

TEXTS

COMMENTARIES

Edited by

NADIA URBINATI

COLUMBIA UNIVERSITY

W. W. NORTON & COMPANY

Celebrating a Century of Independent Publishing

To Alan Ryan

W. W. Norton & Company has been independent since its founding in 1923, when William Warder Norton and Mary D. Herter Norton first published lectures delivered at the People's Institute, the adult education division of New York City's Cooper Union. The firm soon expanded its program beyond the Institute, publishing books by celebrated academics from America and abroad. By mid-century, the two major pillars of Norton's publishing program—trade books and college texts—were firmly established. In the 1950s, the Norton family transferred control of the company to its employees, and today—with a staff of five hundred and hundreds of trade, college, and professional titles published each year—W. W. Norton & Company stands as the largest and oldest publishing house owned wholly by its employees.

Manufacturing by Maple Press
Book design by Antonina Krass
Production manager: Brenda Manzanedo

ISBN: 978-1-324-04575-5 (pbk)

W. W. Norton & Company, Inc., 500 Fifth Avenue, New York, N.Y. 10110
        www.wwnorton.com
W. W. Norton & Company Ltd., 15 Carlisle Street, London W1D 3BS

1 2 3 4 5 6 7 8 9 0

Contents

Preface

The first Norton Critical Edition of Mill's writing was published in 1975 and was edited by David Spitz; the second came out in 1996 and was edited by Alan Ryan. The former focused on the character of Mill's liberty and liberalism, its legacy in the British tradition of the nineteenth century, and the post-totalitarian Popperian theory of an open society. The latter continued the conversation on Mill's liberalism in relation to Romantic and conservative revisions of the Enlightenment and moderate feminist traditions. In the nearly three decades since Ryan's edition was published, there has been a continuous flow of critical work on Mill, particularly on the potential limitations of his theory of liberty and paternalism, on his conception of utility and the idea of happiness, and on his analysis of the nature of liberty in relation to equality. This all-new Norton Critical Edition delves into this new critical work. It concentrates on three book-length essays—*On Liberty, Utilitarianism*, and *The Subjection of Women*—and offers analyses of the place of Mill in contemporary liberalism (Alan Ryan), his conception of liberty of expression (Jonathan Riley), the antipaternalist meaning of his harm principle (Piers Norris Turner), the role of experiments in living in his personal experience and his idea of pleasures (Elizabeth Anderson), the roots and character of his conception of the "inner culture" (Colin Heydt), the meaning of his utilitarianism (Wendy Donner), the radicalism of his feminism in relation to its traditional liberal reading (Martha Nussbaum), a reinterpretation of liberty and its association to the harm principle from the perspective of women's subjection and the inherent quest for equality (David Dyzenhaus), and his conception of "character" contrasted with the period's tendency to biologize human differences (Georgios Varouxakis). Maintaining the standards set by the previous Norton Critical Editions of Mill was a daunting task, but the selected authors make it far less difficult. I thank my colleague David Johnston for his advice and Matthew Cohen and Gregory Conti for their comments on some parts of my introduction.

Introduction

Life

John Stuart Mill was born on May 20, 1806, in London to Harriet Barrow and James Mill and died in Avignon, France, on May 6, 1873, where he was buried next to his wife and long-time companion, Harriet Taylor. The first of nine children, his father educated him to become the leader of the Philosophic Radicals, a group of brilliant minds and political activists gathered around Jeremy Bentham (1758–1842) and James Mill himself, the charismatic mentor. A Scotsman, James Mill was born in 1773 and was educated at Edinburgh University thanks to his benefactor Sir John Stuart of Fettercairn (after whom he named his oldest son). He moved to London in 1802, where instead of becoming a minister (he was licensed to preach in 1789), he became a contributor to the *Anti-Jacobin Review* and a partner of Bentham, who was then principally known as the author of the *Panopticon* (1791), the blueprint for a total and cheap system of prison surveillance. It was James Mill's "intrusion" into Bentham's life that turned the latter into "a democrat."[1]

In the first pages of his *Autobiography*, John Stuart Mill outlined two decisive facts related to his father, one negative and one positive. The downside was that he had married and had nine children, the most contradictory and contrary behavior "which it is impossible not to be struck with."[2] The positive element was his father's temperament and "extraordinary energy," which allowed him to lead a dignified life in the midst of great economic difficulties. Employed

1. Elie Halévy, *The Growth of Philosophical Radicalism*, trans. Mary Morris, with a preface by John Plamenatz (London: Faber and Faber, 1972), p. 255. The best biography of Mill's father is by Alexander Bain (*James Mill: A Biography* [London: Longmans, Green, 1882]), who also published *John Stuart Mill: A Criticism; with Personal Recollections* (London: Longmans, Green, 1882).
2. John Stuart Mill's *Autobiography* (1873), in *The Collected Works of John Stuart Mill* (henceforth *CW*), vol. 1, ed. John M. Robson and Jack Stillinger (Toronto: U of Toronto P, 1981), p. 7. There have been numerous editions of Mill's *Autobiography*, but this is the best, and the introduction by Robson and Stillinger is a remarkable bio-bibliographical reconstruction. This volume also includes Mill's early writings, including the essays on marriage he wrote with Harriet Taylor in 1832–33, and the "early" draft of the *Autobiography* (written between the end of 1853 and the early months of 1854, to be continued after his wedding in 1851 and revised in 1869–70 after Harriet's death).

by the East India Company since 1819 (a job later taken over by his son), the elder Mill was the author of *The History of British India* (which he started writing the year his son was born and published in 1818), which his son praised as one of the most important achievements of his time. Much has been written about the education of the young Mill, which was remarkable for the complete absence of his mother and for the methods of his father. In an early draft of his *Autobiography*, Mill wrote about his lack of a "really warm-hearted mother" with "qualities" that would make her "loved" by her children and capable of balancing his father's severity. In contrast, his relationship with his father was supremely important, surpassed only by that with his future wife. Descriptions of his father's character by some of his contemporaries underline his domineering yet magnetic quality: "He expected to subdue everybody by his domineering tone, to convince everybody by his positiveness. His manner of speaking is oppressive and overbearing."[3] Some of his friends described Harriet Taylor's character as domineering and her influence on Mill as strong as that of his father; they also judged his admiration for her form as "hallucination" and "embarrassing."[4]

Interpretations of Mill's education under a domineering Philosophic Radical and on his sentimental relationship with a spirited Unitarian Radical have flourished since his death, at times insinuating that his celebrated individual autonomy was a desideratum to compensate for what he never had.[5] Yet *On Liberty* (1859) advises us to think *utramque partem* (on both sides of a question), particularly in evaluating the complex relationship between life and thought.

Mill's father was indeed the inspirer of the Philosophic Radicals, a compelling "master of the pen and the speech"[6] who gave them the determination and style of an army well equipped in the struggle against the "reactionaries" on many fronts: ancient history (George Grote), jurisprudence (John Austin), economics (David Ricardo), and philosophy (his son). Some of them, like Ricardo and John Stuart Mill, entered Parliament, thereby fulfilling the main goal of the party.[7] Their basic political ideology, which Members of Parliament

---

3. Description found in W. L. Curtney, *Life of John Stuart Mill* (1898), cited in A. W. Levi, "The 'Mental Crisis' of John Stuart Mill," *Psychoanalytic Review* 32.1 (1945): 90.
4. Richard Garnett, *The Life of W. J. Fox: Public Teacher and Social Reformer* (London and New York: John Lane, 1910), p. 97.
5. "Whereas Harriet took on the role of her own domineering father, coupling it with maternal solicitude, Mill regressed in regard to her into the dependent, obedient role he had played as a child with his father." Bruce Mazlish, *James and John Stuart Mill: Father and Son in the Nineteenth Century* (New York: Basic Books, 1975), p. 309. Unitarian Radicals were Unitarians who, under the leadership of William Johnson Fox (1786–1864), moved toward Romanticism, not Socialism.
6. Harriet Grote cited in Terence Ball, Introduction to *James Mill: Political Writings* (Cambridge: Cambridge UP, 1992), p. xi.
7. The elder Mill hoped for a leader "of philosophic attainment and popular talents" who "could have used the House of Commons as a rostra or a teacher's chair for instructing

(MPs) Henry Fawcett and John Arthur Roebuck exemplified, relied upon an unfaltering "antagonism to the aristocratic habits of privilege."[8] The Radicals were known as democrats for their implacable opposition to aristocracy—they hated the few (for their "sinister interests") more—or rather—than loving the many. Rhetoric and eristic (the ingredients of what critics called "sophistry") were the pillars of the elder Mill's propagandistic method, dissecting adversaries' statements with pugnacity and a determination to win. This was the style of his *Essay on Government* (1820), an attack against the theory of the division of powers, "wild, visionary, chimerical," in the name of democracy (representative, with secret ballot and without universal suffrage).[9] The historian and Whig politician Thomas Babington Macaulay called Mill's essay a travesty of science and a piece of doctrinaire sophistry, which left the elder Mill and his followers in dismay.[1] With similar vehemence, Karl Marx criticized James Mill the economist (*Elements of Political Economy*, published in 1821) for "cloaking 'bourgeois' biases in 'scientific' garb."[2] On the other hand, George Grote, the great historian of ancient Greece who remained a faithful disciple of James Mill all his life, described his mentor as the best example of a Platonist, capable of awakening "the dormant intelligence" with his "earnest convictions, and single-minded devotion to truth."[3] On the occasion of his death in 1836, John Blake, editor of the *Morning Chronicle*, wrote that

> Mr. Mill was eloquent and impressive in conversation. He had a great command of language, which bore the stamp of his earnest and energetic character. Young men were particularly fond of his society. . . . No man could enjoy his society without catching a portion of his elevated enthusiasm. . . . His conversation was so energetic and complete in thought, so succinct, and exact . . . in expression, that, if reported as uttered, his colloquial observations or arguments would have been perfect compositions.[4]

and impelling the public mind." *Autobiography*, CW, vol. 1, p. 205. Halévy's *Growth* (pp. 251–64) offers a succinct and compelling history of the birth of the Philosophic Radicals around 1818, during the campaign for the "radical reform" (which inaugurated the battle over "representative democracy" in Britain, with proposals on voting rights, redistricting, secrecy of ballot), and of how the party distanced itself from the "dangerous" cause of communism.

8. Stefan Collini, *Public Moralists: Political Thought and Intellectual Life in Britain, 1850–1930* (Oxford: Oxford UP, 1991), p. 182.
9. James Mill, "Government," in *Political Writings*, p. 19.
1. Not all Radicals approved of James Mill's essay; as we shall see in presenting *The Subjection of Women*, William Thompson criticized Mill for theorizing the exclusion of women from suffrage.
2. Quoted in Ball, Introduction to Mill, *Political Writings*, p. xii.
3. Quoted in Martin L. Clarke, *George Grote: A Biography* (U London: Athlone P, 1962), pp. 21–22.
4. Quoted in Bain, *James Mill*, p. 457.

Critics of his style and of his radical followers thought otherwise: "they surrender their understanding, with a facility found in no other party, to the meanest and most abject sophisms, provided those sophisms come before them disguised with the externals of demonstration. They do not seem to know that logic has its illusions as well as rhetoric—that a fallacy may lurk in a syllogism as well as in a metaphor."[5] The underlying thrust of these arguments was that James Mill's dogmatism had its roots in his axiomatic and deductive method of reasoning, which would be a major problem for his son, who tried to overcome it starting with *The System of Logic* (1843).

To understand John's remarkable education, it's worth starting with his educator's view of the undertaking. In the essay "Education" (1823), James Mill declared: "if education does not perform everything, there is hardly anything which it does not perform."[6] Education accomplished what no revolution could: it constructed the individual and thus society, by making the mind "an operative cause of happiness."[7] Like Jean-Jacques Rousseau, James Mill was certain that a person was the product of her environment, and that most problems plaguing society originated in a false education. Like the eighteenth-century epistemologists and philosophers Étienne Bonnot de Condillac, Claude Adrien Helvétius, and David Hartley, James Mill believed that general ideas (good and bad, useful and right, etc.) derived from sensations (either directly through the senses, or indirectly as remnants of sensations in recollections or traces) and kindled emotions (that pushed ideas toward action). Helvétius, who gave morals the goal of pursuing the interest "of the greatest number," wished to "treat morals like any other science and to make an experimental morality like an experimental physics."[8] Condillac and Hartley, who continued the tradition of John Locke, conceived of the phenomena of the mind as transformed sensations, or sensations variously combined. Both Bentham and James Mill (like his son) shared in the psychology of association. But only the elder Mill came to be known as its "second founder" and practitioner with his "innovating propaganda."[9] His *Analysis of the Phenomena of the Human Mind* (1829) was a well-known treatise, which his son edited and annotated in 1869. James Mill complemented the science of the mind with an admirable knowledge and love of classical studies, particularly logic and rhetoric (Aristotle's *Art of Rhetoric* was the first treatise on morals and psychology the young Mill studied

5. Thomas Babington Macaulay, "Mill on Government" (March 1829), in *Mill: Political Writings*, pp. 272–73.
6. James Mill, *Political Writings*, p. 160.
7. Ibid., p. 139.
8. From Helvétius's *De l'esprit* (1758), quoted in Halévy, *Growth*, p. 19.
9. Halévy, *Growth*, p. 437.

when he was ten). Mill's inaugural address at the University of St. Andrews in 1867 was a plea on behalf of humanist education, particularly classical languages and cultures, and in effect a tribute to the education he received from his father.

To James Mill, all human beings were equally malleable, and what his son had achieved could be achieved by any other girl or boy; he was proud of the amazing precocity of both John and his sister Wilhelmina, but avoided making them feel superior or exceptional.[1] At the time, home schooling was common among the middle classes and often included strict discipline. John felt torn about this discipline, between paternal affection and the denunciation of despotic subjection ("I . . . grew up in the absence of love and in the presence of fear"),[2] a condition he would later denounce in relations between women and their husbands. However, the strictness of John's education is certainly comprehensible (if not necessarily advisable) when one considers the lofty goals: to manufacture character and infuse a rich knowledge in order to create a "reasoning machine." James took inspiration from two classical texts, Plato's *Republic* and Quintilian's *Institutio Oratoria*.[3] On the model of Quintilian's ideal father, chose his son's career at birth. He also planned to give his son both a theoretical and practical education—for example, combining the study of foreign languages with extensive travel.[4] Like Plato, whose *Republic* was the first textbook on how to fabricate a person, James Mill had a negative view of poetry, particularly the sentimental and Romantic varieties. (His censorship later backfired when John did discover poetry.) At the heart of his philosophy was creating habits of mind and behavior. The stages of his teaching proceeded systematically and combined humanities and sciences, ancient and modern languages: first ancient Greek language and arithmetic (from the age of three), then ancient history (between four and seven), and ancient philosophy and Latin language and literature (seven), along with the orations and tragedies. As a child, John composed a history of Rome (in which he defended the Agrarian Laws based on Livy's narration) and started translating Socratic dialogues (his translations are still

---

1. Graham Wallas, *The Life of Francis Place, 1771–1854* (London: Allen & Unwin, 1925), p. 70.
2. *CW*, vol. 1, p. 612.
3. See James Mill to William Forbes, 8 April 1822, in Anna J. Mill, "The Education of John—Some Further Evidences," *Mill Newsletter* 2 (1976): 10–14; and Bain, *James Mill*, pp. 92–93.
4. When John was ten, James Mill proposed to move to France, then Germany, and then Italy: "We shall then return accomplished people, and men and women of use, I hope, also to do something for the cause of mankind. We shall, at any rate, have plenty of knowledge, the habit of living upon little, and a passion for improvement of the condition of mankind." James Mill to Francis Place, September 6 [1815], in Wallas, *Life*, p. 72.

used in high schools), while deepening his knowledge of algebra, geometry, and the natural sciences.

Mill was educated to become a humanist, inspired by modern exemplary lives no less noble and virtuous than the classical ones.[5] Moreover, like the citizens in Aristotle's *polis*, who learned to rule and be ruled in turn, Mill practiced learning (morning) and teaching (afternoon) by playing with his siblings the role his father was playing with him—important training for the future leader of clubs and journals. John's education was all-encompassing, and his father made sure his son's negligible free time was spent in the sole company of adults and families in Bentham's circle. In 1814, Mill's entire family moved to Fort Abbey, a "huge Devonshire mansion which Bentham had rented" for seven years. The mansion was close to a river and immersed in the countryside, hard to reach and wholly isolated in the winter. Originally a Cistercian monastery, it had a "refectory and two sets of cloisters, one of them almost dark, with the cells on one side . . . resembling very much a ward in a modern mad house."[6] Life at Fort Abbey was spartan: long walks in the early morning, reading and studying until lunch, conversation and reading newspapers in the afternoon, reading and writing until dusk. Communal meals and dialogues on various topics, as in ancient Athens, and a lifetime occupied entirely with books, conversations, solitude, and nature—these formative years shaped Mill's lifelong values and loves.

In 1822, at the age of sixteen, Mill started writing newspaper articles (his first theoretical essay was an attack against aristocracy) and became a Radical propagandist; he also became friends with Sarah Austin (an important presence in his life) and spent two days in prison for campaigning in favor of contraception and birth control, a Malthusian theme central to his future theory of the emancipation of women and the working classes. At the age of seventeen, in 1823, he joined the East India Company, a position he held for thirty-five years, and which was an important professional experience that required "writing dispatches and deciding policy of the so-called Princely States, the Indian states that governed themselves under the general supervision of the company while preserving a nominal independence."[7] He eventually resigned in

5. He was impressed by Condorcet's *Life of Turgot* more than by Plutarch's *Lives*, and described it as "a book well calculated to rouse the best sort of enthusiasm, since it contains one of the wisest and noblest of lives, delineated by one of the wisest and noblest of men." *CW*, vol. 1, p. 115.
6. *Memoirs and Correspondence of Francis Horner*, edited by his brother, Leonard Horner, 2 vols. (Boston: Little, Brown, 1853), vol. 1, pp. 172–73.
7. Alan Ryan, Introduction to *Mill: The Spirit of the Age, On Liberty, The Subjection of Women* (New York and London: Norton, 1975), p. xv.

1858, when the company came under direct control of the British Parliament.[8]

James Mill could rejoice in his successful experiment in education: John was indeed a "reasoning machine" and a devoted leader of the Radical cause. In the spring of 1824, the *Westminster Review* was founded (later renamed the *London and Westminster Review*), which would absorb Mill's time and energy for years; that same year, Mill became friends with John Roebuck, testing his relationship with his father, who disapproved of their friendship. Roebuck, who later became very disappointed with Mill's liaison with Harriet Taylor, was the first close friend of Mill's own age: together, they traveled to Paris in July 1830 to follow the revolution (documented in Mill's letters to his father and his articles for the *Examiner*). Roebuck's description of his first encounter with the Utilitarian Society in 1826 is also worth quoting: "It met in a low, half-furnished, desolate sort of room—I believe the dining-room of the house, not Mr. Bentham's dining room. The place was lighted by a few tallow candles. A desk was drawn across the end of the room, at which we sat in chairs round the room, and formed the society. The essay was a critique for some review of an edition of a Greek author. . . . Mill told me it was a sort of trial piece, and was intended to test the capacity" of the author as a reviewer.[9]

At the time, Mill's entire life was absorbed by his intellectual pursuits. In 1825, the London Debating Society began meeting every Friday, with Mill presiding. The society was an open arena of discussion on philosophical and political questions attracting auditors external to the radical group, and the meetings were a formidable opportunity for the best speakers to emerge, including John Austin, whom Mill praised as a "gladiator." These early experiences were a formidable school to Mill, who learned to appreciate the value of agonism in character formation and politics. One might say that he began to write the second chapter of *On Liberty* in those clubs: "to hear the arguments of adversaries from his own teacher" is not enough; one "must be able to hear them from persons who actually believe them, who defend them in earnest, and to their very utmost for them."[1] In those debating clubs, the young radicals and their conservative peers trained themselves as partisan activists on their way to becoming MPs, journalists, and pamphleteers. With his radical friends, Mill took part enthusiastically in numerous debates at the Cambridge Union, the Oxford United Debating Society, the Co-operative

---

8. Mill signed the petition to defend the administration of the company and thought that putting it under public control would worsen the Indigenous peoples' plight.
9. *Life and Letters of John Arthur Roebuck with Chapters of Autobiography*, ed. Robert E. Leader (London and New York: Edward Arnold, 1897), p. 27.
1. See p. 34 below.

Society of Robert Owen, and the Sterling Club. The London radicals were famous for their rhetorical skills and passions; Mill even depicted participation in Owen's Cooperative Society (wherein he would change his mind on women's social condition in favor of equality) as longing for a *lutte corps-à-corps* (body-to-body combat) and a *bataille* (battle).[2] In addition to those public meetings, Mill attended the "Socratic" club that met in Grote's house, which was strictly devoted to learning. In the former, rhetoric was key as the goal was winning an argument (the debates frequently ended with voting), while in the latter, dialogue was the method for discerning right and wrong interpretations (the meetings ended with consensus).[3]

In addition to participating in discussion clubs, working at the East India Company, and leading the *Westminster Review*, Mill was also editing Bentham's *Rationale of Judicial Evidence*. Later, he depicted his life as follows: "From the winter of 1821, when I first read Bentham, and especially from the commencement of the *Westminster Review*, I had what might truly be called an object in life; to be a reformer of the world. My conception of my own happiness was entirely identified with this object."[4] His father's educational goal—"rendering the human mind to the greatest possible degree the cause of human happiness"—did not require that each member of the human species be happy, nor that the general happiness should be judged from the perspective of each individual person's happiness, and it would be fair to say that Mill's revision of the philosophy of utility in *Utilitarianism* (1863) started in those years of unhappiness.

The melancholic winter of 1826–27 was an awakening in his monochromatic life, whose emotional emptiness Mill rendered with two lines from Coleridge: "Work without hope draws nectar in a sieve / And hope without an object cannot live."[5] His "mental crisis" aroused many and diverse interpretations, some stressing his hard work, others his life's emotional emptiness, still others his pathological relationship with his father. To paraphrase *On Liberty*, each interpretation contains a grain of truth. The last became popular with the growth of psychoanalysis, in conjunction with a page of his *Autobiography* in which Mill narrates how his recovery started:

> I was reading, accidentally, Marmontel's *Memoirs*, and came to the passage which relates his father's death, the distressed position of the family, and the sudden inspiration by which he, then

---

2. *CW*, vol. 1, pp. 129 and 131–33.
3. Along with Mill's *Autobiography*, a good description of these clubs can be found in Richard Monckton Milnes, *The Life, Letters, and Friendships*, 2 vols. (New York: Cassell, 1891), vol. 1, pp. 49–190.
4. *CW*, vol. 1, p. 137.
5. Ibid., p. 145.

a mere boy, felt and made them feel that he would be everything to them—would supply the place of all that they had lost.
A vivid conception of the scene and its feelings came over me,
and I was moved to tears. From this moment my burthen grew
lighter. The oppression of the thought that all feeling was dead
within me, was gone. I was no longer hopeless: I was not a stock
or a stone. I had still, it seemed, some of the material out of which
all worth of character, and all capacity for happiness, are made.
Relieved from my ever present sense of irremediable wretchedness, I gradually found that the ordinary incidents of life could
again give me some pleasure; that I could again find enjoyment,
not intense, but sufficient for cheerfulness, in sunshine and sky, in
books, in conversation, in public affairs; and that there was, once
more, excitement, though of a moderate kind, in exerting myself
for my opinions, and for the public good. Thus the cloud gradually drew off, and I again enjoyed life: and though I had several
relapses, some of which lasted many months, I never again was
as miserable as I had been.[6]

Mill's experiences in these few years, from his hyperactivism in
public life to his "mental crisis" and recovery, trace the evolution of
his philosophy, a gradual reinterpretation of the principle of utility,
including an expansion of the meaning and forms of pleasures and
the identification of happiness with a dignified life—in other words,
his gradual discovery of the value of individuality.[7] Mill's existential
and theoretical transformation was also aided by his encounter
with Romanticism. "The other important change which my opinions
at this time underwent, was that I, for the first time, gave its proper
place, among the prime necessities of human well-being, to the
internal culture of the individual."[8] After all, Mill's unhappiness
mirrored his one-sided life, which he depicted and criticized so effectively in *On Liberty*; the therapy to cure it would be a plurality of
sources of pleasures, as he explained in *Utilitarianism*; and the best
result would be association with others on the basis of moral autonomy and reciprocity, as he argued in *The Subjection of Women*
(1869). Mill gradually emerged from his depression by enriching and
enlarging his intellectual interests to include music, poetry, and fine
arts, and by making new friends outside his tribe, and indeed one
lasting result of the crisis was his thorough rejection of party spirit
(although not partisanship for good causes).

Throughout crisis and discovery, Mill never stopped studying
and writing on logic, political economy, psychology of association,
and utilitarianism, and never repudiated his rationalist stance and

6. Ibid.
7. See Elizabeth Anderson's essay in this Norton Critical Edition.
8. *CW*, vol. 1, p. 147.

political views, but he began to approach all of them differently, and the intellectual and sentimental experiences of those critical years marked his maturity as a philosopher. Mill emerged from his crisis an original scholar, not just a member of the "utilitarian school," and if we continue to read his books today, it is because they elude narrowness and easy classification of any sort.

Mill's personal and intellectual evolution can be seen as stemming from the confrontation of two philosophical traditions: the Enlightenment and Romanticism. In his youth, he experienced the confrontation first-hand through his Coleridgean friends, in particular Frederick Dennison Maurice, John Sterling (Mill's closest friend), and Thomas Carlyle, a genial thinker whose pen smashed and derided almost everything Mill was raised to love and defend, and which he would continue to love and defend, but in his own way. (Very telling in this regard is the position he took—*contra* his radical friends— in favor of Wordsworth and against Byron in a famous debate on poetry.)[9] Through his new acquaintances, Mill became familiar with Johann Wolfgang von Goethe (whose ideal of a modern harmonious self Mill admired, albeit skeptically), Friedrich Schleiermacher (whose essay "On the Worth of Socrates as a Philosopher" made him discover a non-Sophist Socrates), Friedrich Wilhelm von Humboldt (whose idea of individuality and diversity was paramount in his theory of liberty), and Immanuel Kant (whose transcendental principle of morals intrigued him throughout his life).

Mill's youthful disaffection with the style of eighteenth-century rationalism and his appreciation of the Romantic critique of modernity revealed how much he sympathized with "speculative Toryism." He shared with Carlyle the disapproval of commercial values and skepticism of a linear and cumulative progress of knowledge and morality. What Mill admired in Wordsworth's and Coleridge's speculative Toryism was the nostalgia for an ideal England that never existed but served as a criterion to criticize the emerging consumerist society.[1] Predictably, his new friends complicated relations with his radical friends. Roebuck started distancing himself from Mill, perplexed by his appreciation of Wordsworth's poem and his fondness for conservative thinkers. Meanwhile, Mill started feeling that the radical tribe was suffocating and prejudiced against diversity and self-criticism, as Macaulay noted in his critique of James Mill's essay on government. In 1829, the year that critique appeared, Mill stopped participating in the London Debating Society. "I had

---

9. Ibid., pp. 153–55.
1. Mill's letter to John Sterling (20 October 1831), *CW*, vol. 12, pp. 83–84. On the resemblance of Mill's disapproval of consumerism and moral conformity to the discourse of antimodernity, see Joseph Hamburger, *John Stuart Mill on Liberty and Control* (Princeton: Princeton UP, 1999), p. 120.

had enough of speech-making, and was glad to carry on my private studies and meditations without any immediate call for outward assertion of their results. I found the fabric of my old and taught opinions giving way in many fresh places, and I never allowed it to fall to pieces, but was incessantly occupied in weaving it anew."[2]

In this new emotional and intellectual climate, Mill met Harriet Taylor in 1830. The same age as Mill, she was the daughter of a surgeon and like Mill had been schooled at home. She was married to John Taylor and the mother of three children (the youngest, Helen, would live with Mill after the death of her mother, assisting him in the final draft of his *Autobiography*, editing his posthumous *Chapters on Socialism* [1879], and "jealously guarding" all his literary remains).[3] Since her early youth, Harriet had been interested in poetry and committed to "free thinking" ideas (what we would today call civil rights), and when they met, she was associated with the congregation of Unitarian "free thinkers" of Reverend William Fox, in whose magazine the *Monthly Repository* Mill published some of his essays on ancient philosophy under the nom de plume "Antiquus." Just after they met, he was inspired by her to compose two essays on marriage and divorce. They married in 1851, two years after her husband's death.

Predictably, their friendship provoked gossip and harsh criticism. They went on holidays together, "although [they] never went into society as a couple; Harriet Taylor's husband, John, behaves with astonishing self-restraint and forbearance."[4] Less self-restrained were Mill's people: his relationship with his father and his family became very difficult, and the association with his radical friends either broke down or became loose. Roebuck's resentful words about Mill's lack of "courage," first vis-à-vis the Benthamites and now with Harriet ("Mill's intellect bowed down to the feet of Mrs. Taylor"), explain Mill's distress with the oppressive force of social opinions. Some pages of *On Liberty* seem to describe that prolonged and unpleasant situation and explain why Mill insisted on considering it "their" book. Probably, as Alan Ryan observed in his introduction to the 1996 Norton Critical Edition of Mill's writings, if "the substance of the fears [*On Liberty*] expresses was provided by Tocqueville, . . . the intensity of the emotion that went into that expression was provided by Harriet Mill."[5] But perhaps substance and intensity of emotions were mixed in Mill's own mind. Indeed, after the deaths of Bentham and above all of his father, he made public his passionate thoughts on the leader of the Radicals ("Bentham," published in

2. *CW*, vol. 1, p. 163.
3. Friedrich A. von Hayek, introduction to *CW*, vol. 12, p. xviii.
4. Ryan, introduction to the second Norton Critical Edition of Mill's writings (1996), p. xvi.
5. Ibid., p. xviii.

1838) and the Romantics ("Coleridge," 1840), depicting Bentham as Polyphemus (i.e., a one-eyed theorist)—an analogy that would fit several of his radical friends.

The culmination of these formative years came through Mill's encounter with French positivism, and in particular its sociological interpretation of moral and national customs and the idea of progress. The Saint-Simonians reflected both Catholic antimodernity and the Enlightenment belief in progress, combining Joseph de Maistre's attack on individualism and Condorcet's depiction of the march of society toward equality via science, technology, the market economy, and political institutions. Within those parameters, the Saint-Simonians took different directions, some becoming apostles of a new social order based on communal relations among sexes and freedom from institutional constraints (Mill defended their communitarian "utopia" from the accusation of immorality),[6] while others became social scientists seeking the inner logic of social relations (static) and their change (dynamic). Mill was initially enthusiastic about Auguste Comte's *Cours de philosophie positive* (1837) and its theory of progress, but he became gradually more suspicious and finally broke off his correspondence with Comte over a radical disagreement with the latter's biological translation of cultural differences (among races, nations, and sexes), as Mill would explain in *Auguste Comte and Positivism* (1865).

The System of Logic (1843) testifies to Mill's ambition to sketch out a method for social science in the service of emancipation, which he based on two factors: the role of ideas and education in the formation of national characters, and his (unfulfilled) ambition of creating a science of "ethology" to detect the tendencies of social transformation thanks to generalizations from history and empirical observations. In addition, the Saint-Simonians offered Mill (with the enthusiastic support of Harriet) the chance to enlarge the horizon of reformism beyond the legal domains (central to Bentham) to include the critical examination of social relations of power and the denunciation of all forms of subjection. The third edition of his *Principles of Political Economy* (1852; first edition 1848) is a significant document of Mill's social thought, with an added chapter on the future of the working classes, where he criticized the "old school" of economics and countered its one-sided interest in wealth accumulation with the proposal of "good distribution" of wealth in view of improving the "quality of life" for all. (Key issues were finding a solution to the deterioration of the condition of both the working classes and nature.) The text that best demonstrates his ability to

6. "Fontata and Prati's St. Simonism in London" (*Examiner*, 2 February 1834), *CW*, vol. 23, pp. 674–80; see his letter to Emile Honoré Cazelles of May 30, 1869, *CW*, vol. 17, p. 1609.

draw from positivism without succumbing to its full weltanschau-ung is *The Subjection of Women*, which revises French positivism in light of his own idea of progress to be evaluated according to the ideal of an equal distribution of power as a condition of individual autonomy.

These were Mill's main contributions to democracy and democ-ratization, which would amend, without rejecting, the distrust of democratic mediocrity he shared with Alexis de Tocqueville's *Democracy in America* (1835, 1840). Mill reviewed Tocqueville's first volume in 1835, the year his father died, and the second in 1840, the year he published his essay on Coleridge—and the change in tone from the first to the second review is palpable: from enthusiasm to reserved criticism. Tocqueville's work deepened Mill's conviction that the defects of modern democracy lay in civil society; if individ-uals were displaced from political life, if they could not verify the information to which they were exposed and could not shape their choice autonomously, it had to be because of the increasing influ-ence of social classes, especially the middle class. Neither Mill nor Tocqueville thought modern elites bore any resemblance to their ancient counterparts; only military and agricultural societies could produce the flourishing of "that order of virtues in which a commer-cial society is apt to be deficient."[7] Nevertheless, in his second review, Mill blamed the socioeconomic order for this defect rather than democratic equality.

Thus while Tocqueville praised democracy insofar as it was able to incorporate predemocratic elements, Mill criticized democ-racy in the name of its own principles—the primacy of the individ-ual citizen and equal partnership. He challenged democracy on its own terrain, asking not for less democracy but that democracy keep its promises.

Mill's determination to find a counterweight to democratic majoritarianism followed two important events: the publication of Tocqueville's work and the derailment of the 1848 French Revo-lution into plebiscitarianism. A watershed in the evolution of European democratic thought and politics, the French experience induced protodemocrats like Mill to take a more cautious look at democracy. He, like Marx, believed that the fate of European democracy would be decided in France. So Mill strenuously defended the February 1848 revolution from its conservative critics, but harshly condemned its degeneration into Caesarism. Unlike Marx, however, he imputed the victory of Louis Napoléon, and thus the decline of parliamentary democracy, to the unedu-cated masses, "the millions of voters who . . . could neither read

7. Mill, "De Tocqueville on Democracy in America" (1840), *CW*, vol. 18, p. 195.

nor write, and whose knowledge of public men, even by name, was limited to oral tradition."[8] In *Considerations on Representative Government* (1861), he proposed to neutralize those problems by means of bicameralism, proportional representation, and local self-government.[9]

After the death of his wife in 1858, and while in Avignon (where she died and was buried), Mill seemed to be born again to politics and the public life. In the space of a few years, he published some of his most important essays: the three published in this volume, as well as *Considerations on Representative Government*, the principal theoretical essay of the nineteenth century on the quality, institutions, and goals of modern democracy. Finally, in 1865 he decided to run for elected office. He refused to incur personal expense and, consistent with his idea of representation as political service to the citizens, argued that "any particular candidate ought to be borne as a public charge, either by the State or by the locality."[1] He also deemed serving in Parliament a "sacrifice of time and energies" toward "forming a really advanced liberal party."[2]

According to one anecdote, he was confronted under a column in London's Trafalgar Square and asked whether it was true that he defined the lower classes as "habitual liars" (as he did in 1859 in his "Thoughts on Parliamentary Reform"), and one of the working-class leaders publicly endorsed Mill by saying that "my class has no desire not to be told its faults; we want friends, not flatterers."[3] Like his old Radical friends, Mill wanted to use Parliament as a pulpit to advocate for the most advanced causes, including the extension of the right to vote to women and workers, Irish home rule, and freedom to strike. His most important initiative was on women's right to vote, a proposal he introduced during the debate of the 1867 Reform Bill. Mill orchestrated the campaign on female equality with extraordinary care and strategic brilliance by connecting it to the antislavery movement (he put great effort into publicizing *The Slave Power* by John Elliot Cairnes, which he used to denounce all forms of subjection and despotic domination) and the issue of equal treatment (he was one of the most distinguished male participants in the

---

8. Mill, "French Affairs" (9 August 1848), *CW*, vol. 25, pp. 1110–12.
9. The role of local government in the surveillance of the executive was a central issue in Mill's work; he himself solicited Tocqueville to study it in relation to France; the latter's "Political and Social Conditions of France" was a result of that solicitation, which Mill translated and titled for the *London and Westminster Review* in 1836.
1. *CW*, vol. 1, p. 273.
2. To Theodor Gomperz, August 22, 1866, *CW*, vol. 16, p. 1197.
3. Cited in Nicholas Capaldi, *John Stuart Mill: A Biography* (Cambridge: Cambridge UP, 2004), p. 323.

campaign against the Contagious Diseases Acts).[4] Moreover, early
in the 1840s and 1850s, he had written a series of articles exposing
domestic violence against women and demanding voting rights for
educated households "without distinction of sex." The long march
he orchestrated toward emancipation was the synthesis of several
combined initiatives—preparing public opinion with bolder views
that would pave the way toward his greater cause of political equality in Parliament. As he commented to a U.S. magazine after Abra-
ham Lincoln's Emancipation Proclamation of 1863, "the disabilities
of women are now the only remaining national violation of the
principles of your immortal Declaration of Independence."[5] Mill's
proposal was rejected but garnered seventy-three votes, an unpre-
cedented accomplishment. His parliamentary fight for suffrage and
his book (which was published in 1869) became among the most
important arguments for political emancipation in European countries and the United States, galvanizing the young (and then radical) Vilfredo Pareto and keeping the American women's rights
movement kindled in the "difficult post–Civil War years, when some
of the stauncher early male supporters" of suffrage "withdrew their
political support to argue that the vote must first be secured to the
Negro."[6] Even as an active politician, Mill was better at widening the
public debate than winning votes, and after losing his campaign for
reelection in 1868, he was happy to return to his intellectual work,
the only occupation which agreed with his "tastes and habits."

Mill lived in an age of revolutions and great political transformations. He was a contemporary of visionary populists and democratic
nationalists (many of them exiled in London), such as Alexander
Herzen and Giuseppe Mazzini, revolutionary communists such as
Karl Marx and Friedrich Engels, anarchists including Mikhail
Bakunin, social reformers such as Louis Blanc, and utopian social
federalists and cooperativists like Robert Owen and Louis Prou-
dhon. Mill reached his intellectual maturity in the years between

4. The Contagious Diseases Acts were originally passed by Parliament in 1864, with
alterations in 1866 and 1869. In 1862, a committee was established to inquire into
venereal disease (i.e., sexually transmitted infections) in the armed forces. The legislation allowed police officers to arrest women suspected of being prostitutes in certain
ports and army towns. The Act of 1864 stated that women found to be infected could
be interned in locked hospitals for up to three months, a period gradually extended to
one year with the 1869 Act. These measures were justified by medical and military
officials as the most effective method to shield men from venereal disease. Because
military men were often unmarried and homosexuality was criminal, prostitution was
considered a necessary evil. However, no provision was made for the examination of
prostitutes' clientele, which became one of the many points of contention in a campaign to repeal the acts. Mill criticized precisely that unequal treatment of women.
5. Quoted in Ibid., p. 328.
6. Alice S. Rossi, introduction to *The Feminist Papers: From Adams to de Beauvoir*, 1st ed.
(Boston: Northeastern UP, 1973), p. 183.

the French liberal revolution of 1830 (which he chronicled accurately) and the global democratic revolutions of 1848–49, which kindled all European countries and the Americas, sparked expectations of emancipation, and ended with the plebiscitary Bonapartism of Napoleon III in 1852. With the victory of the "strong man" and the decline of the expectation for a new international order based on democratic nations, Mill pinned his hopes on the campaigns for national emancipation in Europe against continental empires, and against slavery in the United States; the latter he supported well before the outbreak of the Civil War, even while the large majority in England remained hostile to the North. Mill treated slavery as "the extreme form of undemocracy"[7] and thought liberty as nonsubjection was the foundation of "good democracy." To achieve this form of democracy, legal reforms were insufficient and "fixed points" in ethical life were needed.

Throughout his life, Mill signed numerous protest documents and petitions, contributed money to causes and movements in various countries, and supported movements of national and social emancipation wherever they arose. But the cause against slavery was the mother of all causes because it put the human condition into absolute jeopardy. It was also the cause that prompted him to clarify his ideas concerning the foundation and limits of politics and political action: against the "sacred doctrine of rebellion" that the Southern states invoked "for the right of burning human creatures alive," Mill opposed the principle of human dignity as the only one sufficient to justify rebellion.

> I am not frightened at the word rebellion. I do not scruple to say that I have sympathized more or less ardently with most of the rebellions, successful and unsuccessful, which have taken place in my time. But I certainly never conceived that there was a sufficient title to my sympathy in the mere fact of being a rebel; that the act of taking arms against one's fellow citizens was so meritorious in itself, was so completely its own justification, that no question need be asked concerning the motive. It seems to me a strange doctrine that the most serious and responsible of all human acts imposes no obligation on those who do it, of showing that they have a real grievance; that those who rebel for the power of oppressing others, exercise as sacred a right as those who do the same thing to resist oppression practiced upon themselves. Neither rebellion, nor any other act which affects the interests of others, is sufficiently legitimated by the mere will to do it.[8]

---

7. Collini, *Public Moralists*, p. 142.
8. Mill, "The Contest in America" (1862), *CW*, vol. 21, p. 137.

On Liberty

In his Preface to the 1975 Norton Critical Edition, David Spitz wrote that *On Liberty* (1859) and Marx's *Communist Manifesto* (1848) were the two essays of the nineteenth century that most "excited attention" and gave rise to "a vast and controversial body of literature." For Spitz, Mill's essay was far more radical than John Milton's *Areopagitica* (1644), which argued for liberty of unlicensed printing, and a formidable statement on "freedom of thought and expression and the right to privacy." And yet, it is noteworthy that Spitz associated this classical liberal text with a republican one. Mill himself would not disdain the association since he emphasized the republican significance of writing it. "I had first planned and written it as a short essay, in 1854. It was in mounting the steps of the Capitol [the Capitoline hill in Rome], in January 1855, that the thought first arose of converting it into a volume."[9] He had announced the decision to his wife in a letter from Rome, adding that "it is a growing need too, for opinion tends to encroach more & more on liberty, & almost all the projects of social reformers in these days are really *liberticide*— Comte, particularly so."[1] Mill offers his readers guidelines to approach what would become the most famous and controversial of his books, harshly criticized for being inconclusive and offensive—"an infidel book"—or ardently praised as "one of the few books that inculcate tolerance in an unalarming and inoffensive way."[2] *On Liberty* has displeased conservatives and irritated radicals because of its supposed privileging of individualism, and it has dissatisfied liberals because it elects utility as the principle of liberty. All things considered, rights-based liberals have been its most persistent critics: to them, it fails to devise a consistent criterion for guiding actions and confronts the individual with the paradox of either waiting for consequences to fully unspool before judging an action, or else relying upon the opinion of the majority. These are not idle objections. But they do not succeed in weakening Mill's arguments in defense of liberty and individuality. "There is no book written in English like *On Liberty*. There was none like it before; there have been none like it since."[3]

9. *CW*, vol. 1, p. 249.
1. To his wife, 15 January 1855, *CW*, vol. 14, p. 294.
2. Respectively, Mill to George Jacob Holyoake, February 1859 (*CW*, vol. 15, p. 593) and a comment by Matthew Arnold quoted in Edward Alexander, *Matthew Arnold and John Stuart Mill* (New York: Columbia UP, 1965), p. 32.
3. George Kateb, "A Reading of *On Liberty*," in John Stuart Mill, *On Liberty*, ed. David Bromwich and George Kateb (New Haven and London: Yale UP, 2003), p. 28.

1. A Manifesto

On Liberty was born as an essay *against* "conservatives" and "misguided progressives" alike,[4] but particularly the latter, whom Mill charged with "liberticide," a word that evokes in reversal the republican foundation of freedom in "tyrannicide." Mill put a new tyranny on trial, a tyranny that Montesquieu and Tocqueville had detected but none knew how to combat, namely the tyranny of a large group over the minority or an individual through "public opinion": to induce "regularity of conduct," mold individual beliefs, and make everyone "conform to the approved standard."[5] According to Mill, modern tyranny takes the form of the "passive imbecility" of the individuals under a "silent" yet overwhelming opinion, and the best resistance would come from the "sovereignty of the individual," which would counteract the "despotism over the mind."[6]

Contemporary social doctrines were inadequate because they were either nostalgic for old aristocratic values of distinction and honor that industrial society had buried forever (Coleridgeans) or programmatically condescending and functional to the new social trend of conformism (French positivists). Traditionalists, critics of modernity, social planners, and eulogists of modernity were all intolerant of individuality and inimical to diversity; but the last were most alarming since they sided with the future and made social progress depend on individual docility. Mill's critique in *On Liberty* was not new: he had discussed the shortcomings of traditional conservatives and radicals in some previous writings, including the essays on Bentham (1838) and Coleridge (1840), and the reviews of Tocqueville's *Democracy in America* (1836; 1840); and he would do so again in *Auguste Comte and Positivism*, which appeared in 1865.

However, *On Liberty* was not simply *against* something. It is also a manifesto *for* individual sovereignty of judgment, which Mill believed was achievable through full liberty of thought and expression. This liberty was desirable and "useful" to society when utility was understood "in the largest sense," as "the utility of man as a

---

4. Ryan, introduction, p. xxvii.
5. Montesquieu had distinguished between "two sorts of tyranny: a real one, which consists in the violence of the government, and one of opinion, which is felt when those who govern establish things that run counter to a nation's way of thinking"; the second sort gestured toward the tyranny of opinion but focused on the violation of "mores" by government. Tocqueville and Mill introduced an important change to the second form of tyranny. Charles de Secondat, Baron de Montesquieu, *The Spirit of the Laws*, trans. Anne M. Cohler, Badia Carolyn Miller, and Harold Samuel Stone (Cambridge: Cambridge UP, 1989), p. 309.
6. See p. 93 below. As he writes in his *Autobiography* (CW, vol. 1, p. 260), he "borrowed" the phrase "Sovereignty of the individual" from Josiah Warren, *Equitable Commerce* (New York: Fowlers and Wells, 1852), p. 26.

progressive being." After drawing a line between "individual independence" and "social control," Mill then interrogates the circumstances under which the interference of society with personal life is warranted, eventually arriving at a simple rule: coercion is only justified to prevent harm to others, and not to directly create social welfare or goodness, which is and should remain the task of individuals. Fairness and justice are the only legitimate limitations on individual free choice.

To Mill, the inhibition of individual spontaneity either through direct coercion or by hindering a person "in his freedom of pursuing his own good" was not a peripheral issue, nor was it unique to certain societies, although many of his readers, past and present, have circumscribed his message to his native country (some critics felt outraged by the illiberal image of British society he advanced) and to his long-term love affair with a married woman, who was also ardently committed to denouncing the prejudices and bigotry of Victorian England. As previously noted, *On Liberty* was John *and* Harriet's book,[7] and it extends the social critique to include not just formal political institutions but also the informal systems, including education, that can either create fertile ground for individual sovereignty, or else throttle it into submission in the cradle: "Human nature is not a machine to be built after a model, and set to do exactly the work prescribed for it."

Unsurprisingly given the scope of its critique, *On Liberty* ends up sketching the model of a society projected toward a distant future, an ideal, like democracy itself, not to be fully realized, but one that can be used as a benchmark against which all existing societies can measure themselves. An unrepentant rationalist and a pessimist on the inevitability of progress, Mill outlined the traits and principles of a society in which individual spontaneity and diversity, communication, and cooperation among autonomous persons would be recognized as valuable and practiced by all. An important lesson he had learned from the English Romantics, particularly Wordsworth and Carlyle, was that "real change comes through changes in human self-consciousness and not by engineering" a new type of society.[8] But Mill was not interested in advocating "heroic self-assertion," although in almost all his political writings he refers to "middle-class complacency" as an obstacle to the moral revolution an enlarged

7. "The *Liberty* was more directly and literally our joint production than anything else which bears my name, for there was not a sentence of it that was not several times gone through by us together, turned over in many ways, and carefully weeded of any faults, either in thought or expression, that we detected in it. It is in consequence of this that, although it never underwent her final revision, it far surpasses, as a mere specimen of composition, anything which has proceeded from me either before or since" (this part of his *Autobiography* was written in 1870). *CW*, vol. 1, pp. 257–59.
8. Capaldi, *John Stuart Mill*, p. 94.

utility would create. Thus, while addressed to the few who could grasp its message, Mill's book was also aimed at a broader audience that would eventually include everyone.

On Liberty is the document of a progressive liberalism that made freedom from subjection the anchor of personal dignity and the mark of an inclusive society, and that competed with other projects of social transformation in an age that was open to different possibilities. It is the text of an intellectual who was passionately engaged in attaining an ideal which was as radical as that of its adversaries. Mill's militant urgency explains the style of this book, passionate and pugnacious, and its genre, a manifesto—all taking place "in a militant age, when those who have thoughts and feelings to impress on the world have a great deal of hard work to do and very little time to do it."[9]

Mill adopted two strategies of argumentation: an eristic and polemical attack with an astute choice of adjectives and exemplary cases of subjection, to win readers to his side; and an inspiring exhortation to endorse his idea that liberty and individuality were the conditions of well-being for all, including those who resisted them. He believed that the arguments of toleration and the harm principle would be especially effective with those who could not be convinced by the sheer desirability of liberty, "those who do not desire liberty." Those "who most need convincing" would be rewarded "for allowing other people to make use of it without hindrance."[1] In sum, liberty and individuality would not hurt anybody and would dispense good to all. If his style was partly eristic, his ultimate goal was not to "win" an argument, but rather to distill the advantages of individual liberty in a way palatable to the greatest number. "None of my writings have been either so carefully composed, or so sedulously corrected as this."[2]

The rhetorical strength of the book lies in its argumentative order: a crescendo from the principle of freedom to the affirmation of individuality, culminating in social progress, with a linearity and "deceptive clarity" that is "unusual in Mill's other writing."[3] The introduction sketches a short history of political liberty, showing that civil liberty was born alongside toleration from the wars of religion, and ends by announcing the "simple principle" of harm that is the sole justification for societal interference in the liberty of expression. Chapter II explains the distinction between actions that pertain solely to ourselves and actions that have a direct impact on others; argues that the latter are the only actions that can be legitimately

---

9. *Diary, CW*, vol. 27, p. 647.
1. See p. 57 below.
2. *CW*, vol. 1, p. 249.
3. Ryan, introduction, pp. xxviii and xxvi.

interfered with; and goes on to demonstrate the utility of liberty to the personal search for truth and social progress. Chapter III is the most controversial, exalting individuality and even eccentricity as a primary good; it aims to prove that a climate of "civil, and social liberty" provides the most conducive environment for happiness and the "utility of man as a progressive being." Chapter IV goes back to the harm principle and analyzes the circumstances and contexts in which the authority of society over the individual is warranted, and in which mode. It argues that a progressive society is held together by communication among people who disagree and publicly express the reasons for their disagreement while treating each other with respect, and that education plays a critical role in forming these individuals. Chapter V proposes a number of cases of the harm principle, where the interests of others should be contemplated in limiting the civil freedom of adult persons.

The main critiques of *On Liberty* have their root in the paragraph that outlines the plan of the book:

> The object of this Essay is to assert one very simple principle, as entitled to govern absolutely the dealings of society with the individual in the way of compulsion and control, whether the means used be physical force in the form of legal penalties, or the moral coercion of public opinion. That principle is, that the sole end for which mankind are warranted, individually or collectively, in interfering with the liberty of action of any of their number, is self-protection. . . . His own good, either physical or moral, is not a sufficient warrant. He cannot rightfully be compelled to do or forbear because it will be better for him to do so, because it will make him happier, because, in the opinions of others, to do so would be wise, or even right. These are good reasons for remonstrating with him, or reasoning with him, or persuading him, or entreating him, but not for compelling him, or visiting him with any evil in case he do otherwise. To justify that, the conduct from which it is desired to deter him, must be calculated to produce evil to some one else. The only part of the conduct of any one, for which he is amenable to society, is that which concerns others. In the part which merely concerns himself, his independence is, of right, absolute. Over himself, over his own body and mind, the individual is sovereign.[4]

2. Liberty, Civil and Political

One common critique casts Mill as the prophet of an aggressive individualism, which is questionable on both historical and theoretical

4. See pp. 10–11 below.

grounds and can be refuted by a close analysis of the relationship
he draws between civil and political liberty.

First, this criticism cannot explain how *On Liberty* became a
political text against fascism. In Italy, a new translation was released
in 1925, the year Benito Mussolini inaugurated his unrestrained
rule, and in his introduction, Luigi Einaudi wrote that after years
of discord,

> minds yearned for peace, tranquility, rest and calmed down at
> the word of those who promised these goods. . . . Woe betide if
> from the natural aspiration to free oneself from the bestial civil
> war into which it had degenerated between 1919 and 1921 the
> political struggle in Italy fell without contrast into absolute con-
> formity to the nationalistic gospel imposed by fascism! It would
> be the death of the nation. With the abolition of freedom of
> the press, with the compression of freedom of thought, with
> the denial of freedom of movement and work by virtue of the
> proclamations and the monopoly of the corporations, the coun-
> try is pushed back toward intolerance and uniformity. They
> want to forcefully impose unanimity of consensus and ideas
> because it is affirmed that it is necessary to defend the truth
> against error, good against evil, the nation against the anti-nation.
> To these mortifying propositions, which Milton already consid-
> ered fatal, Mill's essay opposes the logical justification of the
> right to dissent and the demonstration of the social and spiri-
> tual usefulness of the struggle.[5]

To the fighters against a "liberticide" regime, *On Liberty* proved
that civil liberty and political liberty were parts of "security."

Second, Mill's individual self-reliance must be seen not just as a
good in itself, but as an antidote to conformism and the silencing of
self-inquiry, a means of counteracting the new tyranny of "public
opinion" that fostered individualism and isolation by debilitating the
inner world. To Mill, individuality was not the same as individualism, which had a negative connotation in his time,[6] and was not necessarily inimical to democracy—as long as democracy was not confused
with mass democracy, as Tocqueville explained and Mill restated.
Individualism and individuality were to Mill as opposite as "idiot-
ism" and "communication" or "isolation" and "solitude." Rephrasing
Aristotle's critique of Plato's ideal city in the second book of *Politics*,
Mill argued that passive obedience and conformism do not strengthen
social ties, but rather create selfish characters, "disconnecting each

---

5. Luigi Einaudi, Introduction to J. S. Mill, *Saggio sulla libertà* (Turin: Edizioni Gobetti,
   1925).
6. Koenraad W. Swart, "'Individualism' in the Mid-Nineteenth Century (1826–1860),"
   Journal of the History of Ideas 23 (1962): 77–90.

man's feeling of duty from the interests of his fellow-creatures except so far as a self-interested inducement is offered to him for consulting them."[7] Thus, *On Liberty* is not a tract of self-interested individualism, but rather a powerful argument in favor of sincere and open communication among adult persons, brought about by individuals willing to search within themselves for the source of authority over life. Moreover, individuality was not just a private good, but would positively affect society as a whole.

Mill also fit security within his overall framework of civil liberty, locating a synergy between stable obedience to the law and the limits of state power through "constitutional checks" and the rule of law. A despotic or tyrannical or oligarchic regime could not be the home of "civil" liberty, for it is not sufficient that some individuals enjoy it—which was one reason he admired Giuseppe Mazzini and Louis Blanc, who called for extending what were then privileges of the few to everyone. This is also why he has no desire to return to the past, despite his observation that in the ancient and medieval ages, "the individual was a power in himself. . . . At present individuals are lost in the crowd."[8] But the past cannot serve as a model, because individuality must be extended to all, rather than remaining the privilege of the few, as in Carlyle's cult of the hero as a prophet.[9]

For Mill, individuality and civil liberty go hand in hand in a society that recognizes moral and civic equality and whose government rests on public opinion and the open expression of ideas. Thus while security is indispensable, it does not play the same role as in Hobbes, for it grows stronger along with political emancipation, as we will examine in *The Subjection of Women*.

The claim for "civil, and social liberty" emerges once unaccountable rulers (absolute monarchs or oligarchs) have been replaced with a collective sovereign. Popular sovereignty introduces the problem motivating this essay, because in democracy a "prevailing opinion and feeling" may develop that makes citizens confident that "the tyranny of magistrates" is no longer an issue. To amend Jean-Jacques Rousseau's argument that "the rulers should be identified with the people," Mill stresses the urgency of new immunities capable of devising "other means" of control. Hence the division of labor among his works published in the 1850s and 1860s: *Considerations on Representative Government* sets limits on political power; *On Liberty* sets limits on social authority; and *The Subjection of Women* shows that women's political, civil, and social emancipation from male

7. See p. 45 below.
8. See p. 59 below.
9. Capaldi, *John Stuart Mill*, p. 131.

domination and social customs is the necessary condition for the flourishing of individuality.

Mill was not an antidemocrat. He identified most strongly with the power each citizen has *in relation* to the masses rather than with citizens *as part* of the masses. He did not oppose state intervention in the domains pertaining to other-regarding actions; to him, laws that "recognize and protect common interests, like laws against violence and monopoly, offer no insult to any class or individual; but laws that constrain one man, on the sole ground that he is incompetent to decide what is right for himself, are profoundly insulting to him."[1] An antimonopoly logic is the frame within which to situate his distinction between "other-regarding" and "self-regarding" actions: decisions by state power must enlarge people's sphere of self-regarding actions, while making individuals accountable to those they affect. This entails political inclusion and limited state power. For example, until women can take part in the protection of their private sphere through suffrage, their "civil and social" liberty is not guaranteed and remains a de facto concession or a privilege, much like in the "ancient and medieval ages."[2] Mill extends this prospect to include all disempowered groups, arguing that all persons must be treated as autonomous beings. "What the poor as well as the rich require is not to be indoctrinated, is not to be taught other people's opinions, but to be induced and enabled to think for themselves" and be treated "as equals."[3]

3. *Public Opinion, Dissent, and a Not Very Simple Principle*

Once security was clarified, Mill had to explain the nature of "civil, or social" liberty, which marks the novelty of the essay—extending the republican attack on arbitrary interference (which he calls "coercion") to the authority of society, which "makes itself the organ of the general intolerance of the public."[4] This is the kernel of liberty as nonsubjection (which Mill would later put forth in *The Subjection of Women*) in personal life or "civil, and social liberty." Roughly speaking, this liberty pertains not directly to the body (actions) but to the mind (opinions) which directs those actions, although civil liberty does include the "expression" of ideas and experimentation with different lifestyles. For the sake of analytical clarity, Mill distinguishes ideas and beliefs from actions and treats the latter as "self-regarding": this is the indispensable condition of "civil,

---

1. Ronald Dworkin, *Taking Rights Seriously* (Cambridge, MA.: Harvard UP, 1977), p. 263.
2. As we read in his *Diary* on March 18, 1854, "mixed governments . . . are generally preferred to simple forms of government, or those which establish one power (though it be that of the majority) supreme over all the rest." *CW*, vol. 27, p. 662.
3. See n. 6, p. lxx below.
4. See p. 16 below.

and social liberty." But this distinction works as a general criterion rather than a description; it serves as a guide in practical and political life. We will come back to it after clarifying the meaning of "opinion."

An admirer of Socrates, Mill put public opinion on trial insofar as it acts as an absolute power by silencing contrary views. What he calls "public opinion" is much broader than the contemporary poll-driven idea, and encompasses a complex network of ideas, customs, and beliefs that comprise the character of society. Public opinion is soft power insofar as it cannot be imputed to someone as political domination or coercion. There is no word denoting the killing of a tyrannical opinion. This makes detecting this tyranny complicated, and to some critics Mill was launching a preposterous endeavor because all societies need a substratum of shared beliefs and values to hold themselves together. However, Mill himself was strongly opposed to an atomistic solution (isolation) to the tyranny of opinion.

Some years before writing *On Liberty*, he had reviewed Tocqueville's *Democracy in America*, in which the invisible authority of the "intelligence and wisdom" of society surpassed even the lawmaking power (the democratic sovereign power) and became an irresistible force that "requires the sanction of the time in order to appear legitimate."[5] In the 1840s, Mill was also committed to finding laws of social dynamics and middle laws (the science of ethology or the laws presiding over the formation of national character) to apply to politics and secure the advancement of social progress. But he realized quite soon that he would search in vain. Connecting intentions with actions and explaining social behaviors as a linear convergence of individual decisions in predictive ways was a foolhardy echo of Saint-Simon.

On Liberty goes beyond this simplistic fantasy, and its animosity toward Comte's illiberal system retains the flavor of self-criticism. Mill is no longer certain about the future of society and instead wishes to create the conditions for an endless process of contestation. The new criterion for society is whether or not it expands the domain of personal self-realization and "civil, and social" liberties.[6] As a criterion, it requires a middle principle to bring about good results: this is "the harm principle" and the connected distinction between "self-regarding" and "other-regarding" actions, both of which should guide individuals' judgment and decisions in complex

5. Alexis de Tocqueville, *Democracy in America*, trans. H. Reeve (Boston: Sever, Francis, 1870), p. 326.
6. Piers Norris Turner thus proposes interpreting the harm principle as "merely an anti-paternalism principle, concerned with allocating decisional authority between society and the individual." For more, see his essay in this volume.

and controversial domains, without eliminating the possibility of dissent and conflict.

Mill's harm principle provoked three main lines of criticism: its "simplicity"; the feasibility of the distinction between "self-regarding" and "other-regarding" actions; and the utilitarian justification of an "absolute" freedom of thought and expression. First, was his principle truly simple? To answer this question, we should keep in mind that Mill wanted to apply consequential method to morals and avoid reference to *a priori* principles (among them "natural rights"). The "very simple principle" was not a mere rhetorical device, as he believed that unless our plurality of principles could be made to converge on one "ultimate" principle, our decisions in the practical domain would be shaky and contradictory. In *The System of Logic*, Mill writes (similarly to Kant) that "there must be some standard by which to determine the goodness or badness, absolute and comparative, of ends or objects of desire."[7]

The plurality of pleasures brought about by liberty needs to be ordered for individuals to make reasonable choices. Mill was a pluralist yet not a relativist; his ultimate principle was utility, which was *not* simple, as it could not be reduced to units of pleasure and pain, as we shall see in *Utilitarianism*. "Simple" was predicated on a maxim of practical judgment. "What has to be done?" is the question prompting Mill's simple principle. We are in the domain of practical philosophy, not metaphysics; the final station is the will or decision to act. In his Introduction to the 1996 Norton Critical Edition, Alan Ryan offered a clear example of what Mill meant by a "simple principle" that is not simple at all, as Mill himself knew: "Teachers have great difficulty judging the merit of their students, but the principle that should rank their students in order of merit is a simple principle. In the same way Mill's principle that we cannot interfere with other persons . . . to prevent harm to others is a simple principle but requires a complicated understanding of such ideas as 'harm' and a careful attempt to distinguish between compulsion and other ways of interference."[8]

The harm principle is a pragmatic principle that aims to make actors (state officials and ordinary citizens) good judges who make just decisions. "Justice" refers here to compliance with the goal of

---

7. And he continues: "And whatever that standard is, there can be but one: for if there were several ultimate principles of conduct, the same conduct might be approved by one of those principles and condemned by another; and there would be needed some more general principles, as umpire between them." *The System of Logic*, CW, vol. 8, p. 951. Kant wrote in his *Groundwork of the Metaphysics of Morals* that he concurred with Plato, who proposed "nothing more than the search for the *supreme principle of morality*" in which "the highest and unconditional good alone can be found." *Practical Philosophy*, trans. Mary J. Gregor (Cambridge: Cambridge UP, 1996), pp. 47 and 56.
8. Ryan, Introduction, p. xxxii.

respecting the "permanent interests" of the individual "as a progressive being." Within this pragmatic framework, Mill situated the distinction between "self-regarding" and "other-regarding" actions, and
the formulation that "the sole end" for interfering, individually or
collectively, with liberty of action is "self-protection." His intention
was to put limits on the extension of the harm principle, which could
end up justifying pervasive interference. To protect personal liberty
from interference from external opinion without renouncing consequentialist reasoning and the principle of utility—in effect, without resorting to "natural rights"—Mill had to elect some "permanent
interest," and this interest is the individual and its rich and various
life experience. This enlarged utility puts him in the camp of Kant
and Aristotle and makes Mill a perfectionist who was not truly
opposed to positive liberty or the aspiration to autonomy. This was
the criticism of Isaiah Berlin, who had no doubt that Mill wanted to
protect "the inner citadel," but had no doubt that "the search for freedom was a search for happiness."[9]

Mill's liberalism was certainly perfectionist, since liberty is not
simply a claim of noninterference with one's choice; but its perfectionism came in the form of exhortation rather than a doctrine concerning the best society. "Mill's concern for individual liberty rested
both on self-protection and on a doctrine of self-development."[1]
Self-protection had to be directly guaranteed by the state; self-
development was a prerogative of the single person and a moral
goal. The large immunity Mill grants to individual liberty in the
"inner culture" is an indication of the meaning we should give to
the adjective "progressive," which pertains to habit of mind more
than material well-being. This explains why he embarked on
the controversial distinction between "self-regarding" and "other-
regarding" actions. To traditional utilitarians, the distinction was
of no interest and potentially ludicrous, not only because the utility
of the largest number was their only maxim of practical judgment,
but also because "opinions" and "thoughts" are not actions anyway.

But the inner world Mill depicts is not "a space" in which sensations come and go, and it is not "a state" but rather a temporal pro-
gression of ideas and sensations, passions and opinions, whose
translation into actions is hardly predetermined and should not
interest the public authority. Mill's objection to classical utilitarianism was not simply that it did not offer a safety net for freedom of
thought and expression, but that in paying no attention to a person's
inner life (its complex and endless temporality), utilitarians were
unable to offer any effective justification for containing the possibility

9. See p. 263 below.
1. See Alan Ryan, essay in this volume.

that society interfered *ad libitum* with individuals' choices if the interests of the greater number were at stake. Mill extended this objection to Comte's positivism, whose planners of social progress— "an organized body of spiritual teachers and rulers" engaged in "temporal despotism"—aimed to form the mental habits that would make people not simply act in ways that aligned with progress, but do so with pleasure and enthusiasm, and without objections. Comte's system "stands as a monumental warning to thinkers on society and politics, of what happens when once men lose sight, in their speculations, of the value of Liberty and of Individuality."[2] Freedom of thought and expression is the core of the life of the mind, and respecting this freedom is the foundation of respecting individual judgment and will.

4. *A Liberty That Is Not Rights-Based*

The distinction between self- and other-regarding actions reveals a problem that only a society based on the rule of law and a government ruled by opinion are likely to experience. Mill was not interested in devising an ontology of self-regarding actions, nor was he preaching a moral doctrine of individual indifference. Rather, he was working out general criteria for legislators and judges who had to make decisions about what constituted harmful behavior. He knew all too well that no sphere of life can be disconnected from others and that any act can affect others. Citing the Maine Liquor Law ("prohibition legislation" justified by its supporters on the grounds that no individual action is purely self-regarding because all actions are social), he wrote, "[s]o monstrous a principle is far more dangerous than any single interference with liberty; there is no violation of liberty which it would not justify."[3] Thus although the act of a drunk person can cause pain to family or friends, it is not drinking habits that should concern society but only the subsequent harmful acts, when and if they occur. The decision to drink is self-regarding not because it is without consequences on others, but because it is the result of the personality or judgment of the actor. Society cannot try to eradicate people's desires, no matter how noble the underlying intention. This explains Mill's worry about "liberticide" positivism, whose vision of progress treated individuals like children in need of molding. Precisely because no one is an island, the distinction between "self-regarding" and "other-regarding" actions is a valuable maxim that avoids the language of "rights" but is helpful when rights are applied to specific cases.

2. *CW*, vol. 1, p. 221.
3. See pp. 79–80 below.

Mill's consequentialism has been a persistent source of criticism, particularly after World War Two and the renaissance of the philosophy of human rights and the contractarian justification of political legitimacy. Despite his revision of Bentham's utilitarianism, Mill is accused of evaluating both individual freedom and external interference with it from the perspective of the consequences of liberty rather than its firm deduction from the fountain of rights. To the chagrin of contemporary liberals, Mill's "ultimate" principle is not a substitute for rights. "I forgo," Mill writes, "any advantage from the idea of an abstract right as a thing independent of utility."

In refusing to counter society's arbitrary power with the appeal to "abstract rights," Mill sided with Bentham, who declared natural rights "simple nonsense: natural and imprescriptible rights, rhetorical nonsense—nonsense upon stilts."[4] Mill did not dismiss rights as the historical construction of legal immunities, as he clarified in *Utilitarianism*. He dismissed the "metaphysics" of an imaginary nature as the remnant of a theological approach that wanted people to believe in a value (their freedom) because it came from a superior good endowed with absolute authority (be it God, Nature, or Reason).[5] Reading modern societies as oscillating between the metaphysic of order (conservatives) and the metaphysic of revolution (Jacobins), Mill preferred an antimetaphysical perspective that stressed the practical consequences of actions, which would make people evaluate their actions from the perspective of their responsibility toward themselves and others.

But to believers in rights-based liberalism, Mill's progressive intention and the appeal to responsibility are not enough to make individual liberty safe from the decisions of majorities. One way of defending Mill would be to argue that unharming others would bring us to the same idea that rights entail, namely that the public is justified in intervening "directly" only in order to protect our "security," not to make us good people. Mill would agree with John Rawls's distinction between the right and the good as paramount for individual liberty. The harm principle, Brian Barry wrote, is not necessarily in contradiction with the theory of rights because both can make room for the maxim "Why should one lot of people tell another lot of people what to do if the others aren't hurting them?"[6] Like rights-based liberals, Mill thinks that "mankind" and the "individual" have the same basic interest in security, yet because of their unbalanced power, the basic interests of the individual need to be "protected"

4. Jeremy Bentham, 'Anarchical Fallacies': Nonsense upon Stilts: Bentham, Burke and Marx on the Rights of Man, ed. Jeremy Waldron (London: Methuen, 1987), p. 53.
5. *Auguste Comte and Positivism*, CW, vol. 10, pp. 299–300.
6. Brian Barry, *Political Arguments: A Reissue with a New Introduction* (Berkeley and Los Angeles: U of California P, 1990), p. 71.

against those of "humanity." To liberals, constitutional courts stop power and trump lawmaking assemblies. What is Mill's braking power?

On Liberty held up dissent, control, and surveillance as the primary conditions for containing state power. In *Considerations on Representative Government*, Mill proposed several parliamentary committees that would specialize and articulate (and thus limit) the decisionmaking power of the assembly. One of those committees played the role of a constitutional court (Mill used as his model the *graphē paranómōn*[7] council of lawmaking control in ancient Athens). But in the end, the only substantive protection was a persistent engagement by citizens defending their liberty. The battle would be intellectual and political and point to the formation of citizens' character, an issue extremely important in Mill's liberalism. We read in his *Auguste Comte and Positivism* that the means to overthrow the old hierarchic system of society is assigned to the first article of the liberal doctrine, "the absolute right to free examination and freedom of conscience," together with the "doctrine of equality" and a nondogmatic conception of the role of the state in economic life.[8]

Mill thought that the appeal to the harm principle would convince his readers that personal opinions and lifestyles were not dangerous to society, and that their free expression was a factor in society's advancement. Mill made these arguments on the assumption that people would choose liberty and that the more society allowed individuals to expand their potential, the more individuals would love liberty and be active in sustaining and protecting it.[9] One may infer that relying upon rights and legal immunities would not be sufficient, as the individual element is crucial both in the correct functioning of the institutions and in the selection of the priorities to be pursued. Mill would agree with Thomas Paine that the "interest of the public" does not spring immediately from the aggregate will of individuals, but has to emerge out of a multiplicity of views and interests that are transformed once they are expressed publicly and interact in the making of opinions.[1] Can we be sure that a constitution and a bill of rights are sufficient to secure liberty against those in government? After all, as Paine observed, relying on judges would not be enough, since judges are also human beings.

---

7. *Graphē paranómōn* was, in ancient Athens, public indictment against the proposer of a new decree and against proposals after they had been voted by the popular assembly; thus, both proposals and passed decrees could be indicted of being "against the law" or unconstitutional. A council made of sorted jurors was in charge of this function.
8. *CW*, vol. 10, p. 301.
9. Famously, John Rawls wrote that although there are "forceful arguments," the "liberties of equal citizenship are insecure when founded upon teleological principles," which are precarious because their foundations are unsolvable, "controversial," and "uncertain." *A Theory of Justice* (Cambridge, MA: Harvard UP, 1971), pp. 210–11.
1. Thomas Paine, *The Rights of Man*, in *Political Writings*, ed. Bruce Kuklick (Cambridge: Cambridge UP, 1989), p. 170.

Mill was conscious (this is the reason he wrote *On Liberty*) that "mankind" (society) could use the argument of "security" to include more than individual self-preservation among the things to be preserved, and the possibility worried him. Thus, he opposed any attempt by the state to create good, happy, or dependable citizens, which would be "liberticide." Society behaves like any other tyrant when it imposes itself "over the separate individuals who compose it."[2] It has been observed that the maxim "the sole end for which mankind are warranted . . . in interfering with the liberty of action of any of their number is self-protection" can also be claimed by an inquisitor who wants to protect eternal life or the integrity of the Church. Cardinal Robert Bellarmine, an inquisitor in Galileo Galilei's trial, understood that Galileo had discovered something new with his telescope, but had reasons to believe that the salvation of the soul was more valuable a good than scientific knowledge, and was actually the mark of true individual fulfillment. How to decide which life—physical or eternal—should be put first? "Damnation is harm along exactly the dimension that Mill wanted us to bear in mind: it is the utter absence and the extreme opposite of human excellence and flourishing."[3]

Mill would answer this objection, first with an assertion of plurality and the inability to let one person's or religion's beliefs act as a maxim for all of society, and second with the prospect of a permanent intellectual and political engagement in favor of a culture of respect regardless of the person's faith. Consequentialist reasoning does not make his argument less strong, although it makes it more demanding for the individual. One might say that this holds true also for the principle of rights, which would gain in strength by becoming an undisputed moral culture sufficiently rooted in ethical life to make citizens believe in rights, even when they are poorly applied or violated. Mill's consequentialism helps to strengthen the belief in liberty insofar as it makes each individual responsible for evaluating the effects of their actions.

Thus, more than judges and courts of rights, opinion is the central domain in which the defense of liberty and individuality takes place in *On Liberty*. Mill wanted to convince his readers that a dissenting society would not be unstable and offered a powerful exhortation on the positive way to approach liberty: not through an unconditional conception of freedom that insists on the negative (rights against the state), but through a conception that stresses the positive effects that arise from an individual who does not take refuge in conformism. Mill's argument might be a failure from the

---

2. David Lewis, "Mill and Milquetoast," in *Mill's "On Liberty": Critical Essays*, ed. Gerald Dworkin (Lanham, MD, and New York: Rowman & Littlefield, 1997), p. 10.
3. Ibid.

perspective of rights-based liberalism, but it is amazing that such a failure has been capable of attracting and mobilizing so many generations. It is also amazing that no rights-based liberal has produced such a ringing defense of free speech as Mill did. The best tribute they offer comes from Justice Oliver Wendell Holmes, Jr., who, in dissenting from a majority U.S. Supreme Court ruling that upheld the prosecution of an anarchist for his antiwar views under the Espionage Act of 1917, declared: "But when men have realized that time has upset many fighting faiths, they may come to believe even more than they believe the very foundations of their own conduct that the ultimate good desired is better reached by free trade in ideas—that the best test of truth is the power of the thought to get itself accepted in the competition of the market, and that truth is the only ground upon which their wishes safely can be carried out."[4]

5. *Freedom of Expression, Incitement, Communication*

We now move to the third of the central controversies in *On Liberty*, the utilitarian justification of freedom of thought and expression. Mill used both historical and moral arguments to prove the destabilizing effects of intolerance and the progressive force of dissent and conflict. The history of heretics in their resistance against Church orthodoxy proved that in an unfree environment, a minority can be induced to practice intolerance with its own members in order to strengthen its identity and better resist intolerance from outside. While escalating social divisions and niches of likemindedness, intolerance fosters an exclusionary dynamic that depresses the society as a whole. In *Considerations on Representative Government*, Mill resorts to an argument that recalls Machiavelli's praise of liberty in tumultuous societies when he claims that the greatness of Florence could not be ascribed to the Medicis' Renaissance and despotic pacification, but instead to its prior republican age, when social conflicts were relentless and still capable of making politics the terrain of institutional experimentation and political liberty. It is thus convenient for society that people with different ideas, lifestyles, and faiths are free to express themselves with no fear of being directly or indirectly coerced, even at the risk of generating violence. This is the main topic of Chapter II. "If the arguments of the present chapter are of any validity, there ought to exist the fullest liberty of professing and discussing, as a matter of ethical conviction, any doctrine, however immoral it may be considered."[5]

---

4. *Abrams v. United States*, 250 U.S. 616 (1919), dissenting opinion by Justice Holmes.
5. See n. 3, p. 16 below.

Mill devises several arguments, not all utilitarian, to make his case for free speech. For instance, free speech would be positive even if nothing came from it, as people may want to discuss ideas with no specific goal at hand. The good is not always connected to empirical outcomes and consists also in the climate of openness it creates, which is itself conducive to freedom. Mill derives this argument from Wilhelm von Humboldt, the philosopher of individuality as multiverse potentials. Freedom of speech is itself a source of enjoyment, assuming as Mill does that a public expression of "strong and various faculties" is a source of admiration and learning. With Humboldt, Mill believes that individual development has "two requisites, 'freedom' and 'variety of situations,'" and that "from the union of these arise 'individual vigor and manifold diversity,' which combine themselves in 'originality.'"[6]

Despite this Romantic revision of happiness, the consequentialist argument in favor of free speech retains a place of honor. Freedom of discussion is the soul of the searching habit conducive to progress, because it allows wrongs to amend themselves, and because a truth or a right that is worshipped and goes uncontested becomes a "dogma," detrimental both to itself and society, since it dries up vital energies and favors stagnation. Freedom of discussion is moreover a mark of respect for others: we should learn from the way people "actually reason"—"we should never have known by what process truth is to be ascertained, if we had not previously ascertained many truths."[7] This aspect of Mill's thought is perhaps the closest to democracy, if by democracy we mean a political system and a society in which ordinary citizens have the right to publicly express their minds, not only those who are cultured and competent. In ancient Greece, this liberty was called *parrhēsia*—telling the truth by speaking one's mind. The public cannot be reserved for the best, because this would exclude all those who are not the best. In a democracy, the bad or the wrong must be able to get up and speak.

The meaning of truth and its endogenous connection to error have sparked a huge debate among philosophers. James Fitzjames Stephen, who was Mill's contemporary and wrote the first devastating critique of his moral and political philosophy just after his death, stressed the absurdity of Mill's torment with even "the exhaustibility of musical combination" as an effect of a decline of human diversity. In the 1960s, both conservative and radical thinkers saw Mill's eulogy of disagreement as a prelude to a new homogeneity—the rule of opinions consistent with the liberal and rationalistic religion of humanity. To Herbert Marcuse, Mill's doctrine of toleration

6. See pp. 51–52 below.
7. *CW*, vol. 8, p. 833.

was a trap of conformism, and freedom of speech a strategy for over-coming diversity.

Mill treats "truth" as searching. This is key to his plea for liberty of thought and expression in "the matter of ethical conviction." At times, he uses "truth," "conviction," and "opinion" as synonyms; he claims that every opinion, even those (and indeed particularly those) we carry thoughtlessly, should be checked against experience, and in *The Subjection of Women* he uses this argument to prove the unjustifiability of the belief in women's natural inferiority. Theodor Gomperz, one of Mill's closest friends and a prominent scholar of Greek philosophy, proposed a parallel between the democratic leader of the Sophists, Protagoras, and Mill, since both of them proposed that "on every question there are two speeches, which stand in oppo-sition to one another."[8] *On Liberty*: "There is no such thing as abso-lute certainty, but there is assurance sufficient for the purpose of human life."[9] Several instances of this method appear in *Auguste Comte and Positivism*, when Mill analyzes the main assumed truths of his time, in economics, psychology and morality, and shows how they invariably have more than one side.

Mill's belief in dissent and discussion seems to stem from a belief that these activities keep mental energies in motion; free discussion is a gymnasium, much like Socratic dialogues. But on closer inspec-tion it appears that dissent is more than a training exercise; it is not supposed to instill skepticism but to strengthen beliefs: when an opinion has been tested by observation, experience, and discussion, people have sufficient grounds for holding it with more certainty. As Mill wrote to Henry Samuel Chapman, the main advantage of public opinion's sanction lies "not in compelling or inducing people to act as public opinion dictates, but in making it necessary for them, if they do not, to have a firm ground in their own conviction to stand on, and to be capable of maintaining it against attack."[1] Thus the point is not to test a belief's truth, since one can never be sure of the truth anyway. The point is that free discussion gives a surplus of force to our beliefs and makes us more engaged and less apathetic.

The vitality argument justifies his quest for tolerance in the spheres of politics, morality, religion, and taste, because it presumes that without a free exchange of ideas, good views will become rigid like dogmas and thus weak, insofar as those who believe them do not think they have to put any extra effort into defending them. The

8. Theodor Gomperz, *Greek Thinkers: A History of Ancient Philosophy*, trans. Laurie Magnus (London: John Murray, 1964), vol. 1, p. 463.
9. See p. 18 below.
1. July 8, 1858, *CW*, vol. 15, p. 559.

real target of the vitality argument was self-abnegation, which Mill contrasted with pagan self-assertion, as Ryan explains. Machiavelli would have loved this argument: he accused the established Church of stripping religion of its civic potential by making it a routinized series of rituals and dogmas ("And while, in the morality of the best Pagan nations, duty to the State holds even a disproportionate place . . . in purely Christian ethics, that grand department of duty is scarcely noticed or acknowledged"). However true or good an opinion may be, if it is not fully, frequently, and fearlessly discussed, if it does not have adversaries, it will cease to be held as a "living truth."[2]

According to Mill, intolerance of opinions involves, inevitably, a claim to infallible knowledge. Mill would not share in what today is called "militant democracy," the preemptive exclusion from the public arena of those ideas that the majority judges dangerous to the constitutional order. Silencing an opinion is to Mill like "robbing the human race" and risks freezing contrary ideas, thereby making them even more intolerant and threatening to social stability. It is safer to have "dangerous" political ideas in the open than to make them clandestine.

"Feeling as complete assurance" is what truth searching generates, neither objective truth nor indifference. Recall that Mill thought feeling was pivotal as it moves actions and is moved by actions in turn ("the food of feeling is action"). Thus, freedom of speech and expression are in direct communication with the will to act. If we translate into politics his maxim to never take beliefs as unchangeable truth, we must conclude that no achievement is irreversible, no matter how good and progressive. Thus for women and other subordinated groups, legal and moral equality works as a strategic support to be guarded and furthered. To liberals who consider rights the first and last trench of politics, Mill replies that vindicating rights and having them written in constitutions and bills is not the same thing as fully enjoying them. Thus, for instance, associating a right with an unquestioned truth may systematize it in codes and legalistic practices while demoting citizens' engagement with it. Mill was convinced that truth in the making was invariably coupled with freedom, a radical departure from many contemporary reformers. In this sense, he equally disdained and opposed the tyranny of the majority and the tyranny of the minority (philosopher kings, technocratic guardians, heretics), although scholars have usually stressed the former. Restraining civil liberty can originate at both ends, and

---

2. Niccolò Machiavelli, *The Discourses on the First Ten Books of Titus Livius* (written between 1513 and 1519), also known as *The Discourses*, book 1, chapter 12.

"whatever might be the evils of freedom, they could not be worse than the evils of restraint."

Mill's consequentialist logic works with a long-term perspective, and thus dedicating time to analysis and discussion is good even if the immediate outcome is bad. This is an argument against conformism and the temptation the public has to discriminate against unorthodox opinions. Excluding what the public deems useless, false, or obnoxious would limit public discourse by demoting or excluding a perspective that could actually help clarify people's thinking. To Mill, the good is discussion and rivalry more than any specific opinion or truth; the good is the searching habit of the mind. Hence, censorship is no less alarming than conformism.

When he speaks of "custom" and "opinion," Mill presumes an anthropological disposition to apathy, like surrendering to a view or a doctrine for the sake of psychological relaxation. To counter this habit, Mill is even willing to invent artificial situations of dissent: "So essential is this discipline to a real understanding of moral and human subjects, that if opponents of all important truths do not exist, it is indispensable to imagine them, and supply them with the strongest arguments which the most skillful devil's advocate can conjure up."[3] To conclude, the good of diversity (of lifestyles, sexual choices, religions, ideologies) is connected to that of liberty, as Humboldt argued, and society should reward both of them at the cost of risking some violence.

Having gone through Mill's arguments in favor of "absolute" liberty of thought and discussion, it's worth examining just how absolute this liberty is meant to be. After celebrating individuality as experimentation and an endless and fearless self-revision of ideas and beliefs in Chapter III, Mill goes on to discuss the limits of this liberty in the following chapters. The overall scope for limits is first laid out in Chapters II and III, when Mill discusses the difficulty of regulating competing and overlapping liberties between the different members of society. There would be no need to limit liberty if we were like atoms, just as there is no reason to regulate our liberty when we are alone in our rooms—no matter how heated the imaginary debate unfolding in our imaginations. Communicative relations within ourselves and with others define the immaterial space in which liberty of expression arises.

The space of communication is not owned by those who communicate and cannot be sanitized of contestation and conflict. Mill repeatedly stresses that ideas do not progress or change in isolation, which is one reason that despotic systems try to isolate individuals

3. See pp. 34–35 below.

from one another, and this argument returns in Mill's defense of the public expression of opinions, which nonetheless is not as fully unconstrained as our thinking. Which ideas or opinions are we absolutely free to publicly express? What is the difference, if any, between speech that leads to actions (like persuasion and incitement to action) and expressive acts or acts that are themselves forms of speech?

The U.S. Supreme Court has ruled in favor of flag burning as a protected form of expression; Greta Thunberg sitting outside the Swedish parliament building every Friday in the summer of 2018 to demand policies that address global warming is another recent example. For Mill, these are both actions-as-speech that therefore deserve full protection. But things get complicated as soon as *On Liberty* explores the *mode* and *circumstances* of our speech and uses them as relevant factors in evaluating where our "absolute" freedom ends. Interaction with each other's sensibilities reveals how demanding freedom of speech is and why Mill thinks that we have to be careful imposing limits. Thus according to Jonathan Riley, to Mill "expression" belongs to the "social" part rather than the "self-regarding" part of the conduct of an individual, and this excludes a politics of "free speech absolutism."[4]

Clearly, speech can be restricted if it intentionally incites harmful deeds, such as libels and blackmail, or, in the case of advertising and contract clauses, is deliberately untrue. In all these cases, Mill writes, speech "loses its immunity" because it becomes an action and falls under the harm principle as an "other-regarding" action. There are cases that also pertain to the mode and circumstances in which the speech was delivered and which are judged based on the emotion they arouse. *On Liberty* uses a corn dealer to illustrate: it is acceptable to claim that corn dealers starve the poor in print, in academic seminars, or in conversation among acquaintances and friends; but it is unacceptable to make the same statement to an angry crowd gathered outside the house of a corn dealer. Unlike in the previous cases, where words sought the truth, in this case they incite action, place the interests and even the life of the corn dealer in danger, and thus fall afoul of the harm principle.[5] Mill does not censure any idea without first considering the *mode* and *circumstance* within which it was made public. His argument is precautionary and based on the security of the person rather than the survival of the state. However, this distinction makes his argument not less but more problematic because it seems to limit full

4. See the essay by Jonathan Riley in this volume.
5. See p. 50 below.

freedom of discussion to the domain of truth seeking and exclude it from politics.

This is in line with his broader understanding of the link between speech, emotion, and action. As Mill learned from ancient orators, public speech is attentive to emotions because it is concerned with actions. Consequentially, "[N]o one pretends that actions should be as free as opinions. On the contrary, even opinions lose their immunity, when the circumstances in which they are expressed are such as to constitute their expression a positive instigation to some mischievous act."[6] But he recognizes that the link between speech, emotions, and action is variable. In the corn dealer example, he uses the word "instigation," implying a direct link between speech and action, but in *On Liberty* he also writes that there is "no natural connexion between strong impulses and a weak conscience." [7] We cannot assume that listening to a socialist orator in a crowded square will translate into an uprising against capitalists (although this is Mill's implication in the example of the corn dealer). Suspending freedom of speech would entail in this case applying the harm principle preventatively, blocking words before they reach people's minds.

To some critics, the idea of preventative censorship shows that the harm principle might escalate coercive interventions instead of containing them and should therefore be abandoned. George Kateb wrote that if we want to limit speech because it causes harm, then we will have to ban many forms of speech, starting with political and religious speech, which is frequently deceitful and crafted to incite intolerance and even violence.[8] Would a square packed with socialist demonstrators advocating for the abolition of private property be allowed in Mill's society? The answer is yes, but on condition that the orator does not point the finger at any specific person (especially if they are present in the square).

Again, Mill's solution raises as many problems as it solves and takes us to the principle of offense, which Mill also uses. In 2005, a Danish cartoonist published a series of caricatures of the Prophet Muhammad wearing a bomb-shaped turban, which set off violent protests by Muslims. The author declared that his cartoons were not intended to be "offensive" but to raise questions about self-censorship and the limitations on criticism of Islam in Western societies. Mill would reply: "Again, there are *many* acts which, being directly injurious only to the agents themselves, ought not to be legally interdicted, but which, if done publicly, are a violation of good manners and, coming thus within the category of *offenses* against

6. See p. 50 below.
7. See pp. 53–54 below.
8. George Kateb, "The Freedom of Worthless and Harmful Speech," in *Liberalism Without Illusions*, ed. Bernard Yack (Chicago and London: U of Chicago P, 1996), p. 226.

others, may rightfully be prohibited."[9] But of course, as any religious example demonstrates (and also many contemporary examples of so-called cancel culture), offense is a highly subjective state.

According to Mill, sincere reactions of disapprobation are legitimate free expression by anyone who happens to be offended as long as they are a spontaneous response, without malice, dissimulation, or incitement to further offend. Virtue is required in expressing our reprobation of those we judge unfavorably, for disagreement should never block the possibility of further communication. Thus, the style of our public expression (mode and circumstances) is an important component of freedom of expression. In other words, the public sphere of communication requires different modes of expression than those we use privately or with friends. Expression must not interfere with others' use of the same space, for words too can be a form of coercion.

This desire to avoid offense in the public sphere anticipates John Rawls's "virtue of civility" and fits in nicely with later theories of democratic deliberation. The limits we impose on ourselves are important because the "collision of ideas" can lead to coercion, as Mill pointed out on several occasions in criticizing the Enlightenment's abstract method of analysis and the radical style of disputation—a style he experienced in his youth and came to regard as indoctrinating in rather than emancipating from passivity. Mill's attention to public discourse translates seamlessly to the internet, where the rules of civility might in some ways be even more important given the potential for anonymity.

Full liberty to exchange ideas also implies public forums that are accessible to all and owned by none, and the association of "openness" with a "public" that is not identified with the state is a seminal contribution whose potential implications are even broader in our age than in Mill's. Yet much of its richness seems to rest on the circumvention of the harm principle more than on its literal application. Joel Feinberg made this point when he wrote that the only way Mill can make such claims of limitations of freedom of speech, as he does, is to endorse the "offense principle" and drop the harm principle.[1] Doing so is tantamount to admitting that the latter is not the *only* principle Mill built his argument on.

To explore this, let's return to the issue of "incitement." Incitement refers to words that inflame an audience, but it is complicated when applied to already emotionally charged subjects. Experts discussing how corn dealers increase the market price of wheat might

---

9. See p. 86 below (author's emphases).
1. Joel Feinberg, *Offense to Others: The Moral Limits of the Criminal Law* (Oxford: Oxford University Press, 1985).

be just as excited as the orators who speak to a mass of the poor gathered in front of a corn dealer's home. Mill appreciates and even encourages the former incitement but not the latter; extrapolating, we might say that the further an idea is from direct action, the more passionately involved speech about it can be. Thus, topics without direct implications or applications end up enjoying more latitude, which might seem contradictory in a book that praises individuality and eschews apathy. Enthusiasm is not foreign to incitement or to Mill's ideal society, which possesses a cacophonic public space, a bustling "marketplace of ideas" (a metaphor that Mill did not coin).[2] In such a society, citizens are permanently talking to defend their views and/or to convince others. Clearly, nobody is required to justify her opinions; they can simply assert their opinions, or start a polemical confrontation.

Dialogue is not mandatory, although Mill's progressive society can be measured by its broad acceptance of a dialogical style, nor does disagreement need to conclude with consensus; in fact, it rarely does. A scholar and admirer of ancient Greek philosophy, Mill was aware of the difference between eristic and dialectics, discussion for the sake of victory and dialogue for the sake of truth (as we saw, in his youth he participated intensely in clubs that practiced both styles of discussion). Mill's conception of happiness as the final goal of a progressive society rests on the assumption that in the long run, a society that makes room for pluralism of opinions, deliberation, and disputation is more open and tolerant, and also a society in which "civility" is at a high level and broadly distributed.

In such a society, animosity and incitement are inevitable, although not for mobilizing a crowd against any particular profiteering tradesmen. The form of animosity that discourse takes testifies to the degree of social progress. Mill's contemporary society needed labor unions to balance the unequal bargaining power of the higher classes, but he believed that the further a society progressed, the more complete and individual freedom could become. Mill was not against social conflict and was a sincere and active supporter of countless movements for emancipation and self-determination around the world. But *On Liberty* proposes a society in which material wants are mostly solved and security is not merely legal. In *Principles of Political Economy*, published well before *On Liberty*, he had made it clear that the distribution of wealth was a "matter of human institution solely" and thus an object of political deliberation.[3] In a letter to John Austin in 1847, he wrote that it seemed essential

---

2. The first reference to "free trade of ideas" was by Justice Oliver Wendell Holmes Jr. in *Abrams v. United States* (1919).
3. *CW*, vol. 2, p. 199.

to him that society at large not be "overworked, nor over-anxious about the means of subsistence."[4]

A critic could say that Mill was truly an idealist, since his society would be so socially harmonious that its members could freely and passionately discuss vital matters without using speech instrumentally to incite action. Mill's view of a discursive society uplifted by an open communication between diverse and equal citizens reminds us of Hannah Arendt's, especially since both choose an ideal *polis* as their model of the good society, where individuals discuss freely and are not driven by partisan affiliations tailored to class interests, a condition that would curtail both their individuality and their freedom of expression. Mill depicts a progressive society as a leisure society in the pure sense of the word: a society in which our life is freed from wants and our individuality can freely express itself, resulting in the leisure of experimentation and exploration among opinions and lifestyles. Ideas are never passionless, and their free circulation in public is a condition for stirring people's curiosity. Animosity and enthusiasm are not excluded, but must be unrelated to a cause (hence his hostility to political parties). This is the ideal horizon in which Mill situates his enlarged conception of utility and individuality as autonomy of judgment and the cultivated disposition to create one's life.

6. A Progressive Society

After Friedrich von Hayek published Mill's correspondence with Harriet Taylor in 1951, Mill's mental crisis and love affair with Mrs. Taylor became the object of psychological analysis, his conception of individuality read as a byproduct of sentimental and romantic intoxication, a medicine for healing his machinelike mind. In this light, individuality appeared to be a complication for liberalism and the source of unsolvable contradictions. In recent years, as part of a wave of scholarship on European imperialism and colonialism, a novel interpretation has gained momentum that finds traces of Great Britain's imperialistic ideology in Mill's individualism. Several elements in Mill's work support this interpretation: the distinction between civilized and uncivilized societies, which in effect translates to the differences between Western and non-Western peoples; the association of this distinction not simply with technological and material achievements, but also with the cognitive capacities of individuals; and finally, the use of that distinction to justify colonialism as a form of benevolent despotism with a civilizing mission. In this picture, Mill's conception of civilization and progress resembles a

4. 13 April 1847, *CW*, vol. 13, p. 713.

pyramid whose base was filled with colonized peoples who might slowly climb upwards with the help of their benefactor-colonizers. These charges are not unwarranted; the fact that nineteenth-century thinkers of all stripes, from Hegel to Comte to Tocqueville to Marx, shared a Eurocentric vision of progress does not absolve Mill, who defined and refined principles that could have brought him to more courageous and egalitarian outcomes. Yet as we saw and will more thoroughly explain at the conclusion of the introduction to *The Subjection of Women*, within the European context, ideas of progress were not homogenous and identical, and their differences deserve to be considered when evaluating their respective civilizing ambitions.

In *On Liberty*, "backwardness" was not circumscribed to an area of the world and was a temporal category, not a spatial one: it included European countries, past and present, and in relation to "civil, and social liberty" also encompassed Great Britain. In addition, all individuals start "barbarian" as we slowly liberate ourselves from ready-made opinions and one-sided views, and the goal of civilization is not one mode of thought or life, but the ability to choose them freely. Progress is a way of thinking, and although we may disdain Mill's permanently dissatisfied, quarrelsome individuals, and may dislike the crude and uncensored language he employs to describe states of civilization that do not yet accord to this vision of liberty, it is important to emphasize that Mill did not think this specific "backwardness" belonged exclusively to colonized people, even if he did think colonized peoples could benefit from European tutelage.

All European nations were backward according to his ideal of liberty, and many were "above England" in "moral and intellectual liberty," albeit "inferior to it as to political freedom."[5] Moreover there is no clear link between Mill's self-questioning individual and imperial arrogance; his ideal is more reminiscent of Kant's *sapere aude* ("the transcendent worth of virtue and wisdom . . . and the infinitely superior eligibility of the just life"[6]). Fundamentally, Mill had an egalitarian conception of human potentials, and his idea of freedom from subjection was a work in progress inclusive of the many present and future forms of discrimination and infantilization.

Contrast this with positivism. Comte and the positivist culture in the age of the French Second Empire ascribed "permanent interests" to society first; they rendered the *summum bonum* as the "unity" of the collective, in relation to which the individual's well-being was functional and not extensible to all persons equally.

---

5. To Pasquale Villari, March 9, 1859, *CW*, vol. 15, p. 550 [*Editor's translation from the French*].
6. Mill, "The Gorgias" and "Grote's Plato," *CW*, vol. 11, pp. 97 and 415.

Comte conceived racial, national, and gender differences as embody-
ing biological inequalities, and pushed some of them outside any
discussion of moral progress. His hierarchical society comprised
layers of functional subjections, with acquired competence (the
leaders) on top and the mere reproduction of auxiliary roles (women
and inferior races) below. Historically, this doctrine of progress primarily inspired policies of social and cultural integration in the
early decades after the French revolutions (1789–1852) and subsequently nourished the celebration of industrialization and ethnic
nationalism. This counterrevolutionary vision was particularly important in shaping the ideological culture of European nations that
reached their political independence in the final years of Mill's life. As
historians have documented, the positivist doctrine of social progress
was an important component of the ideological terrain that gave way
to fascism after World War One. Most of the imperial and colonialist
ideology that the European nation-states pursued in those decades
was inspired by a vision of progress which sought to pacify domestic
societies, partly through colonization. Thus, the positivist doctrine
of progress *was* an ideological weapon of colonial imperialism; but
it did not belong to Mill.

Mill overturned the positivist logic by making "the individual as
a progressive being" the *summum bonum*. Such an individual would
not be "progressive" according to a ready-made and homogenous
model insofar as the state and society did not determine the meaning of individual happiness, nor were they in charge of providing it.
Like Kant, Mill opposed state paternalism in societies that had
solved the problem of "security" (which Kant would define as "republican" or constitutional). As mentioned, Mill did not wholly drop
paternalism and applied it to peoples who were not yet capable of
governing themselves through the sole command of the laws and
political institutions based on consent (representative government).
His social philosophy was historicist and contextualist; it assumed
that social and cultural conditions were not indifferent to the stability of political regimes. Mill did not think that the best form of
government for some European states could be imposed everywhere
in the world because of their absolute worth. Moreover, he was not
a determinist and did not think history was driven by natural laws
toward a predetermined end, which helps us understand Mill's conception of the "permanent interests" of the individual as a "progressive being."

He used the term "progress" in relation to the expansion of inner
potential, pertaining to the world of the mind and sentiments first
and foremost. Moreover, this individual was not individualistic but
a cooperator: it "is not a question of quid pro quo in respect to his
cooperation, but of how much the circumstances of society permit

to be assigned to him, consistently with the just claims of others."[7]
Mill never used the word "individualism," which he considered a
defect and a vice. A progressive society would be comprised of and
educate cooperative persons and committed citizens, who entertain a permanent and sincere communication on the most relevant
issues. Communication entails the desire to be part of a conversing
community; moreover, it entails people who listen and are not indifferent or dismissive; and finally, it presumes interference with each
other's minds not for the sake of imposing beliefs but to encourage
critical reflection. This makes us appreciate his revised conception
of utility and happiness, which plays a crucial role in the justification of freedom of speech and expression. The more the "permanent
interests" were identified with external qualities, the more the person would run the risk of becoming a manufactured being, her personality identified with her social functions and the reproduction
of the values of her community or her economic performance. To
counter that view, Mill situated the "permanent interests" in the
process of freedom of discussion and dissent, which resembles
today's ideal of deliberative democracy. Cooperation with others
took the form of communication among free and mature individuals treating themselves with equal respect. The direction of flourishing could not be predetermined, for it was an individual process
and choice.

Mill was not a neutralist. He thought that some goals and some
models of individual life were more valuable than others: as we shall
see below, a dissatisfied Socrates is inherently superior to a satisfied pig in his philosophy. Yet persons are different and their differences will not disappear through communicative intertwining. Mill's
progressive society is not like a state of nirvana in which the final
solution of wants will reward a lifelong struggle. Different stimuli
are a starting point for individuals to develop in various and unpre-
meditated directions, so that no individual's achievement is final, but
is constantly unspooling. A progressive society of this kind is not
spared the risk of decline, and Mill is particularly wary of "dead
dogma," which is any idea that has ceased being questioned and
refined. Not even scientific knowledge can avoid dissent when thrown
in the forum, as we learned during the COVID-19 pandemic.
Even Newton's gravitational principle would find opponents in the
public, Mill wrote. Thus, his idea of a progressive conception of individuality creates a society in which there is a broad acceptance of
the fallible condition of our knowledge, leading to the habit of critical reflection on all issues.

7. *Auguste Comte and Positivism*, CW, vol. 10, p. 341.

Utilitarianism

"Mill's concern with self-development and moral progress is a strand in his philosophy to which almost everything else is subordinate."[8] *Utilitarianism* is a pillar of this strand and a complement to *On Liberty*. It is a clever attempt to reformulate the doctrine of utilitarianism in a way that emancipates it from becoming materialistic and indifferent to "the internal culture of the individual."[9] Like *On Liberty*, *Utilitarianism* was addressed primarily to a "popular audience" and "written with this readership in view" (it appeared in three parts in *Fraser's Magazine* in 1861, and then in book form in 1863).[1] Like *On Liberty*, it was conceived as the tract of a minority position; Mill insisted on several occasions, above all with his friends from the continent, that it was wrong to think that the philosophy of utility was dominant in his country; on the contrary it was "très impopulaire" (very unpopular). "Most English scholars not simply deny it but insult it: and Bentham's school has always been regarded (I say it with regret) as a meaningless minority."[2] But utilitarianism's critics thought otherwise. Bentham and his followers, Carlyle thundered, have imbued popular morality with the belief "that our happiness depends entirely on external circumstances; nay, that the strength and dignity of the mind within us is itself the creature and consequence of these. Were the laws, the government, in good order, all were well with us; the rest would care for itself!"[3]

In fact, consequentialism and the principle of pleasure were the two halves of Bentham's doctrine that Mill discusses and defends in his book, which was not written in the form of a manifesto like *On Liberty*, but as a defense against misconceptions, in particular against those that reinforced the popular image of utility as a "morality of the swine," indifferent to the "inner culture," and essentially preoccupied with outcomes. While perhaps exaggerating utilitarianism's minority position, Mill was right in lamenting its bad reputation. In his country, the repugnance for a "pig philosophy" was widespread among intellectuals: Carlyle mocked it in almost all of

---

8. Alan Ryan, *The Philosophy of John Stuart Mill* (London: Macmillan, 1970), p. 255.
9. *CW*, vol. 1, p. 147.
1. Mill wrote the chapters of *Utilitarianism* when *Considerations on Representative Government* had just been published and while writing *The Subjection of Women*: "Soon after this time I took from their repository a portion of the unpublished papers which I had written during the last years of our married life, and shaped them, with some additional matter, into the little work entitled *Utilitarianism*; which was first published in three parts, in successive numbers of *Fraser's Magazine*, and afterwards reprinted in a volume." *CW*, vol. 1, pp. 265–66.
2. To Charles Dupont-White, 10 October 1861, *CW*, vol. 15, p. 745 [*Editor's translation from the French*].
3. See Colin Heydt's essay in this volume; and Alan Ryan, Introduction to *John Stuart Mill and Jeremy Bentham, Utilitarianism and Other Essays* (London: Penguin, 1987), p. 12.

his writing, from *Sartor Resartus* (1836) to *Latter-Day Pamphlets* (1850); Charles Dickens offered a pitiful image of it in *Hard Times* (1854); and the idealist Francis H. Bradley would some years later devote his *Ethical Studies* (1876) to the task of demystifying the primacy of pleasures and the gospel of hedonism in moral philosophy.

Mill's complaint made sense of his project to a) take utilitarianism out of the corner of eighteenth-century radicalism and b) make it a conception of justice capable of inspiring individual responsibility and conscience without transcending reason and attention to the consequences of action. It is hard to tell whether he succeeded given the massive criticism his revisionist move provoked, and some have written that the book was made important by the "efforts of its opponents rather than those of its friends."[4] Bertrand Russell wrote that Mill, his godfather, failed for the simple reason that his project was wrong: utilitarianism was an art of prudence, not a moral philosophy, because we cannot deduce the desirability of pleasure from the fact that it is desired.[5] The "is" cannot be used to deduce the "ought," and scientific rationality is not the same as ethical rationality.

In *Utilitarianism* Mill grappled with all the critics ("trascendentalists," "theists," and "*a priori* moralists") under the rubric of "intuitionism," an approach that held moral principles self-evident and true *a priori* and whose main English interpreter was the Cambridge philosopher William Whewell, who enlarged the gap, Mill lamented, between the two schools and declared utilitarianism to be against "conscience, duty, rectitude."[6] A typical intuitionist objection runs as follows: since utilitarianism lacks any moral criterion independent of pleasure (or a transcendental law commanding duty) and thus cannot offer the individual any ordering criterion of preferences other than personal pleasure, utilitarians resort to positive laws (coercion) to solve the unavoidable tension between individual and social interests. Moral intuitionism (Whewell) and deontological ethics (Kant) agreed that in order to judge actions morally we should appeal not to their consequences but to the conformity of their motives to certain rules of duties, whose source is theistic (Whewell) or a principle of reason (Kant)—and only on this condition does moral duty exist independent of legal obligation and the analysis of the consequences. "Do the right thing because you have to do it, no other reason attached," Kant would say.

---

4. John Skorupski, *John Stuart Mill* (London: Routledge, 1989), p. 2.
5. "John Stuart Mill, in his *Utilitarianism*, offers an argument which is so fallacious that it is hard to understand how he can have thought it valid." Bertrand Russell, *History of Western Philosophy* (London: Taylor & Francis e-Library, 2005 [1946]), p. 702. Russell reiterated the criticism made by G. E. Moore in *Principia Ethica* (1903).
6. John Stuart Mill, "Whewell on Moral Philosophy" (1852), *CW*, vol. 10, p. 172.

As Colin Heydt demonstrates in "Mill, Bentham and 'Internal Culture,'" Mill tried to rehabilitate utilitarianism by making the "inner culture" a source of duty and judgment of pleasures, without deriving it from religious command or *a priori* assumptions; he made it transcendental as to the disinterestedness of duty and consequentialist as to the ultimate test of what is worth pursuing. However, this revised utilitarianism was a compromise that sounded contradictory to many. To attain his goal, Mill relied essentially on moral culture and the education of character, thus instilling in each person the first virtues of justice—equality and impartiality—which were the maxims of the very meaning of "Utility, or the Greatest Happiness Principle."[7] "The sanction, so far as it is disinterested, is always in the mind itself; and the notion therefore of the transcendental moralists must be, that this sanction will not exist in the mind unless it is believed to have its root out of the mind itself."[8] Mill answered both intuitionists and deontologists, Whewell and Kant, and tried to prove that it is possible to have moral duty without transcending human experience through the command of God, and without proceeding from a pure command of reason independent of outside motives, sentiments, and education. In addition, while "unwilling to acknowledge [*a priori* duty] as the fundamental principle of morality," Mill wanted to prove to "those *a priori* moralists" that the utilitarian arguments were "indispensable" to explain their own doctrine of duty.

The controversy brought him not merely to restate utilitarianism, but to reformulate it: a) by connecting happiness to a theory of moral duty based on empirical evidence; b) by moving from pleasures to happiness and situating "the very meaning of utility" in the happiness of humanity; and c) by making the latter the superior pleasure that each individual could feel as qualitatively superior, thus transforming it into a desired duty. His reformulation pivoted on a reinterpretation of pleasure as a complex experience springing not solely from bodily sensations but also from intellectual and aesthetic faculties, thanks to which individuals acquired the ability to distinguish and prioritize among pleasures. This ordering ability derived not from some *a priori* assumptions but from education: while the rightness of an action is to be judged solely by its consequences, the quality of pleasures can be experienced and appreciated better if intellectual faculties are cultivated.[9] These pleasures make a better life, for the individual and society, and together comprised the Greatest Happiness Principle, which would be "a mere form of words . . .

---

7. See p. 108 below.
8. See p. 128 below.
9. According to Elizabeth Anderson, Mill's cultivation of the nonutilitarian sentiments was one of the chief constituents of the good life." See her essay below.

unless one person's happiness, supposed equal in degree (with the proper allowance made for kind), is counted for exactly as much as another's."[1] Individual responsibility, reciprocity, and equality were the criteria of disinterestedness that Mill applied to his enlarged interpretation of utility. He thought that in starting from "the conception of our own happiness as a unit, neither more nor less valuable than that of another," he brought utilitarianism to concur with "the doctrine of loving one's neighbor as oneself"[2] and to answer the objection that it did not have other resources of obligation except for the coercion of the law.

These are the main themes of *Utilitarianism*, in which Mill first defines utilitarianism, then delineates the main lines of criticism (Chapters I and II), goes on to analyze the external and internal sanctions (Chapter III) and to explain happiness and the parts composing it (Chapter IV), and finally defines the principle of justice not only as a legal expedient but as a moral duty derived from the Greatest Happiness Principle (Chapter V). His overall goal is to make utilitarianism a moral philosophy, capable of inspiring disinterested actions or actions of justice that elect the happiness of humanity as the "great moral duty" that justifies an individual's voluntary sacrifice of her interests. There is room for moral duty in utilitarianism, for choosing to do good not because of an external source of deterrence like legal obligation. This argument was crucial because moral laws, including some prescribing justice, cannot be enforced as positive laws as their moral nature rests precisely in being the expression of a person's voluntary choice and even sacrifice. In a word, Mill's revision of utilitarianism consisted in connecting the morality of the Greatest Happiness Principle to virtues, and only secondarily to legal expedience.

He achieved this outcome without resorting to extra-empirical principles and renouncing consequentialism by turning to the role of opinion and persuasion (moral culture and socialization) as a means of sanctioning wrongdoing and inspiring morally valuable action.[3] As he wrote to Grote in 1862, thanks to education, the sacrifice of individual interest would become a reasoned choice of the individual: "I am very glad that you like the papers on Utilitarianism so much. I am not more sanguine than you are about their converting opponents. The most that writing of that sort can be expected to do, is to place the doctrine in a better light, and prevent

1. See p. 156 below.
2. Mill to Grote, *CW*, vol. 15, p. 762.
3. "There are many acts, and a still greater number of forbearances, the perpetual practice of which by all is so necessary to the general well-being, that people must be held to it compulsorily, either by law, or by social pressure. These acts and forbearances constitute duty." Mill, "Thornton on Labour and Its Claims" (1868–69), *CW*, vol. 5, pp. 650–51.

the other side having everything their own way, and triumphing in their moral and metaphysical superiority as they have done for the last half century."[4]

To understand Mill's project, a reading of *Utilitarianism* should pay attention to some key aspects: his relationship with Bentham's philosophy and its critics; the role he ascribed to education and socialization in the formation of moral habits; his conception of "quality" and "quantity" pleasures, in relation to which he proposed the figure of the competent judge; and finally, the debt of his revised utilitarianism to classical culture and virtue ethics. These aspects, deeply intertwined and hard to disentangle, should help us understand how Mill approached and resolved his basic problem: making utilitarianism a moral philosophy.

1. Questioning the Opposites

Utilitarianism was the culmination of a tormented theoretical and spiritual journey that had started in the early 1830s, along with Mill's criticism of "the commercial spirit" of the age and the exclusive "concern" with material well-being.[5] He never questioned his belonging in Bentham's school, not even when he felt attracted to the anti-Benthamites ("I am still, & am likely to remain, a utilitarian; though not one of 'the people called utilitarians'").[6] If anything, his familiarity with the Romantic school made him determined to rescue utilitarianism from the accusations that it preached selfishness, individualism, and materialism, and this defense takes up the second chapter. Mill situated utilitarianism within the controversy on the criterion of right and wrong, or the method by which principles of morals were derived, whether empirically or intuitionally. Unlike their critics, utilitarians believed that right and wrong were objects of "observation and experience" like true and false and any other verifiable data. Mill applied his method to explain the assumptions of intuitionists and argued that they were also consequentialists, albeit unknowingly, because what they deemed an *a priori* duty was really a residue of reiterated experiences of "favor or aversion" whose genesis was forgotten. *A priori* assumptions were "a consecration of men's actual sentiments," much like "effects of things" on human sensations of pleasure and pain; in addition, they were functional to the status quo. Thus, why not make utilitarianism the object of social education? From the Coleridge school and the French

4. Mill to George Grote, 10 January 1862, *CW*, vol. 15, p. 763.
5. To Gustave d'Eichthal, 15 May 1829, *CW*, vol. 12, pp. 31–32.
6. To Carlyle, 12 January 1834, *CW*, vol. 12, p. 207. And in the *Autobiography*: "I never, indeed, wavered in the conviction that happiness is the test of all rules of conduct, and the end of life. But I now thought that this end was only to be attained by not making it the direct end." *CW*, vol. 1, p. 145.

positivists, Mill learned that society as a whole is like "a system of education" presiding over the formation of moral norms through a multilayered relational structure, from family, schooling, and the workplace to politics and government. As an indirect "restraining discipline," this process of social education of moral sentiments could be oriented toward different (and even conflicting) goals, such as selfish individualism, docility, and subjection—but also individual self-dependence, sympathy, and cooperation.[7] As Georgios Varouxakis writes, Mill attempted "to adapt and translate to the intellectual climate of the nineteenth century a world-view and aspirations rooted in the Enlightenment of the eighteenth century while purging the latter of what he saw as its historical immaturity and naiveté."[8]

The "social feeling of mankind" and the "desire to be in unity with our fellows" have to be instilled by education. But it is surprising that in *Utilitarianism* Mill resorted to opinion as the teacher, which in *On Liberty* was judged tyrannical. The difficulty is perhaps resolved if we clarify that the pressure of opinion on the individual is not oppressive insofar as it is imbued with the values of autonomy and happiness to humanity, and teaches persons to think with their minds and never rely on ready-made beliefs. As we have seen in analyzing the problem of "instigation" in *On Liberty*, the kind of progressive society Mill envisaged was not made up of atomistic selves; it was a society in which social conflicts over scarce resources (and thus the permanent engagement of the many with the satisfaction of quantitative pleasures) would be largely solved and attention to individual autonomy would strengthen social cooperation. Reference to moral customs was thus meant not only to prove that intuitionism was socially constructed, but also to construct a utilitarian ethical culture that would replace the previous one with an enlarged sentiment of happiness. This is the theme of Chapter III, which claims utilitarianism as a progressive ideal promoting the general happiness of humanity by forming moral habits and feelings of obligation.[9] As was evident already in his essays on Coleridge (the representative of the Conservatives) and

---

7. See pp. 128–29 below.
8. See p. 358 below.
9. Education was one of Mill's most persistent topics. In 1834, he defended the motion by Roebuck in the House of Commons for the appointment of a "committee to consider the subject of national education." On that occasion, he strongly supported "schools for all, without distinction of sect, and without imposing upon any sect the creed or observances of another." He defended the method of Pestalozzi and had strong words against the existing system of popular education for "the working classes of England," deficient both in "quantity" (i.e., instruction) and "quality" (i.e., education). Instruction as "repetition by rote" or mental passivity was his main topic, which resonated in all his writings, particularly those collected in this book. See "Reform in Education" (1834), CW, vol. 21, pp. 63–64.

Bentham (the representative of the Philosophic Radicals), Mill was advancing a solution that on the one hand confirmed the validity of the school of Bentham and on the other hand amended the latter's "negative" method of analysis, with a novel sympathy for feelings that were only indirectly derivable from bodily sensations and yet no less real, and a source of even superior pleasures.[1] Mill did not reject the doctrine of pains and pleasures; however, he pluralized the sources and characters of pleasures; more important, as we shall see, he rendered pleasures "both in point of quantity and quality" the name of a permanent search for desirable and refined things, like a habit of the mind that was consistent with the fallibility and searching-for principles he defended in *On Liberty*.

In Chapter IV of *Utilitarianism*, we read that "happiness is a good" but is only "*one* of the ends of conduct and consequently one of the criteria of morality," not the only one; for example, the "desire" of "virtue and the absence of vice" is also a pleasure: "there are other ends of human action besides happiness."[2] Mill's long-standing project of "reconciliation of opposites"[3] reached maturity thanks to a reconceptualization of happiness in terms that resembled Aristotle's virtue ethics more than Bentham's and his father's tallying of pleasure and pain. Mill's theory was more than an endeavor against intuitionism; his new utilitarianism was a progressive ethical culture capable of inspiring individual behavior, general opinion, and political decisions, stretching well beyond the sectarian appeal of the Radicals.

Mill was a reformed Benthamite. "Bentham has been in this age and country the great questioner of things established," who shook "the yoke of authority" and compelled "innumerable opinions, formerly received on tradition as incontestable," to give an account of themselves.[4] A critical thinker like Voltaire in France, no one before Bentham "dared to speak disrespectfully of the British constitution and English law"; he desecrated whatever was assumed sacred and considered mere historical artefact what was thought of as eternal and immutable. His method of argumentation, based on a sharp logical dissection of incongruences and sophistries, fulfilled an invaluable "negative" task against ready-made assumptions. Mill reiterated throughout his entire intellectual career the crucial role

1. "The principle of utility does not mean that any given pleasure, as music, for instance, or any given exemption from pain, as for example health, are to be looked upon as means to a collective something termed happiness, and to be desired on that account." See p. 134 below.
2. See p. 133 below.
3. Capaldi, *John Stuart Mill*, p. 89.
4. "Death of Jeremy Bentham" (*Examiner*, 10 June 1832), *CW*, vol. 23, pp. 467–73; Bentham "attempted to give a rule to all human conduct" without having a comprehensive conception "either of the agencies by which human conduct *is*, or of those by which it *should* be influenced."

Bentham played: a giant who did not only destroy, because in order to "discredit erroneous systems" he needed to refer to principles and could not simply state "mere *results*." His principle was utility; his rule of action was prudence; and his method was evidence. Through his analysis, Bentham denounced and rewrote laws and procedures, making them simpler and their language accessible to all. His Enlightenment made justice of "the rubbish of pretended natural law, natural justice, and the like," which was in effect a system of "imposture."[5]

Mill took over from where Bentham ended, but not before correcting the "one-sidedness" of his basic principle of utility and his deconstructive method.[6] As mentioned earlier, to him Bentham resembled Polyphemus, a "one-eyed" theorist whose deconstructing analysis was as sharp as his understanding of other points of view was inept ("he occupied very little in studying the ideas of others," which he considered wrong and distracting). Mill sought to emend utilitarianism, free it from its sectarian origins, and reach a broader audience. *Utilitarianism* starts with a criticism of the Kantian method (*a priori*), but then gradually orients the idea of a moral life toward Kant's goal: act as if your action be adopted as a maxim of moral obligation by all moral beings, a maxim that commands the respect of the person and its self-development.[7] To Grote, Mill confessed that he considered "happiness as a unit . . . or, in Christian language, the doctrine of loving one's neighbor as oneself," wherein he translated love as "perfect ethical impartiality between the two."[8]

The conversations Mill maintained throughout the years with Benthamites, anti-utilitarians (i.e., Romantics), and French positivists are detectable in the conditions he thought would advance an ethical culture of social progress: a) education, by which he meant the formation of the habit of obedience to moral obligation based on accountable evidence, not blind faith;[9] b) the construction of "something permanent, and not to be called in question," which the conservatives identified with loyalty to maxims of traditional morality and Mill with "some fixed point" in the ethical life of society as anticipated in *On Liberty*; and c) the promotion of "a strong and active principle of cohesion," which French positivists identified with the religion of humanity and Mill with "sympathy" or a sense of

5. *CW*, vol. 23, pp. 470–71.
6. Ibid., p. 472.
7. Mill formulated a "synthesis" of teleology (consequentialism) and deontology (*a priorism*), and his utilitarianism "presupposes a nonutilitarian doctrine that specifies some content to the human good." Capaldi, *John Stuart Mill*, pp. 260 and 262.
8. To Grote, *CW*, vol. 15, 762.
9. Wendy Donner suggests that Mill's work "needs to be read against the background of his more scholarly writing in *A System of Logic* and his editorial footnotes to James Mill's *Analysis of the Phenomena of the Human Mind*." See p. 286 below.

"union" that made no part of society feel foreign to the rest and no part achieve permanent privileges in government. The aim of education was to make individuals choose to behave responsibly, and to construct the sovereignty of individual judgment as the "fixed point" ("[what] men agreed in holding sacred") holding society together, "the common estimation placed beyond discussion," like second nature.[1]

As a result, individuality would gain both legal codification (utilitarianism as expediently enforceable rules of justice) and moral legitimacy (thanks to the stabilization of rational and self-reflective practices); it would permeate the positive laws and ethical life (sentiment of sympathy and cooperation). Mill's utilitarianism embodied Bentham's just as his ethical morality embodied the legal component. These two facets composed the fabric of a progressive culture, with *On Liberty* defining its "fixed point" and *Utilitarianism* translating that point into social morality.

Searching for a common denominator to bridge opposite schools did not require abandoning the utilitarian camp. Mill did not doubt that his conception of happiness could be reinterpreted without betraying utilitarianism. The kernel of his project was spelled out already in his Diary on March 23, 1854:

> The only true or definite rule of conduct or standard of morality is the greatest happiness, but there is needed first a philosophical estimate of happiness. Quality as well as quantity of happiness is to be considered; less of a higher kind in preferable to more of a lower. The test of quality is the preference given by those who are acquainted with both. Socrates would rather choose to be Socrates dissatisfied than to be a pig satisfied. The pig probably would not, but then the pig knows only one side of the question: Socrates knows both.[2]

Notice that Mill does not disclaim "quantitative" pleasures or think that a pig should not seek satisfaction: he prescribes happiness "both in point of quantity and of quality."[3] What he disclaims is the "one-eyed" approach: the problem with the pig is that he is totally concentrated on satisfying one and only one kind of pleasure and deprives himself of the possibility of expanding his experience toward other pleasures. But this also holds true with people who pursue only "qualitative" pleasures and disdain "quantitative" ones. Mill was no ascetic. In all spheres, he was opposed to one-sided models as they tended to be undergirded by assumptions of superiority or infallibility, and thus the adhesion to a creed by only the force of

1. "Coleridge," CW, vol. 10, p. 134.
2. CW, vol. 27, p. 663. He uses similar words in *Utilitarianism*; see p. 111 below.
3. See p. 112 below.

authority. Once again *On Liberty* and *Utilitarianism* reinforce the same theme of independence forged through plurality.

2. *The Competent Judge and the Place of Equality*

An important obstacle to Mill's bridging project, at least from a conservative standpoint, was the egalitarian character of utilitarianism, which did not recognize any representative authority and considered each individual the sole judge of her sensations of pain and pleasure. Carlyle's criticism was vitriolic: in 1849 he charged utilitarianism of erasing the "qualitative" character of labor as service to intelligence and creativity by transforming it into paid labor to be judged according to a "quantitative" criterion (the labor time) in a perfect egalitarian logic.[4] How would Mill fulfill his conciliatory task without sacrificing the egalitarian appeal of Bentham's philosophy and conceding to Carlyle's aristocratism?

First, by introducing the figure of the competent judge. In theory, individuality allows people to become competent judges in morals and thus the best evaluators of what is of superior "quality" among two pleasures. As Bentham famously wrote, only the wearer can tell if her shoe pinches, no one else, no matter whether endowed with superior knowledge. In practice, however, few become competent judges. Neither Bentham nor Mill suggests that all are equally competent to make decisions; knowing where my shoe pinches does not teach me how to fix it.

In the political realm, Mill bridges this divide between democratic potential and aristocratic reality through representation. Political representatives should be chosen from among the best "advocates," and not merely among those who are alike: a fool might not be the best representative of the interests of fools. Although he believed Parliament should be a microcosm of the nation, Mill defended proportional representation not to reproduce society in miniature but to mix the logic of the mirror with that of competence: citizens should choose a good advocate of their cause, a *point d'appui* who needed to be not "like" them but close to them.[5]

Returning to competent judges in morality, Mill and Bentham would agree that the individual is the first judge of her interests (an important acknowledgment of the role of the public and the individual right to suffrage), but they were not fully egalitarian in their administrative solutions. Bentham opposed aristocratic (i.e., unelected) government (which acted as if they knew the needs of the people without

---

4. Thomas Carlyle, "Occasional Discourse on the Negro Question," *Fraser's Magazine* 40 (1849): 670–79. See Mill's answer: "The Negro Question" (1850), *CW*, vol. 21, pp. 85–95.
5. *Considerations on Representative Government* (1861), *CW*, vol. 19, p. 459.

bothering to consult with them) but did not argue for equal participation in government. The example of the pinching shoe was meant
to prove that getting information from the public would allow those
in power to pursue the "universal interest," but it doesn't mean
decisions don't need competent agents.[6] Nonetheless, Bentham gave
a unique authority to citizens' judgment, and in this sense he
opened the path to the idea that "acting for someone else independently and with discretion is not possible."[7] Mill followed Bentham
and in *Considerations on Representative Government* made communication between institutions and society the spirit of representative politics.

Thus, while Mill's idea of the competent judge did go beyond
the radical party, it was not more inegalitarian than Bentham's
theory. However, the difference between the two was not trivial,
and Bentham does appear more egalitarian than Mill when it comes
to judging our sensations and pleasures. "It is not necessary," Bentham wrote, "to consult Plato, nor Aristotle. Pain and pleasure are
what everybody feels to be such—the peasant and the prince, the
unlearned as well as the philosophers."[8] Mill thought that consulting (some) philosophers was a necessary step, a guide and a model
to the unlearned (and also to many philosophers). But consultation
is not deliberation, and Mill was suspicious of a "human life . . . governed by superior beings" and of "an aristocracy of scribblers, dividing social importance with the other aristocracies, or rather receiving
it from them and basking in their beams."[9]

Once again, education is the fulcrum of Mill's singularity, pull-
ing him closer to his father's philosophy than to Bentham's. Echoing Aristotle's idea of happiness, Mill believed that faculties should
be formed with the aim of creating people capable of searching for
higher pleasures, and education had the crucial role of cultivating
the "very tender plant" in each person that would give them the
"capacity for the nobler feelings."[1] Like his father, Mill did not think
a person came into the world with a premade character; but unlike
his father, he did not think that a person was a totally manufactured
being. The role of personal self-culture was as essential as the environment; it was also the factor that induced Mill to focus utilitarianism across domains of life, from the family and the workplace to
the school and political institutions. The entire universe rotated

6. Jeremy Bentham, *Plan of Parliamentary Reform*, in *Works*, vol. 3, ed. W. Stark (London:
   George Allen and Unwin, 1843), pp. 33 and 455.
7. Hanna Fenichel Pitkin, *The Concept of Representation* (Berkeley: U of California P,
   1967), p. 199.
8. Jeremy Bentham, *The Theory of Legislation*, ed. C. K. Odgen (New York: Harcourt,
   Brace and Company, 1931), p. 3.
9. *Diary*, February 14 and February 12, 1854, *CW*, vol. 27, pp. 654 and 653.
1. See p. 111 below.

around the individual, and all progressive potential depended on her capacity to act independently and competently. Since pleasures vary, character formation should aim at making each person a competent judge able to discover within herself the source of obligation to pursue the greatest happiness of humanity. Mill's goal was to make the consequentialist logic work not only to obstruct harmful behavior but also to inspire good behavior: "I feel that I am bound not to rob or murder, betray or deceive; but why am I bound to promote the general happiness?"[2]

On the issue of education, the two Mills were on the same track, but with a crucial difference. James Mill agreed that some pleasures were superior to others, but he was concerned above all with moderation, and thus education had the essentially negative role of training individuals to depress the intensity of passions (hence his aversion to Romanticism and the irrationalism it encouraged). John Stuart Mill agreed up to a point, but he did not rely upon intensity as a criterion and did not think only in obstructive terms.[3] Like Aristotle, he judged pleasures in relation to the faculties they excited and suggested that the goal of education was to develop dominance in the higher faculties that represented the individual at her best.

But questions remain. Should I experience all pleasures in order to distinguish those that give me superior pleasure? And if I don't have such experience, who can assure me that these pleasures are "superior in quality"? The answers to these questions reveal how close Mill came to transcendentalism, with a moral doctrine capable of distinguishing between different desires based on the individual's preference for what was more attached to disinterested duty, with no need to actually experience the associated pains and pleasures. If we assume that everyone will pursue pleasures and give them not only instruments to pursue them (virtues), but also the tools to discriminate between them, then we are *de facto* outside of utilitarianism and close to Kant's doctrine of duty. These are the premises of Mill's inclusive perfectionism, whose steps are, first, that "the test of quality, and the rule for measuring it against quantity" not come simply from our physical sensations; and second, that they come also from "the preference felt by those who, in their opportunities of experience, to which must be added their habits of self-consciousness and self-observation, are best furnished with the means of comparison."[4] Thus the "standard

---

2. See p. 126 below.
3. If we define pleasures and pains in terms of "intensity," Mill wrote, "a pain should differ from a pleasure only by being more (or perhaps less) intense." *An Examination of Sir William Hamilton's Philosophy and of the Principal Political Questions Discussed in His Writings* (1865), CW, vol. 9, p. 433.
4. See p. 112 below.

of morality" is defined as "the rules and precepts for human conduct, by the observance of which an existence such as has been
described might be, to the greatest extent possible, secured to all
mankind."[5] In sum, a liberal progressive society should aim at making the individual the primary good and also the primary agent of
the general happiness of humanity. To this end, the formation of an
expansive, inclusive, and consciously sympathetic individual should
be the goal for the largest possible number of people, and it is within
this progressive perspective that we should situate Mill's competent judge.

3. *Types of Pleasures*

Mill made two steps to perfect his defense of utilitarianism against
critics: first, he claimed that the critics were the creators of the
image of utilitarianism they criticized; and second, he asserted
the honorability of this doctrine by resorting to its ancient origins, "the Epicureans," including Cicero, the Stoics (Marcus Aurelius in particular, but also some Christians), Plato (but in effect
Socrates), and above all Aristotle, whose "judicious utilitarianism"
was pivotal to Mill's philosophy.[6] Mill thought the detractors of
utilitarianism offered a degrading image of the person who seeks
pleasure because they had a degrading image of pleasure as solace
for the swine. They understood pleasure as a defect because they
assumed human beings were incapable of pleasures beyond those of
the swine for the simple reason that pleasures could not be other
than those of the swine.

Thus, defending utilitarianism first required emancipating pleasure from its negative cliché—which originated in the philosophy
of human nature. For Mill, the ultimate goal of education and individuality is to go beyond the primary sensations and desires of
human nature, not in a way that negates them, but so that people
are free to turn their attention to other and superior pleasures. The
General Principle of Utility must be applied to concrete experiences
and integrated with rules that allow people to achieve an equilib-
rium between their individual exigencies and the general interest.
The rule of human conduct requires a "just conception of Utility or
Happiness" that is not simply reducible to "the agent's own greatest
happiness."

Many critical studies have examined whether Mill's utilitarianism
is act- or rule-based.[7] Mill did lean on the latter when he wrote that
"human happiness, even one's own, is in general more successfully

5. See p. 113 below.
6. See p. 23 below.
7. See Wendy Donner's analysis of several interpretations below.

pursued by acting on general rules than by measuring the consequences of each act."[8] As Wendy Donner writes, "Actions are right in
proportion as they tend to promote happiness, wrong as they tend to
produce the reverse of happiness." But it is utilitarianism as a
"theory of life" that makes this rule legitimate. A rule that guides
us in all our actions is not incompatible with case-by-case decisions;
they simply have different purviews. All rules and actions "must be
justified by utility," whose general rule should produce the general
balance of happiness.[9] Thus, while utilitarianism might be a matter
of prudence and expedience in the domain of politics and applied
justice, as a moral theory it goes beyond prudence because it appeals
to a kind of life in which "pleasure, and freedom from pain, are
the only things desirable as ends" and in which "all desirable
things . . . are desirable either for the pleasure inherent in themselves, or as means to the promotion of pleasures and the prevention
of pain."[1] This distinction brings us back to Aristotle's hierarchy
between goods we desire for their own sake and goods we desire for
the sake of something else. It introduces us to what Mill calls the
"art of life"; but since pleasure is the source of our judgment of good
(pleasant) and bad (unpleasant), utilitarianism needs a "theory of
life" to organize the many sensations, emotions, and passions in a
way that facilitates rules for action.

This "theory of life" derives from a humanist theory of human
worth, where things pleasant and unpleasant are distinguished and
organized according to whether they are activated or felt by what the
humanists considered the mental faculties most representative of
human nature. Mill's conception of the individual finds an echo in
Aristotle's view that "pleasures differ in kinds," and that the salient
differences are located in the human faculties, "for those derived
from noble sources are different from those derived from base
sources."[2] Mill concurs: "human beings have faculties more elevated
than the animal appetites" and their gratification gives superior pleasures. "Human beings' conception of happiness" needs to ground
the theory of utility, otherwise utilitarianism would indeed be swine
morality.[3] Mill does not exclude all pleasures that do not produce a
gratification of the "more elevated" faculties. Although he thinks
certain pleasures are qualitatively superior to others, it would be
incorrect to infer that the search for happiness does not include
quantitative pleasures. Quantitative and qualitative pleasures are

8. To Grote, *CW*, vol. 15, p. 762.
9. See Donner's essay below.
1. To Grote, p. 762.
2. Aristotle, *Nicomachean Ethics*, trans. David Ross (Oxford and New York: Oxford UP,
   1990), p. 253.
3. See p. 109 below.

tied together: without satisfying bodily needs, Aristotle wrote, happiness would be simply impossible. Similarly, Mill did not indulge in an ascetic ideal of happiness as total detachment from the external world and bodily sensations, although he does not identify happiness with individualistic hedonism either. "Strikingly similar to Platonic and Aristotelian claims," Mill's distinction between quantitative and qualitative pleasures is rooted in classical moral philosophy and its distinction between bodily pleasures and the pleasures of the mind.[4] To fully appreciate this distinction we have to situate it within the theme of the education of character and the formation of human capacities, a seminal component of Mill's utilitarianism. This makes it closer to Aristotle than to Epicurus, since it is more attentive to action than to the avoidance of action.

Epicurus situated happiness in "the removal of all that causes pain," in the resulting absence of burden, and in independence from the outside world and desire. Aristotle, on the contrary, insisted on action. Pleasures, he wrote, "are activities and ends; nor do they arise when we are acquiring some faculty, but when we are exercising it."[5] When we love an activity for its own sake, we reach the peak of happiness, and only intellectual activity can be loved in this way. Happiness goes with activity because it goes with excellence (in performance) or virtue, and because the superior virtue or excellence is the thinking itself, wherein happiness resides.[6] Mill's evaluation of pleasures and the human faculties that give the highest pleasure to our conscience belongs within this Aristotelian framework—a framework that blurs the distinction between rule ethics and virtue ethics. As T. H. Irwin writes, Mill recognized with Aristotle that a virtuous person chooses virtue for its own sake, so that the relationship between virtue and happiness is not one of external causality but "the development of will and habit" that produces "an attitude to virtue and happiness that cannot be understood if we take the relation between them to be purely external."[7]

The role of education and the legacy of the ancients are key to understanding Mill's distinction between "bodily pleasures" and "mental pleasures," a distinction that exalts his humanist vision of human nature and makes us appreciate the role of moral examples and great characters. Mill thinks that the individual is a unity in which a multiverse (an expression he borrowed from Humboldt) of faculties converge. (In his youth, he had borrowed the term "androgyny" from the Saint-Simonians to understand the simultaneous

---

4. T. H. Irwin, "Mill and the Classical World," in *The Cambridge Companion to Mill*, ed. John Skorupski (Cambridge: Cambridge UP, 1998), pp. 421–63.
5. Aristotle, *Nicomachean Ethics*, pp. 185–86.
6. Ibid., pp. 264–65.
7. Irwin, "Mill and the Classical World," p. 451.

complexity and unity that make each human a microcosm of human-ity.) His humanist teleology assumes the "superiority" of the mental over the bodily faculties and makes a distinction between means and ends. "Superiority" was predicated not on metaphysical premises (for instance, a model of sainthood as transcending the human condi-tion itself) but on empirical criteria: in comparison to bodily plea-sures, mental pleasures are marked by "greater permanency, safety, uncostliness, etc.," writes Mill. The empirical character of these markers should alert us against the mistaken conclusion that Mill ascribed an ontological superiority to "qualitative" pleasures. But his judgment on the character of the "qualitative" pleasures was empiri-cal and in this sense verifiable. Mill did not transgress utilitarianism when he endorsed the difference between "quality" and "quantity," a distinction that was introduced by Epicurus ("when once the pain caused by need has been removed, bodily pleasure will not be increased in amount but only varied in quality"). In Bentham's *Deon-tology*, one finds several observations that would concur with Mill's, including on the value of leisure as mental liberty from "laborious occupation" and "inaction by the pressure of adjacent circumstances," or those about "the ideas be made to spring up in the realms of plea-sure, as far as the will can act upon their production." "Let the mind seek to occupy itself by the solution of questions upon which a large sum of happiness or misery depends." Bentham also distinguished between sensations of "corporeal class" directly employed in the satisfaction of wants (thus not permanent or costless) and those associated with "ideas presented by memory or imagination," which were capable of producing inestimable pleasures. Like Mill in many of his writings, Bentham eulogized "unoccupied or misoccupied" time spent in the "exercise of free thought" once the necessities of life were satisfied.[8]

Yet these similarities entail the novelty that Mill's qualitative plea-sures jump out even more, as Elizabeth Anderson points out in her essay in this volume. Among the evidences for "qualitative" plea-sures, Mill also includes the experience of exemplary individuals. The exemplary few were like a vanguard opening the road to all; yet they were not superior or exceptional beings, otherwise they could not be a model for anybody. Rather, they had shown themselves good judges of which pleasures were worth pursuing.

Competent judges are those who have experienced both quanti-tative and qualitative pleasures and do not disclaim the former but see them as means to ends. Mill borrows almost verbatim

---

8. Jeremy Bentham, *Deontology: Or, The Science of Morality*, 2 vols., ed. John Bowring (London: Longman, 1834), vol. 2, pp. 105–06, 113.

from the passage in Plato's *Republic* where Socrates claims that the philosopher has more intellectual experience of all pleasures because she experiences them "in the company of reason," which obviates the need to experience them directly.[9] To Mill, it is compatible with utilitarianism that "some kinds of pleasure are most desirable and more valuable than others," and it seems obvious that the "estimation" of pleasures does not depend "on quantity alone."[1] Here is where Mill "jettisons" Bentham's happiness calculus and the "intensity" criterion of his father, and where the extraordinary richness and complexity of his utilitarianism manifests itself not simply as a distinction between bodily and intellectual pleasures.

From the perspective of Bentham's *Theory of Legislation*, one might conclude that Mill was hardly a utilitarian and seemed like an "ascetic," one of those who to Bentham "have flattered themselves with the idea of something to rise above humanity, by despising vulgar pleasures." Bentham would also have criticized the anti-animal implications of a theory that raised mental above bodily pleasures. Bentham might put Mill among the Stoics because he tended to prescribe suffering when turning "the implication of pain into a duty,"[2] and would situate Mill closer to Plato because he deemed "estimation" a matter of intellectual appreciation or understanding, a conclusion hardly translatable into arithmetic, and deeply related to mental potentials and education.

Mill's distinction between "desirability" (what is desirable) and what is qualitatively superior was indeed reminiscent of Plato and explicative of his idea of "differences of quality in pleasures." If between two pleasures the large majority judged one superior, the decision would decree the pleasure "more desirable." However, what is *more desirable* is not necessarily what is superior in quality. *More valuable* is what "competent" minds estimate as capable of generating superior pleasures. As anticipated, this unequal "estimation" connects to Mill's humanistic idea of the individual. "Few human creatures would consent to be changed into any of the lower animals, for a promise of the fullest allowance of a beast's pleasures; no intelligent human being would consent to be a fool, no instructed person would be an ignoramus."[3] Since all have the potential to understand what belongs to human beings as a species, a progressive society gives all members the stimuli and opportunities to follow their telos as humans and try to discover and appreciate their

9. Plato, *Republic*, trans. G. M. A. Grube, rev. C. D. C. Reeve (Indianapolis: Hackett, 1992), p. 252.
1. See p. 109 below.
2. Bentham, *Theory of Legislation*, pp. 4, 10, and 5.
3. See p. 110 below.

unexplored potential. To deprive some (in effect a large majority) of this possibility is like robbing them of their humanity.

4. A Practical Example

Since his youth, when he became familiar with socialist utopians and Saint-Simonians, Mill had been convinced that the working people (whose lives were occupied with production and want satisfaction) were deprived of the chance to develop the sensibility of the beautiful "in all its kinds and varieties." In his trip to Paris on the occasion of the July Revolution of 1830, he was impressed by the impact of keeping the gallery of the Louvre open on Sunday and of a country "where the populace, in the height of an armed insurrection, place sentinels to guard their own gallery of statues and pictures from injury, and chalk up in every street the words, 'Respect aux Monuments'."[4] More than thirty years later, running for Parliament, he proposed "opening the British Museum and similar institutions on Sunday under proper regulations."[5] This indirect method of exposing people to beauty shows a delicate sensibility and respect for human beings, with determination never to treat them as means or subjects to be indoctrinated, nor to turn adults into children. It was an extension of his antipaternalism (which also explains why he strenuously opposed any forms of state socialism, yet did not oppose cooperation or using the law to compel moral actions).

His instinct was always to give people the chance to think for themselves, and to make society a cornucopia of opportunities and stimuli that "exposed" members to experiences and emotions that would otherwise remain reserved to a privileged few. Mill applied this maxim to political relations with the working class: "Free discussion with them as equals in speech and writings, seems the best instruction that can be given to them"; they are "not to be indoctrinated" but "to be induced and enabled to think for themselves."[6]

The closing statements of *The System of Logic* introduce *Utilitarianism* and are devoted to the meaning of happiness, the goal that the Doctrines of Ends delivers to the Art of Life, and that the Art of Life employs to devise the maxims and rules that indicate how to use experience toward the attainment of happiness. Not all actions, Mill agrees with Aristotle, should have happiness as their direct and voluntary end, because happiness is the justification that proves or

---

4. Mill, "The Monthly Repository for December 1833," *CW*, vol. 23, p. 655.
5. Mill, "The Westminster Election of 1863 [2]," *CW*, vol. 28, p. 27.
6. Mill to the Rev. Henry William Carr, 7 January 1852, *CW*, vol. 14, pp. 80–81. "In general, those who attempt to correct the errors of the working classes do it as if they were talking to babies:" "Representation of the People [2]," *CW*, vol. 28, p. 65.

legitimizes actions, but not the sole end. There are many virtuous actions whose performance involves sacrifice rather than pleasure, yet they are virtuous because they contribute to the happiness "in the world," which is the final goal of the Doctrine of Ends. Because of the indirect and discrete relationship between the agent and happiness, the cultivation of character and the education of virtues are essential.

Unlike Bentham, who retained the idea of obligation as coercion (institutional or by calculation of interests), Mill's attention was both to external sanction (issues of justice) and the inward culture as a sanctioning force. Socialization and education were paramount. Mill was aware that moral rules, as well as rules of justice, "cannot be expediently enforced as positive laws" and that morality is the result of a complex process of social relations and decisions in a variety of realms, not only politics and the state.[7] "Consequently, the smallest germs of the feelings are laid hold of and nourished by the contagion of sympathy and the influence of education; and a complete web of corroborative association is woven round it, by the powerful agency of the external sanction. This mode of conceiving ourselves and human life, as civilization goes on, is felt to be more and more natural."[8] Consider, for example, Mill's admiration for disinterested engagement and his own engagement in numerous campaigns for emancipation of the working classes, religious liberty, and liberty of the press, and against domestic despotism and slavery. Each effort was an indication of how a progressive project could be furthered and how social engagement could be a school of moral sentiments for both the agents and the people affected by their actions.

Social engagement was the reflection of a virtuous disposition toward a goal that transcended personal interests and could be a model for the citizens to be admired and imitated, although not made into a moral obligation. In a republican mode, Mill made participation an elective choice; he thought that the more a person cultivates virtuous habits, the more her actions are felt by others as generous contributions to a better life for all. The need for behavioral models highlights the role of imagination, a faculty that marks a broad sphere of intellectual and artistic ideations and is connected to aesthetics and beauty, which Mill deemed the most important leverages of the education of sentiments.[9] It is thus clear why Mill made engagement for good causes not a moral command but a

---

7. Jonathan Riley, "Optimal Moral Rules and Supererogatory Acts," in *John Stuart Mill and the Art of Life*, ed. Ben Eggleston, Dale E. Miller, and David Weinstein (Oxford: Oxford UP, 2011), p. 122.
8. See pp. 130–31 below.
9. Mill, "Inaugural Address Delivered to the University of St. Andrews" (1867), *CW*, vol. 21, p. 254.

personal choice to correct the "very imperfect state of the world's arrangements." Virtuous behavior comes with renunciation of personal interests, yet it is also a source of happiness for those who choose it freely.

The Subjection of Women

Of Mill's political writings, *The Subjection of Women* is the most successful at combining ideals with prudence—what is right with what is currently feasible. His pragmatic principle of approximating the real to the ideal is central, which also brilliantly explicates the effective difference between intuitionism and consequentialism, between assertions based on the logic of consistency with shared beliefs and reasons that are based on exhaustive verification of all shared beliefs. Furthermore, *The Subjection of Women* testifies vividly to the role Mill played as an intellectual in civil and political battles, capable of presenting sophisticated arguments to a large public without betraying their meaning and without treating his readers paternalistically. His deliberative style encompassed reason and emotions; his arguments made readers think with their own minds and side with his proposals.

As he did in *On Liberty*, in *The Subjection of Women* Mill criticized the intrusion of majority opinion into personal life. Yet he acknowledged the power of opinion in modern society and believed in the public role of reason—otherwise he might not have written his books. In *Utilitarianism*, he gave critical thinking and scientific knowledge the task of advancing social justice, extinguishing poverty, and fighting against diseases in a language that recalled Condorcet's *Prospectus d'un tableau historique des progrès de l'esprit humain* (1793). Mill and Harriet Taylor did share some traits with Condorcet (1743–1794) and his wife Marie-Louise-Sophie de Grouchy, one of Mill's models of enlightenment, as both couples were committed to transforming the opinion of their society and shattering persistent beliefs such as those on slavery and racial and sexual inequality. To Mill, the issue of women was the issue of humanity, both in its extreme deprivation and in its enormous potential. Women were not unlike the slaves in the United States (*The Subjection of Women* was written in the months before the Civil War erupted) or the working class in Marx's *Manifesto*. As the immediate furious reactions to Mill's text proved, the argument for female equality was effective because it was presented in the language of subjection, inviting readers to call the bluff of contractual marriage. Mill took a position that was decidedly in the minority: as one reviewer put it, "he exactly corresponds to the lunatic who

proved logically that the rest of the world was insane."[1] Sigmund
Freud, who translated *The Subjection of Women* book into German
some years later, expressed a similar dislike in a letter to his fiancée
in which he confessed not to like his "gentle sweet girl as a competi-
tor" to him, and implored her "to withdraw from the struggle into
the calm uncompetitive activity of my home."[2]

The Subjection of Women almost immediately became a feminist
manifesto, translated into many languages (although it remained
neglected and unpopular in Britain),[3] and along with harsh critiques, inspired reformist lawmakers, petitioners, and suffragist
movements all over the world.[4] It was a milestone in the criticism of
sexual roles in family and society, anticipating *Women and Economics* by Charlotte Perkins Gilman (1898) and *The Second Sex* by
Simone de Beauvoir (1951). But *The Subjection of Women* is special
both because it was written when the ideas it defends were deemed
absurd and outrageous and because it was written by a man, who in
this book collected the ideas that had inspired his partnership with
Harriet Taylor since 1831.

Taylor held a more radical position on female equality and marriage than Mill, and "she stood out as a dissenting voice in midcen-
tury Britain, influenced by Owenite feminism, which lost however
much of its intellectual appeal with the collapse of the Owenite
experiment."[5] The document of Taylor's feminism is her 1851 *The
Enfranchisement of Women* (which Mill included in his collection
Dissertations and Discussions in 1859), a text more radical than
The Subjection of Women, which Mill wrote in Avignon between
1860 and 1861, two years after his wife had passed away, but was
only printed in 1869. Why did he wait so long to make it public?
The answer shows Mill's profound comprehension of the extra-
institutional forms of participation in representative government
and the role of advocacy both inside and outside Parliament. His
book was conceived, written, and published as a political pamphlet
to address a specific audience, not a hypothetical humanity, and not
even the *république des lettres*. Mill wrote it expressly to help the
cause of enfranchisement and thought prudently and strategically:

1. Anonymous reviewer signed as "T" in *Blackwood's Edinburgh Magazine* 106 (September 1869): 309.
2. Ernest Jones, *The Life and Work of Sigmund Freud*, ed. Lionel Trilling and Steven
   Marcus (London: Penguin, 1964), pp. 166–67.
3. Alan Ryan, *J. S. Mill* (London: Routledge, 1974), p. 125.
4. For an overview of the global impact of Mill's book and ideas, see Jad Adams, *Women
   and the Vote: A World History* (Oxford: Oxford UP, 2016).
5. Julia Berest, "The Reception of J. S. Mill's Feminist Thought in Imperial Russia," *Russian History* 43 (2016): 106. The Russian translator of Taylor's article, Mikhail
   Mikhailov, was a prominent feminist and radical who ended up in Siberian exile for
   spreading revolutionary propaganda in 1861–62. Taylor's essay (some of whose political language was "muted" by censorship) was part of that propaganda.

he had written it at a time in which opinion was radically hostile to female political emancipation, and Mill was afraid that this text would hurt rather than help the cause. As he wrote to Florence May on March 22, 1868, it was necessary to be "as far as possible invulnerable" on the question of women's equality.[6] Hence in his *Autobiography*: "The intention was to keep this among other unpublished papers, improving it from time to time if I was able, and to publish it at the time when it should seem likely to be most useful."[7]

Things started changing during the debates on the Second Reform Bill, and when Mill decided to enter politics and compete for a seat in Parliament. Woman suffrage was the core of his electoral campaign and once elected, in 1866, he presented a petition to the House of Commons with over 1,500 signatures which had been collected by the Women's Suffrage Committee. Mill used the Second Reform Bill as an opportunity to introduce equal voting rights. His amendment obtained seventy-three votes, but its defeat turned out to be a *de facto* victory since his proposal brought the topic to the attention of public opinion, in Britain and abroad. In a parliamentary speech Mill connected the success of the cause to its failure to become a law: "it is quite certain that its rejection would give a most extraordinary impulse to the movement, which has lately made so much progress, for giving the suffrage to women."[8] Just after his parliamentary defeat, he was able to announce that "a Society has been formed to continue the movement for the admission of women to the suffrage."[9] As his correspondence shows, the news of his parliamentary proposal circulated widely and contributed to making *The Subjection of Women* a turning point in the international movement for suffrage.

Chapter I questions the assumption of natural female inequality and asks whether their nature is truly different from that of men, wherein different means unequal. The chapter is devoted to showing that women's position in society is wholly conventional, rather than natural, and that their subjection to men is simply one of the few remaining results of the rule of force. Like Rousseau in the *Discourse on Inequality* (1754), Mill claimed that women and men have natural differences and concluded that it is absurd to make those differences a reason for social and political inequality. Mill recapped the history of Western societies to show the untenable logic of subordination by birth in all professions and also politics. Chapter II

---

6. *CW*, vol. 16, p. 1342–722.
7. *CW*, vol. 1, p. 265.
8. Mill, "Married Women's Property" (10 June, 1868), *CW*, vol. 28, p. 283.
9. Mill to Mary Thompson, August 4, 1867, *CW*, vol. 16, p. 1300. In 1869, Elizabeth Cady Stanton asked him for a letter of support for the American Equal Rights Association, of which she would soon be elected president (*CW*, vol. 16, p. 1594).

extends this argument to the English marriage and shows how many obstacles existed, in property law and inheritance, that blocked divorce, thus violating the principle of contract upon which marriage was celebrated as a relation based on consent.[1] Once again Rousseau comes to mind, since Mill argued that a contract that makes some dominate others and cannot be rescinded was nothing but a masquerade of contract. Chapter III discusses women's admissibility to all the professions and their occupation outside the family. It adopts a powerful argument: if men and women were naturally thoroughly incompetent and the latter were inferior to men, such an effort in creating and strengthening extra barriers to keep women out would be unjustifiable. In fact, the care with which men excluded women from extra-family occupations was evidence of their natural aptitudes and capacities. Chapter IV argues that educated women would enrich society at large by also enriching domestic life. Given the expanded role of private and domestic life in modern society, it would not be appealing for men to share most of their lives with illiterate women incapable of becoming autonomous persons. Hence, female emancipation represented a condition of happiness for both men and women and progress for all of society. The book ends with a plea for a new relationship between the sexes based on reciprocity and cooperation.

1. Despotism and Freedom from Subjection

Mill rests the claim for women's equality on the category of despotism (whereby he derives the denunciation of their subjection) and on its institutional and ethical antonym, the *polis* as a partnership among equals. His strategy was republican and similar to the one he used in *On Liberty* to denounce Comte's social project as "liberticide." The equation of liberty with nonslavery in the Roman republican tradition was a familiar trope in Mill's time, especially given the debates surrounding the American Civil War. Reading liberty through its opposites—slavery and despotism—indicates that a liberal interpretation of *The Subjection of Women* is narrow and off the mark. Mill did not claim emancipation based on opportunity-based discourse. Moreover, he did not make equality a mere issue of rights distribution and legal reforms. Instead, equality designated a power structure without which liberty could not sustain itself. Mary Lyndon Shanley wrote that the liberal argument for free choice, for marriage as a contractual relation, and for a policy of equal opportunity were all insufficient for Mill's political purposes:

---

1. He took the floor in the House of Commons to argue against the exclusion of women from all rights of property.

he "insisted that the subjection of women could not be ended by law alone, but only by law and the reformation of education, of opinion, of social inculcation, of habits, and finally of the conduct of family life itself."[2] Martha Nussbaum states explicitly that while *The Subjection of Women* is part of "the liberal tradition in its focus on human autonomy, liberty and self-expression, nonetheless this text anticipates the best insights of radical feminism, with its shrewd analysis of power structures in the family and in sexual relationships and its insightful account of the ways in which power deforms desire."[3]

Consistent with *On Liberty* and *Utilitarianism*, *The Subjection of Women* proposed a view of liberty that connects security and moral autonomy, and thus relations of power based on reciprocity and equality; and it suggests that society would be radically transformed by the transformation of gender relations. Mill made the family a political realm, a realm of power relations which impacted the entire society and which therefore law and opinion had a right and duty to interfere with. This disturbed his critics profoundly. They had good reason to worry that Mill's argument for emancipation would entail much more than suffrage; they were right to think that if the law intervened in regulating husband-and-wife relations, the family as it existed would be over.[4] As we shall see below, in desacralizing marriage and family, Mill made the supposedly intimate relationships a mark of abuse, not consent. Justice entailed a system of human relationships based on reciprocity and equal respect and was not merely a matter of legal reform. As he clarified in *Utilitarianism*, the formation of habits of sympathy and cooperation is paramount to complete the work of legal reforms.

Mill was not the first theorist to use a political category like despotism to criticize nonpolitical power relationships like marriage and the family. In *An Enquiry Concerning Political Justice* (1793), William Godwin castigated the existing marital "contract" as a "fraud" and the worst of all monopolies, since it institutionalized a relation of slavery.[5] Mary Wollstonecraft anticipated Godwin's argument and challenged Rousseau's exclusionary republicanism. She claimed—as Mill later would—that by living with pariahs, male citizens were *de facto* condemning themselves to spend most of their life in relationships with semi-humans to whom, in addition, they gave the task of educating the future generation of free male citizens. Wollstonecraft

---

2. Mary Lyndon Shanley, "The subjection of women," in *The Cambridge Companion to Mill*, ed. John Skorupski (Cambridge: Cambridge University Press, 1998), p. 410.
3. See p. 332 below.
4. Anonymous reviewer signed "T," pp. 318–19.
5. "So long as I seek, by despotic and artificial means, to maintain my possession of a woman, I am guilty of the most odious selfishness," William Godwin, *An Enquiry Concerning Political Justice, and Its Influence on General Virtue and Happiness*, ed. K. Codell Carter (Oxford: Clarendon P, 1971), p. 303.

made quality a prerequisite for the dignity of men as well as of women: the subjection of the latter precluded men from achieving recognition as the bearers of the highest human qualities, such as virtue and intelligence.[6] In Mill's time, William Thompson used the analogy of despotism to attack James Mill's article "Government" (1820), which justified the political exclusion of women in the name of the general interest. Thompson published his *Appeal of One Half of the Human Race* the same year the older Mill's essay was reissued as an abstract by the *Encyclopedia Britannica* (1825). The *Appeal* contained the core argument of *The Subjection of Women*, which Locke and Rousseau had also used to refute the doctrine of political power as voluntary subjection by some to the nonrescindable, absolute, and discretionary power of others. Unlike Locke and Rousseau, however, Thompson's scolding blurred any distinction between the criteria for judging and regulating public and private relations. He treated marital relationships as a form of government, the most perverted of all, which made his feminism radical. In similarly poignant language, Harriet Taylor also equated women's enfranchisement with emancipation from despotism and the liberation of the entire society from the logic of possession: "the rights of women are no other than the rights of human beings. The phrase has come into use, and become necessary, only because law and opinion, having been made chiefly by men, have refused to recognize in women the universal claims of humanity."[7] Mill followed in Thompson's footsteps and made freedom from subjection the normative principle with which he pled the cause of women's equality and independence in the private, social, and political domains.[8] As a principle of freedom, it could not be traded off. A benevolent paternalism could not compensate for the suppression of liberty, even if (as James Mill tried to argue) it could satisfy the utilitarian principle of the general welfare of society. Reading relations among sexes as power relations advanced a conception of suffrage that was truly democratic. (The role of debating in his youth was important as Mill changed his view on the unequal political status of women during a public debate with Thompson at the Owenist Club.)[9]

6. Mary Wollstonecraft, *Vindication of the Rights of Woman*, ed. Miriam Brody (London: Penguin, 1988). Godwin and Wollstonecraft were the parents of Mary Shelley, the author of *Frankenstein or, The Modern Prometheus* (1818) and the wife of the poet Percy Bysshe Shelley. In his memoirs, Godwin wrote that he married Wollstonecraft because she was pregnant. The reputation of being an unwed mother cost Wollstonecraft ostracism while she was alive and afterward. Mill never mentions her in his *Subjection of Women*, although he took inspiration from her work.
7. Harriet Taylor and J. S. Mill, "Papers on Women's Rights (1847–50)," CW, vol. 21, p. 386.
8. James Mill, "On Government," 27; Thompson, *Appeal*, pp. 60–67 and 107.
9. CW, vol. 1, pp. 127–29; see also his "Cooperation: Closing Speech" (1825), CW, vol. 26, p. 321.

To James Mill, suffrage was not a personal right but a means to an end, an institution that served to protect the general interests of society. People who did not contribute to social utility did not need to have a political voice, for the simple reason that their interests were more competently taken care of by those who had prominent interests to defend: thus, the interests of women and nonadult men were identified with those of their husbands, fathers, and older brothers, and the interests of workers were comprised within those of their employers.

John Stuart Mill reversed his father's argument and linked voting rights to the protection of personal liberty—and elevated having a voice, advancing a claim, and taking part in public life as vital parts of that liberty. Suffrage was a power, as his father acknowledged; but precisely because it was a power, individuals had to enjoy it equally. This would protect both the broader interest of society and individual liberty. To keep people away from government would encourage and justify their indifference to the general interest; conversely, participation was like a school of "public feeling," and it was paramount for citizens to have the chance to partake of the common life directly.

Mill's argument was a direct response to the common argument that women's participation would do a disservice to society, given their lack of competence on political issues. He also answered his father by linking suffrage to utility, making female suffrage a matter of both personal liberty and civic responsibility. To Mill, suffrage has to be a personal right precisely because it is a power, which is secure in proportion to its equal and universal distribution. Those who are "protected" in their persons by a law they do not participate in making, and cannot check on and judge its implementation, are not protected at all: "we know what legal protection the slaves have, where the laws are made by their masters."[1] Only a conception of voting as a personal right and only its equal distribution could transform the power of suffrage into an instrument of liberty. Hence, women's emancipation was both just and useful, since countering the use of political power for the benefit of some (women) would increase liberty for all, not just for women.

Through female emancipation, Mill was advancing an egalitarian criterion for liberty as nonsubjection. This criterion pertained to both the form of interference and the position of the interfered-with person within the decision-making process, as David Dyzenhaus argues in his essay in the volume. On one hand, it entailed a distinction between decisions "supported by reasons" and decisions based on "personal preferences"; on the other, it called for inclusion

---

1. See p. 204 below.

and reciprocity. This was the criterion Mill used to justify the political enfranchisement of women as well as the reform of the institution of marriage: "society between human beings, except in the relation of master and slave, is manifestly impossible on any other footing than that the interests of all are to be consulted."[2] This is also the core principle on which he situated the difference between simple noninterference and *nonarbitrary* interference.

> Look at the government of Napoleon Bonaparte: if security from robbery and murder constituted good government, there never was a better government than this. But security from robbers and murders is a small part of good government and includes only that very subordinate department called police. Why do we call Bonaparte's government a bad one? Because if person and property were secure against individuals, they were not secure against the despot. He suppressed all robbers and murderers but himself.[3]

Casting marriage as despotism worked both as a critical weapon in itself—like a "brandished sword," in Cicero's words—and as an *a contrario* introduction to the ideal marriage as a miniaturized *polis*. The classical tradition—from Herodotus to Aristotle and Cicero—cast despotism and the *polis* as irreconcilable models: the former implied enmity, mistrust, and selfish individualism; the latter suggested a form of freedom wherein each participated responsibly according to her competence and character. In the latter, voluntary commitment and civil friendship designated a condition of equality as reciprocity, where each played a plurality of roles to contribute to the common good. When *The Subjection of Women* was released, its critics immediately pointed to the "strange" idea of marriage it proposed, which was "inimical to the conception of a wife as a possession" and furthered an idea of independence that made Mill confound marriage with friendship—"each party being able to subsist alone, and seeking a mate, not to supply an essential need, but to be enjoyed as a mere ally, or great moral luxury."[4] This reviewer got it right: Mill did indeed make marriage similar to citizens' friendship. He used the same words in *The Subjection of Women* that he had used many years before in confiding to John Sterling his idea of friendship: "one fellow traveler, or one fellow soldier," a companion "in the pursuit of a common object." These words expressed Mill's vision of life as an intellectual search ("travel"), based on a commitment to a goal that transcended the sphere of individual interests ("war"). It implied mutual responsibility, shared values, and

2. See p. 130 below.
3. "Parliamentary Reform [2]" (August 1824), *CW*, vol. 26, p. 282.
4. Anonymous reviewer signed "T," p. 562.

"helping one another in an arduous undertaking." Equality in friendship meant searching not for one's "own double" but rather for a
friendly emulation that enriched both the individuals and the couple.
It mirrored a communal life as a project according to which personal autonomy would be an "element of happiness" for the whole,
as he argued in *Utilitarianism*. Mill revived *On Liberty*'s ideal of
individual autonomy in the final page of *The Subjection of Women*:

> Whatever has been said or written, from the time of Herodotus
> to the present, of the ennobling influence of free government—
> the nerve and spring which it gives to all the faculties, the larg-
> est and higher objects which it presents to the intellect and
> feelings, the more unselfish public spirit, and calmer and
> broader views of duty, that it engenders, and the generally
> loftier platform on which it elevates the individual as a moral,
> spiritual, and social being—is every particle as true of women
> as of men.[5]

2. *Liberty as Security and as Autonomy*

The connotation of antisubjection Mill gave to individual freedom
created an interesting configuration between liberty as "security"
and liberty as "autonomy," and *The Subjection of Women* allows us
to better understand this configuration—thus completing the analysis we started in *On Liberty*. Mill has been portrayed as an ambiguous liberal with two competing notions of liberty: the first (security)
echoing a moderate and realist liberalism, and the second (autonomy) advancing a perfectionist liberalism with progressive ambitions, such that the latter betrayed the former. Liberty as security
appears as a universal good, while only those with fully developed
characters who appreciate and pursue the higher or qualitative
pleasures enjoy liberty as autonomy. According to some critics,
this makes Mill a cross-eyed liberal: advocating superior liberty for
the few or the civilized Western people, and Hobbesian security
for the rest.[6] Several scholars have tried to correct this binary reading
of Mill's liberty by situating Mill's theory of liberty within a dynamic
vision of individuality that is egalitarian and identifiable not with a
status but rather with a *process*.[7] Joel Feinberg makes a perspica-
cious argument: we all are born with the potential to become self-
dependent beings, which we do not attain only at the moment we
become autonomous; the fact that when we are children we hold our

5. See p. 245 below.
6. John Gray, *Mill on Liberty: A Defense* (London: Routledge, 1983), p. 55.
7. See, among others, Wendy Donner, *The Liberal Self: John Stuart Mill's Moral and
    Political Philosophy* (Ithaca: Cornell UP, 1991); C. L. Ten, *Mill on Liberty* (Oxford:
    Oxford UP, 1980); Joel Feinberg, "The Child's Right to an Open Future," in *Ethical
    Principles for Social Policy*, ed. John Howie (Carbondale: Southern Illinois UP, 1983).

right to an autonomous life "in trust" does not mean that we do not possess the moral right to or are not capable of autonomy; hence, to disrespect our immediate right to security while we are children compromises the possibility of the future enjoyment of our moral right to autonomy. Liberty as security and liberty as autonomy comprise a single liberty that manifests itself in a temporal process and different life circumstances. *The Subjection of Women* allows us to appreciate this complexity because it approaches liberty from the perspective of autonomy deprivation.

For Mill, the power enjoyed by the husband-master is most apparent in the suppression of his wife's mental and moral autonomy. Because men's ultimate aim is to dominate women's minds, they are "averse," Mill remarked astutely, "to instruct women." In order for them to master their wives' right to security (and thus be their guardians), they must first deprive them of "their moral right to autonomy." Wives must be made docile and apathetic so that they are willing to give their masters charge over their security. The husband-master shrinks his wife's autonomy—he undermines her mental and spiritual life—*in order* to make her dependent on him: "To be entirely dependant upon her husband for every pleasure, and for exemption from every pain; to feel secure, only when under his protection."[8] They want women's sentiment so they will be perceived as their protectors, not as their masters. Only in this way can they enjoy an absolute power over their wives, who will eventually see their husbands as the benevolent guardians of their security.

The distinction between despotism and tyranny illuminates this point. Despotism is a form of hegemonic domination over the inner life and the mind of both the subjected and the subjecting because it operates on the emotions, not just on actions.[9] The despot, unlike the tyrant, strikes with fear and love simultaneously as he wants more than obedience; he wants unquestioned obedience. Subjects of the tyrant long to rebel; under a despot they become affectionate "chattel slaves," as in Mill's description of women. In tyranny, freedom is always latent and the subjects are aware of their liberty; in disposition, total surrender, pacification, and "complete abnegation" reign. Tyranny represses action and violates security. Despotism violates the individual's very determination to act, her moral autonomy and self-reliance, and thus both security and autonomy. More perverse than tyranny, despotism induces its subjects to transfer their freedom to formulate choices and make decisions to

---

8. Mill, "Periodical Literature: Edinburgh Review" (published in *Westminster Review*, April 1824), *CW*, vol. 1, p. 312.
9. See Mill's disagreement with Herbert Spencer (letter of June 14, 1869) on the latter's lack of understanding of how despotic relations are prone to distort both male and female, *CW*, vol. 16, p. 1614.

their masters, who eventually will be seen by their subjects as a source of their security. Mill argued that because women are not merely forced to serve their masters but are trained to desire to serve them, the position of women differs from that of all other subjected classes and makes them similar to slaves. "All women are brought up from the very earliest years in the belief that their ideal of character" is "not self-will, and government by self-control," like men, but instead "submission, and yielding to the control of others . . . to live for others; to make complete abnegation of themselves, and to have no life but in their affections."[1] Hence, by annihilating liberty as auton- omy, despotism annihilates *all* liberty.

It is thus hard to say that liberty as autonomy is for the few and liberty as security is for all. The case of women's subjection shows that suppression of the former is a condition for the suppression of the later going uncontested. Had Mill envisaged autonomy as a lib- erty only for the few, had he identified it with a *status* enjoyed only by *actually* autonomous individuals, he would not have been able to criticize marriage as a despotic institution. In fact, one of the most virulent critics of Mill's feminism, the "insolent & domineering" James Fitzjames Stephen, attacked his egalitarian extension of lib- erty as autonomy to women since it legitimated the denunciation of marital patriarchalism and in so doing upset any form of marital and familial hierarchy.[2]

To Mill, despotism and patriarchalism are great evils because they obstruct the path toward independence, and aim at keeping individuals (women in this case) in a status of perennial subalter- nity. In effect, Mill was depicting and condemning infantiliza- tion, which presumes the existence of a two-tiered humanity, a society in which "the moral right to autonomy is possessed, not by all men, but only by those possessing in some degree the capacities of an autonomous agent."[3] Mill explicitly rejected this dualism. As he wrote in his *Principles of Political Economy*, the theory of depen- dence and protection implies that "only those possessing in some degree the capacities of an autonomous agent" have the power to decide the destiny of others. It implies that only some enjoy the moral right of autonomy: "The rich should be *in loco parentis* to the poor, guiding and restraining them like children. Of spontaneous action on their part there should be no need."[4] "Dependence" was Mill's word for a "hostile" environment that involved "a breach of

---

1. See p. 171 below.
2. James Fitzjames Stephen, *Liberty, Equality, Fraternity*, ed. Stuart D. Warner (India- napolis: Liberty Fund, 1993), 133–46. See Mill's expressions of "dislike" in a letter to T. E. Cliffe Leslie, May 8, 1869, *CW*, vol. 17, p. 1600.
3. Gray, *Mill on Liberty*, p. 55.
4. *CW*, vol. 3, p. 759. *In loco parentis* is a Latin legal term still in use and means an adult responsible for children or acting in the place of a parent.

those rules which are necessary to social stability and survival" (or liberty as security).

Thus for Mill nonsubjection demands more than a politics of power limitation; it demands activity—on the part of the subjects themselves (hence the right to vote) and the law—to remove the causes of subjection. Although liberty as nonsubjection is negative (against a condition of domination), it requires positive intervention not only to remove a "hostile" environment to individual autonomy but also to prevent such an environment from returning. That is what distinguishes it from liberty as noninterference, which is negative both in conceptual definition and in practice. But to Mill, an environment can be "hostile" when the distribution of power gives one party disproportionate influence over the destiny and lifestyle of another. Here, a hostile environment is, properly speaking, a "system of inequality of rights" or inequality in power. Mill's notion of freedom from subjection is grounded in his interpretation of rights and liberty as political acquisitions, rather than natural endowments. It is a claim or a vindication, not "a separate element in the composition of the idea and sentiment." As a claim, it defines the way individuals seek to associate; it is a power whose effectiveness implies an obligation, as we read in the last chapter of *Utilitarianism*.

The concept of liberty includes the action of *limiting*: to impose a limit on somebody's action in a specific sphere implies *ispo facto* the extension of somebody *else's* power of action in that sphere. This means two things: first, that liberty needs to be conceived progressively or as a process of gradual (and at times revolutionary) change within a system of social and political relations; and second, that liberty presumes not isolated beings, but communication and inter-actions among individuals.[5] Calls for a "just" distribution of power are predicated on a relational view of liberty and the individual—just as a just distribution of power within the family signals the transition from patriarchalism to partnership, from despotism to co-operation among equals.

3. Differences and Inequalities

The Subjection of Women provides Mill's definitive answer to Comte and the positivists on human nature. The question of female subjection (and emancipation) emerged while an important change was underway among nineteenth-century scholars in the understanding and justification of inequality among races, sexes, nations and classes. In the 1840s, Mill was interested in making ethology a science studying the forces that moved societies and the role of habits

5. See the essay by Wendy Donner below.

and customs in shaping behavior and "national character." But midway through the nineteenth century, "character" came to be translated into a subject of "objective valuations" of the natural dispositions of groups of people. As Mill wrote to Comte, this new course was alarming as it tended to erase the role of the individual by making it a sample of homogenous aggregates and to impress a shift toward the naturalization of what to Mill was instead a complex result of social institutions and education. Whereas the eighteenth century made all human life an artificial or social construction, the nineteenth century tended to naturalize character so as to congeal existing cleavages and power relations. The adaptation of the model of natural evolution to the study of human societies became a weapon against the claims of equality and emancipation among colonized peoples. Rather than searching for the laws that would explain the dynamic of social transformation, through structures (Marx) or socialization and education (Mill), the new scientific trend moved instead to naturalize social phenomena. We must situate *The Subjection of Women* within that shift to fully appreciate its radicality. As Georgios Varouxakis explains in his essay in this volume, race, sex, class, and nation started being employed as hardly modifiable factors, as marks of an unsolvable division within human history and society that global interaction through commerce and colonialism exalted. Eighteenth-century "enlightened despotism" or "paternalism" had given way to nineteenth-century natural domination and subjection. Mill sided with the former, as his writings on the British colonies and India show, and although "accepting vaguely that racial origin is one of the factors influencing the formation of national character," he was explicit in establishing that "racial predisposition in itself could prove nothing."[6]

It was clear to Mill that the naturalization of characters and dispositions would make any project of social progress null. His correspondence with Charles Dupont-White and Auguste Comte testifies to his opposition to the trend and his unambiguous conclusions against the superiority or inferiority of parts of humanity and society. Mill put his finger on each of the supposed natural factors and debunked them. Against the working class, naturalization provided a patina of objectivity to justify aristocratic nostalgia for a hierarchical, pacified society, well represented by Carlyle and the Romantic reaction against the eighteenth century. In "The Negro Question" (1850), a polemical exchange with Carlyle, Mill attacked the idea of servitude by questioning the idea that wisdom or any other virtue could be inborn. Finally, Mill challenged Carlyle's "gospel of work" as service to the "gods" by juxtaposing it to the "gospel of leisure,"

---

6. See p. 351 below.

while disassociating it from self-fulfillment and associating it with pain and necessity for survival instead: "Work, I imagine, is not a good in itself. There is nothing laudable in work for work's sake." Reminiscent of Aristotle's distinction between work and action, Mill translated the distinction between "quantitative" and "qualitative" pleasures into an argument in favor of an equal opportunity for leisure (hence his claim in favor of the "right to work" so as to give everyone the chance to meet their basic needs). "In opposition to the 'gospel' of work, I would assert the gospel of leisure, and maintain that human beings cannot rise to the finer attributes of their nature compatibly with a life filled with labour."[7] Mill interpreted Carlyle's argument as symptomatic of a society that forced a large portion of humankind into a "state of most unmitigated savagery" to seek the "mere preservation of life."[8]

National character was also part of the argument for "natural" inequality, as we can see in Mill's writings on Ireland, which sought to show "that the alleged failings of the Irish were not 'natural' to them, but were due to misgovernment," and argued that "[o]f all vulgar modes of escaping from the consideration of the effect of social and moral influences on the human mind, the most vulgar is that of attributing the diversities of conduct and character to inherent natural differences."[9] He also discussed the naturalization of racial differences, arguing against the trend of ascribing the destiny of countries and nations to "natural" racial dispositions. Regarding the supposed natural inferiority of Black people, Mill advanced a stylization of what some years ago Martin Bernal theorized as "Black Athena."[1] "It is curious withal, that the earliest known civilization was . . . a negro civilization. The original Egyptians are inferred, from the evidence of their sculptures, to have been a negro race: it was from negroes, therefore, that the Greeks learnt their first lessons in civilization."[2]

Yet it was the naturalization of sexual relations that Mill countered with the most vigor. He was full of contempt for efforts to ascribe women's inferior status to their biology, a contempt that he shared not too diplomatically with Comte. He used associational psychology and history to counter the "unspeakable ignorance and inattention of mankind in respect to the influences which form human character." And perhaps the best representation of Mill's ideal of a progressive liberal society as a form of voluntary

---

7. Mill, "The Negro Question," CW, vol. 21, p. 91.
8. Mill, "Inaugural Address," CW, vol. 21, p. 217.
9. Principles of Political Economy, CW, vol. 2, p. 319.
1. Martin Bernal, Black Athena: The Afroasiatic Roots of Classical Civilization, 3 vol. (New Brunswick: Rutgers UP, 1987).
2. CW, vol. 21, p. 93.

cooperation is the document he wrote on the occasion of his own marriage in 1851: "And in the event of marriage between Mrs. Taylor and me I declare it to be my will and intention, and the condition of the engagement between us, that she retains in all respects whatever the same absolute freedom of action, and freedom of disposal of herself and of all that does or may at any time belong to her, as if no such marriage had taken place."[3]

3. *CW*, vol. 21, p. 97.

The Texts of
ON LIBERTY AND
OTHER WRITINGS

On Liberty

> The grand, leading principle, towards which every argument
> unfolded in these pages directly converges, is the absolute and
> essential importance of human development in its richest
> diversity.
> —WILHELM VON HUMBOLDT: *Sphere and Duties of Government.*

To the beloved and deplored memory of her who was the inspirer,
and in part the author, of all that is best in my writings—the friend
and wife whose exalted sense of truth and right was my strongest
incitement, and whose approbation was my chief reward—I dedicate
this volume.[1] Like all that I have written for many years, it belongs
as much to her as to me; but the work as it stands has had, in a
very insufficient degree, the inestimable advantage of her revision; some of the most important portions having been reserved for a
more careful re-examination, which they are now never destined to
receive. Were I but capable of interpreting to the world one half the
great thoughts and noble feelings which are buried in her grave, I
should be the medium of a greater benefit to it, than is ever likely to
arise from anything that I can write, unprompted and unassisted by
her all but unrivalled wisdom.

CHAPTER I

Introductory

The subject of this Essay is not the so-called Liberty of the Will, so
unfortunately opposed to the misnamed doctrine of Philosophical
Necessity; but Civil, or Social Liberty: the nature and limits of the
power which can be legitimately exercised by society over the individual. A question seldom stated, and hardly ever discussed, in
general terms, but which profoundly influences the practical controversies of the age by its latent presence, and is likely soon to

---

1. Dedication to Harriet Taylor Mill, Mill's wife. The epigraph above is from Wilhelm von
   Humboldt, *Sphere and Duties of Government*, trans. Joseph Coulthard (London: Chapman, 1856), p. 65.

make itself recognised as the vital question of the future. It is so far from being new, that in a certain sense, it has divided mankind, almost from the remotest ages; but in the stage of progress into which the more civilized portions of the species have now entered, it presents itself under new conditions, and requires a different and more fundamental treatment.

The struggle between Liberty and Authority is the most conspicuous feature in the portions of history with which we are earliest familiar, particularly in that of Greece, Rome, and England. But in old times this contest was between subjects, or some classes of subjects, and the government. By liberty, was meant protection against the tyranny of the political rulers. The rulers were conceived (except in some of the popular governments of Greece) as in a necessarily antagonistic position to the people whom they ruled. They consisted of a governing One, or a governing tribe or caste, who derived their authority from inheritance or conquest, who, at all events, did not hold it at the pleasure of the governed, and whose supremacy men did not venture, perhaps did not desire, to contest, whatever precautions might be taken against its oppressive exercise. Their power was regarded as necessary, but also as highly dangerous; as a weapon which they would attempt to use against their subjects, no less than against external enemies. To prevent the weaker members of the community from being preyed upon by innumerable vultures, it was needful that there should be an animal of prey stronger than the rest, commissioned to keep them down. But as the king of the vultures would be no less bent upon preying on the flock, than any of the minor harpies, it was indispensable to be in a perpetual attitude of defence against his beak and claws. The aim, therefore, of patriots, was to set limits to the power which the ruler should be suffered to exercise over the community; and this limitation was what they meant by liberty. It was attempted in two ways. First, by obtaining a recognition of certain immunities, called political liberties or rights, which it was to be regarded as a breach of duty in the ruler to infringe, and which if he did infringe, specific resistance, or general rebellion, was held to be justifiable. A second, and generally a later expedient, was the establishment of constitutional checks; by which the consent of the community, or of a body of some sort, supposed to represent its interests, was made a necessary condition to some of the more important acts of the governing power. To the first of these modes of limitation, the ruling power, in most European countries, was compelled, more or less, to submit. It was not so with the second; and to attain this, or when already in some degree possessed, to attain it more completely, became everywhere the principal object of the lovers of liberty. And so long as mankind were content to combat one enemy by another, and to be ruled by a master, on condition of being guaranteed more or less efficaciously against his tyranny, they did not carry their aspirations beyond this point.

A time, however, came, in the progress of human affairs, when men ceased to think it a necessity of nature that their governors should be an independent power, opposed in interest to themselves. It appeared to them much better that the various magistrates of the State should be their tenants or delegates, revocable at their pleasure. In that way alone, it seemed, could they have complete security that the powers of government would never be abused to their disadvantage. By degrees, this new demand for elective and temporary rulers became the prominent object of the exertions of the popular party, wherever any such party existed; and superseded, to a considerable extent, the previous efforts to limit the power of rulers. As the struggle proceeded for making the ruling power emanate from the periodical choice of the ruled, some persons began to think that too much importance had been attached to the limitation of the power itself. *That* (it might seem) was a resource against rulers whose interests were habitually opposed to those of the people. What was now wanted was, that the rulers should be identified with the people; that their interest and will should be the interest and will of the nation. The nation did not need to be protected against its own will. There was no fear of its tyrannizing over itself. Let the rulers be effectually responsible to it, promptly removable by it, and it could afford to trust them with power of which it could itself dictate the use to be made. Their power was but the nation's own power, concentrated, and in a form convenient for exercise. This mode of thought, or rather perhaps of feeling, was common among the last generation of European liberalism, in the Continental section of which, it still apparently predominates. Those who admit any limit to what a government may do, except in the case of such governments as they think ought not to exist, stand out as brilliant exceptions among the political thinkers of the Continent. A similar tone of sentiment might by this time have been prevalent in our own country, if the circumstances which for a time encouraged it, had continued unaltered.

But, in political and philosophical theories, as well as in persons, success discloses faults and infirmities which failure might have concealed from observation. The notion, that the people have no need to limit their power over themselves, might seem axiomatic, when popular government was a thing only dreamed about, or read of as having existed at some distant period of the past. Neither was that notion necessarily disturbed by such temporary aberrations as those of the French Revolution, the worst of which were the work of an usurping few, and which, in any case, belonged, not to the permanent working of popular institutions, but to a sudden and

convulsive outbreak against monarchical and aristocratic despotism. In time, however, a democratic republic[2] came to occupy a
large portion of the earth's surface, and made itself felt as one of
the most powerful members of the community of nations; and elective and responsible government became subject to the observations
and criticisms which wait upon a great existing fact. It was now
perceived that such phrases as 'self-government,' and 'the power of
the people over themselves,' do not express the true state of the case.
The 'people' who exercise the power, are not always the same people
with those over whom it is exercised; and the 'self-government' spoken of, is not the government of each by himself, but of each by all
the rest. The will of the people, moreover, practically means, the
will of the most numerous or the most active *part* of the people;
the majority, or those who succeed in making themselves accepted
as the majority: the people, consequently, *may* desire to oppress a
part of their number; and precautions are as much needed against
this, as against any other abuse of power. The limitation, therefore, of the power of government over individuals, loses none of its
importance when the holders of power are regularly accountable
to the community, that is, to the strongest party therein. This
view of things, recommending itself equally to the intelligence of
thinkers and to the inclination of those important classes in European society to whose real or supposed interests democracy is
adverse, has had no difficulty in establishing itself; and in political speculations 'the tyranny of the majority' is now generally
included among the evils against which society requires to be on
its guard.[3]

Like other tyrannies, the tyranny of the majority was at first, and
is still vulgarly, held in dread, chiefly as operating through the acts
of the public authorities. But reflecting persons perceived that when
society is itself the tyrant—society collectively, over the separate
individuals who compose it—its means of tyrannizing are not
restricted to the acts which it may do by the hands of its political
functionaries. Society can and does execute its own mandates: and
if it issues wrong mandates instead of right, or any mandates at all
in things with which it ought not to meddle, it practises a social tyranny more formidable than many kinds of political oppression,
since, though not usually upheld by such extreme penalties, it leaves
fewer means of escape, penetrating much more deeply into the

2. The United States of America.
3. John Adams used the expression "tyranny of the majority" to oppose "a single sovereign
   assembly" in A *Defense of the Constitutions of Government of the United States of America* (1788); James Madison proposed a similar idea in Federalist 10 (1788), speaking of
   "the superior force of an interested and overbearing majority" on a government; Alexis
   de Tocqueville proposed this idea in *Democracy in America* (vol. 1, part 2, chaps. 5–7),
   whose two volumes Mill reviewed in 1836 and 1840, respectively.

details of life, and enslaving the soul itself. Protection, therefore, against the tyranny of the magistrate is not enough: there needs protection also against the tyranny of the prevailing opinion and feeling; against the tendency of society to impose, by other means than civil penalties, its own ideas and practices as rules of conduct on those who dissent from them; to fetter the development, and, if possible, prevent the formation, of any individuality not in harmony with its ways, and compel all characters to fashion themselves upon the model of its own. There is a limit to the legitimate interference of collective opinion with individual independence: and to find that limit, and maintain it against encroachment, is as indispensable to a good condition of human affairs, as protection against political despotism.

But though this proposition is not likely to be contested in general terms, the practical question, where to place the limit—how to make the fitting adjustment between individual independence and social control—is a subject on which nearly everything remains to be done. All that makes existence valuable to any one, depends on the enforcement of restraints upon the actions of other people. Some rules of conduct, therefore, must be imposed, by law in the first place, and by opinion on many things which are not fit subjects for the operation of law. What these rules should be, is the principal question in human affairs; but if we except a few of the most obvious cases, it is one of those which least progress has been made in resolving. No two ages, and scarcely any two countries, have decided it alike; and the decision of one age or country is a wonder to another. Yet the people of any given age and country no more suspect any difficulty in it, than if it were a subject on which mankind had always been agreed. The rules which obtain among themselves appear to them self-evident and self-justifying. This all but universal illusion is one of the examples of the magical influence of custom, which is not only, as the proverb says, a second nature, but is continually mistaken for the first. The effect of custom, in preventing any misgiving respecting the rules of conduct which mankind impose on one another, is all the more complete because the subject is one on which it is not generally considered necessary that reasons should be given, either by one person to others, or by each to himself. People are accustomed to believe, and have been encouraged in the belief by some who aspire to the character of philosophers, that their feelings, on subjects of this nature, are better than reasons, and render reasons unnecessary. The practical principle which guides them to their opinions on the regulation of human conduct, is the feeling in each person's mind that everybody should be required to act as he, and those with whom he sympathizes, would like them to act. No one, indeed, acknowledges to himself that his standard of judgment is his own liking; but an opinion on a point of conduct, not supported by reasons, can only count as one person's preference; and if the reasons, when given, are a mere appeal to a similar preference felt by other people, it is still only many people's liking instead of one. To an ordinary man, however, his own preference, thus supported, is not only a perfectly satisfactory reason, but the only one he generally has for any of his notions of morality, taste, or propriety, which are not expressly written in his religious creed; and his chief guide in the interpretation even of that. Men's opinions, accordingly, on what is laudable or blameable, are affected by all the multifarious causes which influence their wishes in regard to the conduct of others, and which are as numerous as those which determine their wishes on any other subject. Sometimes their reason—at other times their prejudices or superstitions: often their social affections, not seldom their antisocial ones, their envy or jealousy, their arrogance or contemptuousness: but most commonly, their desires or fears for themselves—their legitimate or illegitimate self-interest. Wherever there is an ascendant class, a large portion of the morality of the country emanates from its class interests, and its feelings of class superiority. The morality between Spartans and Helots, between planters and negroes, between princes and subjects, between nobles and roturiers,[4] between men and women, has been for the most part the creation of these class interests and feelings: and the sentiments thus generated, react in turn upon the moral feelings of the members of the ascendant class, in their relations among themselves. Where, on the other hand, a class, formerly ascendant, has lost its ascendancy, or where its ascendancy is unpopular, the prevailing moral sentiments frequently bear the impress of an impatient dislike of superiority. Another grand determining principle of the rules of conduct, both in act and forbearance, which have been enforced by law or opinion, has been the servility of mankind towards the supposed preferences or aversions of their temporal masters, or of their gods. This servility, though essentially selfish, is not hypocrisy; it gives rise to perfectly genuine sentiments of abhorrence; it made men burn magicians and heretics. Among so many baser influences, the general and obvious interests of society have of course had a share, and a large one, in the direction of the moral sentiments: less, however, as a matter of reason, and on their own account, than as a consequence of the sympathies and antipathies which grew out of them: and sympathies and antipathies which had little or nothing

---

4. *Roturiers:* low-rank persons (French). The helots were a class of serfs or unfree people in ancient Sparta, owned by the state and ranking between the slaves and the citizens.

to do with the interests of society, have made themselves felt in the establishment of moralities with quite as great force.

The likings and dislikings of society, or of some powerful portion of it, are thus the main thing which has practically determined the rules laid down for general observance, under the penalties of law or opinion. And in general, those who have been in advance of society in thought and feeling, have left this condition of things unassailed in principle, however they may have come into conflict with it in some of its details. They have occupied themselves rather in inquiring what things society ought to like or dislike, than in questioning whether its likings or dislikings should be a law to individuals. They preferred endeavouring to alter the feelings of mankind on the particular points on which they were themselves heretical, rather than make common cause in defence of freedom, with heretics generally. The only case in which the higher ground has been taken on principle and maintained with consistency, by any but an individual here and there, is that of religious belief: a case instructive in many ways, and not least so as forming a most striking instance of the fallibility of what is called the moral sense: for the *odium theologicum*,[5] in a sincere bigot, is one of the most unequivocal cases of moral feeling. Those who first broke the yoke of what called itself the Universal Church,[6] were in general as little willing to permit difference of religious opinion as that church itself. But when the heat of the conflict was over, without giving a complete victory to any party, and each church or sect was reduced to limit its hopes to retaining possession of the ground it already occupied; minorities, seeing that they had no chance of becoming majorities, were under the necessity of pleading to those whom they could not convert, for permission to differ. It is accordingly on this battle field, almost solely, that the rights of the individual against society have been asserted on broad grounds of principle, and the claim of society to exercise authority over dissentients, openly controverted. The great writers to whom the world owes what religious liberty it possesses, have mostly asserted freedom of conscience as an indefeasible right, and denied absolutely that a human being is accountable to others for his religious belief. Yet so natural to mankind is intolerance in whatever they really care about, that religious freedom has hardly anywhere been practically realized, except where religious indifference, which dislikes to have its peace disturbed by theological quarrels, has added its weight to the scale. In the minds of almost all religious persons, even in the most tolerant countries, the duty of toleration is admitted with tacit reserves. One person will bear

5. Religious hatred (Latin).
6. The Roman Catholic Church.

with dissent in matters of church government, but not of dogma; another can tolerate everybody, short of a Papist or an Unitarian; another, every one who believes in revealed religion; a few extend their charity a little further, but stop at the belief in a God and in a future state. Wherever the sentiment of the majority is still genuine and intense, it is found to have abated little of its claim to be obeyed.

In England, from the peculiar circumstances of our political history, though the yoke of opinion is perhaps heavier, that of law is lighter, than in most other countries of Europe; and there is considerable jealousy of direct interference, by the legislative or the executive power, with private conduct; not so much from any just regard for the independence of the individual, as from the still subsisting habit of looking on the government as representing an opposite interest to the public. The majority have not yet learnt to feel the power of the government their power, or its opinions their opinions. When they do so, individual liberty will probably be as much exposed to invasion from the government, as it already is from public opinion. But, as yet, there is a considerable amount of feeling ready to be called forth against any attempt of the law to control individuals in things in which they have not hitherto been accustomed to be controlled by it; and this with very little discrimination as to whether the matter is, or is not, within the legitimate sphere of legal control; insomuch that the feeling, highly salutary on the whole, is perhaps quite as often misplaced as well grounded in the particular instances of its application. There is, in fact, no recognised principle by which the propriety or impropriety of government interference is customarily tested. People decide according to their personal preferences. Some, whenever they see any good to be done, or evil to be remedied, would willingly instigate the government to undertake the business; while others prefer to bear almost any amount of social evil, rather than add one to the departments of human interests amenable to governmental control. And men range themselves on one or the other side in any particular case, according to this general direction of their sentiments; or according to the degree of interest which they feel in the particular thing which it is proposed that the government should do, or according to the belief they entertain that the government would, or would not, do it in the manner they prefer; but very rarely on account of any opinion to which they consistently adhere, as to what things are fit to be done by a government. And it seems to me that in consequence of this absence of rule or principle, one side is at present as often wrong as the other; the interference of government is, with about equal frequency, improperly invoked and improperly condemned.

The object of this Essay is to assert one very simple principle, as entitled to govern absolutely the dealings of society with the individual in the way of compulsion and control, whether the means used be physical force in the form of legal penalties, or the moral coercion of public opinion. That principle is, that the sole end for which mankind are warranted, individually or collectively, in interfering with the liberty of action of any of their number, is self-protection. That the only purpose for which power can be rightfully exercised over any member of a civilized community, against his will, is to prevent harm to others. His own good, either physical or moral, is not a sufficient warrant. He cannot rightfully be compelled to do or forbear because it will be better for him to do so, because it will make him happier, because, in the opinions of others, to do so would be wise, or even right. These are good reasons for remonstrating with him, or reasoning with him, or persuading him, or entreating him, but not for compelling him, or visiting him with any evil in case he do otherwise. To justify that, the conduct from which it is desired to deter him, must be calculated to produce evil to some one else. The only part of the conduct of any one, for which he is amenable to society, is that which concerns others. In the part which merely concerns himself, his independence is, of right, absolute. Over himself, over his own body and mind, the individual is sovereign.

It is, perhaps, hardly necessary to say that this doctrine is meant to apply only to human beings in the maturity of their faculties. We are not speaking of children, or of young persons below the age which the law may fix as that of manhood or womanhood. Those who are still in a state to require being taken care of by ethers, must be protected against their own actions as well as against external injury. For the same reason, we may leave out of consideration those backward states of society in which the race itself may be considered as in its nonage. The early difficulties in the way of spontaneous progress are so great, that there is seldom any choice of means for overcoming them; and a ruler full of the spirit of improvement is warranted in the use of any expedients that will attain an end, perhaps otherwise unattainable. Despotism is a legitimate mode of government in dealing with barbarians, provided the end be their improvement, and the means justified by actually effecting that end. Liberty, as a principle, has no application to any state of things anterior to the time when mankind have become capable of being improved by free and equal discussion. Until then, there is nothing for them but implicit obedience to an Akbar or a Charlemagne,[7] if they are so fortunate as to find one. But as soon as mankind have

---

7. Charlemagne (702–814) was the king of the Franks who united a large part of Europe and was crowned Holy Roman Emperor by Pope Leo III in Rome on Christmas Eve 800. Akbar (1542–1605) was the greatest of the Mogul emperors, extending his power over most of the Indian subcontinent.

attained the capacity of being guided to their own improvement by conviction or persuasion (a period long since reached in all nations with whom we need here concern ourselves), compulsion, either in the direct form or in that of pains and penalties for non-compliance, is no longer admissible as a means to their own good, and justifiable only for the security of others.

It is proper to state that I forego any advantage which could be derived to my argument from the idea of abstract right, as a thing independent of utility. I regard utility as the ultimate appeal on all ethical questions; but it must be utility in the largest sense, grounded on the permanent interests of man as a progressive being. Those interests, I contend, authorize the subjection of individual spontaneity to external control, only in respect to those actions of each, which concern the interest of other people. If any one does an act hurtful to others, there is a *primá facie*[8] case for punishing him, by law, or, where legal penalties are not safely applicable, by general disapprobation. There are also many positive acts for the benefit of others, which he may rightfully be compelled to perform; such as, to give evidence in a court of justice; to bear his fair share in the common defence, or in any other joint work necessary to the interest of the society of which he enjoys the protection; and to perform certain acts of individual beneficence, such as saving a fellow-creature's life, or interposing to protect the defenceless against ill-usage, things which whenever it is obviously a man's duty to do, he may rightfully be made responsible to society for not doing. A person may cause evil to others not only by his actions but by his inaction, and in either case he is justly accountable to them for the injury. The latter case, it is true, requires a much more cautious exercise of compulsion than the former. To make any one answerable for doing evil to others, is the rule; to make him answerable for not preventing evil, is, comparatively speaking, the exception. Yet there are many cases clear enough and grave enough to justify that exception. In all things which regard the external relations of the individual, he is *de jure*[9] amenable to those whose interests are concerned, and if need be, to society as their protector. There are often good reasons for not holding him to the responsibility; but these reasons must arise from the special expediencies of the case: either because it is a kind of case in which he is on the whole likely to act better, when left to his own discretion, than when controlled in any way in which society have it in their power to control him; or because the attempt to exercise control would produce other evils, greater than those which it would prevent. When such reasons as these preclude the

8. At first sight (Latin), or "at first appearance," or "based on first impression."
9. By right (Latin).

enforcement of responsibility, the conscience of the agent himself should step into the vacant judgment seat, and protect those interests of others which have no external protection; judging himself all the more rigidly, because the case does not admit of his being made accountable to the judgment of his fellow-creatures.

But there is a sphere of action in which society, as distinguished from the individual, has, if any, only an indirect interest; comprehending all that portion of a person's life and conduct which affects only himself, or if it also affects others, only with their free, voluntary, and undeceived consent and participation. When I say only himself, I mean directly, and in the first instance: for whatever affects himself, may affect others *through* himself; and the objection which may be grounded on this contingency, will receive consideration in the sequel. This, then, is the appropriate region of human liberty. It comprises, first, the inward domain of consciousness; demanding liberty of conscience, in the most comprehensive sense; liberty of thought and feeling; absolute freedom of opinion and sentiment on all subjects, practical or speculative, scientific, moral, or theological. The liberty of expressing and publishing opinions may seem to fall under a different principle, since it belongs to that part of the conduct of an individual which concerns other people; but, being almost of as much importance as the liberty of thought itself, and resting in great part on the same reasons, is practically inseparable from it. Secondly, the principle requires liberty of tastes and pursuits; of framing the plan of our life to suit our own character; of doing as we like, subject to such consequences as may follow: without impediment from our fellow-creatures, so long as what we do does not harm them, even though they should think our conduct foolish, perverse, or wrong. Thirdly, from this liberty of each individual, follows the liberty, within the same limits, of combination among individuals; freedom to unite, for any purpose not involving harm to others: the persons combining being supposed to be of full age, and not forced or deceived.

No society in which these liberties are not, on the whole, respected, is free, whatever may be its form of government; and none is completely free in which they do not exist absolute and unqualified. The only freedom which deserves the name, is that of pursuing our own good in our own way, so long as we do not attempt to deprive others of theirs, or impede their efforts to obtain it. Each is the proper guardian of his own health, whether bodily, or mental and spiritual. Mankind are greater gainers by suffering each other to live as seems good to themselves, than by compelling each to live as seems good to the rest.

Though this doctrine is anything but new, and, to some persons, may have the air of a truism, there is no doctrine which stands more directly opposed to the general tendency of existing opinion and practice. Society has expended fully as much effort in the attempt (according to its lights) to compel people to conform to its notions of personal, as of social excellence. The ancient commonwealths thought themselves entitled to practise, and the ancient philosophers countenanced, the regulation of every part of private conduct by public authority, on the ground that the State had a deep interest in the whole bodily and mental discipline of every one of its citizens; a mode of thinking which may have been admissible in small republics surrounded by powerful enemies, in constant peril of being subverted by foreign attack or internal commotion, and to which even a short interval of relaxed energy and self-command might so easily be fatal, that they could not afford to wait for the salutary permanent effects of freedom. In the modern world, the greater size of political communities, and above all, the separation between spiritual and temporal authority (which placed the direction of men's consciences in other hands than those which controlled their worldly affairs), prevented so great an interference by law in the details of private life; but the engines of moral repression have been wielded more strenuously against divergence from the reigning opinion in self-regarding, than even in social matters; religion, the most powerful of the elements which have entered into the formation of moral feeling, having almost always been governed either by the ambition of a hierarchy, seeking control over every department of human conduct, or by the spirit of Puritanism. And some of those modern reformers who have placed themselves in strongest opposition to the religions of the past, have been noway behind either churches or sects in their assertion of the right of spiritual domination: M. Comte,[1] in particular, whose social system, as unfolded in his *Traité de Politique Positive*, aims at establishing (though by moral more than by legal appliances) a despotism of society over the individual, surpassing anything contemplated in the political ideal of the most rigid disciplinarian among the ancient philosophers.

Apart from the peculiar tenets of individual thinkers, there is also in the world at large an increasing inclination to stretch unduly the powers of society over the individual, both by the force of opinion and even by that of legislation: and as the tendency of all the changes taking place in the world is to strengthen society, and diminish the power of the individual, this encroachment is not one of the evils

---

1. Auguste Comte (1795–1857) was the founder of positivism, a doctrine intended to determine the scientific laws explaining social processes and guiding a sort of secular clergy (an élite of social engineers) in the administration of society toward well-being, with the goal of promoting a harmonious unity and overcoming conflicts and disagreements. Mill referred to Comte's system as "liberticide" (the assassination of liberty) and planned to write *On Liberty* as a confutation of it.

which tend spontaneously to disappear, but, on the contrary, to grow more and more formidable. The disposition of mankind, whether as rulers or as fellow-citizens, to impose their own opinions and inclinations as a rule of conduct on others, is so energetically supported by some of the best and by some of the worst feelings incident to human nature, that it is hardly ever kept under restraint by anything but want of power; and as the power is not declining, but growing, unless a strong barrier of moral conviction can be raised against the mischief, we must expect, in the present circumstances of the world, to see it increase.

It will be convenient for the argument, if, instead of at once entering upon the general thesis, we confine ourselves in the first instance to a single branch of it, on which the principle here stated is, if not fully, yet to a certain point, recognised by the current opinions. This one branch is the Liberty of Thought: from which it is impossible to separate the cognate liberty of speaking and of writing. Although these liberties, to some considerable amount, form part of the political morality of all countries which profess religious toleration and free institutions, the grounds, both philosophical and practical, on which they rest, are perhaps not so familiar to the general mind, nor so thoroughly appreciated by many even of the leaders of opinion, as might have been expected. Those grounds, when rightly understood, are of much wider application than to only one division of the subject, and a thorough consideration of this part of the question will be found the best introduction to the remainder. Those to whom nothing which I am about to say will be new, may therefore, I hope, excuse me, if on a subject which for now three centuries has been so often discussed, I venture on one discussion more.

CHAPTER II

Of the Liberty of Thought and Discussion

The time, it is to be hoped, is gone by, when any defence would be necessary of the 'liberty of the press' as one of the securities against corrupt or tyrannical government. No argument, we may suppose, can now be needed, against permitting a legislature or an executive, not identified in interest with the people, to prescribe opinions to them, and determine what doctrines or what arguments they shall be allowed to hear. This aspect of the question, besides, has been so often and so triumphantly enforced by preceding writers, that it needs not be specially insisted on in this place. Though the law of

England, on the subject of the press, is as servile to this day as it was in the time of the Tudors,[2] there is little danger of its being actually put in force against political discussion, except during some temporary panic, when fear of insurrection drives ministers and judges from their propriety;[3] and, speaking generally, it is not, in constitutional countries, to be apprehended, that the government, whether completely responsible to the people or not, will often attempt to control the expression of opinion, except when in doing so it makes itself the organ of the general intolerance of the public. Let us suppose, therefore, that the government is entirely at one with the people, and never thinks of exerting any power of coercion unless in agreement with what it conceives to be their voice. But I deny the right of the people to exercise such coercion, either by themselves or by their government. The power itself is illegitimate. The best government has no more title to it than the worst. It is as noxious, or more noxious, when exerted in accordance with public opinion, than when in opposition to it. If all mankind minus one, were of one opinion, and only one person were of the contrary opinion, mankind would be no more justified in silencing that one person, than he, if he had the power, would be justified in silencing mankind. Were an opinion a personal possession of no value except to the owner; if to be obstructed in the enjoyment of it were simply a private injury, it would make some difference whether the injury was inflicted only on a few persons or on many. But the peculiar evil of silencing the expression of an opinion is, that it is robbing the human race; posterity as well as the existing generation; those who dissent from the

---

2. The royal family that ruled England from 1486 (Henry VII) to 1603 (Elizabeth I).

3. These words had scarcely been written, when, as if to give them an emphatic contradiction, occurred the Government Press Prosecutions of 1858. That ill-judged interference with the liberty of public discussion has not, however, induced me to alter a single word in the text, nor has it at all weakened my conviction that, moments of panic excepted, the era of pains and penalties for political discussion has, in our own country, passed away. For, in the first place, the prosecutions were not persisted in; and, in the second, they were never, properly speaking, political prosecutions. The offence charged was not that of criticising institutions, or the acts or persons of rulers, but of circulating what was deemed an immoral doctrine, the lawfulness of Tyrannicide.

If the arguments of the present chapter are of any validity, there ought to exist the fullest liberty of professing and discussing, as a matter of ethical conviction, any doctrine, however immoral it may be considered. It would, therefore, be irrelevant and out of place to examine here, whether the doctrine of Tyrannicide deserves that title. I shall content myself with saying, that the subject has been at all times one of the open questions of morals; that the act of a private citizen in striking down a criminal, who, by raising himself above the law, has placed himself beyond the reach of legal punishment or control, has been accounted by whole nations, and by some of the best and wisest of men, not a crime, but an act of exalted virtue; and that, right or wrong, it is not of the nature of assassination, but of civil war. As such, I hold that the instigation to it, in a specific case, may be a proper subject of punishment, but only if an overt act has followed, and at least a probable connexion can be established between the act and the instigation. Even then, it is not a foreign government, but the very government assailed, which alone, in the exercise of self-defence, can legitimately punish attacks directed against its own existence [Mill's note].

opinion, still more than those who hold it. If the opinion is right, they are deprived of the opportunity of exchanging error for truth: if wrong, they lose, what is almost as great a benefit, the clearer perception and livelier impression of truth, produced by its collision with error.

It is necessary to consider separately these two hypotheses, each of which has a distinct branch of the argument corresponding to it. We can never be sure that the opinion we are endeavouring to stifle is a false opinion; and if we were sure, stifling it would be an evil still.

First: the opinion which it is attempted to suppress by authority may possibly be true. Those who desire to suppress it, of course deny its truth; but they are not infallible. They have no authority to decide the question for all mankind, and exclude every other person from the means of judging. To refuse a hearing to an opinion, because they are sure that it is false, is to assume that *their* certainty is the same thing as *absolute* certainty. All silencing of discussion is an assumption of infallibility. Its condemnation may be allowed to rest on this common argument, not the worse for being common.

Unfortunately for the good sense of mankind, the fact of their fallibility is far from carrying the weight in their practical judgment, which is always allowed to it in theory; for while every one well knows himself to be fallible, few think it necessary to take any precautions against their own fallibility, or admit the supposition that any opinion, of which they feel very certain, may be one of the examples of the error to which they acknowledge themselves to be liable. Absolute princes, or others who are accustomed to unlimited deference, usually feel this complete confidence in their own opinions on nearly all subjects. People more happily situated, who sometimes hear their opinions disputed, and are not wholly unused to be set right when they are wrong, place the same unbounded reliance only on such of their opinions as are shared by all who surround them, or to whom they habitually defer: for in proportion to a man's want of confidence in his own solitary judgment, does he usually repose, with implicit trust, on the infallibility of 'the world' in general. And the world, to each individual, means the part of it with which he comes in contact; his party, his sect, his church, his class of society: the man may be called, by comparison, almost liberal and large-minded to whom it means anything so comprehensive as his own country or his own age. Nor is his faith in this collective authority at all shaken by his being aware that other ages, countries, sects, churches, classes, and parties have thought, and even now think, the exact reverse. He devolves upon his own world the responsibility of being in the right against the dissentient worlds of other people; and it never troubles him that mere accident has decided which of these numerous worlds is the object of his reliance, and that the same causes which make him a Churchman in London, would have made him a Buddhist or a Confucian in Pekin. Yet it is as evident in itself, as any amount of argument can make it, that ages are no more infallible than individuals; every age having held many opinions which subsequent ages have deemed not only false but absurd; and it is as certain that many opinions, now general, will be rejected by future ages, as it is that many, once general, are rejected by the present.

The objection likely to be made to this argument, would probably take some such form as the following. There is no greater assumption of infallibility in forbidding the propagation of error, than in any other thing which is done by public authority on its own judgment and responsibility. Judgment is given to men that they may use it. Because it may be used erroneously, are men to be told that they ought not to use it at all? To prohibit what they think pernicious, is not claiming exemption from error, but fulfilling the duty incumbent on them, although fallible, of acting on their conscientious conviction. If we were never to act on our opinions, because those opinions may be wrong, we should leave all our interests uncared for, and all our duties unperformed. An objection which applies to all conduct, can be no valid objection to any conduct in particular. It is the duty of governments, and of individuals, to form the truest opinions they can; to form them carefully, and never impose them upon others unless they are quite sure of being right. But when they are sure (such reasoners may say), it is not conscientiousness but cowardice to shrink from acting on their opinions, and allow doctrines which they honestly think dangerous to the welfare of mankind, either in this life or in another, to be scattered abroad without restraint, because other people, in less enlightened times, have persecuted opinions now believed to be true. Let us take care, it may be said, not to make the same mistake: but governments and nations have made mistakes in other things, which are not denied to be fit subjects for the exercise of authority: they have laid on bad taxes, made unjust wars. Ought we therefore to lay on no taxes, and, under whatever provocation, make no wars? Men, and governments, must act to the best of their ability. There is no such thing as absolute certainty, but there is assurance sufficient for the purposes of human life. We may, and must, assume our opinion to be true for the guidance of our own conduct: and it is assuming no more when we forbid bad men to pervert society by the propagation of opinions which we regard as false and pernicious.

I answer, that it is assuming very much more. There is the greatest difference between presuming an opinion to be true, because, with every opportunity for contesting it, it has not been refuted, and assuming its truth for the purpose of not permitting its refutation. Complete liberty of contradicting and disproving our opinion, is the very condition which justifies us in assuming its truth for purposes of action; and on no other terms can a being with human faculties have any rational assurance of being right.

When we consider either the history of opinion, or the ordinary conduct of human life, to what is it to be ascribed that the one and the other are no worse than they are? Not certainly to the inherent force of the human understanding; for, on any matter not self-evident, there are ninety-nine persons totally incapable of judging of it, for one who is capable; and the capacity of the hundredth person is only comparative; for the majority of the eminent men of every past generation held many opinions now known to be erroneous, and did or approved numerous things which no one will now justify. Why is it, then, that there is on the whole a preponderance among mankind of rational opinions and rational conduct? If there really is this preponderance—which there must be, unless human affairs are, and have always been, in an almost desperate state—it is owing to a quality of the human mind, the source of everything respectable in man either as an intellectual or as a moral being, namely, that his errors are corrigible. He is capable of rectifying his mistakes, by discussion and experience. Not by experience alone. There must be discussion, to show how experience is to be interpreted. Wrong opinions and practices gradually yield to fact and argument: but facts and arguments, to produce any effect on the mind, must be brought before it. Very few facts are able to tell their own story, without comments to bring out their meaning. The whole strength and value, then, of human judgment, depending on the one property, that it can be set right when it is wrong, reliance can be placed on it only when the means of setting it right are kept constantly at hand. In the case of any person whose judgment is really deserving of confidence, how has it become so? Because he has kept his mind open to criticism of his opinions and conduct. Because it has been his practice to listen to all that could be said against him; to profit by as much of it as was just, and expound to himself, and upon occasion to others, the fallacy of what was fallacious. Because he has felt, that the only way in which a human being can make some approach to knowing the whole of a subject, is by hearing what can be said about it by persons of every variety of opinion, and studying all modes in which it can be looked at by every character of mind. No wise man ever acquired his wisdom in any mode but this; nor is it in the nature of human intellect to become wise in any other manner. The steady habit of correcting and completing his own opinion by collating it with those of others, so far from causing doubt and hesitation in carrying it into practice, is the only stable foundation for a just reliance on it: for, being cognisant of all that can, at least obviously, be said against him, and having taken up his position against all gainsayers—knowing that he has sought for objections and difficulties, instead of avoiding them, and has shut out no light which can be thrown upon the subject from any quarter—he has a right to think his judgment better than that of any person, or any multitude, who have not gone through a similar process.

It is not too much to require that what the wisest of mankind, those who are best entitled to trust their own judgment, find necessary to warrant their relying on it, should be submitted to by that miscellaneous collection of a few wise and many foolish individuals, called the public. The most intolerant of churches, the Roman Catholic Church, even at the canonization of a saint, admits, and listens patiently to, a 'devil's advocate.'[4] The holiest of men, it appears, cannot be admitted to posthumous honours, until all that the devil could say against him is known and weighed. If even the Newtonian philosophy were not permitted to be questioned, mankind could not feel as complete assurance of its truth as they now do. The beliefs which we have most warrant for, have no safeguard to rest on, but a standing invitation to the whole world to prove them unfounded. If the challenge is not accepted, or is accepted and the attempt fails, we are far enough from certainty still; but we have done the best that the existing state of human reason admits of; we have neglected nothing that could give the truth a chance of reaching us: if the lists are kept open, we may hope that if there be a better truth, it will be found when the human mind is capable of receiving it; and in the meantime we may rely on having attained such approach to truth, as is possible in our own day. This is the amount of certainty attainable by a fallible being, and this the sole way of attaining it.

Strange it is, that men should admit the validity of the arguments for free discussion, but object to their being 'pushed to an extreme;' not seeing that unless the reasons are good for an extreme case, they are not good for any case. Strange that they should imagine that they are not assuming infallibility, when they acknowledge that there should be free discussion on all subjects which can possibly be *doubtful*, but think that some particular principle or doctrine should be forbidden to be questioned because it is *so certain*, that is, because *they are certain* that it is certain. To call any

---

4. The *avocatus diaboli* (Latin) was an official position in the Catholic Church with the function of testing a candidate for canonization by trying to uncover moral or character flaws.

proposition certain, while there is any one who would deny its certainty if permitted, but who is not permitted, is to assume that we ourselves, and those who agree with us, are the judges of certainty, and judges without hearing the other side.

In the present age—which has been described as 'destitute of faith, but terrified at scepticism'[5]—in which people feel sure, not so much that their opinions are true, as that they should not know what to do without them—the claims of an opinion to be protected from public attack are rested not so much on its truth, as on its importance to society. There are, it is alleged, certain beliefs, so useful, not to say indispensable to well-being, that it is as much the duty of governments to uphold those beliefs, as to protect any other of the interests of society. In a case of such necessity, and so directly in the line of their duty, something less than infallibility may, it is maintained, warrant, and even bind, governments, to act on their own opinion, confirmed by the general opinion of mankind. It is also often argued, and still oftener thought, that none but bad men would desire to weaken these salutary beliefs; and there can be nothing wrong, it is thought, in restraining bad men, and prohibiting what only such men would wish to practise. This mode of thinking makes the justification of restraints on discussion not a question of the truth of doctrines, but of their usefulness; and flatters itself by that means to escape the responsibility of claiming to be an infallible judge of opinions. But those who thus satisfy themselves, do not perceive that the assumption of infallibility is merely shifted from one point to another. The usefulness of an opinion is itself matter of opinion: as disputable, as open to discussion, and requiring discussion as much, as the opinion itself. There is the same need of an infallible judge of opinions to decide an opinion to be noxious, as to decide it to be false, unless the opinion condemned has full opportunity of defending itself. And it will not do to say that the heretic may be allowed to maintain the utility or harmlessness of his opinion, though forbidden to maintain its truth. The truth of an opinion is part of its utility. If we would know whether or not it is desirable that a proposition should be believed, is it possible to exclude the consideration of whether or not it is true? In the opinion, not of bad men, but of the best men, no belief which is contrary to truth can be really useful: and can you prevent such men from urging that plea, when they are charged with culpability for denying some doctrine which they are told is useful, but which they believe to be false? Those who are on the side of received opinions, never fail to take all

5. Thomas Carlyle, "Memoirs of the Life of Scott," published in the *London and Westminster Review* (January 1838) and reprinted in *Critical and Miscellaneous Essays in Five Volumes* (New York: Scribner's, 1900–1901), vol. 4, p. 49.

possible advantage of this plea; you do not find *them* handling the question of utility as if it could be completely abstracted from that of truth: on the contrary, it is, above all, because their doctrine is 'the truth,' that the knowledge or the belief of it is held to be so indispensable. There can be no fair discussion of the question of usefulness, when an argument so vital may be employed on one side, but not on the other. And in point of fact, when law or public feeling do not permit the truth of an opinion to be disputed, they are just as little tolerant of a denial of its usefulness. The utmost they allow is an extenuation of its absolute necessity, or of the positive guilt of rejecting it.

In order more fully to illustrate the mischief of denying a hearing to opinions because we, in our own judgment, have condemned them, it will be desirable to fix down the discussion to a concrete case; and I choose, by preference, the cases which are least favourable to me—in which the argument against freedom of opinion, both on the score of truth and on that of utility, is considered the strongest. Let the opinions impugned be the belief in a God and in a future state, or any of the commonly received doctrines of morality. To fight the battle on such ground, gives a great advantage to an unfair antagonist; since he will be sure to say (and many who have no desire to be unfair will say it internally), Are these the doctrines which you do not deem sufficiently certain to be taken under the protection of law? Is the belief in a God one of the opinions, to feel sure of which, you hold to be assuming infallibility? But I must be permitted to observe, that it is not the feeling sure of a doctrine (be it what it may) which I call an assumption of infallibility. It is the undertaking to decide that question *for others*, without allowing them to hear what can be said on the contrary side. And I denounce and reprobate this pretension not the less, if put forth on the side of my most solemn convictions. However positive any one's persuasion may be, not only of the falsity, but of the pernicious consequences—not only of the pernicious consequences, but (to adopt expressions which I altogether condemn) the immorality and impiety of an opinion; yet if, in pursuance of that private judgment, though backed by the public judgment of his country or his cotemporaries, he prevents the opinion from being heard in its defence, he assumes infallibility. And so far from the assumption being less objectionable or less dangerous because the opinion is called immoral or impious, this is the case of all others in which it is most fatal. These are exactly the occasions on which the men of one generation commit those dreadful mistakes, which excite the astonishment and horror of posterity. It is among such that we find the instances memorable in history, when the arm of the law has been employed to root out the best men and the noblest doctrines;

with deplorable success as to the men, though some of the doctrines have survived to be (as if in mockery) invoked, in defence of similar conduct towards those who dissent from *them*, or from their received interpretation.

Mankind can hardly be too often reminded, that there was once a man named Socrates, between whom and the legal authorities and public opinion of his time, there took place a memorable collision. Born in an age and country abounding in individual greatness, this man has been handed down to us by those who best knew both him and the age, as the most virtuous man in it; while *we* know him as the head and prototype of all subsequent teachers of virtue, the source equally of the lofty inspiration of Plato and the judicious utilitarianism of Aristotle, '*i maëstri di color che sanno,*'[6] the two headsprings of ethical as of all other philosophy. This acknowledged master of all the eminent thinkers who have since lived—whose fame, still growing after more than two thousand years, all but outweighs the whole remainder of the names which make his native city illustrious—was put to death by his countrymen, after a judicial conviction, for impiety and immorality. Impiety, in denying the gods recognised by the State; indeed his accuser asserted (see the 'Apologia')[7] that he believed in no gods at all. Immorality, in being, by his doctrines and instructions, a 'corruptor of youth.' Of these charges the tribunal, there is every ground for believing, honestly found him guilty, and condemned the man who probably of all then born had deserved best of mankind, to be put to death as a criminal.

To pass from this to the only other instance of judicial iniquity, the mention of which, after the condemnation of Socrates, would not be an anti-climax: the event which took place on Calvary[8] rather more than eighteen hundred years ago. The man who left on the memory of those who witnessed his life and conversation, such an impression of his moral grandeur, that eighteen subsequent centuries have done homage to him as the Almighty in person, was ignominiously put to death, as what? As a blasphemer. Men did not merely mistake their benefactor; they mistook him for the exact contrary of what he was, and treated him as that prodigy of impiety, which they themselves are now held to be, for their treatment of

---

6. "The masters of those who know" (Italian); in Dante's *Divine Comedy* ("Inferno," 4.131) indicating the most authoritative classical authors, among others Plato (427–347 B.C.E) and Aristotle (384–322 B.C.E), and their teacher Socrates (?–399 B.C.E.).
7. *The Apology of Socrates,* Plato's dialogue on the speech Socrates made at the trial in which he was charged by the people's tribunal of Athens with denying the gods, proposing new divinities, and corrupting the youth. Socrates was executed in 399 B.C.E. Mill translated *The Apology* and some other Plato dialogues, which appeared in the *Monthly Repository* of 1834–35; reprinted in *CW,* vol. 11.
8. The name of the hill where Jesus Christ was crucified.

him. The feelings with which mankind now regard these lamentable transactions, especially the later of the two, render them extremely unjust in their judgment of the unhappy actors. These were, to all appearance, not bad men—not worse than men commonly are, but rather the contrary; men who possessed in a full, or somewhat more than a full measure, the religious, moral, and patriotic feelings of their time and people: the very kind of men who, in all times, our own included, have every chance of passing through life blameless and respected. The high-priest who rent his garments when the words were pronounced,[9] which, according to all the ideas of his country, constituted the blackest guilt, was in all probability quite as sincere in his horror and indignation, as the generality of respectable and pious men now are in the religious and moral sentiments they profess; and most of those who now shudder at his conduct, if they had lived in his time, and been born Jews, would have acted precisely as he did. Orthodox Christians who are tempted to think that those who stoned to death the first martyrs must have been worse men than they themselves are, ought to remember that one of those persecutors was Saint Paul.[1]

Let us add one more example, the most striking of all, if the impressiveness of an error is measured by the wisdom and virtue of him who falls into it. If ever any one, possessed of power, had grounds for thinking himself the best and most enlightened among his contemporaries, it was the Emperor Marcus Aurelius.[2] Absolute monarch of the whole civilized world, he preserved through life not only the most unblemished justice, but what was less to be expected from his Stoical breeding, the tenderest heart. The few failings which are attributed to him, were all on the side of indulgence: while his writings, the highest ethical product of the ancient mind, differ scarcely perceptibly, if they differ at all, from the most characteristic teachings of Christ. This man, a better Christian in all but the dogmatic sense of the word, than almost any of the ostensibly Christian sovereigns who have since reigned, persecuted Christianity. Placed at the summit of all the previous attainments of humanity, with an open, unfettered intellect, and a character which led him of himself to embody in his moral writings the Christian

9. "The high priest [Caiaphas] tore his clothing to show his horror" when Christ, asked to confirm whether he was the son of God, answered, "You have said it yourself," thus being blasphemous (Matthew 26:25).

1. "The Acts of the Apostles" attests that Paul of Tarsus (67 B.C.E.–5 C.E.) participated in Jerusalem, before his conversion, in the persecution of early disciples of Jesus, a Hellenized diaspora of Jews converted to Christianity.

2. The Roman emperor Marcus Aurelius Antoninus (121–180) was a Stoic. Stoicism was a school of thought founded by Zeno of Citium (c. 336–264 B.C.E.) that became very important in Rome starting in the last decades of the Republic; Seneca was its main representative. Stoicism teaches the mastery of reason over passions, a condition essential to holding a virtuous life and achieving individual autonomy.

ideal, he yet failed to see that Christianity was to be a good and not an evil to the world, with his duties to which he was so deeply penetrated. Existing society he knew to be in a deplorable state. But such as it was, he saw, or thought he saw, that it was held together, and prevented from being worse, by belief and reverence of the received divinities. As a ruler of mankind, he deemed it his duty not to suffer society to fall in pieces; and saw not how, if its existing ties were removed, any others could be formed which could again knit it together. The new religion openly aimed at dissolving these ties: unless, therefore, it was his duty to adopt that religion, it seemed to be his duty to put it down. Inasmuch then as the theology of Christianity did not appear to him true or of divine origin; inasmuch as this strange history of a crucified God was not credible to him, and a system which purported to rest entirely upon a foundation to him so wholly unbelievable, could not be foreseen by him to be that renovating agency which, after all abatements, it has in fact proved to be; the gentlest and most amiable of philosophers and rulers, under a solemn sense of duty, authorized the persecution of Christianity. To my mind this is one of the most tragical facts in all history. It is a bitter thought, how different a thing the Christianity of the world might have been, if the Christian faith had been adopted as the religion of the empire under the auspices of Marcus Aurelius instead of those of Constantine.[3] But it would be equally unjust to him and false to truth, to deny, that no one plea which can be urged for punishing anti-Christian teaching, was wanting to Marcus Aurelius for punishing, as he did, the propagation of Christianity. No Christian more firmly believes that Atheism is false, and tends to the dissolution of society, than Marcus Aurelius believed the same things of Christianity; he who, of all men then living, might have been thought the most capable of appreciating it. Unless any one who approves of punishment for the promulgation of opinions, flatters himself that he is a wiser and better man than Marcus Aurelius—more deeply versed in the wisdom of his time, more elevated in his intellect above it—more earnest in his search for truth, or more single-minded in his devotion to it when found;—let him abstain from that assumption of the joint infallibility of himself and the multitude, which the great Antoninus made with so unfortunate a result.

Aware of the impossibility of defending the use of punishment for restraining irreligious opinions, by any argument which will not justify Marcus Antoninus, the enemies of religious freedom, when

---

3. Emperor Constantine (288–337) issued the Edict of Milan in 313, which legalized Christianity and made it the sole religion of the empire, a decision that prompted intolerance of other beliefs and practices.

hard pressed, occasionally accept this consequence, and say, with
Dr. Johnson,[4] that the persecutors of Christianity were in the right;
that persecution is an ordeal through which truth ought to pass, and
always passes successfully, legal penalties being, in the end, powerless against truth, though sometimes beneficially effective against
mischievous errors. This is a form of the argument for religious intolerance, sufficiently remarkable not to be passed without notice.

A theory which maintains that truth may justifiably be persecuted because persecution cannot possibly do it any harm, cannot be charged with being intentionally hostile to the reception
of new truths; but we cannot commend the generosity of its dealing with the persons to whom mankind are indebted for them. To
discover to the world something which deeply concerns it, and of
which it was previously ignorant; to prove to it that it had been mistaken on some vital point of temporal or spiritual interest, is as
important a service as a human being can render to his fellow-
creatures, and in certain cases, as in those of the early Christians
and of the Reformers, those who think with Dr. Johnson believe it
to have been the most precious gift which could be bestowed on
mankind. That the authors of such splendid benefits should be
requited by martyrdom; that their reward should be to be dealt
with as the vilest of criminals, is not, upon this theory, a deplorable
error and misfortune, for which humanity should mourn in sack-
cloth and ashes, but the normal and justifiable state of things. The
propounder of a new truth, according to this doctrine, should stand,
as stood, in the legislation of the Locrians,[5] the proposer of a new law,
with a halter round his neck, to be instantly tightened if the public
assembly did not, on hearing his reasons, then and there adopt his
proposition. People who defend this mode of treating benefactors,
cannot be supposed to set much value on the benefit; and I believe
this view of the subject is mostly confined to the sort of persons
who think that new truths may have been desirable once, but that
we have had enough of them now.

But, indeed, the dictum that truth always triumphs over persecution, is one of those pleasant falsehoods which men repeat after one
another till they pass into commonplaces, but which all experience
refutes. History teems with instances of truth put down by persecution. If not suppressed for ever, it may be thrown back for centuries.
To speak only of religious opinions: the Reformation broke out at

4. Samuel Johnson, often called Dr. Johnson (1709–1784), was a poet, essayist, moralist,
   editor, and lexicographer, a devout Anglican and a conservative.
5. Locri was a Greek colony in Calabria, southern Italy, established in the seventh century
   B.C.E.; it adopted a very severe code regulating the way women had to live, dress, and
   behave. Michel de Montaigne described it in one of his *Essays*, "Of Sumptuary Laws,"
   published in 1580. A Latin version of the Locrian Code was published in Germany at the
   end of the seventeenth century.

least twenty times before Luther, and was put down. Arnold of Brescia was put down. Fra Dolcino was put down. Savonarola was put down. The Albigeois were put down. The Vaudois were put down. The Lollards were put down. The Hussites were put down.[6] Even after the era of Luther, wherever persecution was persisted in, it was successful. In Spain, Italy, Flanders, the Austrian empire, Protestantism was rooted out; and, most likely, would have been so in England, had Queen Mary lived, or Queen Elizabeth died. Persecution has always succeeded, save where the heretics were too strong a party to be effectually persecuted. No reasonable person can doubt that Christianity might have been extirpated in the Roman Empire. It spread, and became predominant, because the persecutions were only occasional, lasting but a short time, and separated by long intervals of almost undisturbed propagandism. It is a piece of idle sentimentality that truth, merely as truth, has any inherent power denied to error, of prevailing against the dungeon and the stake. Men are not more zealous for truth than they often are for error, and a sufficient application of legal or even of social penalties will generally succeed in stopping the propagation of either. The real advantage which truth has, consists in this, that when an opinion is true, it may be extinguished once, twice, or many times, but in the course of ages there will generally be found persons to rediscover it, until some one of its reappearances falls on a time when from favourable circumstances it escapes persecution until it has made such head as to withstand all subsequent attempts to suppress it.

It will be said, that we do not now put to death the introducers of new opinions: we are not like our fathers who slew the prophets, we even build sepulchres to them. It is true we no longer put heretics to death; and the amount of penal infliction which modern feeling would probably tolerate, even against the most obnoxious opinions,

6. A list of failed reformers who were suppressed before the Dominican friar Martin Luther (1483–1546) succeeded in breaking with the Church of Rome and initiating the Protestant Reformation (1517). Arnold of Brescia (1090–1155), leader of a civil and religious movement against clerical wealth, corruption, and the temporal power of the popes, was declared a heretic and executed. Dolcino (1250–1307), a friar and leader of the Dulcinian reformist movement, was tortured and burned at the stake in Piedmont, northern Italy. Girolamo (Jerome) Savonarola (1452–1498), a Dominican friar from Ferrara, in northern Italy, and a preacher in Renaissance Florence, inspired the citizens to expel the Medici and institute a republic; he was hanged and burned. The Albigeois, better known as Albigenses (or Cathari), were members of a reformist sect in the Languedoc, southern France; Pope Innocent III launched a crusade to exterminate them. The Vaudois were followers of Pierre Waldo (1140–1205), a successful merchant who underwent a religious conversion and became the leader of a reformist sect in Lyon which found refuge in Piedmont, in the valleys of the Alps. The Lollards were followers of the Oxford theologian and philosopher John Wycliffe (1324–1384), who preached evangelical poverty; their ideas inspired the Hussites, followers of the Czech theologian John Huss (1369–1415), who in turn inspired Luther. Elizabeth I (1533–1603), queen of England from 1558 to 1603, secured the survival of the Church of England by putting an end to the realm (and life) of Mary Tudor (1516–1558), her cousin and queen from 1553 to 1558, who had tried to restore Catholicism in England.

is not sufficient to extirpate them. But let us not flatter ourselves
that we are yet free from the stain even of legal persecution. Penalties for opinion, or at least for its expression, still exist by law; and
their enforcement is not, even in these times, so unexampled as to
make it at all incredible that they may some day be revived in full
force. In the year 1857, at the summer assizes of the county of Corn-
wall, an unfortunate man,[7] said to be of unexceptionable conduct in
all relations of life, was sentenced to twenty-one months imprisonment, for uttering, and writing on a gate, some offensive words concerning Christianity. Within a month of the same time, at the Old
Bailey, two persons, on two separate occasions,[8] were rejected as
jurymen, and one of them grossly insulted by the judge and by one
of the counsel, because they honestly declared that they had no theological belief; and a third, a foreigner,[9] for the same reason, was
denied justice against a thief. This refusal of redress took place in
virtue of the legal doctrine, that no person can be allowed to give
evidence in a court of justice, who does not profess belief in a God
(any god is sufficient) and in a future state; which is equivalent to
declaring such persons to be outlaws, excluded from the protection
of the tribunals; who may not only be robbed or assaulted with impunity, if no one but themselves, or persons of similar opinions, be
present, but any one else may be robbed or assaulted with impunity,
if the proof of the fact depends on their evidence. The assumption
on which this is grounded, is that the oath is worthless, of a person
who does not believe in a future state; a proposition which betokens
much ignorance of history in those who assent to it (since it is historically true that a large proportion of infidels in all ages have been
persons of distinguished integrity and honour); and would be maintained by no one who had the smallest conception how many of the
persons in greatest repute with the world, both for virtues and for
attainments, are well known, at least to their intimates, to be
unbelievers. The rule, besides, is suicidal, and cuts away its own
foundation. Under pretence that atheists must be liars, it admits the
testimony of all atheists who are willing to lie, and rejects only those
who brave the obloquy of publicly confessing a detested creed rather
than affirm a falsehood. A rule thus self-convicted of absurdity so
far as regards its professed purpose, can be kept in force only as a
badge of hatred, a relic of persecution; a persecution, too, having
the peculiarity, that the qualification for undergoing it, is the being
clearly proved not to deserve it. The rule, and the theory it implies,
are hardly less insulting to believers than to infidels. For if he who

---

7. Thomas Pooley, Bodmin Assizes, July 31, 1857. In December following, he received a free
   pardon from the Crown [*Mill's note*].
8. George Jacob Holyoake, August 17, 1857; Edward Truelove, July, 1857 [*Mill's note*].
9. Baron de Gleichen, Marlborough-street Police Court, August 4, 1857 [*Mill's note*].

does not believe in a future state, necessarily lies, it follows that they who do believe are only prevented from lying, if prevented they are, by the fear of hell. We will not do the authors and abettors of the rule the injury of supposing, that the conception which they have formed of Christian virtue is drawn from their own consciousness.

These, indeed, are but rags and remnants of persecution, and may be thought to be not so much an indication of the wish to persecute, as an example of that very frequent infirmity of English minds, which makes them take a preposterous pleasure in the assertion of a bad principle, when they are no longer bad enough to desire to carry it really into practice. But unhappily there is no security in the state of the public mind, that the suspension of worse forms of legal persecution, which has lasted for about the space of a generation, will continue. In this age the quiet surface of routine is as often ruffled by attempts to resuscitate past evils, as to introduce new benefits. What is boasted of at the present time as the revival of religion, is always, in narrow and uncultivated minds, at least as much the revival of bigotry; and where there is the strong permanent leaven of intolerance in the feelings of a people, which at all times abides in the middle classes of this country, it needs but little to provoke them into actively persecuting those whom they have never ceased to think proper objects of persecution.[1] For it is this—it is the opinions men entertain, and the feelings they cherish, respecting those who disown the beliefs they deem important, which makes this country not a place of mental freedom. For a long time past, the chief mischief of the legal penalties is that they strengthen the social stigma. It is that stigma which is really effective, and so effective is it, that the profession of opinions which are under the ban of society is much less common in England, than is, in many

---

1. Ample warning may be drawn from the large infusion of the passions of a persecutor, which mingled with the general display of the worst parts of our national character on the occasion of the Sepoy insurrection. The ravings of fanatics or charlatans from the pulpit may be unworthy of notice; but the heads of the Evangelical party have announced as their principle, for the government of Hindoos and Mahomedans, that no schools be supported by public money in which the Bible is not taught, and by necessary consequence that no public employment be given to any but real or pretended Christians. An Under-Secretary of State, in a speech delivered to his constituents on the 12th of November, 1857, is reported to have said: 'Toleration of their faith' (the faith of a hundred millions of British subjects), 'the superstition which they called religion, by the British Government, had had the effect of retarding the ascendancy of the British name, and preventing the salutary growth of Christianity. . . . Toleration was the great corner-stone of the religious liberties of this country; but do not let them abuse that precious word toleration.' As he understood it, it meant the complete liberty to all, freedom of worship, *among Christians, who worshipped upon the same foundation.* It meant toleration of all sects and denominations of *Christians who believed in the one mediation.* I desire to call attention to the fact, that a man who has been deemed fit to fill a high office in the government of this country, under a liberal Ministry, maintains the doctrine that all who do not believe in the divinity of Christ are beyond the pale of toleration. Who, after this imbecile display, can indulge the illusion that religious persecution has passed away, never to return [*Mill's note*]!

other countries, the avowal of those which incur risk of judicial punishment. In respect to all persons but those whose pecuniary circumstances make them independent of the good will of other people, opinion, on this subject, is as efficacious as law; men might as well be imprisoned, as excluded from the means of earning their bread. Those whose bread is already secured, and who desire no favours from men in power, or from bodies of men, or from the public, have nothing to fear from the open avowal of any opinions, but to be ill-thought of and ill-spoken of, and this it ought not to require a very heroic mould to enable them to bear. There is no room for any appeal *ad misericordium*[2] in behalf of such persons. But though we do not now inflict so much evil on those who think differently from us, as it was formerly our custom to do, it may be that we do ourselves as much evil as ever by our treatment of them. Socrates was put to death, but the Socratic philosophy rose like the sun in heaven, and spread its illumination over the whole intellectual firmament. Christians were east to the lions, but the Christian church grew up a stately and spreading tree, overtopping the older and less vigorous growths, and stifling them by its shade. Our merely social intolerance kills no one, roots out no opinions, but induces men to disguise them, or to abstain from any active effort for their diffusion. With us, heretical opinions do not perceptibly gain, or even lose, ground in each decade or generation; they never blaze out far and wide, but continue to smoulder in the narrow circles of thinking and studious persons among whom they originate, without ever lighting up the general affairs of mankind with either a true or a deceptive light. And thus is kept up a state of things very satisfactory to some minds, because, without the unpleasant process of fining or imprisoning anybody, it maintains all prevailing opinions outwardly undisturbed, while it does not absolutely interdict the exercise of reason by dissentients afflicted with the malady of thought. A convenient plan for having peace in the intellectual world, and keeping all things going on therein very much as they do already. But the price paid for this sort of intellectual pacification, is the sacrifice of the entire moral courage of the human mind. A state of things in which a large portion of the most active and inquiring intellects find it advisable to keep the genuine principles and grounds of their convictions within their own breasts, and attempt, in what they address to the public, to fit as much as they can of their own conclusions to premises which they have internally renounced, cannot send forth the open, fearless characters, and logical, consistent intellects who once adorned the thinking world. The sort of men who can be looked for under it, are either mere conformers to

2. For mercy (Latin).

common-place, or time servers for truth, whose arguments on all
great subjects are meant for their hearers, and are not those which
have convinced themselves. Those who avoid this alternative, do so
by narrowing their thoughts and interest to things which can be
spoken of without venturing within the region of principles, that is,
to small practical matters, which would come right of themselves, if
but the minds of mankind were strengthened and enlarged, and
which will never be made effectually right until then: while that
which would strengthen and enlarge men's minds, free and daring
speculation on the highest subjects, is abandoned.

Those in whose eyes this reticence on the part of heretics is no
evil, should consider in the first place, that in consequence of it there
is never any fair and thorough discussion of heretical opinions; and
that such of them as could not stand such a discussion, though they
may be prevented from spreading, do not disappear. But it is not the
minds of heretics that are deteriorated most, by the ban placed on
all inquiry which does not end in the orthodox conclusions. The
greatest harm done is to those who are not heretics, and whose whole
mental development is cramped, and their reason cowed, by the fear
of heresy. Who can compute what the world loses in the multitude
of promising intellects combined with timid characters, who dare
not follow out any bold, vigorous, independent train of thought,
lest it should land them in something which would admit of being
considered irreligious or immoral? Among them we may occasionally
see some man of deep conscientiousness, and subtle and refined
understanding, who spends a life in sophisticating with an intellect
which he cannot silence, and exhausts the resources of ingenuity
in attempting to reconcile the promptings of his conscience and
reason with orthodoxy, which yet he does not, perhaps, to the end
succeed in doing. No one can be a great thinker who does not recognise, that as a thinker it is his first duty to follow his intellect to whatever conclusions it may lead. Truth gains more even by the errors of
one who, with due study and preparation, thinks for himself, than by
the true opinions of those who only hold them because they do not
suffer themselves to think. Not that it is solely, or chiefly, to form
great thinkers, that freedom of thinking is required. On the contrary, it is as much, and even more indispensable, to enable average
human beings to attain the mental stature which they are capable
of. There have been, and may again be, great individual thinkers, in
a general atmosphere of mental slavery. But there never has been,
nor ever will be, in that atmosphere, an intellectually active people.
Where any people has made a temporary approach to such a character, it has been because the dread of heterodox speculation was
for a time suspended. Where there is a tacit convention that principles are not to be disputed; where the discussion of the greatest

questions which can occupy humanity is considered to be closed, we cannot hope to find that generally high scale of mental activity which has made some periods of history so remarkable. Never when controversy avoided the subjects which are large and important enough to kindle enthusiasm, was the mind of a people stirred up from its foundations, and the impulse given which raised even persons of the most ordinary intellect to something of the dignity of thinking beings. Of such we have had an example in the condition of Europe during the times immediately following the Reformation; another, though limited to the Continent and to a more cultivated class, in the speculative movement of the latter half of the eighteenth century; and a third, of still briefer duration, in the intellectual fermentation of Germany during the Goethian and Fichtean[3] period. These periods differed widely in the particular opinions which they developed; but were alike in this, that during all three the yoke of authority was broken. In each, an old mental despotism had been thrown off, and no new one had yet taken its place. The impulse given at these three periods has made Europe what it now is. Every single improvement which has taken place either in the human mind or in institutions, may be traced distinctly to one or other of them. Appearances have for some time indicated that all three impulses are well nigh spent; and we can expect no fresh start, until we again assert our mental freedom.

Let us now pass to the second division of the argument, and dismissing the supposition that any of the received opinions may be false, let us assume them to be true, and examine into the worth of the manner in which they are likely to be held, when their truth is not freely and openly canvassed. However unwillingly a person who has a strong opinion may admit the possibility that his opinion may be false, he ought to be moved by the consideration that however true it may be, if it is not fully, frequently, and fearlessly discussed, it will be held as a dead dogma, not a living truth.

There is a class of persons (happily not quite so numerous as formerly) who think it enough if a person assents undoubtingly to what they think true, though he has no knowledge whatever of the grounds of the opinion, and could not make a tenable defence of it against the most superficial objections. Such persons, if they can once get their creed taught from authority, naturally think that no good, and some harm, comes of its being allowed to be questioned.

3. Johann Gottlieb Fichte (1762–1814), German philosopher and a theorist of national identity, who conceived the development of the individual as possible only in the context of the life of the nation. Johann Wolfgang von Goethe (1749–1832), German poet, playwright, novelist, scientist, statesman, theater director, and critic; important also for his treatises on botany, anatomy, and colors.

Where their influence prevails, they make it nearly impossible for the received opinion to be rejected wisely and considerately, though it may still be rejected rashly and ignorantly; for to shut out discussion entirely is seldom possible, and when it once gets in, beliefs not grounded on conviction are apt to give way before the slightest semblance of an argument. Waving, however, this possibility—assuming that the true opinion abides in the mind, but abides as a prejudice, a belief independent of, and proof against, argument—this is not the way in which truth ought to be held by a rational being. This is not knowing the truth. Truth, thus held, is but one superstition the more, accidentally clinging to the words which enunciate a truth.

If the intellect and judgment of mankind ought to be cultivated, a thing which Protestants at least do not deny, on what can these faculties be more appropriately exercised by any one, than on the things which concern him so much that it is considered necessary for him to hold opinions on them? If the cultivation of the understanding consists in one thing more than in another, it is surely in learning the grounds of one's own opinions. Whatever people believe, on subjects on which it is of the first importance to believe rightly, they ought to be able to defend against at least the common objections. But, some one may say, 'Let them be *taught* the grounds of their opinions. It does not follow that opinions must be merely parroted because they are never heard controverted. Persons who learn geometry do not simply commit the theorems to memory, but understand and learn likewise the demonstrations; and it would be absurd to say that they remain ignorant of the grounds of geometrical truths, because they never hear any one deny, and attempt to disprove them.' Undoubtedly: and such teaching suffices on a subject like mathematics, where there is nothing at all to be said on the wrong side of the question. The peculiarity of the evidence of mathematical truths is, that all the argument is on one side. There are no objections, and no answers to objections. But on every subject on which difference of opinion is possible, the truth depends on a balance to be struck between two sets of conflicting reasons. Even in natural philosophy, there is always some other explanation possible of the same facts; some geocentric theory instead of heliocentric, some phlogiston instead of oxygen; and it has to be shown why that other theory cannot be the true one: and until this is shown, and until we know how it is shown, we do not understand the grounds of our opinion. But when we turn to subjects infinitely more complicated, to morals, religion, politics, social relations, and the business of life, three-fourths of the arguments for every disputed opinion consist in dispelling the appearances which favour some opinion different from it. The greatest orator, save one, of antiquity,[4] has left it on record that he always studied his adversary's case with as great, if not with still greater, intensity than even his own. What Cicero practised as the means of forensic success, requires to be imitated by all who study any subject in order to arrive at the truth. He who knows only his own side of the case, knows little of that. His reasons may be good, and no one may have been able to refute them. But if he is equally unable to refute the reasons on the opposite side; if he does not so much as know what they are, he has no ground for preferring either opinion. The rational position for him would be suspension of judgment, and unless he contents himself with that, he is either led by authority, or adopts, like the generality of the world, the side to which he feels most inclination. Nor is it enough that he should hear the arguments of adversaries from his own teachers, presented as they state them, and accompanied by what they offer as refutations. That is not the way to do justice to the arguments, or bring them into real contact with his own mind. He must be able to hear them from persons who actually believe them; who defend them in earnest, and do their very utmost for them. He must know them in their most plausible and persuasive form; he must feel the whole force of the difficulty which the true view of the subject has to encounter and dispose of; else he will never really possess himself of the portion of truth which meets and removes that difficulty. Ninety-nine in a hundred of what are called educated men are in this condition; even of those who can argue fluently for their opinions. Their conclusion may be true, but it might be false for anything they know: they have never thrown themselves into the mental position of those who think differently from them, and considered what such persons may have to say; and consequently they do not, in any proper sense of the word, know the doctrine which they themselves profess. They do not know those parts of it which explain and justify the remainder; the considerations which show that a fact which seemingly conflicts with another is reconcilable with it, or that, of two apparently strong reasons, one and not the other ought to be preferred. All that part of the truth which turns the scale, and decides the judgment of a completely informed mind, they are strangers to; nor is it ever really known, but to those who have attended equally and impartially to both sides, and endeavoured to see the reasons of both in the strongest light. So essential is this discipline to a real understanding of moral and human subjects, that if opponents of all important truths do not exist, it is indispensable to

4. Mill refers to the Roman orator Marcus Tullius Cicero (106–43 B.C.E.) and implicitly to the Greek Demosthenes (384–322 B.C.E.) as the "greatest" orator.

imagine them, and supply them with the strongest arguments which the most skilful devil's advocate can conjure up.

To abate the force of these considerations, an enemy of free discussion may be supposed to say, that there is no necessity for mankind in general to know and understand all that can be said against or for their opinions by philosophers and theologians. That it is not needful for common men to be able to expose all the misstatements or fallacies of an ingenious opponent. That it is enough if there is always somebody capable of answering them, so that nothing likely to mislead uninstructed persons remains unrefuted. That simple minds, having been taught the obvious grounds of the truths inculcated on them, may trust to authority for the rest, and being aware that they have neither knowledge nor talent to resolve every difficulty which can be raised, may repose in the assurance that all those which have been raised have been or can be answered, by those who are specially trained to the task.

Conceding to this view of the subject the utmost that can be claimed for it by those most easily satisfied with the amount of understanding of truth which ought to accompany the belief of it; even so, the argument for free discussion is no way weakened. For even this doctrine acknowledges that mankind ought to have a rational assurance that all objections have been satisfactorily answered; and how are they to be answered if that which requires to be answered is not spoken? or how can the answer be known to be satisfactory, if the objectors have no opportunity of showing that it is unsatisfactory? If not the public, at least the philosophers and theologians who are to resolve the difficulties, must make themselves familiar with those difficulties in their most puzzling form; and this cannot be accomplished unless they are freely stated, and placed in the most advantageous light which they admit of. The Catholic Church has its own way of dealing with this embarrassing problem. It makes a broad separation between those who can be permitted to receive its doctrines on conviction, and those who must accept them on trust. Neither, indeed, are allowed any choice as to what they will accept; but the clergy, such at least as can be fully confided in, may admissibly and meritoriously make themselves acquainted with the arguments of opponents, in order to answer them, and may, therefore, read heretical books; the laity, not unless by special permission, hard to be obtained. This discipline recognises a knowledge of the enemy's case as beneficial to the teachers, but finds means, consistent with this, of denying it to the rest of the world: thus giving to the *élite* more mental culture, though not more mental freedom, than it allows to the mass. By this device it succeeds in obtaining the kind of mental superiority which its purposes require; for though culture without freedom never made a large and liberal mind, it can make a clever *nisi prius*[5] advocate of a cause. But in countries professing Protestantism, this resource is denied; since Protestants hold, at least in theory, that the responsibility for the choice of a religion must be borne by each for himself, and cannot be thrown off upon teachers. Besides, in the present state of the world, it is practically impossible that writings which are read by the instructed can be kept from the uninstructed. If the teachers of mankind are to be cognisant of all that they ought to know, everything must be free to be written and published without restraint.

If, however, the mischievous operation of the absence of free discussion, when the received opinions are true, were confined to leaving men ignorant of the grounds of those opinions, it might be thought that this, if an intellectual, is no moral evil, and does not affect the worth of the opinions, regarded in their influence on the character. The fact, however, is, that not only the grounds of the opinion are forgotten in the absence of discussion, but too often the meaning of the opinion itself. The words which convey it, cease to suggest ideas, or suggest only a small portion of those they were originally employed to communicate. Instead of a vivid conception and a living belief, there remain only a few phrases retained by rote; or, if any part, the shell and husk only of the meaning is retained, the finer essence being lost. The great chapter in human history which this fact occupies and fills, cannot be too earnestly studied and meditated on.

It is illustrated in the experience of almost all ethical doctrines and religious creeds. They are all full of meaning and vitality to those who originate them, and to the direct disciples of the originators. Their meaning continues to be felt in undiminished strength, and is perhaps brought out into even fuller consciousness, so long as the struggle lasts to give the doctrine or creed an ascendancy over other creeds. At last it either prevails, and becomes the general opinion, or its progress stops; it keeps possession of the ground it has gained, but ceases to spread further. When either of these results has become apparent, controversy on the subject flags, and gradually dies away. The doctrine has taken its place, if not as a received opinion, as one of the admitted sects or divisions of opinion: those who hold it have generally inherited, not adopted it; and conversion from one of these doctrines to another, being now an exceptional fact, occupies little place in the thoughts of their professors. Instead of being, as at first, constantly on the alert either to defend themselves against the world, or to bring the world over to them, they have

5. A Latin term meaning that a law or an opinion counts as valid "unless proved otherwise."

subsided into acquiescence, and neither listen, when they can help it, to arguments against their creed, nor trouble dissentients (if there be such) with arguments in its favour. From this time may usually be dated the decline in the living power of the doctrine. We often hear the teachers of all creeds lamenting the difficulty of keeping up in the minds of believers a lively apprehension of the truth which they nominally recognise, so that it may penetrate the feelings, and acquire a real mastery over the conduct. No such difficulty is complained of while the creed is still fighting for its existence: even the weaker combatants then know and feel what they are fighting for, and the difference between it and other doctrines; and in that period of every creed's existence, not a few persons may be found, who have realized its fundamental principles in all the forms of thought, have weighed and considered them in all their important bearings, and have experienced the full effect on the character, which belief in that creed ought to produce in a mind thoroughly imbued with it. But when it has come to be an hereditary creed, and to be received passively, not actively—when the mind is no longer compelled, in the same degree as at first, to exercise its vital powers on the questions which its belief presents to it, there is a progressive tendency to forget all of the belief except the formularies, or to give it a dull and torpid assent, as if accepting it on trust dispensed with the necessity of realizing it in consciousness, or testing it by personal experience; until it almost ceases to connect itself at all with the inner life of the human being. Then are seen the cases, so frequent in this age of the world as almost to form the majority, in which the creed remains as it were outside the mind, encrusting and petrifying it against all other influences addressed to the higher parts of our nature; manifesting its power by not suffering any fresh and living conviction to get in, but itself doing nothing for the mind or heart, except standing sentinel over them to keep them vacant.

To what an extent doctrines intrinsically fitted to make the deepest impression upon the mind may remain in it as dead beliefs, without being ever realized in the imagination, the feelings, or the understanding, is exemplified by the manner in which the majority of believers hold the doctrines of Christianity. By Christianity I here mean what is accounted such by all churches and sects—the maxims and precepts contained in the New Testament. These are considered sacred, and accepted as laws, by all professing Christians. Yet it is scarcely too much to say that not one Christian in a thousand guides or tests his individual conduct by reference to those laws. The standard to which he does refer it, is the custom of his nation, his class, or his religious profession. He has thus, on the one hand, a collection of ethical maxims, which he believes to have been vouchsafed to him by infallible wisdom as rules for his government; and on the other, a set of every-day judgments and practices, which go a certain length with some of those maxims, not so great a length with others, stand in direct opposition to some, and are, on the whole, a compromise between the Christian creed and the interests and suggestions of worldly life. To the first of these standards he gives his homage; to the other his real allegiance. All Christians believe that the blessed are the poor and humble, and those who are ill-used by the world; that it is easier for a camel to pass through the eye of a needle than for a rich man to enter the kingdom of heaven; that they should judge not, lest they be judged; that they should swear not at all; that they should love their neighbour as themselves; that if one take their cloak, they should give him their coat also; that they should take no thought for the morrow; that if they would be perfect, they should sell all that they have and give it to the poor. They are not insincere when they say that they believe these things. They do believe them, as people believe what they have always heard lauded and never discussed. But in the sense of that living belief which regulates conduct, they believe these doctrines just up to the point to which it is usual to act upon them. The doctrines in their integrity are serviceable to pelt adversaries with; and it is understood that they are to be put forward (when possible) as the reasons for whatever people do that they think laudable. But any one who reminded them that the maxims require an infinity of things which they never even think of doing, would gain nothing but to be classed among those very unpopular characters who affect to be better than other people. The doctrines have no hold on ordinary believers—are not a power in their minds. They have an habitual respect for the sound of them, but no feeling which spreads from the words to the things signified, and forces the mind to take *them* in, and make them conform to the formula. Whenever conduct is concerned, they look round for Mr. A and B to direct them how far to go in obeying Christ.

Now we may be well assured that the case was not thus, but far otherwise, with the early Christians. Had it been thus, Christianity never would have expanded from an obscure sect of the despised Hebrews into the religion of the Roman empire. When their enemies said, 'See how these Christians love one another'[6] (a remark not likely to be made by anybody now), they assuredly had a much livelier feeling of the meaning of their creed than they have ever had since. And to this cause, probably, it is chiefly owing that Christianity now makes so little progress in extending its domain, and after eighteen centuries, is still nearly confined to Europeans and the

---

6. From Tertullian's (late second century C.E.), *Apology*, translated from Latin by T. R. Glover (London: Heinemann; New York: Putnam's Sons, 1931), 39.7.

descendants of Europeans. Even with the strictly religious, who are much in earnest about their doctrines, and attach a greater amount of meaning to many of them than people in general, it commonly happens that the part which is thus comparatively active in their minds is that which was made by Calvin, or Knox,[7] or some such person much nearer in character to themselves. The sayings of Christ coexist passively in their minds, producing hardly any effect beyond what is caused by mere listening to words so amiable and bland. There are many reasons, doubtless, why doctrines which are the badge of a sect retain more of their vitality than those common to all recognised sects, and why more pains are taken by teachers to keep their meaning alive; but one reason certainly is, that the peculiar doctrines are more questioned, and have to be oftener defended against open gainsayers. Both teachers and learners go to sleep at their post, as soon as there is no enemy in the field.

The same thing holds true, generally speaking, of all traditional doctrines—those of prudence and knowledge of life, as well as of morals or religion. All languages and literatures are full of general observations on life, both as to what it is, and how to conduct oneself in it; observations which everybody knows, which everybody repeats, or hears with acquiescence, which are received as truisms, yet of which most people first truly learn the meaning, when experience, generally of a painful kind, has made it a reality to them. How often, when smarting under some unforeseen misfortune or disappointment, does a person call to mind some proverb or common saying, familiar to him all his life, the meaning of which, if he had ever before felt it as he does now, would have saved him from the calamity. There are indeed reasons for this, other than the absence of discussion: there are many truths of which the full meaning *cannot* be realized, until personal experience has brought it home. But much more of the meaning even of these would have been understood, and what was understood would have been far more deeply impressed on the mind, if the man had been accustomed to hear it argued *pro* and *con* by people who did understand it. The fatal tendency of mankind to leave off thinking about a thing when it is no longer doubtful, is the cause of half their errors. A contemporary author has well spoken of 'the deep slumber of a decided opinion.'[8]

---

7. John Knox (1505 or 1514–1572), a Scottish minister and theologian, a leader of the Reformation, and the founder of the Presbyterian Church of Scotland. John Calvin (1508–1564), a French theologian, pastor, and reformer in Geneva during the Protestant Reformation.

8. "The unfortunate Ladurlad did not desire the sleep that for ever fled his weary eyelids with more earnestness than most people seek the deep slumber of a decided opinion." Arthur Helps, *Thoughts in the Cloister and the Crowd*, a book of aphorisms published in 1835 (Glasgow: Wilson & McCormik, 1883), p. 10.

But what! (it may be asked) Is the absence of unanimity an indispensable condition of true knowledge? Is it necessary that some part of mankind should persist in error, to enable any to realize the truth? Does a belief cease to be real and vital as soon as it is generally received—and is a proposition never thoroughly understood and felt unless some doubt of it remains? As soon as mankind have unanimously accepted a truth, does the truth perish within them? The highest aim and best result of improved intelligence, it has hitherto been thought, is to unite mankind more and more in the acknowledgment of all important truths: and does the intelligence only last as long as it has not achieved its object? Do the fruits of conquest perish by the very completeness of the victory?

I affirm no such thing. As mankind improve, the number of doctrines which are no longer disputed or doubted will be constantly on the increase: and the well-being of mankind may almost be measured by the number and gravity of the truths which have reached the point of being uncontested. The cessation, on one question after another, of serious controversy, is one of the necessary incidents of the consolidation of opinion; a consolidation as salutary in the case of true opinions, as it is dangerous and noxious when the opinions are erroneous. But though this gradual narrowing of the bounds of diversity of opinion is necessary in both senses of the term, being at once inevitable and indispensable, we are not therefore obliged to conclude that all its consequences must be beneficial. The loss of so important an aid to the intelligent and living apprehension of a truth, as is afforded by the necessity of explaining it to, or defending it against, opponents, though not sufficient to outweigh, is no trifling drawback from, the benefit of its universal recognition. Where this advantage can no longer be had, I confess I should like to see the teachers of mankind endeavouring to provide a substitute for it; some contrivance for making the difficulties of the question as present to the learner's consciousness, as if they were pressed upon him by a dissentient champion, eager for his conversion.

But instead of seeking contrivances for this purpose, they have lost those they formerly had. The Socratic dialectics, so magnificently exemplified in the dialogues of Plato, were a contrivance of this description. They were essentially a negative discussion of the great questions of philosophy and life, directed with consummate skill to the purpose of convincing any one who had merely adopted the commonplaces of received opinion, that he did not understand the subject—that he as yet attached no definite meaning to the doctrines he professed; in order that, becoming aware of his ignorance, he might be put in the way to attain a stable belief, resting on a clear apprehension both of the meaning of doctrines and of their evidence. The school disputations of the middle ages had a somewhat similar object. They were intended to make sure that the pupil understood his own opinion, and (by necessary correlation) the opinion opposed to it, and could enforce the grounds of the one and confute those of the other. These last-mentioned contests had indeed the incurable defect, that the premises appealed to were taken from authority, not from reason; and, as a discipline to the mind, they were in every respect inferior to the powerful dialectics which formed the intellects of the 'Socratici viri:'[9] but the modern mind owes far more to both than it is generally willing to admit, and the present modes of education contain nothing which in the smallest degree supplies the place either of the one or of the other. A person who derives all his instruction from teachers or books, even if he escape the besetting temptation of contenting himself with cram, is under no compulsion to hear both sides; accordingly it is far from a frequent accomplishment, even among thinkers, to know both sides; and the weakest part of what everybody says in defence of his opinion, is what he intends as a reply to antagonists. It is the fashion of the present time to disparage negative logic—that which points out weaknesses in theory or errors in practice, without establishing positive truths. Such negative criticism would indeed be poor enough as an ultimate result; but as a means to attaining any positive knowledge or conviction worthy the name, it cannot be valued too highly; and until people are again systematically trained to it, there will be few great thinkers, and a low general average of intellect, in any but the mathematical and physical departments of speculation. On any other subject no one's opinions deserve the name of knowledge, except so far as he has either had forced upon him by others, or gone through of himself, the same mental process which would have been required of him in carrying on an active controversy with opponents. That, therefore, which when absent, it is so indispensable, but so difficult, to create, how worse than absurd is it to forego, when spontaneously offering itself! If there are any persons who contest a received opinion, or who will do so if law or opinion will let them, let us thank them for it, open our minds to listen to them, and rejoice that there is some one to do for us what we otherwise ought, if we have any regard for either the certainty or the vitality of our convictions, to do with much greater labour for ourselves.

It still remains to speak of one of the principal causes which make diversity of opinion advantageous, and will continue to do so until

---

9. From Cicero's oration *Ad Atticum* (xiv.9); it refers to the pupils of Socrates, primarily Plato and Aristotle: "Oh Socrates and Socratic philosophers, I shall never be able to thank you enough!"

mankind shall have entered a stage of intellectual advancement which at present seems at an incalculable distance. We have hitherto considered only two possibilities: that the received opinion may be false, and some other opinion, consequently, true; or that, the received opinion being true, a conflict with the opposite error is essential to a clear apprehension and deep feeling of its truth. But there is a commoner case than either of these; when the conflicting doctrines, instead of being one true and the other false, share the truth between them; and the nonconforming opinion is needed to supply the remainder of the truth, of which the received doctrine embodies only a part. Popular opinions, on subjects not palpable to sense, are often true, but seldom or never the whole truth. They are a part of the truth; sometimes a greater, sometimes a smaller part, but exaggerated, distorted, and disjoined from the truths by which they ought to be accompanied and limited. Heretical opinions, on the other hand, are generally some of these suppressed and neglected truths, bursting the bonds which kept them down, and either seeking reconciliation with the truth contained in the common opinion, or fronting it as enemies, and setting themselves up, with similar exclusiveness, as the whole truth. The latter case is hitherto the most frequent, as, in the human mind, one-sidedness has always been the rule, and many-sidedness the exception. Hence, even in revolutions of opinion, one part of the truth usually sets while another rises. Even progress, which ought to superadd, for the most part only substitutes one partial and incomplete truth for another; improvement consisting chiefly in this, that the new fragment of truth is more wanted, more adapted to the needs of the time, than that which it displaces. Such being the partial character of prevailing opinions, even when resting on a true foundation; every opinion which embodies somewhat of the portion of truth which the common opinion omits, ought to be considered precious, with whatever amount of error and confusion that truth may be blended. No sober judge of human affairs will feel bound to be indignant because those who force on our notice truths which we should otherwise have overlooked, overlook some of those which we see. Rather, he will think that so long as popular truth is onesided, it is more desirable than otherwise that unpopular truth should have onesided asserters too; such being usually the most energetic, and the most likely to compel reluctant attention to the fragment of wisdom which they proclaim as if it were the whole.

Thus, in the eighteenth century, when nearly all the instructed, and all those of the uninstructed who were led by them, were lost in admiration of what is called civilization, and of the marvels of modern science, literature, and philosophy, and while greatly overrating the amount of unlikeness between the men of modern and those of ancient times, indulged the belief that the whole of the difference was in their own favour; with what a salutary shock did the paradoxes of Rousseau[1] explode like bombshells in the midst, dislocating the compact mass of onesided opinion, and forcing its elements to recombine in a better form and with additional ingredients. Not that the current opinions were on the whole farther from the truth than Rousseau's were; on the contrary they were nearer to it; they contained more of positive truth, and very much less of error. Nevertheless there lay in Rousseau's doctrine, and has floated down the stream of opinion along with it, a considerable amount of exactly those truths which the popular opinion wanted; and these are the deposit which was left behind when the flood subsided. The superior worth of simplicity of life, the enervating and demoralizing effect of the trammels and hypocrisies of artificial society, are ideas which have never been entirely absent from cultivated minds since Rousseau wrote; and they will in time produce their due effect, though at present needing to be asserted as much as ever, and to be asserted by deeds, for words, on this subject, have nearly exhausted their power.

In politics, again, it is almost a commonplace, that a party of order or stability, and a party of progress or reform, are both necessary elements of a healthy state of political life; until the one or the other shall have so enlarged its mental grasp as to be a party equally of order and of progress, knowing and distinguishing what is fit to be preserved from what ought to be swept away. Each of these modes of thinking derives its utility from the deficiencies of the other; but it is in a great measure the opposition of the other that keeps each within the limits of reason and sanity. Unless opinions favourable to democracy and to aristocracy, to property and to equality, to cooperation and to competition, to luxury and to abstinence, to sociality and individuality, to liberty and discipline, and all the other standing antagonisms of practical life, are expressed with equal freedom, and enforced and defended with equal talent and energy, there is no chance of both elements obtaining their due; one scale is sure to go up, and the other down. Truth, in the great practical concerns of life, is so much a question of the reconciling and combining of opposites, that very few have minds sufficiently capacious and impartial to make the adjustment with an approach to correctness, and it has to be made by the rough process of a struggle between combatants fighting under hostile banners. On any of the great open questions just enumerated, if either of the two opinions has a better claim

---

1. Jean-Jacques Rousseau (1712–1778), Genevan political and moral philosopher, author of *The Social Contract* (1762), which set out the theoretical foundations of popular sovereignty.

than the other, not merely to be tolerated, but to be encouraged and countenanced, it is the one which happens at the particular time and place to be in a minority. That is the opinion which, for the time being, represents the neglected interests, the side of human well-being which is in danger of obtaining less than its share. I am aware that there is not, in this country, any intolerance of differences of opinion on most of these topics. They are adduced to show, by admitted and multiplied examples, the universality of the fact, that only through diversity of opinion is there, in the existing state of human intellect, a chance of fair play to all sides of the truth. When there are persons to be found, who form an exception to the apparent unanimity of the world on any subject, even if the world is in the right, it is always probable that dissentients have something worth hearing to say for themselves, and that truth would lose something by their silence.

It may be objected, 'But *some* received principles, especially on the highest and most vital subjects, are more than half-truths. The Christian morality, for instance, is the whole truth on that subject, and if any one teaches a morality which varies from it, he is wholly in error.' As this is of all cases the most important in practice, none can be fitter to test the general maxim. But before pronouncing what Christian morality is or is not, it would be desirable to decide what is meant by Christian morality. If it means the morality of the New Testament, I wonder that any one who derives his knowledge of this from the book itself, can suppose that it was announced, or intended, as a complete doctrine of morals. The Gospel always refers to a pre-existing morality, and confines its precepts to the particulars in which that morality was to be corrected, or superseded by a wider and higher; expressing itself, moreover, in terms most general, often impossible to be interpreted literally, and possessing rather the impressiveness of poetry or eloquence than the precision of legislation. To extract from it a body of ethical doctrine, has never been possible without eking it out from the Old Testament, that is, from a system elaborate indeed, but in many respects barbarous, and intended only for a barbarous people. St. Paul, a declared enemy to this Judaical mode of interpreting the doctrine and filling up the scheme of his Master, equally assumes a pre-existing morality, namely that of the Greeks and Romans; and his advice to Christians is in a great measure a system of accommodation to that; even to the extent of giving an apparent sanction to slavery. What is called Christian, but should rather be termed theological, morality, was not the work of Christ or the Apostles, but is of much later origin, having been gradually built up by the Catholic church of the first five centuries, and though not implicitly adopted by moderns and Protestants, has been much less modified by them than might have been expected. For the most part, indeed, they have contented themselves with cutting off the additions which had been made to it in the middle ages, each sect supplying the place by fresh additions, adapted to its own character and tendencies. That mankind owe a great debt to this morality, and to its early teachers, I should be the last person to deny; but I do not scruple to say of it, that it is, in many important points, incomplete and onesided, and that unless ideas and feelings, not sanctioned by it, had contributed to the formation of European life and character, human affairs would have been in a worse condition than they now are. Christian morality (so called) has all the characters of a reaction; it is, in great part, a protest against Paganism. Its ideal is negative rather than positive; passive rather than active; Innocence rather than Nobleness; Abstinence from Evil, rather than energetic Pursuit of Good: in its precepts (as has been well said) 'thou shalt not' predominates unduly over 'thou shalt.' In its horror of sensuality, it made an idol of asceticism, which has been gradually compromised away into one of legality. It holds out the hope of heaven and the threat of hell, as the appointed and appropriate motives to a virtuous life; in this falling far below the best of the ancients, and doing what lies in it to give to human morality an essentially selfish character, by disconnecting each man's feelings of duty from the interests of his fellow-creatures, except so far as a self-interested inducement is offered to him for consulting them. It is essentially a doctrine of passive obedience; it inculcates submission to all authorities found established; who indeed are not to be actively obeyed when they command what religion forbids, but who are not to be resisted, far less rebelled against, for any amount of wrong to ourselves. And while, in the morality of the best Pagan nations, duty to the State holds even a disproportionate place, infringing on the just liberty of the individual; in purely Christian ethics, that grand department of duty is scarcely noticed or acknowledged. It is in the Koran, not the New Testament, that we read the maxim—'A ruler who appoints any man to an office, when there is in his dominions another man better qualified for it, sins against God and against the State.'[2] What little recognition the idea of obligation to the public obtains in modern morality, is derived from Greek and Roman sources, not from Christian; as, even in the morality of private life, whatever exists of magnanimity, highmindedness, personal dignity, even the sense of honour, is derived from the purely human, not the religious part of our education, and

---

2. Mill is incorrect; this passage is not in the Koran, but in a commentary by Charles Hamilton, *The Hedàya or Guide: A Commentary on the Mussulman Laws*, 4 vols. (London: Bensley, 1791), vol. 2, p. 615 (see *CW*, vol. 18, p. 255).

never could have grown out of a standard of ethics in which the only worth, professedly recognised, is that of obedience.

I am as far as any one from pretending that these defects are necessarily inherent in the Christian ethics, in every manner in which it can be conceived, or that the many requisites of a complete moral doctrine which it does not contain, do not admit of being reconciled with it. Far less would I insinuate this of the doctrines and precepts of Christ himself. I believe that the sayings of Christ are all, that I can see any evidence of their having been intended to be; that they are irreconcileable with nothing which a comprehensive morality requires; that everything which is excellent in ethics may be brought within them, with no greater violence to their language than has been done to it by all who have attempted to deduce from them any practical system of conduct whatever. But it is quite consistent with this, to believe that they contain, and were meant to contain, only a part of the truth; that many essential elements of the highest morality are among the things which are not provided for, nor intended to be provided for, in the recorded deliverances of the Founder of Christianity, and which have been entirely thrown aside in the system of ethics erected on the basis of those deliverances by the Christian Church. And this being so, I think it a great error to persist in attempting to find in the Christian doctrine that complete rule for our guidance, which its author intended it to sanction and enforce, but only partially to provide. I believe, too, that this narrow theory is becoming a grave practical evil, detracting greatly from the value of the moral training and instruction, which so many well-meaning persons are now at length exerting themselves to promote. I much fear that by attempting to form the mind and feelings on an exclusively religious type, and discarding those secular standards (as for want of a better name they may be called) which heretofore coexisted with and supplemented the Christian ethics, receiving some of its spirit, and infusing into it some of theirs, there will result, and is even now resulting, a low, abject, servile type of character, which, submit itself as it may to what it deems the Supreme Will, is incapable of rising to or sympathizing in the conception of Supreme Goodness. I believe that other ethics than any which can be evolved from exclusively Christian sources, must exist side by side with Christian ethics to produce the moral regeneration of mankind; and that the Christian system is no exception to the rule, that in an imperfect state of the human mind, the interests of truth require a diversity of opinions. It is not necessary that in ceasing to ignore the moral truths not contained in Christianity, men should ignore any of those which it does contain. Such prejudice, or oversight, when it occurs, is altogether an evil; but it is one from which we cannot hope to be always exempt, and must be regarded as the price paid for an inestimable good. The exclusive pretension made by a part of the truth to be the whole, must and ought to be protested against, and if a reactionary impulse should make the protestors unjust in their turn, this onesidedness, like the other, may be lamented, but must be tolerated. If Christians would teach infidels to be just to Christianity, they should themselves be just to infidelity. It can do truth no service to blink the fact, known to all who have the most ordinary acquaintance with literary history, that a large portion of the noblest and most valuable moral teaching has been the work, not only of men who did not know, but of men who knew and rejected, the Christian faith.

I do not pretend that the most unlimited use of the freedom of enunciating all possible opinions would put an end to the evils of religious or philosophical sectarianism. Every truth which men of narrow capacity are in earnest about, is sure to be asserted, inculcated, and in many ways even acted on, as if no other truth existed in the world, or at all events none that could limit or qualify the first. I acknowledge that the tendency of all opinions to become sectarian is not cured by the freest discussion, but is often heightened and exacerbated thereby; the truth which ought to have been, but was not, seen, being rejected all the more violently because proclaimed by persons regarded as opponents. But it is not on the impassioned partisan, it is on the calmer and more disinterested bystander, that this collision of opinions works its salutary effect. Not the violent conflict between parts of the truth, but the quiet suppression of half of it, is the formidable evil: there is always hope when people are forced to listen to both sides; it is when they attend only to one that errors harden into prejudices, and truth itself ceases to have the effect of truth, by being exaggerated into falsehood. And since there are few mental attributes more rare than that judicial faculty which can sit in intelligent judgment between two sides of a question, of which only one is represented by an advocate before it, truth has no chance but in proportion as every side of it, every opinion which embodies any fraction of the truth, not only finds advocates, but is so advocated as to be listened to.

We have now recognised the necessity to the mental well-being of mankind (on which all their other well-being depends) of freedom of opinion, and freedom of the expression of opinion, on four distinct grounds; which we will now briefly recapitulate.

First, if any opinion is compelled to silence, that opinion may, for aught we can certainly know, be true. To deny this is to assume our own infallibility.

Secondly, though the silenced opinion be an error, it may, and very commonly does, contain a portion of truth; and since the general or prevailing opinion on any subject is rarely or never the whole truth, it is only by the collision of adverse opinions that the remainder of the truth has any chance of being supplied.

Thirdly, even if the received opinion be not only true, but the whole truth; unless it is suffered to be, and actually is, vigorously and earnestly contested, it will, by most of those who receive it, be held in the manner of a prejudice, with little comprehension or feeling of its rational grounds. And not only this, but, fourthly, the meaning of the doctrine itself will be in danger of being lost, or enfeebled, and deprived of its vital effect on the character and conduct: the dogma becoming a mere formal profession, inefficacious for good, but cumbering the ground, and preventing the growth of any real and heartfelt conviction, from reason or personal experience.

Before quitting the subject of freedom of opinion, it is fit to take some notice of those who say, that the free expression of all opinions should be permitted, on condition that the manner be temperate, and do not pass the bounds of fair discussion. Much might be said on the impossibility of fixing where these supposed bounds are to be placed; for if the test be offence to those whose opinion is attacked, I think experience testifies that this offence is given whenever the attack is telling and powerful, and that every opponent who pushes them hard, and whom they find it difficult to answer, appears to them, if he shows any strong feeling on the subject, an intemperate opponent. But this, though an important consideration in a practical point of view, merges in a more fundamental objection. Undoubtedly the manner of asserting an opinion, even though it be a true one, may be very objectionable, and may justly incur severe censure. But the principal offences of the kind are such as it is mostly impossible, unless by accidental self-betrayal, to bring home to conviction. The gravest of them is, to argue sophistically, to suppress facts or arguments, to misstate the elements of the case, or misrepresent the opposite opinion. But all this, even to the most aggravated degree, is so continually done in perfect good faith, by persons who are not considered, and in many other respects may not deserve to be considered, ignorant or incompetent, that it is rarely possible on adequate grounds conscientiously to stamp the misrepresentation as morally culpable; and still less could law presume to interfere with this kind of controversial misconduct. With regard to what is commonly meant by intemperate discussion, namely invective, sarcasm, personality, and the like, the denunciation of these weapons would deserve more sympathy if it were ever proposed to interdict them equally to both sides; but it is only desired to restrain the employment of them against the prevailing opinion: against the unprevailing they may not only be used without general disapproval, but will be likely to obtain for him who uses them the praise of honest zeal and righteous indignation. Yet whatever mischief arises from their use, is greatest when they are employed against the comparatively defenceless; and whatever unfair advantage can be derived by any opinion from this mode of asserting it, accrues almost exclusively to received opinions. The worst offence of this kind which can be committed by a polemic, is to stigmatize those who hold the contrary opinion as bad and immoral men. To calumny of this sort, those who hold any unpopular opinion are peculiarly exposed, because they are in general few and uninfluential, and nobody but themselves feels much interest in seeing justice done them; but this weapon is, from the nature of the case, denied to those who attack a prevailing opinion: they can neither use it with safety to themselves, nor, if they could, would it do anything but recoil on their own cause. In general, opinions contrary to those commonly received can only obtain a hearing by studied moderation of language, and the most cautious avoidance of unnecessary offence, from which they hardly ever deviate even in a slight degree without losing ground: while unmeasured vituperation employed on the side of the prevailing opinion, really does deter people from professing contrary opinions, and from listening to those who profess them. For the interest, therefore, of truth and justice, it is far more important to restrain this employment of vituperative language than the other; and, for example, if it were necessary to choose, there would be much more need to discourage offensive attacks on infidelity, than on religion. It is, however, obvious that law and authority have no business with restraining either, while opinion ought, in every instance, to determine its verdict by the circumstances of the individual case; condemning every one, on whichever side of the argument he places himself, in whose mode of advocacy either want of candour, or malignity, bigotry, or intolerance of feeling manifest themselves; but not inferring these vices from the side which a person takes, though it be the contrary side of the question to our own: and giving merited honour to every one, whatever opinion he may hold, who has calmness to see and honesty to state what his opponents and their opinions really are, exaggerating nothing to their discredit, keeping nothing back which tells, or can be supposed to tell, in their favour. This is the real morality of public discussion; and if often violated, I am happy to think that there are many controversialists who to a great extent observe it, and a still greater number who conscientiously strive towards it.

CHAPTER III

Of Individuality, as One of the Elements of Well-Being

Such being the reasons which make it imperative that human beings should be free to form opinions, and to express their opinions without reserve; and such the baneful consequences to the intellectual, and through that to the moral nature of man, unless this liberty is either conceded, or asserted in spite of prohibition; let us next examine whether the same reasons do not require that men should be free to act upon their opinions—to carry these out in their lives, without hindrance, either physical or moral, from their fellow-men, so long as it is at their own risk and peril. This last proviso is of course indispensable. No one pretends that actions should be as free as opinions. On the contrary, even opinions lose their immunity, when the circumstances in which they are expressed are such as to constitute their expression a positive instigation to some mischievous act: An opinion that corn-dealers are starvers of the poor, or that private property is robbery, ought to be unmolested when simply circulated through the press, but may justly incur punishment when delivered orally to an excited mob assembled before the house of a corn-dealer, or when handed about among the same mob in the form of a placard. Acts, of whatever kind, which, without justifiable cause, do harm to others, may be, and in the more important cases absolutely require to be, controlled by the unfavourable sentiments, and, when needful, by the active interference of mankind. The liberty of the individual must be thus far limited; he must not make himself a nuisance to other people. But if he refrains from molesting others in what concerns them, and merely acts according to his own inclination and judgment in things which concern himself, the same reasons which show that opinion should be free, prove also that he should be allowed, without molestation, to carry his opinions into practice at his own cost. That mankind are not infallible; that their truths, for the most part, are only half-truths; that unity of opinion, unless resulting from the fullest and freest comparison of opposite opinions, is not desirable, and diversity not an evil, but a good, until mankind are much more capable than at present of recognising all sides of the truth, are principles applicable to men's modes of action, not less than to their opinions. As it is useful that while mankind are imperfect there should be different opinions, so is it that there should be different experiments of living; that free scope should be given to varieties of character, short of injury to others; and that the worth of different modes of life should be proved practically, when any one thinks fit to try them. It is desirable, in short, that in things which do not primarily concern others, individuality should assert itself. Where, not the person's own character, but the traditions or customs of other people are the rule of conduct, there is wanting one of the principal ingredients of human happiness, and quite the chief ingredient of individual and social progress.

In maintaining this principle, the greatest difficulty to be encountered does not lie in the appreciation of means towards an acknowledged end, but in the indifference of persons in general to the end itself. If it were felt that the free development of individuality is one of the leading essentials of well-being; that is not only a co-ordinate element with all that is designated by the terms civilization, instruction, education, culture, but is itself a necessary part and condition of all those things; there would be no danger that liberty should be undervalued, and the adjustment of the boundaries between it and social control would present no extraordinary difficulty. But the evil is, that individual spontaneity is hardly recognized by the common modes of thinking, as having any intrinsic worth, or deserving any regard on its own account. The majority, being satisfied with the ways of mankind as they now are (for it is they who make them what they are), cannot comprehend why those ways should not be good enough for everybody; and what is more, spontaneity forms no part of the ideal of the majority of moral and social reformers, but is rather looked on with jealousy, as a troublesome and perhaps rebellious obstruction to the general acceptance of what these reformers, in their own judgment, think would be best for mankind. Few persons, out of Germany, even comprehend the meaning of the doctrine which Wilhelm Von Humboldt, so eminent both as a *savant*[3] and as a politician, made the text of a treatise—that 'the end of man, or that which is prescribed by the eternal or immutable dictates of reason, and not suggested by vague and transient desires, is the highest and most harmonious developement of his powers to a complete and consistent whole;' that, therefore, the object 'towards which every human being must ceaselessly direct his efforts, and on which especially those who design to influence their fellow-men must ever keep their eyes, is the individuality of power and developement;' that for this there are two requisites, 'freedom, and a variety of situations;' and that from the union of these arise 'individual

3. A person of learning (French).

vigour and manifold diversity,' which combine themselves in 'originality.'[4]

Little, however, as people are accustomed to a doctrine like that of Von Humboldt, and surprising as it may be to them to find so high a value attached to individuality, the question, one must nevertheless think, can only be one of degree. No one's idea of excellence in conduct is that people should do absolutely nothing but copy one another. No one would assert that people ought not to put into their mode of life, and into the conduct of their concerns, any impress whatever of their own judgment, or of their own individual character. On the other hand, it would be absurd to pretend that people ought to live as if nothing whatever had been known in the world before they came into it; as if experience had as yet done nothing towards showing that one mode of existence, or of conduct, is preferable to another. Nobody denies that people should be so taught and trained in youth, as to know and benefit by the ascertained results of human experience. But it is the privilege and proper condition of a human being, arrived at the maturity of his faculties, to use and interpret experience in his own way. It is for him to find out what part of recorded experience is properly applicable to his own circumstances and character. The traditions and customs of other people are, to a certain extent, evidence of what their experience has taught *them*; presumptive evidence, and as such, have a claim to his deference: but, in the first place, their experience may be too narrow; or they may not have interpreted it rightly. Secondly, their interpretation of experience may be correct, but unsuitable to him. Customs are made for customary circumstances, and customary characters: and his circumstances or his character may be uncustomary. Thirdly, though the customs be both good as customs, and suitable to him, yet to conform to custom, merely *as* custom, does not educate or develop in him any of the qualities which are the distinctive endowment of a human being. The human faculties of perception, judgment, discriminative feeling, mental activity, and even moral preference, are exercised only in making a choice. He who does anything because it is the custom, makes no choice. He gains no practice either in discerning or in desiring what is best. The mental and moral, like the muscular powers, are improved only by being used. The faculties are called into no exercise by doing a thing merely because others do it, no more than by believing a thing only because others believe it. If the grounds of an opinion are not conclusive to the person's own reason, his reason cannot be strengthened, but is likely to be weakened by his adopting it: and if the

4. *The Sphere and Duties of Government*, from the German of Baron Wilhelm von Humboldt, pp. 11–13 [*Mill's note*].

inducements to an act are not such as are consentaneous to his own feelings and character (where affection, or the rights of others, are not concerned) it is so much done towards rendering his feelings and character inert and torpid, instead of active and energetic.

He who lets the world, or his own portion of it, choose his plan of life for him, has no need of any other faculty than the ape-like one of imitation. He who chooses his plan for himself, employs all his faculties. He must use observation to see, reasoning and judgment to foresee, activity to gather materials for decision, discrimination to decide, and when he has decided, firmness and self-control to hold to his deliberate decision. And these qualities he requires and exercises exactly in proportion as the part of his conduct which he determines according to his own judgment and feelings is a large one. It is possible that he might be guided in some good path, and kept out of harm's way, without any of these things. But what will be his comparative worth as a human being? It really is of importance, not only what men do, but also what manner of men they are that do it. Among the works of man, which human life is rightly employed in perfecting and beautifying, the first in importance surely is man himself. Supposing it were possible to get houses built, corn grown, battles fought, causes tried, and even churches erected and prayers said, by machinery—by automatons in human form—it would be a considerable loss to exchange for these automatons even the men and women who at present inhabit the more civilized parts of the world, and who assuredly are but starved specimens of what nature can and will produce. Human nature is not a machine to be built after a model, and set to do exactly the work prescribed for it, but a tree, which requires to grow and develope itself on all sides, according to the tendency of the inward forces which make it a living thing.

It will probably be conceded that it is desirable people should exercise their understandings, and that an intelligent following of custom, or even occasionally an intelligent deviation from custom, is better than a blind and simply mechanical adhesion to it. To a certain extent it is admitted, that our understanding should be our own: but there is not the same willingness to admit that our desires and impulses should be our own likewise; or that to possess impulses of our own, and of any strength, is anything but a peril and a snare. Yet desires and impulses are as much a part of a perfect human being, as beliefs and restraints: and strong impulses are only perilous when not properly balanced; when one set of aims and inclinations is developed into strength, while others, which ought to co-exist with them, remain weak and inactive. It is not because men's desires are strong that they act ill; it is because their consciences are weak. There is no natural connexion between strong impulses and a weak conscience. The natural connexion is the other way. To say that one person's desires and feelings are stronger and more various than those of another, is merely to say that he has more of the raw material of human nature, and is therefore capable, perhaps of more evil, but certainly of more good. Strong impulses are but another name for energy. Energy may be turned to bad uses; but more good may always be made of an energetic nature, than of an indolent and impassive one. Those who have most natural feeling, are always those whose cultivated feelings may be made the strongest. The same strong susceptibilities which make the personal impulses vivid and powerful, are also the source from whence are generated the most passionate love of virtue, and the sternest self-control. It is through the cultivation of these, that society both does its duty and protects its interests: not by rejecting the stuff of which heroes are made, because it knows not how to make them. A person whose desires and impulses are his own—are the expression of his own nature, as it has been developed and modified by his own culture— is said to have a character. One whose desires and impulses are not his own, has no character, no more than a steam-engine has a character. If, in addition to being his own, his impulses are strong, and are under the government of a strong will, he has an energetic character. Whoever thinks that individuality of desires and impulses should not be encouraged to unfold itself, must maintain that society has no need of strong natures—is not the better for containing many persons who have much character—and that a high general average of energy is not desirable.

In some early states of society, these forces might be, and were, too much ahead of the power which society then possessed of disciplining and controlling them. There has been a time when the element of spontaneity and individuality was in excess, and the social principle had a hard struggle with it. The difficulty then was, to induce men of strong bodies or minds to pay obedience to any rules which required them to control their impulses. To overcome this difficulty, law and discipline, like the Popes struggling against the Emperors, asserted a power over the whole man, claiming to control all his life in order to control his character—which society had not found any other sufficient means of binding. But society has now fairly got the better of individuality; and the danger which threatens human nature is not the excess, but the deficiency, of personal impulses and preferences. Things are vastly changed, since the passions of those who were strong by station or by personal endowment were in a state of habitual rebellion against laws and ordinances, and required to be rigorously chained up to enable the persons within their reach to enjoy any particle of security. In our times, from the highest class of society down to the lowest, every one lives as under

the eye of a hostile and dreaded censorship. Not only in what concerns others, but in what concerns only themselves, the individual, or the family, do not ask themselves—what do I prefer? or,
what would suit my character and disposition? or, what would allow
the best and highest in me to have fair play, and enable it to grow
and thrive? They ask themselves, what is suitable to my position?
what is usually done by persons of my station and pecuniary circumstances? or (worse still) what is usually done by persons of a
station and circumstances superior to mine? I do not mean that they
choose what is customary, in preference to what suits their own
inclination. It does not occur to them to have any inclination, except
for what is customary. Thus the mind itself is bowed to the yoke:
even in what people do for pleasure, conformity is the first thing
thought of; they like in crowds; they exercise choice only among
things commonly done: peculiarity of taste, eccentricity of conduct,
are shunned equally with crimes: until by dint of not following their
own nature, they have no nature to follow: their human capacities
are withered and starved: they become incapable of any strong
wishes or native pleasures, and are generally without either opinions or feelings of home growth, or properly their own. Now is this,
or is it not, the desirable condition of human nature?

It is so, on the Calvinistic theory. According to that, the one great
offence of man is Self-will. All the good of which humanity is capable, is comprised in Obedience. You have no choice; thus you must
do, and no otherwise: 'whatever is not a duty, is a sin.' Human nature
being radically corrupt, there is no redemption for any one until
human nature is killed within him. To one holding this theory of
life, crushing out any of the human faculties, capacities, and susceptibilities, is no evil: man needs no capacity, but that of surrendering himself to the will of God: and if he uses any of his faculties
for any other purpose but to do that supposed will more effectually,
he is better without them. That is the theory of Calvinism; and it is
held, in a mitigated form, by many who do not consider themselves
Calvinists; the mitigation consisting in giving a less ascetic interpretation to the alleged will of God; asserting it to be his will that
mankind should gratify some of their inclinations; of course not in
the manner they themselves prefer, but in the way of obedience, that
is, in a way prescribed to them by authority; and, therefore, by the
necessary conditions of the case, the same for all.

In some such insidious form there is at present a strong tendency
to this narrow theory of life, and to the pinched and hidebound type
of human character which it patronizes. Many persons, no doubt,
sincerely think that human beings thus cramped and dwarfed, are
as their Maker designed them to be; just as many have thought that
trees are a much finer thing when clipped into pollards, or cut out

into figures of animals, than as nature made them. But if it be any part of religion to believe that man was made by a good being, it is more consistent with that faith to believe, that this Being gave all human faculties that they might be cultivated and unfolded, not rooted out and consumed, and that he takes delight in every nearer approach made by his creatures to the ideal conception embodied in them, every increase in any of their capabilities of comprehension, of action, or of enjoyment. There is a different type of human excellence from the Calvinistic; a conception of humanity as having its nature bestowed on it for other purposes than merely to be abnegated. 'Pagan self-assertion' is one of the elements of human worth, as well as 'Christian self-denial.'[5] There is a Greek ideal of self-development, which the Platonic and Christian ideal of self-government blends with, but does not supersede. It may be better to be a John Knox than an Alcibiades, but it is better to be a Pericles[6] than either; nor would a Pericles, if we had one in these days, be without anything good which belonged to John Knox.

It is not by wearing down into uniformity all that is individual in themselves, but by cultivating it and calling it forth, within the limits imposed by the rights and interests of others, that human beings become a noble and beautiful object of contemplation; and as the works partake the character of those who do them, by the same process human life also becomes rich, diversified, and animating, furnishing more abundant aliment to high thoughts and elevating feelings, and strengthening the tie which binds every individual to the race, by making the race infinitely better worth belonging to. In proportion to the development of his individuality, each person becomes more valuable to himself, and is therefore capable of being more valuable to others. There is a greater fulness of life about his own existence, and when there is more life in the units there is more in the mass which is composed of them. As much compression as is necessary to prevent the stronger specimens of human nature from encroaching on the rights of others, cannot be dispensed with; but for this there is ample compensation even in the point of view of human development. The means of development which the individual loses by being prevented from gratifying his inclinations to the injury of others, are chiefly obtained at the expense of the development of other people. And even to himself there is a full equivalent in the better development of the social part of his nature, rendered

5. Sterling's *Essays* [Mill's note].
6. Pericles (495–429 B.C.E.) was an Athenian statesman and general during the Golden Age of Athens, famous for his wisdom in war and peace; Thucydides called him "the first citizen of Athens." Alcibiades (450–404 B.C.E.) was an Athenian statesman, military commander, and politician, famous for his impetuous character and above all his campaign in favor of the expedition to Sicily, which resulted in a massive defeat and the beginning of the decline of the Athenian Empire.

possible by the restraint put upon the selfish part. To be held to rigid rules of justice for the sake of others, developes the feelings and capacities which have the good of others for their object. But to be restrained in things not affecting their good, by their mere displeasure, developes nothing valuable, except such force of character as may unfold itself in resisting the restraint. If acquiesced in, it dulls and blunts the whole nature. To give any fair play to the nature of each, it is essential that different persons should be allowed to lead different lives. In proportion as this latitude has been exercised in any age, has that age been noteworthy to posterity. Even despotism does not produce its worst effects, so long as individuality exists under it; and whatever crushes individuality is despotism, by whatever name it may be called, and whether it professes to be enforcing the will of God or the injunctions of men.

Having said that individuality is the same thing with development, and that it is only the cultivation of individuality which produces, or can produce, well-developed human beings, I might here close the argument: for what more or better can be said of any condition of human affairs, than that it brings human beings themselves nearer to the best thing they can be? or what worse can be said of any obstruction to good, than that it prevents this? Doubtless, however, these considerations will not suffice to convince those who most need convincing; and it is necessary further to show, that these developed human beings are of some use to the undeveloped—to point out to those who do not desire liberty, and would not avail themselves of it, that they may be in some intelligible manner rewarded for allowing other people to make use of it without hindrance.

In the first place, then, I would suggest that they might possibly learn something from them. It will not be denied by anybody, that originality is a valuable element in human affairs. There is always need of persons not only to discover new truths, and point out when what were once truths are true no longer, but also to commence new practices, and set the example of more enlightened conduct, and better taste and sense in human life. This cannot well be gainsaid by anybody who does not believe that the world has already attained perfection in all its ways and practices. It is true that this benefit is not capable of being rendered by everybody alike: there are but few persons, in comparison with the whole of mankind, whose experiments, if adopted by others, would be likely to be any improvement on established practice. But these few are the salt of the earth; without them, human life would become a stagnant pool. Not only is it they who introduce good things which did not before exist; it is they who keep the life in those which already existed. If there were nothing new to be done, would human intellect cease to be necessary?

Would it be a reason why those who do the old things should forget why they are done, and do them like cattle, not like human beings? There is only too great a tendency in the best beliefs and practices to degenerate into the mechanical; and unless there were a succession of persons whose ever-recurring originality prevents the grounds of those beliefs and practices from becoming merely traditional, such dead matter would not resist the smallest shock from anything really alive, and there would be no reason why civilization should not die out, as in the Byzantine Empire. Persons of genius, it is true, are, and are always likely to be, a small minority; but in order to have them, it is necessary to preserve the soil in which they grow. Genius can only breathe freely in an *atmosphere* of freedom. Persons of genius are, *ex vi termini*,[7] *more* individual than any other people—less capable, consequently, of fitting themselves, without hurtful compression, into any of the small number of moulds which society provides in order to save its members the trouble of forming their own character. If from timidity they consent to be forced into one of these moulds, and to let all that part of themselves which cannot expand under the pressure remain unexpanded, society will be little the better for their genius. If they are of a strong character, and break their fetters, they become a mark for the society which has not succeeded in reducing them to commonplace, to point at with solemn warning as 'wild,' 'erratic,' and the like; much as if one should complain of the Niagara river for not flowing smoothly between its banks like a Dutch canal.

I insist thus emphatically on the importance of genius, and the necessity of allowing it to unfold itself freely both in thought and in practice, being well aware that no one will deny the position in theory, but knowing also that almost every one, in reality, is totally indifferent to it. People think genius a fine thing if it enables a man to write an exciting poem, or paint a picture. But in its true sense, that of originality in thought and action, though no one says that it is not a thing to be admired, nearly all, at heart, think that they can do very well without it. Unhappily this is too natural to be wondered at. Originality is the one thing which unoriginal minds cannot feel the use of. They cannot see what it is to do for them: how should they? If they could see what it would do for them, it would not be originality. The first service which originality has to render them, is that of opening their eyes: which being once fully done, they would have a chance of being themselves original. Meanwhile, recollecting that nothing was ever yet done which some one was not the first to do, and that all good things which exist are the fruits of originality, let them be modest enough to believe that there is something

---

7. By definition (Latin).

still left for it to accomplish, and assure themselves that they are more in need of originality, the less they are conscious of the want.

In sober truth, whatever homage may be professed, or even paid, to real or supposed mental superiority, the general tendency of things throughout the world is to render mediocrity the ascendant power among mankind. In ancient history, in the middle ages, and in a diminishing degree through the long transition from feudality to the present time, the individual was a power in himself; and if he had either great talents or a high social position, he was a considerable power. At present individuals are lost in the crowd. In politics it is almost a triviality to say that public opinion now rules the world. The only power deserving the name is that of masses, and of governments while they make themselves the organ of the tendencies and instincts of masses. This is as true in the moral and social relations of private life as in public transactions. Those whose opinions go by the name of public opinion, are not always the same sort of public: in America they are the whole white population; in England, chiefly the middle class. But they are always a mass, that is to say, collective mediocrity. And what is a still greater novelty, the mass do not now take their opinions from dignitaries in Church or State, from ostensible leaders, or from books. Their thinking is done for them by men much like themselves, addressing them or speaking in their name, on the spur of the moment, through the newspapers. I am not complaining of all this. I do not assert that anything better is compatible, as a general rule, with the present low state of the human mind. But that does not hinder the government of mediocrity from being mediocre government. No government by a democracy or a numerous aristocracy, either in its political acts or in the opinions, qualities, and tone of mind which it fosters, ever did or could rise above mediocrity, except in so far as the sovereign. Many have let themselves be guided (which in their best times they always have done) by the counsels and influence of a more highly gifted and instructed One or Few. The initiation of all wise or noble things, comes and must come from individuals; generally at first from some one individual. The honour and glory of the average man is that he is capable of following that initiative; that he can respond internally to wise and noble things, and be led to them with his eyes open. I am not countenancing the sort of 'hero-worship' which applauds the strong man of genius for forcibly seizing on the government of the world and making it do his bidding in spite of itself. All he can claim is, freedom to point out the way. The power of compelling others into it, is not only inconsistent with the freedom and development of all the rest, but corrupting to the strong man himself. It does seem, however, that when the opinions of masses of merely average men are everywhere become or becoming the dominant power, the counterpoise and corrective to that tendency would be, the more and more pronounced individuality of those who stand on the higher eminences of thought. It is in these circumstances most especially, that exceptional individuals, instead of being deterred, should be encouraged in acting differently from the mass. In other times there was no advantage in their doing so, unless they acted not only differently, but better. In this age the mere example of non-conformity, the mere refusal to bend the knee to custom, is itself a service. Precisely because the tyranny of opinion is such as to make eccentricity a reproach, it is desirable, in order to break through that tyranny, that people should be eccentric. Eccentricity has always abounded when and where strength of character has abounded; and the amount of eccentricity in a society has generally been proportional to the amount of genius, mental vigour, and moral courage which it contained. That so few now dare to be eccentric, marks the chief danger of the time.

I have said that it is important to give the freest scope possible to uncustomary things, in order that it may in time appear which of these are fit to be converted into customs. But independence of action, and disregard of custom are not solely deserving of encouragement for the chance they afford that better modes of action, and customs more worthy of general adoption, may be struck out; nor is it only persons of decided mental superiority who have a just claim to carry on their lives in their own way. There is no reason that all human existences should be constructed on some one, or some small number of patterns. If a person possesses any tolerable amount of common sense and experience, his own mode of laying out his existence is the best, not because it is the best in itself, but because it is his own mode. Human beings are not like sheep; and even sheep are not undistinguishably alike. A man cannot get a coat or a pair of boots to fit him, unless they are either made to his measure, or he has a whole warehouseful to choose from: and is it easier to fit him with a life than with a coat, or are human beings more like one another in their whole physical and spiritual conformation than in the shape of their feet? If it were only that people have diversities of taste, that is reason enough for not attempting to shape them all after one model. But different persons also require different conditions for their spiritual development; and can no more exist healthily in the same moral, than all the variety of plants can in the same physical, atmosphere and climate. The same things which are helps to one person towards the cultivation of his higher nature, are hindrances to another. The same mode of life is a healthy excitement to one, keeping all his faculties of action and enjoyment in their best order, while to another it is a distracting burthen, which suspends or crushes all internal life. Such are the differences among human beings in their sources of pleasure, their susceptibilities of pain, and the operation on them of different physical and moral agencies, that unless there is a corresponding diversity in their modes of life, they neither obtain their fair share of happiness, nor grow up to the mental, moral, and æsthetic stature of which their nature is capable. Why then should tolerance, as far as the public sentiment is concerned, extend only to tastes and modes of life which extort acquiescence by the multitude of their adherents? Nowhere (except in some monastic institutions) is diversity of taste entirely unrecognised; a person may, without blame, either like or dislike rowing, or smoking, or music, or athletic exercises, or chess, or cards, or study, because both those who like each of these things, and those who dislike them, are too numerous to be put down. But the man, and still more the woman, who can be accused either of doing 'what nobody does,' or of not doing 'what everybody does,' is the subject of as much depreciatory remark as if he or she had committed some grave moral delinquency. Persons require to possess a title, or some other badge of rank, or of the consideration of people of rank, to be able to indulge somewhat in the luxury of doing as they like without detriment to their estimation. To indulge somewhat, I repeat: for whoever allow themselves much of that indulgence, incur the risk of something worse than disparaging speeches—they are in peril of a commission *de lunatico*,[8] and of having their property taken from them and given to their relations.[9]

There is one characteristic of the present direction of public opinion, peculiarly calculated to make it intolerant of any marked demonstration of individuality. The general average of mankind are not only moderate in intellect, but also moderate in inclinations: they have no tastes or wishes strong enough to incline them to do

---

8. A commission to ascertain the presence of insanity.
9. There is something both contemptible and frightful in the sort of evidence on which, of late years, any person can be judicially declared unfit for the management of his affairs; and after his death, his disposal of his property can be set aside, if there is enough of it to pay the expenses of litigation—which are charged on the property itself. All the minute details of his daily life are pried into, and whatever is found which, seen through the medium of the perceiving and describing faculties of the lowest of the low, bears an appearance unlike absolute commonplace, is laid before the jury as evidence of insanity, and often with success; the jurors being little, if at all, less vulgar and ignorant than the witnesses; while the judges, with that extraordinary want of knowledge of human nature and life which continually astonishes us in English lawyers, often help to mislead them. These trials speak volumes as to the state of feeling and opinion among the vulgar with regard to human liberty. So far from setting any value on individuality—so far from respecting the rights of each individual to act, in things indifferent, as seems good to his own judgment and inclinations, judges and juries cannot even conceive that a person in a state of sanity can desire such freedom. In former days, when it was proposed to burn atheists, charitable people used to suggest putting them in a madhouse instead: it would be nothing surprising now-a-days were we to see this done, and the doers applauding themselves, because, instead of persecuting for religion, they had adopted so humane and Christian a mode of treating these unfortunates, not without a silent satisfaction at their having thereby obtained their deserts [*Mill's note*].

anything unusual, and they consequently do not understand those who have, and class all such with the wild and intemperate whom they are accustomed to look down upon. Now, in addition to this fact which is general, we have only to suppose that a strong movement has set in towards the improvement of morals, and it is evident what we have to expect. In these days such a movement has set in; much has actually been effected in the way of increased regularity of conduct, and discouragement of excesses; and there is a philanthropic spirit abroad, for the exercise of which there is no more inviting field than the moral and prudential improvement of our fellow-creatures. These tendencies of the times cause the public to be more disposed than at most former periods to prescribe general rules of conduct, and endeavour to make every one conform to the approved standard. And that standard, express or tacit, is to desire nothing strongly. Its ideal of character is to be without any marked character; to maim by compression, like a Chinese lady's foot, every part of human nature which stands out prominently, and tends to make the person markedly dissimilar in outline to commonplace humanity.

As is usually the case with ideals which exclude one-half of what is desirable, the present standard of approbation produces only an inferior imitation of the other half. Instead of great energies guided by vigorous reason, and strong feelings strongly controlled by a conscientious will, its result is weak feelings and weak energies, which therefore can be kept in outward conformity to rule without any strength either of will or of reason. Already energetic characters on any large scale are becoming merely traditional. There is now scarcely any outlet for energy in this country except business. The energy expended in that may still be regarded as considerable. What little is left from that employment, is expended on some hobby; which may be a useful, even a philanthropic hobby, but is always some one thing, and generally a thing of small dimensions. The greatness of England is now all collective: individually small, we only appear capable of anything great by our habit of combining; and with this our moral and religious philanthropists are perfectly contented. But it was men of another stamp than this that made England what it has been; and men of another stamp will be needed to prevent its decline.

The despotism of custom is everywhere the standing hindrance to human advancement, being in unceasing antagonism to that disposition to aim at something better than customary, which is called, according to circumstances, the spirit of liberty, or that of progress or improvement. The spirit of improvement is not always a spirit of liberty, for it may aim at forcing improvements on an unwilling people; and the spirit of liberty, in so far as it resists such attempts, may ally itself locally and temporarily with the opponents of improvement; but the only unfailing and permanent source of improvement is liberty, since by it there are as many possible independent centres of improvement as there are individuals. The progressive principle, however, in either shape, whether as the love of liberty or of improvement, is antagonistic to the sway of Custom, involving at least emancipation from that yoke; and the contest between the two constitutes the chief interest of the history of mankind. The greater part of the world has, properly speaking, no history, because the despotism of Custom is complete. This is the case over the whole East. Custom is there, in all things, the final appeal; justice and right mean conformity to custom; the argument of custom no one, unless some tyrant intoxicated with power, thinks of resisting. And we see the result. Those nations must once have had originality; they did not start out of the ground populous, lettered, and versed in many of the arts of life; they made themselves all this, and were then the greatest and most powerful nations in the world. What are they now? The subjects or dependents of tribes whose forefathers wandered in the forests when theirs had magnificent palaces and gorgeous temples, but over whom custom exercised only a divided rule with liberty and progress. A people, it appears, may be progressive for a certain length of time, and then stop: when does it stop? When it ceases to possess individuality. If a similar change should befall the nations of Europe, it will not be in exactly the same shape: the despotism of custom with which these nations are threatened is not precisely stationariness. It proscribes singularity, but it does not preclude change, provided all change together. We have discarded the fixed costumes of our forefathers; every one must still dress like other people, but the fashion may change once or twice a year. We thus take care that when there is change, it shall be for change's sake, and not from any idea of beauty or convenience; for the same idea of beauty or convenience would not strike all the world at the same moment, and be simultaneously thrown aside by all at another moment. But we are progressive as well as changeable: we continually make new inventions in mechanical things, and keep them until they are again superseded by better; we are eager for improvement in politics, in education, even in morals, though in this last our idea of improvement chiefly consists in persuading or forcing other people to be as good as ourselves. It is not progress that we object to; on the contrary, we flatter ourselves that we are the most progressive people who ever lived. It is individuality that we war against: we should think we had done wonders if we had made ourselves all alike; forgetting that the unlikeness of one person to another is generally the first thing which draws the attention of either to the imperfection of his own type, and the superiority of another, or the possibility, by combining the advantages of both, of producing something better than either. We have a warning example in China—a nation of much talent, and, in some respects, even wisdom, owing to the rare good fortune of having been provided at an early period with a particularly good set of customs, the work, in some measure, of men to whom even the most enlightened European must accord, under certain limitations, the title of sages and philosophers. They are remarkable, too, in the excellence of their apparatus for impressing, as far as possible, the best wisdom they possess upon every mind in the community, and securing that those who have appropriated most of it shall occupy the posts of honour and power. Surely the people who did this have discovered the secret of human progressiveness, and must have kept themselves steadily at the head of the movement of the world. On the contrary, they have become stationary—have remained so for thousands of years; and if they are ever to be farther improved, it must be by foreigners. They have succeeded beyond all hope in what English philanthropists are so industriously working at—in making a people all alike, all governing their thoughts and conduct by the same maxims and rules; and these are the fruits. The modern *régime* of public opinion is, in an unorganized form, what the Chinese educational and political systems are in an organized; and unless individuality shall be able successfully to assert itself against this yoke, Europe, notwithstanding its noble antecedents and its professed Christianity, will tend to become another China.[1]

What is it that has hitherto preserved Europe from this lot? What has made the European family of nations an improving, instead of a stationary portion of mankind? Not any superior excellence in them, which, when it exists, exists as the effect, not as the cause; but their remarkable diversity of character and culture. Individuals, classes, nations, have been extremely unlike one another: they have struck out a great variety of paths, each leading to something valuable; and although at every period those who travelled in different paths have been intolerant of one another, and each would have thought it an excellent thing if all the rest could have been compelled to travel his road, their attempts to thwart each other's development have rarely had any permanent success, and each has in time endured to receive the good which the others have offered. Europe is, in my judgment, wholly indebted to this plurality of paths for its progressive and many-sided development. But it already begins to possess this benefit in a considerably less degree. It is decidedly advancing

---

1. Mill refers to China as the example of a stationary state and applies the eighth-century identification of "Asian despotism" with stagnation to modern societies in that it tends to suffocate the individual through conformism to opinions and customs.

towards the Chinese ideal of making all people alike. M. de Tocqueville, in his last important work,[2] remarks how much more the Frenchmen of the present day resemble one another, than did those even of the last generation. The same remark might be made of Englishmen in a far greater degree. In a passage already quoted from Wilhelm von Humboldt, he points out two things as necessary conditions of human development, because necessary to render people unlike one another; namely, freedom, and variety of situations. The second of these two conditions is in this country every day diminishing. The circumstances which surround different classes and individuals, and shape their characters, are daily becoming more assimilated. Formerly, different ranks, different neighbourhoods, different trades and professions, lived in what might be called different worlds; at present, to a great degree in the same. Comparatively speaking, they now read the same things, listen to the same things, see the same things, go to the same places, have their hopes and fears directed to the same objects, have the same rights and liberties, and the same means of asserting them. Great as are the differences of position which remain, they are nothing to those which have ceased. And the assimilation is still proceeding. All the political changes of the age promote it, since they all tend to raise the low and to lower the high. Every extension of education promotes it, because education brings people under common influences, and gives them access to the general stock of facts and sentiments. Improvements in the means of communication promote it, by bringing the inhabitants of distant places into personal contact, and keeping up a rapid flow of changes of residence between one place and another. The increase of commerce and manufactures promotes it, by diffusing more widely the advantages of easy circumstances, and opening all objects of ambition, even the highest, to general competition, whereby the desire of rising becomes no longer the character of a particular class, but of all classes. A more powerful agency than even all these, in bringing about a general similarity among mankind, is the complete establishment, in this and other free countries, of the ascendancy of public opinion in the State. As the various social eminences which enabled persons entrenched on them to disregard the opinion of the multitude, gradually become levelled; as the very idea of resisting the will of the public, when it is positively known that they have a will, disappears more and more from the minds of practical politicians; there ceases to be any social support for non-conformity—any substantive power in society, which, itself opposed to the ascendancy of numbers, is interested in

2. Alexis de Tocqueville, *L'ancien régime et la revolution* (1856).

taking under its protection opinions and tendencies at variance with those of the public.

The combination of all these causes forms so great a mass of influences hostile to Individuality, that it is not easy to see how it can stand its ground. It will do so with increasing difficulty, unless the intelligent part of the public can be made to feel its value—to see that it is good there should be differences, even though not for the better, even though, as it may appear to them, some should be for the worse. If the claims of Individuality are ever to be asserted, the time is now, while much is still wanting to complete the enforced assimilation. It is only in the earlier stages that any stand can be successfully made against the encroachment. The demand that all other people shall resemble ourselves, grows by what it feeds on. If resistance waits till life is reduced *nearly* to one uniform type, all deviations from that type will come to be considered impious, immoral, even monstrous and contrary to nature. Mankind speedily become unable to conceive diversity, when they have been for some time unaccustomed to see it.

CHAPTER IV

Of the Limits to the Authority of Society over the Individual

What, then, is the rightful limit to the sovereignty of the individual over himself? Where does the authority of society begin? How much of human life should be assigned to individuality, and how much to society?

Each will receive its proper share, if each has that which more particularly concerns it. To individuality should belong the part of life in which it is chiefly the individual that is interested; to society, the part which chiefly interests society.

Though society is not founded on a contract, and though no good purpose is answered by inventing a contract in order to deduce social obligations from it, every one who receives the protection of society owes a return for the benefit, and the fact of living in society renders it indispensable that each should be bound to observe a certain line of conduct towards the rest. This conduct consists, first, in not injuring the interests of one another; or rather certain interests, which, either by express legal provision or by tacit understanding, ought to be considered as rights; and secondly, in each person's bearing his share (to be fixed on some equitable principle) of the labours and sacrifices incurred for defending the society or its members from injury and molestation. These conditions society is justified in enforcing, at all costs to those who endeavour to withhold fulfilment. Nor is this all that society may do. The acts of an individual may be hurtful to others, or wanting in due consideration for their welfare, without going the length of violating any of their constituted rights. The offender may then be justly punished by opinion, though not by law. As soon as any part of a person's conduct affects prejudicially the interests of others, society has jurisdiction over it, and the question whether the general welfare will or will not be promoted by interfering with it, becomes open to discussion. But there is no room for entertaining any such question when a person's conduct affects the interests of no persons besides himself, or needs not affect them unless they like (all the persons concerned being of full age, and the ordinary amount of understanding). In all such cases there should be perfect freedom, legal and social, to do the action and stand the consequences.

It would be a great misunderstanding of this doctrine, to suppose that it is one of selfish indifference, which pretends that human beings have no business with each other's conduct in life, and that they should not concern themselves about the well-doing or well-being of one another, unless their own interest is involved. Instead of any diminution, there is need of a great increase of disinterested exertion to promote the good of others. But disinterested benevolence can find other instruments to persuade people to their good, than whips and scourges, either of the literal or the metaphorical sort. I am the last person to undervalue the self-regarding virtues; they are only second in importance, if even second, to the social. It is equally the business of education to cultivate both. But even education works by conviction and persuasion as well as by compulsion, and it is by the former only that, when the period of education is past, the self-regarding virtues should be inculcated. Human beings owe to each other help to distinguish the better from the worse, and encouragement to choose the former and avoid the latter. They should be for ever stimulating each other to increased exercise of their higher faculties, and increased direction of their feelings and aims towards wise instead of foolish, elevating instead of degrading, objects and contemplations. But neither one person, nor any number of persons, is warranted in saying to another human creature of ripe years, that he shall not do with his life for his own benefit what he chooses to do with it. He is the person most interested in his own well-being: the interest which any other person, except in cases of strong personal attachment, can have in it, is trifling, compared with that which he himself has; the interest which society has in him individually (except as to his conduct to others) is fractional, and altogether indirect: while, with respect to his own feelings and circumstances, the most ordinary man or woman has means of knowledge immeasurably surpassing those that can be possessed by any one else. The interference of society to overrule his judgment and purposes in what only regards himself, must be grounded on general presumptions; which may be altogether wrong, and even if right, are as likely as not to be misapplied to individual cases, by persons no better acquainted with the circumstances of such cases than those are who look at them merely from without. In this department, therefore, of human affairs, Individuality has its proper field of action. In the conduct of human beings towards one another, it is necessary that general rules should for the most part be observed, in order that people may know what they have to expect; but in each person's own concerns, his individual spontaneity is entitled to free exercise. Considerations to aid his judgment, exhortations to strengthen his will, may be offered to him, even obtruded on him, by others; but he himself is the final judge. All errors which he is likely to commit against advice and warning, are far outweighed by the evil of allowing others to constrain him to what they deem his good.

I do not mean that the feelings with which a person is regarded by others, ought not to be in any way affected by his self-regarding qualities or deficiencies. This is neither possible nor desirable. If he is eminent in any of the qualities which conduce to his own good, he is, so far, a proper object of admiration. He is so much the nearer to the ideal perfection of human nature. If he is grossly deficient in those qualities, a sentiment the opposite of admiration will follow. There is a degree of folly, and a degree of what may be called (though the phrase is not unobjectionable) lowness or depravation of taste, which, though it cannot justify doing harm to the person who manifests it, renders him necessarily and properly a subject of distaste, or, in extreme cases, even of contempt: a person could not have the opposite qualities in due strength without entertaining these feelings. Though doing no wrong to any one, a person may so act as to compel us to judge him, and feel to him, as a fool, or as a being of an inferior order: and since this judgment and feeling are a fact which he would prefer to avoid, it is doing him a service to warn him of it beforehand, as of any other disagreeable consequence to which he exposes himself. It would be well, indeed, if this good office were much more freely rendered than the common notions of politeness at present permit, and if one person could honestly point out to another that he thinks him in fault, without being considered unmannerly or presuming. We have a right, also, in various ways, to act upon our unfavourable opinion of any one, not to the oppression of his individuality, but in the exercise of ours. We are not bound, for example, to seek his society; we have a right to avoid it (though not to parade the avoidance), for we have a right to choose the society most acceptable to us. We have a right, and it may be our duty, to caution others against him, if we think his example or conversation likely to have a pernicious effect on those with whom he associates. We may give others a preference over him in optional good offices, except those which tend to his improvement. In these various modes a person may suffer very severe penalties at the hands of others, for faults which directly concern only himself; but he suffers these penalties only in so far as they are the natural, and, as it were, the spontaneous consequences of the faults themselves, not because they are purposely inflicted on him for the sake of punishment. A person who shows rashness, obstinacy, self-conceit—who cannot live within moderate means—who cannot restrain himself from hurtful indulgences—who pursues animal pleasures at the expense of those of feeling and intellect—must expect to be lowered in the opinion of others, and to have a less share of their favourable sentiments; but of this he has no right to complain, unless he has merited their favour by special excellence in his social relations, and has thus established a title to their good offices, which is not affected by his demerits towards himself.

What I contend for is, that the inconveniences which are strictly inseparable from the unfavourable judgment of others, are the only ones to which a person should ever be subjected for that portion of his conduct and character which concerns his own good, but which does not affect the interests of others in their relations with him. Acts injurious to others require a totally different treatment. Encroachment on their rights; infliction on them of any loss or damage not justified by his own rights; falsehood or duplicity in dealing with them; unfair or ungenerous use of advantages over them; even selfish abstinence from defending them against injury— these are fit objects of moral reprobation, and, in grave cases, of moral retribution and punishment. And not only these acts, but the dispositions which lead to them, are properly immoral, and fit sub-jects of disapprobation which may rise to abhorrence. Cruelty of disposition; malice and ill-nature; that most anti-social and odious of all passions, envy; dissimulation and insincerity; irascibility on insufficient cause, and resentment disproportioned to the provoca-tion; the love of domineering over others; the desire to engross more than one's share of advantages (the πλεονεξία[3] of the Greeks); the pride which derives gratification from the abasement of others; the egotism which thinks self and its concerns more important than everything else, and decides all doubtful questions in its own favour;—these are moral vices, and constitute a bad and odious

3. Pleonexia means at the same time, desire, insolence, and lust for domination.

moral character: unlike the self-regarding faults previously mentioned, which are not properly immoralities, and to whatever pitch they may be carried, do not constitute wickedness. They may be proofs of any amount of folly, or want of personal dignity and self-respect; but they are only a subject of moral reprobation when they involve a breach of duty to others, for whose sake the individual is bound to have care for himself. What are called duties to ourselves are not socially obligatory, unless circumstances render them at the same time duties to others. The term duty to oneself, when it means anything more than prudence, means self-respect or self-development; and for none of these is any one accountable to his fellow creatures, because for none of them is it for the good of mankind that he be held accountable to them.

The distinction between the loss of consideration which a person may rightly incur by defect of prudence or of personal dignity, and the reprobation which is due to him for an offence against the rights of others, is not a merely nominal distinction. It makes a vast difference both in our feelings and in our conduct towards him, whether he displeases us in things in which we think we have a right to control him, or in things in which we know that we have not. If he displeases us, we may express our distaste, and we may stand aloof from a person as well as from a thing that displeases us; but we shall not therefore feel called on to make his life uncomfortable. We shall reflect that he already bears, or will bear, the whole penalty of his error; if he spoils his life by mismanagement, we shall not, for that reason, desire to spoil it still further: instead of wishing to punish him, we shall rather endeavour to alleviate his punishment, by showing him how he may avoid or cure the evils his conduct tends to bring upon him. He may be to us an object of pity, perhaps of dislike, but not of anger or resentment; we shall not treat him like an enemy of society: the worst we shall think ourselves justified in doing is leaving him to himself, if we do not interfere benevolently by showing interest or concern for him. It is far otherwise if he has infringed the rules necessary for the protection of his fellow-creatures, individually or collectively. The evil consequences of his acts do not then fall on himself, but on others; and society, as the protector of all its members, must retaliate on him; must inflict pain on him for the express purpose of punishment, and must take care that it be sufficiently severe. In the one case, he is an offender at our bar, and we are called on not only to sit in judgment on him, but, in one shape or another, to execute our own sentence: in the other case, it is not our part to inflict any suffering on him, except what may incidentally follow from our using the same liberty in the regulation of our own affairs, which we allow to him in his.

The distinction here pointed out between the part of a person's life which concerns only himself, and that which concerns others, many persons will refuse to admit. How (it may be asked) can any part of the conduct of a member of society be a matter of indifference to the other members? No person is an entirely isolated being; it is impossible for a person to do anything seriously or permanently hurtful to himself, without mischief reaching at least to his near connexions, and often far beyond them. If he injures his property, he does harm to those who directly or indirectly derived support from it, and usually diminishes, by a greater or less amount, the general resources of the community. If he deteriorates his bodily or mental faculties, he not only brings evil upon all who depended on him for any portion of their happiness, but disqualifies himself for rendering the services which he owes to his fellow creatures generally; perhaps becomes a burthen on their affection or benevolence; and if such conduct were very frequent, hardly any offence that is committed would detract more from the general sum of good. Finally, if by his vices or follies a person does no direct harm to others, he is nevertheless (it may be said) injurious by his example; and ought to be compelled to control himself, for the sake of those whom the sight or knowledge of his conduct might corrupt or mislead.

And even (it will be added) if the consequences of misconduct could be confined to the vicious or thoughtless individual, ought society to abandon to their own guidance those who are manifestly unfit for it? If protection against themselves is confessedly due to children and persons under age, is not society equally bound to afford it to persons of mature years who are equally incapable of self-government? If gambling, or drunkenness, or incontinence, or idleness, or uncleanliness, are as injurious to happiness, and as great a hindrance to improvement, as many or most of the acts prohibited by law, why (it may be asked) should not law, so far as is consistent with practicability and social convenience, endeavour to repress these also? And as a supplement to the unavoidable imperfections of law, ought not opinion at least to organize a powerful police against these vices, and visit rigidly with social penalties those who are known to practise them? There is no question here (it may be said) about restricting individuality, or impeding the trial of new and original experiments in living. The only things it is sought to prevent are things which have been tried and condemned from the beginning of the world until now; things which experience has shown not to be useful or suitable to any person's individuality. There must be some length of time and amount of experience, after which a moral or prudential truth may be regarded as established: and it is merely desired to prevent generation after generation from falling over the same precipice which has been fatal to their predecessors.

I fully admit that the mischief which a person does to himself, may seriously affect, both through their sympathies and their interests, those nearly connected with him, and in a minor degree, society at large. When, by conduct of this sort, a person is led to violate a distinct and assignable obligation to any other person or persons, the case is taken out of the self-regarding class, and becomes amenable to moral disapprobation in the proper sense of the term. If, for example, a man, through intemperance or extravagance, becomes unable to pay his debts, or, having undertaken the moral responsibility of a family, becomes from the same cause incapable of supporting or educating them, he is deservedly reprobated, and might be justly punished; but it is for the breach of duty to his family or creditors, not for the extravagance. If the resources which ought to have been devoted to them, had been diverted from them for the most prudent investment, the moral culpability would have been the same. George Barnwell[4] murdered his uncle to get money for his mistress, but if he had done it to set himself up in business, he would equally have been hanged. Again, in the frequent case of a man who causes grief to his family by addiction to bad habits, he deserves reproach for his unkindness or ingratitude; but so he may for cultivating habits not in themselves vicious, if they are painful to those with whom he passes his life, or who from personal ties are dependent on him for their comfort. Whoever fails in the consideration generally due to the interests and feelings of others, not being compelled by some more imperative duty, or justified by allowable self-preference, is a subject of moral disapprobation for that failure, but not for the cause of it, nor for the errors, merely personal to himself, which may have remotely led to it. In like manner, when a person disables himself, by conduct purely self-regarding, from the performance of some definite duty incumbent on him to the public, he is guilty of a social offence. No person ought to be punished simply for being drunk; but a soldier or a policeman should be punished for being drunk on duty. Whenever, in short, there is a definite damage, or a definite risk of damage, either to an individual or to the public, the case is taken out of the province of liberty, and placed in that of morality or law.

But with regard to the merely contingent, or, as it may be called, constructive injury which a person causes to society, by conduct which neither violates any specific duty to the public, nor occasions perceptible hurt to any assignable individual except himself;

---

4. The lead character in George Lillo's play *The London Merchant*, representing the misfortunes of an ambitious young apprentice.

the inconvenience is one which society can afford to bear, for the sake of the greater good of human freedom. If grown persons are to be punished for not taking proper care of themselves, I would rather it were for their own sake, than under pretence of preventing them from impairing their capacity of rendering to society benefits which society does not pretend it has a right to exact. But I cannot consent to argue the point as if society had no means of bringing its weaker members up to its ordinary standard of rational conduct, except waiting till they do something irrational, and then punishing them, legally or morally, for it. Society has had absolute power over them during all the early portion of their existence: it has had the whole period of childhood and nonage in which to try whether it could make them capable of rational conduct in life. The existing generation is master both of the training and the entire circumstances of the generation to come; it cannot indeed make them perfectly wise and good, because it is itself so lamentably deficient in goodness and wisdom; and its best efforts are not always, in individual cases, its most successful ones; but it is perfectly well able to make the rising generation, as a whole, as good as, and a little better than, itself. If society lets any considerable number of its members grow up mere children, incapable of being acted on by rational consideration of distant motives, society has itself to blame for the consequences. Armed not only with all the powers of education, but with the ascendancy which the authority of a received opinion always exercises over the minds who are least fitted to judge for themselves; and aided by the *natural* penalties which cannot be prevented from falling on those who incur the distaste or the contempt of those who know them; let not society pretend that it needs, besides all this, the power to issue commands and enforce obedience in the personal concerns of individuals, in which, on all principles of justice and policy, the decision ought to rest with those who are to abide the consequences. Nor is there anything which tends more to discredit and frustrate the better means of influencing conduct, than a resort to the worse. If there be among those whom it is attempted to coerce into prudence or temperance, any of the material of which vigorous and independent characters are made, they will infallibly rebel against the yoke. No such person will ever feel that others have a right to control him in his concerns, such as they have to prevent him from injuring them in theirs; and it easily comes to be considered a mark of spirit and courage to fly in the face of such usurped authority, and do with ostentation the exact opposite of what it enjoins; as in the fashion of grossness which succeeded, in the time of Charles II.,[5] to the fanatical moral intolerance of the Puritans.

5. King of England from 1660 to 1685, famous for his many mistresses.

With respect to what is said of the necessity of protecting society from the bad example set to others by the vicious or the self-indulgent; it is true that bad example may have a pernicious effect, especially the example of doing wrong to others with impunity to the wrong-doer. But we are now speaking of conduct which, while it does no wrong to others, is supposed to do great harm to the agent himself; and I do not see how those who believe this, can think otherwise than that the example, on the whole, must be more salutary than hurtful, since, if it displays the misconduct, it displays also the painful or degrading consequences which, if the conduct is justly censured, must be supposed to be in all or most cases attendant on it.

But the strongest of all the arguments against the interference of the public with purely personal conduct, is that when it does interfere, the odds are that it interferes wrongly, and in the wrong place. On questions of social morality, of duty to others, the opinion of the public, that is, of an overruling majority, though often wrong, is likely to be still oftener right; because on such questions they are only required to judge of their own interests; of the manner in which some mode of conduct, if allowed to be practised, would affect themselves. But the opinion of a similar majority, imposed as a law on the minority, on questions of self-regarding conduct, is quite as likely to be wrong as right; for in these cases public opinion means, at the best, some people's opinion of what is good or bad for other people; while very often it does not even mean that; the public, with the most perfect indifference, passing over the pleasure or convenience of those whose conduct they censure, and considering only their own preference. There are many who consider as an injury to themselves any conduct which they have a distaste for, and resent it as an outrage to their feelings; as a religious bigot, when charged with disregarding the religious feelings of others, has been known to retort that they disregard his feelings, by persisting in their abominable worship or creed. But there is no parity between the feeling of a person for his own opinion, and the feeling of another who is offended at his holding it; no more than between the desire of a thief to take a purse, and the desire of the right owner to keep it. And a person's taste is as much his own peculiar concern as his opinion or his purse. It is easy for any one to imagine an ideal public, which leaves the freedom and choice of individuals in all uncertain matters undisturbed, and only requires them to abstain from modes of conduct which universal experience has condemned. But where has there been seen a public which set any such limit to its censorship? or when does the public trouble itself about universal experience? In its interferences with personal conduct it is seldom thinking of anything but the enormity of acting or feeling differently from itself; and this standard of judgment, thinly disguised, is held up to mankind as the dictate of religion and philosophy, by nine-tenths of all moralists and speculative writers. These teach that things are right because they are right; because we feel them to be so. They tell us to search in our own minds and hearts for laws of conduct binding on ourselves and on all others. What can the poor public do but apply these instructions, and make their own personal feelings of good and evil, if they are tolerably unanimous in them, obligatory on all the world?

The evil here pointed out is not one which exists only in theory; and it may perhaps be expected that I should specify the instances in which the public of this age and country improperly invests its own preferences with the character of moral laws. I am not writing an essay on the aberrations of existing moral feeling. That is too weighty a subject to be discussed parenthetically, and by way of illustration. Yet examples are necessary, to show that the principle I maintain is of serious and practical moment, and that I am not endeavouring to erect a barrier against imaginary evils. And it is not difficult to show, by abundant instances, that to extend the bounds of what may be called moral police, until it encroaches on the most unquestionably legitimate liberty of the individual, is one of the most universal of all human propensities.

As a first instance, consider the antipathies which men cherish on no better grounds than that persons whose religious opinions are different from theirs, do not practise their religious observances, especially their religious abstinences. To cite a rather trivial example, nothing in the creed or practice of Christians does more to envenom the hatred of Mahomedans against them, than the fact of their eating pork. There are few acts which Christians and Europeans regard with more unaffected disgust, than Mussulmans regard this particular mode of satisfying hunger. It is, in the first place, an offence against their religion; but this circumstance by no means explains either the degree or the kind of their repugnance; for wine also is forbidden by their religion, and to partake of it is by all Mussulmans accounted wrong, but not disgusting. Their aversion to the flesh of the 'unclean beast' is, on the contrary, of that peculiar character, resembling an instinctive antipathy, which the idea of uncleanness, when once it thoroughly sinks into the feelings, seems always to excite even in those whose personal habits are anything but scrupulously cleanly, and of which the sentiment of religious impurity, so intense in the Hindoos, is a remarkable example. Suppose now that in a people, of whom the majority were Mussulmans, that majority should insist upon not permitting pork to be eaten within the limits of the country. This would be nothing new in Mahomedan countries.[6] Would it be a legitimate exercise of the moral authority of public opinion? and if not, why not? The practice is really revolting to such a public. They also sincerely think that it is forbidden and abhorred by the Deity. Neither could the prohibition be censured as religious persecution. It might be religious in its origin, but it would not be persecution for religion, since nobody's religion makes it a duty to eat pork. The only tenable ground of condemnation would be, that with the personal tastes and self-regarding concerns of individuals the public has no business to interfere.

To come somewhat nearer home: the majority of Spaniards consider it a gross impiety, offensive in the highest degree to the Supreme Being, to worship him in any other manner than the Roman Catholic; and no other public worship is lawful on Spanish soil. The people of all Southern Europe look upon a married clergy as not only irreligious, but unchaste, indecent, gross, disgusting. What do Protestants think of these perfectly sincere feelings, and of the attempt to enforce them against non-Catholics? Yet, if mankind are justified in interfering with each other's liberty in things which do not concern the interests of others, on what principle is it possible consistently to exclude these cases? or who can blame people for desiring to suppress what they regard as a scandal in the sight of God and man? No stronger case can be shown for prohibiting anything which is regarded as a personal immorality, than is made out for suppressing these practices in the eyes of those who regard them as impieties; and unless we are willing to adopt the logic of persecutors, and to say that we may persecute others because we are right, and that they must not persecute us because they are wrong, we must beware of admitting a principle of which we should resent as a gross injustice the application to ourselves.

The preceding instances may be objected to, although unreasonably, as drawn from contingencies impossible among us: opinion, in this country, not being likely to enforce abstinence from meats, or to interfere with people for worshipping, and for either marrying or not marrying, according to their creed or inclination. The next example, however, shall be taken from an interference with liberty which

6. The case of the Bombay Parsees is a curious instance in point. When this industrious and enterprising tribe, the descendants of the Persian fire-worshippers, flying from their native country before the Caliphs, arrived in Western India, they were admitted to toleration by the Hindoo sovereigns, on condition of not eating beef. When those regions afterwards fell under the dominion of Mahomedan conquerors, the Parsees obtained from them a continuance of indulgence, on condition of refraining from pork. What was at first obedience to authority became a second nature, and the Parsees to this day abstain both from beef and pork. Though not required by their religion, the double abstinence has had time to grow into a custom of their tribe; and custom, in the East, is a religion [*Mill's note*].

we have by no means passed all danger of. Wherever the Puritans have been sufficiently powerful, as in New England, and in Great Britain at the time of the Commonwealth, they have endeavoured, with considerable success, to put down all public, and nearly all private, amusements: especially music, dancing, public games, or other assemblages for purposes of diversion, and the theatre. There are still in this country large bodies of persons by whose notions of morality and religion these recreations are condemned; and those persons belonging chiefly to the middle class, who are the ascendant power in the present social and political condition of the kingdom, it is by no means impossible that persons of these sentiments may at some time or other command a majority in Parliament. How will the remaining portion of the community like to have the amusements that shall be permitted to them regulated by the religious and moral sentiments of the stricter Calvinists and Methodists?[7] Would they not, with considerable peremptoriness, desire these intrusively pious members of society to mind their own business? This is precisely what should be said to every government and every public, who have the pretension that no person shall enjoy any pleasure which they think wrong. But if the principle of the pretension be admitted, no one can reasonably object to its being acted on in the sense of the majority, or other preponderating power in the country; and all persons must be ready to conform to the idea of a Christian commonwealth, as understood by the early settlers in New England, if a religious profession similar to theirs should ever succeed in regaining its lost ground, as religions supposed to be declining have so often been known to do.

To imagine another contingency, perhaps more likely to be realized than the one last mentioned. There is confessedly a strong tendency in the modern world towards a democratic constitution of society, accompanied or not by popular political institutions. It is affirmed that in the country where this tendency is most completely realized—where both society and the government are most democratic—the United States—the feeling of the majority, to whom any appearance of a more showy or costly style of living than they can hope to rival is disagreeable, operates as a tolerably effectual sumptuary law, and that in many parts of the Union it is really difficult for a person possessing a very large income, to find any mode of spending it, which will not incur popular disapprobation. Though such statements as these are doubtless much exaggerated as a representation of existing facts, the state of things they describe is not only a conceivable and possible, but a probable result of

---

7. A revival of Christianity within the Church of England inspired by John Wesley (1703–1791), who initiated an independent movement called Methodism.

democratic feeling, combined with the notion that the public has a
right to a veto on the manner in which individuals shall spend
their incomes. We have only further to suppose a considerable
diffusion of Socialist opinions, and it may become infamous in the
eyes of the majority to possess more property than some very small
amount, or any income not earned by manual labour. Opinions similar in principle to these, already prevail widely among the artizan
class, and weigh oppressively on those who are amenable to the
opinion chiefly of that class, namely, its own members. It is known
that the bad workmen who form the majority of the operatives in
many branches of industry, are decidedly of opinion that bad
workmen ought to receive the same wages as good, and that no one
ought to be allowed, through piecework or otherwise, to earn by
superior skill or industry more than others can without it. And they
employ a moral police, which occasionally becomes a physical one,
to deter skilful workmen from receiving, and employers from giving, a larger remuneration for a more useful service. If the public
have any jurisdiction over private concerns, I cannot see that these
people are in fault, or that any individual's particular public can be
blamed for asserting the same authority over his individual conduct, which the general public asserts over people in general.

But, without dwelling upon supposititious cases, there are, in our
own day, gross usurpations upon the liberty of private life actually
practised, and still greater ones threatened with some expectation
of success, and opinions proposed which assert an unlimited right
in the public not only to prohibit by law everything which it thinks
wrong, but in order to get at what it thinks wrong, to prohibit any
number of things which it admits to be innocent.

Under the name of preventing intemperance, the people of one
English colony, and of nearly half the United States, have been
interdicted by law from making any use whatever of fermented
drinks, except for medical purposes: for prohibition of their sale is
in fact, as it is intended to be, prohibition of their use.[8] And though
the impracticability of executing the law has caused its repeal in several of the States which had adopted it, including the one from
which it derives its name, an attempt has notwithstanding been commenced, and is prosecuted with considerable zeal by many of the
professed philanthropists, to agitate for a similar law in this country. The association, or 'Alliance' as it terms itself,[9] which has been

---

8. The Maine Liquor Law, enacted in 1851, prohibited the sale of alcoholic spirits except for
   those considered "medicinal and mechanical"; it had a precedent in the Total Abstinence
   Society, founded in Portland, Maine, in 1815, and remained basically in effect until the
   repeal of national Prohibition in 1934.
9. The United Kingdom Alliance for the Legislative Suppression of the Sale of Intoxicat-
   ing Liquor was founded in 1853.

formed for this purpose, has acquired some notoriety through the publicity given to a correspondence between its Secretary and one of the very few English public men who hold that a politician's opinions ought to be founded on principles. Lord Stanley's[1] share in this correspondence is calculated to strengthen the hopes already built on him, by those who know how rare such qualities as are manifested in some of his public appearances, unhappily are among those who figure in political life. The organ of the Alliance, who would 'deeply deplore the recognition of any principle which could be wrested to justify bigotry and persecution,' undertakes to point out the 'broad and impassable barrier' which divides such principles from those of the association. 'All matters relating to thought, opinion, conscience, appear to me,' he says, 'to be without the sphere of legislation; all pertaining to social act, habit, relation, subject only to a discretionary power vested in the State itself, and not in the individual, to be within it.' No mention is made of a third class, different from either of these, viz. acts and habits which are not social, but individual; although it is to this class, surely, that the act of drinking fermented liquors belongs. Selling fermented liquors, however, is trading, and trading is a social act. But the infringement complained of is not on the liberty of the seller, but on that of the buyer and consumer; since the State might just as well forbid him to drink wine, as purposely make it impossible for him to obtain it. The Secretary, however, says, 'I claim, as a citizen, a right to legislate whenever my social rights are invaded by the social act of another.' And now for the definition of these 'social rights.' 'If anything invades my social rights, certainly the traffic in strong drink does. It destroys my primary right of security, by constantly creating and stimulating social disorder. It invades my right of equality, by deriving a profit from the creation of a misery, I am taxed to support. It impedes my right to free moral and intellectual development, by surrounding my path with dangers, and by weakening and demoralizing society, from which I have a right to claim mutual aid and intercourse.' A theory of 'social rights,' the like of which probably never before found its way into distinct language—being nothing short of this—that it is the absolute social right of every individual, that every other individual shall act in every respect exactly as he ought; that whosoever fails thereof in the smallest particular, violates my social right, and entitles me to demand from the legislature the removal of the grievance. So monstrous a principle is far more dangerous than any single interference with liberty;

---

1. Edward Henry Stanley (1826–1893) was a British statesman who served as Secretary of State for Foreign Affairs in the 1860s and 1870s, and also as Colonial Secretary in the late 1850s and mid-1880s.

there is no violation of liberty which it would not justify; it acknowledges no right to any freedom whatever, except perhaps to that of
holding opinions in secret, without ever disclosing them: for the
moment an opinion which I consider noxious, passes any one's lips,
it invades all the 'social rights' attributed to me by the Alliance. The
doctrine ascribes to all mankind a vested interest in each other's
moral, intellectual, and even physical perfection, to be defined by
each claimant according to his own standard.

Another important example of illegitimate interference with the
rightful liberty of the individual, not simply threatened, but long
since carried into triumphant effect, is Sabbatarian legislation.
Without doubt, abstinence on one day in the week, so far as the exigencies of life permit, from the usual daily occupation, though in
no respect religiously binding on any except Jews, is a highly beneficial custom. And inasmuch as this custom cannot be observed
without a general consent to that effect among the industrious
classes, therefore, in so far as some persons by working may impose
the same necessity on others, it may be allowable and right that the
law should guarantee to each, the observance by others of the custom, by suspending the greater operations of industry on a particular day. But this justification, grounded on the direct interest which
others have in each individual's observance of the practice, does not
apply to the self-chosen occupations in which a person may think fit
to employ his leisure; nor does it hold good, in the smallest degree,
for legal restrictions on amusements. It is true that the amusement
of some is the day's work of others; but the pleasure, not to say the
useful recreation, of many, is worth the labour of a few, provided
the occupation is freely chosen, and can be freely resigned. The
operatives are perfectly right in thinking that if all worked on Sunday, seven days' work would have to be given for six days' wages: but
so long as the great mass of employments are suspended, the small
number who for the enjoyment of others must still work, obtain a
proportional increase of earnings; and they are not obliged to follow those occupations, if they prefer leisure to emolument. If a further remedy is sought, it might be found in the establishment by
custom of a holiday on some other day of the week for those particular classes of persons. The only ground, therefore, on which
restrictions on Sunday amusements can be defended, must be
that they are religiously wrong; a motive of legislation which never
can be too earnestly protested against. 'Deorum injuriæ Diis curæ.'[2]
It remains to be proved that society or any of its officers holds a

---

2. "Injuries to the gods will be remedied by the gods" (Latin); from Tacitus's *Annals*, quoting
the emperor Tiberius. In Mill's text, the maxim indicates a distinction between things that
pertain mostly to the individual and things that pertain mostly to society.

commission from on high to avenge any supposed offence to Omnipotence, which is not also a wrong to our fellow creatures. The notion that it is one man's duty that another should be religious, was the foundation of all the religious persecutions ever perpetrated, and if admitted, would fully justify them. Though the feeling which breaks out in the repeated attempts to stop railway travelling on Sunday, in the resistance to the opening of Museums, and the like, has not the cruelty of the old persecutors, the state of mind indicated by it is fundamentally the same. It is a determination not to tolerate others in doing what is permitted by their religion, because it is not permitted by the persecutor's religion. It is a belief that God not only abominates the act of the misbeliever, but will not hold us guiltless if we leave him unmolested.

I cannot refrain from adding to these examples of the little account commonly made of human liberty, the language of downright persecution which breaks out from the press of this country, whenever it feels called on to notice the remarkable phenomenon of Mormonism.[3] Much might be said on the unexpected and instructive fact, that an alleged new revelation, and a religion founded on it, the product of palpable imposture, not even supported by the *prestige* of extraordinary qualities in its founder, is believed by hundreds of thousands, and has been made the foundation of a society, in the age of newspapers, railways, and the electric telegraph. What here concerns us is, that this religion, like other and better religions, has its martyrs; that its prophet and founder was, for his teaching, put to death by a mob; that others of its adherents lost their lives by the same lawless violence; that they were forcibly expelled, in a body, from the country in which they first grew up; while, now that they have been chased into a solitary recess in the midst of a desert, many in this country openly declare that it would be right (only that it is not convenient) to send an expedition against them, and compel them by force to conform to the opinions of other people. The article of the Mormonite doctrine which is the chief provocative to the antipathy which thus breaks through the ordinary restraints of religious tolerance, is its sanction of polygamy; which, though permitted to Mahomedans, and Hindoos, and Chinese, seems to excite unquenchable animosity when practised by persons who speak English, and profess to be a kind of Christians. No one has a deeper disapprobation than I have of this Mormon institution; both for other reasons, and because, far from being in any way countenanced by the principle of liberty, it is a direct infraction of that principle,

---

3. The religion of the Church of Latter-Day Saints, founded by Joseph Smith (1805–1844). Brigham Young (1801–1877) led the Mormons to the west of America, what is now Utah, to escape persecution.

being a mere rivetting of the chains of one half of the community, and an emancipation of the other from reciprocity of obligation towards them. Still, it must be remembered that this relation is as much voluntary on the part of the women concerned in it, and who may be deemed the sufferers by it, as is the case with any other form of the marriage institution; and however surprising this fact may appear, it has its explanation in the common ideas and customs of the world, which teaching women to think marriage the one thing needful, make it intelligible that many a woman should prefer being one of several wives, to not being a wife at all. Other countries are not asked to recognise such unions, or release any portion of their inhabitants from their own laws on the score of Mormonite opinions. But when the dissentients have conceded to the hostile sentiments of others, far more than could justly be demanded; when they have left the countries to which their doctrines were unacceptable, and established themselves in a remote corner of the earth, which they have been the first to render habitable to human beings; it is difficult to see on what principles but those of tyranny they can be prevented from living there under what laws they please, provided they commit no aggression on other nations, and allow perfect freedom of departure to those who are dissatisfied with their ways. A recent writer, in some respects of considerable merit, proposes (to use his own words,) not a crusade, but a *civilizade*, against this polygamous community, to put an end to what seems to him a retrograde step in civilization. It also appears so to me, but I am not aware that any community has a right to force another to be civilized. So long as the sufferers by the bad law do not invoke assistance from other communities, I cannot admit that persons entirely unconnected with them ought to step in and require that a condition of things with which all who are directly interested appear to be satisfied, should be put an end to because it is a scandal to persons some thousands of miles distant, who have no part or concern in it. Let them send missionaries, if they please, to preach against it; and let them, by any fair means (of which silencing the teachers is not one,) oppose the progress of similar doctrines among their own people. If civilization has got the better of barbarism when barbarism had the world to itself, it is too much to profess to be afraid lest barbarism, after having been fairly got under, should revive and conquer civilization. A civilization that can thus succumb to its vanquished enemy, must first have become so degenerate, that neither its appointed priests and teachers, nor anybody else, has the capacity, or will take the trouble, to stand up for it. If this be so, the sooner such a civilization receives notice to quit, the better. It can only go on from bad to worse, until destroyed and regenerated (like the Western Empire) by energetic barbarians.

CHAPTER V

Applications

The principles asserted in these pages must be more generally admitted as the basis for discussion of details, before a consistent application of them to all the various departments of government and morals can be attempted with any prospect of advantage. The few observations I propose to make on questions of detail, are designed to illustrate the principles, rather than to follow them out to their consequences. I offer, not so much applications, as specimens of application; which may serve to bring into greater clearness the meaning and limits of the two maxims which together form the entire doctrine of this Essay, and to assist the judgment in holding the balance between them, in the cases where it appears doubtful which of them is applicable to the case.

The maxims are, first, that the individual is not accountable to society for his actions, in so far as these concern the interests of no person but himself. Advice, instruction, persuasion, and avoidance by other people if thought necessary by them for their own good, are the only measures by which society can justifiably express its dislike or disapprobation of his conduct. Secondly, that for such actions as are prejudicial to the interests of others, the individual is accountable, and may be subjected either to social or to legal punishments, if society is of opinion that the one or the other is requisite for its protection.

In the first place, it must by no means be supposed, because damage, or probability of damage, to the interests of others, can alone justify the interference of society, that therefore it always does justify such interference. In many cases, an individual, in pursuing a legitimate object, necessarily and therefore legitimately causes pain or loss to others, or intercepts a good which they had a reasonable hope of obtaining. Such oppositions of interest between individuals often arise from bad social institutions, but are unavoidable while those institutions last; and some would be unavoidable under any institutions. Whoever succeeds in an overcrowded profession, or in a competitive examination; whoever is preferred to another in any contest for an object which both desire, reaps benefit from the loss of others, from their wasted exertion and their disappointment. But it is, by common admission, better for the general interest of mankind, that persons should pursue their objects undeterred by this sort of consequences. In other words, society admits no right, either legal or moral, in the disappointed competitors, to immunity from this kind of suffering; and feels called on to interfere, only when means of success have been employed which it is contrary to the general interest to permit—namely, fraud or treachery, and force.

Again, trade is a social act. Whoever undertakes to sell any description of goods to the public, does what affects the interest of other persons, and of society in general; and thus his conduct, in principle, comes within the jurisdiction of society: accordingly, it was once held to be the duty of governments, in all cases which were considered of importance, to fix prices, and regulate the processes of manufacture. But it is now recognised, though not till after a long struggle, that both the cheapness and the good quality of commodities are most effectually provided for by leaving the producers and sellers perfectly free, under the sole check of equal freedom to the buyers for supplying themselves elsewhere. This is the so-called doctrine of Free Trade, which rests on grounds different from, though equally solid with, the principle of individual liberty asserted in this Essay. Restrictions on trade, or on production for purposes of trade, are indeed restraints; and all restraint, *quâ* restraint, is an evil: but the restraints in question affect only that part of conduct which society is competent to restrain, and are wrong solely because they do not really produce the results which it is desired to produce by them. As the principle of individual liberty is not involved in the doctrine of Free Trade, so neither is it in most of the questions which arise respecting the limits of that doctrine: as for example, what amount of public control is admissible for the prevention of fraud by adulteration; how far sanitary precautions, or arrangements to protect workpeople employed in dangerous occupations, should be enforced on employers. Such questions involve considerations of liberty, only in so far as leaving people to themselves is always better, *cæteris paribus*,[4] than controlling them: but that they may be legitimately controlled for these ends, is in principle undeniable. On the other hand, there are questions relating to interference with trade, which are essentially questions of liberty; such as the Maine Law, already touched upon; the prohibition of the importation of opium into China; the restriction of the sale of poisons; all cases, in short, where the object of the interference is to make it impossible or difficult to obtain a particular commodity. These interferences are objectionable, not as infringements on the liberty of the producer or seller, but on that of the buyer.

One of these examples, that of the sale of poisons, opens a new question; the proper limits of what may be called the functions of police; how far liberty may legitimately be invaded for the prevention of crime, or of accident. It is one of the undisputed functions of government to take precautions against crime before it has been

4. Other things being equal (Latin).

committed, as well as to detect and punish it afterwards. The preventive function of government, however, is far more liable to be abused, to the prejudice of liberty, than the punitory function; for there is hardly any part of the legitimate freedom of action of a human being which would not admit of being represented, and fairly too, as increasing the facilities for some form or other of delinquency. Nevertheless, if a public authority, or even a private person, sees any one evidently preparing to commit a crime, they are not bound to look on inactive until the crime is committed, but may interfere to prevent it. If poisons were never bought or used for any purpose except the commission of murder, it would be right to prohibit their manufacture and sale. They may, however, be wanted not only for innocent but for useful purposes, and restrictions cannot be imposed in the one case without operating in the other. Again, it is a proper office of public authority to guard against accidents. If either a public officer or any one else saw a person attempting to cross a bridge which had been ascertained to be unsafe, and there were no time to warn him of his danger, they might seize him and turn him back, without any real infringement of his liberty; for liberty consists in doing what one desires, and he does not desire to fall into the river. Nevertheless, when there is not a certainty, but only a danger of mischief, no one but the person himself can judge of the sufficiency of the motive which may prompt him to incur the risk: in this case, therefore, (unless he is a child, or delirious, or in some state of excitement or absorption incompatible with the full use of the reflecting faculty), he ought, I conceive, to be only warned of the danger; not forcibly prevented from exposing himself to it. Similar considerations, applied to such a question as the sale of poisons, may enable us to decide which among the possible modes of regulation are or are not contrary to principle. Such a precaution, for example, as that of labelling the drug with some word expressive of its dangerous character, may be enforced without violation of liberty: the buyer cannot wish not to know that the thing he possesses has poisonous qualities. But to require in all cases the certificate of a medical practitioner, would make it sometimes impossible, always expensive, to obtain the article for legitimate uses. The only mode apparent to me, in which difficulties may be thrown in the way of crime committed through this means, without any infringement, worth taking into account, upon the liberty of those who desire the poisonous substance for other purposes, consists in providing what, in the apt language of Bentham, is called 'preappointed evidence.' This provision is familiar to every one in the case of contracts. It is usual and right that the law, when a contract is entered into, should require as the condition of its enforcing performance, that certain formalities should be observed, such as signatures, attestation of witnesses, and the like, in order that in case of subsequent dispute, there may be evidence to prove that the contract was really entered into, and that there was nothing in the circumstances to render it legally invalid: the effect being, to throw great obstacles in the way of fictitious contracts, or contracts made in circumstances which, if known, would destroy their validity. Precautions of a similar nature might be enforced in the sale of articles adapted to be instruments of crime. The seller, for example, might be required to enter in a register the exact time of the transaction, the name and address of the buyer, the precise quality and quantity sold; to ask the purpose for which it was wanted, and record the answer he received. When there was no medical prescription, the presence of some third person might be required, to bring home the fact to the purchaser, in case there should afterwards be reason to believe that the article had been applied to criminal purposes. Such regulations would in general be no material impediment to obtaining the article, but a very considerable one to making an improper use of it without detection.

The right inherent in society, to ward off crimes against itself by antecedent precautions, suggests the obvious limitations to the maxim, that purely self-regarding misconduct cannot properly be meddled with in the way of prevention or punishment. Drunkenness, for example, in ordinary cases, is not a fit subject for legislative interference; but I should deem it perfectly legitimate that a person, who had once been convicted of any act of violence to others under the influence of drink, should be placed under a special legal restriction, personal to himself; that if he were afterwards found drunk, he should be liable to a penalty, and that if when in that state he committed another offence, the punishment to which he would be liable for that other offence should be increased in severity. The making himself drunk, in a person whom drunkenness excites to do harm to others, is a crime against others. So, again, idleness, except in a person receiving support from the public, or except when it constitutes a breach of contract, cannot without tyranny be made a subject of legal punishment; but if either from idleness or from any other avoidable cause, a man fails to perform his legal duties to others, as for instance to support his children, it is no tyranny to force him to fulfil that obligation, by compulsory labour, if no other means are available.

Again, there are many acts which, being directly injurious only to the agents themselves, ought not to be legally interdicted, but which, if done publicly, are a violation of good manners, and coming thus within the category of offences against others, may rightfully be prohibited. Of this kind are offences against decency; on which it is unnecessary to dwell, the rather as they are only connected indirectly with our subject, the objection to publicity being equally strong in the case of many actions not in themselves condemnable, nor supposed to be so.

There is another question to which an answer must be found, consistent with the principles which have been laid down. In cases of personal conduct supposed to be blameable, but which respect for liberty precludes society from preventing or punishing, because the evil directly resulting falls wholly on the agent; what the agent is free to do, ought other persons to be equally free to counsel or instigate? This question is not free from difficulty. The case of a person who solicits another to do an act, is not strictly a case of self-regarding conduct. To give advice or offer inducements to any one, is a social act, and may therefore, like actions in general which affect others, be supposed amenable to social control. But a little reflection corrects the first impression, by showing that if the case is not strictly within the definition of individual liberty, yet the reasons on which the principle of individual liberty is grounded, are applicable to it. If people must be allowed, in whatever concerns only themselves, to act as seems best to themselves at their own peril, they must equally be free to consult with one another about what is fit to be so done; to exchange opinions, and give and receive suggestions. Whatever it is permitted to do, it must be permitted to advise to do. The question is doubtful, only when the instigator derives a personal benefit from his advice; when he makes it his occupation, for subsistence or pecuniary gain, to promote what society and the state consider to be an evil. Then, indeed, a new element of complication is introduced; namely, the existence of classes of persons with an interest opposed to what is considered as the public weal, and whose mode of living is grounded on the counteraction of it. Ought this to be interfered with, or not? Fornication, for example, must be tolerated, and so must gambling; but should a person be free to be a pimp, or to keep a gambling-house? The case is one of those which lie on the exact boundary line between two principles, and it is not at once apparent to which of the two it properly belongs. There are arguments on both sides. On the side of toleration it may be said, that the fact of following anything as an occupation, and living or profiting by the practice of it, cannot make that criminal which would otherwise be admissible; that the act should either be consistently permitted or consistently prohibited; that if the principles which we have hitherto defended are true, society has no business, *as* society, to decide anything to be wrong which concerns only the individual; that it cannot go beyond dissuasion, and that one person should be as free to persuade, as another to dissuade. In opposition to this it may be contended, that although the public, or the State, are not warranted in authoritatively deciding, for purposes of repression or punishment, that such or such conduct affecting only the interests of the individual is good or bad, they are fully justified in assuming, if they regard it as bad, that its being so or not is at least a disputable question: That, this being supposed, they cannot be acting wrongly in endeavouring to exclude the influence of solicitations which are not disinterested, of instigators who cannot possibly be impartial—who have a direct personal interest on one side, and that side the one which the State believes to be wrong, and who confessedly promote it for personal objects only. There can surely, it may be urged, be nothing lost, no sacrifice of good, by so ordering matters that persons shall make their election, either wisely or foolishly, on their own prompting, as free as possible from the arts of persons who stimulate their inclinations for interested purposes of their own. Thus (it may be said) though the statutes respecting unlawful games are utterly indefensible—though all persons should be free to gamble in their own or each other's houses, or in any place of meeting established by their own subscriptions, and open only to the members and their visitors—yet public gambling-houses should not be permitted. It is true that the prohibition is never effectual, and that whatever amount of tyrannical power is given to the police, gambling-houses can always be maintained under other pretences; but they may be compelled to conduct their operations with a certain degree of secrecy and mystery, so that nobody knows anything about them but those who seek them; and more than this, society ought not to aim at. There is considerable force in these arguments; I will not venture to decide whether they are sufficient to justify the moral anomaly of punishing the accessary, when the principal is (and must be) allowed to go free; of fining or imprisoning the procurer, but not the fornicator, the gambling-house keeper, but not the gambler. Still less ought the common operations of buying and selling to be interfered with on analogous grounds. Almost every article which is bought and sold may be used in excess, and the sellers have a pecuniary interest in encouraging that excess; but no argument can be founded on this, in favour, for instance, of the Maine Law; because the class of dealers in strong drinks, though interested in their abuse, are indispensably required for the sake of their legitimate use. The interest, however, of these dealers in promoting intemperance is a real evil, and justifies the State in imposing restrictions and requiring guarantees, which but for that justification would be infringements of legitimate liberty.

A further question is, whether the State, while it permits, should nevertheless indirectly discourage conduct which it deems contrary to the best interests of the agent; whether, for example, it should take measures to render the means of drunkenness more costly, or add to the difficulty of procuring them, by limiting the number of the places of sale. On this as on most other practical questions, many distinctions require to be made. To tax stimulants for the sole purpose of making them more difficult to be obtained, is a measure differing only in degree from their entire prohibition; and would be justifiable only if that were justifiable. Every increase of cost is a prohibition, to those whose means do not come up to the augmented price; and to those who do, it is a penalty laid on them for gratifying a particular taste. Their choice of pleasures, and their mode of expending their income, after satisfying their legal and moral obligations to the State and to individuals, are their own concern, and must rest with their own judgment. These considerations may seem at first sight to condemn the selection of stimulants as special subjects of taxation for purposes of revenue. But it must be remembered that taxation for fiscal purposes is absolutely inevitable; that in most countries it is necessary that a considerable part of that taxation should be indirect; that the State, therefore, cannot help imposing penalties, which to some persons may be prohibitory, on the use of some articles of consumption. It is hence the duty of the State to consider, in the imposition of taxes, what commodities the consumers can best spare; and *à fortiori*,[5] to select in preference those of which it deems the use, beyond a very moderate quantity, to be positively injurious. Taxation, therefore, of stimulants, up to the point which produces the largest amount of revenue (supposing that the State needs all the revenue which it yields) is not only admissible, but to be approved of.

The question of making the sale of these commodities a more or less exclusive privilege, must be answered differently, according to the purposes to which the restriction is intended to be subservient. All places of public resort require the restraint of a police, and places of this kind peculiarly, because offences against society are especially apt to originate there. It is, therefore, fit to confine the power of selling these commodities (at least for consumption on the spot) to persons of known or vouched-for respectability of conduct; to make such regulations respecting hours of opening and closing as may be requisite for public surveillance, and to withdraw the licence if breaches of the peace repeatedly take place through the connivance or incapacity of the keeper of the house, or if it becomes a rendezvous for concocting and preparing offences against the law. Any further restriction I do not conceive to be, in principle, justifiable. The limitation in number, for instance, of beer and spirit-houses, for the express purpose of rendering them more difficult of access, and diminishing the occasions of temptation, not only exposes all to an inconvenience because there are some by whom

5. With even stronger reason (Latin).

the facility would be abused, but is suited only to a state of society in which the labouring classes are avowedly treated as children or savages, and placed under an education of restraint, to fit them for future admission to the privileges of freedom. This is not the principle on which the labouring classes are professedly governed in any free country; and no person who sets due value on freedom will give his adhesion to their being so governed, unless after all efforts have been exhausted to educate them for freedom and govern them as freemen, and it has been definitively proved that they can only be governed as children. The bare statement of the alternative shows the absurdity of supposing that such efforts have been made in any case which needs be considered here. It is only because the institutions of this country are a mass of inconsistencies, that things find admittance, into our practice which belong to the system of despotic, or what is called paternal, government, while the general freedom of our institutions precludes the exercise of the amount of control necessary to render the restraint of any real efficacy as a moral education.

It was pointed out in an early part of this Essay, that the liberty of the individual, in things wherein the individual is alone concerned, implies a corresponding liberty in any number of individuals to regulate by mutual agreement such things as regard them jointly, and regard no persons but themselves. This question presents no difficulty, so long as the will of all the persons implicated remains unaltered; but since that will may change, it is often necessary, even in things in which they alone are concerned, that they should enter into engagements with one another; and when they do, it is fit, as a general rule, that those engagements should be kept. Yet in the laws, probably, of every country, this general rule has some exceptions. Not only persons are not held to engagements which violate the rights of third parties, but it is sometimes considered a sufficient reason for releasing them from an engagement, that it is injurious to themselves. In this and most other civilized countries, for example, an engagement by which a person should sell himself, or allow himself to be sold, as a slave, would be null and void; neither enforced by law nor by opinion. The ground for thus limiting his power of voluntarily disposing of his own lot in life, is apparent, and is very clearly seen in this extreme case. The reason for not interfering, unless for the sake of others, with a person's voluntary acts, is consideration for his liberty. His voluntary choice is evidence that what he so chooses is desirable, or at the least endurable, to him, and his good is on the whole best provided for by allowing him to take his own means of pursuing it. But by selling himself for a slave, he abdicates his liberty; he foregoes any future use of it, beyond that single act. He therefore defeats, in his own case, the very purpose which is the justification of allowing him to dispose of himself. He is no longer free; but is thenceforth in a position which has no longer the presumption in its favour, that would be afforded by his voluntarily remaining in it. The principle of freedom cannot require that he should be free not to be free. It is not freedom, to be allowed to alienate his freedom. These reasons, the force of which is so conspicuous in this peculiar case, are evidently of far wider application; yet a limit is everywhere set to them by the necessities of life, which continually require, not indeed that we should resign our freedom, but that we should consent to this and the other limitation of it. The principle, however, which demands uncontrolled freedom of action in all that concerns only the agents themselves, requires that those who have become bound to one another, in things which concern no third party, should be able to release one another from the engagement: and even without such voluntary release, there are perhaps no contracts or engagements, except those that relate to money or money's worth, of which one can venture to say that there ought to be no liberty whatever of retractation. Baron Wilhelm von Humboldt, in the excellent essay from which I have already quoted, states it as his conviction, that engagements which involve personal relations or services, should never be legally binding beyond a limited duration of time; and that the most important of these engagements, marriage, having the peculiarity that its objects are frustrated unless the feelings of both the parties are in harmony with it, should require nothing more than the declared will of either party to dissolve it. This subject is too important, and too complicated, to be discussed in a parenthesis, and I touch on it only so far as is necessary for purposes of illustration. If the conciseness and generality of Baron Humboldt's dissertation had not obliged him in this instance to content himself with enunciating his conclusion without discussing the premises, he would doubtless have recognised that the question cannot be decided on grounds so simple as those to which he confines himself. When a person, either by express promise or by conduct, has encouraged another to rely upon his continuing to act in a certain way—to build expectations and calculations, and stake any part of his plan of life upon that supposition, a new series of moral obligations arises on his part towards that person, which may possibly be overruled, but cannot be ignored. And again, if the relation between two contracting parties has been followed by consequences to others; if it has placed third parties in any peculiar position, or, as in the case of marriage, has even called third parties into existence, obligations arise on the part of both the contracting parties towards those third persons, the fulfilment of which, or at all events the mode of fulfilment, must be greatly affected by the continuance or disruption of the relation between the original parties to the contract. It does not follow, nor can I admit, that these obligations extend to requiring the fulfilment of the contract at all costs to the happiness of the reluctant party; but they are a necessary element in the question; and even if, as Von Humboldt maintains, they ought to make no difference in the *legal* freedom of the parties to release themselves from the engagement (and I also hold that they ought not to make *much* difference), they necessarily make a great difference in the *moral* freedom. A person is bound to take all these circumstances into account, before resolving on a step which may affect such important interests of others; and if he does not allow proper weight to those interests, he is morally responsible for the wrong. I have made these obvious remarks for the better illustration of the general principle of liberty, and not because they are at all needed on the particular question, which, on the contrary, is usually discussed as if the interest of children was everything, and that of grown persons nothing.

I have already observed that, owing to the absence of any recognised general principles, liberty is often granted where it should be withheld, as well as withheld where it should be granted; and one of the cases in which, in the modern European world, the sentiment of liberty is the strongest, is a case where, in my view, it is altogether misplaced. A person should be free to do as he likes in his own concerns; but he ought not to be free to do as he likes in acting for another, under the pretext that the affairs of another are his own affairs. The State, while it respects the liberty of each in what specially regards himself, is bound to maintain a vigilant control over his exercise of any power which it allows him to possess over others. This obligation is almost entirely disregarded in the case of the family relations, a case, in its direct influence on human happiness, more important than all others taken together. The almost despotic power of husbands over wives needs not be enlarged upon here, because nothing more is needed for the complete removal of the evil, than that wives should have the same rights, and should receive the protection of law in the same manner, as all other persons; and because, on this subject, the defenders of established injustice do not avail themselves of the plea of liberty, but stand forth openly as the champions of power. It is in the case of children, that misapplied notions of liberty are a real obstacle to the fulfilment by the State of its duties. One would almost think that a man's children were supposed to be literally, and not metaphorically, a part of himself, so jealous is opinion of the smallest interference of law with his absolute and exclusive control over them; more jealous than of almost any interference with his own freedom of action: so much less do the generality of mankind value liberty than power. Consider, for example, the case of education. Is it not almost a self-evident axiom, that the State should require and compel the education, up to a certain standard, of every human being who is born its citizen? Yet who is there that is not afraid to recognise and assert this truth? Hardly any one indeed will deny that it is one of the most sacred duties of the parents (or, as law and usage now stand, the father), after summoning a human being into the world, to give to that being an education fitting him to perform his part well in life towards others and towards himself. But while this is unanimously declared to be the father's duty, scarcely anybody, in this country, will bear to hear of obliging him to perform it. Instead of his being required to make any exertion or sacrifice for securing education to the child, it is left to his choice to accept it or not when it is provided gratis! It still remains unrecognised, that to bring a child into existence without a fair prospect of being able, not only to provide food for its body, but instruction and training for its mind, is a moral crime, both against the unfortunate offspring and against society; and that if the parent does not fulfil this obligation, the State ought to see it fulfilled, at the charge, as far as possible, of the parent.

Were the duty of enforcing universal education once admitted, there would be an end to the difficulties about what the State should teach, and how it should teach, which now convert the subject into a mere battle-field for sects and parties, causing the time and labour which should have been spent in educating, to be wasted in quarrelling about education. If the government would make up its mind to *require* for every child a good education, it might save itself the trouble of *providing* one. It might leave to parents to obtain the education where and how they pleased, and content itself with helping to pay the school fees of the poorer class of children, and defraying the entire school expenses of those who have no one else to pay for them. The objections which are urged with reason against State education, do not apply to the enforcement of education by the State, but to the State's taking upon itself to direct that education; which is a totally different thing. That the whole or any large part of the education of the people should be in State hands, I go as far as any one in deprecating. All that has been said of the importance of individuality of character, and diversity in opinions and modes of conduct, involves, as of the same unspeakable importance, diversity of education. A general State education is a mere contrivance for moulding people to be exactly like one another; and as the mould in which it casts them is that which pleases the predominant power in the government, whether this be a monarch, a priesthood, an aristocracy, or the majority of the existing generation, in proportion as it is efficient and successful, it establishes a despotism over the mind, leading by natural tendency to one over the body. An education established and controlled by the State, should only exist, if it exist at all, as one among many competing experiments, carried on for the purpose of example and stimulus, to keep the others up to a certain standard of excellence. Unless, indeed, when society in general is in so backward a state that it could not or would not provide for itself any proper institutions of education, unless the government undertook the task; then, indeed, the government may, as the less of two great evils, take upon itself the business of schools and universities, as it may that of joint stock companies, when private enterprise, in a shape fitted for undertaking great works of industry, does not exist in the country. But in general, if the country contains a sufficient number of persons qualified to provide education under government auspices, the same persons would be able and willing to give an equally good education on the voluntary principle, under the assurance of remuneration afforded by a law rendering education compulsory, combined with State aid to those unable to defray the expense.

The instrument for enforcing the law could be no other than public examinations, extending to all children, and beginning at an early age. An age might be fixed at which every child must be examined, to ascertain if he (or she) is able to read. If a child proves unable, the father, unless he has some sufficient ground of excuse, might be subjected to a moderate fine, to be worked out, if necessary, by his labour, and the child might be put to school at his expense. Once in every year the examination should be renewed, with a gradually extending range of subjects, so as to make the universal acquisition, and what is more, retention, of a certain minimum of general knowledge, virtually compulsory. Beyond that minimum, there should be voluntary examinations on all subjects, at which all who come up to a certain standard of proficiency might claim a certificate. To prevent the State from exercising, through these arrangements, an improper influence over opinion, the knowledge required for passing an examination (beyond the merely instrumental parts of knowledge, such as languages and their use) should, even in the higher class of examinations, be confined to facts and positive science exclusively. The examinations on religion, politics, or other disputed topics, should not turn on the truth or falsehood of opinions, but on the matter of fact that such and such an opinion is held, on such grounds, by such authors, or schools, or churches. Under this system, the rising generation would be no worse off in regard to all disputed truths, than they are at present; they would be brought up either churchmen or dissenters as they now are, the state merely taking care that they should be instructed churchmen, or instructed dissenters. There would be nothing to hinder them from being taught religion, if their parents chose, at the same schools where they were taught other things. All attempts by the state to bias the conclusions of its citizens on disputed subjects, are evil; but it may very properly offer to ascertain and certify that a person possesses the knowledge, requisite to make his conclusions, on any given subject, worth attending to. A student of philosophy would be the better for being able to stand an examination both in Locke and in Kant, whichever of the two he takes up with, or even if with neither: and there is no reasonable objection to examining an atheist in the evidences of Christianity, provided he is not required to profess a belief in them. The examinations, however, in the higher branches of knowledge should, I conceive, be entirely voluntary. It would be giving too dangerous a power to governments, were they allowed to exclude any one from professions, even from the profession of teacher, for alleged deficiency of qualifications: and I think, with Wilhelm von Humboldt, that degrees, or other public certificates of scientific or professional acquirements, should be given to all who present themselves for examination, and stand the test; but that such certificates should confer no advantage over competitors, other than the weight which may be attached to their testimony by public opinion.

It is not in the matter of education only, that misplaced notions of liberty prevent moral obligations on the part of parents from being recognised, and legal obligations from being imposed, where there are the strongest grounds for the former always, and in many cases for the latter also. The fact itself, of causing the existence of a human being, is one of the most responsible actions in the range of human life. To undertake this responsibility—to bestow a life which may be either a curse or a blessing—unless the being on whom it is to be bestowed will have at least the ordinary chances of a desirable existence, is a crime against that being. And in a country either over-peopled, or threatened with being so, to produce children, beyond a very small number, with the effect of reducing the reward of labour by their competition, is a serious offence against all who live by the remuneration of their labour. The laws which, in many countries on the Continent, forbid marriage unless the parties can show that they have the means of supporting a family, do not exceed the legitimate powers of the state: and whether such laws be expedient or not (a question mainly dependent on local circumstances and feelings), they are not objectionable as violations of liberty. Such laws are interferences of the state to prohibit a mischievous act—an act injurious to others, which ought to be a subject of reprobation, and social stigma, even when it is not deemed expedient to superadd legal punishment. Yet the current ideas of liberty, which bend so easily to real infringements of the freedom of the individual, in things which concern only himself, would repel the attempt to put any restraint upon his inclinations when the consequence of their indulgence is a life, or lives, of wretchedness and depravity to the off-spring, with manifold evils to those sufficiently within reach to be in any way affected by their actions. When we compare the strange respect of mankind for liberty, with their strange want of respect for it, we might imagine that a man had an indispensable right to do harm to others, and no right at all to please himself without giving pain to any one.

I have reserved for the last place a large class of questions respecting the limits of government interference, which, though closely connected with the subject of this Essay, do not, in strictness, belong to it. These are cases in which the reasons against interference do not turn upon the principle of liberty: the question is not about restraining the actions of individuals, but about helping them: it is asked whether the government should do, or cause to be done, something for their benefit, instead of leaving it to be done by themselves, individually, or in voluntary combination.

The objections to government interference, when it is not such as to involve infringement of liberty, may be of three kinds.

The first is, when the thing to be done is likely to be better done by individuals than by the government. Speaking generally, there is no one so fit to conduct any business, or to determine how or by whom it shall be conducted, as those who are personally interested in it. This principle condemns the interferences, once so common, of the legislature, or the officers of government, with the ordinary processes of industry. But this part of the subject has been sufficiently enlarged upon by political economists, and is not particularly related to the principles of this Essay.

The second objection is more nearly allied to our subject. In many cases, though individuals may not do the particular thing so well, on the average, as the officers of government, it is nevertheless desirable that it should be done by them, rather than by the government, as a means to their own mental education—a mode of strengthening their active faculties, exercising their judgment, and giving them a familiar knowledge of the subjects with which they are thus left to deal. This is a principal, though not the sole, recommendation of jury trial (in cases not political); of free and popular local and municipal institutions; of the conduct of industrial and philanthropic enterprises by voluntary associations. These are not questions of liberty, and are connected with that subject only by remote tendencies; but they are questions of development. It belongs to a different occasion from the present to dwell on these things as parts of national education; as being, in truth, the peculiar training of a citizen, the practical part of the political education of a free people, taking them out of the narrow circle of personal and family selfishness, and accustoming them to the comprehension of joint interests, the management of joint concerns—habituating them to act from public or semi-public motives, and guide their conduct by aims which unite instead of isolating them from one another. Without these habits and powers, a free constitution can neither be worked nor preserved, as is exemplified by the too-often transitory nature of political freedom in countries where it does not rest upon a sufficient basis of local liberties. The management of purely local business by the localities, and of the great enterprises of industry by the union of those who voluntarily supply the pecuniary means, is further recommended by all the advantages which have been set forth in this Essay as belonging to individuality of development, and diversity of modes of action. Government operations tend to be everywhere alike. With individuals and voluntary associations, on the contrary, there are varied experiments, and endless diversity of experience. What the State can usefully do, is to make itself a central depository, and active circulator and diffuser, of the experience resulting from many trials. Its business is to enable each experimentalist to benefit by the experiments of others, instead of tolerating no experiments but its own.

The third, and most cogent reason for restricting the interference of government, is the great evil of adding unnecessarily to its power. Every function superadded to those already exercised by the government, causes its influence over hopes and fears to be more widely diffused, and converts, more and more, the active and ambitious part of the public into hangers-on of the government, or of some party which aims at becoming the government. If the roads, the railways, the banks, the insurance offices, the great joint-stock companies, the universities, and the public charities, were all of them branches of the government; if, in addition, the municipal corporations and local boards, with all that now devolves on them, became departments of the central administration; if the employés of all these different enterprises were appointed and paid by the government, and looked to the government for every rise in life; not all the freedom of the press and popular constitution of the legislature would make this or any other country free otherwise than in name. And the evil would be greater, the more efficiently and scientifically the administrative machinery was constructed—the more skilful the arrangements for obtaining the best qualified hands and heads with which to work it. In England it has of late been proposed that all the members of the civil service of government should be selected by competitive examination, to obtain for those employments the most intelligent and instructed persons procurable; and much has been said and written for and against this proposal. One of the arguments most insisted on by its opponents, is that the occupation of a permanent official

servant of the State does not hold out sufficient prospects of emolument and importance to attract the highest talents, which will
always be able to find a more inviting career in the professions, or in
the service of companies and other public bodies. One would not
have been surprised if this argument had been used by the friends
of the proposition, as an answer to its principal difficulty. Coming
from the opponents it is strange enough. What is urged as an objection is the safety-valve of the proposed system. If indeed all the
high talent of the country *could* be drawn into the service of the
government, a proposal tending to bring about that result might well
inspire uneasiness. If every part of the business of society which
required organized concert, or large and comprehensive views, were in
the hands of the government, and if government offices were universally filled by the ablest men, all the enlarged culture and practised
intelligence in the country, except the purely speculative, would be
concentrated in a numerous bureaucracy, to whom alone the rest of
the community would look for all things: the multitude for direction and dictation in all they had to do; the able and aspiring for
personal advancement. To be admitted into the ranks of this bureaucracy, and when admitted, to rise therein, would be the sole objects
of ambition. Under this régime, not only is the outside public ill-
qualified, for want of practical experience, to criticize or check the
mode of operation of the bureaucracy, but even if the accidents of
despotic or the natural working of popular institutions occasionally
raise to the summit a ruler or rulers of reforming inclinations, no
reform can be effected which is contrary to the interest of the bureaucracy. Such is the melancholy condition of the Russian empire, as is
shown in the accounts of those who have had sufficient opportunity
of observation. The Czar himself is powerless against the bureaucratic body; he can send any one of them to Siberia, but he cannot
govern without them, or against their will. On every decree of his
they have a tacit veto, by merely refraining from carrying it into
effect. In countries of more advanced civilization and of a more
insurrectionary spirit, the public, accustomed to expect everything
to be done for them by the State, or at least to do nothing for themselves without asking from the State not only leave to do it, but
even how it is to be done, naturally hold the State responsible for all
evil which befals them, and when the evil exceeds their amount of
patience, they rise against the government and make what is called
a revolution; whereupon somebody else, with or without legitimate
authority from the nation, vaults into the seat, issues his orders to
the bureaucracy, and everything goes on much as it did before;
the bureaucracy being unchanged, and nobody else being capable of
taking their place.

A very different spectacle is exhibited among a people accustomed to transact their own business. In France, a large part of the people having been engaged in military service, many of whom have held at least the rank of non-commissioned officers, there are in every popular insurrection several persons competent to take the lead, and improvise some tolerable plan of action. What the French are in military affairs, the Americans are in every kind of civil business; let them be left without a government, every body of Americans is able to improvise one, and to carry on that or any other public business with a sufficient amount of intelligence, order, and decision. This is what every free people ought to be: and a people capable of this is certain to be free; it will never let itself be enslaved by any man or body of men because these are able to seize and pull the reins of the central administration. No bureaucracy can hope to make such a people as this do or undergo anything that they do not like. But where everything is done through the bureaucracy, nothing to which the bureaucracy is really adverse can be done at all. The constitution of such countries is an organization of the experience and practical ability of the nation, into a disciplined body for the purpose of governing the rest; and the more perfect that organization is in itself, the more successful in drawing to itself and educating for itself the persons of greatest capacity from all ranks of the community, the more complete is the bondage of all, the members of the bureaucracy included. For the governors are as much the slaves of their organization and discipline, as the governed are of the governors. A Chinese mandarin is as much the tool and creature of a despotism as the humblest cultivator. An individual Jesuit is to the utmost degree of abasement the slave of his order, though the order itself exists for the collective power and importance of its members.

It is not, also, to be forgotten, that the absorption of all the principal ability of the country into the governing body is fatal, sooner or later, to the mental activity and progressiveness of the body itself. Banded together as they are—working a system which, like all systems, necessarily proceeds in a great measure by fixed rules—the official body are under the constant temptation of sinking into indolent routine, or, if they now and then desert that mill-horse round, of rushing into some half-examined crudity which has struck the fancy of some leading member of the corps: and the sole check to these closely allied, though seemingly opposite, tendencies, the only stimulus which can keep the ability of the body itself up to a high standard, is liability to the watchful criticism of equal ability outside the body. It is indispensable, therefore, that the means should exist, independently of the government, of forming such ability, and furnishing it with the opportunities and experience necessary

for a correct judgment of great practical affairs. If we would possess
permanently a skilful and efficient body of functionaries—above all,
a body able to originate and willing to adopt improvements; if we
would not have our bureaucracy degenerate into a pedantocracy,
this body must not engross all the occupations which form and
cultivate the faculties required for the government of mankind.

To determine the point at which evils, so formidable to human
freedom and advancement, begin, or rather at which they begin to
predominate over the benefits attending the collective application of
the force of society, under its recognised chiefs, for the removal
of the obstacles which stand in the way of its well-being; to secure
as much of the advantages of centralized power and intelligence, as
can be had without turning into governmental channels too great a
proportion of the general activity, is one of the most difficult and
complicated questions in the art of government. It is, in a great
measure, a question of detail, in which many and various considerations must be kept in view, and no absolute rule can be laid down.
But I believe that the practical principle in which safety resides, the
ideal to be kept in view, the standard by which to test all arrangements intended for overcoming the difficulty, may be conveyed in
these words: the greatest dissemination of power consistent with
efficiency; but the greatest possible centralization of information,
and diffusion of it from the centre. Thus, in municipal administration, there would be, as in the New England States, a very minute
division among separate officers, chosen by the localities, of all business which is not better left to the persons directly interested; but
besides this, there would be, in each department of local affairs, a
central superintendence, forming a branch of the general government. The organ of this superintendence would concentrate, as in
a focus, the variety of information and experience derived from
the conduct of that branch of public business in all the localities, from
everything analogous which is done in foreign countries, and from the
general principles of political science. This central organ should
have a right to know all that is done, and its special duty should be
that of making the knowledge acquired in one place available for
others. Emancipated from the petty prejudices and narrow views of
a locality by its elevated position and comprehensive sphere of observation, its advice would naturally carry much authority; but its
actual power, as a permanent institution, should, I conceive, be
limited to compelling the local officers to obey the laws laid down
for their guidance. In all things not provided for by general rules,
those officers should be left to their own judgment, under responsibility to their constituents. For the violation of rules, they should be
responsible to law, and the rules themselves should be laid down by
the legislature; the central administrative authority only watching

over their execution, and if they were not properly carried into effect, appealing, according to the nature of the case, to the tribunal to enforce the law, or to the constituencies to dismiss the functionaries who had not executed it according to its spirit. Such, in its general conception, is the central superintendence which the Poor Law Board[6] is intended to exercise over the administrators of the Poor Rate throughout the country. Whatever powers the Board exercises beyond this limit, were right and necessary in that peculiar case, for the cure of rooted habits of maladministration in matters deeply affecting not the localities merely, but the whole community; since no locality has a moral right to make itself by mismanagement a nest of pauperism, necessarily overflowing into other localities, and impairing the moral and physical condition of the whole labouring community. The powers of administrative coercion and subordinate legislation possessed by the Poor Law Board (but which, owing to the state of opinion on the subject, are very scantily exercised by them), though perfectly justifiable in a case of first-rate national interest, would be wholly out of place in the superintendence of interests purely local. But a central organ of information and instruction for all the localities, would be equally valuable in all departments of administration. A government cannot have too much of the kind of activity which does not impede, but aids and stimulates, individual exertion and development. The mischief begins when, instead of calling forth the activity and powers of individuals and bodies, it substitutes its own activity for theirs; when, instead of informing, advising, and, upon occasion, denouncing, it makes them work in fetters, or bids them stand aside and does their work instead of them. The worth of a State, in the long run, is the worth of the individuals composing it; and a State which postpones the interests of *their* mental expansion and elevation, to a little more of administrative skill, or of that semblance of it which practice gives, in the details of business; a State which dwarfs its men, in order that they may be more docile instruments in its hands even for beneficial purposes, will find that with small men no great thing can really be accomplished; and that the perfection of machinery to which it has sacrificed everything, will in the end avail it nothing, for want of the vital power which, in order that the machine might work more smoothly, it has preferred to banish.

THE END

---

6. The agency supervising the administration of the Poor Law of 1834.

Utilitarianism

CHAPTER I

General Remarks

There are few circumstances among those which make up the present condition of human knowledge, more unlike what might have been expected, or more significant of the backward state in which speculation on the most important subjects still lingers, than the little progress which has been made in the decision of the controversy respecting the criterion of right and wrong. From the dawn of philosophy, the question concerning the *summum bonum*,[1] or, what is the same thing, concerning the foundation of morality, has been accounted the main problem in speculative thought, has occupied the most gifted intellects, and divided them into sects and schools, carrying on a vigorous warfare against one another. And after more than two thousand years the same discussions continue, philosophers are still ranged under the same contending banners, and neither thinkers nor mankind at large seem nearer to being unanimous on the subject, than when the youth Socrates listened to the old Protagoras,[2] and asserted (if Plato's dialogue be grounded on a real conversation) the theory of utilitarianism against the popular morality of the so-called sophist.

It is true that similar confusion and uncertainty, and in some cases similar discordance, exist respecting the first principles of all the sciences, not excepting that which is deemed the most certain of them, mathematics; without much impairing, generally indeed without impairing at all, the trustworthiness of the conclusions of those sciences. An apparent anomaly, the explanation of which is, that the detailed doctrines of a science are not usually deduced from,

1. The highest or ultimate good (Latin).
2. Protagoras (481–411 B.C.E.), a leading Sophist in ancient Athens, after whom Plato named one of his dialogues, which Mill translated in his youth (*CW*, vol. 11). Mill relies upon Protagoras to defend utilitarianism from the accusation of preaching selfishness, yet in the dialogue Protagoras proposes an egoistic version of hedonism according to which each person should pursue first of all her own personal interest, which is what Mill wants to confute against his critics.

nor depend for their evidence upon, what are called its first principles. Were it not so, there would be no science more precarious, or
whose conclusions were more insufficiently made out, than algebra;
which derives none of its certainty from what are commonly taught
to learners as its elements, since these, as laid down by some of its
most eminent teachers, are as full of fictions as English law, and of
mysteries as theology. The truths which are ultimately accepted as
the first principles of a science, are really the last results of metaphysical analysis, practised on the elementary notions with which
the science is conversant; and their relation to the science is not
that of foundations to an edifice, but of roots to a tree, which may
perform their office equally well though they be never dug down to
and exposed to light. But though in science the particular truths
precede the general theory, the contrary might be expected to be the
case with a practical art, such as morals or legislation. All action is
for the sake of some end, and rules of action, it seems natural to
suppose, must take their whole character and colour from the end
to which they are subservient. When we engage in a pursuit, a clear
and precise conception of what we are pursuing would seem to be
the first thing we need, instead of the last we are to look forward to.
A test of right and wrong must be the means, one would think, of
ascertaining what is right or wrong, and not a consequence of having
already ascertained it.

The difficulty is not avoided by having recourse to the popular
theory of a natural faculty, a sense or instinct, informing us of right
and wrong. For—besides that the existence of such a moral instinct
is itself one of the matters in dispute—those believers in it who have
any pretensions to philosophy, have been obliged to abandon the idea
that it discerns what is right or wrong in the particular case in hand,
as our other senses discern the sight or sound actually present. Our
moral faculty, according to all those of its interpreters who are entitled to the name of thinkers, supplies us only with the general principles of moral judgments; it is a branch of our reason, not of our
sensitive faculty; and must be looked to for the abstract doctrines of
morality, not for perception of it in the concrete. The intuitive, no
less than what may be termed the inductive, school of ethics, insists
on the necessity of general laws.[3] They both agree that the morality
of an individual action is not a question of direct perception, but of
the application of a law to an individual case. They recognise also,
to a great extent, the same moral laws; but differ as to their evidence,
and the source from which they derive their authority. According to

---

3. Mill is here referring to the "intuitionists" and particularly William Whewell, whose
   thought he criticized in "Whewell on Moral Philosophy" (1852), *CW*, vol. 10,
   pp. 167–200.

the one opinion, the principles of morals are evident *à priori*.[4] requiring nothing to command assent, except that the meaning of the terms be understood. According to the other doctrine, right and wrong, as well as truth and falsehood, are questions of observation and experience. But both hold equally that morality must be deduced from principles; and the intuitive school affirm as strongly as the inductive, that there is a science of morals. Yet they seldom attempt to make out a list of the *à priori* principles which are to serve as the premises of the science; still more rarely do they make any effort to reduce those various principles to one first principle, or common ground of obligation. They either assume the ordinary precepts of morals as of *à priori* authority, or they lay down as the common groundwork of those maxims, some generality much less obviously authoritative than the maxims themselves, and which has never succeeded in gaining popular acceptance. Yet to support their pretensions there ought either to be some one fundamental principle or law, at the root of all morality, or if there be several, there should be a determinate order of precedence among them; and the one principle, or the rule for deciding between the various principles when they conflict, ought to be self-evident.

To inquire how far the bad effects of this deficiency have been mitigated in practice, or to what extent the moral beliefs of mankind have been vitiated or made uncertain by the absence of any distinct recognition of an ultimate standard, would imply a complete survey and criticism of past and present ethical doctrine. It would, however, be easy to show that whatever steadiness or consistency these moral beliefs have attained, has been mainly due to the tacit influence of a standard not recognised. Although the non-existence of an acknowledged first principle has made ethics not so much a guide as a consecration of men's actual sentiments, still, as men's sentiments, both of favour and of aversion, are greatly influenced by what they suppose to be the effects of things upon their happiness, the principle of utility, or as Bentham latterly called it, the greatest happiness principle, has had a large share in forming the moral doctrines even of those who most scornfully reject its authority. Nor is there any school of thought which refuses to admit that the influence of actions on happiness is a most material and even predominant consideration in many of the details of morals, however unwilling to acknowledge it as the fundamental principle of morality, and the source of moral obligation. I might go much further, and say that to all those *à priori* moralists who deem it necessary to argue at all, utilitarian arguments are indispensable.

4. Latin term meaning arguments or justifications independent of experience; opposite to *a posteriori*, or arguments and judgments relying on experience.

It is not my present purpose to criticize these thinkers; but I cannot help referring, for illustration, to a systematic treatise by one of the most illustrious of them, the *Metaphysics of Ethics*, by Kant.[5] This remarkable man, whose system of thought will long remain one of the landmarks in the history of philosophical speculation, does, in the treatise in question, lay down an universal first principle as the origin and ground of moral obligation; it is this:—'So act, that the rule on which thou actest would admit of being adopted as a law by all rational beings.' But when he begins to deduce from this precept any of the actual duties of morality, he fails, almost grotesquely, to show that there would be any contradiction, any logical (not to say physical) impossibility, in the adoption by all rational beings of the most outrageously immoral rules of conduct. All he shows is that the *consequences* of their universal adoption would be such as no one would choose to incur.

On the present occasion, I shall, without further discussion of the other theories, attempt to contribute something towards the understanding and appreciation of the Utilitarian or Happiness theory, and towards such proof as it is susceptible of. It is evident that this cannot be proof in the ordinary and popular meaning of the term. Questions of ultimate ends are not amenable to direct proof. Whatever can be proved to be good, must be so by being shown to be a means to something admitted to be good without proof. The medical art is proved to be good, by its conducing to health; but how is it possible to prove that health is good? The art of music is good, for the reason, among others, that it produces pleasure; but what proof is it possible to give that pleasure is good? If, then, it is asserted that there is a comprehensive formula, including all things which are in themselves good, and that whatever else is good, is not so as an end, but as a mean, the formula may be accepted or rejected, but is not a subject of what is commonly understood by proof. We are not, however, to infer that its acceptance or rejection must depend on blind impulse, or arbitrary choice. There is a larger meaning of the word proof, in which this question is as amenable to it as any other of the disputed questions of philosophy. The subject is within the cognizance of the rational faculty; and neither does that faculty deal with it solely in the way of intuition. Considerations may be presented capable of determining the intellect either to give or withhold its assent to the doctrine; and this is equivalent to proof.

We shall examine presently of what nature are these considerations; in what manner they apply to the case, and what rational

---

5. "Act on a maxim which at the same time contains in itself its own universal validity for every rational being." Immanuel Kant, *Groundwork for the Metaphysics of Morals* (1785), trans. James W. Ellington (Indianapolis and Cambridge: Hackett, 1994), pp. 42–43. Mill referred to the German edition of 1797.

grounds, therefore, can be given for accepting or rejecting the utilitarian formula. But it is a preliminary condition of rational acceptance or rejection, that the formula should be correctly understood. I believe that the very imperfect notion ordinarily formed of its meaning, is the chief obstacle which impedes its reception; and that could it be cleared, even from only the grosser misconceptions, the question would be greatly simplified, and a large proportion of its difficulties removed. Before, therefore, I attempt to enter into the philosophical grounds which can be given for assenting to the utilitarian standard, I shall offer some illustrations of the doctrine itself; with the view of showing more clearly what it is, distinguishing it from what it is not, and disposing of such of the practical objections to it as either originate in, or are closely connected with, mistaken interpretations of its meaning. Having thus prepared the ground, I shall afterwards endeavour to throw such light as I can upon the question, considered as one of philosophical theory.

CHAPTER II

What Utilitarianism Is

A passing remark is all that needs be given to the ignorant blunder of supposing that those who stand up for utility as the test of right and wrong, use the term in that restricted and merely colloquial sense in which utility is opposed to pleasure. An apology is due to the philosophical opponents of utilitarianism, for even the momentary appearance of confounding them with any one capable of so absurd a misconception; which is the more extraordinary, inasmuch as the contrary accusation, of referring everything to pleasure, and that too in its grossest form, is another of the common charges against utilitarianism: and, as has been pointedly remarked by an able writer, the same sort of persons, and often the very same persons, denounce the theory 'as impracticably dry when the word utility precedes the word pleasure, and as too practicably voluptuous when the word pleasure precedes the word utility.' Those who know anything about the matter are aware that every writer, from Epicurus[6] to Bentham, who maintained the theory of utility, meant by it, not something to be contradistinguished from pleasure, but pleasure

---

6. Epicurus (341–270 B.C.E.), a Greek philosopher from the island of Samos, turned against Platonism and inaugurated his own school, known as "the Garden," in Athens; his teaching aimed at educating people to make them capable of attaining happiness by containing both desires and pains and achieving freedom from fear. Most knowledge of his ideas Mill derived (like us) from later authors, particularly Diogenes Laertius (180–240), Sextus Empiricus (c. 2 or 3 C.E.), the Roman poet Lucretius (c. 99–c. 55 B.C.E.), and Marcus Tullius Cicero (106 B.C.E.–43 B.C.E.).

itself, together with exemption from pain; and instead of opposing the useful to the agreeable or the ornamental, have always declared that the useful means these, among other things. Yet the common herd, including the herd of writers, not only in newspapers and periodicals, but in books of weight and pretension, are perpetually falling into this shallow mistake. Having caught up the word utilitarian, while knowing nothing whatever about it but its sound, they habitually express by it the rejection, or the neglect, of pleasure in some of its forms; of beauty, of ornament, or of amusement. Nor is the term thus ignorantly misapplied solely in disparagement, but occasionally in compliment; as though it implied superiority to frivolity and the mere pleasures of the moment. And this perverted use is the only one in which the word is popularly known, and the one from which the new generation are acquiring their sole notion of its meaning. Those who introduced the word, but who had for many years discontinued it as a distinctive appellation, may well feel themselves called upon to resume it, if by doing so they can hope to contribute anything towards rescuing it from this utter degradation.[7]

The creed which accepts as the foundation of morals, Utility, or the Greatest Happiness Principle, holds that actions are right in proportion as they tend to promote happiness, wrong as they tend to produce the reverse of happiness. By happiness is intended pleasure, and the absence of pain; by unhappiness, pain, and the privation of pleasure. To give a clear view of the moral standard set up by the theory, much more requires to be said; in particular, what things it includes in the ideas of pain and pleasure; and to what extent this is left an open question. But these supplementary explanations do not affect the theory of life on which this theory of morality is grounded—namely, that pleasure, and freedom from pain, are the only things desirable as ends: and that all desirable things (which are as numerous in the utilitarian as in any other scheme) are desirable either for the pleasure inherent in themselves, or as means to the promotion of pleasure and the prevention of pain.

Now, such a theory of life excites in many minds, and among them in some of the most estimable in feeling and purpose, inveterate dislike. To suppose that life has (as they express it) no higher end than pleasure—no better and nobler object of desire and pursuit—they designate as utterly mean and grovelling; as a doctrine

7. The author of this essay has reason for believing himself to be the first person who brought the word utilitarian into use. He did not invent it, but adopted it from a passing expression in Mr. Galt's *Annals of the Parish*. After using it as a designation for several years, he and others abandoned it from a growing dislike to anything resembling a badge or watchword of sectarian distinction. But as a name for one single opinion, not a set of opinions—to denote the recognition of utility as a standard, not any particular way of applying it—the term supplies a want in the language, and offers, in many cases, a convenient mode of avoiding tiresome circumlocution [*Mill's note*].

worthy only of swine, to whom the followers of Epicurus were, at a
very early period, contemptuously likened;[8] and modern holders of
the doctrine are occasionally made the subject of equally polite
comparisons by its German, French, and English assailants.

When thus attacked, the Epicureans have always answered, that
it is not they, but their accusers, who represent human nature in a
degrading light; since the accusation supposes human beings to be
capable of no pleasures except those of which swine are capable. If
this supposition were true, the charge could not be gainsaid, but
would then be no longer an imputation; for if the sources of pleasure were precisely the same to human beings and to swine, the rule
of life which is good enough for the one would be good enough for
the other. The comparison of the Epicurean life to that of beasts is
felt as degrading, precisely because a beast's pleasures do not satisfy a human being's conceptions of happiness. Human beings have
faculties more elevated than the animal appetites, and when once
made conscious of them, do not regard anything as happiness which
does not include their gratification. I do not, indeed, consider the
Epicureans to have been by any means faultless in drawing out their
scheme of consequences from the utilitarian principle. To do this
in any sufficient manner, many Stoic, as well as Christian elements
require to be included. But there is no known Epicurean theory of
life which does not assign to the pleasures of the intellect, of the
feelings and imagination, and of the moral sentiments, a much
higher value as pleasures than to those of mere sensation. It must
be admitted, however, that utilitarian writers in general have placed
the superiority of mental over bodily pleasures chiefly in the greater
permanency, safety, uncostliness, &c., of the former—that is, in
their circumstantial advantages rather than in their intrinsic nature.
And on all these points utilitarians have fully proved their case; but
they might have taken the other, and, as it may be called, higher
ground, with entire consistency. It is quite compatible with the
principle of utility to recognise the fact, that some *kinds* of pleasure
are more desirable and more valuable than others. It would be absurd
that while, in estimating all other things, quality is considered as
well as quantity, the estimation of pleasures should be supposed to
depend on quantity alone.

If I am asked, what I mean by difference of quality in pleasures, or
what makes one pleasure more valuable than another, merely as a
pleasure, except its being greater in amount, there is but one possible
answer. Of two pleasures, if there be one to which all or almost all

---

8. Reference is to Thomas Carlyle's definition of utilitarianism as "Pig-Philosophy" in
   Latter-Day Pamphlets (London: Chapman and Hall, 1850), section on "Pig-Philosophy,"
   chap. 8, "Jesuitism" (1 August 1850), pp. 268–70.

who have experience of both give a decided preference, irrespective of any feeling of moral obligation to prefer it, that is the more desirable pleasure. If one of the two is, by those who are competently acquainted with both, placed so far above the other that they prefer it, even though knowing it to be attended with a greater amount of discontent, and would not resign it for any quantity of the other pleasure which their nature is capable of, we are justified in ascribing to the preferred enjoyment a superiority in quality, so far outweighing quantity as to render it, in comparison, of small account.

Now it is an unquestionable fact that those who are equally acquainted with, and equally capable of appreciating and enjoying, both, do give a most marked preference to the manner of existence which employs their higher faculties. Few human creatures would consent to be changed into any of the lower animals, for a promise of the fullest allowance of a beast's pleasures; no intelligent human being would consent to be a fool, no instructed person would be an ignoramus, no person of feeling and conscience would be selfish and base, even though they should be persuaded that the fool, the dunce, or the rascal is better satisfied with his lot than they are with theirs. They would not resign what they possess more than he, for the most complete satisfaction of all the desires which they have in common with him. If they ever fancy they would, it is only in cases of unhappiness so extreme, that to escape from it they would exchange their lot for almost any other, however undesirable in their own eyes. A being of higher faculties requires more to make him happy, is capable probably of more acute suffering, and is certainly accessible to it at more points, than one of an inferior type; but in spite of these liabilities, he can never really wish to sink into what he feels to be a lower grade of existence. We may give what explanation we please of this unwillingness; we may attribute it to pride, a name which is given indiscriminately to some of the most and to some of the least estimable feelings of which mankind are capable; we may refer it to the love of liberty and personal independence, an appeal to which was with the Stoics one of the most effective means for the inculcation of it; to the love of power, or to the love of excitement, both of which do really enter into and contribute to it: but its most appropriate appellation is a sense of dignity, which all human beings possess in one form or other, and in some, though by no means in exact, proportion to their higher faculties, and which is so essential a part of the happiness of those in whom it is strong, that nothing which conflicts with it could be, otherwise than momentarily, an object of desire to them. Whoever supposes that this preference takes place at a sacrifice of happiness—that the superior being, in anything like equal circumstances, is not happier than the inferior—confounds the two very different ideas, of happiness, and content. It is indisputable that the being whose capacities of enjoyment are low, has the greatest chance of having them fully satisfied; and a highly-endowed being will always feel that any happiness which he can look for, as the world is constituted, is imperfect. But he can learn to bear its imperfections, if they are at all bearable; and they will not make him envy the being who is indeed unconscious of the imperfections, but only because he feels not at all the good which those imperfections qualify. It is better to be a human being dissatisfied than a pig satisfied; better to be Socrates dissatisfied than a fool satisfied. And if the fool, or the pig, is of a different opinion, it is because they only know their own side of the question. The other party to the comparison knows both sides.

It may be objected, that many who are capable of the higher pleasures, occasionally, under the influence of temptation, postpone them to the lower. But this is quite compatible with a full appreciation of the intrinsic superiority of the higher. Men often, from infirmity of character, make their election for the nearer good, though they know it to be the less valuable; and this no less when the choice is between two bodily pleasures, than when it is between bodily and mental. They pursue sensual indulgences to the injury of health, though perfectly aware that health is the greater good. It may be further objected, that many who begin with youthful enthusiasm for everything noble, as they advance in years sink into indolence and selfishness. But I do not believe that those who undergo this very common change, voluntarily choose the lower description of pleasures in preference to the higher. I believe that before they devote themselves exclusively to the one, they have already become incapable of the other. Capacity for the nobler feelings is in most natures a very tender plant, easily killed, not only by hostile influences, but by mere want of sustenance; and in the majority of young persons it speedily dies away if the occupations to which their position in life has devoted them, and the society into which it has thrown them, are not favourable to keeping that higher capacity in exercise. Men lose their high aspirations as they lose their intellectual tastes, because they have not time or opportunity for indulging them; and they addict themselves to inferior pleasures, not because they deliberately prefer them, but because they are either the only ones to which they have access, or the only ones which they are any longer capable of enjoying. It may be questioned whether any one who has remained equally susceptible to both classes of pleasures, ever knowingly and calmly preferred the lower; though many, in all ages, have broken down in an ineffectual attempt to combine both.

From this verdict of the only competent judges, I apprehend there can be no appeal. On a question which is the best worth having of two pleasures, or which of two modes of existence is the most grateful to the feelings, apart from its moral attributes and from its consequences, the judgment of those who are qualified by knowledge of both, or, if they differ, that of the majority among them, must be admitted as final. And there needs be the less hesitation to accept this judgment respecting the quality of pleasures, since there is no other tribunal to be referred to even on the question of quantity. What means are there of determining which is the acutest of two pains, or the intensest of two pleasurable sensations, except the general suffrage of those who are familiar with both? Neither pains nor pleasures are homogeneous, and pain is always heterogeneous with pleasure. What is there to decide whether a particular pleasure is worth purchasing at the cost of a particular pain, except the feelings and judgment of the experienced? When, therefore, those feelings and judgment declare the pleasures derived from the higher faculties to be preferable *in kind*, apart from the question of intensity, to those of which the animal nature, disjoined from the higher faculties, is susceptible, they are entitled on this subject to the same regard.

I have dwelt on this point, as being a necessary part of a perfectly just conception of Utility or Happiness, considered as the directive rule of human conduct. But it is by no means an indispensable condition to the acceptance of the utilitarian standard; for that standard is not the agent's own greatest happiness, but the greatest amount of happiness altogether; and if it may possibly be doubted whether a noble character is always the happier for its nobleness, there can be no doubt that it makes other people happier, and that the world in general is immensely a gainer by it. Utilitarianism, therefore, could only attain its end by the general cultivation of nobleness of character, even if each individual were only benefited by the nobleness of others, and his own, so far as happiness is concerned, were a sheer deduction from the benefit. But the bare enunciation of such an absurdity as this last, renders refutation superfluous.

According to the Greatest Happiness Principle, as above explained, the ultimate end, with reference to and for the sake of which all other things are desirable (whether we are considering our own good or that of other people), is an existence exempt as far as possible from pain, and as rich as possible in enjoyments, both in point of quantity and quality; the test of quality, and the rule for measuring it against quantity, being the preference felt by those who, in their opportunities of experience, to which must be added their habits of self-consciousness and self-observation, are best furnished with the means of comparison. This, being, according to the utilitarian opinion, the end of human action, is necessarily also the standard of morality; which may accordingly be defined, the rules and precepts for human conduct, by the observance of which an existence such as has been described might be, to the greatest extent possible, secured to all mankind; and not to them only, but, so far as the nature of things admits, to the whole sentient creation.

Against this doctrine, however, arises another class of objectors, who say that happiness, in any form, cannot be the rational purpose of human life and action; because, in the first place, it is unattainable: and they contemptuously ask, What right hast thou to be happy? a question which Mr. Carlyle clenches by the addition, What right, a short time ago, hadst thou even *to be*?[9] Next, they say, that men can do *without* happiness; that all noble human beings have felt this, and could not have become noble but by learning the lesson of Entsagen, or renunciation; which lesson, thoroughly learnt and submitted to, they affirm to be the beginning and necessary condition of all virtue.[1]

The first of these objections would go to the root of the matter were it well founded; for if no happiness is to be had at all by human beings, the attainment of it cannot be the end of morality, or of any rational conduct. Though, even in that case, something might still be said for the utilitarian theory; since utility includes not solely the pursuit of happiness, but the prevention or mitigation of unhappiness; and if the former aim be chimerical, there will be all the greater scope and more imperative need for the latter, so long at least as mankind think fit to live, and do not take refuge in the simultaneous act of suicide recommended under certain conditions by Novalis.[2] When, however, it is thus positively asserted to be impossible that human life should be happy, the assertion, if not something like a verbal quibble, is at least an exaggeration. If by happiness be meant a continuity of highly pleasurable excitement, it is evident enough that this is impossible. A state of exalted pleasure lasts only moments, or in some cases, and with some intermissions, hours or days, and is the occasional brilliant flash of enjoyment, not its permanent and steady flame. Of this the philosophers who have taught that happiness is the end of life were as fully aware as those who taunt them. The happiness which they meant was not a life of rapture; but moments of such, in an existence made up of few and transitory pains, many and various pleasures, with a decided predominance of

9. Thomas Carlyle, *Sartor Resartus* (1836), ed. Archibald MacMechan (Boston: Ginn & Company; London: Athenaeum P, 1902), p. 174.

1. "It is only with Renunciation (*Entsagen*) that Life, properly speaking, can be said to begin," Carlyle, *Sartor Resartus*, pp. 173–74. See next footnote.

2. Novalis (1772–1801), an early Romantic mystic poet and philosopher. Carlyle discussed his work in "Novalis" (*Foreign Review*, 1829), repr. in *The Works of Thomas Carlyle in Thirty Volumes*, vol. 18: *Critical and Miscellaneous Essays*, t. II, pp. 1–55; Carlyle described Novalis as the teacher of "the great doctrine of *Entsagen*, of 'Renunciation'" (p. 15).

the active over the passive, and having as the foundation of the whole, not to expect more from life than it is capable of bestowing. A life thus composed, to those who have been fortunate enough to obtain it, has always appeared worthy of the name of happiness. And such an existence is even now the lot of many, during some considerable portion of their lives. The present wretched education, and wretched social arrangements, are the only real hindrance to its being attainable by almost all.

The objectors perhaps may doubt whether human beings, if taught to consider happiness as the end of life, would be satisfied with such a moderate share of it. But great numbers of mankind have been satisfied with much less. The main constituents of a satisfied life appear to be two, either of which by itself is often found sufficient for the purpose: tranquillity, and excitement. With much tranquillity, many find that they can be content with very little pleasure: with much excitement, many can reconcile themselves to a considerable quantity of pain. There is assuredly no inherent impossibility in enabling even the mass of mankind to unite both; since the two are so far from being incompatible that they are in natural alliance, the prolongation of either being a preparation for, and exciting a wish for, the other. It is only those in whom indolence amounts to a vice, that do not desire excitement after an interval of repose; it is only those in whom the need of excitement is a disease, that feel the tranquillity which follows excitement dull and insipid, instead of pleasurable in direct proportion to the excitement which preceded it. When people who are tolerably fortunate in their outward lot do not find in life sufficient enjoyment to make it valuable to them, the cause generally is, caring for nobody but themselves. To those who have neither public nor private affections, the excitements of life are much curtailed, and in any case dwindle in value as the time approaches when all selfish interests must be terminated by death: while those who leave after them objects of personal affection, and especially those who have also cultivated a fellow-feeling with the collective interests of mankind, retain as lively an interest in life on the eve of death as in the vigour of youth and health. Next to selfishness, the principal cause which makes life unsatisfactory, is want of mental cultivation. A cultivated mind—I do not mean that of a philosopher, but any mind to which the fountains of knowledge have been opened, and which has been taught, in any tolerable degree, to exercise its faculties—finds sources of inexhaustible interest in all that surrounds it; in the objects of nature, the achievements of art, the imaginations of poetry, the incidents of history, the ways of mankind past and present, and their prospects in the future. It is possible, indeed, to become indifferent to all this, and that too without having exhausted a thousandth part of it; but only when one has had from the beginning no moral or human interest in these things, and has sought in them only the gratification of curiosity.

Now there is absolutely no reason in the nature of things why an amount of mental culture sufficient to give an intelligent interest in these objects of contemplation, should not be the inheritance of every one born in a civilized country. As little is there an inherent necessity that any human being should be a selfish egotist, devoid of every feeling or care but those which centre in his own miserable individuality. Something far superior to this is sufficiently common even now, to give ample earnest of what the human species may be made. Genuine private affections, and a sincere interest in the public good, are possible, though in unequal degrees, to every rightly brought up human being. In a world in which there is so much to interest, so much to enjoy, and so much also to correct and improve, every one who has this moderate amount of moral and intellectual requisites is capable of an existence which may be called enviable; and unless such a person, through bad laws, or subjection to the will of others, is denied the liberty to use the sources of happiness within his reach, he will not fail to find this enviable existence, if he escape the positive evils of life, the great sources of physical and mental suffering—such as indigence, disease, and the unkindness, worthlessness, or premature loss of objects of affection. The main stress of the problem lies, therefore, in the contest with these calamities, from which it is a rare good fortune entirely to escape; which, as things now are, cannot be obviated, and often cannot be in any material degree mitigated. Yet no one whose opinion deserves a moment's consideration can doubt that most of the great positive evils of the world are in themselves removable, and will, if human affairs continue to improve, be in the end reduced within narrow limits. Poverty, in any sense implying suffering, may be completely extinguished by the wisdom of society, combined with the good sense and providence of individuals. Even that most intractable of enemies, disease, may be indefinitely reduced in dimensions by good physical and moral education, and proper control of noxious influences; while the progress of science holds out a promise for the future of still more direct conquests over this detestable foe. And every advance in that direction relieves us from some, not only of the chances which cut short our own lives, but, what concerns us still more, which deprives us of those in whom our happiness is wrapt up. As for vicissitudes of fortune, and other disappointments connected with worldly circumstances, these are principally the effect either of gross imprudence, of ill-regulated desires, or of bad or imperfect social institutions. All the grand sources, in short, of human suffering are in a great degree, many of them almost entirely, conquerable by human care and effort; and though their removal is grievously slow—though a long succession of generations will perish in the breach before the conquest is completed, and this world becomes all that if will and knowledge were not wanting, it might easily be made—yet every mind sufficiently intelligent and generous to bear a part, however small and unconspicuous, in the endeavour, will draw a noble enjoyment from the contest itself, which he would not for any bribe in the form of selfish indulgence consent to be without.

And this leads to the true estimation of what is said by the objectors concerning the possibility, and the obligation, of learning to do without happiness. Unquestionably it is possible to do without happiness; it is done involuntarily by nineteen-twentieths of mankind, even in those parts of our present world which are least deep in barbarism; and it often has to be done voluntarily by the hero or the martyr, for the sake of something which he prizes more than his individual happiness. But this something, what is it, unless the happiness of others, or some of the requisites of happiness? It is noble to be capable of resigning entirely one's own portion of happiness, or chances of it: but, after all, this self-sacrifice must be for some end; it is not its own end; and if we are told that its end is not happiness, but virtue, which is better than happiness, I ask, would the sacrifice be made if the hero or martyr did not believe that it would earn for others immunity from similar sacrifices? Would it be made, if he thought that his renunciation of happiness for himself would produce no fruit for any of his fellow creatures, but to make their lot like his, and place them also in the condition of persons who have renounced happiness? All honour to those who can abnegate for themselves the personal enjoyment of life, when by such renunciation they contribute worthily to increase the amount of happiness in the world; but he who does it, or professes to do it, for any other purpose, is no more deserving of admiration than the ascetic mounted on his pillar. He may be an inspiriting proof of what men *can* do, but assuredly not an example of what they *should*.

Though it is only in a very imperfect state of the world's arrangements that any one can best serve the happiness of others by the absolute sacrifice of his own, yet so long as the world is in that imperfect state, I fully acknowledge that the readiness to make such a sacrifice is the highest virtue which can be found in man. I will add, that in this condition of the world, paradoxical as the assertion may be, the conscious ability to do without happiness gives the best prospect of realizing such happiness as is attainable. For nothing except that consciousness can raise a person above the chances of life, by making him feel that, let fate and fortune do their worst, they have not power to subdue him: which, once felt, frees him from excess of anxiety concerning the evils of life, and enables him, like many a

Stoic in the worst times of the Roman Empire, to cultivate in tranquillity the sources of satisfaction accessible to him, without concerning himself about the uncertainty of their duration, any more
than about their inevitable end.

Meanwhile, let utilitarians never cease to claim the morality of
self-devotion as a possession which belongs by as good a right to
them, as either to the Stoic or to the Transcendentalist. The utilitarian morality does recognise in human beings the power of sacrificing their own greatest good for the good of others. It only refuses
to admit that the sacrifice is itself a good. A sacrifice which does
not increase, or tend to increase, the sum total of happiness, it considers as wasted. The only self-renunciation which it applauds, is
devotion to the happiness, or to some of the means of happiness, of
others; either of mankind collectively, or of individuals within the
limits imposed by the collective interests of mankind.

I must again repeat, what the assailants of utilitarianism seldom
have the justice to acknowledge, that the happiness which forms the
utilitarian standard of what is right in conduct, is not the agent's
own happiness, but that of all concerned. As between his own happiness and that of others, utilitarianism requires him to be as strictly
impartial as a disinterested and benevolent spectator. In the golden
rule of Jesus of Nazareth, we read the complete spirit of the ethics
of utility. To do as one would be done by, and to love one's neighbour as oneself, constitute the ideal perfection of utilitarian morality. As the means of making the nearest approach to this ideal, utility
would enjoin, first, that laws and social arrangements should place
the happiness, or (as speaking practically it may be called) the interest, of every individual, as nearly as possible in harmony with the
interest of the whole; and secondly, that education and opinion,
which have so vast a power over human character, should so use that
power as to establish in the mind of every individual an indissoluble
association between his own happiness and the good of the whole;
especially between his own happiness and the practice of such modes
of conduct, negative and positive, as regard for the universal happiness prescribes: so that not only he may be unable to conceive the
possibility of happiness to himself, consistently with conduct opposed
to the general good, but also that a direct impulse to promote the
general good may be in every individual one of the habitual motives
of action, and the sentiments connected therewith may fill a large
and prominent place in every human being's sentient existence. If
the impugners of the utilitarian morality represented it to their own
minds in this its true character, I know not what recommendation
possessed by any other morality they could possibly affirm to be
wanting to it: what more beautiful or more exalted developments of
human nature any other ethical system can be supposed to foster,

or what springs of action, not accessible to the utilitarian, such systems rely on for giving effect to their mandates.

The objectors to utilitarianism cannot always be charged with representing it in a discreditable light. On the contrary, those among them who entertain anything like a just idea of its disinterested character, sometimes find fault with its standard as being too high for humanity. They say it is exacting too much to require that people shall always act from the inducement of promoting the general interests of society. But this is to mistake the very meaning of a standard of morals, and to confound the rule of action with the motive of it. It is the business of ethics to tell us what are our duties, or by what test we may know them; but no system of ethics requires that the sole motive of all we do shall be a feeling of duty; on the contrary, ninety-nine hundredths of all our actions are done from other motives, and rightly so done, if the rule of duty does not condemn them. It is the more unjust to utilitarianism that this particular misapprehension should be made a ground of objection to it, inasmuch as utilitarian moralists have gone beyond almost all others in affirming that the motive has nothing to do with the morality of the action, though much with the worth of the agent. He who saves a fellow creature from drowning does what is morally right, whether his motive be duty, or the hope of being paid for his trouble: he who betrays the friend that trusts him, is guilty of a crime, even if his object be to serve another friend to whom he is under greater obligations.[3] But to speak only of actions done from the motive of duty,

---

3. An opponent, whose intellectual and moral fairness it is a pleasure to acknowledge (the Rev. J. Llewellyn Davies), has objected to this passage, saying, "Surely the rightness or wrongness of saving a man from drowning does depend very much upon the motive with which it is done. Suppose that a tyrant, when his enemy jumped into the sea to escape from him, saved him from drowning simply in order that he might inflict upon him more exquisite tortures, would it tend to clearness to speak of that rescue as 'a morally right action?' Or suppose again, according to one of the stock illustrations of ethical inquiries, that a man betrayed a trust received from a friend, because the discharge of it would fatally injure that friend himself or some one belonging to him, would utilitarianism compel one to call the betrayal 'a crime' as much as if it had been done from the meanest motive?"

I submit, that he who saves another from drowning in order to kill him by torture afterwards, does not differ only in motive from him who does the same thing from duty or benevolence; the act itself is different. The rescue of the man is, in the case supposed, only the necessary first step of an act far more atrocious than leaving him to drown would have been. Had Mr. Davies said, "The rightness or wrongness of saving a man from drowning does depend very much"—not upon the motive, but—"upon the *intention*," no utilitarian would have differed from him. Mr. Davies, by an oversight too common not to be quite venial, has in this case confounded the very different ideas of Motive and Intention. There is no point which utilitarian thinkers (and Bentham preeminently) have taken more pains to illustrate than this. The morality of the action depends entirely upon the intention—that is, upon what the agent *wills to do*. But the motive, that is, the feeling which makes him will so to do, when it makes no difference in the act, makes none in the morality: though it makes a great difference in our moral estimation of the agent, especially if it indicates a good or a bad habitual *disposition*—a bent of character from which useful, or from which hurtful actions are likely to arise [*Mill's note*].

and in direct obedience to principle: it is a misapprehension of the utilitarian mode of thought, to conceive it as implying that people should fix their minds upon so wide a generality as the world, or society at large. The great majority of good actions are intended, not for the benefit of the world, but for that of individuals, of which the good of the world is made up; and the thoughts of the most virtuous man need not on these occasions travel beyond the particular persons concerned, except so far as is necessary to assure himself that in benefiting them he is not violating the rights—that is, the legitimate and authorized expectations—of any one else. The multiplication of happiness is, according to the utilitarian ethics, the object of virtue: the occasions on which any person (except one in a thousand) has it in his power to do this on an extended scale, in other words, to be a public benefactor, are but exceptional; and on these occasions alone is he called on to consider public utility; in every other case, private utility, the interest or happiness of some few persons, is all he has to attend to. Those alone the influence of whose actions extends to society in general, need concern themselves habitually about so large an object. In the case of abstinences indeed—of things which people forbear to do, from moral considerations, though the consequences in the particular case might be beneficial—it would be unworthy of an intelligent agent not to be consciously aware that the action is of a class which, if practised generally, would be generally injurious, and that this is the ground of the obligation to abstain from it. The amount of regard for the public interest implied in this recognition, is no greater than is demanded by every system of morals; for they all enjoin to abstain from whatever is manifestly pernicious to society.

The same considerations dispose of another reproach against the doctrine of utility, founded on a still grosser misconception of the purpose of a standard of morality, and of the very meaning of the words right and wrong. It is often affirmed that utilitarianism renders men cold and unsympathizing; that it chills their moral feelings towards individuals; that it makes them regard only the dry and hard consideration of the consequences of actions, not taking into their moral estimate the qualities from which those actions emanate. If the assertion means that they do not allow their judgment respecting the rightness or wrongness of an action to be influenced by their opinion of the qualities of the person who does it, this is a complaint not against utilitarianism, but against having any standard of morality at all; for certainly no known ethical standard decides an action to be good or bad because it is done by a good or a bad man, still less because done by an amiable, a brave, or a benevolent man, or the contrary. These considerations are relevant, not to the estimation of actions, but of persons; and there is nothing in the utilitarian theory inconsistent with the fact that there are other things which interest us in persons besides the rightness and wrongness of their actions. The Stoics, indeed, with the paradoxical misuse of language which was part of their system, and by which they strove to raise themselves above all concern about anything but virtue, were fond of saying that he who has that has everything; that he, and only he, is rich, is beautiful, is a king. But no claim of this description is made for the virtuous man by the utilitarian doctrine. Utilitarians are quite aware that there are other desirable possessions and qualities besides virtue, and are perfectly willing to allow to all of them their full worth. They are also aware that a right action does not necessarily indicate a virtuous character, and that actions which are blameable often proceed from qualities entitled to praise. When this is apparent in any particular case, it modifies their estimation, not certainly of the act, but of the agent. I grant that they are, notwithstanding, of opinion, that in the long run the best proof of a good character is good actions; and resolutely refuse to consider any mental disposition as good, of which the predominant tendency is to produce bad conduct. This makes them unpopular with many people; but it is an unpopularity which they must share with every one who regards the distinction between right and wrong in a serious light; and the reproach is not one which a conscientious utilitarian need be anxious to repel.

If no more be meant by the objection than that many utilitarians look on the morality of actions, as measured by the utilitarian standard, with too exclusive a regard, and do not lay sufficient stress upon the other beauties of character which go towards making a human being loveable or admirable, this may be admitted. Utilitarians who have cultivated their moral feelings, but not their sympathies nor their artistic perceptions, do fall into this mistake; and so do all other moralists under the same conditions. What can be said in excuse for other moralists is equally available for them, namely, that if there is to be any error, it is better that it should be on that side. As a matter of fact, we may affirm that among utilitarians as among adherents of other systems, there is every imaginable degree of rigidity and of laxity in the application of their standard: some are even puritanically rigorous, while others are as indulgent as can possibly be desired by sinner or by sentimentalist. But on the whole, a doctrine which brings prominently forward the interest that mankind have in the repression and prevention of conduct which violates the moral law, is likely to be inferior to no other in turning the sanctions of opinion against such violations. It is true, the question, What does violate the moral law? is one on which those who recognise different standards of morality are likely now and then to differ. But difference of opinion on moral questions was not first introduced into the world by utilitarianism, while that doctrine does supply, if not always an easy, at all events a tangible and intelligible mode of deciding such differences.

It may not be superfluous to notice a few more of the common misapprehensions of utilitarian ethics, even those which are so obvious and gross that it might appear impossible for any person of candour and intelligence to fall into them: since persons, even of considerable mental endowments, often give themselves so little trouble to understand the bearings of any opinion against which they entertain a prejudice, and men are in general so little conscious of this voluntary ignorance as a defect, that the vulgarest misunderstandings of ethical doctrines are continually met with in the deliberate writings of persons of the greatest pretensions both to high principle and to philosophy. We not uncommonly hear the doctrine of utility inveighed against as a *godless* doctrine. If it be necessary to say anything at all against so mere an assumption, we may say that the question depends upon what idea we have formed of the moral character of the Deity. If it be a true belief that God desires, above all things, the happiness of his creatures, and that this was his purpose in their creation, utility is not only not a godless doctrine, but more profoundly religious than any other. If it be meant that utilitarianism does not recognise the revealed will of God as the supreme law of morals, I answer, that an utilitarian who believes in the perfect goodness and wisdom of God, necessarily believes that whatever God has thought fit to reveal on the subject of morals, must fulfil the requirements of utility in a supreme degree. But others besides utilitarians have been of opinion that the Christian revelation was intended, and is fitted, to inform the hearts and minds of mankind with a spirit which should enable them to find for themselves what is right, and incline them to do it when found, rather than to tell them, except in a very general way, what it is: and that we need a doctrine of ethics, carefully followed out, to *interpret* to us the will of God. Whether this opinion is correct or not, it is superfluous here to discuss; since whatever aid religion, either natural or revealed, can afford to ethical investigation, is as open to the utilitarian moralist as to any other. He can use it as the testimony of God to the usefulness or hurtfulness of any given course of action, by as good a right as others can use it for the indication of a transcendental law, having no connexion with usefulness or with happiness.

Again, Utility is often summarily stigmatized as an immoral doctrine by giving it the name of Expediency, and taking advantage of the popular use of that term to contrast it with Principle. But the Expedient, in the sense in which it is opposed to the Right, generally means that which is expedient for the particular interest of the agent himself; as when a minister sacrifices the interest of his country to keep himself in place. When it means anything better than this, it means that which is expedient for some immediate object, some temporary purpose, but which violates a rule whose observance is expedient in a much higher degree. The Expedient, in this sense, instead of being the same thing with the useful, is a branch of the hurtful. Thus, it would often be expedient, for the purpose of getting over some momentary embarrassment, or attaining some object immediately useful to ourselves or others, to tell a lie. But inasmuch as the cultivation in ourselves of a sensitive feeling on the subject of veracity, is one of the most useful, and the enfeeblement of that feeling one of the most hurtful, things to which our conduct can be instrumental; and inasmuch as any, even unintentional, deviation from truth, does that much towards weakening the trustworthiness of human assertion, which is not only the principal support of all present social well-being, but the insufficiency of which does more than any one thing that can be named to keep back civilization, virtue, everything on which human happiness on the largest scale depends; we feel that the violation, for a present advantage, of a rule of such transcendant expediency, is not expedient, and that he who, for the sake of a convenience to himself or to some other individual, does what depends on him to deprive mankind of the good, and inflict upon them the evil, involved in the greater or less reliance which they can place in each other's word, acts the part of one of their worst enemies. Yet that even this rule, sacred as it is, admits of possible exceptions, is acknowledged by all moralists; the chief of which is when the withholding of some fact (as of information from a malefactor, or of bad news from a person dangerously ill) would preserve some one (especially a person other than oneself) from great and unmerited evil, and when the withholding can only be effected by denial. But in order that the exception may not extend itself beyond the need, and may have the least possible effect in weakening reliance on veracity, it ought to be recognised, and, if possible, its limits defined; and if the principle of utility is good for anything, it must be good for weighing these conflicting utilities against one another, and marking out the region within which one or the other preponderates.

Again, defenders of utility often find themselves called upon to reply to such objections as this—that there is not time, previous to action, for calculating and weighing the effects of any line of conduct on the general happiness. This is exactly as if any one were to say that it is impossible to guide our conduct by Christianity, because there is not time, on every occasion on which anything has to be done, to read through the Old and New Testaments. The answer to the objection is, that there has been ample time, namely, the whole past duration of the human species. During all that time mankind have been learning by experience the tendencies of actions; on which experience all the prudence, as well as all the morality of life, is dependent. People talk as if the commencement of this course of experience had hitherto been put off, and as if, at the moment when some man feels tempted to meddle with the property or life of another, he had to begin considering for the first time whether murder and theft are injurious to human happiness. Even then I do not think that he would find the question very puzzling; but, at all events, the matter is now done to his hand. It is truly a whimsical supposition that if mankind were agreed in considering utility to be the test of morality, they would remain without any agreement as to what *is* useful, and would take no measures for having their notions on the subject taught to the young, and enforced by law and opinion. There is no difficulty in proving any ethical standard whatever to work ill, if we suppose universal idiocy to be conjoined with it; but on any hypothesis short of that, mankind must by this time have acquired positive beliefs as to the effects of some actions on their happiness; and the beliefs which have thus come down are the rules of morality for the multitude, and for the philosopher until he has succeeded in finding better. That philosophers might easily do this, even now, on many subjects; that the received code of ethics is by no means of divine right; and that mankind have still much to learn as to the effects of actions on the general happiness, I admit, or rather, earnestly maintain. The corollaries from the principle of utility, like the precepts of every practical art, admit of indefinite improvement, and, in a progressive state of the human mind, their improvement is perpetually going on. But to consider the rules of morality as improvable, is one thing; to pass over the intermediate generalizations entirely, and endeavour to test each individual action directly by the first principle, is another. It is a strange notion that the acknowledgment of a first principle is inconsistent with the admission of secondary ones. To inform a traveller respecting the place of his ultimate destination, is not to forbid the use of landmarks and direction-posts on the way. The proposition that happiness is the end and aim of morality, does not mean that no road ought to be laid down to that goal, or that persons going thither should not be advised to take one direction rather than another. Men really ought to leave off talking a kind of nonsense on this subject, which they would neither talk nor listen to on other matters of practical concernment. Nobody argues that the art of navigation is not founded on astronomy, because sailors cannot wait to calculate the Nautical Almanack.[4] Being rational creatures, they go to sea with it ready calculated; and all rational creatures go out upon the sea of life with their minds made up on the common questions of right and wrong, as well as on many of the far more difficult questions of wise and foolish. And this, as long as foresight is a human quality, it is to be presumed they will continue to do. Whatever we adopt as the fundamental principle of morality, we require subordinate principles to apply it by: the impossibility of doing without them, being common to all systems, can afford no argument against any one in particular: but gravely to argue as if no such secondary principles could be had, and as if mankind had remained till now, and always must remain, without drawing any general conclusions from the experience of human life, is as high a pitch, I think, as absurdity has ever reached in philosophical controversy.

The remainder of the stock arguments against utilitarianism mostly consist in laying to its charge the common infirmities of human nature, and the general difficulties which embarrass conscientious persons in shaping their course through life. We are told that an utilitarian will be apt to make his own particular case an exception to moral rules, and, when under temptation, will see an utility in the breach of a rule, greater than he will see in its observance. But is utility the only creed which is able to furnish us with excuses for evil doing, and means of cheating our own conscience? They are afforded in abundance by all doctrines which recognise as a fact in morals the existence of conflicting considerations; which all doctrines do, that have been believed by sane persons. It is not the fault of any creed, but of the complicated nature of human affairs, that rules of conduct cannot be so framed as to require no exceptions, and that hardly any kind of action can safely be laid down as either always obligatory or always condemnable. There is no ethical creed which does not temper the rigidity of its laws, by giving a certain latitude, under the moral responsibility of the agent, for accommodation to peculiarities of circumstances; and under every creed, at the opening thus made, self-deception and dishonest casuistry get in. There exists no moral system under which there do not arise unequivocal cases of conflicting obligation. These are the real difficulties, the knotty points both in the theory of ethics, and in the conscientious guidance of personal conduct. They are overcome practically with greater or with less success according to the intellect and virtue of the individual; but it can hardly be pretended

---

4. A publication describing the positions of celestial bodies to enable navigators to determine the position of their ships while at sea; in Britain, it has been published annually ever since 1767.

that any one will be the less qualified for dealing with them, from possessing an ultimate standard to which conflicting rights and duties can be referred. If utility is the ultimate source of moral obligations, utility may be invoked to decide between them when their demands are incompatible. Though the application of the standard may be difficult, it is better than none at all: while in other systems, the moral laws all claiming independent authority, there is no common umpire entitled to interfere between them; their claims to precedence one over another rest on little better than sophistry, and unless determined, as they generally are, by the unacknowledged influence of considerations of utility, afford a free scope for the action of personal desires and partialities. We must remember that only in these cases of conflict between secondary principles is it requisite that first principles should be appealed to. There is no case of moral obligation in which some secondary principle is not involved; and if only one, there can seldom be any real doubt which one it is, in the mind of any person by whom the principle itself is recognised.

CHAPTER III

Of the Ultimate Sanction of the Principle of Utility

The question is often asked, and properly so, in regard to any supposed moral standard—What is its sanction?[5] what are the motives to obey it? or more specifically, what is the source of its obligation? whence does it derive its binding force? It is a necessary part of moral philosophy to provide the answer to this question; which, though frequently assuming the shape of an objection to the utilitarian morality, as if it had some special applicability to that above others, really arises in regard to all standards. It arises, in fact, whenever a person is called on to *adopt* a standard, or refer morality to any basis on which he has not been accustomed to rest it. For the customary morality, that which education and opinion have consecrated, is the only one which presents itself to the mind with the feeling of being *in itself* obligatory; and when a person is asked to believe that this morality *derives* its obligation from some general principle round which custom has not thrown the same halo, the assertion is to him a paradox; the supposed corollaries seem to have a more binding

---

5. "Sanctions" play a key role in utilitarianism; Bentham considered them sources of pain and pleasure and listed four kinds: physical, political, moral, and religious (to which he later added sympathy); they guided the decision of the legislator and the conduct of the individual, pivoting on the assumption that a person is motivated by self-interest.

force than the original theorem; the superstructure seems to stand better without, than with, what is represented as its foundation. He says to himself, I feel that I am bound not to rob or murder, betray or deceive; but why am I bound to promote the general happiness? If my own happiness lies in something else, why may I not give that the preference?

If the view adopted by the utilitarian philosophy of the nature of the moral sense be correct, this difficulty will always present itself, until the influences which form moral character have taken the same hold of the principle which they have taken of some of the consequences—until, by the improvement of education, the feeling of unity with our fellow creatures shall be (what it cannot be doubted that Christ intended it to be) as deeply rooted in our character, and to our own consciousness as completely a part of our nature, as the horror of crime is in an ordinarily well-brought up young person. In the mean time, however, the difficulty has no peculiar application to the doctrine of utility, but is inherent in every attempt to analyse morality and reduce it to principles; which, unless the principle is already in men's minds invested with as much sacredness as any of its applications, always seems to divest them of a part of their sanctity.

The principle of utility either has, or there is no reason why it might not have, all the sanctions which belong to any other system of morals. Those sanctions are either external or internal. Of the external sanctions it is not necessary to speak at any length. They are, the hope of favour and the fear of displeasure from our fellow creatures or from the Ruler of the Universe, along with whatever we may have of sympathy or affection for them, or of love and awe of Him, inclining us to do his will independently of selfish consequences. There is evidently no reason why all these motives for observance should not attach themselves to the utilitarian morality, as completely and as powerfully as to any other. Indeed, those of them which refer to our fellow creatures are sure to do so, in proportion to the amount of general intelligence; for whether there be any other ground of moral obligation than the general happiness or not, men do desire happiness; and however imperfect may be their own practice, they desire and commend all conduct in others towards themselves, by which they think their happiness is promoted. With regard to the religious motive, if men believe, as most profess to do, in the goodness of God, those who think that conduciveness to the general happiness is the essence, or even only the criterion, of good, must necessarily believe that it is also that which God approves. The whole force therefore of external reward and punishment, whether physical or moral, and whether proceeding from God or from our fellow men, together with all that the capacities of human nature admit, of disinterested devotion to either, become available to enforce the utilitarian morality, in proportion as that morality is recognised; and the more powerfully, the more the appliances of education and general cultivation are bent to the purpose.

So far as to external sanctions. The internal sanction of duty, whatever our standard of duty may be, is one and the same—a feeling in our own mind; a pain, more or less intense, attendant on violation of duty, which in properly-cultivated moral natures rises, in the more serious cases, into shrinking from it as an impossibility. This feeling, when disinterested, and connecting itself with the pure idea of duty, and not with some particular form of it, or with any of the merely accessory circumstances, is the essence of Conscience; though in that complex phenomenon as it actually exists, the simple fact is in general all encrusted over with collateral associations, derived from sympathy, from love, and still more from fear; from all the forms of religious feeling; from the recollections of childhood and of all our past life; from self-esteem, desire of the esteem of others, and occasionally even self-abasement. This extreme complication is, I apprehend, the origin of the sort of mystical character which, by a tendency of the human mind of which there are many other examples, is apt to be attributed to the idea of moral obligation, and which leads people to believe that the idea cannot possibly attach itself to any other objects than those which, by a supposed mysterious law, are found in our present experience to excite it. Its binding force, however, consists in the existence of a mass of feeling which must be broken through in order to do what violates our standard of right, and which, if we do nevertheless violate that standard, will probably have to be encountered afterwards in the form of remorse. Whatever theory we have of the nature or origin of conscience, this is what essentially constitutes it.

The ultimate sanction, therefore, of all morality (external motives apart) being a subjective feeling in our own minds, I see nothing embarrassing to those whose standard is utility, in the question, what is the sanction of that particular standard? We may answer, the same as of all other moral standards—the conscientious feelings of mankind. Undoubtedly this sanction has no binding efficacy on those who do not possess the feelings it appeals to; but neither will these persons be more obedient to any other moral principle than to the utilitarian one. On them morality of any kind has no hold but through the external sanctions. Meanwhile the feelings exist, a fact in human nature, the reality of which, and the great power with which they are capable of acting on those in whom they have been duly cultivated, are proved by experience. No reason has ever been shown why they may not be cultivated to as great intensity in connexion with the utilitarian, as with any other rule of morals.

There is, I am aware, a disposition to believe that a person who sees in moral obligation a transcendental fact, an objective reality belonging to the province of 'Things in themselves,' is likely to be more obedient to it than one who believes it to be entirely subjective, having its seat in human consciousness only. But whatever a person's opinion may be on this point of Ontology, the force he is really urged by is his own subjective feeling, and is exactly measured by its strength. No one's belief that Duty is an objective reality is stronger than the belief that God is so; yet the belief in God apart from the expectation of actual reward and punishment, only operates on conduct through, and in proportion to, the subjective religious feeling. The sanction, so far as it is disinterested, is always in the mind itself; and the notion therefore of the transcendental moralists must be, that this sanction will not exist *in* the mind unless it is believed to have its root out of the mind; and that if a person is able to say to himself, This which is restraining me, and which is called my conscience, is only a feeling in my own mind, he may possibly draw the conclusion that when the feeling ceases the obligation ceases, and that if he find the feeling inconvenient, he may disregard it, and endeavour to get rid of it. But is this danger confined to the utilitarian morality? Does the belief that moral obligation has its seat outside the mind make the feeling of it too strong to be got rid of? The fact is so far otherwise, that all moralists admit and lament the ease with which, in the generality of minds, conscience can be silenced or stifled. The question, Need I obey my conscience? is quite as often put to themselves by persons who never heard of the principle of utility, as by its adherents. Those whose conscientious feelings are so weak as to allow of their asking this question, if they answer it affirmatively, will not do so because they believe in the transcendental theory, but because of the external sanctions.

It is not necessary, for the present purpose, to decide whether the feeling of duty is innate or implanted. Assuming it to be innate, it is an open question to what objects it naturally attaches itself; for the philosophic supporters of that theory are now agreed that the intuitive perception is of principles of morality, and not of the details. If there be anything innate in the matter, I see no reason why the feeling which is innate should not be that of regard to the pleasures and pains of others. If there is any principle of morals which is intuitively obligatory, I should say it must be that. If so, the intuitive ethics would coincide with the utilitarian, and there would be no further quarrel between them. Even as it is, the intuitive moralists, though they believe that there are other intuitive moral obligations, do already believe this to be one; for they unanimously hold that a large *portion* of morality turns upon the consideration due to the interests of our fellow creatures. Therefore, if the belief in the transcendental origin of moral obligation gives any additional efficacy to the internal sanction, it appears to me that the utilitarian principle has already the benefit of it.

On the other hand, if, as is my own belief, the moral feelings are not innate, but acquired, they are not for that reason the less natural. It is natural to man to speak, to reason, to build cities, to cultivate the ground, though these are acquired faculties. The moral feelings are not indeed a part of our nature, in the sense of being in any perceptible degree present in all of us; but this, unhappily, is a fact admitted by those who believe the most strenuously in their transcendental origin. Like the other acquired capacities above referred to, the moral faculty, if not a part of our nature, is a natural outgrowth from it; capable, like them, in a certain small degree, of springing up spontaneously; and susceptible of being brought by cultivation to a high degree of development. Unhappily it is also susceptible, by a sufficient use of the external sanctions and of the force of early impressions, of being cultivated in almost any direction: so that there is hardly anything so absurd or so mischievous that it may not, by means of these influences, be made to act on the human mind with all the authority of conscience. To doubt that the same potency might be given by the same means to the principle of utility, even if it had no foundation in human nature, would be flying in the face of all experience.

But moral associations which are wholly of artificial creation, when intellectual culture goes on, yield by degrees to the dissolving force of analysis: and if the feeling of duty, when associated with utility, would appear equally arbitrary; if there were no leading department of our nature, no powerful class of sentiments, with which that association would harmonize, which would make us feel it congenial, and incline us not only to foster it in others (for which we have abundant interested motives), but also to cherish it in ourselves; if there were not, in short, a natural basis of sentiment for utilitarian morality, it might well happen that this association also, even after it had been implanted by education, might be analysed away.

But there *is* this basis of powerful natural sentiment; and this it is which, when once the general happiness is recognised as the ethical standard, will constitute the strength of the utilitarian morality. This firm foundation is that of the social feelings of mankind; the desire to be in unity with our fellow creatures, which is already a powerful principle in human nature, and happily one of those which tend to become stronger, even without express inculation, from the influences of advancing civilization. The social state is at once so natural, so necessary, and so habitual to man, that, except in some unusual circumstances or by an effort of voluntary abstraction, he never conceives himself otherwise than as a member of a body; and this association is riveted more and more, as mankind are further removed from the state of savage independence. Any condition, therefore, which is essential to a state of society, becomes more and more an inseparable part of every person's conception of the state of things which he is born into, and which is the destiny of a human being. Now, society between human beings, except in the relation of master and slave, is manifestly impossible on any other footing than that the interests of all are to be consulted. Society between equals can only exist on the understanding that the interests of all are to be regarded equally. And since in all states of civilization, every person, except an absolute monarch, has equals, every one is obliged to live on these terms with somebody; and in every age some advance is made towards a state in which it will be impossible to live permanently on other terms with anybody. In this way people grow up unable to conceive as possible to them a state of total disregard of other people's interests. They are under a necessity of conceiving themselves as at least abstaining from all the grosser injuries, and (if only for their own protection) living in a state of constant protest against them. They are also familiar with the fact of co-operating with others, and proposing to themselves a collective, not an individual, interest, as the aim (at least for the time being) of their actions. So long as they are co-operating, their ends are identified with those of others; there is at least a temporary feeling that the interests of others are their own interests. Not only does all strengthening of social ties, and all healthy growth of society, give to each individual a stronger personal interest in practically consulting the welfare of others; it also leads him to identify his *feelings* more and more with their good, or at least with an ever greater degree of practical consideration for it. He comes, as though instinctively, to be conscious of himself as a being who *of course* pays regard to others. The good of others becomes to him a thing naturally and necessarily to be attended to, like any of the physical conditions of our existence. Now, whatever amount of this feeling a person has, he is urged by the strongest motives both of interest and of sympathy to demonstrate it, and to the utmost of his power encourage it in others; and even if he has none of it himself, he is as greatly interested as any one else that others should have it. Consequently, the smallest germs of the feeling are laid hold of and nourished by the contagion of sympathy and the influences of education; and a complete web of corroborative association is woven round it, by the powerful agency of the external sanctions. This mode of conceiving ourselves and human life, as civilization goes on, is felt to be more and more natural. Every step in political improvement renders it more so, by removing the sources of opposition of interest, and levelling those inequalities of legal privilege between individuals or classes, owing to which there are large portions of mankind whose happiness it is still practicable to disregard. In an improving state of the human mind, the influences are constantly on the increase, which tend to generate in each individual a feeling of unity with all the rest; which feeling, if perfect, would make him never think of, or desire, any beneficial condition for himself, in the benefits of which they are not included. If we now suppose this feeling of unity to be taught as a religion, and the whole force of education, of institutions, and of opinion, directed, as it once was in the case of religion, to make every person grow up from infancy surrounded on all sides both by the profession and by the practice of it, I think that no one, who can realize this conception, will feel any misgiving about the sufficiency of the ultimate sanction for the Happiness morality. To any ethical student who finds the realization difficult, I recommend, as a means of facilitating it, the second of M. Comte's two principal works, the *Système de Politique Positive*.[6] I entertain the strongest objections to the system of politics and morals set forth in that treatise; but I think it has superabundantly shown the possibility of giving to the service of humanity, even without the aid of belief in a Providence, both the psychical power and the social efficacy of a religion; making it take hold of human life, and colour all thought, feeling, and action, in a manner of which the greatest ascendancy ever exercised by any religion may be but a type and foretaste; and of which the danger is, not that it should be insufficient, but that it should be so excessive as to interfere unduly with human freedom and individuality.[7]

Neither is it necessary to the feeling which constitutes the binding force of the utilitarian morality on those who recognise it, to wait for those social influences which would make its obligation felt by mankind at large. In the comparatively early state of human advancement in which we now live, a person cannot indeed feel that entireness of sympathy with all others, which would make any real discordance in the general direction of their conduct in life impossible; but already a person in whom the social feeling is at all developed, cannot bring himself to think of the rest of his fellow creatures as struggling rivals with him for the means of happiness, whom he

6. Auguste Comte, *Système de politique positive, ou Traité de sociologie, instituant la religion de l'humanité* (1851–54).
7. In *The System of Logic*, bk. 6, chap. 2, sect. 4 (*CW*, vol. 8).

must desire to see defeated in their object in order that he may succeed in his. The deeply-rooted conception which every individual
even now has of himself as a social being, tends to make him feel it
one of his natural wants that there should be harmony between his
feelings and aims and those of his fellow creatures. If differences of
opinion and of mental culture make it impossible for him to share
many of their actual feelings—perhaps make him denounce and defy
those feelings—he still needs to be conscious that his real aim and
theirs do not conflict; that he is not opposing himself to what they
really wish for, namely, their own good, but is, on the contrary, promoting it. This feeling in most individuals is much inferior in
strength to their selfish feelings, and is often wanting altogether. But
to those who have it, it possesses all the characters of a natural feeling. It does not present itself to their minds as a superstition of
education, or a law despotically imposed by the power of society, but
as an attribute which it would not be well for them to be without.
This conviction is the ultimate sanction of the greatest-happiness
morality. This it is which makes any mind, of well-developed feelings, work with, and not against, the outward motives to care for
others, afforded by what I have called the external sanctions; and
when those sanctions are wanting, or act in an opposite direction,
constitutes in itself a powerful internal binding force, in proportion
to the sensitiveness and thoughtfulness of the character; since few
but those whose mind is a moral blank, could bear to lay out their
course of life on the plan of paying no regard to others except so far
as their own private interest compels.

CHAPTER IV

Of What Sort of Proof the Principle
of Utility Is Susceptible

It has already been remarked, that questions of ultimate ends do not
admit of proof, in the ordinary acceptation of the term. To be incapable of proof by reasoning is common to all first principles; to the
first premises of our knowledge, as well as to those of our conduct.
But the former, being matters of fact, may be the subject of a direct
appeal to the faculties which judge of fact—namely, our senses, and
our internal consciousness. Can an appeal be made to the same faculties on questions of practical ends? Or by what other faculty is
cognizance taken of them?

Questions about ends are, in other words, questions what things
are desirable. The utilitarian doctrine is, that happiness is desirable,

and the only thing desirable, as an end; all other things being only desirable as means to that end. What ought to be required of this doctrine—what conditions is it requisite that the doctrine should fulfil—to make good its claim to be believed?

The only proof capable of being given that an object is visible, is that people actually see it. The only proof that a sound is audible, is that people hear it: and so of the other sources of our experience. In like manner, I apprehend, the sole evidence it is possible to produce that anything is desirable, is that people do actually desire it. If the end which the utilitarian doctrine proposes to itself were not, in theory and in practice, acknowledged to be an end, nothing could ever convince any person that it was so. No reason can be given why the general happiness is desirable, except that each person, so far as he believes it to be attainable, desires his own happiness. This, however, being a fact, we have not only all the proof which the case admits of, but all which it is possible to require, that happiness is a good: that each person's happiness is a good to that person, and the general happiness, therefore, a good to the aggregate of all persons. Happiness has made out its title as *one* of the ends of conduct, and consequently one of the criteria of morality.

But it has not, by this alone, proved itself to be the sole criterion. To do that, it would seem, by the same rule, necessary to show, not only that people desire happiness, but that they never desire anything else. Now it is palpable that they do desire things which, in common language, are decidedly distinguished from happiness. They desire, for example, virtue, and the absence of vice, no less really than pleasure and the absence of pain. The desire of virtue is not as universal, but it is as authentic a fact, as the desire of happiness. And hence the opponents of the utilitarian standard deem that they have a right to infer that there are other ends of human action besides happiness, and that happiness is not the standard of approbation and disapprobation.

But does the utilitarian doctrine deny that people desire virtue, or maintain that virtue is not a thing to be desired? The very reverse. It maintains not only that virtue is to be desired, but that it is to be desired disinterestedly, for itself. Whatever may be the opinion of utilitarian moralists as to the original conditions by which virtue is made virtue; however they may believe (as they do) that actions and dispositions are only virtuous because they promote another end than virtue; yet this being granted, and it having been decided, from considerations of this description, what *is* virtuous, they not only place virtue at the very head of the things which are good as means to the ultimate end, but they also recognise as a psychological fact the possibility of its being, to the individual, a good in itself, without looking to any end beyond it; and hold, that the mind is not in a right state, not in a state conformable to Utility, not in the state most conducive to the general happiness, unless it does love virtue in this manner—as a thing desirable in itself, even although, in the individual instance, it should not produce those other desirable consequences which it tends to produce, and on account of which it is held to be virtue. This opinion is not, in the smallest degree, a departure from the Happiness principle. The ingredients of happiness are very various, and each of them is desirable in itself, and not merely when considered as swelling an aggregate. The principle of utility does not mean that any given pleasure, as music, for instance, or any given exemption from pain, as for example health, are to be looked upon as means to a collective something termed happiness, and to be desired on that account. They are desired and desirable in and for themselves; besides being means, they are a part of the end. Virtue, according to the utilitarian doctrine, is not naturally and originally part of the end, but it is capable of becoming so; and in those who love it disinterestedly it has become so, and is desired and cherished, not as a means to happiness, but as a part of their happiness.

To illustrate this farther, we may remember that virtue is not the only thing, originally a means, and which if it were not a means to anything else, would be and remain indifferent, but which by association with what it is a means to, comes to be desired for itself, and that too with the utmost intensity. What, for example, shall we say of the love of money? There is nothing originally more desirable about money than about any heap of glittering pebbles. Its worth is solely that of the things which it will buy; the desires for other things than itself, which it is a means of gratifying. Yet the love of money is not only one of the strongest moving forces of human life, but money is, in many cases, desired in and for itself; the desire to possess it is often stronger than the desire to use it, and goes on increasing when all the desires which point to ends beyond it, to be compassed by it, are falling off. It may be then said truly, that money is desired not for the sake of an end, but as part of the end. From being a means to happiness, it has come to be itself a principal ingredient of the individual's conception of happiness. The same may be said of the majority of the great objects of human life—power, for example, or fame; except that to each of these there is a certain amount of immediate pleasure annexed, which has at least the semblance of being naturally inherent in them; a thing which cannot be said of money. Still, however, the strongest natural attraction, both of power and of fame, is the immense aid they give to the attainment of our other wishes; and it is the strong association thus generated between them and all our objects of desire, which gives to the direct desire of them the intensity it often assumes, so as in some characters to surpass in strength all other desires. In these cases the means have become a part of the end, and a more important part of it than any of the things which they are means to. What was once desired as an instrument for the attainment of happiness, has come to be desired for its own sake. In being desired for its own sake it is, however, desired as *part* of happiness. The person is made, or thinks he would be made, happy by its mere possession; and is made unhappy by failure to obtain it. The desire of it is not a different thing from the desire of happiness, any more than the love of music, or the desire of health. They are included in happiness. They are some of the elements of which the desire of happiness is made up. Happiness is not an abstract idea, but a concrete whole; and these are some of its parts. And the utilitarian standard sanctions and approves their being so. Life would be a poor thing, very ill provided with sources of happiness, if there were not this provision of nature, by which things originally indifferent, but conducive to, or otherwise associated with, the satisfaction of our primitive desires, become in themselves sources of pleasure more valuable than the primitive pleasures, both in permanency, in the space of human existence that they are capable of covering, and even in intensity.

Virtue, according to the utilitarian conception, is a good of this description. There was no original desire of it, or motive to it, save its conduciveness to pleasure, and especially to protection from pain. But through the association thus formed, it may be felt a good in itself, and desired as such with as great intensity as any other good; and with this difference between it and the love of money, of power, or of fame, that all of these may, and often do, render the individual noxious to the other members of the society to which he belongs, whereas there is nothing which makes him so much a blessing to them as the cultivation of the disinterested love of virtue. And consequently, the utilitarian standard, while it tolerates and approves those other acquired desires, up to the point beyond which they would be more injurious to the general happiness than promotive of it, enjoins and requires the cultivation of the love of virtue up to the greatest strength possible, as being above all things important to the general happiness.

It results from the preceding considerations, that there is in reality nothing desired except happiness. Whatever is desired otherwise than as a means to some end beyond itself, and ultimately to happiness, is desired as itself a part of happiness, and is not desired for itself until it has become so. Those who desire virtue for its own sake, desire it either because the consciousness of it is a pleasure, or because the consciousness of being without it is a pain, or for both reasons united; as in truth the pleasure and pain seldom exist

separately, but almost always together, the same person feeling pleasure in the degree of virtue attained, and pain in not having attained
more. If one of these gave him no pleasure, and the other no pain,
he would not love or desire virtue, or would desire it only for the
other benefits which it might produce to himself or to persons whom
he cared for.

We have now, then, an answer to the question, of what sort of
proof the principle of utility is susceptible. If the opinion which I
have now stated is psychologically true—if human nature is so constituted as to desire nothing which is not either a part of happiness
or a means of happiness, we can have no other proof, and we require
no other, that these are the only things desirable. If so, happiness is
the sole end of human action, and the promotion of it the test by
which to judge of all human conduct; from whence it necessarily follows that it must be the criterion of morality, since a part is included
in the whole.

And now to decide whether this is really so; whether mankind
do desire nothing for itself but that which is a pleasure to them, or
of which the absence is a pain; we have evidently arrived at a
question of fact and experience, dependent, like all similar questions, upon evidence. It can only be determined by practised self-
consciousness and self-observation, assisted by observation of others.
I believe that these sources of evidence, impartially consulted, will
declare that desiring a thing and finding it pleasant, aversion to it
and thinking of it as painful, are phenomena entirely inseparable,
or rather two parts of the same phenomenon; in strictness of language, two different modes of naming the same psychological fact:
that to think of an object as desirable (unless for the sake of its
consequences), and to think of it as pleasant, are one and the same
thing; and that to desire anything, except in proportion as the idea
of it is pleasant, is a physical and metaphysical impossibility.

So obvious does this appear to me, that I expect it will hardly be
disputed: and the objection made will be, not that desire can possibly be directed to anything ultimately except pleasure and exemption from pain, but that the will is a different thing from desire; that
a person of confirmed virtue, or any other person whose purposes
are fixed, carries out his purposes without any thought of the pleasure he has in contemplating them, or expects to derive from their
fulfilment; and persists in acting on them, even though these
pleasures are much diminished, by changes in his character or decay
of his passive sensibilities, or are outweighed by the pains which the
pursuit of the purposes may bring upon him. All this I fully admit,
and have stated it elsewhere, as positively and emphatically as any
one. Will, the active phenomenon, is a different thing from desire,
the state of passive sensibility, and though originally an offshoot

from it, may in time take root and detach itself from the parent stock; so much so, that in the case of an habitual purpose, instead of willing the thing because we desire it, we often desire it only because we will it. This, however, is but an instance of that familiar fact, the power of habit, and is nowise confined to the case of virtuous actions. Many indifferent things, which men originally did from a motive of some sort, they continue to do from habit. Sometimes this is done unconsciously, the consciousness coming only after the action: at other times with conscious volition, but volition which has become habitual, and is put into operation by the force of habit, in opposition perhaps to the deliberate preference, as often happens with those who have contracted habits of vicious or hurtful indulgence. Third and last comes the case in which the habitual act of will in the individual instance is not in contradiction to the general intention prevailing at other times, but in fulfilment of it; as in the case of the person of confirmed virtue, and of all who pursue deliberately and consistently any determinate end. The distinction between will and desire thus understood, is an authentic and highly important psychological fact; but the fact consists solely in this— that will, like all other parts of our constitution, is amenable to habit, and that we may will from habit what we no longer desire for itself, or desire only because we will it. It is not the less true that will, in the beginning, is entirely produced by desire; including in that term the repelling influence of pain as well as the attractive one of pleasure. Let us take into consideration, no longer the person who has a confirmed will to do right, but him in whom that virtuous will is still feeble, conquerable by temptation, and not to be fully relied on; by what means can it be strengthened? How can the will to be virtuous, where it does not exist in sufficient force, be implanted or awakened? Only by making the person *desire* virtue— by making him think of it in a pleasurable light, or of its absence in a painful one. It is by associating the doing right with pleasure, or the doing wrong with pain, or by eliciting and impressing and bringing home to the person's experience the pleasure naturally involved in the one or the pain in the other, that it is possible to call forth that will to be virtuous, which, when confirmed, acts without any thought of either pleasure or pain. Will is the child of desire, and passes out of the dominion of its parent only to come under that of habit. That which is the result of habit affords no presumption of being intrinsically good; and there would be no reason for wishing that the purpose of virtue should become independent of pleasure and pain, were it not that the influence of the pleasurable and painful associations which prompt to virtue is not sufficiently to be depended on for unerring constancy of action until it has acquired the support of habit. Both in feeling and in conduct, habit is the

only thing which imparts certainty; and it is because of the importance to others of being able to rely absolutely on one's feelings and
conduct, and to oneself of being able to rely on one's own, that the
will to do right ought to be cultivated into this habitual independence. In other words, this state of the will is a means to good, not
intrinsically a good; and does not contradict the doctrine that
nothing is a good to human beings but in so far as it is either itself
pleasurable, or a means of attaining pleasure or averting pain.

But if this doctrine be true, the principle of utility is proved.
Whether it is so or not, must now be left to the consideration of the
thoughtful reader.

CHAPTER V

On the Connexion between Justice and Utility

In all ages of speculation, one of the strongest obstacles to the reception of the doctrine that Utility or Happiness is the criterion of
right and wrong, has been drawn from the idea of Justice. The
powerful sentiment, and apparently clear perception, which that
word recalls with a rapidity and certainty resembling an instinct,
have seemed to the majority of thinkers to point to an inherent quality in things; to show that the Just must have an existence in Nature
as something absolute—generically distinct from every variety of the
Expedient, and, in idea, opposed to it, though (as is commonly
acknowledged) never, in the long run, disjoined from it in fact.

In the case of this, as of our other moral sentiments, there is no
necessary connexion between the question of its origin, and that
of its binding force. That a feeling is bestowed on us by Nature,
does not necessarily legitimate all its promptings. The feeling of
justice might be a peculiar instinct, and might yet require, like
our other instincts, to be controlled and enlightened by a higher
reason. If we have intellectual instincts, leading us to judge in a
particular way, as well as animal instincts that prompt us to act in
a particular way, there is no necessity that the former should be
more infallible in their sphere than the latter in theirs: it may
as well happen that wrong judgments are occasionally suggested
by those, as wrong actions by these. But though it is one thing
to elieve that we have natural feelings of justice, and another to
acknowledge them as an ultimate criterion of conduct, these two
opinions are very closely connected in point of fact. Mankind are
always predisposed to believe that any subjective feeling, not otherwise accounted for, is a revelation of some objective reality. Our
present object is to determine whether the reality, to which the

feeling of justice corresponds, is one which needs any such special revelation; whether the justice or injustice of an action is a thing intrinsically peculiar, and distinct from all its other qualities, or only a combination of certain of those qualities, presented under a peculiar aspect. For the purpose of this inquiry, it is practically important to consider whether the feeling itself, of justice and injustice, is *sui generis*[8] like our sensations of colour and taste, or a derivative feeling, formed by a combination of others. And this it is the more essential to examine, as people are in general willing enough to allow, that objectively the dictates of justice coincide with a part of the field of General Expediency; but inasmuch as the subjective mental feeling of Justice is different from that which commonly attaches to simple expediency, and, except in extreme cases of the latter, is far more imperative in its demands, people find it difficult to see, in Justice, only a particular kind or branch of general utility, and think that its superior binding force requires a totally different origin.

To throw light upon this question, it is necessary to attempt to ascertain what is the distinguishing character of justice, or of injustice: what is the quality, or whether there is any quality, attributed in common to all modes of conduct designated as unjust (for justice, like many other moral attributes, is best defined by its opposite), and distinguishing them from such modes of conduct as are disapproved, but without having that particular epithet of disapprobation applied to them. If, in everything which men are accustomed to characterize as just or unjust, some one common attribute or collection of attributes is always present, we may judge whether this particular attribute or combination of attributes would be capable of gathering round it a sentiment of that peculiar character and intensity by virtue of the general laws of our emotional constitution, or whether the sentiment is inexplicable, and requires to be regarded as a special provision of Nature. If we find the former to be the case, we shall, in resolving this question, have resolved also the main problem: if the latter, we shall have to seek for some other mode of investigating it.

To find the common attributes of a variety of objects, it is necessary to begin by surveying the objects themselves in the concrete. Let us therefore advert successively to the various modes of action, and arrangements of human affairs, which are classed, by universal or widely spread opinion, as Just or as Unjust. The things well known to excite the sentiments associated with those names, are of

8. Unique or in a class by itself (Latin).

a very multifarious character. I shall pass them rapidly in review, without studying any particular arrangement.

In the first place, it is mostly considered unjust to deprive any one of his personal liberty, his property, or any other thing which belongs to him by law. Here, therefore, is one instance of the application of the terms just and unjust in a perfectly definite sense, namely, that it is just to respect, unjust to violate, the *legal rights* of any one. But this judgment admits of several exceptions, arising from the other forms in which the notions of justice and injustice present themselves. For example, the person who suffers the deprivation may (as the phrase is) have *forfeited* the rights which he is so deprived of: a case to which we shall return presently. But also,

Secondly; the legal rights of which he is deprived, may be rights which *ought* not to have belonged to him; in other words, the law which confers on him these rights, may be a bad law. When it is so, or when (which is the same thing for our purpose) it is supposed to be so, opinions will differ as to the justice or injustice of infringing it. Some maintain that no law, however bad, ought to be disobeyed by an individual citizen; that his opposition to it, if shown at all, should only be shown in endeavouring to get it altered by competent authority. This opinion (which condemns many of the most illustrious benefactors of mankind, and would often protect pernicious institutions against the only weapons which, in the state of things existing at the time, have any chance of succeeding against them) is defended, by those who hold it, on grounds of expediency; principally on that of the importance, to the common interest of mankind, of maintaining inviolate the sentiment of submission to law. Other persons, again, hold the directly contrary opinion, that any law, judged to be bad, may blamelessly be disobeyed, even though it be not judged to be unjust, but only inexpedient; while others would confine the licence of disobedience to the case of unjust laws: but again, some say, that all laws which are inexpedient are unjust; since every law imposes some restriction on the natural liberty of mankind, which restriction is an injustice, unless legitimated by tending to their good. Among these diversities of opinion, it seems to be universally admitted that there may be unjust laws, and that law, consequently, is not the ultimate criterion of justice, but may give to one person a benefit, or impose on another an evil, which justice condemns. When, however, a law is thought to be unjust, it seems always to be regarded as being so in the same way in which a breach of law is unjust, namely, by infringing somebody's right; which, as it cannot in this case be a legal right, receives a different appellation, and is called a moral right. We may say, therefore, that a second case of injustice consists in taking or withholding from any person that to which he has a *moral right*.

Thirdly, it is universally considered just that each person should obtain that (whether good or evil) which he *deserves;* and unjust that he should obtain a good, or be made to undergo an evil, which he does not deserve. This is, perhaps, the clearest and most emphatic form in which the idea of justice is conceived by the general mind. As it involves the notion of desert, the question arises, what constitutes desert? Speaking in a general way, a person is understood to deserve good if he does right, evil if he does wrong; and in a more particular sense, to deserve good from those to whom he does or has done good, and evil from those to whom he does or has done evil. The precept of returning good for evil has never been regarded as a case of the fulfilment of justice, but as one in which the claims of justice are waved, in obedience to other considerations.

Fourthly, it is confessedly unjust to *break faith* with any one: to violate an engagement, either express or implied, or disappoint expectations raised by our own conduct, at least if we have raised those expectations knowingly and voluntarily. Like the other obligations of justice already spoken of, this one is not regarded as absolute, but as capable of being overruled by a stronger obligation of justice on the other side; or by such conduct on the part of the person concerned as is deemed to absolve us from our obligation to him, and to constitute a *forfeiture* of the benefit which he has been led to expect.

Fifthly, it is, by universal admission, inconsistent with justice to be *partial*; to show favour or preference to one person over another, in matters to which favour and preference do not properly apply. Impartiality, however, does not seem to be regarded as a duty in itself, but rather as instrumental to some other duty; for it is admitted that favour and preference are not always censurable, and indeed the cases in which they are condemned are rather the exception than the rule. A person would be more likely to be blamed than applauded for giving his family or friends no superiority in good offices over strangers, when he could do so without violating any other duty; and no one thinks it unjust to seek one person in preference to another as a friend, connexion, or companion. Impartiality where rights are concerned is of course obligatory, but this is involved in the more general obligation of giving to every one his right. A tribunal, for example, must be impartial, because it is bound to award, without regard to any other consideration, a disputed object to the one of two parties who has the right to it. There are other cases in which impartiality means, being solely influenced by desert; as with those who, in the capacity of judges, preceptors, or parents, administer reward and punishment as such. There are cases, again, in which it means, being solely influenced by consideration for the public interest; as in making a selection among candidates for a government employment. Impartiality, in short, as an obligation of justice, may be said to mean, being exclusively influenced by the considerations which it is supposed ought to influence the particular case in hand; and resisting the solicitation of any motives which prompt to conduct different from what those considerations would dictate.

Nearly allied to the idea of impartiality, is that of *equality*; which often enters as a component part both into the conception of justice and into the practice of it, and, in the eyes of many persons, constitutes its essence. But in this, still more than in any other case, the notion of justice varies in different persons, and always conforms in its variations to their notion of utility. Each person maintains that equality is the dictate of justice, except where he thinks that expediency requires inequality. The justice of giving equal protection to the rights of all, is maintained by those who support the most outrageous inequality in the rights themselves. Even in slave countries it is theoretically admitted that the rights of the slave, such as they are, ought to be as sacred as those of the master; and that a tribunal which fails to enforce them with equal strictness is wanting in justice; while, at the same time, institutions which leave to the slave scarcely any rights to enforce, are not deemed unjust, because they are not deemed inexpedient. Those who think that utility requires distinctions of rank, do not consider it unjust that riches and social privileges should be unequally dispensed; but those who think this inequality inexpedient, think it unjust also. Whoever thinks that government is necessary, sees no injustice in as much inequality as is constituted by giving to the magistrate powers not granted to other people. Even among those who hold levelling doctrines, there are as many questions of justice as there are differences of opinion about expediency. Some Communists consider it unjust that the produce of the labour of the community should be shared on any other principle than that of exact equality; others think it just that those should receive most whose needs are greatest; while others hold that those who work harder, or who produce more, or whose services are more valuable to the community, may justly claim a larger quota in the division of the produce. And the sense of natural justice may be plausibly appealed to in behalf of every one of these opinions.

Among so many diverse applications of the term Justice, which yet is not regarded as ambiguous, it is a matter of some difficulty to seize the mental link which holds them together, and on which the moral sentiment adhering to the term essentially depends. Perhaps, in this embarrassment, some help may be derived from the history of the word, as indicated by its etymology.

In most, if not in all, languages, the etymology of the word which corresponds to Just, points to an origin connected either with positive law, or with that which was in most cases the primitive form of law—authoritative custom. *Justum* is a form of *jussum*, that which has been ordered. *Jus* is of the same origin. *Δίκαιον* comes from *δίκη*, of which the principal meaning, at least in the historical ages of Greece, was a suit at law. Originally, indeed, it meant only the mode or *manner* of doing things, but it early came to mean the *prescribed* manner; that which the recognised authorities, patriarchal, judicial, or political, would enforce. *Recht*, from which came *right* and *righteous*, is synonymous with law. The original meaning indeed of *recht* did not point to law, but to physical straightness; as *wrong* and its Latin equivalents meant twisted or *tortuous*; and from this it is argued that right did not originally mean law, but on the contrary law meant right. But however this may be, the fact that *recht* and *droit* became restricted in their meaning to positive law, although much which is not required by law is equally necessary to moral straightness or rectitude, is as significant of the original character of moral ideas as if the derivation had been the reverse way. The courts of justice, the administration of justice, are the courts and the administration of law. *La justice*, in French, is the established term for judicature. There can, I think, be no doubt that the *idée mère*,[9] the primitive element, in the formation of the notion of justice, was conformity to law. It constituted the entire idea among the Hebrews, up to the birth of Christianity; as might be expected in the case of a people whose laws attempted to embrace all subjects on which precepts were required, and who believed those laws to be a direct emanation from the Supreme Being. But other nations, and in particular the Greeks and Romans, who knew that their laws had been made originally, and still continued to be made, by men, were not afraid to admit that those men might make bad laws; might do, by law, the same things, and from the same motives, which, if done by individuals without the sanction of law, would be called unjust. And hence the sentiment of injustice came to be attached, not to all violations of law, but only to violations of such laws as *ought* to exist, including such as ought to exist but do not; and to laws themselves, if supposed to be contrary to what ought to be law. In this manner the idea of law and of its injunctions was still predominant in the notion of justice, even when the laws actually in force ceased to be accepted as the standard of it.

It is true that mankind consider the idea of justice and its obligations as applicable to many things which neither are, nor is it desired that they should be, regulated by law. Nobody desires that laws should interfere with the whole detail of private life; yet every one

9. Basic notion (French); literally, "mother idea."

allows that in all daily conduct a person may and does show himself to be either just or unjust. But even here, the idea of the breach of what ought to be law, still lingers in a modified shape. It would always give us pleasure, and chime in with our feelings of fitness, that acts which we deem unjust should be punished, though we do not always think it expedient that this should be done by the tribunals. We forego that gratification on account of incidental inconveniences. We should be glad to see just conduct enforced and injustice repressed, even in the minutest details, if we were not, with reason, afraid of trusting the magistrate with so unlimited an amount of power over individuals. When we think that a person is bound in justice to do a thing, it is an ordinary form of language to say, that he ought to be compelled to do it. We should be gratified to see the obligation enforced by anybody who had the power. If we see that its enforcement by law would be inexpedient, we lament the impossibility, we consider the impunity given to injustice as an evil, and strive to make amends for it by bringing a strong expression of our own and the public disapprobation to bear upon the offender. Thus the idea of legal constraint is still the generating idea of the notion of justice, though undergoing several transformations before that notion, as it exists in an advanced state of society, becomes complete.

The above is, I think, a true account, as far as it goes, of the origin and progressive growth of the idea of justice. But we must observe, that it contains, as yet, nothing to distinguish that obligation from moral obligation in general. For the truth is, that the idea of penal sanction, which is the essence of law, enters not only into the conception of injustice, but into that of any kind of wrong. We do not call anything wrong, unless we mean to imply that a person ought to be punished in some way or other for doing it; if not by law, by the opinion of his fellow creatures; if not by opinion, by the reproaches of his own conscience. This seems the real turning point of the distinction between morality and simple expediency. It is a part of the notion of Duty in every one of its forms, that a person may rightfully be compelled to fulfil it. Duty is a thing which may be *exacted* from a person, as one exacts a debt. Unless we think that it might be exacted from him, we do not call it his duty. Reasons of prudence, or the interest of other people, may militate against actually exacting it; but the person himself, it is clearly understood, would not be entitled to complain. There are other things, on the contrary, which we wish that people should do, which we like or admire them for doing, perhaps dislike or despise them for not doing, but yet admit that they are not bound to do; it is not a case of moral obligation; we do not blame them, that is, we do not think that they are proper objects of punishment. How we come by these ideas of deserving and not deserving punishment, will appear, perhaps, in the sequel; but I think there is no doubt that this distinction lies at the bottom of the notions of right and wrong; that we call any conduct wrong, or employ, instead, some other term of dislike or disparagement, according as we think that the person ought, or ought not, to be punished for it; and we say that it would be right to do so and so, or merely that it would be desirable or laudable, according as we would wish to see the person whom it concerns, compelled, or only persuaded and exhorted, to act in that manner.[1]

This, therefore, being the characteristic difference which marks off, not justice, but morality in general, from the remaining provinces of Expediency and Worthiness; the character is still to be sought which distinguishes justice from other branches of morality. Now it is known that ethical writers divide moral duties into two classes, denoted by the ill-chosen expressions, duties of perfect and of imperfect obligation; the latter being those in which, though the act is obligatory, the particular occasions of performing it are left to our choice; as in the case of charity or beneficence, which we are indeed bound to practise, but not towards any definite person, nor at any prescribed time. In the more precise language of philosophic jurists, duties of perfect obligation are those duties in virtue of which a correlative *right* resides in some person or persons; duties of imperfect obligation are those moral obligations which do not give birth to any right. I think it will be found that this distinction exactly coincides with that which exists between justice and the other obligations of morality. In our survey of the various popular acceptations of justice, the term appeared generally to involve the idea of a personal right—a claim on the part of one or more individuals, like that which the law gives when it confers a proprietary or other legal right. Whether the injustice consists in depriving a person of a possession, or in breaking faith with him, or in treating him worse than he deserves, or worse than other people who have no greater claims, in each case the supposition implies two things—a wrong done, and some assignable person who is wronged. Injustice may also be done by treating a person better than others; but the wrong in this case is to his competitors, who are also assignable persons. It seems to me that this feature in the case—a right in some person, correlative to the moral obligation—constitutes the specific difference between justice, and generosity or beneficence. Justice implies something which it is not only right to do, and wrong not to do, but which some individual person can claim from us as his moral right. No one has

---

1. See this point enforced and illustrated by Professor Bain, in an admirable chapter (entitled "The Ethical Emotions, or the Moral Sense"), of the second of the two treatises composing his elaborate and profound work on the Mind [*Mill's note*]. [The reference is to Alexander Bain, *The Emotions and the Will* (London: Parker, 1859)—*Editor's note*.]

a moral right to our generosity or beneficence, because we are not morally bound to practise those virtues towards any given individual. And it will be found with respect to this as with respect to every correct definition, that the instances which seem to conflict with it are those which most confirm it. For if a moralist attempts, as some have done, to make out that mankind generally, though not any given individual, have a right to all the good we can do them, he at once, by that thesis, includes generosity and beneficence within the category of justice. He is obliged to say, that our utmost exertions are *due* to our fellow creatures, thus assimilating them to a debt; or that nothing less can be a sufficient *return* for what society does for us, thus classing the case as one of gratitude; both of which are acknowledged cases of justice. Wherever there is a right, the case is one of justice, and not of the virtue of beneficence: and whoever does not place the distinction between justice and morality in general where we have now placed it, will be found to make no distinction between them at all, but to merge all morality in justice.

Having thus endeavoured to determine the distinctive elements which enter into the composition of the idea of justice, we are ready to enter on the inquiry, whether the feeling, which accompanies the idea, is attached to it by a special dispensation of nature, or whether it could have grown up, by any known laws, out of the idea itself; and in particular, whether it can have originated in considerations of general expediency.

I conceive that the sentiment itself does not arise from anything which would commonly, or correctly, be termed an idea of expediency; but that though, the sentiment does not, whatever is moral in it does.

We have seen that the two essential ingredients in the sentiment of justice are, the desire to punish a person who has done harm, and the knowledge or belief that there is some definite individual or individuals to whom harm has been done.

Now it appears to me, that the desire to punish a person who has done harm to some individual, is a spontaneous outgrowth from two sentiments, both in the highest degree natural, and which either are or resemble instincts; the impulse of self-defence, and the feeling of sympathy.

It is natural to resent, and to repel or retaliate, any harm done or attempted against ourselves, or against those with whom we sympathize. The origin of this sentiment it is not necessary here to discuss. Whether it be an instinct or a result of intelligence, it is, we know, common to all animal nature; for every animal tries to hurt those who have hurt, or who it thinks are about to hurt, itself or its young. Human beings, on this point, only differ from other animals in two particulars. First, in being capable of sympathizing, not solely with their offspring, or, like some of the more noble animals, with some superior animal who is kind to them, but with all human, and even with all sentient, beings. Secondly, in having a more developed intelligence, which gives a wider range to the whole of their sentiments, whether self-regarding or sympathetic. By virtue of his superior intelligence, even apart from his superior range of sympathy, a human being is capable of apprehending a community of interest between himself and the human society of which he forms a part, such that any conduct which threatens the security of the society generally, is threatening to his own, and calls forth his instinct (if instinct it be) of self-defence. The same superiority of intelligence, joined to the power of sympathizing with human beings generally, enables him to attach himself to the collective idea of his tribe, his country, or mankind, in such a manner that any act hurtful to them rouses his instinct of sympathy, and urges him to resistance.

The sentiment of justice, in that one of its elements which consists of the desire to punish, is thus, I conceive, the natural feeling of retaliation or vengeance, rendered by intellect and sympathy applicable to those injuries, that is, to those hurts, which wound us through, or in common with, society at large. This sentiment, in itself, has nothing moral in it; what is moral is, the exclusive subordination of it to the social sympathies, so as to wait on and obey their call. For the natural feeling tends to make us resent indiscriminately whatever any one does that is disagreeable to us; but when moralized by the social feeling, it only acts in the directions conformable to the general good: just persons resenting a hurt to society, though not otherwise a hurt to themselves, and not resenting a hurt to themselves, however painful, unless it be of the kind which society has a common interest with them in the repression of.

It is no objection against this doctrine to say, that when we feel our sentiment of justice outraged, we are not thinking of society at large, or of any collective interest, but only of the individual case. It is common enough certainly, though the reverse of commendable, to feel resentment merely because we have suffered pain; but a person whose resentment is really a moral feeling, that is, who considers whether an act is blameable before he allows himself to resent it—such a person, though he may not say expressly to himself that he is standing up for the interest of society, certainly does feel that he is asserting a rule which is for the benefit of others as well as for his own. If he is not feeling this—if he is regarding the act solely as it affects him individually—he is not consciously just; he is not concerning himself about the justice of his actions. This is admitted even by anti-utilitarian moralists. When Kant (as before remarked) propounds as the fundamental principle of morals, 'So act, that thy rule of conduct might be adopted as a law by all rational beings,' he virtually acknowledges that the interest of mankind collectively, or at least of mankind indiscriminately, must be in the mind of the agent when conscientiously deciding on the morality of the act. Otherwise he uses words without a meaning: for, that a rule even of utter selfishness could not *possibly* be adopted by all rational beings—that there is any insuperable obstacle in the nature of things to its adoption—cannot be even plausibly maintained. To give any meaning to Kant's principle, the sense put upon it must be, that we ought to shape our conduct by a rule which all rational beings might adopt *with benefit to their collective interest*.

To recapitulate: the idea of justice supposes two things; a rule of conduct, and a sentiment which sanctions the rule. The first must be supposed common to all mankind, and intended for their good. The other (the sentiment) is a desire that punishment may be suffered by those who infringe the rule. There is involved, in addition, the conception of some definite person who suffers by the infringement; whose rights (to use the expression appropriated to the case) are violated by it. And the sentiment of justice appears to me to be, the animal desire to repel or retaliate a hurt or damage to oneself, or to those with whom one sympathizes, widened so as to include all persons, by the human capacity of enlarged sympathy, and the human conception of intelligent self-interest. From the latter elements, the feeling derives its morality; from the former, its peculiar impressiveness, and energy of self-assertion.

I have, throughout, treated the idea of a *right* residing in the injured person, and violated by the injury, not as a separate element in the composition of the idea and sentiment, but as one of the forms in which the other two elements clothe themselves. These elements are, a hurt to some assignable person or persons on the one hand, and a demand for punishment on the other. An examination of our own minds, I think, will show, that these two things include all that we mean when we speak of violation of a right. When we call anything a person's right, we mean that he has a valid claim on society to protect him in the possession of it, either by the force of law, or by that of education and opinion. If he has what we consider a sufficient claim, on whatever account, to have something guaranteed to him by society, we say that he has a right to it. If we desire to prove that anything does not belong to him by right, we think this done as soon as it is admitted that society ought not to take measures for securing it to him, but should leave it to chance, or to his own exertions. Thus, a person is said to have a right to what he can earn in fair professional competition; because society ought not to allow any other person to hinder him from endeavouring to earn in that manner as much as he can. But he has not a right to three hundred a-year, though he may happen to be earning it; because society is not called on to provide that he shall earn that sum. On the contrary, if he owns ten thousand pounds three per cent stock he *has* a right to three hundred a-year; because society has come under an obligation to provide him with an income of that amount.

To have a right, then, is, I conceive, to have something which society ought to defend me in the possession of. If the objector goes on to ask why it ought, I can give him no other reason than general utility. If that expression does not seem to convey a sufficient feeling of the strength of the obligation, nor to account for the peculiar energy of the feeling, it is because there goes to the composition of the sentiment, not a rational only but also an animal element, the thirst for retaliation; and this thirst derives its intensity, as well as its moral justification, from the extraordinarily important and impressive kind of utility which is concerned. The interest involved is that of security, to every one's feelings the most vital of all interests. Nearly all other earthly benefits are needed by one person, not needed by another; and many of them can, if necessary, be cheerfully foregone, or replaced by something else; but security no human being can possibly do without; on it we depend for all our immunity from evil, and for the whole value of all and every good, beyond the passing moment; since nothing but the gratification of the instant could be of any worth to us, if we could be deprived of everything the next instant by whoever was momentarily stronger than ourselves. Now this most indispensable of all necessaries, after physical nutriment, cannot be had, unless the machinery for providing it is kept unintermittedly in active play. Our notion, therefore, of the claim we have on our fellow-creatures to join in making safe for us the very groundwork of our existence, gathers feelings round it so much more intense than those concerned in any of the more common cases of utility, that the difference in degree (as is often the case in psychology) becomes a real difference in kind. The claim assumes that character of absoluteness, that apparent infinity, and incommensurability with all other considerations, which constitute the distinction between the feeling of right and wrong and that of ordinary expediency and inexpediency. The feelings concerned are so powerful, and we count so positively on finding a responsive feeling in others (all being alike interested), that *ought* and *should* grow into *must*, and recognised indispensability becomes a moral necessity, analogous to physical, and often not inferior to it in binding force.

If the preceding analysis, or something resembling it, be not the correct account of the notion of justice; if justice be totally independent of utility, and be a standard *per se*, which the mind can recognise by simple introspection of itself; it is hard to understand why that internal oracle is so ambiguous, and why so many things appear either just or unjust, according to the light in which they are regarded.

We are continually informed that Utility is an uncertain standard, which every different person interprets differently, and that there is no safety but in the immutable, ineffaceable, and unmistakeable dictates of Justice, which carry their evidence in themselves, and are independent of the fluctuations of opinion. One would suppose from this that on questions of justice there could be no controversy; that if we take that for our rule, its application to any given case could leave us in as little doubt as a mathematical demonstration. So far is this from being the fact, that there is as much difference of opinion, and as fierce discussion, about what is just, as about what is useful to society. Not only have different nations and individuals different notions of justice, but, in the mind of one and the same individual, justice is not some one rule, principle, or maxim, but many, which do not always coincide in their dictates, and in choosing between which, he is guided either by some extraneous standard, or by his own personal predilections.

For instance, there are some who say, that it is unjust to punish any one for the sake of example to others; that punishment is just, only when intended for the good of the sufferer himself. Others maintain the extreme reverse, contending that to punish persons who have attained years of discretion, for their own benefit, is despotism and injustice, since if the matter at issue is solely their own good, no one has a right to control their own judgment of it; but that they may justly be punished to prevent evil to others, this being an exercise of the legitimate right of self-defence. Mr. Owen,[2] again, affirms that it is unjust to punish at all; for the criminal did not make his own character; his education, and the circumstances which surround him, have made him a criminal, and for these he is not responsible. All these opinions are extremely plausible; and so long as the question is argued as one of justice simply, without going down to the principles which lie under justice and are the source of its authority, I am unable to see how any of these reasoners can be refuted. For, in truth, every one of the three builds upon rules of justice confessedly true. The first appeals to the acknowledged injustice of singling out an individual, and making him a sacrifice, without his consent, for other people's benefit. The second relies on the acknowledged justice of self-defence, and the admitted injustice of forcing one person to conform to another's notions of what constitutes his good. The

2. Robert Owen (1771–1858), a Welsh textile manufacturer, philanthropist, reformer, and utopian socialist who advocated a society based on cooperatives; Mill criticized his social determinism in *The System of Logic*, bk. 6, chaps. 2 and 3 (*CW*, vol. 8).

Owenite invokes the admitted principle, that it is unjust to punish any one for what he cannot help. Each is triumphant so long as he is not compelled to take into consideration any other maxims of justice than the one he has selected; but as soon as their several maxims are brought face to face, each disputant seems to have exactly as much to say for himself as the others. No one of them can carry out his own notion of justice without trampling upon another equally binding. These are difficulties; they have always been felt to be such; and many devices have been invented to turn rather than to overcome them. As a refuge from the last of the three, men imagined what they called the freedom of the will; fancying that they could not justify punishing a man whose will is in a thoroughly hateful state, unless it be supposed to have come into that state through no influence of anterior circumstances. To escape from the other difficulties, a favourite contrivance has been the fiction of a contract, whereby at some unknown period all the members of society engaged to obey the laws, and consented to be punished for any disobedience to them; thereby giving to their legislators the right, which it is assumed they would not otherwise have had, of punishing them, either for their own good or for that of society. This happy thought was considered to get rid of the whole difficulty, and to legitimate the infliction of punishment, in virtue of another received maxim of justice, *volenti non fit injuria*; that is not unjust which is done with the consent of the person who is supposed to be hurt by it. I need hardly remark, that even if the consent were not a mere fiction, this maxim is not superior in authority to the others which it is brought in to supersede. It is, on the contrary, an instructive specimen of the loose and irregular manner in which supposed principles of justice grow up. This particular one evidently came into use as a help to the coarse exigencies of courts of law, which are sometimes obliged to be content with very uncertain presumptions, on account of the greater evils which would often arise from any attempt on their part to cut finer. But even courts of law are not able to adhere consistently to the maxim, for they allow voluntary engagements to be set aside on the ground of fraud, and sometimes on that of mere mistake or misinformation.

Again, when the legitimacy of inflicting punishment is admitted, how many conflicting conceptions of justice come to light in discussing the proper apportionment of punishment to offences. No rule on this subject recommends itself so strongly to the primitive and spontaneous sentiment of justice, as the *lex talionis*, an eye for an eye and a tooth for a tooth. Though this principle of the Jewish and of the Mahomedan law has been generally abandoned in Europe as a practical maxim, there is, I suspect, in most minds, a secret hankering after it; and when retribution accidentally falls on an offender in that precise shape, the general feeling of satisfaction evinced, bears witness how natural is the sentiment to which this repayment in kind is acceptable. With many the test of justice in penal infliction is that the punishment should be proportioned to the offence; meaning that it should be exactly measured by the moral guilt of the culprit (whatever be their standard for measuring moral guilt): the consideration, what amount of punishment is necessary to deter from the offence, having nothing to do with the question of justice, in their estimation: while there are others to whom that consideration is all in all; who maintain that it is not just, at least for man, to inflict on a fellow-creature, whatever may be his offences, any amount of suffering beyond the least that will suffice to prevent him from repeating, and others from imitating, his misconduct.

To take another example from a subject already once referred to. In a co-operative industrial association, is it just or not that talent or skill should give a title to superior remuneration? On the negative side of the question it is argued, that whoever does the best he can, deserves equally well, and ought not in justice to be put in a position of inferiority for no fault of his own; that superior abilities have already advantages more than enough, in the admiration they excite, the personal influence they command, and the internal sources of satisfaction attending them, without adding to these a superior share of the world's goods; and that society is bound in justice rather to make compensation to the less favoured, for this unmerited inequality of advantages, than to aggravate it. On the contrary side it is contended, that society receives more from the more efficient labourer; that his services being more useful, society owes him a larger return for them; that a greater share of the joint result is actually his work, and not to allow his claim to it is a kind of robbery; that if he is only to receive as much as others, he can only be justly required to produce as much, and to give a smaller amount of time and exertion, proportioned to his superior efficiency. Who shall decide between these appeals to conflicting principles of justice? Justice has in this case two sides to it, which it is impossible to bring into harmony, and the two disputants have chosen opposite sides; the one looks to what it is just that the individual should receive, the other to what it is just that the community should give. Each, from his own point of view, is unanswerable; and any choice between them, on grounds of justice, must be perfectly arbitrary. Social utility alone can decide the preference.

How many, again, and how irreconcileable, are the standards of justice to which reference is made in discussing the repartition of taxation. One opinion is, that payment to the State should be in numerical proportion to pecuniary means. Others think that justice dictates what they term graduated taxation; taking a higher percentage from those who have more to spare. In point of natural justice a strong case might be made for disregarding means altogether, and taking the same absolute sum (whenever it could be got) from every one: as the subscribers to a mess, or to a club, all pay the same sum for the same privileges, whether they can all equally afford it or not.[3] Since the protection (it might be said) of law and government is afforded to, and is equally required by, all, there is no injustice in making all buy it at the same price. It is reckoned justice, not injustice, that a dealer should charge to all customers the same price for the same article, not a price varying according to their means of payment. This doctrine, as applied to taxation, finds no advocates, because it conflicts strongly with men's feelings of humanity and perceptions of social expediency; but the principle of justice which it invokes is as true and as binding as those which can be appealed to against it. Accordingly, it exerts a tacit influence on the line of defence employed for other modes of assessing taxation. People feel obliged to argue that the State does more for the rich than for the poor, as a justification for its taking more from them: though this is in reality not true, for the rich would be far better able to protect themselves, in the absence of law or government, than the poor, and indeed would probably be successful in converting the poor into their slaves. Others, again, so far defer to the same conception of justice, as to maintain that all should pay an equal capitation tax for the protection of their persons (these being of equal value to all), and an unequal tax for the protection of their property, which is unequal. To this others reply, that the all of one man is as valuable to him as the all of another. From these confusions there is no other mode of extrication than the utilitarian.

Is, then, the difference between the Just and the Expedient a merely imaginary distinction? Have mankind been under a delusion in thinking that justice is a more sacred thing than policy, and that the latter ought only to be listened to after the former has been satisfied? By no means. The exposition we have given of the nature and origin of the sentiment, recognises a real distinction; and no one of those who profess the most sublime contempt for the consequences of actions as an element in their morality, attaches more importance to the distinction than I do.[4] While I dispute the pretensions of any

3. Mill had discussed criteria of fair taxation in his *Principles of Political Economy*, vol. 2, bk. 5, chaps. 2–6 (*CW*, vol. 3).
4. To be read as an introduction to Mill's idea of the affirmation of individuality as the goal of justice; this chapter was drafted in 1854 (although published in 1861), before he started writing *On Liberty*, as one reads in some of his letters to Harriet Taylor in June of that year (*CW*, vol. 14: "I employed the five hours of steamboat partly in conning over the subject of justice for the essay").

theory which sets up an imaginary standard of justice not grounded on utility, I account the justice which is grounded on utility to be the chief part, and incomparably the most sacred and binding part, of all morality. Justice is a name for certain classes of moral rules, which concern the essentials of human well-being more nearly, and are therefore of more absolute obligation, than any other rules for the guidance of life; and the notion which we have found to be of the essence of the idea of justice, that of a right residing in an individual, implies and testifies to this more binding obligation.

The moral rules which forbid mankind to hurt one another (in which we must never forget to include wrongful interference with each other's freedom) are more vital to human well-being than any maxims, however important, which only point out the best mode of managing some department of human affairs. They have also the peculiarity, that they are the main element in determining the whole of the social feelings of mankind. It is their observance which alone preserves peace among human beings: if obedience to them were not the rule, and disobedience the exception, every one would see in every one else a probable enemy, against whom he must be perpetually guarding himself. What is hardly less important, these are the precepts which mankind have the strongest and the most direct inducements for impressing upon one another. By merely giving to each other prudential instruction or exhortation, they may gain, or think they gain, nothing: in inculcating on each other the duty of positive beneficence they have an unmistakeable interest, but far less in degree: a person may possibly not need the benefits of others; but he always needs that they should not do him hurt. Thus the moralities which protect every individual from being harmed by others, either directly or by being hindered in his freedom of pursuing his own good, are at once those which he himself has most at heart, and those which he has the strongest interest in publishing and enforcing by word and deed. It is by a person's observance of these, that his fitness to exist as one of the fellowship of human beings, is tested and decided; for on that depends his being a nuisance or not to those with whom he is in contact. Now it is these moralities primarily, which compose the obligations of justice. The most marked cases of injustice, and those which give the tone to the feeling of repugnance which characterizes the sentiment, are acts of wrongful aggression, or wrongful exercise of power over some one; the next are those which consist in wrongfully withholding from him something which is his due; in both cases, inflicting on him a positive hurt, either in the form of direct suffering, or of the privation of some good which he had reasonable ground, either of a physical or of a social kind, for counting upon.

The same powerful motives which command the observance of these primary moralities, enjoin the punishment of those who violate them; and as the impulses of self-defence, of defence of others, and of vengeance, are all called forth against such persons, retribution, or evil for evil, becomes closely connected with the sentiment of justice, and is universally included in the idea. Good for good is also one of the dictates of justice; and this, though its social utility is evident, and though it carries with it a natural human feeling, has not at first sight that obvious connexion with hurt or injury, which, existing in the most elementary cases of just and unjust, is the source of the characteristic intensity of the sentiment. But the connexion, though less obvious, is not less real. He who accepts benefits, and denies a return of them when needed, inflicts a real hurt, by disappointing one of the most natural and reasonable of expectations, and one which he must at least tacitly have encouraged, otherwise the benefits would seldom have been conferred. The important rank, among human evils and wrongs, of the disappointment of expectation, is shown in the fact that it constitutes the principal criminality of two such highly immoral acts as a breach of friendship and a breach of promise. Few hurts which human beings can sustain are greater, and none wound more, than when that on which they habitually and with full assurance relied, fails them in the hour of need; and few wrongs are greater than this mere withholding of good; none excite more resentment, either in the person suffering, or in a sympathizing spectator. The principle, therefore, of giving to each what they deserve, that is, good for good as well as evil for evil, is not only included within the idea of Justice as we have defined it, but is a proper object of that intensity of sentiment, which places the Just, in human estimation, above the simply Expedient.

Most of the maxims of justice current in the world, and commonly appealed to in its transactions, are simply instrumental to carrying into effect the principles of justice which we have now spoken of. That a person is only responsible for what he has done voluntarily, or could voluntarily have avoided; that it is unjust to condemn any person unheard; that the punishment ought to be proportioned to the offence, and the like, are maxims intended to prevent the just principle of evil for evil from being perverted to the infliction of evil without that justification. The greater part of these common maxims have come into use from the practice of courts of justice, which have been naturally led to a more complete recognition and elaboration than was likely to suggest itself to others, of the rules necessary to enable them to fulfil their double function, of inflicting punishment when due, and of awarding to each person his right.

That first of judicial virtues, impartiality, is an obligation of justice, partly for the reason last mentioned; as being a necessary condition of the fulfilment of the other obligations of justice. But this is not the only source of the exalted rank, among human obligations, of those maxims of equality and impartiality, which, both in popular estimation and in that of the most enlightened, are included among the precepts of justice. In one point of view, they may be considered as corollaries from the principles already laid down. If it is a duty to do to each according to his deserts, returning good for good as well as repressing evil by evil, it necessarily follows that we should treat all equally well (when no higher duty forbids) who have deserved equally well of us, and that society should treat all equally well who have deserved equally well of it, that is, who have deserved equally well absolutely. This is the highest abstract standard of social and distributive justice; towards which all institutions, and the efforts of all virtuous citizens, should be made in the utmost possible degree to converge. But this great moral duty rests upon a still deeper foundation, being a direct emanation from the first principle of morals, and not a mere logical corollary from secondary or derivative doctrines. It is involved in the very meaning of Utility, or the Greatest-Happiness Principle. That principle is a mere form of words without rational signification, unless one person's happiness, supposed equal in degree (with the proper allowance made for kind), is counted for exactly as much as another's. Those conditions being supplied, Bentham's dictum, 'everybody to count for one, nobody for more than one,' might be written under the principle of utility as an explanatory commentary.[5] The equal claim of everybody to happiness in the

5. This implication, in the first principle of the utilitarian scheme, of perfect impartiality between persons, is regarded by Mr. Herbert Spencer (in his 'Social Statics') as a disproof of the pretensions of utility to be a sufficient guide to right; since (he says) the principle of utility presupposes the anterior principle, that everybody has an equal right to happiness. It may be more correctly described as supposing that equal amounts of happiness are equally desirable, whether felt by the same or by different persons. This, however, is not a presupposition; not a premise needful to support the principle of utility, but the very principle itself; for what is the principle of utility, if it be not that 'happiness' and 'desirable' are synonymous terms? If there is any anterior principle implied, it can be no other than this, that the truths of arithmetic are applicable to the valuation of happiness, as of all other measurable quantities.

    [Mr. Herbert Spencer, in a private communication on the subject of the preceding Note, objects to being considered an opponent of Utilitarianism, and states that he regards happiness as the ultimate end of morality; but deems that end only partially attainable by empirical generalizations from the observed results of conduct, and completely attainable only by deducing, from the laws of life and the conditions of existence, what kinds of action necessarily tend to produce happiness, and what kinds to produce unhappiness. With the exception of the word "necessarily," I have no dissent to express from this doctrine; and (omitting that word) I am not aware that any modern advocate of utilitarianism is of a different opinion. Bentham, certainly, to whom in the *Social Statics* Mr. Spencer particularly referred, is, least of all writers, chargeable with unwillingness to deduce the effect of actions on happiness from the laws of human nature and the universal conditions of human life. The common charge against him is of relying too exclusively upon such deductions, and declining altogether to be bound by the generalizations

estimation of the moralist and the legislator, involves an equal claim to all the means of happiness, except in so far as the inevitable conditions of human life, and the general interest, in which that of every individual is included, set limits to the maxim; and those limits ought to be strictly construed. As every other maxim of justice, so this, is by no means applied or held applicable universally; on the contrary, as I have already remarked, it bends to every person's ideas of social expediency. But in whatever case it is deemed applicable at all, it is held to be the dictate of justice. All persons are deemed to have a *right* to equality of treatment, except when some recognised social expediency requires the reverse. And hence all social inequalities which have ceased to be considered expedient, assume the character not of simple inexpediency, but of injustice, and appear so tyrannical, that people are apt to wonder how they ever could have been tolerated; forgetful that they themselves perhaps tolerate other inequalities under an equally mistaken notion of expediency, the correction of which would make that which they approve seem quite as monstrous as what they have at last learnt to condemn. The entire history of social improvement has been a series of transitions, by which one custom or institution after another, from being a supposed primary necessity of social existence, has passed into the rank of an universally stigmatized injustice and tyranny. So it has been with the distinctions of slaves and freemen, nobles and serfs, patricians and plebeians; and so it will be, and in part already is, with the aristocracies of colour, race, and sex.

It appears from what has been said, that justice is a name for certain moral requirements, which, regarded collectively, stand higher in the scale of social utility, and are therefore of more paramount obligation, than any others; though particular cases may occur in which some other social duty is so important, as to overrule any one of the general maxims of justice. Thus, to save a life, it may not only be allowable, but a duty, to steal, or take by force, the necessary food or medicine, or to kidnap, and compel to officiate, the only qualified medical practitioner. In such cases, as we do not call anything justice which is not a virtue, we usually say, not that justice must give way to some other moral principle, but that what is just in ordinary

---

from specific experience which Mr. Spencer thinks that utilitarians generally confine themselves to. My own opinion (and, as I collect, Mr. Spencer's) is, that in ethics, as in all other branches of scientific study, the consilience of the results of both these processes, each corroborating and verifying the other, is requisite to give to any general proposition the kind and degree of evidence which constitutes scientific proof.] [*Mill's note*]. [Herbert Spencer (1820–1903), English philosopher and anthropologist, initiator of social Darwinism, which interpreted Darwin's principle of natural selection as a force operating in history and society. Mill refers to his *Social Statics, or Conditions Essential to Human Happiness specified, and The First of Them Developed* (London: Chapman, 1851), 94. As to their private communication see Herbert Spencer, *Autobiography* (London: Williams and Norgate, 1904), vol. 2, pp. 87–90—*Editor's note*.]

cases is, by reason of that other principle, not just in the particular case. By this useful accommodation of language, the character of indefeasibility attributed to justice is kept up, and we are saved from the necessity of maintaining that there can be laudable injustice.

The considerations which have now been adduced resolve, I conceive, the only real difficulty in the utilitarian theory of morals. It has always been evident that all cases of justice are also cases of expediency: the difference is in the peculiar sentiment which attaches to the former, as contradistinguished from the latter. If this characteristic sentiment has been sufficiently accounted for; if there is no necessity to assume for it any peculiarity of origin; if it is simply the natural feeling of resentment, moralized by being made coextensive with the demands of social good; and if this feeling not only does but ought to exist in all the classes of cases to which the idea of justice corresponds; that idea no longer presents itself as a stumbling-block to the utilitarian ethics. Justice remains the appropriate name for certain social utilities which are vastly more important, and therefore more absolute and imperative, than any others are as a class (though not more so than others may be in particular cases); and which, therefore, ought to be, as well as naturally are, guarded by a sentiment not only different in degree, but also in kind; distinguished from the milder feeling which attaches to the mere idea of promoting human pleasure or convenience, at once by the more definite nature of its commands, and by the sterner character of its sanctions.

THE END

The Subjection of Women

CHAPTER I

The object of this Essay is to explain as clearly as I am able, the grounds of an opinion which I have held from the very earliest period when I had formed any opinions at all on social or political matters, and which, instead of being weakened or modified, has been constantly growing stronger by the progress of reflection and the experience of life: That the principle which regulates the existing social relations between the two sexes—the legal subordination of one sex to the other—is wrong in itself, and now one of the chief hindrances to human improvement; and that it ought to be replaced by a principle of perfect equality, admitting no power or privilege on the one side, nor disability on the other.[1]

The very words necessary to express the task I have undertaken, show how arduous it is. But it would be a mistake to suppose that the difficulty of the case must lie in the insufficiency or obscurity of the grounds of reason on which my conviction rests. The difficulty is that which exists in all cases in which there is a mass of feeling to be contended against. So long as an opinion is strongly rooted in the feelings, it gains rather than loses in stability by having a preponderating weight of argument against it. For if it were accepted as a result of argument, the refutation of the argument might shake the solidity of the conviction; but when it rests solely on feeling, the worse it fares in argumentative contest, the more persuaded its adherents are that their feeling must have some deeper ground, which the arguments do not reach; and while the feeling remains, it is always throwing up fresh intrenchments of argument to repair any breach made in the old. And there are so many causes tending to make the feelings connected with this subject the most intense and most deeply-rooted of all those which gather round and protect old institutions and customs, that we need not wonder to find them as yet less undermined and loosened than any of the rest by the progress of the great modern spiritual and social transition; nor

---

1. See above, *On Liberty*, p. 67.

suppose that the barbarisms to which men cling longest must be less barbarisms than those which they earlier shake off.

In every respect the burthen is hard on those who attack an almost universal opinion. They must be very fortunate as well as unusually capable if they obtain a hearing at all. They have more difficulty in obtaining a trial, than any other litigants have in getting a verdict. If they do extort a hearing, they are subjected to a set of logical requirements totally different from those exacted from other people. In all other cases, the burthen of proof is supposed to lie with the affirmative. If a person is charged with a murder, it rests with those who accuse him to give proof of his guilt, not with himself to prove his innocence. If there is a difference of opinion about the reality of any alleged historical event, in which the feelings of men in general are not much interested, as the Siege of Troy for example, those who maintain that the event took place are expected to produce their proofs, before those who take the other side can be required to say anything; and at no time are these required to do more than show that the evidence produced by the others is of no value. Again, in practical matters, the burthen of proof is supposed to be with those who are against liberty; who contend for any restriction or prohibition; either any limitation of the general freedom of human action, or any disqualification or disparity of privilege affecting one person or kind of persons, as compared with others. The *à priori* presumption is in favour of freedom and impartiality. It is held that there should be no restraint not required by the general good, and that the law should be no respecter of persons, but should treat all alike, save where dissimilarity of treatment is required by positive reasons, either of justice or of policy. But of none of these rules of evidence will the benefit be allowed to those who maintain the opinion I profess. It is useless for me to say that those who maintain the doctrine that men have a right to command and women are under an obligation to obey, or that men are fit for government and women unfit, are on the affirmative side of the question, and that they are bound to show positive evidence for the assertions, or submit to their rejection. It is equally unavailing for me to say that those who deny to women any freedom or privilege rightly allowed to men, having the double presumption against them that they are opposing freedom and recommending partiality, must be held to the strictest proof of their case, and unless their success be such as to exclude all doubt, the judgment ought to go against them. These would be thought good pleas in any common case; but they will not be thought so in this instance. Before I could hope to make any impression, I should be expected not only to answer all that has ever been said by those who take the other side of the question, but to imagine all that could be said by them—to find them in reasons, as well as answer all I find: and besides refuting all arguments for the affirmative, I shall be called upon for invincible positive arguments to prove a negative. And even if I could do all this, and leave the opposite party with a host of unanswered arguments against them, and not a single unrefuted one on their side, I should be thought to have done little; for a cause supported on the one hand by universal usage, and on the other by so great a preponderance of popular sentiment, is supposed to have a presumption in its favour, superior to any conviction which an appeal to reason has power to produce in any intellects but those of a high class.

I do not mention these difficulties to complain of them; first, because it would be useless; they are inseparable from having to contend through people's understandings against the hostility of their feelings and practical tendencies: and truly the understandings of the majority of mankind would need to be much better cultivated than has ever yet been the case, before they can be asked to place such reliance in their own power of estimating arguments, as to give up practical principles in which they have been born and bred and which are the basis of much of the existing order of the world, at the first argumentative attack which they are not capable of logically resisting. I do not therefore quarrel with them for having too little faith in argument, but for having too much faith in custom and the general feeling. It is one of the characteristic prejudices of the reaction of the nineteenth century against the eighteenth, to accord to the unreasoning elements in human nature the infallibility which the eighteenth century is supposed to have ascribed to the reasoning elements. For the apotheosis of Reason we have substituted that of Instinct; and we call everything instinct which we find in ourselves and for which we cannot trace any rational foundation. This idolatry, infinitely more degrading than the other, and the most pernicious of the false worships of the present day, of all of which it is now the main support, will probably hold its ground until it gives way before a sound psychology, laying bare the real root of much that is bowed down to as the intention of Nature and the ordinance of God. As regards the present question, I am willing to accept the unfavourable conditions which the prejudice assigns to me. I consent that established custom, and the general feeling, should be deemed conclusive against me, unless that custom and feeling from age to age can be shown to have owed their existence to other causes than their soundness, and to have derived their power from the worse rather than the better parts of human nature. I am willing that judgment should go against me, unless I can show that my judge has been tampered with. The concession is not so great as it might appear; for to prove this, is by far the easiest portion of my task.

The generality of a practice is in some cases a strong presumption that it is, or at all events once was, conducive to laudable ends. This is the case, when the practice was first adopted, or afterwards kept up, as a means to such ends, and was grounded on experience of the mode in which they could be most effectually attained. If the authority of men over women, when first established, had been the result of a conscientious comparison between different modes of constituting the government of society; if, after trying various other modes of social organization—the government of women over men, equality between the two, and such mixed and divided modes of government as might be invented—it had been decided, on the testimony of experience, that the mode in which women are wholly under the rule of men, having no share at all in public concerns, and each in private being under the legal obligation of obedience to the man with whom she has associated her destiny, was the arrangement most conducive to the happiness and well being of both; its general adoption might then be fairly thought to be some evidence that, at the time when it was adopted, it was the best: though even then the considerations which recommended it may, like so many other primeval social facts of the greatest importance, have subsequently, in the course of ages, ceased to exist. But the state of the case is in every respect the reverse of this. In the first place, the opinion in favour of the present system, which entirely subordinates the weaker sex to the stronger, rests upon theory only; for there never has been trial made of any other: so that experience, in the sense in which it is vulgarly opposed to theory, cannot be pretended to have pronounced any verdict. And in the second place, the adoption of this system of inequality never was the result of deliberation, or forethought, or any social ideas, or any notion whatever of what conduced to the benefit of humanity or the good order of society. It arose simply from the fact that from the very earliest twilight of human society, every woman (owing to the value attached to her by men, combined with her inferiority in muscular strength) was found in a state of bondage to some man. Laws and systems of polity always begin by recognising the relations they find already existing between individuals. They convert what was a mere physical fact into a legal right, give it the sanction of society, and principally aim at the substitution of public and organized means of asserting and protecting these rights, instead of the irregular and lawless conflict of physical strength. Those who had already been compelled to obedience became in this manner legally bound to it. Slavery, from being a mere affair of force between the master and the slave, became regularized and a matter of compact among the masters, who, binding themselves to one another for common protection, guaranteed by their collective strength the private possessions of each, including his slaves. In early times, the great majority of the male sex were slaves, as well as the whole of the female. And many ages elapsed, some of them ages of high cultivation, before any thinker was bold enough to question the rightfulness, and the absolute social necessity, either of the one slavery or of the other. By degrees such thinkers did arise: and (the general progress of society assisting) the slavery of the male sex has, in all the countries of Christian Europe at least (though, in one of them, only within the last few years)[2] been at length abolished, and that of the female sex has been gradually changed into a milder form of dependence. But this dependence, as it exists at present, is not an original institution, taking a fresh start from considerations of justice and social expediency—it is the primitive state of slavery lasting on, through successive mitigations and modifications occasioned by the same causes which have softened the general manners, and brought all human relations more under the control of justice and the influence of humanity. It has not lost the taint of its brutal origin. No presumption in its favour, therefore, can be drawn from the fact of its existence. The only such presumption which it could be supposed to have, must be grounded on its having lasted till now, when so many other things which came down from the same odious source have been done away with. And this, indeed, is what makes it strange to ordinary ears, to hear it asserted that the inequality of rights between men and women has no other source than the law of the strongest.

That this statement should have the effect of a paradox, is in some respects creditable to the progress of civilization, and the improvement of the moral sentiments of mankind. We now live—that is to say, one or two of the most advanced nations of the world now live—in a state in which the law of the strongest seems to be entirely abandoned as the regulating principle of the world's affairs: nobody professes it, and, as regards most of the relations between human beings, nobody is permitted to practise it. When any one succeeds in doing so, it is under cover of some pretext which gives him the semblance of having some general social interest on his side. This being the ostensible state of things, people flatter themselves that the rule of mere force is ended; that the law of the strongest cannot be the reason of existence of anything which has remained in full operation down to the present time. However any of our present institutions may have begun, it can only, they think, have been preserved to this period of advanced civilization by a well-grounded feeling of its adaptation to human nature, and conduciveness to the general good. They do not understand the great vitality and

2. The reference is to the abolition of serfdom in Russia in 1861 by Emperor Alexander II.

durability of institutions which place right on the side of might; how intensely they are clung to; how the good as well as the bad propensities and sentiments of those who have power in their hands, become identified with retaining it; how slowly these bad institutions give way, one at a time, the weakest first, beginning with those which are least interwoven with the daily habits of life; and how very rarely those who have obtained legal power because they first had physical, have ever lost their hold of it until the physical power had passed over to the other side. Such shifting of the physical force not having taken place in the case of women; this fact, combined with all the peculiar and characteristic features of the particular case, made it certain from the first that this branch of the system of right founded on might, though softened in its most atrocious features at an earlier period than several of the others, would be the very last to disappear. It was inevitable that this one case of a social relation grounded on force, would survive through generations of institutions grounded on equal justice, an almost solitary exception to the general character of their laws and customs; but which, so long as it does not proclaim its own origin, and as discussion has not brought out its true character, is not felt to jar with modern civilization, any more than domestic slavery among the Greeks jarred with their notion of themselves as a free people.

The truth is, that people of the present and the last two or three generations have lost all practical sense of the primitive condition of humanity; and only the few who have studied history accurately, or have much frequented the parts of the world occupied by the living representatives of ages long past, are able to form any mental picture of what society then was. People are not aware how entirely, in former ages, the law of superior strength was the rule of life; how publicly and openly it was avowed, I do not say cynically or shamelessly—for these words imply a feeling that there was something in it to be ashamed of, and no such notion could find a place in the faculties of any person in those ages, except a philosopher or a saint. History gives a cruel experience of human nature, in shewing how exactly the regard due to the life, possessions, and entire earthly happiness of any class of persons, was measured by what they had the power of enforcing; how all who made any resistance to authorities that had arms in their hands, however dreadful might be the provocation, had not only the law of force but all other laws, and all the notions of social obligation against them; and in the eyes of those whom they resisted, were not only guilty of crime, but of the worst of all crimes, deserving the most cruel chastisement which human beings could inflict. The first small vestige of a feeling of obligation in a superior to acknowledge any right in inferiors, began when he had been induced, for convenience, to make some promise to them. Though these promises, even when sanctioned by the most solemn oaths, were for many ages revoked or violated on the most trifling provocation or temptation, it is probable that this, except by persons of still worse than the average morality, was seldom done without some twinges of conscience. The ancient republics, being mostly grounded from the first upon some kind of mutual compact, or at any rate formed by an union of persons not very unequal in strength, afforded, in consequence, the first instance of a portion of human relations fenced round, and placed under the dominion of another law than that of force. And though the original law of force remained in full operation between them and their slaves, and also (except so far as limited by express compact) between a commonwealth and its subjects, or other independent commonwealths; the banishment of that primitive law even from so narrow a field, commenced the regeneration of human nature, by giving birth to sentiments of which experience soon demonstrated the immense value even for material interests, and which thenceforward only required to be enlarged, not created. Though slaves were no part of the commonwealth, it was in the free states that slaves were first felt to have rights as human beings. The Stoics[3] were, I believe, the first (except so far as the Jewish law constitutes an exception) who taught as a part of morality that men were bound by moral obligations to their slaves. No one, after Christianity became ascendant, could ever again have been a stranger to this belief, in theory; nor, after the rise of the Catholic Church, was it ever without persons to stand up for it. Yet to enforce it was the most arduous task which Christianity ever had to perform. For more than a thousand years the Church kept up the contest, with hardly any perceptible success. It was not for want of power over men's minds. Its power was prodigious. It could make kings and nobles resign their most valued possessions to enrich the Church. It could make thousands, in the prime of life and the height of worldly advantages, shut themselves up in convents to work out their salvation by poverty, fasting, and prayer. It could send hundreds of thousands across land and sea, Europe and Asia, to give their lives for the deliverance of the Holy Sepulchre. It could make kings relinquish wives who were the object of their passionate attachment, because the Church declared that they were within the seventh (by our calculation the fourteenth) degree of relationship. All this it did; but it could not make men fight less with one another, nor tyrannize less cruelly over the serfs, and when they were able, over burgesses. It

---

3. One of the most influential philosophical schools in antiquity (founded in Greece by Zeno of Citium in the early third century B.C.E.), particularly from the last decades of the Roman Republic until the third century of the Christian era. See n. 2 (p. 24) in *On Liberty*.

could not make them renounce either of the applications of force; force militant, or force triumphant. This they could never be induced to do until they were themselves in their turn compelled by superior force. Only by the growing power of kings was an end put to fighting except between kings, or competitors for kingship; only by the growth of a wealthy and warlike bourgeoisie in the fortified towns, and of a plebeian infantry which proved more powerful in the field than the undisciplined chivalry, was the insolent tyranny of the nobles over the bourgeoisie and peasantry brought within some bounds. It was persisted in not only until, but long after, the oppressed had obtained a power enabling them often to take conspicuous vengeance; and on the Continent much of it continued to the time of the French Revolution, though in England the earlier and better organization of the democratic classes put an end to it sooner, by establishing equal laws and free national institutions.

If people are mostly so little aware how completely, during the greater part of the duration of our species, the law of force was the avowed rule of general conduct, any other being only a special and exceptional consequence of peculiar ties—and from how very recent a date it is that the affairs of society in general have been even pretended to be regulated according to any moral law; as little do people remember or consider, how institutions and customs which never had any ground but the law of force, last on into ages and states of general opinion which never would have permitted their first establishment. Less than forty years ago, Englishmen might still by law hold human beings in bondage as saleable property: within the present century they might kidnap them and carry them off, and work them literally to death. This absolutely extreme case of the law of force, condemned by those who can tolerate almost every other form of arbitrary power, and which, of all others, presents features the most revolting to the feelings of all who look at it from an impartial position, was the law of civilized and Christian England within the memory of persons now living:[4] and in one half of Anglo-Saxon America three or four years ago, not only did slavery exist, but the slave trade, and the breeding of slaves expressly for it, was a general practice between slave states. Yet not only was there a greater strength of sentiment against it, but, in England at least, a less amount either of feeling or of interest in favour of it, than of any other of the customary abuses of force: for its motive was the love of gain, unmixed and undisguised; and those who profited by it were a very small numerical fraction of the country, while the natural feeling of all who were not personally interested

---

4. The slave trade was abolished in Britain in 1807 (Slavery Abolition Act), and in the British West Indies in 1833 (Slave Emancipation Act).

in it, was unmitigated abhorrence. So extreme an instance makes it almost superfluous to refer to any other: but consider the long duration of absolute monarchy. In England at present it is the almost universal conviction that military despotism is a case of the law of force, having no other origin or justification. Yet in all the great nations of Europe except England it either still exists, or has only just ceased to exist, and has even now a strong party favourable to it in all ranks of the people, especially among persons of station and consequence. Such is the power of an established system, even when far from universal; when not only in almost every period of history there have been great and well-known examples of the contrary system, but these have almost invariably been afforded by the most illustrious and most prosperous communities. In this case, too, the possessor of the undue power, the person directly interested in it, is only one person, while those who are subject to it and suffer from it are literally all the rest. The yoke is naturally and necessarily humiliating to all persons, except the one who is on the throne, together with, at most, the one who expects to succeed to it. How different are these cases from that of the power of men over women! I am not now prejudging the question of its justifiableness. I am showing how vastly more permanent it could not but be, even if not justifiable, than these other dominations which have nevertheless lasted down to our own time. Whatever gratification of pride there is in the possession of power, and whatever personal interest in its exercise, is in this case not confined to a limited class, but common to the whole male sex. Instead of being, to most of its supporters, a thing desirable chiefly in the abstract, or, like the political ends usually contended for by factious, of little private importance to any but the leaders; it comes home to the person and hearth of every male head of a family, and of every one who looks forward to being so. The clodhopper exercises, or is to exercise, his share of the power equally with the highest nobleman. And the case is that in which the desire of power is the strongest: for every one who desires power, desires it most over those who are nearest to him, with whom his life is passed, with whom he has most concerns in common, and in whom any independence of his authority is oftenest likely to interfere with his individual preferences. If, in the other cases specified, powers manifestly grounded only on force, and having so much less to support them, are so slowly and with so much difficulty got rid of, much more must it be so with this, even if it rests on no better foundation than those. We must consider, too, that the possessors of the power have facilities in this case, greater than in any other, to prevent any uprising against it. Every one of the subjects lives under the very eye, and almost, it may be said, in the hands, of one of the masters—in closer intimacy with

him than with any of her fellow-subjects; with no means of combining against him, no power of even locally over-mastering him,
and, on the other hand, with the strongest motives for seeking his
favour and avoiding to give him offence. In struggles for political
emancipation, everybody knows how often its champions are bought
off by bribes, or daunted by terrors. In the case of women, each
individual of the subject-class is in a chronic state of bribery and
intimidation combined. In setting up the standard of resistance, a
large number of the leaders, and still more of the followers, must
make an almost complete sacrifice of the pleasures or the allevia-
tions of their own individual lot. If ever any system of privilege and
enforced subjection had its yoke tightly riveted on the necks of
those who are kept down by it, this has. I have not yet shown that it
is a wrong system: but every one who is capable of thinking on the
subject must see that even if it is, it was certain to outlast all other
forms of unjust authority. And when some of the grossest of the
other forms still exist in many civilized countries, and have only
recently been got rid of in others, it would be strange if that which
is so much the deepest-rooted had yet been perceptibly shaken anywhere. There is more reason to wonder that the protests and testi-
monies against it should have been so numerous and so weighty as
they are.

Some will object, that a comparison cannot fairly be made between
the government of the male sex and the forms of unjust power which
I have adduced in illustration of it, since these are arbitrary, and the
effect of mere usurpation, while it on the contrary is natural. But
was there ever any domination which did not appear natural to those
who possessed it? There was a time when the division of mankind
into two classes, a small one of masters and a numerous one of
slaves, appeared, even to the most cultivated minds, to be a natural,
and the only natural, condition of the human race. No less an
intellect, and one which contributed no less to the progress of
human thought, than Aristotle, held this opinion without doubt
or misgiving; and rested it on the same premises on which the same
assertion in regard to the dominion of men over women is usually
based, namely that there are different natures among mankind,
free natures, and slave natures; that the Greeks were of a free
nature, the barbarian races of Thracians and Asiatics of a slave
nature.[5] But why need I go back to Aristotle? Did not the slaveowners of the Southern United States maintain the same doctrine,
with all the fanaticism with which men cling to the theories that
justify their passions and legitimate their personal interests? Did

---

5. Aristotle defined natural slavery in his *Politics* (I, ii), where he discussed the hierarchal
   forms of authority in the household (*oikos*).

they not call heaven and earth to witness that the dominion of the
white man over the black is natural, that the black race is by nature
incapable of freedom, and marked out for slavery? some even going
so far as to say that the freedom of manual labourers is an unnatural order of things anywhere. Again, the theorists of absolute
monarchy have always affirmed it to be the only natural form of
government; issuing from the patriarchal, which was the primitive
and spontaneous form of society, framed on the model of the paternal, which is anterior to society itself, and, as they contend, the
most natural authority of all. Nay, for that matter, the law of force
itself, to those who could not plead any other, has always seemed
the most natural of all grounds for the exercise of authority. Conquering races hold it to be Nature's own dictate that the conquered
should obey the conquerors, or, as they euphoniously paraphrase it,
that the feebler and more unwarlike races should submit to the
braver and manlier. The smallest acquaintance with human life in
the middle ages, shows how supremely natural the dominion of the
feudal nobility over men of low condition appeared to the nobility
themselves, and how unnatural the conception seemed, of a person
of the inferior class claiming equality with them, or exercising
authority over them. It hardly seemed less so to the class held in
subjection. The emancipated serfs and burgesses, even in their most
vigorous struggles, never made any pretension to a share of authority; they only demanded more or less of limitation to the power of
tyrannizing over them. So true is it that unnatural generally means
only uncustomary, and that everything which is usual appears
natural. The subjection of women to men being a universal custom, any departure from it quite naturally appears unnatural. But
how entirely, even in this case, the feeling is dependent on custom,
appears by ample experience. Nothing so much astonishes the
people of distant parts of the world, when they first learn anything
about England, as to be told that it is under a queen: the thing seems
to them so unnatural as to be almost incredible. To Englishmen this
does not seem in the least degree unnatural, because they are used
to it; but they do feel it unnatural that women should be soldiers or
members of parliament. In the feudal ages, on the contrary, war
and politics were not thought unnatural to women, because not
unusual; it seemed natural that women of the privileged classes
should be of manly character, inferior in nothing but bodily strength
to their husbands and fathers. The independence of women seemed
rather less unnatural to the Greeks than to other ancients, on
account of the fabulous Amazons (whom they believed to be historical), and the partial example afforded by the Spartan women;
who, though no less subordinate by law than in other Greek states,
were more free in fact, and being trained to bodily exercises in the

same manner with men, gave ample proof that they were not naturally disqualified for them. There can be little doubt that Spartan
experience suggested to Plato, among many other of his doctrines,
that of the social and political equality of the two sexes.[6]

But, it will be said, the rule of men over women differs from all
these others in not being a rule of force: it is accepted voluntarily;
women make no complaint, and are consenting parties to it. In the
first place, a great number of women do not accept it. Ever since
there have been women able to make their sentiments known
by their writings (the only mode of publicity which society permits
to them), an increasing number of them have recorded protests
against their present social condition: and recently many thousands
of them, headed by the most eminent women known to the public,
have petitioned Parliament for their admission to the Parliamentary Suffrage.[7] The claim of women to be educated as solidly, and in
the same branches of knowledge, as men, is urged with growing
intensity, and with a great prospect of success; while the demand for
their admission into professions and occupations hitherto closed
against them, becomes every year more urgent. Though there are
not in this country, as there are in the United States, periodical
Conventions and an organized party to agitate for the Rights of
Women, there is a numerous and active Society organized and
managed by women, for the more limited object of obtaining the
political franchise.[8] Nor is it only in our own country and in America that women are beginning to protest, more or less collectively,
against the disabilities under which they labour. France, and Italy,
and Switzerland, and Russia now afford examples of the same
thing. How many more women there are who silently cherish similar aspirations, no one can possibly know; but there are abundant
tokens how many *would* cherish them, were they not so strenuously
taught to repress them as contrary to the proprieties of their sex. It
must be remembered, also, that no enslaved class ever asked for
complete liberty at once. When Simon de Montfort called the depu-
ties of the commons to sit for the first time in Parliament,[9] did any
of them dream of demanding that an assembly, elected by their

6. *The Republic* 5.449–57.
7. Mill had actually petitioned for the extension of the right to vote to women in 1866, while
   an MP. The petition to the House of Commons came with over 1,500 signatures and had
   been collected by the Women's Suffrage Committee. Mill used the Second Reform Bill
   (then being debated in Parliament) as an opportunity to introduce equal voting rights; his
   amendment obtained 73 votes.
8. The Manchester National Society for Women's Suffrage was established in 1865 by Elizabeth Wolstenholme-Elmy; the National Society for Women's Suffrage was founded in
   1867 by Lydia Becker. In Great Britain woman suffrage was first advocated by Mary Wollstonecraft in *A Vindication of the Rights of Woman* (1792) and demanded by the Chartist
   movement in the 1840s.
9. Simon de Montfort, The Earl of Leicester (1208–1265), led the baronial resistance to
   King Henry III (1207–1272) and called the first English Parliament in 1265.

constituents, should make and destroy ministries, and dictate to the king in affairs of state? No such thought entered into the imagination of the most ambitious of them. The nobility had already these pretensions; the commons pretended to nothing but to be exempt from arbitrary taxation, and from the gross individual oppression of the king's officers. It is a political law of nature that those who are under any power of ancient origin, never begin by complaining of the power itself, but only of its oppressive exercise. There is never any want of women who complain of ill usage by their husbands. There would be infinitely more, if complaint were not the greatest of all provocatives to a repetition and increase of the ill usage. It is this which frustrates all attempts to maintain the power but protect the woman against its abuses. In no other case (except that of a child) is the person who has been proved judicially to have suffered an injury, replaced under the physical power of the culprit who inflicted it. Accordingly wives, even in the most extreme and protracted cases of bodily ill usage, hardly ever dare avail themselves of the laws made for their protection: and if, in a moment of irrepressible indignation, or by the interference of neighbours, they are induced to do so, their whole effort afterwards is to disclose as little as they can, and to beg off their tyrant from his merited chastisement.

All causes, social and natural, combine to make it unlikely that women should be collectively rebellious to the power of men. They are so far in a position different from all other subject classes, that their masters require something more from them than actual service. Men do not want solely the obedience of women, they want their sentiments. All men, except the most brutish, desire to have, in the woman most nearly connected with them, not a forced slave but a willing one, not a slave merely, but a favourite. They have therefore put everything in practice to enslave their minds. The masters of all other slaves rely, for maintaining obedience, on fear; either fear of themselves, or religious fears. The masters of women wanted more than simple obedience, and they turned the whole force of education to effect their purpose. All women are brought up from the very earliest years in the belief that their ideal of character is the very opposite to that of men; not self-will, and government by self-control, but submission, and yielding to the control of others. All the moralities tell them that it is the duty of women, and all the current sentimentalities that it is their nature, to live for others; to make complete abnegation of themselves, and to have no life but in their affections. And by their affections are meant the only ones they are allowed to have—those to the men with whom they are connected, or to the children who constitute an additional and indefeasible tie between them and a man. When we put together three things—first, the natural attraction between opposite sexes; secondly, the wife's entire dependence on the husband, every privilege or pleasure she has being either his gift, or depending entirely on his will; and lastly, that the principal object of human pursuit, consideration, and all objects of social ambition, can in general be sought or obtained by her only through him, it would be a miracle if the object of being attractive to men had not become the polar star of feminine education and formation of character. And, this great means of influence over the minds of women having been acquired, an instinct of selfishness made men avail themselves of it to the utmost as a means of holding women in subjection, by representing to them meekness, submissiveness, and resignation of all individual will into the hands of a man, as an essential part of sexual attractiveness. Can it be doubted that any of the other yokes which mankind have succeeded in breaking, would have subsisted till now if the same means had existed, and had been as sedulously used, to bow down their minds to it? If it had been made the object of the life of every young plebeian to find personal favour in the eyes of some patrician, of every young serf with some seigneur;[1] if domestication with him, and a share of his personal affections, had been held out as the prize which they all should look out for, the most gifted and aspiring being able to reckon on the most desirable prizes; and if, when this prize had been obtained, they had been shut out by a wall of brass from all interests not centering in him, all feelings and desires but those which he shared or inculcated; would not serfs and seigneurs, plebeians and patricians, have been as broadly distinguished at this day as men and women are? and would not all but a thinker here and there, have believed the distinction to be a fundamental and unalterable fact in human nature?

The preceding considerations are amply sufficient to show that custom, however universal it may be, affords in this case no presumption, and ought not to create any prejudice, in favour of the arrangements which place women in social and political subjection to men. But I may go farther, and maintain that the course of history, and the tendencies of progressive human society, afford not only no presumption in favour of this system of inequality of rights, but a strong one against it; and that, so far as the whole course of human improvement up to this time, the whole stream of modern tendencies, warrants any inference on the subject, it is, that this relic of the past is discordant with the future, and must necessarily disappear.

1. Lord (French).

For, what is the peculiar character of the modern world—the difference which chiefly distinguishes modern institutions, modern social ideas, modern life itself, from those of times long past? It is, that human beings are no longer born to their place in life, and chained down by an inexorable bond to the place they are born to, but are free to employ their faculties, and such favourable chances as offer, to achieve the lot which may appear to them most desirable. Human society of old was constituted on a very different principle. All were born to a fixed social position, and were mostly kept in it by law, or interdicted from any means by which they could emerge from it. As some men are born white and others black, so some were born slaves and others freemen and citizens; some were born patricians, others plebeians; some were born feudal nobles, others commoners and *roturiers*.[2] A slave or serf could never make himself free, nor, except by the will of his master, become so. In most European countries it was not till towards the close of the middle ages, and as a consequence of the growth of regal power, that commoners could be ennobled. Even among nobles, the eldest son was born the exclusive heir to the paternal possessions, and a long time elapsed before it was fully established that the father could disinherit him. Among the industrious classes, only those who were born members of a guild, or were admitted into it by its members, could lawfully practise their calling within its local limits; and nobody could practise any calling deemed important, in any but the legal manner—by processes authoritatively prescribed. Manufacturers have stood in the pillory for presuming to carry on their business by new and improved methods. In modern Europe, and most in those parts of it which have participated most largely in all other modern improvements, diametrically opposite doctrines now prevail. Law and government do not undertake to prescribe by whom any social or industrial operation shall or shall not be conducted, or what modes of conducting them shall be lawful. These things are left to the unfettered choice of individuals. Even the laws which required that workmen should serve an apprenticeship, have in this country been repealed: there being ample assurance that in all cases in which an apprenticeship is necessary, its necessity will suffice to enforce it. The old theory was, that the least possible should be left to the choice of the individual agent; that all he had to do should, as far as practicable, be laid down for him by superior wisdom. Left to himself he was sure to go wrong. The modern conviction, the fruit of a thousand years of experience, is, that things in which the individual is the person directly interested, never go right but as they are left to his own discretion; and that any

2. Low-rank persons (French).

regulation of them by authority, except to protect the rights of others, is sure to be mischievous. This conclusion, slowly arrived at, and not adopted until almost every possible application of the contrary theory had been made with disastrous result, now (in the industrial department) prevails universally in the most advanced countries, almost universally in all that have pretensions to any sort of advancement. It is not that all processes are supposed to be equally good, or all persons to be equally qualified for everything; but that freedom of individual choice is now known to be the only thing which procures the adoption of the best processes, and throws each operation into the hands of those who are best qualified for it. Nobody thinks it necessary to make a law that only a strong-armed man shall be a blacksmith. Freedom and competition suffice to make blacksmiths strong-armed men, because the weak-armed can earn more by engaging in occupations for which they are more fit. In consonance with this doctrine, it is felt to be an overstepping of the proper bounds of authority to fix beforehand, on some general presumption, that certain persons are not fit to do certain things. It is now thoroughly known and admitted that if some such presumptions exist, no such presumption is infallible. Even if it be well grounded in a majority of cases, which it is very likely not to be, there will be a minority of exceptional cases in which it does not hold: and in those it is both an injustice to the individuals, and a detriment to society, to place barriers in the way of their using their faculties for their own benefit and for that of others. In the cases, on the other hand, in which the unfitness is real, the ordinary motives of human conduct will on the whole suffice to prevent the incompetent person from making, or from persisting in, the attempt.

If this general principle of social and economical science is not true; if individuals, with such help as they can derive from the opinion of those who know them, are not better judges than the law and the government, of their own capacities and vocation; the world cannot too soon abandon this principle, and return to the old system of regulations and disabilities. But if the principle is true, we ought to act as if we believed it, and not to ordain that to be born a girl instead of a boy, any more than to be born black instead of white, or a commoner instead of a nobleman, shall decide the person's position through all life—shall interdict people from all the more elevated social positions, and from all, except a few, respectable occupations. Even were we to admit the utmost that is ever pretended as to the superior fitness of men for all the functions now reserved to them, the same argument applies which forbids a legal qualification for members of Parliament. If only once in a dozen years the conditions of eligibility exclude a fit person, there is a real loss, while the exclusion of thousands of unfit persons is no gain; for if the constitution of the electoral body disposes them to choose unfit persons, there are always plenty of such persons to choose from. In all things of any difficulty and importance, those who can do them well are fewer than the need, even with the most unrestricted latitude of choice: and any limitation of the field of selection deprives society of some chances of being served by the competent, without ever saving it from the incompetent.

At present, in the more improved countries, the disabilities of women are the only case, save one, in which laws and institutions take persons at their birth, and ordain that they shall never in all their lives be allowed to compete for certain things. The one exception is that of royalty. Persons still are born to the throne; no one, not of the reigning family, can ever occupy it, and no one even of that family can, by any means but the course of hereditary succession, attain it. All other dignities and social advantages are open to the whole male sex: many indeed are only attainable by wealth, but wealth may be striven for by any one, and is actually obtained by many men of the very humblest origin. The difficulties, to the majority, are indeed insuperable without the aid of fortunate accidents; but no male human being is under any legal ban: neither law nor opinion superadd artificial obstacles to the natural ones. Royalty, as I have said, is excepted: but in this case every one feels it to be an exception—an anomaly in the modern world, in marked opposition to its customs and principles, and to be justified only by extraordinary special expediencies, which, though individuals and nations differ in estimating their weight, unquestionably do in fact exist. But in this exceptional case, in which a high social function is, for important reasons, bestowed on birth instead of being put up to competition, all free nations contrive to adhere in substance to the principle from which they nominally derogate; for they circumscribe this high function by conditions avowedly intended to prevent the person to whom it ostensibly belongs from really performing it; while the person by whom it is performed, the responsible minister, does obtain the post by a competition from which no full-grown citizen of the male sex is legally excluded. The disabilities, therefore, to which women are subject from the mere fact of their birth, are the solitary examples of the kind in modern legislation. In no instance except this, which comprehends half the human race, are the higher social functions closed against any one by a fatality of birth which no exertions, and no change of circumstances, can overcome; for even religious disabilities (besides that in England and in Europe they have practically almost ceased to exist) do not close any career to the disqualified person in case of conversion.

The social subordination of women thus stands out an isolated fact in modern social institutions; a solitary breach of what has become their fundamental law; a single relic of an old world of thought and practice exploded in everything else, but retained in the one thing of most universal interest; as if a gigantic dolmen, or a vast temple of Jupiter Olympius,[3] occupied the site of St. Paul's and received daily worship, while the surrounding Christian churches were only resorted to on fasts and festivals. This entire discrepancy between one social fact and all those which accompany it, and the radical opposition between its nature and the progressive movement which is the boast of the modern world, and which has successively swept away everything else of an analogous character, surely affords, to a conscientious observer of human tendencies, serious matter for reflection. It raises a primâ facie presumption on the unfavourable side, far outweighing any which custom and usage could in such circumstances create on the favourable; and should at least suffice to make this, like the choice between republicanism and royalty, a balanced question.

The least that can be demanded is, that the question should not be considered as prejudged by existing fact and existing opinion, but open to discussion on its merits, as a question of justice and expediency: the decision on this, as on any of the other social arrangements of mankind, depending on what an enlightened estimate of tendencies and consequences may show to be most advantageous to humanity in general, without distinction of sex. And the discussion must be a real discussion, descending to foundations, and not resting satisfied with vague and general assertions. It will not do, for instance, to assert in general terms, that the experience of mankind has pronounced in favour of the existing system. Experience cannot possibly have decided between two courses, so long as there has only been experience of one. If it be said that the doctrine of the equality of the sexes rests only on theory, it must be remembered that the contrary doctrine also has only theory to rest upon. All that is proved in its favour by direct experience, is that mankind have been able to exist under it, and to attain the degree of improvement and prosperity which we now see; but whether that prosperity has been attained sooner, or is now greater, than it would have been under the other system, experience does not say. On the other hand, experience does say, that every step in improvement has been so invariably accompanied by a step made in raising the social position of women, that historians and philosophers have been led to adopt their elevation or debasement as on the whole the surest test and

---

3. Jupiter was the supreme god in ancient Rome. *dolmen*: a megalith tomb dating to the Neolithic age, part of Druidic rituals.

most correct measure of the civilization of a people or an age. Through all the progessive period of human history, the condition of women has been approaching nearer to equality with men. This does not of itself prove that the assimilation must go on to complete equality; but it assuredly affords some presumption that such is the case.

Neither does it avail anything to say that the *nature* of the two sexes adapts them to their present functions and position, and renders these appropriate to them. Standing on the ground of common sense and the constitution of the human mind, I deny that any one knows, or can know, the nature of the two sexes, as long as they have only been seen in their present relation to one another. If men had ever been found in society without women, or women without men, or if there had been a society of men and women in which the women were not under the control of the men, something might have been positively known about the mental and moral differences which may be inherent in the nature of each. What is now called the nature of women is an eminently artificial thing—the result of forced repression in some directions, unnatural stimulation in others. It may be asserted without scruple, that no other class of dependents have had their character so entirely distorted from its natural proportions by their relation with their masters; for, if conquered and slave races have been, in some respects, more forcibly repressed, whatever in them has not been crushed down by an iron heel has generally been let alone, and if left with any liberty of development, it has developed itself according to its own laws; but in the case of women, a hot-house and stove cultivation has always been carried on of some of the capabilities of their nature, for the benefit and pleasure of their masters. Then, because certain products of the general vital force sprout luxuriantly and reach a great development in this heated atmosphere and under this active nurture and watering, while other shoots from the same root, which are left outside in the wintry air, with ice purposely heaped all round them, have a stunted growth, and some are burnt off with fire and disappear; men, with that inability to recognise their own work which distinguishes the un-analytic mind, indolently believe that the tree grows of itself in the way they have made it grow, and that it would die if one half of it were not kept in a vapour bath and the other half in the snow.

Of all difficulties which impede the progress of thought, and the formation of well-grounded opinions on life and social arrangements, the greatest is now the unspeakable ignorance and inattention of mankind in respect to the influences which form human character. Whatever any portion of the human species now are, or seem to be, such, it is supposed, they have a natural tendency to be:

even when the most elementary knowledge of the circumstances in which they have been placed, clearly points out the causes that made them what they are. Because a cottier[4] deeply in arrears to his landlord is not industrious, there are people who think that the Irish are naturally idle. Because constitutions can be overthrown when the authorities appointed to execute them turn their arms against them, there are people who think the French incapable of free government. Because the Greeks cheated the Turks, and the Turks only plundered the Greeks, there are persons who think that the Turks are naturally more sincere: and because women, as is often said, care nothing about politics except their personalities, it is supposed that the general good is naturally less interesting to women than to men. History, which is now so much better understood than formerly, teaches another lesson: if only by showing the extraordinary susceptibility of human nature to external influences, and the extreme variableness of those of its manifestations which are supposed to be most universal and uniform. But in history, as in travelling, men usually see only what they already had in their own minds; and few learn much from history, who do not bring much with them to its study.

Hence, in regard to that most difficult question, what are the natural differences between the two sexes—a subject on which it is impossible in the present state of society to obtain complete and correct knowledge—while almost everybody dogmatizes upon it, almost all neglect and make light of the only means by which any partial insight can be obtained into it. This is, an analytic study of the most important department of psychology, the laws of the influence of circumstances on character. For, however great and apparently ineradicable the moral and intellectual differences between men and women might be, the evidence of their being natural differences could only be negative. Those only could be inferred to be natural which could not possibly be artificial—the residuum, after deducting every characteristic of either sex which can admit of being explained from education or external circumstances. The profoundest knowledge of the laws of the formation of character is indispensable to entitle any one to affirm even that there is any difference, much more what the difference is, between the two sexes considered as moral and rational beings; and since no one, as yet, has that knowledge, (for there is hardly any subject which, in proportion to

4. An Irish tenant farmer subjected to cultivating a piece of land for a proprietor and receiving a portion of the produce, a practice similar to *métayage* in France and *mezzadria* in Italy. In *Principles of Political Economy* (3rd ed., 1852) Mill dedicated several chapters to an attack on the "wretched cottier system," according to which "[i]f the landlord at any time exerted his full legal rights, the cottier would not be able even to live" (*CW*, vol. 2, pp. 183 and 326).

its importance, has been so little studied), no one is thus far entitled to any positive opinion on the subject. Conjectures are all that
can at present be made; conjectures more or less probable, according as more or less authorized by such knowledge as we yet have of
the laws of psychology, as applied to the formation of character.

Even the preliminary knowledge, what the differences between
the sexes now are, apart from all question as to how they are made
what they are, is still in the crudest and most incomplete state.
Medical practitioners and physiologists have ascertained, to some
extent, the differences in bodily constitution; and this is an important element to the psychologist: but hardly any medical practitioner is a psychologist. Respecting the mental characteristics of
women, their observations are of no more worth than those of common men. It is a subject on which nothing final can be known, so
long as those who alone can really know it, women themselves, have
given but little testimony, and that little, mostly suborned. It is easy
to know stupid women. Stupidity is much the same all the world
over. A stupid person's notions and feelings may confidently be
inferred from those which prevail in the circle by which the person
is surrounded. Not so with those whose opinions and feelings are
an emanation from their own nature and faculties. It is only a man
here and there who has any tolerable knowledge of the character
even of the women of his own family. I do not mean, of their capabilities; these nobody knows, not even themselves, because most of
them have never been called out. I mean their actually existing
thoughts and feelings. Many a man thinks he perfectly understands
women, because he has had amatory relations with several, perhaps
with many of them. If he is a good observer, and his experience
extends to quality as well as quantity, he may have learnt something
of one narrow department of their nature—an important department, no doubt. But of all the rest of it, few persons are generally
more ignorant, because there are few from whom it is so carefully
hidden. The most favourable case which a man can generally have
for studying the character of a woman, is that of his own wife: for
the opportunities are greater, and the cases of complete sympathy
not so unspeakably rare. And in fact, this is the source from which
any knowledge worth having on the subject has, I believe, generally
come. But most men have not had the opportunity of studying in
this way more than a single case: accordingly one can, to an almost
laughable degree, infer what a man's wife is like, from his opinions
about women in general. To make even this one case yield any result,
the woman must be worth knowing, and the man not only a competent judge, but of a character so sympathetic in itself, and so well
adapted to hers, that he can either read her mind by sympathetic
intuition, or has nothing in himself which makes her shy of

disclosing it. Hardly anything, I believe, can be more rare than this conjunction. It often happens that there is the most complete unity of feeling and community of interests as to all external things, yet the one has as little admission into the internal life of the other as if they were common acquaintance. Even with true affection, authority on the one side and subordination on the other prevent perfect confidence. Though nothing may be intentionally withheld, much is not shown. In the analogous relation of parent and child, the corresponding phenomenon must have been in the observation of every one. As between father and son, how many are the cases in which the father, in spite of real affection on both sides, obviously to all the world does not know, nor suspect, parts of the son's character familiar to his companions and equals. The truth is, that the position of looking up to another is extremely unpropitious to complete sincerity and openness with him. The fear of losing ground in his opinion or in his feelings is so strong, that even in an upright character, there is an unconscious tendency to show only the best side, or the side which, though not the best, is that which he most likes to see: and it may be confidently said that thorough knowledge of one another hardly ever exists, but between persons who, besides being intimates, are equals. How much more true, then, must all this be, when the one is not only under the authority of the other, but has it inculcated on her as a duty to reckon everything else subordinate to his comfort and pleasure, and to let him neither see nor feel anything coming from her, except what is agreeable to him. All these difficulties stand in the way of a man's obtaining any thorough knowledge even of the one woman whom alone, in general, he has sufficient opportunity of studying. When we further consider that to understand one woman is not necessarily to understand any other woman; that even if he could study many women of one rank, or of one country, he would not thereby understand women of other ranks or countries; and even if he did, they are still only the women of a single period of history; we may safely assert that the knowledge which men can acquire of women, even as they have been and are, without reference to what they might be, is wretchedly imperfect and superficial, and always will be so, until women themselves have told all that they have to tell.

And this time has not come; nor will it come otherwise than gradually. It is but of yesterday that women have either been qualified by literary accomplishments, or permitted by society, to tell anything to the general public. As yet very few of them dare tell anything, which men, on whom their literary success depends, are unwilling to hear. Let us remember in what manner, up to a very recent time, the expression, even by a male author, of uncustomary opinions, or what are deemed eccentric feelings, usually was, and in some degree still is, received; and we may form some faint conception under what impediments a woman, who is brought up to think custom and opinion her sovereign rule, attempts to express in books anything drawn from the depths of her own nature. The greatest woman who has left writings behind her sufficient to give her an eminent rank in the literature of her country, thought it necessary to prefix as a motto to her boldest work, "Un homme peut braver l'opinion; une femme doit s'y soumettre."[5] The greater part of what women write about women is mere sycophancy to men. In the case of unmarried women, much of it seems only intended to increase their chance of a husband. Many, both married and unmarried, overstep the mark, and inculcate a servility beyond what is desired or relished by any man, except the very vulgarest. But this is not so often the case as, even at a quite late period, it still was. Literary women are becoming more freespoken, and more willing to express their real sentiments. Unfortunately, in this country especially, they are themselves such artificial products, that their sentiments are compounded of a small element of individual observation and consciousness, and a very large one of acquired associations. This will be less and less the case, but it will remain true to a great extent, as long as social institutions do not admit the same free development of originality in women which is possible to men. When that time comes, and not before, we shall see, and not merely hear, as much as it is necessary to know of the nature of women, and the adaptation of other things to it.

I have dwelt so much on the difficulties which at present obstruct any real knowledge by men of the true nature of women, because in this as in so many other things "opinio copiæ inter maximas causas inopiæ est;"[6] and there is little chance of reasonable thinking on the matter, while people flatter themselves that they perfectly understand a subject of which most men know absolutely nothing, and of which it is at present impossible that any man, or all men taken together, should have knowledge which can qualify them to lay down the law to women as to what is, or is not, their vocation. Happily, no such knowledge is necessary for any practical purpose connected with the position of women in relation to society and life. For, according to all the principles involved in modern society, the question rests with women themselves—to be decided by their own experience, and by the use of their own faculties. There are no means of finding what either one person or many can do, but by trying—and

---

5. Title-page of Mme. de Stael's "Delphine" [*Mill's note*]. ["A man can defy public opinion, but a woman must subject herself to it" (French)—*Editor's note*.]
6. "Thinking one is wealthy is among the chief causes of poverty" (Latin); from Francis Bacon, *Novum Organum,* Pars II ("The Great Instauration"), published in 1620.

no means by which any one else can discover for them what it is for their happiness to do or leave undone.

One thing we may be certain of—that what is contrary to women's nature to do, they never will be made to do by simply giving their nature free play. The anxiety of mankind to interfere in behalf of nature, for fear lest nature should not succeed in effecting its purpose, is an altogether unnecessary solicitude. What women by nature cannot do, it is quite superfluous to forbid them from doing. What they can do, but not so well as the men who are their competitors, competition suffices to exclude them from; since nobody asks for protective duties and bounties in favour of women; it is only asked that the present bounties and protective duties in favour of men should be recalled. If women have a greater natural inclination for some things than for others, there is no need of laws or social inculcation to make the majority of them do the former in preference to the latter. Whatever women's services are most wanted for, the free play of competition will hold out the strongest inducements to them to undertake. And, as the words imply, they are most wanted for the things for which they are most fit; by the apportionment of which to them, the collective faculties of the two sexes can be applied on the whole with the greatest sum of valuable result.

The general opinion of men is supposed to be, that the natural vocation of a woman is that of a wife and mother. I say, is supposed to be, because, judging from acts—from the whole of the present constitution of society—one might infer that their opinion was the direct contrary. They might be supposed to think that the alleged natural vocation of women was of all things the most repugnant to their nature; insomuch that if they are free to do anything else—if any other means of living, or occupation of their time and faculties, is open, which has any chance of appearing desirable to them—there will not be enough of them who will be willing to accept the condition said to be natural to them. If this is the real opinion of men in general, it would be well that it should be spoken out. I should like to hear somebody openly enunciating the doctrine (it is already implied in much that is written on the subject)—"It is necessary to society that women should marry and produce children. They will not do so unless they are compelled. Therefore it is necessary to compel them." The merits of the case would then be clearly defined. It would be exactly that of the slaveholders of South Carolina and Louisiana. "It is necessary that cotton and sugar should be grown. White men cannot produce them. Negroes will not, for any wages which we choose to give. *Ergo* they must be compelled." An illustration still closer to the point is that of impressment. Sailors must absolutely be had to defend the country. It often happens that they will not voluntarily enlist. Therefore there must be the power of forcing them. How often has this logic been used! and, but for one flaw in it, without doubt it would have been successful up to this day. But it is open to the retort—First pay the sailors the honest value of their labour. When you have made it as well worth their while to serve you, as to work for other employers, you will have no more difficulty than others have in obtaining their services. To this there is no logical answer except "I will not:" and as people are now not only ashamed, but are not desirous, to rob the labourer of his hire, impressment is no longer advocated. Those who attempt to force women into marriage by closing all other doors against them, lay themselves open to a similar retort. If they mean what they say, their opinion must evidently be, that men do not render the married condition so desirable to women, as to induce them to accept it for its own recommendations. It is not a sign of one's thinking the boon one offers very attractive, when one allows only Hobson's choice,[7] "that or none." And here, I believe, is the clue to the feelings of those men, who have a real antipathy to the equal freedom of women. I believe they are afraid, not lest women should be unwilling to marry, for I do not think that any one in reality has that apprehension; but lest they should insist that marriage should be on equal conditions; lest all women of spirit and capacity should prefer doing almost anything else, not in their own eyes degrading, rather than marry, when marrying is giving themselves a master, and a master too of all their earthly possessions. And truly, if this consequence were necessarily incident to marriage, I think that the apprehension would be very well founded. I agree in thinking it probable that few women, capable of anything else, would, unless under an irresistible *entrainement*,[8] rendering them for the time insensible to anything but itself, choose such a lot, when any other means were open to them of filling a conventionally honourable place in life: and if men are determined that the law of marriage shall be a law of despotism, they are quite right, in point of mere policy, in leaving to women only Hobson's choice. But, in that case, all that has been done in the modern world to relax the chain on the minds of women, has been a mistake. They never should have been allowed to receive a literary education. Women who read, much more women who write, are, in the existing constitution of things, a contradiction and a disturbing element: and it was wrong

---

7. Meaning "taking it or leave it." According to tradition, the expression originated with Thomas Hobson (1544–1631), a livery stable owner in Cambridge, England, who offered customers no other choice but either taking the horse in his stall nearest to the door or taking none at all. This was to prevent the best horses from always being chosen, which would have caused those horses to become overused.
8. Allurement (French).

to bring women up with any acquirements but those of an odalisque,[9] or of a domestic servant.

CHAPTER II

It will be well to commence the detailed discussion of the subject by the particular branch of it to which the course of our observations has led us: the conditions which the laws of this and all other countries annex to the marriage contract. Marriage being the destination appointed by society for women, the prospect they are brought up to, and the object which it is intended should be sought by all of them, except those who are too little attractive to be chosen by any man as his companion; one might have supposed that everything would have been done to make this condition as eligible to them as possible, that they might have no cause to regret being denied the option of any other. Society, however, both in this, and, at first, in all other cases, has preferred to attain its object by foul rather than fair means: but this is the only case in which it has substantially persisted in them even to the present day. Originally women were taken by force, or regularly sold by their father to the husband. Until a late period in European history, the father had the power to dispose of his daughter in marriage at his own will and pleasure, without any regard to hers. The Church, indeed, was so far faithful to a better morality as to require a formal "yes" from the woman at the marriage ceremony; but there was nothing to shew that the consent was other than compulsory; and it was practically impossible for the girl to refuse compliance if the father persevered, except perhaps when she might obtain the protection of religion by a determined resolution to take monastic vows. After marriage, the man had anciently (but this was anterior to Christianity) the power of life and death over his wife. She could invoke no law against him; he was her sole tribunal and law. For a long time he could repudiate her, but she had no corresponding power in regard to him. By the old laws of England, the husband was called the *lord* of the wife; he was literally regarded as her sovereign, inasmuch that the murder of a man by his wife was called treason (*petty* as distinguished from *high* treason), and was more cruelly avenged than was usually the case with high treason, for the penalty was burning to death. Because these various enormities have fallen into disuse (for most of them were never formally abolished, or not until they had long ceased to be practised) men suppose that all is now as

---

9. Either a sexual object ("odalisque" meaning a sexual slave or concubine in a harem) or a servant.

it should be in regard to the marriage contract; and we are continually told that civilization and Christianity have restored to the
woman her just rights. Meanwhile the wife is the actual bond-
servant of her husband: no less so, as far as legal obligation goes,
than slaves commonly so called. She vows a lifelong obedience to
him at the altar, and is held to it all through her life by law. Casu-
ists may say that the obligation of obedience stops short of participation in crime, but it certainly extends to everything else. She can
do no act whatever but by his permission, at least tacit. She can
acquire no property but for him; the instant it becomes hers, even if
by inheritance, it becomes *ipso facto*[1] his. In this respect the wife's
position under the common law of England is worse than that of
slaves in the laws of many countries: by the Roman law, for example, a slave might have his peculium, which to a certain extent the
law guaranteed to him for his exclusive use. The higher classes in
this country have given an analogous advantage to their women,
through special contracts setting aside the law, by conditions of
pin-money, &c.: since parental feeling being stronger with fathers
than the class feeling of their own sex, a father generally prefers his
own daughter to a son-in-law who is a stranger to him. By means of
settlements, the rich usually contrive to withdraw the whole or part
of the inherited property of the wife from the absolute control of
the husband: but they do not succeed in keeping it under her own
control; the utmost they can do only prevents the husband from
squandering it, at the same time debarring the rightful owner
from its use. The property itself is out of the reach of both; and as
to the income derived from it, the form of settlement most favourable to the wife (that called "to her separate use") only precludes
the husband from receiving it instead of her: it must pass through
her hands, but if he takes it from her by personal violence as soon
as she receives it, he can neither be punished, nor compelled to
restitution. This is the amount of the protection which, under the
laws of this country, the most powerful nobleman can give to his
own daughter as respects her husband. In the immense majority of
cases there is no settlement: and the absorption of all rights, all
property, as well as all freedom of action, is complete. The two are
called "one person in law," for the purpose of inferring that whatever is hers is his, but the parallel inference is never drawn that
whatever is his is hers; the maxim is not applied against the man,
except to make him responsible to third parties for her acts, as a
master is for the acts of his slaves or of his cattle. I am far from
pretending that wives are in general no better treated than slaves;
but no slave is a slave to the same lengths, and in so full a sense of

1. By the fact itself (Latin).

the word, as a wife is. Hardly any slave, except one immediately attached to the master's person, is a slave at all hours and all minutes; in general he has, like a soldier, his fixed task, and when it is done, or when he is off duty, he disposes, within certain limits, of his own time, and has a family life into which the master rarely intrudes. "Uncle Tom" under his first master had his own life in his "cabin,"[2] almost as much as any man whose work takes him away from home, is able to have in his own family. But it cannot be so with the wife. Above all, a female slave has (in Christian countries) an admitted right, and is considered under a moral obligation, to refuse to her master the last familiarity. Not so the wife: however brutal a tyrant she may unfortunately be chained to—though she may know that he hates her, though it may be his daily pleasure to torture her, and though she may feel it impossible not to loathe him—he can claim from her and enforce the lowest degradation of a human being, that of being made the instrument of an animal function contrary to her inclinations. While she is held in this worst description of slavery as to her own person, what is her position in regard to the children in whom she and her master have a joint interest? They are by law *his* children. He alone has any legal rights over them. Not one act can she do towards or in relation to them, except by delegation from him. Even after he is dead she is not their legal guardian, unless he by will has made her so. He could even send them away from her, and deprive her of the means of seeing or corresponding with them, until this power was in some degree restricted by Serjeant Talfourd's Act.[3] This is her legal state. And from this state she has no means of withdrawing herself. If she leaves her husband, she can take nothing with her, neither her children nor anything which is rightfully her own. If he chooses, he can compel her to return, by law, or by physical force; or he may content himself with seizing for his own use anything which she may earn, or which may be given to her by her relations. It is only legal separation by a decree of a court of justice, which entitles her to live apart, without being forced back into the custody of an exasperated jailer—or which empowers her to apply any earnings to her own use, without fear that a man whom perhaps she has not seen for twenty years will pounce upon her some day and carry all off. This legal separation, until lately, the courts of justice would only give at an expense which made it inaccessible to any one out of the higher ranks. Even now it is only given in cases of desertion, or of the extreme of cruelty; and yet complaints are made every day that it is granted too easily. Surely,

---

2. Reference to Harriet Beecher Stowe's *Uncle Tom's Cabin* (1852).
3. The emendation of the law regulating the custody of infants (1839), from Sir Thomas Noon Talfourd (1795–1854), an English judge and radical politician.

if a woman is denied any lot in life but that of being the personal body-servant of a despot, and is dependent for everything upon the chance of finding one who may be disposed to make a favourite of her instead of merely a drudge, it is a very cruel aggravation of her fate that she should be allowed to try this chance only once. The natural sequel and corollary from this state of things would be, that since her all in life depends upon obtaining a good master, she should be allowed to change again and again until she finds one. I am not saying that she ought to be allowed this privilege. That is a totally different consideration. The question of divorce, in the sense involving liberty of remarriage, is one into which it is foreign to my purpose to enter. All I now say is, that to those to whom nothing but servitude is allowed, the free choice of servitude is the only, though a most insufficient, alleviation. Its refusal completes the assimilation of the wife to the slave—and the slave under not the mildest form of slavery: for in some slave codes the slave could, under certain circumstances of ill usage, legally compel the master to sell him. But no amount of ill usage, without adultery superadded, will in England free a wife from her tormentor.

I have no desire to exaggerate, nor does the case stand in any need of exaggeration. I have described the wife's legal position, not her actual treatment. The laws of most countries are far worse than the people who execute them, and many of them are only able to remain laws by being seldom or never carried into effect. If married life were all that it might be expected to be, looking to the laws alone, society would be a hell upon earth. Happily there are both feelings and interests which in many men exclude, and in most, greatly temper, the impulses and propensities which lead to tyranny: and of those feelings, the tie which connects a man with his wife affords, in a normal state of things, incomparably the strongest example. The only tie which at all approaches to it, that between him and his children, tends, in all save exceptional cases, to strengthen, instead of conflicting with, the first. Because this is true; because men in general do not inflict, nor women suffer, all the misery which could be inflicted and suffered if the full power of tyranny with which the man is legally invested were acted on; the defenders of the existing form of the institution think that all its iniquity is justified, and that any complaint is merely quarrelling with the evil which is the price paid for every great good. But the mitigations in practice, which are compatible with maintaining in full legal force this or any other kind of tyranny, instead of being any apology for despotism, only serve to prove what power human nature possesses of reacting against the vilest institutions, and with what vitality the seeds of good as well as those of evil in human character diffuse and propagate themselves. Not a word can be said for despotism in the family which

cannot be said for political despotism. Every absolute king does not
sit at his window to enjoy the groans of his tortured subjects, nor
strips them of their last rag and turns them out to shiver in the road.
The despotism of Louis XVI. was not the despotism of Philippe le
Bel, or of Nadir Shah, or of Caligula;[4] but it was bad enough to justify the French Revolution, and to palliate even its horrors. If an
appeal be made to the intense attachments which exist between
wives and their husbands, exactly as much may be said of domestic
slavery. It was quite an ordinary fact in Greece and Rome for slaves
to submit to death by torture rather than betray their masters. In
the proscriptions of the Roman civil wars it was remarked that wives
and slaves were heroically faithful, sons very commonly treacherous.
Yet we know how cruelly many Romans treated their slaves. But in
truth these intense individual feelings nowhere rise to such a luxu-
riant height as under the most atrocious institutions. It is part of
the irony of life, that the strongest feelings of devoted gratitude of
which human nature seems to be susceptible, are called forth in
human beings towards those who, having the power entirely to crush
their earthly existence, voluntarily refrain from using that power.
How great a place in most men this sentiment fills, even in religious
devotion, it would be cruel to inquire. We daily see how much their
gratitude to Heaven appears to be stimulated by the contemplation
of fellow-creatures to whom God has not been so merciful as he has
to themselves.

Whether the institution to be defended is slavery, political absolutism, or the absolutism of the head of a family, we are always
expected to judge of it from its best instances; and we are presented
with pictures of loving exercise of authority on one side, loving submission to it on the other—superior wisdom ordering all things for
the greatest good of the dependents, and surrounded by their smiles
and benedictions. All this would be very much to the purpose if any
one pretended that there are no such things as good men. Who
doubts that there may be great goodness, and great happiness, and
great affection, under the absolute government of a good man?
Meanwhile, laws and institutions require to be adapted, not to good
men, but to bad. Marriage is not an institution designed for a select
few. Men are not required, as a preliminary to the marriage ceremony, to prove by testimonials that they are fit to be trusted with
the exercise of absolute power. The tie of affection and obligation

4. Caligula (r. 37–41 C.E.) was one of the cruelest Roman emperors; murdered by the soldiers who elevated him, he became the epitome of tyranny. *Louis XVI*: (b. 1754) the last
absolute king of France before the French Revolution (1789), who was guillotined (along
with his wife, Marie Antoinette [b. 1755]) in 1793. *Philippe le Bel*: (1268–1314), famous
for being handsome (*le Bel* means "The Beautiful") and autocratic (he was also known as
the Iron King). *Nadir Shah Afshar* (1688–1747), the founder of the Afsharid dynasty of
Iran, who ruled until he was assassinated during a rebellion.

to a wife and children is very strong with those whose general social feelings are strong, and with many who are little sensible to any other social ties; but there are all degrees of sensibility and insensibility to it, as there are all grades of goodness and wickedness in men, down to those whom no ties will bind, and on whom society has no action but through its *ultima ratio*, the penalties of the law. In every grade of this descending scale are men to whom are committed all the legal powers of a husband. The vilest malefactor has some wretched woman tied to him, against whom he can commit any atrocity except killing her, and, if tolerably cautious, can do that without much danger of the legal penalty. And how many thousands are there among the lowest classes in every country, who, without being in a legal sense malefactors in any other respect, because in every other quarter their aggressions meet with resistance, indulge the utmost habitual excesses of bodily violence towards the unhappy wife, who alone, at least of grown persons, can neither repel nor escape from their brutality; and towards whom the excess of dependence inspires their mean and savage natures, not with a generous forbearance, and a point of honour to behave well to one whose lot in life is trusted entirely to their kindness, but on the contrary with a notion that the law has delivered her to them as their thing, to be used at their pleasure, and that they are not expected to practise the consideration towards her which is required from them towards everybody else. The law, which till lately left even these atrocious extremes of domestic oppression practically unpunished, has within these few years made some feeble attempts to repress them. But its attempts have done little, and cannot be expected to do much, because it is contrary to reason and experience to suppose that there can be any real check to brutality, consistent with leaving the victim still in the power of the executioner. Until a conviction for personal violence, or at all events a repetition of it after a first conviction, entitles the woman *ipso facto* to a divorce, or at least to a judicial separation, the attempt to repress these "aggravated assaults" by legal penalties will break down for want of a prosecutor, or for want of a witness.

When we consider how vast is the number of men, in any great country, who are little higher than brutes, and that this never prevents them from being able, through the law of marriage, to obtain a victim, the breadth and depth of human misery caused in this shape alone by the abuse of the institution swells to something appalling. Yet these are only the extreme cases. They are the lowest abysses, but there is a sad succession of depth after depth before reaching them. In domestic as in political tyranny, the case of absolute monsters chiefly illustrates the institution by showing that there is scarcely any horror which may not occur under it if the despot pleases, and thus setting in a strong light what must be the terrible frequency of things only a little less atrocious. Absolute fiends are as rare as angels, perhaps rarer: ferocious savages, with occasional touches of humanity, are however very frequent: and in the wide interval which separates these from any worthy representatives of the human species, how many are the forms and gradations of animalism and selfishness, often under an outward varnish of civilization and even cultivation, living at peace with the law, maintaining a creditable appearance to all who are not under their power, yet sufficient often to make the lives of all who are so, a torment and a burthen to them! It would be tiresome to repeat the commonplaces about the unfitness of men in general for power, which, after the political discussions of centuries, every one knows by heart, were it not that hardly any one thinks of applying these maxims to the case in which above all others they are applicable, that of power, not placed in the hands of a man here and there, but offered to every adult male, down to the basest and most ferocious. It is not because a man is not known to have broken any of the Ten Commandments, or because he maintains a respectable character in his dealings with those whom he cannot compel to have intercourse with him, or because he does not fly out into violent bursts of ill-temper against those who are not obliged to bear with him, that it is possible to surmise of what sort his conduct will be in the unrestraint of home. Even the commonest men reserve the violent, the sulky, the undisguisedly selfish side of their character for those who have no power to withstand it. The relation of superiors to dependents is the nursery of these vices of character, which, wherever else they exist, are an overflowing from that source. A man who is morose or violent to his equals, is sure to be one who has lived among inferiors, whom he could frighten or worry into submission. If the family in its best forms is, as it is often said to be, a school of sympathy, tenderness, and loving forgetfulness of self, it is still oftener, as respects its chief, a school of wilfulness, overbearingness, unbounded self-indulgence, and a double-dyed and idealized selfishness, of which sacrifice itself is only a particular form: the care for the wife and children being only care for them as parts of the man's own interests and belongings, and their individual happiness being immolated in every shape to his smallest preferences. What better is to be looked for under the existing form of the institution? We know that the bad propensities of human nature are only kept within bounds when they are allowed no scope for their indulgence. We know that from impulse and habit, when not from deliberate purpose, almost every one to whom others yield, goes on encroaching upon them, until a point is reached at which they are compelled to resist. Such being the common tendency of human nature; the almost unlimited power which present social institutions give to the man over at least one human being—the one with whom he resides, and whom he has always present—this power seeks out and evokes the latent germs of selfishness in the remotest corners of his nature—fans its faintest sparks and smouldering embers—offers to him a license for the indulgence of those points of his original character which in all other relations he would have found it necessary to repress and conceal, and the repression of which would in time have become a second nature. I know that there is another side to the question. I grant that the wife, if she cannot effectually resist, can at least retaliate; she, too, can make the man's life extremely uncomfortable, and by that power is able to carry many points which she ought, and many which she ought not, to prevail in. But this instrument of self-protection—which may be called the power of the scold, or the shrewish sanction—has the fatal defect, that it avails most against the least tyrannical superiors, and in favour of the least deserving dependents. It is the weapon of irritable and self-willed women; of those who would make the worst use of power if they themselves had it, and who generally turn this power to a bad use. The amiable cannot use such an instrument, the highminded disdain it. And on the other hand, the husbands against whom it is used most effectively are the gentler and more inoffensive; those who cannot be induced, even by provocation, to resort to any very harsh exercise of authority. The wife's power of being disagreeable generally only establishes a counter-tyranny, and makes victims in their turn chiefly of those husbands who are least inclined to be tyrants.

What is it, then, which really tempers the corrupting effects of the power, and makes it compatible with such amount of good as we actually see? Mere feminine blandishments, though of great effect in individual instances, have very little effect in modifying the general tendencies of the situation; for their power only lasts while the woman is young and attractive, often only while her charm is new, and not dimmed by familiarity; and on many men they have not much influence at any time. The real mitigating causes are, the personal affection which is the growth of time, in so far as the man's nature is susceptible of it, and the woman's character sufficiently congenial with his to excite it; their common interests as regards the children, and their general community of interest as concerns third persons (to which however there are very great limitations); the real importance of the wife to his daily comforts and enjoyments, and the value he consequently attaches to her on his personal account, which, in a man capable of feeling for others, lays the foundation of caring for her on her own; and lastly, the influence naturally acquired over almost all human beings by those near to their persons (if not actually disagreeable to them): who, both by their direct entreaties, and by the insensible contagion of their feelings and dispositions, are often able, unless counteracted by some equally strong personal influence, to obtain a degree of command over the conduct of the superior, altogether excessive and unreasonable. Through these various means, the wife frequently exercises even too much power over the man; she is able to affect his conduct in things in which she may not be qualified to influence it for good—in which her influence may be not only unenlightened, but employed on the morally wrong side; and in which he would act better if left to his own prompting. But neither in the affairs of families nor in those of states is power a compensation for the loss of freedom. Her power often gives her what she has no right to, but does not enable her to assert her own rights. A Sultan's favourite slave has slaves under her, over whom she tyrannizes; but the desirable thing would be that she should neither have slaves nor be a slave. By entirely sinking her own existence in her husband; by having no will (or persuading him that she has no will) but his, in anything which regards their joint relation, and by making it the business of her life to work upon his sentiments, a wife may gratify herself by influencing, and very probably perverting, his conduct, in those of his external relations which she has never qualified herself to judge of, or in which she is herself wholly influenced by some personal or other partiality or prejudice. Accordingly, as things now are, those who act most kindly to their wives, are quite as often made worse, as better, by the wife's influence, in respect to all interests extending beyond the family. She is taught that she has no business with things out of that sphere; and accordingly she seldom has any honest and conscientious opinion on them; and therefore hardly ever meddles with them for any legitimate purpose, but generally for an interested one. She neither knows nor cares which is the right side in politics, but she knows what will bring in money or invitations, give her husband a title, her son a place, or her daughter a good marriage.

But how, it will be asked, can any society exist without government? In a family, as in a state, some one person must be the ultimate ruler. Who shall decide when married people differ in opinion? Both cannot have their way, yet a decision one way or the other must be come to.

It is not true that in all voluntary association between two people, one of them must be absolute master: still less that the law must determine which of them it shall be. The most frequent case of voluntary association, next to marriage, is partnership in business: and it is not found or thought necessary to enact that in every partnership, one partner shall have entire control over the concern, and the others shall be bound to obey his orders. No one would enter into partnership on terms which would subject him to the responsibilities of a principal, with only the powers and privileges of a clerk or agent. If the law dealt with other contracts as it does with marriage, it would ordain that one partner should administer the common business as if it was his private concern; that the others should have only delegated powers; and that this one should be designated by some general presumption of law, for example as being the eldest. The law never does this: nor does experience show it to be necessary that any theoretical inequality of power should exist between the partners, or that the partnership should have any other conditions than what they may themselves appoint by their articles of agreement. Yet it might seem that the exclusive power might be conceded with less danger to the rights and interests of the inferior, in the case of partnership than in that of marriage, since he is free to cancel the power by withdrawing from the connexion. The wife has no such power, and even if she had, it is almost always desirable that she should try all measures before resorting to it.

It is quite true that things which have to be decided every day, and cannot adjust themselves gradually, or wait for a compromise, ought to depend on one will: one person must have their sole control. But it does not follow that this should always be the same person. The natural arrangement is a division of powers between the two; each being absolute in the executive branch of their own department, and any change of system and principle requiring the consent of both. The division neither can nor should be pre-established by the law, since it must depend on individual capacities and suitabilities. If the two persons chose, they might pre-appoint it by the marriage contract, as pecuniary arrangements are now often pre-appointed. There would seldom be any difficulty in deciding such things by mutual consent, unless the marriage was one of those unhappy ones in which all other things, as well as this, become subjects of bickering and dispute. The division of rights would naturally follow the division of duties and functions; and that is already made by consent, or at all events not by law, but by general custom, modified and modifiable at the pleasure of the persons concerned.

The real practical decision of affairs, to whichever may be given the legal authority, will greatly depend, as it even now does, upon comparative qualifications. The mere fact that he is usually the eldest, will in most cases give the preponderance to the man; at least until they both attain a time of life at which the difference in their years is of no importance. There will naturally also be a more potential voice on the side, whichever it is, that brings the means of support. Inequality from this source does not depend on the law of marriage, but on the general conditions of human society, as

now constituted. The influence of mental superiority, either general or special, and of superior decision of character, will necessarily tell for much. It always does so at present. And this fact shows
how little foundation there is for the apprehension that the powers
and responsibilities of partners in life (as of partners in business),
cannot be satisfactorily apportioned by agreement between themselves. They always are so apportioned, except in cases in which
the marriage institution is a failure. Things never come to an issue
of downright power on one side, and obedience on the other, except
where the connexion altogether has been a mistake, and it would be
a blessing to both parties to be relieved from it. Some may say that
the very thing by which an amicable settlement of differences
becomes possible, is the power of legal compulsion known to be in
reserve; as people submit to an arbitration because there is a court of
law in the background, which they know that they can be forced to
obey. But to make the cases parallel, we must suppose that the rule
of the court of law was, not to try the cause, but to give judgment
always for the same side, suppose the defendant. If so, the amena-
bility to it would be a motive with the plaintiff to agree to almost
any arbitration, but it would be just the reverse with the defendant.
The despotic power which the law gives to the husband may be a
reason to make the wife assent to any compromise by which power
is practically shared between the two, but it cannot be the reason
why the husband does. That there is always among decently conducted people a practical compromise, though one of them at least
is under no physical or moral necessity of making it, shows that
the natural motives which lead to a voluntary adjustment of the
united life of two persons in a manner acceptable to both, do on the
whole, except in unfavourable cases, prevail. The matter is certainly
not improved by laying down as an ordinance of law, that the superstructure of free government shall be raised upon a legal basis of
despotism on one side and subjection on the other, and that every
concession which the despot makes may, at his mere pleasure, and
without any warning, be recalled. Besides that no freedom is worth
much when held on so precarious a tenure, its conditions are not
likely to be the most equitable when the law throws so prodigious a
weight into one scale; when the adjustment rests between two persons one of whom is declared to be entitled to everything, the other
not only entitled to nothing except during the good pleasure of the
first, but under the strongest moral and religious obligation not to
rebel under any excess of oppression.

A pertinacious adversary, pushed to extremities, may say, that
husbands indeed are willing to be reasonable, and to make fair concessions to their partners without being compelled to it, but that
wives are not: that if allowed any rights of their own, they will

acknowledge no rights at all in any one else, and never will yield in anything, unless they can be compelled, by the man's mere authority, to yield in everything. This would have been said by many persons some generations ago, when satires on women were in vogue, and men thought it a clever thing to insult women for being what men made them. But it will be said by no one now who is worth replying to. It is not the doctrine of the present day that women are less susceptible of good feeling, and consideration for those with whom they are united by the strongest ties, than men are. On the contrary, we are perpetually told that women are better than men, by those who are totally opposed to treating them as if they were as good; so that the saying has passed into a piece of tiresome cant, intended to put a complimentary face upon an injury, and resembling those celebrations of royal clemency which, according to Gulliver, the king of Lilliput always prefixed to his most sanguinary decrees.[5] If women are better than men in anything, it surely is in individual self-sacrifice for those of their own family. But I lay little stress on this, so long as they are universally taught that they are born and created for self-sacrifice. I believe that equality of rights would abate the exaggerated self-abnegation which is the present artificial ideal of feminine character, and that a good woman would not be more self-sacrificing than the best man: but on the other hand, men would be much more unselfish and self-sacrificing than at present, because they would no longer be taught to worship their own will as such a grand thing that it is actually the law for another rational being. There is nothing which men so easily learn as this self-worship: all privileged persons, and all privileged classes, have had it. The more we descend in the scale of humanity, the intenser it is; and most of all in those who are not, and can never expect to be, raised above any one except an unfortunate wife and children. The honourable exceptions are proportionally fewer than in the case of almost any other human infirmity. Philosophy and religion, instead of keeping it in check, are generally suborned to defend it; and nothing controls it but that practical feeling of the equality of human beings, which is the theory of Christianity, but which Christianity will never practically teach, while it sanctions institutions grounded on an arbitrary preference of one human being over another.

There are, no doubt, women, as there are men, whom equality of consideration will not satisfy; with whom there is no peace while any will or wish is regarded but their own. Such persons are a proper subject for the law of divorce. They are only fit to live alone, and no human beings ought to be compelled to associate their lives with

5. Reference to Jonathan Swift's *Gulliver's Travels* (1726).

them. But the legal subordination tends to make such characters among women more, rather than less, frequent. If the man exerts his whole power, the woman is of course crushed: but if she is treated with indulgence, and permitted to assume power, there is no rule to set limits to her encroachments. The law, not determining her rights, but theoretically allowing her none at all, practically declares that the measure of what she has a right to, is what she can contrive to get.

The equality of married persons before the law, is not only the sole mode in which that particular relation can be made consistent with justice to both sides, and conducive to the happiness of both, but it is the only means of rendering the daily life of mankind, in any high sense, a school of moral cultivation. Though the truth may not be felt or generally acknowledged for generations to come, the only school of genuine moral sentiment is society between equals. The moral education of mankind has hitherto emanated chiefly from the law of force, and is adapted almost solely to the relations which force creates. In the less advanced states of society, people hardly recognise any relation with their equals. To be an equal is to be an enemy. Society, from its highest place to its lowest, is one long chain, or rather ladder, where every individual is either above or below his nearest neighbour, and wherever he does not command he must obey. Existing moralities, accordingly, are mainly fitted to a relation of command and obedience. Yet command and obedience are but unfortunate necessities of human life: society in equality is its normal state. Already in modern life, and more and more as it progressively improves, command and obedience become exceptional facts in life, equal association its general rule. The morality of the first ages rested on the obligation to submit to power; that of the ages next following, on the right of the weak to the forbearance and protection of the strong. How much longer is one form of society and life to content itself with the morality made for another? We have had the morality of submission, and the morality of chivalry and generosity; the time is now come for the morality of justice. Whenever, in former ages, any approach has been made to society in equality, Justice has asserted its claims as the foundation of virtue. It was thus in the free republics of antiquity. But even in the best of these, the equals were limited to the free male citizens; slaves, women, and the unenfranchised residents were under the law of force. The joint influence of Roman civilization and of Christianity obliterated these distinctions, and in theory (if only partially in practice) declared the claims of the human being, as such, to be paramount to those of sex, class, or social position. The barriers which had begun to be levelled were raised again by the northern conquests; and the whole of modern history consists of the slow process by which they have since been wearing away. We are entering into an order of things in which justice will again be the primary virtue; grounded as before on equal, but now also on sympathetic association; having its root no longer in the instinct of equals for self-protection, but in a cultivated sympathy between them; and no one being now left out, but an equal measure being extended to all. It is no novelty that mankind do not distinctly foresee their own changes, and that their sentiments are adapted to past, not to coming ages. To see the futurity of the species has always been the privilege of the intellectual élite, or of those who have learnt from them; to have the feelings of that futurity has been the distinction, and usually the martyrdom, of a still rarer élite. Institutions, books, education, society, all go on training human beings for the old, long after the new has come; much more when it is only coming. But the true virtue of human beings is fitness to live together as equals; claiming nothing for themselves but what they as freely concede to every one else; regarding command of any kind as an exceptional necessity, and in all cases a temporary one; and preferring, whenever possible, the society of those with whom leading and following can be alternate and reciprocal. To these virtues, nothing in life as at present constituted gives cultivation by exercise. The family is a school of despotism, in which the virtues of despotism, but also its vices, are largely nourished. Citizenship, in free countries, is partly a school of society in equality; but citizenship fills only a small place in modern life, and does not come near the daily habits or inmost sentiments. The family, justly constituted, would be the real school of the virtues of freedom. It is sure to be a sufficient one of everything else. It will always be a school of obedience for the children, of command for the parents. What is needed is, that it should be a school of sympathy in equality, of living together in love, without power on one side or obedience on the other. This it ought to be between the parents. It would then be an exercise of those virtues which each requires to fit them for all other association, and a model to the children of the feelings and conduct which their temporary training by means of obedience is designed to render habitual, and therefore natural, to them. The moral training of mankind will never be adapted to the conditions of the life for which all other human progress is a preparation, until they practise in the family the same moral rule which is adapted to the normal constitution of human society. Any sentiment of freedom which can exist in a man whose nearest and dearest intimacies are with those of whom he is absolute master, is not the genuine or Christian love of freedom, but, what the love of freedom generally was in the ancients and in the middle ages—an intense feeling of the dignity and importance of his own personality; making him disdain a yoke for himself, of which he has no abhorrence whatever in the abstract, but which he is abundantly ready to impose on others for his own interest or glorification.

I readily admit (and it is the very foundation of my hopes) that numbers of married people even under the present law, (in the higher classes of England probably a great majority,) live in the spirit of a just law of equality. Laws never would be improved, if there were not numerous persons whose moral sentiments are better than the existing laws. Such persons ought to support the principles here advocated; of which the only object is to make all other married couples similar to what these are now. But persons even of considerable moral worth, unless they are also thinkers, are very ready to believe that laws or practices, the evils of which they have not personally experienced, do not produce any evils, but (if seeming to be generally approved of) probably do good, and that it is wrong to object to them. It would, however, be a great mistake in such married people to suppose, because the legal conditions of the tie which unites them do not occur to their thoughts once in a twelvemonth, and because they live and feel in all respects as if they were legally equals, that the same is the case with all other married couples, wherever the husband is not a notorious ruffian. To suppose this, would be to show equal ignorance of human nature and of fact. The less fit a man is for the possession of power—the less likely to be allowed to exercise it over any person with that person's voluntary consent—the more does he hug himself in the consciousness of the power the law gives him, exact its legal rights to the utmost point which custom (the custom of men like himself) will tolerate, and take pleasure in using the power, merely to enliven the agreeable sense of possessing it. What is more; in the most naturally brutal and morally uneducated part of the lower classes, the legal slavery of the woman, and something in the merely physical subjection to their will as an instrument, causes them to feel a sort of disrespect and contempt towards their own wife which they do not feel towards any other woman, or any other human being, with whom they come in contact; and which makes her seem to them an appropriate subject for any kind of indignity. Let an acute observer of the signs of feeling, who has the requisite opportunities, judge for himself whether this is not the case: and if he finds that it is, let him not wonder at any amount of disgust and indignation that can be felt against institutions which lead naturally to this depraved state of the human mind.

We shall be told, perhaps, that religion imposes the duty of obedience; as every established fact which is too bad to admit of any other defence, is always presented to us as an injunction of religion. The Church, it is very true, enjoins it in her formularies, but it would be difficult to derive any such injunction from Christianity. We are told that St. Paul said, "Wives, obey your husbands:" but he also said, "Slaves, obey your masters."[6] It was not St. Paul's business, nor was it consistent with his object, the propagation of Christianity, to incite any one to rebellion against existing laws. The apostle's acceptance of all social institutions as he found them, is no more to be construed as a disapproval of attempts to improve them at the proper time, than his declaration, "The powers that be are ordained of God," gives his sanction to military despotism, and to that alone, as the Christian form of political government, or commands passive obedience to it. To pretend that Christianity was intended to stereotype existing forms of government and society, and protect them against change, is to reduce it to the level of Islamism or of Brahminism. It is precisely because Christianity has not done this, that it has been the religion of the progressive portion of mankind, and Islamism, Brahminism, &c., have been those of the stationary portions; or rather (for there is no such thing as a really stationary society) of the declining portions. There have been abundance of people, in all ages of Christianity, who tried to make it something of the same kind; to convert us into a sort of Christian Mussulmans, with the Bible for a Koran, prohibiting all improvement: and great has been their power, and many have had to sacrifice their lives in resisting them. But they have been resisted, and the resistance has made us what we are, and will yet make us what we are to be.

After what has been said respecting the obligation of obedience, it is almost superfluous to say anything concerning the more special point included in the general one—a woman's right to her own property; for I need not hope that this treatise can make any impression upon those who need anything to convince them that a woman's inheritance or gains ought to be as much her own after marriage as before. The rule is simple: whatever would be the husband's or wife's if they were not married, should be under their exclusive control during marriage; which need not interfere with the power to tie up property by settlement, in order to preserve it for children. Some people are sentimentally shocked at the idea of a separate interest in money matters, as inconsistent with the ideal fusion of two lives into one. For my own part, I am one of the strongest supporters of community of goods, when resulting from an entire unity of feeling in the owners, which makes all things common between them. But I have no relish for a community of goods resting on the doctrine, that what is mine is yours but what is yours is not mine; and I should prefer to decline entering into such a compact with any one, though I were myself the person to profit by it.

6. St. Paul, *Letter to the Colossians* 3:18: "Wives, submit yourselves unto your husbands, as is fit in the Lord"; 3:22: "Servants, obey your masters according to the flesh."

This particular injustice and oppression to women, which is, to common apprehensions, more obvious than all the rest, admits of remedy without interfering with any other mischiefs: and there can be little doubt that it will be one of the earliest remedied. Already, in many of the new and several of the old States of the American Confederation, provisions have been inserted even in the written Constitutions, securing to women equality of rights in this respect: and thereby improving materially the position, in the marriage relation, of those women at least who have property, by leaving them one instrument of power which they have not signed away; and preventing also the scandalous abuse of the marriage institution, which is perpetrated when a man entraps a girl into marrying him without a settlement, for the sole purpose of getting possession of her money. When the support of the family depends, not on property, but on earnings, the common arrangement, by which the man earns the income and the wife superintends the domestic expenditure, seems to me in general the most suitable division of labour between the two persons. If, in addition to the physical suffering of bearing children, and the whole responsibility of their care and education in early years, the wife undertakes the careful and economical application of the husband's earnings to the general comfort of the family; she takes not only her fair share, but usually the larger share, of the bodily and mental exertion required by their joint existence. If she undertakes any additional portion, it seldom relieves her from this, but only prevents her from performing it properly. The care which she is herself disabled from taking of the children and the household, nobody else takes; those of the children who do not die, grow up as they best can, and the management of the household is likely to be so bad, as even in point of economy to be a great drawback from the value of the wife's earnings. In an otherwise just state of things, it is not, therefore, I think, a desirable custom, that the wife should contribute by her labour to the income of the family. In an unjust state of things, her doing so may be useful to her, by making her of more value in the eyes of the man who is legally her master; but, on the other hand, it enables him still farther to abuse his power, by forcing her to work, and leaving the support of the family to her exertions, while he spends most of his time in drinking and idleness. The *power* of earning is essential to the dignity of a woman, if she has not independent property. But if marriage were an equal contract, not implying the obligation of obedience; if the connexion were no longer enforced to the oppression of those to whom it is purely a mischief, but a separation, on just terms (I do not now speak of a divorce), could be obtained by any woman who was morally entitled to it; and if she would then find all honourable employments as freely open to her as to men; it would not be necessary for her protection, that during marriage she should make this particular use of her faculties. Like a man when he chooses a profession, so, when a woman marries, it may in general be understood that she makes choice of the management of a household, and the bringing up of a family, as the first call upon her exertions, during as many years of her life as may be required for the purpose; and that she renounces, not all other objects and occupations, but all which are not consistent with the requirements of this. The actual exercise, in a habitual or systematic manner, of outdoor occupations, or such as cannot be carried on at home, would by this principle be practically interdicted to the greater number of married women. But the utmost latitude ought to exist for the adaptation of general rules to individual suitabilities; and there ought to be nothing to prevent faculties exceptionally adapted to any other pursuit, from obeying their vocation notwithstanding marriage: due provision being made for supplying otherwise any falling-short which might become inevitable, in her full performance of the ordinary functions of mistress of a family. These things, if once opinion were rightly directed on the subject, might with perfect safety be left to be regulated by opinion, without any interference of law.

CHAPTER III

On the other point which is involved in the just equality of women, their admissibility to all the functions and occupations hitherto retained as the monopoly of the stronger sex, I should anticipate no difficulty in convincing any one who has gone with me on the subject of the equality of women in the family. I believe that their disabilities elsewhere are only clung to in order to maintain their subordination in domestic life; because the generality of the male sex cannot yet tolerate the idea of living with an equal. Were it not for that, I think that almost every one, in the existing state of opinion in politics and political economy, would admit the injustice of excluding half the human race from the greater number of lucrative occupations, and from almost all high social functions; ordaining from their birth either that they are not, and cannot by any possibility become, fit for employments which are legally open to the stupidest and basest of the other sex, or else that however fit they may be, those employments shall be interdicted to them, in order to be preserved for the exclusive benefit of males. In the last two centuries, when (which was seldom the case) any reason beyond the mere existence of the fact was thought to be required to justify the disabilities of women, people seldom assigned as a reason their inferior mental capacity; which, in times when there was a real trial of personal faculties (from which all women were not excluded) in the struggles of public life, no one really believed in. The reason given in those days was not women's unfitness, but the interest of society, by which was meant the interest of men: just as the *raison d'état*, meaning the convenience of the government, and the support of existing authority, was deemed a sufficient explanation and excuse for the most flagitious crimes. In the present day, power holds a smoother language, and whomsoever it oppresses, always pretends to do so for their own good: accordingly, when anything is forbidden to women, it is thought necessary to say, and desirable to believe, that they are incapable of doing it, and that they depart from their real path of success and happiness when they aspire to it. But to make this reason plausible (I do not say valid), those by whom it is urged must be prepared to carry it to a much greater length than any one ventures to do in the face of present experience. It is not sufficient to maintain that women on the average are less gifted than men on the average, with certain of the higher mental faculties, or that a smaller number of women than of men are fit for occupations and functions of the highest intellectual character. It is necessary to maintain that no women at all are fit for them, and that the most eminent women are inferior in mental faculties to the most medio-cre of the men on whom those functions at present devolve. For if the performance of the function is decided either by competition, or by any mode of choice which secures regard to the public inter-est, there needs be no apprehension that any important employments will fall into the hands of women inferior to average men, or to the average of their male competitors. The only result would be that there would be fewer women than men in such employments; a result certain to happen in any case, if only from the preference always likely to be felt by the majority of women for the one vocation in which there is nobody to compete with them. Now, the most deter-mined depreciator of women will not venture to deny, that when we add the experience of recent times to that of ages past, women, and not a few merely, but many women, have proved themselves capable of everything, perhaps without a single exception, which is done by men, and of doing it successfully and creditably. The utmost that can be said is, that there are many things which none of them have succeeded in doing as well as they have been done by some men— many in which they have not reached the very highest rank. But there are extremely few, dependent only on mental faculties, in which they have not attained the rank next to the highest. Is not this enough, and much more than enough, to make it a tyranny to them, and a detriment to society, that they should not be allowed to compete with men for the exercise of these functions? Is it not a mere truism to say, that such functions are often filled by men far less fit for them than numbers of women, and who would be beaten by women in any fair field of competition? What difference does it make that there may be men somewhere, fully employed about other things, who may be still better qualified for the things in question than these women? Does not this take place in all competitions? Is there so great a superfluity of men fit for high duties, that society can afford to reject the service of any competent person? Are we so certain of always finding a man made to our hands for any duty or function of social importance which falls vacant, that we lose nothing by putting a ban upon one-half of mankind, and refusing beforehand to make their faculties available, however distinguished they may be? And even if we could do without them, would it be consistent with justice to refuse to them their fair share of honour and distinction, or to deny to them the equal moral right of all human beings to choose their occupation (short of injury to others) according to their own preferences, at their own risk? Nor is the injustice confined to them: it is shared by those who are in a position to benefit by their services. To ordain that any kind of persons shall not be physicians, or shall not be advocates, or shall not be members of parliament, is to injure not them only, but all who employ physicians or advocates, or elect members of parliament, and who are deprived of the stimulating effect of greater competition on the exertions of the competitors, as well as restricted to a narrower range of individual choice.

It will perhaps be sufficient if I confine myself, in the details of my argument, to functions of a public nature: since, if I am successful as to those, it probably will be readily granted that women should be admissible to all other occupations to which it is at all material whether they are admitted or not. And here let me begin by marking out one function, broadly distinguished from all others, their right to which is entirely independent of any question which can be raised concerning their faculties. I mean the suffrage, both parliamentary and municipal. The right to share in the choice of those who are to exercise a public trust, is altogether a distinct thing from that of competing for the trust itself. If no one could vote for a member of parliament who was not fit to be a candidate, the government would be a narrow oligarchy indeed. To have a voice in choosing those by whom one is to be governed, is a means of self-protection due to every one, though he were to remain for ever excluded from the function of governing: and that women are considered fit to have such a choice, may be presumed from the fact, that the law already gives it to women in the most important of all cases to themselves: for the choice of the man who is to govern a woman to the end of life, is always supposed to be voluntarily made by herself. In the case of election to public trusts, it is the business

of constitutional law to surround the right of suffrage with all needful securities and limitations; but whatever securities are sufficient
in the case of the male sex, no others need be required in the case
of women. Under whatever conditions, and within whatever limits,
men are admitted to the suffrage, there is not a shadow of justification for not admitting women under the same. The majority of the
women of any class are not likely to differ in political opinion
from the majority of the men of the same class, unless the question
be one in which the interests of women, as such, are in some way
involved; and if they are so, women require the suffrage, as their
guarantee of just and equal consideration. This ought to be obvious
even to those who coincide in no other of the doctrines for which I
contend. Even if every woman were a wife, and if every wife ought
to be a slave, all the more would these slaves stand in need of legal
protection: and we know what legal protection the slaves have, where
the laws are made by their masters.

    With regard to the fitness of women, not only to participate in
elections, but themselves to hold offices or practise professions
involving important public responsibilities; I have already observed
that this consideration is not essential to the practical question in
dispute: since any woman, who succeeds in an open profession,
proves by that very fact that she is qualified for it. And in the case
of public offices, if the political system of the country is such as to
exclude unfit men, it will equally exclude unfit women: while if it
is not, there is no additional evil in the fact that the unfit persons
whom it admits may be either women or men. As long therefore
as it is acknowledged that even a few women may be fit for these
duties, the laws which shut the door on those exceptions cannot be
justified by any opinion which can be held respecting the capacities
of women in general. But, though this last consideration is not
essential, it is far from being irrelevant. An unprejudiced view of it
gives additional strength to the arguments against the disabilities
of women, and reinforces them by high considerations of practical
utility.

    Let us at first make entire abstraction of all psychological consid-
erations tending to show, that any of the mental differences supposed to exist between women and men are but the natural effect
of the differences in their education and circumstances, and indicate no radical difference, far less radical inferiority, of nature. Let
us consider women only as they already are, or as they are known to
have been; and the capacities which they have already practically
shown. What they have done, that at least, if nothing else, it is proved
that they can do. When we consider how sedulously they are all
trained away from, instead of being trained towards, any of the occupations or objects reserved for men, it is evident that I am taking a

very humble ground for them, when I rest their case on what they have actually achieved. For, in this case, negative evidence is worth little, while any positive evidence is conclusive. It cannot be inferred to be impossible that a woman should be a Homer, or an Aristotle, or a Michael Angelo, or a Beethoven, because no woman has yet actually produced works comparable to theirs in any of those lines of excellence. This negative fact at most leaves the question uncertain, and open to psychological discussion. But it is quite certain that a woman can be a Queen Elizabeth, or a Deborah, or a Joan of Arc,[7] since this is not inference, but fact. Now it is a curious consideration, that the only things which the existing law excludes women from doing, are the things which they have proved that they are able to do. There is no law to prevent a woman from having written all the plays of Shakspeare, or composed all the operas of Mozart. But Queen Elizabeth or Queen Victoria,[8] had they not inherited the throne, could not have been intrusted with the smallest of the political duties, of which the former showed herself equal to the greatest.

If anything conclusive could be inferred from experience, without psychological analysis, it would be that the things which women are not allowed to do are the very ones for which they are peculiarly qualified; since their vocation for government has made its way, and become conspicuous, through the very few opportunities which have been given; while in the lines of distinction which apparently were freely open to them, they have by no means so eminently distinguished themselves. We know how small a number of reigning queens history presents, in comparison with that of kings. Of this smaller number a far larger proportion have shown talents for rule; though many of them have occupied the throne in difficult periods. It is remarkable, too, that they have, in a great number of instances, been distinguished by merits the most opposite to the imaginary and conventional character of women: they have been as much remarked for the firmness and vigour of their rule, as for its intelligence. When, to queens and empresses, we add regents, and viceroys of provinces, the list of women who have been eminent rulers of mankind swells to a great length.[9] This fact is so undeniable,

7. Joan of Arc (1412–1431), a French peasant (known also as "The Maid of Orléans") who became a heroine in the Hundred Years' War and was made a saint. Elizabeth I (1533–1603), queen of England. *Deborah:* prophetess of the God of the Israelites and the only female judge mentioned in the Old Testament (Book of Judges 4–5).
8. Victoria (1819–1901), the longest-reigning British monarch (1837–1901) before Queen Elizabeth II.
9. Especially is this true if we take into consideration Asia as well as Europe. If a Hindoo principality is strongly, vigilantly, and economically governed; if order is preserved without oppression; if cultivation is extending, and the people prosperous, in three cases out of four that principality is under a woman's rule. This fact, to me an entirely unexpected one, I have collected from a long official knowledge of Hindoo governments. There are

that some one, long ago, tried to retort the argument, and turned the admitted truth into an additional insult, by saying that queens are better than kings, because under kings women govern, but under queens, men.

It may seem a waste of reasoning to argue against a bad joke; but such things do affect people's minds; and I have heard men quote this saying, with an air as if they thought that there was something in it. At any rate, it will serve as well as anything else for a starting point in discussion. I say, then, that it is not true that under kings, women govern. Such cases are entirely exceptional: and weak kings have quite as often governed ill through the influence of male favourites, as of female. When a king is governed by a woman merely through his amatory propensities, good government is not probable, though even then there are exceptions. But French history counts two kings who have voluntarily given the direction of affairs during many years, the one to his mother, the other to his sister: one of them, Charles VIII., was a mere boy, but in doing so he followed the intentions of his father Louis XI., the ablest monarch of his age. The other, Saint Louis,[1] was the best, and one of the most vigorous rulers, since the time of Charlemagne. Both these princesses ruled in a manner hardly equalled by any prince among their cotemporaries. The emperor Charles the Fifth,[2] the most politic prince of his time, who had as great a number of able men in his service as a ruler ever had, and was one of the least likely of all sovereigns to sacrifice his interest to personal feelings, made two princesses of his family successively Governors of the Netherlands, and kept one or other of them in that post during his whole life, (they were afterwards succeeded by a third). Both ruled very successfully, and one of them, Margaret of Austria, was one of the ablest politicians of the age. So much for one side of the question. Now as to the other. When it is said that under queens men govern, is the same meaning to be understood as when kings are said to be governed by women? Is it meant that queens choose as their instruments of government, the associates of their personal pleasures? The case is rare even with those who are as unscrupulous on

---

many such instances: for though, by Hindoo institutions, a woman cannot reign, she is the legal regent of a kingdom during the minority of the heir; and minorities are frequent, the lives of the male rulers being so often prematurely terminated through the effect of inactivity and sensual excesses. When we consider that these princesses have never been seen in public, have never conversed with any man not of their own family except from behind a curtain, that they do not read, and if they did, there is no book in their languages which can give them the smallest instruction on political affairs; the example they afford of the natural capacity of women for government is very striking [Mill's note].

1. Louis IX (1214–1270). *Charles VIII:* (1470–1498); he was just a boy when he ascended to the throne of France; until 1491 his sister Anne was regent.

2. Charles V (1500–1558), king of Spain and Holy Roman Emperor. He was brought up by his aunt, Margaret of Austria, who acted also as regent of the Netherlands.

the latter point as Catherine II.:[3] and it is not in these cases that the good government, alleged to arise from male influence, is to be found. If it be true, then, that the administration is in the hands of better men under a queen than under an average king, it must be that queens have a superior capacity for choosing them; and women must be better qualified than men both for the position of sovereign, and for that of chief minister; for the principal business of a prime minister is not to govern in person, but to find the fittest persons to conduct every department of public affairs. The more rapid insight into character, which is one of the admitted points of superiority in women over men, must certainly make them, with anything like parity of qualifications in other respects, more apt than men in that choice of instruments, which is nearly the most important business of every one who has to do with governing mankind. Even the unprincipled Catherine de' Medici could feel the value of a Chancellor de l'Hôpital.[4] But it is also true that most great queens have been great by their own talents for government, and have been well served precisely for that reason. They retained the supreme direction of affairs in their own hands: and if they listened to good advisers, they gave by that fact the strongest proof that their judgment fitted them for dealing with the great questions of government.

Is it reasonable to think that those who are fit for the greater functions of politics, are incapable of qualifying themselves for the less? Is there any reason in the nature of things, that the wives and sisters of princes should, whenever called on, be found as competent as the princes themselves to *their* business, but that the wives and sisters of statesmen, and administrators, and directors of companies, and managers of public institutions, should be unable to do what is done by their brothers and husbands? The real reason is plain enough; it is that princesses, being more raised above the generality of men by their rank than placed below them by their sex, have never been taught that it was improper for them to concern themselves with politics; but have been allowed to feel the liberal interest natural to any cultivated human being, in the great transactions which took place around them, and in which they might be called on to take a

3. Catherine II (1722–1796), empress of Russia, known as "Catherine the Great"; she came to power following the assassination of her husband and second cousin, Peter III.
4. Michel de l'Hôpital (1507–1573), prime minister under Catherine de' Medici (1519–1589), the wife of King Henry II of France (r. 1547–59); mother of Kings Francis II, Charles IX, and Henry III. When Francis II died in 1560, she became regent on behalf of her 10-year-old son Charles and was thus granted sweeping powers. After Charles died in 1574, Catherine played a key role in the reign of her third son, Henry III. She succeeded in preserving the monarchy and the unity of the state in a time of great uncertainty. With de l'Hôpital, she tried to solve the country's religious controversies peacefully by convening the Colloquy of Poissy (1561), with representatives of the religious factions. That attempt failed. The St. Bartholomew's Day Massacre in 1572 (a Catholic mob violence directed against the Protestant Huguenots) marked a turning point in the French Wars of Religion.

part. The ladies of reigning families are the only women who are
allowed the same range of interests and freedom of development as
men; and it is precisely in their case that there is not found to be
any inferiority. Exactly where and in proportion as women's capacities for government have been tried, in that proportion have they
been found adequate.

This fact is in accordance with the best general conclusions which
the world's imperfect experience seems as yet to suggest, concerning the peculiar tendencies and aptitudes characteristic of women,
as women have hitherto been. I do not say, as they will continue to
be; for, as I have already said more than once, I consider it presumption in any one to pretend to decide what women are or are not, can
or cannot be, by natural constitution. They have always hitherto
been kept, as far as regards spontaneous development, in so unnatural a state, that their nature cannot but have been greatly distorted
and disguised; and no one can safely pronounce that if women's
nature were left to choose its direction as freely as men's, and if no
artificial bent were attempted to be given to it except that required
by the conditions of human society, and given to both sexes alike,
there would be any material difference, or perhaps any difference
at all, in the character and capacities which would unfold themselves. I shall presently show, that even the least contestable of the
differences which now exist, are such as may very well have been
produced merely by circumstances, without any difference of natural capacity. But, looking at women as they are known in experience,
it may be said of them, with more truth than belongs to most other
generalizations on the subject, that the general bent of their talents
is towards the practical. This statement is conformable to all the
public history of women, in the present and the past. It is no less
borne out by common and daily experience. Let us consider the special nature of the mental capacities most characteristic of a woman
of talent. They are all of a kind which fits them for practice, and
makes them tend towards it. What is meant by a woman's capacity
of intuitive perception? It means, a rapid and correct insight into
present fact. It has nothing to do with general principles. Nobody
ever perceived a scientific law of nature by intuition, nor arrived at
a general rule of duty or prudence by it. These are results of slow
and careful collection and comparison of experience; and neither the
men nor the women of intuition usually shine in this department,
unless, indeed, the experience necessary is such as they can acquire
by themselves. For what is called their intuitive sagacity makes them
peculiarly apt in gathering such general truths as can be collected
from their individual means of observation. When, consequently,
they chance to be as well provided as men are with the results of
other people's experience, by reading and education, (I use the word

chance advisedly, for, in respect to the knowledge that tends to fit them for the greater concerns of life, the only educated women are the self-educated) they are better furnished than men in general with the essential requisites of skilful and successful practice. Men who have been much taught, are apt to be deficient in the sense of present fact; they do not see, in the facts which they are called upon to deal with, what is really there, but what they have been taught to expect. This is seldom the case with women of any ability. Their capacity of "intuition" preserves them from it. With equality of experience and of general faculties, a woman usually sees much more than a man of what is immediately before her. Now this sensibility to the present, is the main quality on which the capacity for practice, as distinguished from theory, depends. To discover general principles, belongs to the speculative faculty: to discern and discriminate the particular cases in which they are and are not applicable, constitutes practical talent: and for this, women as they now are have a peculiar aptitude. I admit that there can be no good practice without principles, and that the predominant place which quickness of observation holds among a woman's faculties, makes her particularly apt to build over-hasty generalizations upon her own observation; though at the same time no less ready in rectifying those generalizations, as her observation takes a wider range. But the corrective to this defect, is access to the experience of the human race; general knowledge—exactly the thing which education can best supply. A woman's mistakes are specifically those of a clever self-educated man, who often sees what men trained in routine do not see, but falls into errors for want of knowing things which have long been known. Of course he has acquired much of the pre-existing knowledge, or he could not have got on at all; but what he knows of it he has picked up in fragments and at random, as women do.

But this gravitation of women's minds to the present, to the real, to actual fact, while in its exclusiveness it is a source of errors, is also a most useful counteractive of the contrary error. The principal and most characteristic aberration of speculative minds as such, consists precisely in the deficiency of this lively perception and ever-present sense of objective fact. For want of this, they often not only overlook the contradiction which outward facts oppose to their theories, but lose sight of the legitimate purpose of speculation altogether, and let their speculative faculties go astray into regions not peopled with real beings, animate or inanimate, even idealized, but with personified shadows created by the illusions of metaphysics or by the mere entanglement of words, and think these shadows the proper objects of the highest, the most transcendant, philosophy. Hardly anything can be of greater value to a man of theory and speculation who employs himself not in collecting materials of knowledge by observation, but in working them up by processes of thought into comprehensive truths of science and laws of conduct, than to carry on his speculations in the companionship, and under the criticism, of a really superior woman. There is nothing comparable to it for keeping his thoughts within the limits of real things, and the actual facts of nature. A woman seldom runs wild after an abstraction. The habitual direction of her mind to dealing with things as individuals rather than in groups, and (what is closely connected with it) her more lively interest in the present feelings of persons, which makes her consider first of all, in anything which claims to be applied to practice, in what manner persons will be affected by it—these two things make her extremely unlikely to put faith in any speculation which loses sight of individuals, and deals with things as if they existed for the benefit of some imaginary entity, some mere creation of the mind, not resolvable into the feelings of living beings. Women's thoughts are thus as useful in giving reality to those of thinking men, as men's thoughts in giving width and largeness to those of women. In depth, as distinguished from breadth, I greatly doubt if even now, women, compared with men, are at any disadvantage.

If the existing mental characteristics of women are thus valuable even in aid of speculation, they are still more important, when speculation has done its work, for carrying out the results of speculation into practice. For the reasons already given, women are comparatively unlikely to fall into the common error of men, that of sticking to their rules in a case whose specialities either take it out of the class to which the rules are applicable, or require a special adaptation of them. Let us now consider another of the admitted superiorities of clever women, greater quickness of apprehension. Is not this preeminently a quality which fits a person for practice? In action, everything continually depends upon deciding promptly. In speculation, nothing does. A mere thinker can wait, can take time to consider, can collect additional evidence; he is not obliged to complete his philosophy at once, lest the opportunity should go by. The power of drawing the best conclusion possible from insufficient data is not indeed useless in philosophy; the construction of a provisional hypothesis consistent with all known facts is often the needful basis for further inquiry. But this faculty is rather serviceable in philosophy, than the main qualification for it: and, for the auxiliary as well as for the main operation, the philosopher can allow himself any time he pleases. He is in no need of the capacity of doing rapidly what he does; what he rather needs is patience, to work on slowly until imperfect lights have become perfect, and a conjecture has ripened into a theorem. For those, on the contrary, whose business is with the fugitive and perishable—with individual facts, not kinds of facts—rapidity of thought is a qualification next only in importance to the power of thought itself. He who has not his faculties under immediate command, in the contingencies of action, might as well not have them at all. He may be fit to criticize, but he is not fit to act. Now it is in this that women, and the men who are most like women, confessedly excel. The other sort of man, however pre-eminent may be his faculties, arrives slowly at complete command of them: rapidity of judgment and promptitude of judicious action, even in the things he knows best, are the gradual and late result of strenuous effort grown into habit.

It will be said, perhaps, that the greater nervous susceptibility of women is a disqualification for practice, in anything but domestic life, by rendering them mobile, changeable, too vehemently under the influence of the moment, incapable of dogged perseverance, unequal and uncertain in the power of using their faculties. I think that these phrases sum up the greater part of the objections commonly made to the fitness of women for the higher class of serious business. Much of all this is the mere overflow of nervous energy run to waste, and would cease when the energy was directed to a definite end. Much is also the result of conscious or unconscious cultivation; as we see by the almost total disappearance of "hysterics" and fainting fits, since they have gone out of fashion. Moreover, when people are brought up, like many women of the higher classes (though less so in our own country than in any other) a kind of hothouse plants, shielded from the wholesome vicissitudes of air and temperature, and untrained in any of the occupations and exercises which give stimulus and development to the circulatory and muscular system, while their nervous system, especially in its emotional department, is kept in unnaturally active play; it is no wonder if those of them who do not die of consumption, grow up with constitutions liable to derangement from slight causes, both internal and external, and without stamina to support any task, physical or mental, requiring continuity of effort. But women brought up to work for their livelihood show none of these morbid characteristics, unless indeed they are chained to an excess of sedentary work in confined and unhealthy rooms. Women who in their early years have shared in the healthful physical education and bodily freedom of their brothers, and who obtain a sufficiency of pure air and exercise in after-life, very rarely have any excessive susceptibility of nerves which can disqualify them for active pursuits. There is indeed a certain proportion of persons, in both sexes, in whom an unusual degree of nervous sensibility is constitutional, and of so marked a character as to be the feature of their organization which exercises the greatest influence over the whole character of the vital phenomena. This constitution, like other physical conformations, is hereditary, and is transmitted to sons as well as daughters; but it is possible, and probable, that the nervous temperament (as it is called) is inherited by a greater number of women than of men. We will assume this as a fact: and let me then ask, are men of nervous temperament found to be unfit for the duties and pursuits usually followed by men? If not, why should women of the same temperament be unfit for them? The peculiarities of the temperament are, no doubt, within certain limits, an obstacle to success in some employments, though an aid to it in others. But when the occupation is suitable to the temperament, and sometimes even when it is unsuitable, the most brilliant examples of success are continually given by the men of high nervous sensibility. They are distinguished in their practical manifestations chiefly by this, that being susceptible of a higher degree of excitement than those of another physical constitution, their powers when excited differ more than in the case of other people, from those shown in their ordinary state: they are raised, as it were, above themselves, and do things with ease which they are wholly incapable of at other times. But this lofty excitement is not, except in weak bodily constitutions, a mere flash, which passes away immediately, leaving no permanent traces, and incompatible with persistent and steady pursuit of an object. It is the character of the nervous temperament to be capable of *sustained* excitement, holding out through long continued efforts. It is what is meant by *spirit*. It is what makes the high-bred racehorse run without slackening speed till he drops down dead. It is what has enabled so many delicate women to maintain the most sublime constancy not only at the stake, but through a long preliminary succession of mental and bodily tortures. It is evident that people of this temperament are particularly apt for what may be called the executive department of the leadership of mankind. They are the material of great orators, great preachers, impressive diffusers of moral influences. Their constitution might be deemed less favourable to the qualities required from a statesman in the cabinet, or from a judge. It would be so, if the consequence necessarily followed that because people are excitable they must always be in a state of excitement. But this is wholly a question of training. Strong feeling is the instrument and element of strong self-control: but it requires to be cultivated in that direction. When it is, it forms not the heroes of impulse only, but those also of self-conquest. History and experience prove that the most passionate characters are the most fanatically rigid in their feelings of duty, when their passion has been trained to act in that direction. The judge who gives a just decision in a case where his feelings are intensely interested on the other side, derives from that same strength of feeling the determined sense of the obligation of justice, which enables him to achieve this victory over himself. The capability of that lofty enthusiasm which takes the human being out of his every-day character, reacts upon the daily character itself. His aspirations and powers when he is in this exceptional state, become the type with which he compares, and by which he estimates, his sentiments and proceedings at other times: and his habitual purposes assume a character moulded by and assimilated to the moments of lofty excitement, although those, from the physical nature of a human being, can only be transient. Experience of races, as well as of individuals, does not show those of excitable temperament to be less fit, on the average, either for speculation or practice, than the more unexcitable. The French, and the Italians, are undoubtedly by nature more nervously excitable than the Teutonic races, and, compared at least with the English, they have a much greater habitual and daily emotional life: but have they been less great in science, in public business, in legal and judicial eminence, or in war? There is abundant evidence that the Greeks were of old, as their descendants and successors still are, one of the most excitable of the races of mankind. It is superfluous to ask, what among the achievements of men they did not excel in. The Romans, probably, as an equally southern people, had the same original temperament: but the stern character of their national discipline, like that of the Spartans, made them an example of the opposite type of national character; the greater strength of their natural feelings being chiefly apparent in the intensity which the same original temperament made it possible to give to the artificial. If these cases exemplify what a naturally excitable people may be made, the Irish Celts afford one of the aptest examples of what they are when left to themselves; (if those can be said to be left to themselves who have been for centuries under the indirect influence of bad government, and the direct training of a Catholic hierarchy and of a sincere belief in the Catholic religion). The Irish character must be considered, therefore, as an unfavourable case: yet, whenever the circumstances of the individual have been at all favourable, what people have shown greater capacity for the most varied and multifarious individual eminence? Like the French compared with the English, the Irish with the Swiss, the Greeks or Italians compared with the German races, so women compared with men may be found, on the average, to do the same things with some variety in the particular kind of excellence. But, that they would do them fully as well on the whole, if their education and cultivation were adapted to correcting instead of aggravating the infirmities incident to their temperament, I see not the smallest reason to doubt.

Supposing it, however, to be true that women's minds are by nature more mobile than those of men, less capable of persisting long in the same continuous effort, more fitted for dividing their faculties among many things than for travelling in any one path to the highest point which can be reached by it: this may be true of women as they now are (though not without great and numerous exceptions), and may account for their having remained behind the highest order of men in precisely the things in which this absorption of the whole mind in one set of ideas and occupations may seem to be most requisite. Still, this difference is one which can only affect the kind of excellence, not the excellence itself, or its practical worth: and it remains to be shown whether this exclusive working of a part of the mind, this absorption of the whole thinking faculty in a single subject, and concentration of it on a single work, is the normal and healthful condition of the human faculties, even for speculative uses. I believe that what is gained in special development by this concentration, is lost in the capacity of the mind for the other purposes of life; and even in abstract thought, it is my decided opinion that the mind does more by frequently returning to a difficult problem, than by sticking to it without interruption. For the purposes, at all events, of practice, from its highest to its humblest departments, the capacity of passing promptly from one subject of consideration to another, without letting the active spring of the intellect run down between the two, is a power far more valuable; and this power women pre-eminently possess, by virtue of the very mobility of which they are accused. They perhaps have it from nature, but they certainly have it by training and education; for nearly the whole of the occupations of women consist in the management of small but multitudinous details, on each of which the mind cannot dwell even for a minute, but must pass on to other things, and if anything requires longer thought, must steal time at odd moments for thinking of it. The capacity indeed which women show for doing their thinking in circumstances and at times which almost any man would make an excuse to himself for not attempting it, has often been noticed: and a woman's mind, though it may be occupied only with small things, can hardly ever permit itself to be vacant, as a man's so often is when not engaged in what he chooses to consider the business of his life. The business of a woman's ordinary life is things in general, and can as little cease to go on as the world to go round.

But (it is said) there is anatomical evidence of the superior mental capacity of men compared with women: they have a larger brain. I reply, that in the first place the fact itself is doubtful. It is by no means established that the brain of a woman is smaller than that of a man. If it is inferred merely because a woman's bodily frame generally is of less dimensions than a man's, this criterion would lead to strange consequences. A tall and large-boned man must on this showing be wonderfully superior in intelligence to a small man, and an elephant or a whale must prodigiously excel mankind. The size of the brain in human beings, anatomists say, varies much less than the size of the body, or even of the head, and the one cannot be at all inferred from the other. It is certain that some women have as large a brain as any man. It is within my knowledge that a man who had weighed many human brains, said that the heaviest he knew of, heavier even than Cuvier's (the heaviest previously recorded), was that of a woman. Next, I must observe that the precise relation which exists between the brain and the intellectual powers is not yet well understood, but is a subject of great dispute. That there is a very close relation we cannot doubt. The brain is certainly the material organ of thought and feeling: and (making abstraction of the great unsettled controversy respecting the appropriation of different parts of the brain to different mental faculties) I admit that it would be an anomaly, and an exception to all we know of the general laws of life and organization, if the size of the organ were wholly indifferent to the function; if no accession of power were derived from the greater magnitude of the instrument. But the exception and the anomaly would be fully as great if the organ exercised influence by its magnitude *only*. In all the more delicate operations of nature—of which those of the animated creation are the most delicate, and those of the nervous system by far the most delicate of these—differences in the effect depend as much on differences of quality in the physical agents, as on their quantity: and if the quality of an instrument is to be tested by the nicety and delicacy of the work it can do, the indications point to a greater average fineness of quality in the brain and nervous system of women than of men. Dismissing abstract difference of quality, a thing difficult to verify, the efficiency of an organ is known to depend not solely on its size but on its activity: and of this we have an approximate measure in the energy with which the blood circulates through it, both the stimulus and the reparative force being mainly dependent on the circulation. It would not be surprising—it is indeed an hypothesis which accords well with the differences actually observed between the mental operations of the two sexes—if men on the average should have the advantage in the size of the brain, and women in activity of cerebral circulation. The results which conjecture, founded on analogy, would lead us to expect from this difference of organization, would correspond to some of those which we most commonly see. In the first place, the mental operations of men might be expected to be slower. They would neither be so prompt as women in thinking, nor so quick to feel. Large bodies take more time to get into full action. On the other hand, when once got thoroughly into play, men's brain would bear more work. It would be more persistent in the line first taken; it would have more difficulty in changing from one mode of action to another, but, in the one thing it was doing, it could go on longer without loss of power or sense of fatigue. And do we not find that the things in which men most excel women are those which require most plodding and long hammering at a single thought, while women do best what must be done rapidly? A woman's brain is sooner fatigued, sooner exhausted; but give the degree of exhaustion, we should expect to find that it would recover itself sooner. I repeat that this speculation is entirely hypothetical; it pretends to no more than to suggest a line of enquiry. I have before repudiated the notion of its being yet certainly known that there is any natural difference at all in the average strength or direction of the mental capacities of the two sexes, much less what that difference is. Nor is it possible that this should be known, so long as the psychological laws of the formation of character have been so little studied, even in a general way, and in the particular case never scientifically applied at all; so long as the most obvious external causes of difference of character are habitually disregarded—left unnoticed by the observer, and looked down upon with a kind of supercilious contempt by the prevalent schools both of natural history and of mental philosophy: who, whether they look for the source of what mainly distinguishes human beings from one another, in the world of matter or in that of spirit, agree in running down those who prefer to explain these differences by the different relations of human beings to society and life.

To so ridiculous an extent are the notions formed of the nature of women, mere empirical generalizations, framed, without philosophy or analysis, upon the first instances which present themselves, that the popular idea of it is different in different countries, according as the opinions and social circumstances of the country have given to the women living in it any speciality of development or non-development. An Oriental[5] thinks that women are by nature peculiarly voluptuous; see the violent abuse of them on this ground in Hindoo writings. An Englishman usually thinks that they are by nature cold. The sayings about women's fickleness are mostly of French origin; from the famous distich of Francis the First,[6] upward and downward. In England it is a common remark, how much more

---

5. The noun "Oriental" has a long history of association with language depicting the "exotic" races of the various Asian identities and China in particular; beginning with Aristotle (384 B.C.E.–322 B.C.E.), it has been associated with despotism; the Baron of Montesquieu (1689–1755) also associated it with the absence of progress and stagnation; following in the footsteps of Georg Wilhelm Hegel (1770–1831), Karl Marx (1818–1883) spoke of the Asian mode of production as lacking private property. Mill also used it in this meaning.
6. Francis I (1494–1547), king of France; renowned for being a "man of letters," he made his court an intellectual center of the Renaissance in Europe and commissioned several paintings by Leonardo da Vinci, including the *Mona Lisa* (known in France as *La Joconde*). The distich Mill refers to is probably "Souvent femme varie, / Bien fol est qui s'y fie" (Woman often varies, / Very foolish is the man who trusts her).

constant women are than men. Inconstancy has been longer reckoned discreditable to a woman, in England than in France; and
Englishwomen are besides, in their inmost nature, much more subdued to opinion. It may be remarked by the way, that Englishmen
are in peculiarly unfavourable circumstances for attempting to judge
what is or is not natural, not merely to women, but to men, or to
human beings altogether, at least if they have only English experience to go upon: because there is no place where human nature
shows so little of its original lineaments. Both in a good and a bad
sense, the English are farther from a state of nature than any other
modern people. They are, more than any other people, a product of
civilization and discipline. England is the country in which social
discipline has most succeeded, not so much in conquering, as in suppressing, whatever is liable to conflict with it. The English, more
than any other people, not only act but feel according to rule. In
other countries, the taught opinion, or the requirement of society,
may be the stronger power, but the promptings of the individual
nature are always visible under it, and often resisting it: rule may
be stronger than nature, but nature is still there. In England, rule
has to a great degree substituted itself for nature. The greater part
of life is carried on, not by following inclination under the control
of rule, but by having no inclination but that of following a rule. Now
this has its good side doubtless, though it has also a wretchedly bad
one; but it must render an Englishman peculiarly ill-qualified to
pass a judgment on the original tendencies of human nature from
his own experience. The errors to which observers elsewhere are
liable on the subject, are of a different character. An Englishman
is ignorant respecting human nature, a Frenchman is prejudiced.
An Englishman's errors are negative, a Frenchman's positive. An
Englishman fancies that things do not exist, because he never sees
them; a Frenchman thinks they must always and necessarily exist,
because he does see them. An Englishman does not know nature,
because he has had no opportunity of observing it; a Frenchman
generally knows a great deal of it, but often mistakes it, because he
has only seen it sophisticated and distorted. For the artificial state
superinduced by society disguises the natural tendencies of the thing
which is the subject of observation, in two different ways: by extinguishing the nature, or by transforming it. In the one case there is but
a starved residuum of nature remaining to be studied; in the other
case there is much, but it may have expanded in any direction rather
than that in which it would spontaneously grow.

I have said that it cannot now be known how much of the existing mental differences between men and women is natural, and how
much artificial; whether there are any natural differences at all;
or, supposing all artificial causes of difference to be withdrawn,

what natural character would be revealed. I am not about to attempt what I have pronounced impossible: but doubt does not forbid conjecture, and where certainty is unattainable, there may yet be the means of arriving at some degree of probability. The first point, the origin of the differences actually observed, is the one most accessible to speculation; and I shall attempt to approach it, by the only path by which it can be reached; by tracing the mental consequences of external influences. We cannot isolate a human being from the circumstances of his condition, so as to ascertain experimentally what he would have been by nature; but we can consider what he is, and what his circumstances have been, and whether the one would have been capable of producing the other.

Let us take, then, the only marked case which observation affords, of apparent inferiority of women to men, if we except the merely physical one of bodily strength. No production in philosophy, science, or art, entitled to the first rank, has been the work of a woman. Is there any mode of accounting for this, without supposing that women are naturally incapable of producing them?

In the first place, we may fairly question whether experience has afforded sufficient grounds for an induction. It is scarcely three generations since women, saving very rare exceptions, have begun to try their capacity in philosophy, science, or art. It is only in the present generation that their attempts have been at all numerous; and they are even now extremely few, everywhere but in England and France. It is a relevant question, whether a mind possessing the requisites of first-rate eminence in speculation or creative art could have been expected, on the mere calculation of chances, to turn up during that lapse of time, among the women whose tastes and personal position admitted of their devoting themselves to these pursuits. In all things which there has yet been time for—in all but the very highest grades in the scale of excellence, especially in the department in which they have been longest engaged, literature (both prose and poetry)—women have done quite as much, have obtained fully as high prizes and as many of them, as could be expected from the length of time and the number of competitors. If we go back to the earlier period when very few women made the attempt, yet some of those few made it with distinguished success. The Greeks always accounted Sappho among their great poets; and we may well suppose that Myrtis, said to have been the teacher of Pindar, and Corinna, who five times bore away from him the prize of poetry, must at least have had sufficient merit to admit of being compared with that great name. Aspasia[7] did not leave

7. Mistress of Pericles (see n. 6 on p. 56); they lived together until his death of the plague in 429 B.C.E. *Sappho*: (610–580 B.C.E.), a Greek poet from the island of Lesbos, renowned for her poems written as texts to be sung and accompanied by music; she was widely admired as one of the greatest lyric poets, also known as the "Tenth Muse" and "The

any philosophical writings; but it is an admitted fact that Socrates resorted to her for instruction, and avowed himself to have obtained it.

If we consider the works of women in modern times, and contrast them with those of men, either in the literary or the artistic department, such inferiority as may be observed resolves itself essentially into one thing: but that is a most material one; deficiency of originality. Not total deficiency; for every production of mind which is of any substantive value, has an originality of its own—is a conception of the mind itself, not a copy of something else. Thoughts original, in the sense of being unborrowed—of being derived from the thinker's own observations or intellectual processes—are abundant in the writings of women. But they have not yet produced any of those great and luminous new ideas which form an era in thought, nor those fundamentally new conceptions in art, which open a vista of possible effects not before thought of, and found a new school. Their compositions are mostly grounded on the existing fund of thought, and their creations do not deviate widely from existing types. This is the sort of inferiority which their works manifest: for in point of execution, in the detailed application of thought, and the perfection of style, there is no inferiority. Our best novelists in point of composition, and of the management of detail, have mostly been women; and there is not in all modern literature a more eloquent vehicle of thought than the style of Madame de Stael, nor, as a specimen of purely artistic excellence, anything superior to the prose of Madame Sand,[8] whose style acts upon the nervous system like a symphony of Haydn or Mozart. High originality of conception is, as I have said, what is chiefly wanting. And now to examine if there is any manner in which this deficiency can be accounted for.

Let us remember, then, so far as regards mere thought, that during all that period in the world's existence, and in the progress of

Poetess." *Myrtis*: Myrtis of Anthedon (sixth century B.C.E.), an ancient Greek poet, perhaps the teacher of Pindar of Thebes (518–439) and Corinna of Tanagra in Boeotia; some scholars consider her the most important ancient Greek poet after Sappho.

8. George Sand (1804–1876), the pseudonym of Amandine Dupin, a French novelist greatly appreciated by Mill, who corresponded with her. She chose a male name and dressed in male clothes in public. In 1800, the French police issued an order requiring women to apply for a permit in order to wear male clothing; several women like Sand followed the rule in such a precise way that they subverted the dominant male and female stereotypes. Sand was also a journalist and political activist who sided with the poor and working class as well as advocating for women's rights; a republican engaged in the revolution of February 1848, she started her own newspaper, *La voix des femmes* (The Voice of Women). *Madame de Stael*: German de Staël (1766–1817), a prominent French intellectual, novelist, and journalist; her book *Germany* (1813), which Napoleon ordered to be destroyed (he also banned her from Paris), played a crucial role in promoting Romantic literature in European countries and the United States. The daughter of Swiss banker and pre-Revolutionary French minister of finance Jacques Necker, she mingled with, among others, the liberal thinker Benjamin Constant and promoted a debating club in Coppet, Switzerland, which the novelist Stendhal defined as "the general headquarters of European thought" against Napoleon.

cultivation, in which great and fruitful new truths could be arrived at by mere force of genius, with little previous study and accumulation of knowledge—during all that time women did not concern themselves with speculation at all. From the days of Hypatia to those of the Reformation, the illustrious Heloisa[9] is almost the only woman to whom any such achievement might have been possible; and we know not how great a capacity of speculation in her may have been lost to mankind by the misfortunes of her life. Never since any considerable number of women have began to cultivate serious thought, has originality been possible on easy terms. Nearly all the thoughts which can be reached by mere strength of original faculties, have long since been arrived at; and originality, in any high sense of the word, is now scarcely ever attained but by minds which have undergone elaborate discipline, and are deeply versed in the results of previous thinking. It is Mr. Maurice,[1] I think, who has remarked on the present age, that its most original thinkers are those who have known most thoroughly what had been thought by their predecessors: and this will always henceforth be the case. Every fresh stone in the edifice has now to be placed on the top of so many others, that a long process of climbing, and of carrying up materials, has to be gone through by whoever aspires to take a share in the present stage of the work. How many women are there who have gone through any such process? Mrs. Somerville,[2] alone perhaps of women, knows as much of mathematics as is now needful for making any considerable mathematical discovery: is it any proof of inferiority in women, that she has not happened to be one of the two or three persons who in her lifetime have associated their names with some striking advancement of the science? Two women, since political economy has been made a science, have known enough of it to write usefully on the subject:[3] of how many of the innumerable men who have written on it during the same time, is it possible with truth to say more? If no woman has hitherto been a great historian, what woman has had the necessary erudition? If no woman is a great philologist, what woman has studied Sanscrit and Slavonic, the Gothic of

9. Héloise (1098–1164), a renowned teacher in medieval France and the lover of the philosopher Peter Abelard. *Hypatia*: (370–415), a Neoplatonic philosopher, the first notable woman mathematician and astronomer; she taught in Alexandria in Egypt, where she was murdered by a mob of Christians.

1. John Frederick Denison Maurice (1805–1872) lived in London, contributed to the *Westminster Review* edited by Mill, had sympathized with the Radicals, and was later known as a Christian socialist.

2. Mary Summerville (1780–1872), after whom one of Oxford's colleges was named, was an English mathematician and astronomer; she and Caroline Herschel were the first female honorary members of the Royal Astronomical Society. She put her signature first on Mill's petition to Parliament to extend the suffrage to women.

3. Probably referring to Jane Marcet, author of *Conversations on Political Economy* (London: Longman, 1816), and Harriet Martineau, author of *Illustrations of Political Economy*, 9 vols. (London: Fox, 1832–34).

Ulphila and the Persic of the Zendavesta?[4] Even in practical matters we all know what is the value of the originality of untaught geniuses. It means, inventing over again in its rudimentary form something already invented and improved upon by many successive inventors. When women have had the preparation which all men now require to be eminently original, it will be time enough to begin judging by experience of their capacity for originality.

It no doubt often happens that a person, who has not widely and accurately studied the thoughts of others on a subject, has by natural sagacity a happy intuition, which he can suggest, but cannot prove, which yet when matured may be an important addition to knowledge: but even then, no justice can be done to it until some other person, who does possess the previous acquirements, takes it in hand, tests it, gives it a scientific or practical form, and fits it into its place among the existing truths of philosophy or science. Is it supposed that such felicitous thoughts do not occur to women? They occur by hundreds to every woman of intellect. But they are mostly lost, for want of a husband or friend who has the other knowledge which can enable him to estimate them properly and bring them before the world: and even when they are brought before it, they generally appear as his ideas, not their real author's. Who can tell how many of the most original thoughts put forth by male writers, belong to a woman by suggestion, to themselves only by verifying and working out? If I may judge by my own case, a very large proportion indeed.[5]

If we turn from pure speculation to literature in the narrow sense of the term, and the fine arts, there is a very obvious reason why women's literature is, in its general conception and in its main features, an imitation of men's. Why is the Roman literature, as critics proclaim to satiety, not original, but an imitation of the Greek? Simply because the Greeks came first. If women lived in a different country from men, and had never read any of their writings, they would have had a literature of their own. As it is, they have not created one, because they found a highly advanced literature already created. If there had been no suspension of the knowledge of antiquity, or if the Renaissance had occurred before the Gothic cathedrals were built, they never would have been built. We see that, in France and Italy, imitation of the ancient literature stopped the original development even after it had commenced. All women who

<hr/>

4. The rendering in Mill's time of what is known now as Avestan, the archaic Iranian language, in which the sacred texts of Zoroastrianism were written. *Ulphila*: all Latinized forms of the unattested Gothic language, devised by Ulfilas (fourth century, from Cappadocian Greek origins), a bishop who devised the Gothic alphabet and presided over the translation of the Bible from Greek into the Gothic language.
5. See Mill's encomium to his wife in *On Liberty*, p. 3 above.

write are pupils of the great male writers. A painter's early pictures, even if he be a Raffaelle,[6] are undistinguishable in style from those of his master. Even a Mozart does not display his powerful originality in his earliest pieces. What years are to a gifted individual, generations are to a mass. If women's literature is destined to have a different collective character from that of men, depending on any difference of natural tendencies, much longer time is necessary than has yet elapsed, before it can emancipate itself from the influence of accepted models, and guide itself by its own impulses. But if, as I believe, there will not prove to be any natural tendencies common to women, and distinguishing their genius from that of men, yet every individual writer among them has her individual tendencies, which at present are still subdued by the influence of precedent and example: and it will require generations more, before their individuality is sufficiently developed to make head against that influence.

It is in the fine arts, properly so called, that the *primâ facie* evidence of inferior original powers in women at first sight appears the strongest: since opinion (it may be said) does not exclude them from these, but rather encourages them, and their education, instead of passing over this department, is in the affluent classes mainly composed of it. Yet in this line of exertion they have fallen still more short than in many others, of the highest eminence attained by men. This shortcoming, however, needs no other explanation than the familiar fact, more universally true in the fine arts than in anything else; the vast superiority of professional persons over amateurs. Women in the educated classes are almost universally taught more or less of some branch or other of the fine arts, but not that they may gain their living or their social consequence by it. Women artists are all amateurs. The exceptions are only of the kind which confirm the general truth. Women are taught music, but not for the purpose of composing, only of executing it: and accordingly it is only as composers, that men, in music, are superior to women. The only one of the fine arts which women do follow, to any extent, as a profession, and an occupation for life, is the histrionic; and in that they are confessedly equal, if not superior, to men. To make the comparison fair, it should be made between the productions of women in any branch of art, and those of men not following it as a profession. In musical composition, for example, women surely have produced fully as good things as have ever been produced by male amateurs. There are now a few women, a very few, who practise painting as a profession, and these are already beginning to show

6. Raffaello or Raffaello Sanzio (1483–1520), also known as Raphael; from Urbino, Italy; one of the greatest painters of the late Renaissance, he was particularly loved by Mill, as we learn from the letter Mill wrote to Harriet Taylor from Rome (see p. xxv above).

quite as much talent as could be expected. Even male painters (*pace* Mr. Ruskin)[7] have not made any very remarkable figure these last centuries, and it will be long before they do so. The reason why the old painters were so greatly superior to the modern, is that a greatly superior class of men applied themselves to the art. In the fourteenth and fifteenth centuries the Italian painters were the most accomplished men of their age. The greatest of them were men of encyclopædical acquirements and powers, like the great men of Greece. But in their times fine art was, to men's feelings and conceptions, among the grandest things in which a human being could excel; and by it men were made, what only political or military distinction now makes them, the companions of sovereigns, and the equals of the highest nobility. In the present age, men of anything like similar calibre find something more important to do, for their own fame and the uses of the modern world, than painting: and it is only now and then that a Reynolds or a Turner[8] (of whose relative rank among eminent men I do not pretend to an opinion) applies himself to that art. Music belongs to a different order of things; it does not require the same general powers of mind, but seems more dependant on a natural gift: and it may be thought surprising that no one of the great musical composers has been a woman. But even this natural gift, to be made available for great creations, requires study, and professional devotion to the pursuit. The only countries which have produced first-rate composers, even of the male sex, are Germany and Italy—countries in which, both in point of special and of general cultivation, women have remained far behind France and England, being generally (it may be said without exaggeration) very little educated, and having scarcely cultivated at all any of the higher faculties of mind. And in those countries the men who are acquainted with the principles of musical composition must be counted by hundreds, or more probably by thousands, the women barely by scores: so that here again, on the doctrine of averages, we cannot reasonably expect to see more than one eminent woman to fifty eminent men; and the last three centuries have not produced fifty eminent male composers either in Germany or in Italy.

There are other reasons, besides those which we have now given, that help to explain why women remain behind men, even in the pursuits which are open to both. For one thing, very few women have

---

7. John Ruskin (1818–1900), author of *Modern Painters* (1843) and supporter of the Pre-Raphaelites.
8. J. M. W. Turner (1775–1851), English Romantic painter famous for his dramatic, contemplative, and often violent, landscapes, particularly marine; his style was defended by Ruskin. *Reynolds:* Sir Joshua Reynolds (1723–1792) was an English painter who specialized in portraits and promoted a style idealizing the imperfect.

time for them. This may seem a paradox; it is an undoubted social
fact. The time and thoughts of every woman have to satisfy great
previous demands on them for things practical. There is, first, the
superintendence of the family and the domestic expenditure, which
occupies at least one woman in every family, generally the one of
mature years and acquired experience; unless the family is so
rich as to admit of delegating that task to hired agency, and sub-
mitting to all the waste and malversation[9] inseparable from that
mode of conducting it. The superintendence of a household, even
when not in other respects laborious, is extremely onerous to the
thoughts; it requires incessant vigilance, an eye which no detail
escapes, and presents questions for consideration and solution,
foreseen and unforeseen, at every hour of the day, from which the
person responsible for them can hardly ever shake herself free. If a
woman is of a rank and circumstances which relieve her in a measure from these cares, she has still devolving on her the management for the whole family of its intercourse with others—of what is
called society, and the less the call made on her by the former duty,
the greater is always the development of the latter: the dinner parties, concerts, evening parties, morning visits, letter writing, and
all that goes with them. All this is over and above the engrossing
duty which society imposes exclusively on women, of making themselves charming. A clever woman of the higher ranks finds nearly a
sufficient employment of her talents in cultivating the graces of
manner and the arts of conversation. To look only at the outward
side of the subject: the great and continual exercise of thought
which all women who attach any value to dressing well (I do not
mean expensively, but with taste, and perception of natural and of
artificial *convenance*[1]) must bestow upon their own dress, perhaps
also upon that of their daughters, would alone go a great way
towards achieving respectable results in art, or science, or literature, and does actually exhaust much of the time and mental power
they might have to spare for either.[2] If it were possible that all this
number of little practical interests (which are made great to them)
should leave them either much leisure, or much energy and freedom

9. Corrupt behavior.
1. Suitability, propriety.
2. "It appears to be the same right turn of mind which enables a man to acquire the *truth*,
   or the just idea of what is right, in the ornaments, as in the more stable principles of art.
   It has still the same centre of perfection, though it is the centre of a smaller circle.—To
   illustrate this by the fashion of dress, in which there is allowed to be a good or bad taste.
   The component parts of dress are continually changing from great to little, from short to
   long; but the general form still remains: it is still the same general dress which is comparatively fixed, though on a very slender foundation; but it is on this which fashion must
   rest. He who invents with the most success, or dresses in the best taste, would probably,
   from the same sagacity employed to greater purposes, have discovered equal skill, or
   have formed the same correct taste, in the highest labours of art."—*Sir Joshua Reynolds'
   Discourses*, Disc. vii [*Mill's note*].

of mind, to be devoted to art or speculation, they must have a much greater original supply of active faculty than the vast majority of men. But this is not all. Independently of the regular offices of life which devolve upon a woman; she is expected to have her time and faculties always at the disposal of everybody. If a man has not a profession to exempt him from such demands, still, if he has a pursuit, he offends nobody by devoting his time to it; occupation is received as a valid excuse for his not answering to every casual demand which may be made on him. Are a woman's occupations, especially her chosen and voluntary ones, ever regarded as excusing her from any of what are termed the calls of society? Scarcely are her most necessary and recognised duties allowed as an exemption. It requires an illness in the family, or something else out of the common way, to entitle her to give her own business the precedence over other people's amusement. She must always be at the beck and call of somebody, generally of everybody. If she has a study or a pursuit, she must snatch any short interval which accidentally occurs to be employed in it. A celebrated woman, in a work which I hope will some day be published, remarks truly that everything a woman does is done at odd times. Is it wonderful, then, if she does not attain the highest eminence in things which require consecutive attention, and the concentration on them of the chief interest of life? Such is philosophy, and such, above all, is art, in which, besides the devotion of the thoughts and feelings, the hand also must be kept in constant exercise to attain high skill.

There is another consideration to be added to all these. In the various arts and intellectual occupations, there is a degree of proficiency sufficient for living by it, and there is a higher degree on which depend the great productions which immortalize a name. To the attainment of the former, there are adequate motives in the case of all who follow the pursuit professionally: the other is hardly ever attained where there is not, or where there has not been at some period of life, an ardent desire of celebrity. Nothing less is commonly a sufficient stimulus to undergo the long and patient drudgery, which, in the case even of the greatest natural gifts, is absolutely required for great eminence in pursuits in which we already possess so many splendid memorials of the highest genius. Now, whether the cause be natural or artificial, women seldom have this eagerness for fame. Their ambition is generally confined within narrower bounds. The influence they seek is over those who immediately surround them. Their desire is to be liked, loved, or admired, by those whom they see with their eyes: and the proficiency in knowledge, arts, and accomplishments, which is sufficient for that, almost always contents them. This is a trait of character which cannot be left out of the account in judging of women as they are. I do not at all believe that it is inherent in women. It is only the natural result of their circumstances. The love of fame in men is encouraged by education and opinion: to "scorn delights and live laborious days" for its sake, is accounted the part of "noble minds," even if spoken of as their "last infirmity,"[3] and is stimulated by the access which fame gives to all objects of ambition, including even the favour of women; while to women themselves all these objects are closed, and the desire of fame itself considered daring and unfeminine. Besides, how could it be that a woman's interests should not be all concentrated upon the impressions made on those who come into her daily life, when society has ordained that all her duties should be to them, and has contrived that all her comforts should depend on them? The natural desire of consideration from our fellow creatures is as strong in a woman as in a man; but society has so ordered things that public consideration is, in all ordinary cases, only attainable by her through the consideration of her husband or of her male relations, while her private consideration is forfeited by making herself individually prominent, or appearing in any other character than that of an appendage to men. Whoever is in the least capable of estimating the influence on the mind of the entire domestic and social position and the whole habit of a life, must easily recognise in that influence a complete explanation of nearly all the apparent differences between women and men, including the whole of those which imply any inferiority.

As for moral differences, considered as distinguished from intellectual, the distinction commonly drawn is to the advantage of women. They are declared to be better than men; an empty compliment, which must provoke a bitter smile from every woman of spirit, since there is no other situation in life in which it is the established order, and considered quite natural and suitable, that the better should obey the worse. If this piece of idle talk is good for anything, it is only as an admission by men, of the corrupting influence of power; for that is certainly the only truth which the fact, if it be a fact, either proves or illustrates. And it *is* true that servitude, except when it actually brutalizes, though corrupting to both, is less so to the slaves than to the slave-masters. It is wholesomer for the moral nature to be restrained, even by arbitrary power, than to be allowed to exercise arbitrary power without restraint. Women, it is said, seldomer fall under the penal law—contribute a much smaller number of offenders to the criminal calendar, than men. I doubt not that the same thing may be said, with the same truth, of negro slaves. Those who are under the control of others cannot often commit crimes, unless at the command and for the purposes of their masters.

3. From John Milton's *Lycidas* (1638).

I do not know a more signal instance of the blindness with which the world, including the herd of studious men, ignore and pass over all the influences of social circumstances, than their silly depreciation of the intellectual, and silly panegyrics on the moral, nature of women.

The complimentary dictum about women's superior moral goodness may be allowed to pair off with the disparaging one respecting their greater liability to moral bias. Women, we are told, are not capable of resisting their personal partialities: their judgment in grave affairs is warped by their sympathies and antipathies. Assuming it to be so, it is still to be proved that women are oftener misled by their personal feelings than men by their personal interests. The chief difference would seem in that case to be, that men are led from the course of duty and the public interest by their regard for themselves, women (not being allowed to have private interests of their own) by their regard for somebody else. It is also to be considered, that all the education which women receive from society inculcates on them the feeling that the individuals connected with them are the only ones to whom they owe any duty—the only ones whose interest they are called upon to care for; while, as far as education is concerned, they are left strangers even to the elementary ideas which are presupposed in any intelligent regard for larger interests or higher moral objects. The complaint against them resolves itself merely into this, that they fulfil only too faithfully the sole duty which they are taught, and almost the only one which they are permitted to practise.

The concessions of the privileged to the unprivileged are so seldom brought about by any better motive than the power of the unprivileged to extort them, that any arguments against the prerogative of sex are likely to be little attended to by the generality, as long as they are able to say to themselves that women do not complain of it. That fact certainly enables men to retain the unjust privilege some time longer; but does not render it less unjust. Exactly the same thing may be said of the women in the harem of an Oriental: they do not complain of not being allowed the freedom of European women. They think our women insufferably bold and unfeminine. How rarely it is that even men complain of the general order of society; and how much rarer still would such complaint be, if they did not know of any different order existing anywhere else. Women do not complain of the general lot of women; or rather they do, for plaintive elegies on it are very common in the writings of women, and were still more so as long as the lamentations could not be suspected of having any practical object. Their complaints are like the complaints which men make of the general unsatisfactoriness of human life; they are not meant to imply blame, or to plead for any

change. But though women do not complain of the power of husbands, each complains of her own husband, or of the husbands of
her friends. It is the same in all other cases of servitude, at least in
the commencement of the emancipatory movement. The serfs did
not at first complain of the power of their lords, but only of their
tyranny. The Commons[4] began by claiming a few municipal privileges; they next asked an exemption for themselves from being taxed
without their own consent; but they would at that time have thought
it a great presumption to claim any share in the king's sovereign
authority. The case of women is now the only case in which to rebel
against established rules is still looked upon with the same eyes as
was formerly a subject's claim to the right of rebelling against his
king. A woman who joins in any movement which her husband dis-
approves, makes herself a martyr, without even being able to be an
apostle, for the husband can legally put a stop to her apostleship.
Women cannot be expected to devote themselves to the emancipation of women, until men in considerable number are prepared to
join with them in the undertaking.

CHAPTER IV

There remains a question, not of less importance than those already
discussed, and which will be asked the most importunately by those
opponents whose conviction is somewhat shaken on the main point.
What good are we to expect from the changes proposed in our customs and institutions? Would mankind be at all better off if women
were free? If not, why disturb their minds, and attempt to make a
social revolution in the name of an abstract right?

It is hardly to be expected that this question will be asked in
respect to the change proposed in the condition of women in marriage. The sufferings, immoralities, evils of all sorts, produced in
innumerable cases by the subjection of individual women to individual men, are far too terrible to be overlooked. Unthinking or un-
candid persons, counting those cases alone which are extreme, or
which attain publicity, may say that the evils are exceptional; but
no one can be blind to their existence, nor, in many cases, to their
intensity. And it is perfectly obvious that the abuse of the power cannot be very much checked while the power remains. It is a power
given, or offered, not to good men, or to decently respectable men,
but to all men; the most brutal, and the most criminal. There is no
check but that of opinion, and such men are in general within the

---

4. The House of Commons, the lower house of the British Parliament, which gets its name
because it represents communities (commons).

reach of no opinion but that of men like themselves. If such men did not brutally tyrannize over the one human being whom the law compels to bear everything from them, society must already have reached a paradisiacal state. There could be no need any longer of laws to curb men's vicious propensities. Astræa[5] must not only have returned to earth, but the heart of the worst man must have become her temple. The law of servitude in marriage is a monstrous contradiction to all the principles of the modern world, and to all the experience through which those principles have been slowly and painfully worked out. It is the sole case, now that negro slavery has been abolished, in which a human being in the plenitude of every faculty is delivered up to the tender mercies of another human being, in the hope forsooth that this other will use the power solely for the good of the person subjected to it. Marriage is the only actual bondage known to our law. There remain no legal slaves, except the mistress of every house.

It is not, therefore, on this part of the subject, that the question is likely to be asked, *Cui bono?*[6] We may be told that the evil would outweigh the good, but the reality of the good admits of no dispute. In regard, however, to the larger question, the removal of women's disabilities—their recognition as the equals of men in all that belongs to citizenship—the opening to them of all honourable employments, and of the training and education which qualifies for those employments—there are many persons for whom it is not enough that the inequality has no just or legitimate defence; they require to be told what express advantage would be obtained by abolishing it.

To which let me first answer, the advantage of having the most universal and pervading of all human relations regulated by justice instead of injustice. The vast amount of this gain to human nature, it is hardly possible, by any explanation or illustration, to place in a stronger light than it is placed by the bare statement, to any one who attaches a moral meaning to words. All the selfish propensities, the self-worship, the unjust self-preference, which exist among mankind, have their source and root in, and derive their principal nourishment from, the present constitution of the relation between men and women. Think what it is to a boy, to grow up to manhood in the belief that without any merit or any exertion of his own, though he may be the most frivolous and empty or the most ignorant and stolid of mankind, by the mere fact of being born a male he is by right the superior of all and every one of an entire half of the human race: including probably some whose real superiority to himself he has

5. "Storming night" in ancient Greek religion was the virgin goddess of justice, purity, precision, innocence.
6. A benefit to whom? (Latin).

daily or hourly occasion to feel; but even if in his whole conduct he
habitually follows a woman's guidance, still, if he is a fool, she thinks
that of course she is not, and cannot be, equal in ability and judgment to himself; and if he is not a fool, he does worse—he sees
that she is superior to him, and believes that, notwithstanding her
superiority, he is entitled to command and she is bound to obey.
What must be the effect on his character, of this lesson? And men of
the cultivated classes are often not aware how deeply it sinks into the
immense majority of male minds. For, among right-feeling and well-
bred people, the inequality is kept as much as possible out of sight;
above all, out of sight of the children. As much obedience is required
from boys to their mother as to their father: they are not permitted
to domineer over their sisters, nor are they accustomed to see these
postponed to them, but the contrary; the compensations of the chivalrous feeling being made prominent, while the servitude which
requires them is kept in the background. Well brought-up youths in
the higher classes thus often escape the bad influences of the situation in their early years, and only experience them when, arrived
at manhood, they fall under the dominion of facts as they really
exist. Such people are little aware, when a boy is differently brought
up, how early the notion of his inherent superiority to a girl arises
in his mind; how it grows with his growth and strengthens with his
strength; how it is inoculated by one schoolboy upon another; how
early the youth thinks himself superior to his mother, owing her perhaps forbearance, but no real respect; and how sublime and sultan-
like a sense of superiority he feels, above all, over the woman whom
he honours by admitting her to a partnership of his life. Is it imagined
that all this does not pervert the whole manner of existence of the
man, both as an individual and as a social being? It is an exact parallel to the feeling of a hereditary king that he is excellent above
others by being born a king, or a noble by being born a noble. The
relation between husband and wife is very like that between lord and
vassal, except that the wife is held to more unlimited obedience than
the vassal was. However the vassal's character may have been
affected, for better and for worse, by his subordination, who can help
seeing that the lord's was affected greatly for the worse? whether
he was led to believe that his vassals were really superior to himself, or to feel that he was placed in command over people as good
as himself, for no merits or labours of his own, but merely for having, as Figaro[7] says, taken the trouble to be born. The self-worship
of the monarch, or of the feudal superior, is matched by the

---

7. The servant in *The Marriage of Figaro* (1784) by Pierre Beaumarchais; in 1786 the play
   was made into an *opera buffa* (comic opera) by Wolfgang Amadeus Mozart, with a libretto
   by Lorenzo Da Ponte.

self-worship of the male. Human beings do not grow up from child-hood in the possession of unearned distinctions, without pluming themselves upon them. Those whom privileges not acquired by their merit, and which they feel to be disproportioned to it, inspire with additional humility, are always the few, and the best few. The rest are only inspired with pride, and the worst sort of pride, that which values itself upon accidental advantages, not of its own achieving. Above all, when the feeling of being raised above the whole of the other sex is combined with personal authority over one individual among them; the situation, if a school of conscientious and affectionate forbearance to those whose strongest points of character are conscience and affection, is to men of another qual-ity a regularly constituted Academy or Gymnasium[8] for training them in arrogance and overbearingness; which vices, if curbed by the certainty of resistance in their intercourse with other men, their equals, break out towards all who are in a position to be obliged to tolerate them, and often revenge themselves upon the unfortunate wife for the involuntary restraint which they are obliged to submit to elsewhere.

The example afforded, and the education given to the sentiments, by laying the foundation of domestic existence upon a relation con-tradictory to the first principles of social justice, must, from the very nature of man, have a perverting influence of such magnitude, that it is hardly possible with our present experience to raise our imagi-nations to the conception of so great a change for the better as would be made by its removal. All that education and civilization are doing to efface the influences on character of the law of force, and replace them by those of justice, remains merely on the surface, as long as the citadel of the enemy is not attacked. The principle of the mod-ern movement in morals and politics, is that conduct, and conduct alone, entitles to respect: that not what men are, but what they do, constitutes their claim to deference; that, above all, merit, and not birth, is the only rightful claim to power and authority. If no author-ity, not in its nature temporary, were allowed to one human being over another, society would not be employed in building up propen-sities with one hand which it has to curb with the other. The child would really, for the first time in man's existence on earth, be trained in the way he should go, and when he was old there would be a chance that he would not depart from it. But so long as the right of the strong to power over the weak rules in the very heart of society, the attempt to make the equal right of the weak the principle of its outward actions will always be an uphill struggle; for the law of

8. A training facility for competitors in public games in ancient Greece. *Academy*: an insti-tution for secondary education; its name traces back to Plato's school of philosophy.

justice, which is also that of Christianity, will never get possession of men's inmost sentiments; they will be working against it, even when bending to it.

The second benefit to be expected from giving to women the free use of their faculties, by leaving them the free choice of their employments, and opening to them the same field of occupation and the same prizes and encouragements as to other human beings, would be that of doubling the mass of mental faculties available for the higher service of humanity. Where there is now one person qualified to benefit mankind and promote the general improvement, as a public teacher, or an administrator of some branch of public or social affairs, there would then be a chance of two. Mental superiority of any kind is at present everywhere so much below the demand; there is such a deficiency of persons competent to do excellently anything which it requires any considerable amount of ability to do; that the loss to the world, by refusing to make use of one-half of the whole quantity of talent it possesses, is extremely serious. It is true that this amount of mental power is not totally lost. Much of it is employed, and would in any case be employed, in domestic management, and in the few other occupations open to women; and from the remainder indirect benefit is in many individual cases obtained, through the personal influence of individual women over individual men. But these benefits are partial; their range is extremely circumscribed; and if they must be admitted, on the one hand, as a deduction from the amount of fresh social power that would be acquired by giving freedom to one-half of the whole sum of human intellect, there must be added, on the other, the benefit of the stimulus that would be given to the intellect of men by the competition; or (to use a more true expression) by the necessity that would be imposed on them of deserving precedency before they could expect to obtain it.

This great accession to the intellectual power of the species, and to the amount of intellect available for the good management of its affairs, would be obtained, partly, through the better and more complete intellectual education of women, which would then improve *pari passu*[9] with that of men. Women in general would be brought up equally capable of understanding business, public affairs, and the higher matters of speculation, with men in the same class of society; and the select few of the one as well as of the other sex, who were qualified not only to comprehend what is done or thought by others, but to think or do something considerable themselves, would meet with the same facilities for improving and training their

9. With an equal step, or "on equal footing" (Latin).

capacities in the one sex as in the other. In this way, the widening of the sphere of action for women would operate for good, by raising their education to the level of that of men, and making the one participate in all improvements made in the other. But independently of this, the mere breaking down of the barrier would of itself have an educational virtue of the highest worth. The mere getting rid of the idea that all the wider subjects of thought and action, all the things which are of general and not solely of private interest, are men's business, from which women are to be warned off—positively interdicted from most of it, coldly tolerated in the little which is allowed them—the mere consciousness a woman would then have of being a human being like any other, entitled to choose her pursuits, urged or invited by the same inducements as any one else to interest herself in whatever is interesting to human beings, entitled to exert the share of influence on all human concerns which belongs to an individual opinion, whether she attempted actual participation in them or not—this alone would effect an immense expansion of the faculties of women, as well as enlargement of the range of their moral sentiments.

Besides the addition to the amount of individual talent available for the conduct of human affairs, which certainly are not at present so abundantly provided in that respect that they can afford to dispense with one-half of what nature proffers; the opinion of women would then possess a more beneficial, rather than a greater, influence upon the general mass of human belief and sentiment. I say a more beneficial, rather than a greater influence; for the influence of women over the general tone of opinion has always, or at least from the earliest known period, been very considerable. The influence of mothers on the early character of their sons, and the desire of young men to recommend themselves to young women, have in all recorded times been important agencies in the formation of character, and have determined some of the chief steps in the progress of civilization. Even in the Homeric age, $\alpha i \delta \omega \varsigma$ towards the $T \rho \omega \alpha \delta \alpha \varsigma$ $\dot{\epsilon} \lambda \kappa \epsilon \sigma \iota \pi \epsilon \pi \lambda o \upsilon \varsigma$ is an acknowledged and powerful motive of action in the great Hector.[1] The moral influence of women has had two modes of operation. First, it has been a softening influence. Those who were most liable to be the victims of violence, have naturally tended as

1. The son of Troy's King Priam and Queen Hecuba and the hero of the Trojan War; brother of Paris (who kidnapped Helena, wife of the Greek king Menelaus, and caused the war), he was killed by Achilles in a duel. The two Greek expressions mean, respectively, "modesty" and "Trojans' wives, with trailing robes"; from Homer's *Iliad* VI, 441–42: "Then spake to her great Hector of the flashing helm: 'Woman, I too take thought of all this, but wondrously have I shame of the Trojans, and the Trojans' wives, with trailing robes, if like a coward I skulk apart from the battle," (trans. Richmond Lattimore [Chicago: U of Chicago P, 1960]).

much as they could towards limiting its sphere and mitigating its excesses. Those who were not taught to fight, have naturally inclined in favour of any other mode of settling differences rather than that of fighting. In general, those who have been the greatest sufferers by the indulgence of selfish passion, have been the most earnest supporters of any moral law which offered a means of bridling passion. Women were powerfully instrumental in inducing the northern conquerors to adopt the creed of Christianity, a creed so much more favourable to women than any that preceded it. The conversion of the Anglo-Saxons and of the Franks may be said to have been begun by the wives of Ethelbert and Clovis.[2] The other mode in which the effect of women's opinion has been conspicuous, is by giving a powerful stimulus to those qualities in men, which, not being themselves trained in, it was necessary for them that they should find in their protectors. Courage, and the military virtues generally, have at all times been greatly indebted to the desire which men felt of being admired by women: and the stimulus reaches far beyond this one class of eminent qualities, since, by a very natural effect of their position, the best passport to the admiration and favour of women has always been to be thought highly of by men. From the combination of the two kinds of moral influence thus exercised by women, arose the spirit of chivalry: the peculiarity of which is, to aim at combining the highest standard of the warlike qualities with the cultivation of a totally different class of virtues—those of gentleness, generosity, and self-abnegation, towards the non-military and defenceless classes generally, and a special submission and worship directed towards women; who were distinguished from the other defenceless classes by the high rewards which they had it in their power voluntarily to bestow on those who endeavoured to earn their favour, instead of extorting their subjection. Though the practice of chivalry fell even more sadly short of its theoretic standard than practice generally falls below theory, it remains one of the most precious monuments of the moral history of our race; as a remarkable instance of a concerted and organized attempt by a most disorganized and distracted society, to raise up and carry into practice a moral ideal greatly in advance of its social condition and institutions; so much so as to have been completely frustrated in the main object, yet never entirely inefficacious, and which has left a most sensible, and for the most part a highly valuable impress on the ideas and feelings of all subsequent times.

2. Clovis I (d. 511), the first king of the Franks to unite all of the tribes under one ruler, thus changing the form of leadership from a group of petty kings to rule by a single king by ensuring that the kingship was passed down to his heir. *Ethelbert*: (560–616), the third king to rule over the Anglo-Saxon Kingdom.

The chivalrous ideal is the acme of the influence of women's sentiments on the moral cultivation of mankind: and if women are to remain in their subordinate situation, it were greatly to be lamented that the chivalrous standard should have passed away, for it is the only one at all capable of mitigating the demoralizing influences of that position. But the changes in the general state of the species rendered inevitable the substitution of a totally different ideal of morality for the chivalrous one. Chivalry was the attempt to infuse moral elements into a state of society in which everything depended for good or evil on individual prowess, under the softening influences of individual delicacy and generosity. In modern societies, all things, even in the military department of affairs, are decided, not by individual effort, but by the combined operations of numbers; while the main occupation of society has changed from fighting to business, from military to industrial life. The exigencies of the new life are no more exclusive of the virtues of generosity than those of the old, but it no longer entirely depends on them. The main foundations of the moral life of modern times must be justice and prudence; the respect of each for the rights of every other, and the ability of each to take care of himself. Chivalry left without legal check all forms of wrong which reigned unpunished throughout society; it only encouraged a few to do right in preference to wrong, by the direction it gave to the instruments of praise and admiration. But the real dependence of morality must always be upon its penal sanctions—its power to deter from evil. The security of society cannot rest on merely rendering honour to right, a motive so comparatively weak in all but a few, and which on very many does not operate at all. Modern society is able to repress wrong through all departments of life, by a fit exertion of the superior strength which civilization has given it, and thus to render the existence of the weaker members of society (no longer defenceless but protected by law) tolerable to them, without reliance on the chivalrous feelings of those who are in a position to tyrannize. The beauties and graces of the chivalrous character are still what they were, but the rights of the weak, and the general comfort of human life, now rest on a far surer and steadier support; or rather, they do so in every relation of life except the conjugal.

At present the moral influence of women is no less real, but it is no longer of so marked and definite a character: it has more nearly merged in the general influence of public opinion. Both through the contagion of sympathy, and through the desire of men to shine in the eyes of women, their feelings have great effect in keeping alive what remains of the chivalrous ideal—in fostering the sentiments and continuing the traditions of spirit and generosity. In these points of character, their standard is higher than that of men; in the quality of justice, somewhat lower. As regards the relations of private life it may be said generally, that their influence is, on the whole, encouraging to the softer virtues, discouraging to the sterner: though the statement must be taken with all the modifications dependent on individual character. In the chief of the greater trials to which virtue is subject in the concerns of life—the conflict between interest and principle—the tendency of women's influence is of a very mixed character. When the principle involved happens to be one of the very few which the course of their religious or moral education has strongly impressed upon themselves, they are potent auxiliaries to virtue: and their husbands and sons are often prompted by them to acts of abnegation which they never would have been capable of without that stimulus. But, with the present education and position of women, the moral principles which have been impressed on them cover but a comparatively small part of the field of virtue, and are, moreover, principally negative; forbidding particular acts, but having little to do with the general direction of the thoughts and purposes. I am afraid it must be said, that disinterestedness in the general conduct of life—the devotion of the energies to purposes which hold out no promise of private advantages to the family—is very seldom encouraged or supported by women's influence. It is small blame to them that they discourage objects of which they have not learnt to see the advantage, and which withdraw their men from them, and from the interests of the family. But the consequence is that women's influence is often anything but favourable to public virtue.

Women have, however, some share of influence in giving the tone to public moralities since their sphere of action has been a little widened, and since a considerable number of them have occupied themselves practically in the promotion of objects reaching beyond their own family and household. The influence of women counts for a great deal in two of the most marked features of modern European life—its aversion to war, and its addiction to philanthropy. Excellent characteristics both; but unhappily, if the influence of women is valuable in the encouragement it gives to these feelings in general, in the particular applications the direction it gives to them is at least as often mischievous as useful. In the philanthropic department more particularly, the two provinces chiefly cultivated by women are religious proselytism and charity. Religious proselytism at home, is but another word for embittering of religious animosities: abroad, it is usually a blind running at an object, without either knowing or heeding the fatal mischiefs—fatal to the religious object itself as well as to all other desirable objects—which may be produced by the means employed. As for charity, it is a matter in which the immediate effect on the persons directly concerned, and the ultimate consequence to the general good, are apt to be at complete war with one another: while the education given to women—an education of the sentiments rather than of the understanding—and the habit inculcated by their whole life, of looking to immediate effects on persons, and not to remote effects on classes of persons—make them both unable to see, and unwilling to admit, the ultimate evil tendency of any form of charity or philanthropy which commends itself to their sympathetic feelings. The great and continually increasing mass of unenlightened and shortsighted benevolence, which, taking the care of people's lives out of their own hands, and relieving them from the disagreeable consequences of their own acts, saps the very foundations of the self-respect, self-help, and self-control which are the essential conditions both of individual prosperity and of social virtue—this waste of resources and of benevolent feelings in doing harm instead of good, is immensely swelled by women's contributions, and stimulated by their influence. Not that this is a mistake likely to be made by women, where they have actually the practical management of schemes of beneficence. It sometimes happens that women who administer public charities—with that insight into present fact, and especially into the minds and feelings of those with whom they are in immediate contact, in which women generally excel men—recognise in the clearest manner the demoralizing influence of the alms given or the help afforded, and could give lessons on the subject to many a male political economist. But women who only give their money, and are not brought face to face with the effects it produces, how can they be expected to foresee them? A woman born to the present lot of women, and content with it, how should she appreciate the value of self-dependence? She is not self-dependent; she is not taught self-dependence; her destiny is to receive everything from others, and why should what is good enough for her be bad for the poor? Her familiar notions of good are of blessings descending from a superior. She forgets that she is not free, and that the poor are; that if what they need is given to them unearned, they cannot be compelled to earn it: that everybody cannot be taken care of by everybody, but there must be some motive to induce people to take care of themselves; and that to be helped to help themselves, if they are physically capable of it, is the only charity which proves to be charity in the end.

These considerations shew how usefully the part which women take in the formation of general opinion, would be modified for the better by that more enlarged instruction, and practical conversancy with the things which their opinions influence, that would necessarily arise from their social and political emancipation. But the improvement it would work through the influence they exercise, each in her own family, would be still more remarkable.

It is often said that in the classes most exposed to temptation, a man's wife and children tend to keep him honest and respectable, both by the wife's direct influence, and by the concern he feels for their future welfare. This may be so, and no doubt often is so, with those who are more weak than wicked; and this beneficial influence would be preserved and strengthened under equal laws; it does not depend on the woman's servitude, but is, on the contrary, diminished by the disrespect which the inferior class of men always at heart feel towards those who are subject to their power. But when we ascend higher in the scale, we come among a totally different set of moving forces. The wife's influence tends, as far as it goes, to prevent the husband from falling below the common standard of approbation of the country. It tends quite as strongly to hinder him from rising above it. The wife is the auxiliary of the common public opinion. A man who is married to a woman his inferior in intelligence, finds her a perpetual dead weight, or, worse than a dead weight, a drag, upon every aspiration of his to be better than public opinion requires him to be. It is hardly possible for one who is in these bonds, to attain exalted virtue. If he differs in his opinion from the mass—if he sees truths which have not yet dawned upon them, or if, feeling in his heart truths which they nominally recognise, he would like to act up to those truths more conscientiously than the generality of mankind—to all such thoughts and desires, marriage is the heaviest of drawbacks, unless he be so fortunate as to have a wife as much above the common level as he himself is.

For, in the first place, there is always some sacrifice of personal interest required; either of social consequence, or of pecuniary means; perhaps the risk of even the means of subsistence. These sacrifices and risks he may be willing to encounter for himself; but he will pause before he imposes them on his family. And his family in this case means his wife and daughters; for he always hopes that his sons will feel as he feels himself, and that what he can do without, they will do without, willingly, in the same cause. But his daughters—their marriage may depend upon it: and his wife, who is unable to enter into or understand the objects for which these sacrifices are made—who, if she thought them worth any sacrifice, would think so on trust, and solely for his sake—who can participate in none of the enthusiasm or the self-approbation he himself may feel, while the things which he is disposed to sacrifice are all in all to her; will not the best and most unselfish man hesitate the longest before bringing on her this consequence? If it be not the comforts of life, but only social consideration, that is at stake, the burthen upon his conscience and feelings is still very severe. Whoever has a wife and children has given hostages to

Mrs. Grundy.[3] The approbation of that potentate may be a matter of indifference to him, but it is of great importance to his wife. The man himself may be above opinion, or may find sufficient compensation in the opinion of those of his own way of thinking. But to the women connected with him, he can offer no compensation. The almost invariable tendency of the wife to place her influence in the same scale with social consideration, is sometimes made a reproach to women, and represented as a peculiar trait of feebleness and childishness of character in them: surely with great injustice. Society makes the whole life of a woman, in the easy classes, a continued self-sacrifice; it exacts from her an unremitting restraint of the whole of her natural inclinations, and the sole return it makes to her for what often deserves the name of a martyrdom, is consideration. Her consideration is inseparably connected with that of her husband, and after paying the full price for it, she finds that she is to lose it, for no reason of which she can feel the cogency. She has sacrificed her whole life to it, and her husband will not sacrifice to it a whim, a freak, an eccentricity; something not recognised or allowed for by the world, and which the world will agree with her in thinking a folly, if it thinks no worse! The dilemma is hardest upon that very meritorious class of men, who, without possessing talents which qualify them to make a figure among those with whom they agree in opinion, hold their opinion from conviction, and feel bound in honour and conscience to serve it, by making profession of their belief, and giving their time, labour, and means, to anything undertaken in its behalf. The worst case of all is when such men happen to be of a rank and position which of itself neither gives them, nor excludes them from, what is considered the best society; when their admission to it depends mainly on what is thought of them personally—and however unexceptionable their breeding and habits, their being identified with opinions and public conduct unacceptable to those who give the tone to society would operate as an effectual exclusion. Many a woman flatters herself (nine times out of ten quite erroneously) that nothing prevents her and her husband from moving in the highest society of her neighbourhood—society in which others well known to her, and in the same class of life, mix freely—except that her husband is unfortunately a Dissenter,[4] or has the reputation of mingling in low radical politics. That it is, she thinks, which hinders George from

3. A figure in Thomas Morton's play *Speed the Plough* (1789). Her name became a figure of speech meaning the tyranny of conventional propriety; Mill epitomizes critically the morality of domesticity, hypocrisy, and self-deception.
4. A member of a non-established or Nonconformist church; the word "dissenter" comes from Latin *dissentire* (to disagree) or [to come] of opinions and ideas.

getting a commission or a place, Caroline from making an advantageous match, and prevents her and her husband from obtaining
invitations, perhaps honours, which, for aught she sees, they are as
well entitled to as some folks. With such an influence in every
house, either exerted actively, or operating all the more powerfully
for not being asserted, is it any wonder that people in general are
kept down in that mediocrity of respectability which is becoming a
marked characteristic of modern times?

There is another very injurious aspect in which the effect, not of
women's disabilities directly, but of the broad line of difference
which those disabilities create between the education and character
of a woman and that of a man, requires to be considered. Nothing
can be more unfavourable to that union of thoughts and inclinations which is the ideal of married life. Intimate society between
people radically dissimilar to one another, is an idle dream. Unlikeness may attract, but it is likeness which retains; and in proportion
to the likeness is the suitability of the individuals to give each
other a happy life. While women are so unlike men, it is not wonderful that selfish men should feel the need of arbitrary power in
their own hands, to arrest *in limine*[5] the life-long conflict of inclinations, by deciding every question on the side of their own preference. When people are extremely unlike, there can be no real identity
of interest. Very often there is conscientious difference of opinion
between married people, on the highest points of duty. Is there any
reality in the marriage union where this takes place? Yet it is not
uncommon anywhere, when the woman has any earnestness of character; and it is a very general case indeed in Catholic countries,
when she is supported in her dissent by the only other authority to
which she is taught to bow, the priest. With the usual barefaced-
ness of power not accustomed to find itself disputed, the influence
of priests over women is attacked by Protestant and Liberal writers,
less for being bad in itself, than because it is a rival authority to the
husband, and raises up a revolt against his infallibility. In England,
similar differences occasionally exist when an Evangelical wife has
allied herself with a husband of a different quality; but in general
this source at least of dissension is got rid of, by reducing the minds
of women to such a nullity, that they have no opinions but those of
Mrs. Grundy, or those which the husband tells them to have. When
there is no difference of opinion, differences merely of taste may be
sufficient to detract greatly from the happiness of married life. And
though it may stimulate the amatory propensities of men, it does not
conduce to married happiness, to exaggerate by differences of education whatever may be the native differences of the sexes. If the

5. On the threshold (Latin).

married pair are well-bred and well-behaved people, they tolerate each other's tastes; but is mutual toleration what people look forward to, when they enter into marriage? These differences of inclination will naturally make their wishes different, if not restrained by affection or duty, as to almost all domestic questions which arise. What a difference there must be in the society which the two persons will wish to frequent, or be frequented by! Each will desire associates who share their own tastes: the persons agreeable to one, will be indifferent or positively disagreeable to the other; yet there can be none who are not common to both, for married people do not now live in different parts of the house and have totally different visiting lists, as in the reign of Louis XV.[6] They cannot help having different wishes as to the bringing up of the children: each will wish to see reproduced in them their own tastes and sentiments: and there is either a compromise, and only a half-satisfaction to either, or the wife has to yield—often with bitter suffering; and, with or without intention, her occult influence continues to counterwork the husband's purposes.

It would of course be extreme folly to suppose that these differences of feeling and inclination only exist because women are brought up differently from men, and that there would not be differences of taste under any imaginable circumstances. But there is nothing beyond the mark in saying that the distinction in bringing-up immensely aggravates those differences, and renders them wholly inevitable. While women are brought up as they are, a man and a woman will but rarely find in one another real agreement of tastes and wishes as to daily life. They will generally have to give it up as hopeless, and renounce the attempt to have, in the intimate associate of their daily life, that *idem velle, idem nolle*,[7] which is the recognised bond of any society that is really such: or if the man succeeds in obtaining it, he does so by choosing a woman who is so complete a nullity that she has no *velle* or *nolle* at all, and is as ready to comply with one thing as another if anybody tells her to do so. Even this calculation is apt to fail; dulness and want of spirit are not always a guarantee of the submission which is so confidently expected from them. But if they were, is this the ideal of marriage? What, in this case, does the man obtain by it, except an upper servant, a nurse, or a mistress? On the contrary, when each of two persons, instead of being a nothing, is a something; when they are attached to one another, and are not too much unlike to begin with; the constant partaking in the same things, assisted by their sympathy, draws out the latent capacities of each for being interested in the things

6. King of France from 1715 to 1774.
7. To like and dislike at the same time (Latin).

which were at first interesting only to the other; and works a gradual assimilation of the tastes and characters to one another, partly by the insensible modification of each, but more by a real enriching of the two natures, each acquiring the tastes and capacities of the other in addition to its own. This often happens between two friends of the same sex, who are much associated in their daily life: and it would be a common, if not the commonest, case in marriage, did not the totally different bringing-up of the two sexes make it next to an impossibility to form a really well-assorted union. Were this remedied, whatever differences there might still be in individual tastes, there would at least be, as a general rule, complete unity and unanimity as to the great objects of life. When the two persons both care for great objects, and are a help and encouragement to each other in whatever regards these, the minor matters on which their tastes may differ are not all-important to them; and there is a foundation for solid friendship, of an enduring character, more likely than anything else to make it, through the whole of life, a greater pleasure to each to give pleasure to the other, than to receive it.

I have considered, thus far, the effects on the pleasures and benefits of the marriage union which depend on the mere unlikeness between the wife and the husband: but the evil tendency is prodigiously aggravated when the unlikeness is inferiority. Mere unlikeness, when it only means difference of good qualities, may be more a benefit in the way of mutual improvement, than a drawback from comfort. When each emulates, and desires and endeavours to acquire, the other's peculiar qualities, the difference does not produce diversity of interest, but increased identity of it, and makes each still more valuable to the other. But when one is much the inferior of the two in mental ability and cultivation, and is not actively attempting by the other's aid to rise to the other's level, the whole influence of the connexion upon the development of the superior of the two is deteriorating: and still more so in a tolerably happy marriage than in an unhappy one. It is not with impunity that the superior in intellect shuts himself up with an inferior, and elects that inferior for his chosen, and sole completely intimate, associate. Any society which is not improving, is deteriorating: and the more so, the closer and more familiar it is. Even a really superior man almost always begins to deteriorate when he is habitually (as the phrase is) king of his company: and in his most habitual company the husband who has a wife inferior to him is always so. While his self-satisfaction is incessantly ministered to on the one hand, on the other he insensibly imbibes the modes of feeling, and of looking at things, which belong to a more vulgar or a more limited mind than his own. This evil differs from many of those which have hitherto been dwelt on, by being an increasing one. The association of men with women in daily life is much closer and more complete than it ever was before. Men's life is more domestic. Formerly, their pleasures and chosen occupations were among men, and in men's company: their wives had but a fragment of their lives. At the present time, the progress of civilization, and the turn of opinion against the rough amusements and convivial excesses which formerly occupied most men in their hours of relaxation—together with (it must be said) the improved tone of modern feeling as to the reciprocity of duty which binds the husband towards the wife—have thrown the man very much more upon home and its inmates, for his personal and social pleasures: while the kind and degree of improvement which has been made in women's education, has made them in some degree capable of being his companions in ideas and mental tastes, while leaving them, in most cases, still hopelessly inferior to him. His desire of mental communion is thus in general satisfied by a communion from which he learns nothing. An unimproving and unstimulating companionship is substituted for (what he might otherwise have been obliged to seek) the society of his equals in powers and his fellows in the higher pursuits. We see, accordingly, that young men of the greatest promise generally cease to improve as soon as they marry, and, not improving, inevitably degenerate. If the wife does not push the husband forward, she always holds him back. He ceases to care for what she does not care for; he no longer desires, and ends by disliking and shunning, society congenial to his former aspirations, and which would now shame his falling-off from them; his higher faculties both of mind and heart cease to be called into activity. And this change coinciding with the new and selfish interests which are created by the family, after a few years he differs in no material respect from those who have never had wishes for anything but the common vanities and the common pecuniary objects.

What marriage may be in the case of two persons of cultivated faculties, identical in opinions and purposes, between whom there exists that best kind of equality, similarity of powers and capacities with reciprocal superiority in them—so that each can enjoy the luxury of looking up to the other, and can have alternately the pleasure of leading and of being led in the path of development—I will not attempt to describe. To those who can conceive it, there is no need; to those who cannot, it would appear the dream of an enthusiast. But I maintain, with the profoundest conviction, that this, and this only, is the ideal of marriage; and that all opinions, customs, and institutions which favour any other notion of it, or turn the conceptions and aspirations connected with it into any other direction, by whatever pretences they may be coloured, are relics of primitive barbarism. The moral regeneration of mankind will only really commence, when the most fundamental of the social relations is placed under the rule of equal justice, and when human beings learn to cultivate their strongest sympathy with an equal in rights and in cultivation.

Thus far, the benefits which it has appeared that the world would gain by ceasing to make sex a disqualification for privileges and a badge of subjection, are social rather than individual; consisting in an increase of the general fund of thinking and acting power, and an improvement in the general conditions of the association of men with women. But it would be a grievous understatement of the case to omit the most direct benefit of all, the unspeakable gain in private happiness to the liberated half of the species; the difference to them between a life of subjection to the will of others, and a life of rational freedom. After the primary necessities of food and raiment, freedom is the first and strongest want of human nature. While mankind are lawless, their desire is for lawless freedom. When they have learnt to understand the meaning of duty and the value of reason, they incline more and more to be guided and restrained by these in the exercise of their freedom; but they do not therefore desire freedom less; they do not become disposed to accept the will of other people as the representative and interpreter of those guiding principles. On the contrary, the communities in which the reason has been most cultivated, and in which the idea of social duty has been most powerful, are those which have most strongly asserted the freedom of action of the individual—the liberty of each to govern his conduct by his own feelings of duty, and by such laws and social restraints as his own conscience can subscribe to.

He who would rightly appreciate the worth of personal independence as an element of happiness, should consider the value he himself puts upon it as an ingredient of his own. There is no subject on which there is a greater habitual difference of judgment between a man judging for himself, and the same man judging for other people. When he hears others complaining that they are not allowed freedom of action—that their own will has not sufficient influence in the regulation of their affairs—his inclination is, to ask, what are their grievances? what positive damage they sustain? and in what respect they consider their affairs to be mismanaged? and if they fail to make out, in answer to these questions, what appears to him a sufficient case, he turns a deaf ear, and regards their complaint as the fanciful querulousness of people whom nothing reasonable will satisfy. But he has a quite different standard of judgment when he is deciding for himself. Then, the most unexceptionable administration of his interests by a tutor set over him, does not satisfy his feelings: his personal exclusion from the deciding authority appears itself the greatest grievance of all, rendering it superfluous even to enter into the question of mismanagement. It is the same with nations. What citizen of a free country would listen to any offers of good and skilful administration, in return for the abdication of freedom? Even if he could believe that good and skilful administration can exist among a people ruled by a will not their own, would not the consciousness of working out their own destiny under their own moral responsibility be a compensation to his feelings for great rudeness and imperfection in the details of public affairs? Let him rest assured that whatever he feels on this point, women feel in a fully equal degree. Whatever has been said or written, from the time of Herodotus[8] to the present, of the ennobling influence of free government—the nerve and spring which it gives to all the faculties, the larger and higher objects which it presents to the intellect and feelings, the more unselfish public spirit, and calmer and broader views of duty, that it engenders, and the generally loftier platform on which it elevates the individual as a moral, spiritual, and social being—is every particle as true of women as of men. Are these things no important part of individual happiness? Let any man call to mind what he himself felt on emerging from boyhood—from the tutelage and control of even loved and affectionate elders—and entering upon the responsibilities of manhood. Was it not like the physical effect of taking off a heavy weight, or releasing him from obstructive, even if not otherwise painful, bonds? Did he not feel twice as much alive, twice as much a human being, as before? And does he imagine that women have none of these feelings? But it is a striking fact, that the satisfactions and mortifications of personal pride, though all in all to most men when the case is their own, have less allowance made for them in the case of other people, and are less listened to as a ground or a justification of conduct, than any other natural human feelings; perhaps because men compliment them in their own case with the names of so many other qualities, that they are seldom conscious how mighty an influence these feelings exercise in their own lives. No less large and powerful is their part, we may assure ourselves, in the lives and feelings of women. Women are schooled into suppressing them in their most natural and most healthy direction, but the internal principle remains, in a different outward form. An active and energetic mind, if denied liberty, will seek for power: refused the command of itself, it will assert its personality by attempting to control others. To allow to any human beings no existence of their own but what depends on others, is giving far too high a premium on bending others to their purposes. Where liberty cannot be hoped for, and power can, power becomes

---

8. Greek historian (480–430/420 B.C.E.) from Halicarnassus; he wrote a detailed account of the Greco-Persian Wars and was the first writer to attain a systematic investigation of historical events and peoples' customs and institutions, political and religious.

the grand object of human desire; those to whom others will not leave the undisturbed management of their own affairs, will compensate themselves, if they can, by meddling for their own purposes with the affairs of others. Hence also women's passion for personal beauty, and dress and display; and all the evils that flow from it, in the way of mischievous luxury and social immorality. The love of power and the love of liberty are in eternal antagonism. Where there is least liberty, the passion for power is the most ardent and unscrupulous. The desire of power over others can only cease to be a depraving agency among mankind, when each of them individually is able to do without it: which can only be where respect for liberty in the personal concerns of each is an established principle.

But it is not only through the sentiment of personal dignity, that the free direction and disposal of their own faculties is a source of individual happiness, and to be fettered and restricted in it, a source of unhappiness, to human beings, and not least to women. There is nothing, after disease, indigence, and guilt, so fatal to the pleasurable enjoyment of life as the want of a worthy outlet for the active faculties. Women who have the cares of a family, and while they have the cares of a family, have this outlet, and it generally suffices for them: but what of the greatly increasing number of women, who have had no opportunity of exercising the vocation which they are mocked by telling them is their proper one? What of the women whose children have been lost to them by death or distance, or have grown up, married, and formed homes of their own? There are abundant examples of men who, after a life engrossed by business, retire with a competency to the enjoyment, as they hope, of rest, but to whom, as they are unable to acquire new interests and excitements that can replace the old, the change to a life of inactivity brings ennui, melancholy, and premature death. Yet no one thinks of the parallel case of so many worthy and devoted women, who, having paid what they are told is their debt to society—having brought up a family blamelessly to manhood and womanhood—having kept a house as long as they had a house needing to be kept—are deserted by the sole occupation for which they have fitted themselves; and remain with undiminished activity but with no employment for it, unless perhaps a daughter or daughter-in-law is willing to abdicate in their favour the discharge of the same functions in her younger household. Surely a hard lot for the old age of those who have worthily discharged, as long as it was given to them to discharge, what the world accounts their only social duty. Of such women, and of those others to whom this duty has not been committed at all—many of whom pine through life with the consciousness of thwarted vocations, and activities which are not suffered to expand—the only resources, speaking generally, are religion and charity. But their religion, though it may be one of feeling, and of ceremonial observance, cannot be a religion of action, unless in the form of charity. For charity many of them are by nature admirably fitted; but to practise it usefully, or even without doing mischief, requires the education, the manifold preparation, the knowledge and the thinking powers, of a skilful administrator. There are few of the administrative functions of government for which a person would not be fit, who is fit to bestow charity usefully. In this as in other cases (pre-eminently in that of the education of children), the duties permitted to women cannot be performed properly, without their being trained for duties which, to the great loss of society, are not permitted to them. And here let me notice the singular way in which the question of women's disabilities is frequently presented to view, by those who find it easier to draw a ludicrous picture of what they do not like, than to answer the arguments for it. When it is suggested that women's executive capacities and prudent counsels might sometimes be found valuable in affairs of state, these lovers of fun hold up to the ridicule of the world, as sitting in parliament or in the cabinet, girls in their teens, or young wives of two or three and twenty, transported bodily, exactly as they are, from the drawing-room to the House of Commons. They forget that males are not usually selected at this early age for a seat in Parliament, or for responsible political functions. Common sense would tell them that if such trusts were confided to women, it would be to such as having no special vocation for married life, or preferring another employment of their faculties (as many women even now prefer to marriage some of the few honourable occupations within their reach), have spent the best years of their youth in attempting to qualify themselves for the pursuits in which they desire to engage; or still more frequently perhaps, widows or wives of forty or fifty, by whom the knowledge of life and faculty of government which they have acquired in their families, could by the aid of appropriate studies be made available on a less contracted scale. There is no country of Europe in which the ablest men have not frequently experienced, and keenly appreciated, the value of the advice and help of clever and experienced women of the world, in the attainment both of private and of public objects; and there are important matters of public administration to which few men are equally competent with such women; among others, the detailed control of expenditure. But what we are now discussing is not the need which society has of the services of women in public business, but the dull and hopeless life to which it so often condemns them, by forbidding them to exercise the practical abilities which many of them are conscious of, in any wider field than one which to some of them never was, and to others is no longer, open. If there is anything vitally important to the happiness of human beings, it is that they should relish their habitual pursuit. This requisite of an enjoyable life is very imperfectly granted, or altogether denied, to a large part of mankind; and by its absence many a life is a failure, which is provided, in appearance, with every requisite of success. But if circumstances which society is not yet skilful enough to overcome, render such failures often for the present inevitable, society need not itself inflict them. The injudiciousness of parents, a youth's own inexperience, or the absence of external opportunities for the congenial vocation, and their presence for an uncongenial, condemn numbers of men to pass their lives in doing one thing reluctantly and ill, when there are other things which they could have done well and happily. But on women this sentence is imposed by actual law, and by customs equivalent to law. What, in unenlightened societies, colour, race, religion, or in the case of a conquered country, nationality, are to some men, sex is to all women; a peremptory exclusion from almost all honourable occupations, but either such as cannot be fulfilled by others, or such as those others do not think worthy of their acceptance. Sufferings arising from causes of this nature usually meet with so little sympathy, that few persons are aware of the great amount of unhappiness even now produced by the feeling of a wasted life. The case will be even more frequent, as increased cultivation creates a greater and greater disproportion between the ideas and faculties of women, and the scope which society allows to their activity.

When we consider the positive evil caused to the disqualified half of the human race by their disqualification—first in the loss of the most inspiriting and elevating kind of personal enjoyment, and next in the weariness, disappointment, and profound dissatisfaction with life, which are so often the substitute for it; one feels that among all the lessons which men require for carrying on the struggle against the inevitable imperfections of their lot on earth, there is no lesson which they more need, than not to add to the evils which nature inflicts, by their jealous and prejudiced restrictions on one another. Their vain fears only substitute other and worse evils for those which they are idly apprehensive of: while every restraint on the freedom of conduct of any of their human fellow creatures, (otherwise than by making them responsible for any evil actually caused by it), dries up *pro tanto*[9] the principal fountain of human happiness, and leaves the species less rich, to an inappreciable degree, in all that makes life valuable to the individual human being.

THE END

9. To that extent (Latin).

COMMENTARIES

ALAN RYAN

Mill in a Liberal Landscape[†]

Mill's essay *On Liberty* had both the good and the ill fortune to become a "classic" on first publication. The immediate success of the book, dedicated as it was to preserving the memory of Harriet Taylor, could only gratify its author. Yet its friends and foes alike fell upon it with such enthusiasm that the essay itself has ever since been hard to see for the smoke of battle.[1] *That* it is a liberal manifesto is clear beyond doubt; *what* the liberalism is that it defends and *how* it defends it remain matters of controversy. Given the lucidity of Mill's prose and the seeming simplicity and transparency of his arguments, this is astonishing; ought we not to know by now whether the essay's main target is the hold of Christianity on the Victorian mind[2] or rather the hold of a monolithic public opinion of whatever kind; whether its intellectual basis lies in utility as Mill claimed or in a covert appeal to natural right; whether the ideal of individual moral and intellectual autonomy is supposed to animate everyone, or only an elite; and so indefinitely on?

* * *

Like that of *Utilitarianism*, the argument of Mill's essay is not so much familiar as notorious. Mill writes that "The object of this Essay is to assert one very simple principle, as entitled to govern absolutely the dealings of society with the individual in the way of compulsion and control. . . ."[3] Commentators have complained about Mill's appeal to one very *simple* principle, they have said that little in human life is simple, and the question of when to interfere with each other's liberty is not part of that little. This complaint may be mistaken, simple principles are often complicated to apply—a planning minister or his civil servants may be required not to withhold consent "unreasonably" when a citizen applies for permission to build a house or a garage, but that simple requirement leads to complicated lawsuits. Mill's simple principle is that we may coerce others into doing what they do not choose to do only for the sake of self-defence,

---

† From *The Cambridge Companion to Mill*, ed. John Skorupski (Cambridge: Cambridge University Press, 1998), pp. 497, 499–502, 505–14, 532–34, 536–40. Copyright © 1998 by Cambridge University Press. Reprinted by permission of the licensor through PLSClear.
1. See the interesting collection of the first reviews of *On Liberty* assembled in [Andrew Pyle, ed. *Liberty: Contemporary Responses to John Stuart Mill* (Bristol: Theommes Press, 1994)].
2. As Joseph Hamburger [in *Intellectuals in Politics: John Stuart Mill and the Philosophic Radicals* (New Haven: Yale U Press, 1991)] is the latest of a long line of critics to argue.
3. *On Liberty*, CW XVIII:225.

and by extension to make them perform a small number of good
offices (such as giving evidence in a court of law) required if others
are not to be harmed by their inaction. It *is* a simple principle, however complicated it may be to apply.

Mill was less interested in employing the principle to restrain coercion by single individuals than to restrain the coercive actions of
groups. It is not the fear that we shall individually assault or incarcer-
ate others when we ought not that motivated him, but the fear that we
shall collectively gang up on eccentric individuals when we ought not.
The fear is based on two things. The first and more obvious is Tocqueville's observation that Americans had less freedom of thought and
speech than one might suppose from their constitutional arrangements; Americans were notably bad at thinking for themselves, and
were vulnerable to the desire to think like everyone else and to the
desire that everyone else should think like them.[4] The second and less
obvious is an idea that Mill picked up from the Saint-Simonians during the late 1820s and early 1830s. This is the view that the progress of
modern civilisation is a movement away from individual genius and
towards action *en masse*.[5] Mill largely relied on the first thought. It was
a corollary to the view of the history of democracy that he had come
to, partly under Tocqueville's tutelage, but quite largely independently
of that influence. The ordinary people of a country like Britain had successfully altered the balance of power between themselves and their
rulers, until the country was in practice, though not in constitutional
principle, democratic, but they had not noticed that in fending off the
tyranny of monarchs and aristocrats, they rendered themselves vulnerable to a different and more insidious tyranny, the tyranny of all
collectively over each individually.

The insidiousness of this tyranny was not only that "self-government"
often meant in practice the government of each by all the rest, but that
this was a soft, constant social pressure for conformity rather than
a visible political tyranny. The consequence was that they tyrannised
over themselves as well as over each other:

*   *   *

There was nothing to be done about the movement towards political democracy. It was a movement that Mill thought inevitable, and
like Tocqueville Mill thought it was on balance morally desirable on
the grounds of justice and liberty alike. All the same, a new view of
liberty was needed to counter the threat posed by the tendency of
the public to suppose that once its mind was made up, dissentients
should defer to public opinion. Mill's "very simple principle" was

4. [Alexis de Tocqueville, *Democracy in America* (London: Dent, 1994).]
5. "Civilization," *CW* XVIII: 121.

intended to provide part of that counter. Individuals must acknowledge the right of society to coerce them out of behaviour that harmed other people, that violated their rights, that damaged their legitimate interests; over all else, each individual remained sovereign.

Critics have complained, not only that Mill's principle was too simple, but that he had no business offering it as an "absolute" principle. Mill himself was aware that it was dangerous for a utilitarian to offer any other principle than utility as "entitled to govern absolutely" the dealings of society with its members. Utilitarians prided themselves on having reduced morality to principle: ethics had been rationalised when the principle of utility justified the everyday morality that utilitarians accepted and the non-everyday morality with which they wished to improve everyday morality. The status of any other principle was thus a delicate matter. Mill was ready with his answer. The individual's sovereignty over him- or herself was not based on natural right; it was derived from utility. It was absolute not in the sense that the liberty principle is "ultimate," but in the sense that it is exceptionless. This claim, however, raised another difficulty. The impetus to the writing of *On Liberty* was to protect freedom from the assaults of illiberal do-gooders—as it were an advance warning against the "bourgeois, benevolent and bureaucratic" Sidney and Beatrice Webb when they should arrive on the scene, and perhaps a warning against his own good-friend Edwin Chadwick, with his enthusiasm for Prussian efficiency. This supposed a conflict between the pursuit of freedom and the pursuit of the general welfare; but Mill proposed to defend freedom in terms of its contribution to the general welfare.

In essence, the rest of *On Liberty* spelled out the way in which the principle of *no coercion save to prevent harm to others* promoted utility. The first step was to point out that the utility involved had to be taken "in its largest sense": it was the utility of "man as a progressive being" that was at stake, not only the bread-and-butter utility of man as a consumer, with fixed tastes and desires.[6] Giving a persuasive account of what the utility of such a person was based on, as most critics have seen, forms the substance of the work.[7] It is worth noting that Mill's expansive conception of the utility of a progressive being rested on a sober basis. In terms of recent discussion, Mill's liberalism is "perfectionist" in the sense that it proposes an

---

6. "It is proper to state that I forego any advantage which could be derived to my argument from the idea of abstract right, as a thing independent of utility. I regard utility as the ultimate appeal on all ethical questions, but it must be utility in the largest sense, grounded on the permanent interests of man as a progressive being. Those interests, I contend, authorize the subjection of individual spontaneity to external control, only in respect to those actions of each, which concern the interest of other people." CW XVIII:224.

7. See, for instance, [John Gray, *Mill and Liberty: A Defense* (London: Routledge and Kegan Paul, 1983)].

ideal way of life; in the sense in which his contemporaries would
have understood such terms, it was more nearly "anti-perfectionist"
inasmuch as it repudiated the idea that the state or society generally had a right to *make* individuals conform to some existing ideal
of good character. In any case, Mill's concern for individual liberty
rested both on a doctrine of self-protection and on a doctrine of self-
development. We have two great needs that rights protect: the first
and most basic is for security, and the second is for room to expand
and flourish according to our own conception of what that entails.[8]
In *Utilitarianism*, Mill went on to explain the achievement of security as the province of *justice*, and to tie the notion of justice to the
notion of rights. Our interest in security has the character of a right
that must be protected against threats from other persons.

Although Mill was not a functionalist, he plainly thought that
organised human society and its legal and political arrangements
existed in order to provide each individual with a collective defence
against such threats. One of the ways in which the principle of no
coercion save to prevent harm to others is glossed by Mill, therefore, is to include the right of society to make each of us bear our
share of the burden of sustaining the institutions that provide collective security. The refusal to give evidence at a trial is not a matter
of our making a legitimate decision to withhold a kindness to the
person whom that evidence would help, but a threat to the arrangements on which everyone's security depends, and so a case of harm
to others, we may therefore be coerced into giving evidence.

✳ ✳ ✳

It is sometimes suggested that a utilitarian defence of liberty is a
non-starter; utilitarianism would license any degree of interference
that gave enough pleasure to the majority. If people *want* to believe
in a shared morality, the majority has a right to have a common
morality enforced, on the utilitarian basis that the enforcement will
provide pleasure to the majority. Mill's response to this vulgar but
not implausible argument was offered glancingly, in several places,
and in three instalments. One was an appeal to the intuitive idea
that any claim that others should behave as I wish *just because* I wish
them to do so, has no merit. Mill knew that nobody *avowed* such a
view. The buried premise of Mill's argument against it therefore was
that where enough moral discord existed to excite the desire for uniformity, the demand that others should do anything in particular
for the sake of a "shared morality" is tantamount to the claim that
they should think like me and act like me, because I want them to.

8. See Gray 1983 for a book-length elaboration of that claim, and *Utilitarianism*, CW
   X:250–51, for Mill's explanation of rights.

This is what Mill denounced as his contemporaries' belief that their "likings and dislikings" should be a universal guide.[9] The second was sketched in the previous paragraph: the content of the "common morality" that any society must enforce was essentially limited to the defence of each of its members against a limited range of harms, and the enforcement of the common rules of interaction that made life more prosperous and more rationally controllable—the morality that underlies the making and keeping of contracts, the doing of jury duty, recognising the obligation to go to work and earn a living, and so on. Any greater uniformity would do more harm than good. The third was essentially an elaboration of the conception of "more harm" that was involved in such a response, that elaboration supplied the bulk of the positive argument of *On Liberty*. Mill denied that enforcing uniformity would be a good bargain in utilitarian terms; the entire essay was an argument to that effect, since it was an argument against yielding to the desire for uniformity of sentiment, whether for its own sake or for the sake of the general welfare.

Mill's concluding admonition to beware of creating a society whose animating spirit has been sacrificed to the perfection of a bureaucratic machine summed up Mill's underlying theme: a society of what Tocqueville had called "industrious sheep" was the only alternative to the lively and flexible (and emotionally uncomfortable) society that Mill was arguing for. * * *

                              *   *   *

Some of Mill's elaborations of what follows from his very simple principle have become justly famous. Others have languished in an unwarranted obscurity, among them his insistence that it was no illicit interference with liberty for the state to demand that young people who proposed to marry should demonstrate that they had the means and the intention to look after the probable children of their union;[1] others, such as his insistence that the state should on no account take a large part in the provision of education, have been much less attended to than one might have expected, perhaps because modern liberals both British and American take public education for granted, while enthusiasts for the privatisation of education have not generally been Millian liberals in other respects.[2] In the contemporary United States, enthusiasts for "home schooling" are overwhelmingly concerned to keep their children at home in order to indoctrinate them in creationism or some other quirk of fundamentalist Protestantism; they are not natural allies of Mill.

9. *On Liberty*, CW XVIII:222.
1. CW XVIII:302–04.
2. CW XVIII:302.

It is a matter for regret that commentators have been so eager to
assimilate Mill's ideas to those of mainstream twentieth-century
liberalism that they have not seen what a very awkward ally of
twentieth-century liberals he is.

The same cross purposes have been visible in much subsequent
commentary on Mill's defence of an almost absolute freedom of
speech. Characteristically, attention has been divided between two
different modern concerns. On the one hand, Mill's insistence that
such a freedom is the best route to the discovery of the truth has
been subjected to some anxious scrutiny in the light of a more scep-
tical view of the lessons of the history of science, while on the other
his view that speech was intrinsically not a source of harm to others
has been scrutinised equally anxiously in the light of American First
Amendment jurisprudence and both British and American obscen-
ity law. What emerges most clearly, however, is that Mill's concern
with truth has more to do with religious "truth" than scientific
truth, and that he had almost nothing to say about indecency and
nothing at all to say about pornography. Mill's arguments are interesting just because his concerns were so unlike the concerns of
recent theorists.

It is perhaps more surprising that Mill not only has little or nothing to say about sexual freedom, but nothing to say about the concept of privacy, the basis of most modern arguments. This is, I
think, a real defect in his treatment of the subject. For one thing,
it is because we mind so much about privacy and about the near-
sanctity of intimate relationships that we flinch from Mill's insistence that society should impose financial requirements on people
intending to marry and have children. Again, many of us would think
that the same considerations were a powerful argument for abolishing penal laws against homosexuality—and that even if some harm
were to be done by their abolition the argument that their enforcement was an outrage against privacy would be a powerful argument in the other direction. For Mill's own purposes, a simpler case
sufficed. He drew a distinction that good sense requires, between
arguments from decency and arguments from harm, and left it at
that. The distinction is simple enough and best illustrated by an
imaginary example. A married couple having sexual intercourse in
Piccadilly Circus in broad daylight engage in an indecent act, but
not one that violates any obligation they owe to one another. Conversely, an adulterous liaison may be objectionable because it violates the trust that the injured spouses had placed in their errant
partners, but if conducted discreetly, it could not be condemned
as indecent. Decency is essentially a matter of obtruding offensive
displays upon others. A moment's thought about our insistence on
the privacy of defecation shows plainly how often decency is not

concerned with the *moral* content of acts that nobody has ever suggested are immoral in themselves, but is concerned with the fact that they would be indecent if done obtrusively in public:

*   *   *

One might regret that Mill so cavalierly waves away arguments about decency, but he had other fish to fry. Most of Mill's argument about freedom of thought and speech had two aims. The first was to establish that freedom was an essential condition for discovering truth, the second was to elaborate an account of what sort of truth he had in mind. Much of the argument was negative, in the sense that many of Mill's arguments were devoted to repudiating familiar arguments against freedom. Thus Mill denied that the defence of free speech amounted to the acceptance of the war of all against all; he thought himself entitled to the conventional distinction between mere speech and incitement, as in his famous claim that we must be free to publish the opinion that corn dealers are thieves but not to put it on a placard and wave it at an angry mob outside a corn dealer's house: *   *   *

More interestingly, at least in the sense that his seeming espousal of a "proto-Popperian" position was in some tension with his usual inductivist views, Mill argued that truth was internally related to controvertibility. The only ground we have for believing in the truth of what we believe is that it has been or can be exposed to attempted refutation and that it has survived or will survive it. To believe something, properly speaking, is to understand what would controvert one's belief in it, and to have confidence in that belief's ability to withstand test. This appears to be Mill in proto-Popperian mode rather than Mill the inductivist. Yet even here, Mill's interest did not lie where Popper's lay. Mill did not offer an empirical claim to the effect that scientific progress depends on an intellectual regime of "conjecture and refutation."[3] What he put forward was a strongly *normative* conception of belief that entailed among other things that most of what we describe as our "beliefs" are not so much "believed" as acquiesced in. Much the greater part of Mill's chapter on freedom of thought was concerned with religion; as this might suggest, Mill's concern was with strong conviction and lively belief, and much of his argument was an argument for trying to maximise the liveliness of our beliefs. A mere recording machine could pick up and reiterate the ideas of others, and might by coincidence reiterate

3. [Karl Popper, *Conjectures and Refutations* (London: Routledge and Kegan Paul, 1974)] is, perhaps surprisingly, not the classic source for the doctrine that science progresses by the process of making hypotheses and testing them against the evidence; [Karl Popper, *The Logic of Scientific Discovery* (London: Hutchinson, 1954)], first published in German in 1937, is that.

the truth; a human mind might do much more.[4] The question how far Mill's conception of the self allowed him to appeal as unself-consciously as he did to the importance of making our beliefs "our own" is a difficult and underexplored one, but that is what animates his argument. It is one of many arguments in the essay that rests upon a "positive" conception of liberty.[5] Mental freedom is a form of positive possession of our ideas.

The argument is plainly more persuasive when applied to moral and religious beliefs than when applied to scientific ideas. This is yet another field in which Mill's argument was directed not towards our anxieties but towards his own. We have become used to the arguments of T. S. Kuhn and Paul Feyerabend, who have claimed that scientific truth is established in a more coercive and non-consensual fashion than previous philosophers of science supposed. So far from making bold conjectures and accepting painful refutations, scientists habitually preserve orthodoxies and run dissenters out of the lab.[6] But Mill was not interested in what made science "special," nor in discussing the difference between establishing low-level facts and high-level theories. He was interested in the degree of conviction with which people held their beliefs about the ends of life. Unless they were in the habit of arguing for their views, they were not in full command of them: "However unwillingly a person who has a strong opinion may admit the possibility that his opinion may be false, he ought to be moved by the consideration that however true it may be, if it is not fully, frequently, and fearlessly discussed, it will be held as a dead dogma, not a living truth."[7]

When we turn to the argument for freedom of action in the forming of our own plans of life, the considerations Mill adduces remain within the same framework. In part Mill was concerned to deny that society was in the condition of an armed camp where everyone must devote all their efforts to the well-being of their fellow creatures. There were emergency situations in which individual claims to freedom had to be more or less denied, but everyday life was not such a situation. A man on sentry duty might be shot for falling asleep; in everyday life, we may choose our own bedtimes. A sentry might be shot for drunkenness on watch; in everyday life, we may generally drink as we like. The rationale for the distinction is the familiar one; we are answerable for the predictable harm we cause others: "No

4. CW XVIII:245.
5. For the distinction between "negative" and "positive" liberty see [Isaiah Berlin, *Two Concepts of Liberty* (Oxford: Clarendon Press, 1969)].
6. [Thomas Kuhn, *The Structure of Scientific Revolution* (Chicago: U of Chicago Press, 1962); Paul Feyerabend, *Against Method* (London: New Left Books, 1975); Ala Musgrave et al., eds., *Criticism and the Growth of Knowledge*, 4 vols. (London: Cambridge U Press, 1970).]
7. CW XVIII:245.

person ought to be punished simply for being drunk; but a soldier or a policeman should be punished for being drunk on duty. Whenever, in short, there is definite damage, or a definite risk of damage, either to an individual or to the public, the case is taken out of the province of liberty, and placed in that of morality or law."[8]

Mill was particularly concerned to deny that a proper concern for the moral welfare of our fellows must take the form of censoring their thoughts and inclinations. This is a feature of his argument that has received less attention than it deserves. He drew a very careful distinction between coercive and uncoercive means of altering other people's behaviour, and was anxious to insist that where coercion was illicit, non-coercive measures might well be appropriate. Mill knew that he was vulnerable to the objection that *On Liberty* put forward a doctrine of ethical laissez-faire that encouraged pure self-centredness and an unconcern with the well-being of others—and he duly denied in several places that he was doing anything of the sort.

* * *

He was eager to point out that it was absurd to suppose that the choice lay between indifference on the one hand and force on the other. "But disinterested benevolence can find other instruments to persuade people to their good, than whips and scourges, either of the literal or the metaphorical sort."[9] This is an echo of Locke's sardonic observation in his *Letter on Toleration* that we can concern ourselves with other people's spiritual welfare without throwing them in jail or burning them at the stake.

Mill argued that we must think of ways of non-coercively encouraging other people's highest aspirations, carefully distinguishing between even the most strenuous exhortation on the one hand and punishment on the other; we may, and we should, tell other people exactly what we think of their behaviour in matters that reflect on their character. If we deplore their drinking, we should say so. If we think their literary tastes are vulgar, we should say so. Ordinary standards of politeness militate against this, but so much the worse for ordinary notions of politeness.

* * *

Mill's contemporaries were puzzled by his insistence on the difference between penalties strictly speaking and the accidental misfortunes that might befall us as a result of differences in taste. To Mill it was of the greatest importance because he saw moral

8. *CW* XVIII:281.
9. *CW* XVIII:276.

coercion as the opinion-based shadow or background of legal coercion. In a democratic *society*, even in the absence of a democratic political system, public opinion was an organised force. Mill absorbed Tocqueville's conviction that what made the force so impressive was its silent and unobtrusive quality; where physical penalties aroused resistance in the person punished, the penalties of opinion worked in his soul. He might, indeed, become his own mental jailer.[1]

Mill's argument in *On Liberty* was deliberately repetitive. He was laying siege to a frame of mind that he thought permeated English society, and he set about driving it from one position after another. He also believed that few people had thought about the problems he had identified, and thus that it was particularly difficult to make the argument he wished to make.[2] This was not always in the interest of extending freedom. It was sometimes, and quite startlingly, in the interest of restricting it. Too few critics attend to the fact that Mill was not attacking only the habit of interfering with harmless conduct. He was equally concerned to attack the absence of rational and publicly understood principle that allowed harmful conduct to flourish unchecked while harmless conduct was repressed. "I have already observed that, owing to the absence of any recognised general principles, liberty is often granted where it should be withheld, as well as withheld where it should be granted," wrote Mill in the context of his claim that society took too little interest in the improvidence and fecklessness with which young people contracted marriage and brought children into the world without having any idea how they were to be reared and educated.[3] His argument was squarely in line with the basic principles underlying *On Liberty*; to produce children who could not be brought up properly was a double offence, once against the wretched children, and secondly against society at large:

> It still remains unrecognised, that to bring a child into existence without a fair prospect of being able, not only to provide food for its body, but instruction and training for its mind, is a moral crime, both against the unfortunate offspring and against society; and that if the parent does not fulfil this obligation, the State ought to see it fulfilled, at the charge, as far as possible, of the parent.[4]

To throw unproductive extra bodies onto the labour market was an anti-social act.

Mill's unconcern with twentieth-century anxieties about privacy and intimacy is a striking feature of his bleakly high-principled

1. Tocqueville 1994, I:264; *CW* XVIII:219.
2. *CW* XVIII:226.
3. *CW* XVIII:302–04.
4. *CW* XVIII:302.

acceptance of restrictions on marriage as well as on the parents' rights over their children.

*   *   *

The concluding chapter of "applications" added little to the argument of *On Liberty* in the narrow sense, but much to one's sense of what Mill was after. He faced difficulties familiar to later generations. One awkward question was whether it was right to prevent people getting together to do collectively what they had an individual right to do; running a brothel would be an example—for fornication is not illegal or to be repressed by the collective censoriousness that he described as the "penalties of opinion"; but one might wish to prevent people living off immoral earnings or trading in sexual services. The same thought applies to gambling houses; one might not object to individuals getting together in an informal fashion to gamble, but still fear the effects of gambling dens.[5] Mill's approach generally concentrated on detaching genuine offences from their non-punishable causes. A man who gambled away his family's housekeeping money was to be blamed, and if necessary forced to look after his family; but he ought not to be treated worse than if he had spent the housekeeping money on failed attempts to invent electric lighting. Still, Mill also understood the problem of attractive nuisances, and he hesitated to put his name to the principle that what a person is allowed to do another person must be allowed to advise him to do.[6]

Mill also reminded his readers of a view that he made rather more of in his *Principles of Political Economy* and *Representative Government*. There he argued that just as private individuals may exhort and encourage where they may not coerce, so governments may take a position on matters where they may neither forbid nor require any particular line of conduct. Moreover, governments may act on such views when they consider how to distribute the burden of taxation. Mill was ferociously opposed to temperance agitation, partly because temperance reformers claimed that drinkers violated their "social rights," and Mill thought the appeal to social rights tyrannical. Yet he was ready to agree that while governments were not entitled to tax alcoholic drink at a level designed to stop its consumption, they were entitled to put a tax on alcoholic drink rather than on tea or bread; supposing the tax to be necessary at all, its incidence would be less damaging if it fell on drink than if it fell on tea or bread.[7]

*   *   *

5. *CW* XVIII:296.
6. *CW* XVIII:296.
7. *CW* XVIII:297.

To a degree Mill weakened the force of the claim that there were right answers to moral problems by suggesting that even though the "right answer" was right for utilitarian reasons, it was delivered by the judgment of a suitably sensitive critic, and not by any very simple utilitarian algorithm.[8] This might imply that there could be several incompatible "right answers" to a given question, an idea not as odd as it sounds: the paintings of Monet and Cézanne provide right but different answers to the question of how to render a landscape for late nineteenth-century sensibilities. If one thinks of ultimate moral questions as having much in common with, and perhaps even as being identical with, aesthetic questions about the shape of a life, it is not foolish to think that discussion of the ends of life will result in plural answers.

Pluralism and liberalism—at any rate, some liberalisms—are thus awkward allies. One form of pluralism, indeed, is consistent with thoroughgoing illiberalism, namely the form in which an overarching, unconstitutional, undemocratic, and anything-but-liberal political authority allows specified social groups to handle the affairs of their own members. The Ottoman Empire was not a liberal enterprise, but operated after such a fashion. Another form is liberal, in the sense that it amounts to the creation of a peace treaty between groups, in order to give each group the freedom to conduct its life as it chooses; but the establishment of a peace treaty does not secure the prevalence of liberal values outside anything other than the political realm, nor does it secure to group members more freedom than their group cares to grant. A pluralism of this kind might be consistent with the Roman Catholic church being able to visit heretics with sanctions, perhaps to deprive them of their livelihoods, so long as the church does not attempt to control the lives of non-Catholics and does not prevent members leaving the church. The Dutch state is more liberal than most, yet it financially aids Catholic universities that can dismiss theologians whose doctrines they dislike.

Such a peace treaty presupposes a liberal state in the background, since that allows members of the church to leave without suffering civil disabilities. A theocratic state, as opposed to a liberal state, might tolerate more diversity than we would suppose likely, but would not offer legal guarantees of this kind. One view of the transformation of the Catholic church in the United States is that it has been forced to become more liberal, and to be more liberal than it is elsewhere, precisely because its members are guaranteed an unsanctioned exit. The theory put forward in John Rawls's *Political Liberalism* is liberal in this fashion; the requirement that they do not

8. *Utilitarianism,* CW X:211.

violate the human rights of their members constrains the authority
any group can exercise over its members. But the theory is not com-
prehensively liberal; there is no suggestion that the group should be
urged or encouraged to adopt liberal conceptions of authority or liberal arrangements for its internal government. Catholics may not
chase after their departed members to do them ill, but they may violate equal opportunity in recruiting for the priesthood, and impose
burdens that liberals would disapprove of: they are not obliged to
accept women as candidates for the priesthood, and they can impose
the requirement of celibacy.

The moment of truth for a pluralist comes when he is asked
whether he is happy to see a great variety of non-liberal ways of life
flourish for the sake of variety, or whether he really wishes to see
only a variety of liberal ways of life even if the result is less variety
than there would be by admitting non-liberal ways of life. Mill
ducked that question by insisting that as things stood, we had too
much to lose by curtailing anything but grossly illiberal ways of life;
we knew too little about what would in the end suit human beings
to be justified in curbing all but the most approved liberal ways of
life. Isaiah Berlin's liberalism causes his critics some difficulty
because Berlin's pluralism is straightforward and his liberalism
therefore not; Berlin would rather see vivid, non-liberal ways of life
flourish than see them suppressed for the sake of the spread of liberal principles. The question, then, is not whether there are non-
liberal forms of moral and political pluralism, but whether liberalism
entails pluralism at all, and whether Mill believed that it did.

Mill thought it entailed one kind of pluralism, about which he and
Berlin agree. We have no definitive, unchallengeable answer to the
question of what the good life consists in, and we must allow experiment to winnow out the mistakes and refine the better answers.
There is one kind of pluralism over which Mill and Berlin disagree.
Mill thought that in the last resort a rational morality reduced to a
single principle, and Berlin dissents. Berlin is, and Mill was not, an
ethical pluralist. Berlin holds the common sense view that freedom
is one thing and happiness another; Mill argued that the search for
freedom was a search for happiness.[9] What is left standing is two
puzzles. The first is whether Mill thought that answers to the question How shall we live? would eventually converge and so eliminate
diversity; the second whether Mill thought that irrespective of the
answer to that question, sheer variety was something to be valued
for its own sake. We know that Berlin's answer to the two questions
is no and yes—that answers to How shall I live? do not converge,
and that variety is intrinsically worth preserving.

9. See, for instance, "Two Concepts of Liberty," in Berlin 1969.

✳   ✳   ✳

I am inclined to believe that Mill held the following view. There *is* an answer to the question what ways of life best suit human beings; it is not a unitary answer, because human nature varies a good deal from one person to another, and therefore yields diverse answers— though these are answers that have a common form, since they will be answers about what conduces to the long-term well-being of the people in question. To reach those answers, we need experiments in living because human nature is exceedingly ill-understood. What we see is the manifestations of human nature as it has been socialised in a variety of ways, of which many are inimical to human flourishing. Mill argued more continuously in *The Subjection of Women* than in *On Liberty* that we have little idea of what we might achieve if we adjusted the ways we socialise the young so as to enable them to live more flourishing and self-actualised existences thereafter, but the thought plainly sustains *On Liberty*, too.[1] Women might be the most immediate beneficiaries of a deeper understanding of how far the interaction of socialisation and human nature distorts or hides the possibility of new forms of happiness, but humankind generally would be the ultimate beneficiaries of such an understanding. Hence Mill's never-realised hopes for the science of ethology.

Human nature is malleable, and as we work on our own characters, so we open up some indeterminacy in the answer to the question of how best to live. We do not only come to be better at pursuing happiness, we change our view of what happiness is. We can also change our own characters so as to be better able to live by the views we come to. Mill, as I have argued elsewhere, suggested that the answer to ultimate questions about what sort of happiness to pursue lay in the realm of aesthetic judgment.[2] Aesthetic judgment has a tendency not to converge in any very straightforward way; it is, in that sense, the antithesis of scientific judgment. Mill is hard to interpret because he wanted both to emphasise the place of scientific rationality and to leave space for aesthetic judgment in determining the ends of life. The experimental life would, if this is a proper interpretation of Mill, have a tendency to settle some questions while opening up others. It would thus promote and destroy pluralism at the same time.

How much pluralism does this yield? It yields as many distinctive and therefore different lives as there are different people; it does not yield as many different political systems as there are human communities. There are many common tasks that governments must perform, and any society concerned with efficiency will have them performed in the same way. It does not yield an infinity of cultural

1. *Subjection of Women*, CW XXI:259–340; *On Liberty*, CW XVIII:260.
2. Ryan 1970, chs. XII–XIII.

options (in the anthropological sense of "cultural"), since many cultures now visible will vanish, because they rest on superstitious beliefs that cannot withstand inspection. In other senses of "cultural" it yields room for infinite variety; there is no sign that the number of available musical, sculptural, literary, and other aesthetic *formulae* will soon diminish, and no sign that we shall soon settle down to repetitively re-creating works of art to a single pattern. Since Mill's borrowings from von Humboldt and Goethe imply that aesthetic invention is the model of experiments in living, we should have no fear that Mill's liberalism is likely to reduce the number of available cultural options to one. Mill's pluralism remains less hospitable to non-liberal and illiberal ways of life than Berlin's pluralism, though perhaps not very much less hospitable. The reason why the gap may not be as great as one would imagine at first sight is that vivid, fully-realised lives for the sake of which Mill, like Berlin, defends freedom, may also be realised in non-liberal settings. Where they are, the liberal will face a familiar transition problem: how much of the vividness and commitment can be kept when beliefs and attitudes change in a liberal direction? It is every moderniser's question. That Mill was more inclined than Berlin to sacrifice vivid traditional societies to less vivid modern ones goes without saying. That he was wrong to make that choice is a more contentious claim. It is also one that there is no space to discuss any further.

JONATHAN RILEY

J. S. Mill's Doctrine of Freedom of Expression[†]

* * *

Millian Censorship

A. WHERE FULL CENSORSHIP IS JUSTIFIABLE

Mill makes it clear that society and government do have legitimate authority to ban the sale of any commodity that can only be used to harm others directly and immediately. Evidently, if a commodity has no self-regarding uses (a powerful nuclear bomb with severe radiation effects that cannot be confined, perhaps, or a vial of killer disease agents that cannot be prevented from spreading), the central principle of self-regarding liberty does not give the individual any

---

† From *Utilitas* 17.2 (July 2005): 165–74. Copyright © 2005 by Cambridge University Press. Reprinted by permission. Unless otherwise indicated, notes are by the author. Some of the author's notes have been omitted.

moral right to use or buy it as she pleases.[1] Similarly, society and government have the authority to prohibit the expression of any opinion whose content necessarily harms others (or poses a risk of doing so). Such opinions include threats of violence or other harms against others, for example, and perhaps certain forms of 'hate speech' that can reasonably be construed as threats to individuals. But I wish to focus attention on another type of opinion that cannot be expressed without direct and immediate harm to others, namely, informed opinions about the intimate details of another's private life which she wishes kept from public view. Expression of an opinion of this sort to third parties necessarily harms her, whatever the context, by invading her self-regarding sphere and thus damaging her ability to pursue her own good in her own way.

B. EXPRESSION THAT INVADES ANOTHER'S SELF-REGARDING SPHERE

Such an invasion of another's privacy might damage her reputation, of course. But, apart from that, it also directly and immediately harms her by reducing her control of the purely self-regarding portion of her life. She can no longer choose to release or withhold information about the intimate details of her life as seems best to her own judgement and inclinations. There is never a context in which the release of this private information into the public arena against her wishes can be permitted without the risk of harm to her.

This form of perceptible damage to her, that is, interfering with her liberty in the sense of her acting and presenting herself as she pleases, is not a moralized conception of harm. It does not presuppose that she has a moral right to complete liberty of self-regarding conduct, or that the violation of this right constitutes the harm. Indeed, she would suffer similar perceptible damage if others published opinions about the social or other-regarding portion of her life without her consent. In the latter case, however, any harm to her may be more than offset by benefits to others: Her social conduct in her position as a police officer may cause serious harms to others, for example, and its public exposure may benefit society far more than it hurts her by preventing her from seriously injuring other people. Thus, society has legitimate authority to permit speech that

---

1. It might be objected that there are really no such commodities. Perhaps, for example, even the vial of killer disease agents as described may have uses other than harming others. Somebody might merely wish to possess it for the sense of power or security it gives, without ever releasing the disease agents. But mere possession without a credible threat of releasing the agents will not provide the feelings of power or security. Mere possession without any threat of release is a purely hypothetical use among humans, given our experience of them. In the real world, there is always a risk that such a vial will be opened and, if it is, fatal diseases will by assumption spread among the human population. I thank Leif Wenar for raising this objection.

exposes such harmful social behaviour by corrupt or incompetent public officials. The individual has no moral right to do as she pleases in social matters.

But Mill's central liberty principle says that the individual does, on utilitarian grounds, have a moral right to individuality in her purely self-regarding matters. Society has no legitimate authority to permit expression that impinges on her self-regarding liberty by exposing the details of her private life against her wishes. Her self-regarding conduct poses no risk of direct and immediate harm to others, so that publicizing it without her permission causes direct and immediate harm to her alone. The interference with her individuality cannot be offset by any perceptible social benefits. It does not prevent any direct and immediate harm to others because there are no such harms to prevent, and Mill implies that her individuality outweighs any mere dislike that others may feel at being denied the relevant expression. True, the invasive publication may titillate meddlesome people and relieve their desires for gossip that is none of their business. But the satisfaction of such 'mere likes' does not constitute a perceptible benefit, in Mill's view, just as the production of 'mere dislikes' does not constitute a perceptible injury. Mere likes and dislikes have no parity with perceptible benefits and harms, including the individual's loss of control over her private life. Some such utilitarian calculation apparently underlies Mill's justification of the moral right to absolute liberty of self-regarding conduct in the first place.[2] The benefits and harms that enter into this calculation cannot already be moralized entities. Rather, the relevant utilitarian calculation is the moral basis of the right to self-regarding liberty. For that reason, he can consistently maintain that violation of the right is a *morally important or severe* kind of harm in terms of his utilitarian liberal morality. To enforce the right and its correlative obligations, society and government must have authority to suppress expression that violates it.[3]

2. For further discussion of Mill's complex utilitarian procedure as I understand it, see my *Liberal Utilitarianism* (Cambridge: Cambridge University Press, 1988), part II; and *Mill's Radical Liberalism* (London: Routledge, 2003), chs. 2–3. It cannot be denied that publishing the details of another's private life may cause third parties to feel some types of enjoyment. As Leif Wenar pointed out in his written comments, some people may be delighted to learn that 'Madonna has sex with badgers, or whatever.' Indeed, I am intrigued myself by the possibilities of 'whatever'! But such mere titillation is a lower kind of enjoyment which counts for very little in comparison to perceptible harms (or benefits) in Mill's utilitarianism as I understand it.

3. Of course, in Mill's approach, others have an equal right to avoid what causes them dislike, and their dislike at being denied access to somebody's private information might lead them voluntarily to incur self-harm in their pursuit of their own individualities. But the person who wants to protect her privacy is not responsible for that indirect and remote harm which others may cause to themselves in response to her self-regarding choice.

Consider an example in which a woman's former partner sells to the media a true story (with accompanying photographs) of their sex life together without her permission. The communication of these opinions and pictures to third parties against her wishes is *coercive interference with her self-regarding liberty*. She is forced to share her personal concerns with others against her will, and thereby loses some of her freedom to choose as she pleases whether to release to others information about her private life.[4] This partial loss of control is direct and immediate harm to her, even if the public exposure should happen to bring her unanticipated benefits such as an increase in prospective sex partners, for example, or offers of employment as a porn star.[5] According to Mill's central argument, a liberal government has moral authority to enforce her right to complete self-regarding liberty, by enacting suitable legislation to ban the publication *without her consent* of any such story and photographs. In short, the promotion of her individuality underwrites society's coercive interference with the former partner's act of expressing and publishing without her consent his sincere and undistorted opinions about their sex life. Her individuality conflicts with his in this case, and hers rightfully wins out because she does not wish to act outside her self-regarding domain whereas he does wish to act outside his and cause direct and immediate harm to another. If she *wishes* to have more sex partners or work in porn films, of course, then, with due caveats about the need to prevent harm to others, she is free to release the relevant information in order to promote her own good in her own way. Her moral right to self-regarding liberty guarantees

4. It might be objected that there is no coercion or forcing in this case since the former partner makes no threat and the woman is not actually forced to do anything. But I maintain that she is forced to participate in her former partner's act of publishing information about their private life together. Strictly speaking, his action is a joint action of theirs over which she has no control. In acting as he does, he makes her release information about her private life to people with whom she does not wish to share that information. Moreover, it seems odd to suggest that there is no coercion unless he threatens to do this. How can it make sense to say that his threatening to release the information is coercive, whereas his actually doing it is not coercive interference with her self-regarding liberty? By his action, he is obstructing her control over her private life: the information he has released constitutes an external impediment to her freedom to choose among self-regarding acts and omissions. I thank Leif Wenar for raising this objection.

5. It is quite possible that the publication of the details of her private life might produce so many putative benefits for her that the outcome seems 'better' for her than what would have happened if she had retained complete control of her private affairs. But Mill claims that her interest in retaining such control, in being able to choose among self-regarding actions as seems best in terms of her own judgement and inclinations, is so valuable that it outweighs these other putative benefits. So long as outcomes are conceived to include the individual's self-development or individuality, it will never be the case that publication of her private details against her wishes results in a 'better' outcome for her than an alternative in which she retains control. Even if she experiments and makes mistakes that others would not make if they controlled her private life for her, she will learn from her mistakes, Mill suggests, given that she is a minimally competent human being.

to her rather than her former partner such control over her own individuality.

It must be admitted that Mill does not spell out in the *Liberty* that a liberal society has authority to censor this type of public expression. But he does make clear in an early work that he thinks truth should not be a justification for any libel relating to another's self-regarding conduct. Truth should be a justification if the libel relates to any act 'in its nature public':

> Where, indeed, the imputation is not upon the private, but upon the public character of a public man; or where the act imputed, though belonging to private life, is in its nature public, (for instance, any violation of decency in a public place,) or has already received publicity, (for instance, by the proceedings of a Court of Justice,) we think . . . that the truth of the charge ought to be a sufficient defence; and we would even allow the alleged libeller to clear himself, though the charge be false, by showing that he had good grounds for believing it to be true.[6]

But truth should not be a defence when somebody publishes without consent details of another's 'acts which are in their nature private', even in the case of a public official:

> [W]e would not permit the press to impute, even truly, acts, however discreditable, which are in their nature private. We would not allow the truth of such imputation to be even pleaded in mitigation. The very attempt to establish the charge by evidence, would often be a gross aggravation of the original injury [more speech is not the solution here]. We see insuperable objections to allowing the details of a person's private conduct to be made the subject of a judicial investigation, at the pleasure of any malignant accuser.[7]

'Acts which are in their nature private' are apparently those later labelled purely self-regarding acts in the *Liberty*. Allowing the details of her self-regarding conduct to be investigated in open court would merely aggravate the original injury of publication. It would simply exacerbate her loss of control over her own private life, her loss of freedom to develop in her own way.

More generally, the threat of such publication would tend to curtail most people's ability to experiment with different personal life-styles as they like, at least so long as people believed what was published, a point made in his letter of 22 February 1834 to William J. Fox. If people who publish the details of others' private lives without consent are permitted to go to court to establish the truth

6. Mill, 'Mr. O'Connell's Bill for the Liberty of the Press' [1834], CW, vi. 166–7.
7. 'Mr. O'Connell's Bill', CW, vi. 167.

of their published imputations as a defence, Mill says, 'I should expect one of two results':

> that the lives of all but the independent in fortune & brave in heart, would be thoroughly artificialized, by becoming one continued struggle to save appearances & escape misinterpretation, or else that freedom would work itself out by what seems to have happened in America, calumny and scandal carried to such a length that nobody believes anything which appears in print, & as none can escape such imputations, nobody regards them.[8]

Mill does not actually say in 1834 that publication of the details of another's self-regarding conduct without her consent can never be utilitarian simply because it directly and immediately reduces her control over her private lifestyle. He does not yet announce explicitly as he does in the *Liberty* that the individual must be given *complete* control over self-regarding matters because what she does in her self-regarding sphere can never be properly described as immoral. Rather, he says merely that it is too difficult for a court to determine whether the published imputations are true or false. As he puts it in his letter to Fox, 'truth, in any rational sense of the term, cannot in such cases be *got at* by the public' and 'true charges *cannot* be distinguished from false ones by such a tribunal'.[9] Still, what Mill says here can be connected to what he emphasizes in *Liberty*. Given that the court can never settle whether one person's opinion of another's private life is warranted or not, he may be interpreted as saying that self-regarding conduct cannot reasonably be regulated by social (legal or moral) authority. The agent ought to have complete liberty of self-regarding conduct because it is too difficult for even a court (let alone other public bodies) to ascertain the moral rightness or wrongness of the conduct in question.

It seems clear that by 1834 Mill is prepared to claim that government has legitimate authority to enact laws forbidding public expression of even sincere and accurate opinions about the intimate details of another's private life against her wishes. This appears to be a change from his view in an 1825 article, where he speaks against legal coercion despite his admission that 'it would be desirable, in such cases, that the truth should be suppressed':

> There is one case, and only one, in which there might appear to be some doubt of the propriety of permitting the truth to be told without reserve. This is, when the truth, without being of any advantage to the public, is calculated to give annoyance to private individuals. That there are such cases must be allowed;

8. Letter of 22 February 1834 to Fox, CW, xiii. 214.
9. Letter to Fox, p. 214.

and also that it would be desirable, in such cases, that the truth should be suppressed, if it could be done by any other means than law, or arbitrary power.[1]

If he really did mean in 1825 to reject legal suppression of such truthful invasions of privacy, however, he was going even further than his radical father recommended in an influential *Encyclopaedia Britannica* article published a couple of years earlier. For James Mill himself recognized that publishing warranted opinions (not merely malicious lies) about another's private life against her wishes was an uncompensated evil:

> It very often happens that men's antipathies are excited to actions from which no evil ensues, either to him who performs them, or to any body else. If any man derives a pleasure from such actions, it is to limit his sphere of innocent enjoyment, to debar him from them. And if the press exposes him to the antipathies, the hatred and contempt of his fellow-creatures, on account of those actions, it produces an evil, uncompensated by the smallest portion of good.[2]

Although he is obviously reluctant to rely on legal coercion and fears that people will often disagree over where to draw the line between acts that are harmful and those that are not, James is 'persuaded' that some clear cases can be marked out where 'all would agree' that legal penalties ought to be used to forbid speech that does nothing but excite popular disapproval of an individual's harmless acts.[3] Given that there are kinds of 'actions which, though injurious to nobody, excite antipathies', he concludes,

> the exercise of truth, with regard to them, might, on the express ground that they were actions innoxious, . . . be forbidden, when injurious, under the penalty of at least making reparation for all the injury of which it had been the cause.[4]

Even if John meant to exclude legal coercion in 1825, he had apparently changed his mind by 1834 and agreed with his father that

---

1. Mill, 'Law of Libel and Liberty of the Press' [1825], CW, xxi. 15.
2. James Mill, 'Liberty of the Press' [1823], in *James Mill: Political Writings*, ed. Terence Ball (Cambridge: Cambridge University Press, 1991), p. 107.
3. James Mill illustrates the point by calling attention to the social stigma that would befall a Mahomedan who drank wine or a Catholic who ate meat on forbidden days if accounts of these harmless acts were published in the press ('Liberty of the Press', pp. 107–8). It should be noted that harmless acts as he defines them differ from purely self-regarding acts as his son defines them, in so far as the latter but not the former may involve direct injury to self.
4. James Mill, 'Liberty of the Press', p. 110. James also argues that there are some facts, 'as those of birth, for which, though a man was in no respect worse, he might be regarded as worse', whose publication might similarly be suppressed by the threat of legal punishment, 'on the express ground that they were . . . facts which ought to be of no importance in the estimate of human worth' (ibid.).

legal coercion against privacy-invading speech was justifiable. True, what he says in 1834 is not repeated explicitly in the *Liberty*, so it might be concluded that he reverts in the 1850s to his 1825 position against legal coercion. Even if he did, he may have meant consistently to allow for coercive regulation by social stigma in these cases rather than endorsing liberty of expression.

But there is really no warrant for the claim that his considered view is against the use of legal sanctions in these cases. He does emphasize in the *Liberty* the propriety of legal and social enforcement of the duty correlative to the individual's moral right to complete liberty in self-regarding matters. This ties in with his suggestion in 1834 that publication of the intimate details of another's life without her consent can properly be suppressed by *law and stigma*. Indeed, his apparent abandonment of the 1825 position against using the law may well be due to the special influence of Harriet Taylor, whom he met in 1830 and married in 1852[5] shortly after the death of her first husband. If she had lived to put her finishing touches on the *Liberty* (which Mill regarded as their joint production), perhaps she would have brought out more explicitly the position Mill seems to have consistently maintained from 1834 onwards, after hearing and discussing her opinions, a position, it should be noted, that James Mill had always endorsed.[6]

In any case, the theory of freedom of expression outlined in the *Liberty* is sufficiently rich to make sense of Mill's various remarks. Given that society has legitimate authority to prohibit the expression of opinions about the details of another's private life against her wishes, it is a separate question how that social authority may be expediently exercised. In some situations, society and government may even recognize that general expediency calls for laissez-faire, despite the fact that a general policy of censorship is legitimate for this invasive type of expression. In effect, a general policy of censorship with laissez-faire exceptions may be expedient in this already special context.

C. WHERE CENSORSHIP OF INVASIVE SPEECH BECOMES INEXPEDIENT

An individual might forfeit her right to privacy in some situations by performing a harmful social act. If she chooses to run for political office and deliberately distorts the facts of her own private life

---

5. The correct date is 1851 [*Editor's note*].
6. If this is right, the remarkable implication is that Harriet persuaded Mill that his father had been correct all along on the issue of using legal coercion to suppress privacy-invading speech. In my view, Mill's considered approach to freedom of expression is highly similar to the approach James had outlined earlier. But I cannot argue the point here.

by expressing her love of traditional family values when she is known to be a prostitute, for example, then society might legitimately decide to permit others to express their sincere and accurate opinions in order to counteract her distortions and thereby benefit the voters. After all, she has willingly initiated a public conversation on this aspect of her private life in the context of an election campaign. By introducing lies about her own self-regarding conduct into the public arena, she has arguably forfeited in her own case the legal protection that society ought generally to provide for the individual's self-regarding sphere. Instead of being required to fulfil obligations to respect her privacy, other people with relevant information about her case might expediently be permitted to rebut her otherwise misleading expression, with the caveat that malicious libels of her private life and character would be subject to the standard punishments in the courts.

Even in situations where a person has done nothing that warrants forefeiture of his right to control his self-regarding sphere, so that others continue to have obligations not to invade his privacy, society might find it generally inexpedient to enforce externally those obligations by law or custom. The costs of external enforcement may simply be too high in some cases. Perhaps an individual engages in kinky sex with other consenting adults in the privacy of his home or club, for example, and word about it gets around to third parties who are disgusted by his self-regarding activity. Even though the information has been received from his sex partners without his consent, society may decide that it is inexpedient to try to prevent the third parties from receiving this information and freely warning their friends and acquaintances about his behaviour. If so, that freedom of invasive expression would become 'practically inseparable' from any person's self-regarding liberty to avoid his company.[7] Any protection afforded to the individual's right to privacy in this type of case would be left to the other individuals' feelings of conscience about just how to express their disapproval of his self-regarding lifestyle. More specifically, their expressions of disgust could not properly call on government or organized pressure groups to employ coercion to prevent or punish his kinky sexual lifestyle. They still have moral obligations correlative to his right to self-regarding liberty.

Laissez-faire may be an expedient policy towards invasive speech if the speech is confined within a relatively small circle of friends

---

7. Note that in this case the individual who engages in kinky sex does suffer perceptible damage without his consent as a direct result of the warnings given to friends and acquaintances. Mill includes the relevant harms (loss of friendship and associated perks) among the 'natural penalties' that he suffers unavoidably as a result of others' exercise of their self-regarding liberty to avoid him (*On Liberty*, CW, xviii. 277–9). But, strictly speaking, society could prevent such harm from befalling him, although general expediency dictates against doing so.

and acquaintances, who remain free to disagree with each other's opinions of kinky sex. But it ceases to be expedient if others attempt to 'parade' invasive speech widely among the public, by using the media or staging public demonstrations and other events, with a view to publicly humiliating the individual and/or forcing him to give up his self-regarding lifestyle. General expediency then calls for the development of social customs enforced by stigma to discourage these attempts and thereby prevent the more severe and widespread direct harm caused to the victim. General expediency can even prescribe the enactment of laws enforced by government officials to prohibit such severely harmful forms of invasive expression.

In some cases, general expediency may recommend the use of social stigma but not legal penalties to suppress the more harmful forms of invasive speech. It may well be inexpedient to use the law to prohibit people from maliciously spreading gossip about their former sex partners in the media, for example, at least in cases where people receive no payments for providing the gossip. Rather than incur the costs of enacting and enforcing general laws, society might decide instead to establish social customs against publication in the media of gossip about another's private affairs. Malicious gossipers and those in the media who give them a platform to publish their gossip would be stigmatized. Mill might even have believed for a time that this form of social coercion was the only effective way for society to suppress the more harmful forms of privacy-invading speech. Needless to add, stigma seems no longer to operate very effectively (if it ever did) against gossip in Britain or the United States.[8]

But general expediency does seem to recommend using *legal* sanctions to suppress privacy-invading expression in at least some situations, even if Mill himself remained dubious that the law could ever be as effective as stigma (I do not say that he did). It seems expedient to prohibit legally one person from selling to the media his accurate account (supported by photographs) of another's sex life against her wishes, with suitable penalties (including reparations, fines and perhaps imprisonment) for those who break the law. This commercial exploitation of the ex-partner's private life directly results in a very serious degree of harm to her. Even if her reputation is not

---

8. Evidently, stigma can only be effective if there are social customs of privacy in place to be enforced. Such customs may well have eroded in societies like Britain and the United States since Mill's time. Perhaps these societies might eventually reach a stage at which nobody wants privacy in any context, including their sexual relationships with other people. In that case, there would cease to be any harm of 'invasion of privacy'. But, in that event, Mill may think that the members of such a society would have sunk to the level of barbarians who are incapable of recognizing that this is a genuine form of harm, that is, a form of perceptible damage (loss of privacy) that any civilized individual capable of rational persuasion would suffer only against his wishes.

damaged, she loses a great deal of control over her self-regarding life by this unauthorized release of private information to a large audience of strangers. Their titillation at what is none of their business, together with any profits made by the media and her ex-partner from the publication, seem, by comparison, to provide trivial offsetting benefits in terms of the promotion of others' individualities. If this is right, then a liberal society may well view the costs of enacting and enforcing suitable laws as being justified in these types of situations. Such laws are needed to prevent the rise of a class of dealers whose business is the publication of any and all invasive speech for profit, and to prevent the net social harm (net loss of liberty of self-regarding conduct) which would otherwise occur.

Legal sanctions also seem expedient to discourage people who deliberately intend seriously to injure their former associates by blackmailing them, or depriving them of employment, or otherwise ruining their reputations through the unauthorized publication of private information that plays to the illiberal prejudices of third parties. If some employers in a certain community are prejudiced against homosexuality, for example, the public exposure of an ex-partner's homosexual lifestyle without his consent might expediently be subjected to legal punishment if he is fired as a result of the exposure. Legal punishment should also be used to discourage public demonstrations calling for the boycott of a business because it employs known homosexuals who are identified by name without their consent.

PIERS NORRIS TURNER

"Harm" and Mill's Harm Principle[†]

I. Introduction

A central problem for John Stuart Mill's liberalism is the specification of "harm" in his famous harm principle. The canonical formulation of the harm principle in *On Liberty* states "that the only purpose for which power can be rightfully exercised over any member of a civilized community, against his will, is to prevent harm to others."[1] It articulates a principled limit on the intrusions of society

---

[†] From *Ethics* 124.2 (January 2014): 299–302, 319–26. © 2014 by The University of Chicago Press. All rights reserved.

1. CW:18, 223 (I.9). Citations marked "CW:18, 223" (or the like) refer to the volume and page numbers of *Collected Works of John Stuart Mill*, 33 vols., ed. John M. Robson (Toronto: University of Toronto Press, 1963–91), 91). * * *

by allowing only considerations of "harm to others" to contribute to the justification of social interference with the individual's control over his own actions.[2] The problem is that Mill never clearly indicates where to draw the line on "harm." Because most any action threatens "harm to others" understood in an *expansive* sense (including any negative consequence for others), it has seemed that either Mill must restrict what counts as "harm," or the harm principle would fail utterly as a shield against society's intrusions. * * *

* * *

* * * I defend the expansive conception of "harm." I argue that accounts of Mill's defense of liberty have expected too much of the harm principle and, as a result, have been forced down unproductive paths with regard to the interpretation of "harm" and the distinction between self-regarding and other-regarding actions. These have in turn led to well-known interpretive difficulties concerning the nature of Mill's liberal commitments. I argue that the first step toward a coherent account of *On Liberty* is to accept that Mill does not explicitly specify what counts as "harm" because he uses it as a general term for bad consequences, requiring no further specification. I then argue that this expansive conception of "harm" grounds an account of the harm principle in which it plays a limited but crucial role in his overall defense of individual liberty.

While the undoubted aim of *On Liberty* is to protect individual liberty against the interference of social authority, my programmatic suggestion is to avoid reading the whole of Mill's defense of liberty into the harm principle itself. The harm principle is one part of that broader defense.[3] In my view, the harm principle is merely an anti-paternalism principle, concerned with allocating decisional authority between society and the individual on the basis of what sorts of reasons are in play.[4] The first stage of Mill's defense of liberty, constituted by the harm principle, is to rule out paternalistic reasons from the justification of social interference. The second stage, going beyond the harm principle, involves a tally of the specific social costs and benefits of interference, which fall under society's rightful authority. Both stages contribute to the overall effort to secure a substantial realm of individual liberty. If Mill would

2. Mill restricts consideration to nonconsensual harm to others. The harm to competent adults from purely consensual activities is treated as harm to oneself (for each of those consensually taking part).
3. D. G. Brown makes the same programmatic suggestion, though he rejects the expansive conception of "harm," in "Mill on Harm to Others' Interests," *Political Studies* 26 (1978): 395–99, see 396–97.
4. Here I endorse the claim that the harm principle is fundamentally about which reasons (concerning the social or individual good) may figure into society's deliberations. See C. L. Ten, *Mill on Liberty* (New York: Oxford University Press, 1980), 40.

reject interference with offensive (but consensual) private sexual practices, then we should not assume that he takes the harm principle alone to be sufficient for this conclusion and thus attempt to characterize "harm" so that it excludes mere offense. Rather, he would first rule out, via the harm principle, potentially weighty paternalistic reasons for interfering in private sexual matters, and second, he would argue that mere offense is relatively insignificant in the tally of social costs and benefits that is within the jurisdiction of social authority. Instead of vitiating *On Liberty*, this reading gives the harm principle a specific and important role, while it also accepts that Mill's defense of liberty is based largely on utilitarian considerations about the great social value of individuality and progress. And by not making the harm principle secure individual liberty all on its own, it allows us to understand why Mill failed to specify a restricted conception of "harm": he didn't need one (by his lights).[5]

This account challenges a widely held and attractive view of the harm principle, according to which it works, on its own, as a rigid barrier against interference by marking out a significant set of other-regarding effects as not properly part of social authority's deliberations. On the view I am proposing, Mill may appear as a less robust liberal than the widely held view would suggest, for the defense of individual liberty depends heavily on certain utilitarian considerations. Interpretively, however, it is worth recalling his explicit commitment to "forego any advantage which could be derived" to his argument from nonutilitarian sources.[6] We should not be surprised to find Mill the author of *Utilitarianism* as well as *On Liberty* relying fundamentally on the principle of utility. And, although my interpretation does not support restricted readings of "harm," I argue that it does allow Mill to remain committed to a relatively robust scheme of liberal rights by appealing, in his words, to "utility in the largest sense, grounded on the permanent interests of man as a progressive being."[7] The two-stage defense of liberty offered here puts the harm principle to work as a vital part of Mill's utilitarian defense of individual liberty, while avoiding the interpretive difficulties

5. There is a complication I am putting off until the end of Sec. IV: in my view, society's right to consider interference may be triggered not only by negative social consequences but also by positive social consequences. Ultimately, "harm principle" is a misnomer. But, given standard accounts of Mill's principle, the crucial step to appreciating this point is to accept that he does not restrict the kinds of negative social consequences that may figure in the justification of social interference. Thus, my focus is on this latter claim.

6. CW:18, 224 (I.11).

7. Ibid. Mill argues that it is often better not to interfere if society wants to develop the individuality of the people within it, and in *Principles of Political Economy* (1848) he proposes a general (though defeasible) laissez-faire policy (CW:3, 944–47). Such arguments, while not strictly applications of the harm principle itself, are part of the overall defense of liberty.

encountered by other accounts. As a result, it offers an attractive alternative that merits further consideration, not only as an interpretation of Mill but, for its own sake, as a defense of individual liberty.

* * *

IV. The Expansive Conception and the
Defense of Liberty

In the previous two sections, I argued that restricted conceptions of "harm" face serious interpretive challenges. Here I argue that an expansive conception of "harm"—according to which any negative consequence counts as "harm"—is more consistent with the textual evidence and can answer the charge that it vitiates the argument of *On Liberty* by failing to provide any defense against social interference.

Earlier, I suggested that we ought to take seriously the thought that the reason Mill does not provide a specification of "harm" is that it should be understood in an expansive way, as a general term for bad consequence. Given the ambiguity surrounding "harm" in *On Liberty* itself, it is instructive that a survey of Mill's *Collected Works* reveals "harm" to be consistently used in practical contexts as simply a companion term for "good," just as "cost" is now a companion to "benefit." For instance, in an 1835 review, Mill writes: "Morality . . . consists in *doing good and refraining from harm*."[8] Thirty years later, in a letter to Henry Brandreth, he writes: "The duty of truth as a positive duty is also to be considered on the ground of *whether more good or harm would follow* to mankind in general if it were generally disregarded."[9] A search for "good than harm," "harm than good," "good or harm," "good rather than harm," "good nor harm," and related phrases reveals numerous other examples. These uses of "harm" are so mundanely nontechnical, they provide no evidence that "harm" is a term of art in the sense commonly supposed, and—perhaps more importantly—no essay by Mill (outside of *On Liberty*, which is the text in dispute) supplies evidence of its being so. We therefore have independent reason to believe that "harm" should be regarded as a general term for bad consequence, and no independent reason to believe that "harm" implies a bad effect of a certain kind or of a certain degree of intensity.

Moreover, the expansive conception is much more consistent with those many formulations of the harm principle in which Mill suggests that "the external relations of the individual" or the mere

8. "Sedgwick's Discourse," CW:10, 59. Emphasis added.
9. CW:16, 1234. Emphasis added.

sociality of an act brings it under society's jurisdiction. Even Riley's weakly restricted definition, by excluding emotional distress, clearly conflicts with a number of them. To understand the harm principle, then, what is crucial in the phrase "harm to others" is less *harm* than *to others*, so that with any action that runs a reasonable risk of affecting others negatively, social authority has jurisdiction and may engage in the further calculation of good and harm.

If it is assumed that the harm principle does its work in defense of liberty partly by restricting the set of negative consequences for others that trigger society's jurisdiction, then the expansive conception of "harm" might seem to make the harm principle almost toothless. But, first, I have suggested already that we should not expect the harm principle alone to encompass Mill's total strategy in defense of liberty. The strategy I propose will depend more on society's being impressed by certain Millian admonitions (e.g., to allow wide scope for individuality) within its jurisdiction rather than on severely restricting that jurisdiction in the first place. Second, on this account the harm principle's sole purpose—to remove paternalistic reasons from society's deliberations—remains significant, given that paternalistic reasons are often weighty reasons addressing the good of human beings in quite fundamental ways. One need only recall that one of Mill's targets is the Church, for whom the paternalistic reason of saving souls figures as an extremely weighty reason (the absence of which would radically alter the interference calculation). The restriction on paternalism is, given the tendencies of his time, a powerful protection for individual liberty. In an 1853 article on Grote's *History of Greece,* he observes:

> In the greatest Greek commonwealth . . . the public interest was held of paramount obligation in all things which concerned it; but, with that part of the conduct of individuals which concerned only themselves, public opinion did not interfere: while in the ethical practice of the moderns, this is exactly reversed, and no one is required by opinion to pay any regard to the public, except by conducting his own private concerns in conformity to its expectations.[1]

The exclusion of paternalistic reasons from any justification of social interference would, on Mill's view, significantly change the way we think about the limits of social interference and would foster much greater social tolerance and diversity.

Once paternalistic reasons are removed from social deliberation about interference, two points follow. First, shorn of any consideration for the well-being of the individual himself, mere offense at

1. CW:11, 319.

one's "experiment of living" is revealed as a weak consideration.[2] While offense counts as "harm," it may not be represented (honestly or dishonestly) by more weighty paternalistic considerations in the interference calculation. Second, important social considerations are to be recommended in all their strength to a well-organized and public-spirited social authority in those matters over which it has rightful control. Much of *On Liberty* concerns Mill's views on the sorts of considerations (e.g., individuality, free discussion, and security) that he believes social authority ought to weigh heavily within its jurisdiction when considering interference, and which on balance often favor individual liberty. But these recommendations about when social interference is or is not justified should not be read back into the harm principle itself.

On this view of the harm principle, then, "harm to others" includes any bad consequence for others, and the purpose of the harm principle is only to exclude paternalistic considerations from social deliberation. This view accords best with the various formulations of the harm principle and other evidence of what Mill means by "harm," but it also need not undermine the overall aim of *On Liberty* if the harm principle is understood as just one (important) part of Mill's defense of individual liberty.

Let us now further clarify this strategy by addressing four possible worries. First, my account of Mill's defense of liberty depends heavily on social authority's effectively performing utility calculations within its jurisdiction. This, one might worry, makes him less robustly liberal than on other accounts. But while this may make some of us nervous, there is no reason to think that Mill—who is, at bottom, a utilitarian—could not have proposed such a view. As an interpretive matter, I worry that this concern stands in the way of potentially fruitful attempts to reread his texts in a more unified way. We might prefer the image of Mill as a robust, principled liberal, but that might not be his view.

Nevertheless, I also want to emphasize that even the presence of widespread feelings of disgust at some offending conduct need not immediately lead to the conclusion that restrictions on the offending conduct would be justified. My view admits mere offense into the interference calculation, but a number of considerations block illiberal restrictions. It is not just that, for Mill, the value of free discussion and individuality is far more significant or weighty than the disvalue of mere offense, though that is *the* crucial consideration (he writes that there is "no parity" between them).[3] It would also need to be the case that restrictions would succeed in diminishing the

---

2. For Mill's discussion of "experiments of living" see CW:18, 260–61 (III.1).
3. CW:18, 283 (IV.12).

offended feelings. Imposing restrictions or punishments might fail to alleviate many of the offended feelings (such as those resulting simply from the knowledge that others are engaging in the offending conduct) or might simply redirect people's attention to other actions that also offend their sensibilities. If people would not be happier as a result of the prohibition or punishment, then such impositions might not be justified. Moreover, the enforcement of a prohibition will have monetary costs to society that might not be worth it or that redirect resources that might better be spent otherwise. Bear in mind that in the cases under consideration, such as restrictions on private sexual conduct, the restrictions would affect millions of individuals, not simply one couple in a room somewhere. The same consideration applies to calculating the nonmonetary costs of loss of liberty or individuality. All things considered, it might be less costly, both monetarily and nonmonetarily, to diminish the offended feelings by educating or acculturating those who felt offended so that they no longer feel offended. The presence of offense or disgust need not be treated as a given. My point is simply that we should not presume that Mill is no longer a liberal if he accepts the expansive conception of harm. Many assumptions are needed to get from the claim that mere offense counts as a relevant interference consideration to the conclusion that it is justified to prohibit or punish those who engage in the offending conduct.[4]

Second, one might object that in my view the overall defense of liberty has two stages and so fails to respect Mill's assertion that "the object of this Essay is to assert one very simple principle."[5] But I contend that my account, by reading the harm principle as merely an antipaternalism principle, makes it simpler than all those accounts that ask it do much more work—and more complicated work—in light of a restricted conception of "harm." It is also very unlikely that Mill means to suggest that every argument in *On Liberty* can be explained as an application of that one principle. One need only turn to chapter II, where he defends the liberty of discussion not by applying the harm principle—that is, he does not argue that "harm to others" considerations are absent in cases of the expression of opinion—but by arguing that the harms associated with free discussion are always outweighed by the benefits. Moreover, in his *Autobiography*, Mill reports that *On Liberty* is "a kind of philosophic text-book of a single truth," namely, "the importance, to man and society, of a large variety in types of character, and of giving full freedom to human nature to expand itself in innumerable

---

4. I am grateful to Don Hubin for a helpful conversation on these issues.
5. CW:18, 223 (I.9).

and conflicting directions."[6] This broader statement of the aims of that work strikes me as more accurate, capturing not just the work of the harm principle but also Mill's claims about the importance of personal liberty even within society's jurisdiction.

Third, it might be objected that the harm principle prohibits legal moralism, that is, legal restrictions against harmless wrongdoing, and so it must be more than a mere antipaternalism principle. Elsewhere I address this issue at length.[7] In brief, I reject the claim that the harm principle expresses the traditional liberal strategy against legal moralism, according to which non-harm-related moral considerations are deemed unfit to justify legal prohibitions. In Mill's view, appeals to harmless wrongdoing are ruled out already by his basic utilitarian commitments, according to which the category of harmless wrongdoing is empty. If harm is understood in an expansive sense, then there will be no wrongdoings that are harmless (one can imagine a limiting case where the wrong action causes no harm but only less good than some other action, but this is not a realistic case).

To be clear, Mill has no sympathy with the sorts of legal prohibitions that are presented as instances of legal moralism. He certainly would have wanted to protect the liberty of individuals to engage in consensual activities that cause no harm to others (such as consensual homosexual intercourse between adults) even if deemed morally bad by a prevailing morality. What is at issue is not whether Mill in some way rules out the instances of interference that concern liberal opponents of legal moralism but how exactly he does so. I believe a close reading of the relevant passages shows that Mill does not explicitly employ the liberal argument against legal moralism but relies only on his antipaternalism and utilitarian commitments to respond to those objectionable cases.

Fourth, my view may still seem incompatible with Mill's statements of the jurisdictional trigger that do not mention bad consequences at all, but only "the external relations of the individual," "the conduct of human beings towards one another," or that the action is a "social act." Moreover, I have thus far ignored Mill's claim that there are "positive acts for the benefit of others," apparently involving no harm to others, that an individual "may rightfully be compelled to perform."[8] These acts include not only core legal responsibilities, such as providing evidence in court or serving in the military during wartime, but also "acts of individual beneficence, such as saving a fellow-creature's life, or interposing to protect the defenceless against ill-usage, things which whenever it is obviously man's duty

6. CW:1, 259.
7. See Piers Norris Turner, "Mill and the Liberal Rejection of Legal Moralism" [in *History of Philosophy Quarterly* 32 n. 1 (2015): 79–99].
8. CW:18, 224–25 (I.11).

to do, he may rightfully be made responsible to society for not doing."[9] Mill notes that society should be more "cautious" about interfering in such cases than in cases of harmful conduct, but they nevertheless fall under society's rightful authority. His attention elsewhere to "harm to others" has led D. G. Brown to argue that social coercion in these "positive" cases cannot be reconciled with the harm principle.[1]

In addressing such cases, I first accept—following David Lyons— that "positive acts" may be socially enforced on harm prevention grounds. On Lyons's view it is consistent with the harm principle that "I might be required to come to another's aid, in order to prevent harm to him, even if I may not be said to have caused the harm that he will suffer if I should fail to help him when I can."[2] In all of these cases, there is an identifiable harm, which we would not normally say is the individual's fault but which would be averted if the individual acted—and that is enough to justify coercion. This is in the spirit of Mill's characterization of cases of failing to act. Thus, although he classifies cases of inaction as examples of "not preventing evil" rather than of "doing evil" (or "causing harm" in Lyons's sense), he subsumes both the failure to prevent and the doing under the heading of "cause" of evil (in a mechanistic sense).[3] The failure to perform these beneficial acts does contribute to the existence of evil. It seems, then, that Mill is focused on harm prevention and not on harmful-conduct prevention—which should be expected, given his utilitarianism. That is enough to treat "positive" cases.

But it remains that the mere "external relations" or "social act" formulations of the harm principle seem to allow considerations of the social good alone to trigger society's jurisdiction. I think this is ultimately correct, but given the overwhelming tendency to read "harm" in a restricted sense, it has been necessary to focus on that issue. I believe Mill does not mean to exclude social good considerations from the justification of social interference in the absence of "harm to others."[4] This is partly because it is difficult to imagine cases where the social good is at stake but there is little or no risk of harm to others understood in the expansive sense, and so it is not clear what cases are distinguished by focusing on harm alone as the jurisdictional trigger. Recall that "social act" for Mill implies effects on nonconsenting others; purely consensual interactions between

---

9. Ibid., 225 (I.11).
1. D. G. Brown, "Mill on Liberty and Morality," *Philosophical Review* 81 (1972): 133–58, 158.
2. David Lyons, *Rights, Welfare, and Mill's Moral Theory* (New York: Oxford University Press, 1994), 92.
3. CW:18, 225 (I.11).
4. This suggests that "harm principle" is a misnomer and that "liberty principle," which is also common usage, is more appropriate.

rational adults remain self-regarding for each of those involved. Thus "trade is a social act," he writes, because of the effects of seemingly private transactions on nonconsenting others and society more generally.[5] Rather, I believe Mill offers the "harm"-oriented formulations in order to focus our attention on what he regards as the most pressing signal to society to consider some matter, namely, that some nonconsenting other person has been adversely affected. It also seems clear that the competence considerations—raised earlier in favor of social authority's rightful control when society might be negatively affected—would apply just as well in cases when the good of others is affected, but where there is no harm to others (were there such cases).

Only the expansive conception of "harm" can be made practically consistent with "external relations" formulations if, as a matter of contingent fact, social acts—in all practical cases—have some harmful consequences in the expansive sense. Mill might then understandably render the jurisdictional trigger as "social act" in one passage and as "harm to others" in another. In my view, the harm principle is simply an antipaternalism principle. It is consistent with that claim to argue that any negative effect for others would trigger society's jurisdiction, just so long as we do not thereby exclude positive effects for others from also triggering society's jurisdiction. This may not sit well with the "harm" formulations of the principle considered alone, but it best respects the whole set of formulations, especially in the context of Mill's utilitarian commitments. Even if this is wrong, however, it does not affect my critical claims concerning Mill's conception of "harm" in *On Liberty*.

V. Conclusion

In order to understand Mill's defense of individual liberty, we needn't carve out a sphere of self-regarding behavior that can be negatively other-affecting in certain ways. We need only follow C. L. Ten in reading the harm principle as being fundamentally about reasons.[6] In this view, what matters to society's deliberations is whether a reason, and not a whole action, is self-regarding. As the canonical formulation states: "the *only purpose* for which power can be rightfully exercised over any member of a civilized community, against his will, is to prevent harm to others. His own good, either physical or moral, is not a sufficient warrant."[7] The

---

5. CW:18, 293 (V.4). Mill continues: "Whoever undertakes to sell any description of goods to the public, does what affects the interest of other persons, and of society in general; and thus his conduct, in principle, comes within the jurisdiction of society."
6. Ten, *Mill on Liberty* 40.
7. CW:18, 223 (I.9). Emphasis added.

reason-restricting reading allows "self-regarding" to mean what it colloquially means, while granting the harm principle its important antipaternalistic function. Once the paternalistic reasons have been removed (because they are not social authority's business), Mill can then argue that remaining considerations of mere offense or outrage are insignificant when compared to the importance of permitting individuals to develop their capacities by living as they see fit.

The harm principle is thus crucial for making the balance of reasons clearly weigh on one side of the account. But it does not make the case all on its own. Much of *On Liberty* concerns Mill's recommendations to social authority not to interfere even when it has jurisdiction, because of the great value of free discussion and individuality. But those recommendations should not be read back into the harm principle itself. Rather than undermine Mill's defense of liberty, the expansive conception of "harm" simply changes our understanding of how that defense proceeds. If all of the foregoing is correct, then our understanding of the harm principle, at least as it appears in Mill, needs to be significantly revised. It does not, by itself, secure a sphere of personal liberty by employing a restricted conception of "harm to others." Rather, it plays the more limited but crucial role of removing paternalistic considerations from society's deliberations, leaving social authority to consider only the social good and harm (in the expansive sense) of interfering in some matter.

WENDY DONNER

Mill's Utilitarianism[†]

Introduction

Mill's *Utilitarianism* was not written as a scholarly treatise but as a series of essays for a popular audience. It was first published in three instalments in *Fraser's Magazine* in 1861 and appeared in book form in 1863. *Fraser's Magazine* was a magazine with a general audience and the essay was written with this readership in view. Although many commentators have examined the arguments Mill puts forward in this work in isolation from his other writings, in fact it cannot be properly appreciated unless it is placed in the context of the

---

† From *The Cambridge Companion to Mill*, ed. John Skorupski (Cambridge: Cambridge University Press, 1998), pp. 255–59, 261–64, 267–69, 272–78, 282–90, 292. Copyright © 1998 by Cambridge University Press. Reprinted by permission of the licensor through PLSClear.

larger body of his work. In particular, this work needs to be read against the background of his more scholarly writing in *A System of Logic* and in his editorial footnotes to James Mill's *Analysis of the Phenomena of the Human Mind* (*Logic*, CW VII and VIII; James[, *An Analysis of the Phenomena of the Human Mind* (1829), ed. J. S. Mill (London: Longmans, Green and Dyer, 1869)].

John Stuart Mill is rightly considered to be a major figure in the history of utilitarianism; his theory is a touchstone to which contemporary ethical theorists regularly return for insights. Yet at the same time, Mill's utilitarianism is boldly revisionist, breaking free of many of the constraints and confines of the narrower and simpler utilitarianism of his predecessors Jeremy Bentham and his father James Mill. Although John Stuart Mill was carefully educated and prepared by his father to be the transmitter and torch bearer of Benthamite utilitarianism, he instead radically transformed it. The result is a theory which is both inspiring and frustrating in its sophistication, richness and complexity. While I argue that Mill's theory is consistent and unified, there is no doubt that it expands and enlarges the familiar boundaries of his predecessors' utilitarianism at times almost to the breaking point. But his theory also shares with theirs some familiar foundations.

Although utilitarianism as a moral theory has many faces, a core idea informs all of them. Utilitarianism makes utility or intrinsic value the foundation of morality. Utilitarianism "evaluates actions in terms of their utility" [L. W. Sumner, "The Good and the Right," in Wesley Cooper, Kay Nielsen, and Steven C. Patter, eds. *New Essays on John Stuart Mill and Utilitarianism. Canadian Journal of Philosophy*, suppl. vol. 5 (1979), 100] rather than in terms of any intrinsic properties of the actions. Utilitarianism is distinguished from moral theories which hold that certain kinds of acts are right or wrong in themselves, and we are obliged to perform them or refrain from doing them for that very reason. According to utilitarianism, on the other hand, concepts of the good are more basic than or prior to concepts of right and obligation, and obligations are determined by reference to intrinsic value. This core idea leaves much room for differing interpretations of the nature of the good to be produced as well as the method of determining obligations on the basis of this good. This latter issue is often formulated as the dispute which divides act utilitarianism and rule utilitarianism. Bentham, James Mill and John Stuart Mill all hold to mental state accounts of utility, that is, accounts which maintain that the good we seek to promote consists in mental states such as pleasure, happiness, enjoyment or satisfaction. The attractive intuitive idea of utilitarianism is the importance of the promotion of well-being in its many forms. But this still leaves open the questions: what is the best account of utility or welfare? and what is the best method for maximizing or promoting (utilitarians can differ over this) utility or welfare, however construed?

The nature of the Good

Classical utilitarians have usually agreed that human good consists in the experience of pleasure or happiness or that pleasure or happiness is the one thing desirable in itself. But utilitarians disagree about the nature of utility. John Stuart Mill holds that the principle of utility is the supreme or foundational principle of morality, which plays the role of justifying all obligations and secondary principles or standards. He says that

> The creed which accepts as the foundation of morals, Utility, or the Greatest Happiness Principle, holds that actions are right in proportion as they tend to promote happiness, wrong as they tend to produce the reverse of happiness. (*Utilitarianism, CW* X:210)

In this formulation Mill's theory puts forward a single standard for morality. However, the principle of utility is most directly a principle of the good which is the foundation for all practical reasoning, including moral reasoning, and so provides the grounding for the moral evaluation of action. In another formulation, the principle of utility is more clearly advanced as a principle of good: "The utilitarian doctrine is, that happiness is desirable, and the only thing desirable, as an end; all other things being only desirable as means to that end" (*CW* X:234). He expands: "By happiness is intended pleasure, and the absence of pain; by unhappiness, pain, and the privation of pleasure" (*CW* X:210). This "theory of morality" is grounded on "the theory of life" that

> pleasure, and freedom from pain, are the only things desirable as ends; and that all desirable things (which are as numerous in the utilitarian as in any other scheme) are desirable either for the pleasure inherent in themselves, or as means to the promotion of pleasure and the prevention of pain. (*CW* X:210)

These quotes signal some important breaks from the Benthamite utilitarian tradition. Good resides in internal mental states of pleasure or happiness. But while for Bentham these mental states are sensations of pleasure, for Mill they are far more complex states of experience. Mill thought that Bentham's conception of the good, his quantitative hedonism, was narrow and misconceived and made him vulnerable to the criticism that utilitarianism is "a doctrine worthy only of swine" (*CW* X:210). Mill expands the conception of the good in two separate but related respects. He takes value to reside in complex mental experiences rather than sensations and he takes the quality of happiness as well as the quantity to be productive of its value. Mill's qualitative hedonism is a complex mental state account of utility which takes into account the quality as well as the quantity of pleasurable experiences in measuring their value and stands as a sophisticated alternative to Bentham's quantitative hedonism. I first explore the views on complex mental states before turning to the question of what makes these experiences valuable.

Mill's qualitative hedonism is intended to fend off criticisms that utilitarianism is a narrow theory appropriate for swine; nevertheless it has drawn more than its share of criticism. Mill stands accused of a list of inconsistencies because he defends a complex mental state account which expands the good-making properties of pleasures to encompass quality as well as quantity of states of experience. Mill concurs with Bentham that pleasurable mental states are what have value or are the things that are valuable. However, Mill dissents from Bentham over the issues both of the nature of these valuable states and of which properties produce their value. Many mistaken or mis-guided objections to Mill's position arise from the failure of critics to keep separate the quite distinct issues of what things are valuable— pleasurable mental states—and what properties of these states are their good-making properties. A position on the issue of what things have value still does not settle the question of what properties of those things produce or create their value.

John Stuart Mill, James Mill and Bentham all share an associationist psychology.[1] When Mill says that "by happiness is intended pleasure, and the absence of pain", he indicates that happiness consists of a composite in which pleasures outbalance pains over time (*Utilitarianism*, CW X:210).[2] Mill's empiricism and psychological associationism provide the impetus for his claim that our mental life is created out of the basic data of sense experience. Sensations are the basic original mental entities and are defined as "the feelings which we have by the five senses—Smell, Taste, Hearing, Touch, and Sight" (James Mill 1869 I:3). Sensations and ideas, which are the subsequent mental copies of sensations, become linked through association and in the normal course of psychological development what were originally simple mental states are turned into much more complex states of experience. Moreover, Mill thinks that association often operates as a quasi-chemical process to create chemical unions of elements in which the original parts or elements merge into a new and complex whole (*Logic*, CW VIII:852–56). He says,

1. James Mill's *An Analysis of the Phenomena of the Human Mind* sets out this association-ist psychology. John Stuart Mill's editorial notes to the 1869 edition set down the few points of dispute with his father's discussions.
2. See also [L. W. Sumner, "Welfare, Happiness, and Pleasure," *Utilitas* 4 (1992): 199–206].

> When many impressions or ideas are operating in the mind together, there sometimes takes place a process of a similar kind to chemical combination. When impressions have been so often experienced in conjunction, that each of them calls up readily and instantaneously the ideas of the whole group, those ideas sometimes melt and coalesce into one another, and appear not several ideas, but one. (CW VIII:853)

The complexes that result occupy an important place in Mill's moral psychology, for they are bearers of value, rather than the simple ideas which generate them.

While Mill's theory can be classified as a sophisticated kind of hedonism because of the role that pleasures and pains play in generating complex pleasurable experiences, it would be a mistake to view his theory as primarily focussed on the evaluation of pleasures. Out of the building blocks of pleasures are built human happiness and satisfaction, and on this base is erected the edifice of human beings of firm and distinctive character freely choosing the projects and activities of meaningful life. Mill's fundamental purpose is to promote human self-development and so he is centrally occupied with exploring the forms of character that allow humans to pursue meaningful lives.

*   *   *

Qualitative Hedonism

In propounding qualitative hedonism, Mill moves beyond Benthamite quantitative hedonism in a decisive and notable way. His insistence that the quality of states of happiness is crucial to their value justly earns for him the reputation of revisionary utilitarian. This break with orthodox Benthamism provides an opening for his radical expansion of the conception of the good at the heart of his moral philosophy. It allows him a means to counter decisively the objections of opponents that hedonistic utilitarianism is worthy only of swine; it also enables him to set out an attractive and plausible alternative.

Mill has been subjected to a good deal of less than sympathetic treatment because of his inclusion of quality as a good-making characteristic. The recent excellent revisionary scholarship which has countered many earlier distorted interpretations of aspects of Mill's thought has still tended to accept what I claim are mistaken interpretations of Mill's qualitative hedonism. Many of the harshest criticisms of Mill take him to task for including quality in the assessment of value. Mill's views on quality are taken to be inconsistent with hedonism, and he is accused of abandoning both utilitarianism and hedonism.

Before I delve into the question of the alleged inconsistency of Mill's recognition of quality with hedonism, I will look at what Mill means by the quality of pleasurable states. Many commentators treat quality and value as synonymous, but this is seriously mistaken. Confusion over just what Mill means by quality has led to misconstruals; it is instructive to clarify this question first. In *Utilitarianism* Mill is insistent that pleasures differ in quality as well as quantity:

> It is quite compatible with the principle of utility to recognize the fact, that some *kinds* of pleasure are more desirable and more valuable than others. It would be absurd that while, in estimating all other things, quality is considered as well as quantity, the estimation of pleasures should be supposed to depend on quantity alone. (*CW* X:211)

*　*　*

The obstacle to a correct interpretation of what Mill means by quality is that he uses the term ambiguously to mean either a kind or a normative property. This vacillation has made him vulnerable to criticisms and misinterpretations. By choosing a consistent sense of quality we can demystify this dimension and put Mill's view of value in clearer perspective. Many interpretations of Mill place quantity (intensity and duration) on one side as a straightforward empirical property and quality on the other side as a mysterious, obscure, normative property [Rem Edwards, *Pleasures and Pains: A Theory of Qualitative Hedonism* (Ithaca: Cornell U Press, 1979)]. This interpretation misses the point of what both Mill and Bentham are doing. Bentham regards the quantities of pleasures as empirical, but he also regards them as normative, that is, productive of good, or that in virtue of which the pleasures that have them are good. Mill does not regard only the quality as normative; he regards both quantity and quality of pleasures and satisfactions as normative or productive of good. He also regards both as empirical. He simply adds one further property, quality, as a normative property. It is often assumed that by including quality as productive of good Mill introduces a radically new and mysterious kind of dimension. This is not the case. In Mill's view, quality is just another ordinary property, and so in all of my discussions of quality of pleasurable experiences I use quality to mean that additional good-making characteristic of pleasures. Quality is thus assigned a consistent meaning, and notions that quality is the only normative aspect of pleasurable experiences should be dispelled. Quality is clearly not synonymous with overall value. Overall value or good-ness is produced by quantity and quality, the two basic good-making characteristics. When competent agents express preferences for different pleasurable experiences, they are ranking these experiences on a scale of value. What is being measured is value of experience. The properties that contribute to value are quantity and quality.

In *Utilitarianism* Mill equates the quality of pleasure with its kind. He says, for example, that "the pleasures derived from the higher faculties [are] preferable *in kind* (CW X:213). Thus intellectual pleasures can be a kind. But kinds of pleasure are not categorized solely by the faculty affected; they are also classified by cause and by phenomenal differences in the pleasurable experiences themselves. Thus causal and intentional properties enter the picture. Mill's notion that quality of pleasurable experiences is roughly equivalent to kind and his particular view of kind give his view a flexibility that Bentham's lacks.

Many critics have not accepted Mill's bold revisionism. Mill's inclusion of quality raises special problems because of its very complexity, and it calls for a more complicated method for measuring value. But many of the common criticisms of Mill's qualitative hedonism are misdirected and insubstantial and confuse the issues at stake. Some of the worst offenders in this regard are historical critics such as G. E. Moore and F. H. Bradley. * * *

*   *   *

The important questions that remain after these objections and alternative interpretations are cleared away are: How are the scales of value to be constructed (conceived of) and what measurement procedure is to be substituted for Bentham's felicific calculus? Mill must also explain how degrees and scales of quantity and quality are put together on the central scale of value. In all of this it must be remembered that the scale we are working with is the scale of value. This scale measures the value of pleasures. A look back at Bentham's felicific calculus, which is a quantitative approach, is instructive as background and in comparison with Mill's measurement procedure.

Both Mill and Bentham require methods of measuring the value of different mental states, but they come up with very different procedures. Bentham's felicific calculus is a method designed to measure the total quantity of pleasure and pain caused by an action. The method calls for a calculation of the quantity of each pleasure and pain of every person whose interests are affected. Then the balance of quantity of all the pleasures and pains is worked out to determine which action will produce the greatest balance of pleasure over pain.

The method quantifies intensity and duration and integrates them into the scale of value. Since value is a function of quantity, the higher on the scale of quantity each pleasure is placed, the greater is its value. Since Benthamite scales are cardinal, units that can be added and multiplied and so aggregated are required for each of the dimensions.

Mill's measurement procedure for value of pleasurable experience thus does not break with Bentham in taking the key step from uni-dimensional to multidimensional measure, since Bentham has already done this with the dimensions of intensity and duration, combined into quantity. But Mill's theory does have more dimensions of value to contend with and is more complicated. Applying Mill's procedure, after intensity and duration have been synthesized, the resulting scale of quantity must in turn be integrated with that of quality to form an overall judgment of value. Some kinds or qualities of pleasurable experience are judged to be more valuable and thus placed higher on the scale of quality by competent agents. Competent agents rank pleasurable experiences on scales that measure their value. * * *

Mill's method of value measurement, as I interpret it, is a general and inclusive procedure for assessing the worth of all enjoyments. Significantly, it allows in principle for the inclusion and comparability of all good-making properties of enjoyments, and does not restrict the domain of the sorts of enjoyments that may be scrutinized and compared for value or disvalue. While there is little doubt that Mill himself regards the enjoyments of intellectual activity and pursuits of justice as the prime examples of highly valuable kinds of pleasures, it is a mistake, I contend, to read his comments on the value of these kinds of enjoyments as doing any more than providing enduring examples of valuable satisfactions. I claim that it is mistaken to restrict the good-making features that may be assessed and compared and to interpret Mill as holding that some kinds of enjoyments are lexically preferable to other kinds, in the sense that a quantity of the lexically preferable kind of enjoyment will always outweigh any quantity of the other.

* * *

In summary, Mill's qualitative hedonism is an appealing and plausible alternative to the Benthamite utilitarian aggregative approach. I have argued that Mill differs from Bentham in regarding valuable things as being complex pleasurable states of experience and in claiming that both quantity and quality or kind are good-making properties which produce value. Mill quite clearly maintains that these two properties are separate, independent good-making features. It is consistent with hedonism to maintain that the kind of pleasure is relevant to its overall value and it begs the question simply to assume without argument that the only relevant good-making property is quantity. Mill's own words apply here aptly: "It would be absurd that while, in estimating all other things, quality is considered as well as quantity, the estimation of pleasures should be supposed to depend on quantity alone" (*Utilitarianism*, *CW* X:211). * * *

* * *

Development and Self-Development

Mill's reliance upon the preference rankings of competent agents to assess value signals some other profound differences with Benthamite utilitarianism. Many twentieth-century commentators focus on the treatment of action and of moral rules and obligations in Mill's utilitarianism. But Mill himself seems to be as concerned about issues of good character and good lives as he is about right action. Instead of focussing primarily on calculations of consequences of actions, he also turns his attention to the proper education and socialization of moral agents, believing that agents who are self-developed are much more likely to promote good in the world as well as lead satisfying lives. More good will come about if self-developed agents act in character or out of habit, and questions of character take on a much weightier role in Mill's theory than in Bentham's. So it is important to give due place to his discussion of the ways in which people are appropriately socialized.

Mill jettisons the Benthamite felicific calculus; he offers in its place a method employing the preferences of self-developed agents. In the relevant passage in *Utilitarianism*, he refers to agents who "have experience of" or "are competently acquainted with" those pleasurable experiences which are being evaluated and ranked (*CW* X:211). But in making this remark, as in the case of many other points of his argument in *Utilitarianism*, Mill draws upon a wealth of background detail and argumentation worked out in other writings. Mill's point is that if such agents prefer or judge more valuable certain enjoyments, then these enjoyments should be taken to be more valuable. The test is the preferences of agents who are in the best position to know.

The first stage of the education and socialization of competent agents is the process of development. During this part of the process, generic human intellectual, affective and moral capacities are nurtured, usually as part of childhood socialization. Mill's doctrine of development, formulated and explained in many writings, sets out the educative process by which these capacities are fostered. Mill's doctrine of development is multifaceted; it plays more than one role in his theory. This doctrine describes a form of education which is foundational in the sense that someone who has undergone it is the kind of person who is in a position to be maximally happy, and in addition has achieved a perspective appropriate to evaluate the experiences, pursuits, character and ways of life which are worth pursuing.

Thus developed and self-developed agents are the pivot of Mill's theory, because their preferences provide the best indicators of value of different kinds of happiness. They are at the same time both the best judges of value and the source and locus of value. The most valuable forms of happiness are those which involve the development and active use of generic human capacities which are the focus of development. The sort of educative process which concerns Mill is one of character formation. Using his psychological theory of association, Mill argues that if our educational goal is to create certain features of character, or to nurture certain human capacities, we must take care to use the laws of association to further these educational goals, creating the right associations to encourage certain forms of character. Our education should encourage the character traits that would produce the most utility if manifested by members of a community (*Logic*, *CW* VIII:869–70).

Mill regards affective development, or the development of feelings, as the foundation of all types of development. This puts his theory in the lineage of Hume and historical utilitarians who regard morality as the domain of feeling as well as of reason. In the *Autobiography* Mill says that he felt that his own education had focussed too narrowly on intellectual training, and when, in early adulthood, he suffered his well-known "mental crisis", a bout of severe depression, he later traced his problems to deficiencies in his education, including the deprecation of internal culture and the lack of nurturing of feeling. He was determined to rectify this imbalance in his own philosophy and to find an appropriate place for "internal culture" (*Autobiography*, *CW* I:147). In his personal experience, encounters with writings of romantic poets such as Wordsworth and Shelley helped to pull him out of his depression and revitalize his feelings. * * *

* * *

The process of moral development teaches children to feel sympathetic connection with others and to take pleasure in their happiness. Cultivation of sympathy with others is the foundation of moral development. Many of Mill's concerns are echoed in contemporary claims about the need for the capacity of empathy for moral agency.

*   *   *

Mill harshly criticizes Bentham for holding to a belief in the "predominance of the selfish principle in human nature" ("Remarks on Bentham's Philosophy," *CW* X:14). The original basis of moral feelings is explained:

> The idea of the pain of another is naturally painful; the idea of the pleasure of another is naturally pleasurable. From this fact in our natural constitution, all our affections both of love and aversion towards human beings . . . originate. In this, the unselfish part of our nature, lies a foundation, even independently of inculcation from without, for the generation of moral feelings. ("Sedgwick's Discourse," *CW* X:60)

Our moral/social side is an element of our nature that needs development along with our intellectual/individualist side, and Mill's refusal to create a hierarchy among these capacities and his insistence upon a balance among them has important consequences for his conception of self-development, as well as for his liberal political theory. On Mill's account, moral development is the appropriate accompaniment to mental development, and one without the other is a caricature of development.

*   *   *

This picture of the process of development prepares the way for the next stage of self-development. In the usual course of events, when children mature and reach adulthood they assume control of the development process and continue it as one of self-development. In the continuation, the higher-order capacities of individuality, autonomy and sociality and cooperativeness are constructed on the groundwork of the generic human capacities. These capacities of sociality/cooperativeness and autonomy/individuality must all be balanced against each other; none must be allowed to take over a dominant role. Individuality is the capacity to discover our own unique mix of the generic human capacities. Autonomy is the capacity to reflect critically upon, choose and endorse the character, projects and pursuits in harmony with our nature. While we do not have one fixed and unchangeable essence, we do have a range of potential and a range of characters, lifestyles and pursuits in harmony with this. The greatest happiness results from seeking out and discovering this range and then choosing and creating traits of character, lifestyles and commitments on this foundation. *   *   *

*   *   *

Mill's concept of individualism is centered around the value he places on the individual as the generator, focus and evaluator of value. Value is located in each and every individual, and whatever value groups or communities have flows only from the value of its members. Such individuality requires that persons are in control of their own lives, that they are accustomed to making and carrying through on their own choices and that their own ideas, activities and projects are an expression of their own particularity.

* * * To deny someone the opportunity of development and self-development is thus to deny that person the status of full moral agency. Although much goes into the socialization and educational experience of self-development, almost everybody, in Mill's view, has the potential to attain such status, and it is usually their social circumstances that determine whether their potential unfolds. Thus Mill's ideals and commitments require that all adult members of society have the opportunity and social resources effectively to gain the status of self-developed agent. I claim then that Mill's utilitarianism, with its fundamental commitment to and dependence upon self-developed competent moral agents, inclines his moral theory towards a form of radical egalitarianism. According to the fundamental tenets of Mill's utilitarianism, people have a right to liberty of self-development and their rights are violated if their social circumstances bar them or do not provide adequate resources for them to attain and exercise self-development. To elaborate in great detail upon these matters would be to stray beyond the confines of this chapter and into the territory of other essays on Mill's political philosophy. However, to conclude the subject of Mill's utilitarianism, it is necessary to survey some issues regarding his views on moral rules and in particular on rules of justice and rights.

*   *   *

Justice, Rights and Utility

* * * Until the recent wave of revisionary scholarship, the chapter of *Utilitarianism* entitled "On the Connexion between Justice and Utility" tended to be ignored. (Indeed, all but a few pages of this work shared this fate.) In this chapter Mill responds to the sorts of objections I have raised in the previous section, namely, those objections which claim that justice and utility are opposed or can conflict. In the course of this he offers an account of the origin of the sentiment of justice, an issue which I sidestep here, as well as an analysis of the concept of a right and a utilitarian defence of rights. In this final section I concentrate on these latter two issues. While Mill's utilitarian justification of rights does not provide as secure a grounding for rights as some might wish, because utilitarian rights are not foundational and so are not "trumps", it is nonetheless a robust defence.[3] The issue, once again, concerns the strength and foundation of rights. Mill's moral theory is not rights-based, because, as his rights are utilitarian rights, they are grounded in well-being. But Mill argues effectively that utilitarianism can strongly support rights and retain a central place for them in the theory. Thus, while rights are not foundational, nonetheless they are weighty and not easily overturned.

* * *

Mill's moral theory thus separates moral rules of obligation from the broader class of rules of expediency or general promotion of the good. But Mill also differentiates rules of justice from moral rules of obligation; the former also constitute a sub-class within the class of moral rules. Mill claims that rules of justice "involve the idea of a personal right—a claim on the part of one or more individuals" (*Utilitarianism, CW* X:247). Injustice "implies two things—a wrong done, and some assignable person who is wronged" (*CW* X:247). This leads to the definition of a right:

> When we call anything a person's right, we mean that he has a valid claim on society to protect him in the possession of it, either by the force of law, or by that of education and opinion. If he has what we consider a sufficient claim, on whatever account, to have something guaranteed to him by society, we say that he has a right to it. (*CW* X:250)

Elaborating on this, he continues, "To have a right, then, is, I conceive, to have something which society ought to defend me in the possession of" (*CW* X:250).

Recent commentators have pointed out that in this first part of the passage Mill analyzes the concept of a right in general, and that this analysis is distinct from his utilitarian defence of rights and could be accepted by thinkers even if they are not committed to utilitarianism ([David Lyons, *Rights, Welfare, and Mill's Moral Theory* (Oxford: Clarendon Press, 1994)], 51). Now Mill sets out his utilitarian justification of rights. He says that "if the objector goes on to ask why it ought, I can give him no other reason than general utility". The moral justification is based on "the extraordinarily important and impressive kind of utility which is concerned" (*Utilitarianism, CW* X:250–51). Mill's substantive theory of justice goes beyond both the analysis of the concept of a right and the utilitarian justification to discuss particular rights. The two most basic rights, according to Mill, are the right to security and the

---

3. See [Ronald Dworkin, *Taking Rights Seriously* (Cambridge, Mass.: Harvard University Press, 1977), 184–205].

right to liberty (including the right to liberty of self-development).[4]
But Mill reiterates his claim that justice and utility are not in
conflict, but on the contrary rules of justice must be based on
well-being.

* * *

Rights protect the most vital human interests. Since they are specifically designed to protect and guarantee such interests, rights
claims ward off casual trade-offs which would permit some people's
important interests being overridden to promote unimportant or
moderately important interests of others, even large groups of others.
Mill analyzes rights as involving claims which are socially guaranteed by institutions collectively set up and maintained to carry out
these guarantees effectively (*Utilitarianism*, CW X:251). Thus, it
would be inconsistent to maintain on the one hand that rights
ought to be effectively protected and guaranteed, and on the other
hand that they can easily be traded off for unimportant or moderately important gains to others. Mill obviously does not intend to
endorse such inconsistencies, but instead intends to propound a
robust view of rights which can give this protection.

* * *

So utilitarianism has strong resources to counter this common
complaint. But other issues remain. The painful dilemmas occur in
cases which involve conflicts among the rights or vital interests of a
number of persons, in which choices concerning whose rights are
to be protected and whose overridden are unavoidable. Although
such dilemmas are sometimes presented as objections to utilitarianism, I claim that such cases on the contrary reveal the strength
of utilitarianism in allowing a method to attempt to resolve such
painful dilemmas. * * *

* * *

Mill's moral theory, with its central and strong place for rights
grounded on well-being, does not permit trade-offs of persons' vital
interests, those very interests protected by rights and backed by
social institutions designed to secure and guarantee their effective
protection, for small increases in the good of even large numbers
of others. When the vital interests enshrined in rights of a number of persons conflict, and when it is impossible to protect all of
these rights, then Mill's utilitarianism provides a method for trying

---

4. For a careful and comprehensive treatment of Mill's theory of justice, see [Fred Berger,
   Happiness, Justice, and Freedom: The Moral and Political Philosophy of John Stuart Mill
   (Berkeley: U of California Press, 1984)], 123–225.

to minimize the harm to interests. John Skorupski, whose nuanced discussion of Mill's views of justice and rights takes full note of the complexities and difficulties involved, puts the point this way:

> There *are* situations—call them cases of 'abnormal peril' in which we are willing to accept sacrifices of individuals' primary utilities to safeguard the primary utilities of others, sacrifices which would in the normal case, the case in which ordinary life is going on, be considered unacceptable. [John Skorupski, *John Stuart Mill* (London: Routledge, 1989), 330]

This is not to say that there is a blueprint set out to resolve such dilemmas. Reflective Millian utilitarians will disagree about how to approach particular cases. But what they will agree on is the obligation to decide in ways which protect fundamental interests from being traded off. This leads into a final point about *Mill's* utilitarianism which needs to be highlighted. Many of the usual cases brought forward as objections to utilitarianism are based upon a conception of moral agents which is firmly rejected by Mill. The sorts of cases which are commonly discussed, in which agents are quite content to sacrifice the vital interests or rights of minorities in order to advance the trivial or moderately important interests of others, depend upon a view of moral agents as rational self-interested agents, concerned primarily to promote their own interests and unconcerned or uncaring about the serious harm inflicted upon others by their pursuit of their own interests. Although this conception of moral agents is commonly and uncritically accepted in twentieth-century discussions, it is a view of agents from which Mill would recoil in horror. It is not sufficiently appreciated, I believe, in contemporary discussions which blithely talk about how easy it is to sacrifice minority interests, that the objectors are accepting without question that this is how moral agents normally go about their deliberations. Moral agents must be *constrained* from sacrificing or ignoring the interests of others by recognizing through reason the *force* of their rights claims. But in Mill's conception of moral agents as self-developed, agents are appropriately socialized spontaneously to take account of the good and interests of others and to care about their well-being without being *forced* to do so. It would be degrading for such a self-developed agent to come to the sorts of decisions that these counterexamples assume is the appropriate utilitarian response.

*   *   *

ELIZABETH ANDERSON

John Stuart Mill and Experiments in Living[†]

* * *

Mill's Experiment in Living

John Stuart Mill led his early life strictly according to Benthamite principles. Mill's father, James Mill, gave Mill an intensive, highly disciplined education, following Bentham's belief that the happiest life was a life of rational calculation. James Mill agreed with Bentham that the sentiments were potentially dangerous dispositions which should not be stimulated, so he did not express strong feelings toward his son or encourage the development of his son's imagination.[1] He conceived of the education of the sentiments as a matter of training, not of cultivation. The association of ideas explained how sentiments could be trained to cling to the right objects through a program of conditioned reinforcement. If an object were frequently paired with a pleasurable (or painful) consequence, eventually the mind would raise the idea of pleasure (or pain) upon the presentation of the object, even if the actual consequence no longer followed—that is, the object would become pleasurable or painful in itself. It was thought that by conditioning, a child could be raised to desire and take pleasure in nearly anything.[2] John Mill was raised to desire the maximization of social utility as his primary end and became an enthusiastic propagandist for it.

Mill's life came as close as any experiment in living could to fulfilling the conditions for a valid test of a conception of the good. It was nearly free from all contrary influences to Bentham's view, such as religion.[3] Mill possessed all of the faculties needed for successfully living out Bentham's conception of the good, and lived in secure circumstances highly favorable to calculation and the pursuit of pleasure. He was zealously committed to Bentham's view, so no doubts of the validity of the experiment could be brought on grounds of lack of dedication to it.

[†] From *Ethics* 102.1 (October 1991): 15–20, 23–26. © 1991 by The University of Chicago Press. All rights reserved.

1. Mill, *Autobiography* [*CW*, vol. 1], pp. 31, 67–68.
2. Ibid., p. 82. Compare "Utilitarianism," *CW*, vol. 10, 4. 5–7, where Mill gives a similar account of the origin of the desire for virtue.
3. An exception to this claim may be found in Mill's recollection that his father rated intellectual enjoyments above all others as pleasures, even discounting their circumstantial advantages (Mill, *Autobiography*, [*CW*, vol. 10], p. 31). This suggests that James Mill implicitly taught his son that there was a distinction between higher and lower pleasures, a clear deviation from Bentham's teachings. I thank Richard Dees for pointing out this exception to me.

Mill's experiment encountered a crisis when he fell into a depression in 1826. Mill saw his subjection to and recovery from depression as the crucial experiences which gave him evidence for the superiority of his mature conception of the good over Bentham's.[4] Most conceptions of the good depend on psychological claims of the following sort: if one follows the view under reasonably favorable conditions, then, barring identifiable problems, one will experience one's life as flourishing. And if one encounters a particular problem, one may overcome it by following a remedy prescribed by the view. If these psychological claims can be undermined in experience, then their associated theories of the good will also be undermined. To improve one's conception of the good, one must engage in a joint quest for a new way of life which overcomes the problems inexplicable and insoluble on the old theory and for a new psychological theory which explains the success of the new way of life in overcoming these problems as the result of its superior grasp of the good.[5]

Mill's experiences disconfirmed Bentham's psychology in two ways. First, Bentham's theory could neither explain the onset of Mill's depression nor offer a successful remedy. Bentham's psychology predicted that a person could lift his spirits by engaging in the pursuits which habitually please him. Mill tried every such pursuit, to no avail.[6] Second, Bentham's psychology failed to explain Mill's recovery from depression through reading poetry. Mill's experiences in reading poetry could be explained only by a more sophisticated theory of the sentiments than Bentham's.

While seeking a recovery from his depression, Mill also sought a superior psychological theory which could explain his predicament. Mill's first attempt to explain his ailment by modifying Bentham's psychology generated the grim prediction that he would be incapable of recovering from depression. He saw his depression as the product of a conflict between the habits of analysis and the sentiments. His well-developed habits of analysis were "a perpetual worm at the root both of the passions and of the virtues." They "fearfully undermine all desires, and all pleasures, which are the effects of

4. This account is found in ibid., pp. 80–90.
5. A successful psychological adjustment is evidence of acquisition of a better set of values only if we have a theory which explains its success in these terms. An alternative explanation of successful adjustment could explain a depression as the result of trying to live out a worthwhile conception of the good in unfavorable circumstances, and recovery as the result of cultivating a certain callousness toward higher ends.
6. A more relaxed Benthamite than James Mill could object that John Mill's life was not a proper test of Benthamite hedonism because his father worked him too hard. An excessively harsh and disciplined upbringing could bring on a depression in later life. Nevertheless, Bentham's view failed to guide Mill out of his depression, or to explain how Mill's own techniques succeeded.

association," by "enabl[ing] us mentally to separate ideas which have only casually clung together."[7]

Mill says just enough to permit us to speculate on the mechanism by which he thought analysis tended to undermine his desires. Analysis makes us separate the idea of an end from the idea of its pleasantness, and hence makes us think of it without being motivated to pursue it. Analysis suggests that the object sought may not really have worth in itself: we desire it only because its attainment was artificially associated with pleasures during our earlier upbringing, not because it is intrinsically valuable. So analysis eats away at our final ends by making us view them in an entirely indifferent light and destroying any thoughts of their intrinsic worth.

Mill's modified psychological theory thus accepted Bentham's account of the origins and training of the desires but added to it the un-Benthamite hypothesis that attachment to some of our final ends depends on viewing them as intrinsically valuable. This new theory predicted that his deeply entrenched habits of analysis would unnerve all of his nonphysical desires, and hence that he would never recover from depression. Mill discovered that his new theory was mistaken when, reading a maudlin memoir of Marmontel, he was brought to tears and came to recognize that he still possessed capacities for human feeling. He was "not a stock or a stone," not a mere "reasoning machine," but a human being who retained the capacity to feel as others felt.[8] His recognition of this fact started him on the path to recovery.

Mill's self-discovery also led him to formulate a new theory of psychology and happiness. Once he realized that he still had human sentiments, Mill had to determine which of the claims of his modified Benthamite psychology were mistaken. Three hypotheses were candidates for rejection: (1) that analysis tends to undermine sentiments born of artificial association; (2) that a lasting attachment to objects of pleasure (besides physical ones) depends on viewing them as intrinsically valuable; and (3) that the only sentiments we have are either instinctive (physical) or brought about through association. Mill would not reject the first hypothesis. It accounted too well for the onset of his depression.

Mill's experiences in reading Wordsworth's poetry convinced him to reject the third hypothesis and retain the second: for poetry alerted him to the higher sentiments, which enabled him to take lasting pleasure in things seen to be intrinsically valuable, apart from the merely "casual" associations they had with external pleasures. Mill had read poetry earlier in his life, but did so in a utilitarian

7. Mill, *Autobiography*, p. 83.
8. Ibid., pp. 85, 66.

spirit, for amusement and instruction.[9] Only when he came to see poetry as cultivating his sensibilities to dimensions of nonhedonic value did he find real inspiration in it. A Benthamite would claim that Mill's pleasure in reading Wordsworth's poetry came from its presentation of images of rural landscapes, images which had given Mill pleasure since childhood. Mill observed, however, that even though second-rate landscapes presented more vivid images, Wordsworth's poetry gave him a special pleasure which real landscapes did not. This pleasure did not result just from an image but from arousing "states of feeling, and of thought coloured by feeling, under the excitement of beauty."[1]

According to Mill, poetry depicts and addresses itself to feelings. If it depicts outward objects, it is as they are felt by the poet's mind.[2] Poetry alerts us to and arouses in us the poet's feelings for what he depicts. The image of a landscape does not immediately cause a pleasure of beauty in us. When a poet depicts it, this image is mediated by a sentiment of beauty, an aesthetic sensibility, which arouses our own feeling for the landscape through our feeling for the qualities of mind the poet depicts. Aesthetic sentiments attune us to non-hedonic values of beauty and nobility and make us take pleasure in and desire them. In reflecting on his reaction to poetry, Mill had thus discovered that some pleasures are mediated by recognitions of nonhedonic worth and that some nonphysical pleasures could be founded on sentiments, not just by artificial association.

Mill thus rejected the third hypothesis of his modified Benthamite psychology: the claim that all sentiments are either instinctive or acquired by association. There is a third kind of sentiment, resulting from "cultivation" through poetry and the other imaginative arts.[3] They do not dissolve under the habits of analysis because

---

9. Ibid., p. 11.
1. Ibid., p. 89.
2. J. S. Mill, "What Is Poetry?" in *Essays on Poetry by John Stuart Mill*, ed. F. P. Sharpless (Columbia: University of South Carolina Press, 1976), pp. 6, 11.
3. Aesthetic education differs from scientific education by the sentiments it arouses and the way these sentiments are linked with ideas. In persons of scientific or business education, "objects group themselves according to the artificial classifications which the understanding has voluntarily made for the convenience of thought or practice." But in persons of aesthetic education, "emotions are the links of association by which their ideas, both sensuous and spiritual, are connected together" (J. S. Mill, "The Two Kinds of Poetry," in *Essays on Poetry by John Stuart Mill*, pp. 33, 31–32). Mill thought it essential that a person's moral training appeal to sentiments cultivated by aesthetic and not just scientific training. For "moral associations, which are wholly of artificial creation . . . yield by degrees to the dissolving force of analysis." To be firm and lasting, they must be connected by the natural social sentiment of "unity with our fellow creatures" ("Utilitarianism," [*CW*, vol. 10], 3:9). Aesthetic education provides this connection, linking the moral sentiments with the sympathetic sentiments through the aesthetic ones. Aesthetic education cultivates our desire for ideal aims, giving us a "higher conception of what constitutes success [happiness] in life." Since the nobler pleasures are shared, not competitive, poetic cultivation "brings home to us all those aspects of life which take hold of our nature on its unselfish side and lead us to identify our joy and grief with the good or

they continue to present their characteristic objects under aspects of intrinsic worth which cannot be unnerved by any representation of empirical facts.[4] Their arousal explained Mill's ability to recover from his depression without abandoning his analytical habits.

Mill's psychology thus departed in significant ways from Bentham's. To explain his depression and his manner of recovery, Mill postulated psychological states and causal processes not found in Bentham's theory. First, there was a new kind of sentiment whose characteristics and causal properties differed from the sentiments born of association. The new sentiments aroused a recognition of values distinct from pleasure; they were cultivated through the imaginative arts, and they were resistant to the force of analysis. Cultivation aroused the sentiments, not by associating their objects with external pleasures but by attuning the agent to dimensions of value internal to the sentiments—values which could not be experienced apart from the sentiments. These sentiments lifted him out of depression by enabling him to recognize himself as a person who had fellow-feeling. Second, there was a new kind of pleasure, consisting in the pleasures we take in the conscious realization of other values. These were the pleasures which gratified the new sentiments—the higher pleasures.

Mill's psychology proved superior to Bentham's in its ability to explain his experiences in living out Bentham's conception of the good. But what implications did this scientific superiority have for their rival ethical theories? First, it caused Mill to change his views of how to attain happiness. Mill's psychology predicted that the sentiments had to be cultivated if one were to lead a happy life while exercising analytical skills. The impersonal, artificially induced zeal for the improvement of humanity could not survive analysis unless it was reinforced by a genuine, cultivated feeling of unity with other people. Mill's psychology also explained why happiness could not be attained by attempting to directly pursue pleasure— that is, by interested behavior, which sees actions as merely instrumental to pleasure. Interested behavior misses out entirely on the higher pleasures, which are pleasing only because they are seen to be valuable in some other respect. Since the higher pleasures consist in pleasurable recognitions of the achievement of distinct excellences, one cannot experience these pleasures without aiming

---

ill of the system of which we form a part" (Mill, "Inaugural Address at the University of St. Andrews," [in *John Stuart Mill on Education* (New York: Teachers College Press), 1971,] p. 224). Thus, aesthetic education inspires the feeling of unity with mankind which Mill thought necessary to support a utilitarian morality. It ties together the higher sentiments underlying the three evaluative perspectives he distinguished in "Bentham."

4. See Mill, *Autobiography*, [*CW*, vol. 1], pp. 91–92, where Mill argues that there is no inconsistency between "the intensest feeling of the beauty of a cloud" and a full understanding of the laws of nature which account for its physical characteristics.

at and recognizing the intrinsic worth of excellence. To aim at excellent action for its own sake, apart from any idea of its pleasurable consequences, is to be motivated by feeling, not interest. On this more Aristotelian view, (higher) pleasure is an unintended byproduct of the passionate pursuit of other ends, considered worthy in themselves.[5]

Every theory of the good is vulnerable to criticism insofar as it misconceives the things it identifies as good. Mill charged Bentham's ethical theory with such a misconception. Against Bentham, he contended that pleasure is not homogeneous in quality and does not motivate solely in respect of its quantity. Pleasures differ in quality because they embody recognitions of distinct dimensions of intrinsic value. People experiencing these pleasures understand themselves to be enjoying other values. Mill's psychology thus forces Bentham to concede that to have certain kinds of pleasure, people must understand themselves to be experiencing nonhedonic values, for these pleasures are inextricably bound up with experiences understood in this way.

*   *   *

Experiments in Living, Empiricism, and Intuitionism

Mill's analysis of his transition from Bentham's to his own conception of the good offers a general model of how experiments in living bear upon conceptions of the good. This model views conceptions of the good as dependent upon empirical theories in several ways. These theories explain the nature of the things the ethical theory identifies as good, the means by which people achieve the good, how they come to appreciate and seek the good, and so forth. A person may enter a period of crisis if, having faithfully followed the recommendations of the conception of the good under reasonably favorable conditions, she experiences her life as one of suffering rather than one of flourishing. This crisis has two dimensions: it is a crisis of life, since she is not realizing what she can recognize as good; and it is a theoretical crisis, since the theories linked with her conception of the good cannot account for her felt suffering. The experience of crisis prompts a twofold quest, for a way of life which relieves the suffering and sets new goals she recognizes as worthwhile, and for a new theory which can explain the failures of the old way of life and the successes of the new.

This quest is largely a quest for self-understanding. To discover her good, a person must come to terms with her experiences and

5. Ibid., pp. 85–86. Compare Aristotle *Nicomachean Ethics* 1174b20–1175a21.

motivations—with what she finds to be good according to under-standings which she finds compelling.[6] The crucial test for a con-ception of the good is that it provide a perspective of self-understanding which is both personally compelling (has normative force for the agent) and capable of explaining and resolving her predicament—the reasons for crisis and for recovery from it. Mill's conception of the good, with its associated psychology, met these conditions for superiority over Bentham's conception of the good. Mill adopted an expansive understanding of what was intrinsically valuable and sought out these new goods. By adopting this new conception of the good, he was able to overcome his depression and lead a life he found to be fulfilling.

If Mill had succeeded only on a practical and not on a theoretical plane, one could have charged that he had only shown that believ-ing his theory has instrumental value, not that it was better. The theoretical success of Mill's conception of the good consisted in its ability to account for the defects of Bentham's view and the suc-cesses of his own. It showed that Bentham's view was insensitive to the fundamental human needs to cultivate and gratify the higher sentiments. Mill's failure to tend to these needs accounted for his lapse into depression, and his fulfillment of the need, for his recov-ery from it. Bentham's psychology could not even describe this need, much less explain it. Hence, Mill could explain the practical suc-cess of his new conception of the good as coming about in virtue of its superior account of and sensitivity to fundamental human needs which could be described and recognized only within the perspec-tive of his conception of the good.

My elaboration of Mill's theory of experiments in living has both exploratory and critical parts.[7] The critical part determines if and how a conception of the good is defective, by testing its underlying empirical claims. It makes comparative assessments of two given conceptions of the good. But it does not by itself lead us to a supe-rior theory. To discover a superior conception of the good, we must be free to explore different ways of life under conditions of tolera-tion, as Mill outlined in *On Liberty*. I have emphasized the critical part of Mill's views because the exploratory part is more familiar. Yet the exploratory part is apt to be more crucial for many people. As a pluralist, Mill thought that even after defective conceptions of the good such as Bentham's were eliminated, there would remain numerous rival views compatible with empirical psychology. Not every choice among conceptions of the good can be resolved on the basis of underlying empirical disagreements. At this level, an

6. This is a central theme of Mill's *On Liberty* [*CW*, vol. 18]. See esp. pp. 260–67.
7. I am indebted to Andrew Levine for raising some of the issues in these paragraphs.

individual trying to decide between rivals can only explore both and consult her decided preference. But if she comes to question whether her decided preferences are based upon authentic evaluative distinctions, then she must use the critical theory.

One might object to the critical theory that it is incompatible with a credible philosophy of science. How could Mill draw definite conclusions about the good from just one experiment (his own life), and for human beings generally? And isn't a life too messy to count as a good test of any conception of the good? To be sure, Mill cannot lay claim to a definitive refutation of Bentham's conception of the good, but only to reasonable grounds for rejecting it. However, few empirically based theories are ever decisively refuted. They usually contain resources for evading refutation, and the more resources, the more complex the conditions of experiment are. Mill's life was no more complex than the phenomena upon which social scientific theories are routinely built. Nor did it contain just a single test of Bentham's views; it contained numerous tests which repeatedly failed to solve his overriding problem of depression. As with any other theory, at some point, certainly reached by Mill, it becomes reasonable to try a new conception of the good rather than to continue tinkering with an old one which has repeatedly failed to deliver on its promises.

Nevertheless, the demands of Mill's critical theory are daunting. Critical theory requires an extraordinary degree of self-understanding. Mill supposed that people can make themselves relatively self-transparent through determined and thoughtful introspection. A credible critical theory today must provide a more complex account of how people can gain access to their unconscious motivations, and will likely be less sanguine about the prospects for success. Mill's critical theory also demands that the principles underlying people's conceptions of the good be precise and articulate enough to be undermined through scientific inquiry. Most people's conceptions of the good are vague and unsystematic, and hence difficult to bring into contact with empirical theory.

Even if Mill should not be faulted for drawing unreasonable conclusions about his own good, what about his generalizations to other people? Mill would agree that his conception of the good is not valid for people incapable of cultivating the higher sentiments. Mill could reasonably apply his theory only to those who share his psychology, and it is an open question how many people do. * * *

COLIN HEYDT

Mill, Bentham and "Internal Culture"†

In well-known lines from his *Autobiography*, Mill identifies two 'very marked effects' on his 'opinions and character' brought about by the period of his mental crisis. The first involved no longer making happiness 'the direct end' of conduct and life. The second effect, which will consume our attention here, was that Mill 'gave its proper place, among the prime necessities of human well-being, to the internal culture of the individual', i.e. the cultivation of the feelings.[1] He had, he says, ceased to attach 'almost exclusive importance to the ordering of outward circumstances, and the training of the human being for speculation and for action'.[2]

The contrast of internal culture with speculation, action, and 'the ordering of outward circumstances', draws on a vigorous literature of protest against the tenets of utilitarianism and political economy. Again and again in critics of utilitarianism such as Carlyle, Coleridge, Dickens and Mackintosh, one finds defences of the 'inner', 'internal', 'interior', 'inward' and 'inmost' against the 'external', 'outward', 'outer' and the closely related 'mechanical'. * * *

* * *

* * * Thus, critics oppose the Philosophic Radicals in politics, which the radicals attempt to rationalize and turn into a science on the basis of controversial psychological premises, and in ethics, which, as Mackintosh put it, they treat 'too juridically'.[3]

These criticisms resonated strongly with Mill. Though he never fully abandons the tradition of his teachers, he worries about the lack of attention in Bentham's and his father's work to the quality of psychic life. The emphasis on internal culture in the passage from his *Autobiography* reflects Mill's reconsideration of philosophical radicalism in the face of intelligent, aggressive and hostile analysis.[4]

---

† From *British Journal for the History of Philosophy* 14.2 (August 2006): 275–76, 284–300. Copyright © 2006 BSHP, reprinted by permission of Taylor and Francis Ltd. on behalf of BSHP. Some of the author's notes have been omitted.
1. John Stuart Mill, *The Collected Works of John Stuart Mill*, edited by John M. Robson, 33 vols. (Toronto: University of Toronto Press, 1963–91), Vol. I, p. 147.
2. Ibid.
3. James Mackintosh, *Dissertation Second; Exhibiting a General View of the Progress of Ethical Philosophy, Chiefly During the Seventeenth and Eighteenth Centuries*, prefixed to the seventh edition of the *Encyclopedia Britannica* [1830] 384.
4. Mill was not alone among the friends of utilitarianism on this score. In his *Autobiography* (I: 185), he talks about his affinities with the elder Austin who had spent time in Germany: 'He attached much less importance than formerly to outward changes; unless accompanied by a better cultivation of the inward nature. He had a strong distaste for the general meanness of English life, the absence of enlarged thoughts and unselfish desires, the low objects on which the faculties of all classes of the English are intent'.

This reconsideration focuses on character (or, more broadly, the self) and its education. Mill outlines a place for character in utilitarian theory and provides new goals for the development of various dispositions, especially those of feeling.

*   *   *

* * * Carlyle argued that his age was a 'mechanical' one in which thinkers such as Bentham treated humans as components to be fitted into a smoothly working machine. They are thereby seen only from the outside, from an external point of view. The criticisms of Bentham's and others' 'mechanical' thought play an important role in the period's discussion of internal culture.

In using this disparaging term, intellectuals such as Carlyle were influenced by, among other things, German Romanticism, Idealism, *Naturphilosophie*, and more home-grown intellectual movements.[5] A number of oppositions were built into this accusation, all of which depended on characterizing the mechanical as an imposition on something more authentic. First, there were basic contrasts of the mechanical with the organic and living. In epistemology and philosophy of mind/psychology these contrasts manifest in the distinction between the analytic understanding and synthetic reason, with only the latter supplying the genuine knowledge of the whole needed fully to comprehend the parts grasped by understanding. Coleridge, who brought this distinction into prominence in Britain, consistently speaks of the 'dead' or 'abstract' understanding in contrast to 'living' reason. The methodological criticisms of associationism and of the Lockean tradition in psychology relate to this, as does the rejection of self-interest as the key to interpreting action and institutions.

The necessity of knowing the whole if the part is to make sense also played out in historiography. Coleridge criticizes the 'histories and political economy of the present and preceding century' that 'partake in the general contagion of its mechanic philosophy, and are the product of an unenlivened generalizing understanding'.[6] * * *

*   *   *

5. The opposition between inner and outer can be found in the German contrast of *'Kultur'* (and the associated *'Bildung'*), which expresses the value placed on the inner, spiritual sphere and its development, with *'Zivilisation'*, which is something of secondary importance, namely, the outward appearance and form of human beings. For the seminal treatment of this distinction, see Norbert Elias, *The Civilizing Process* (Oxford: Blackwell Publishers, 1994), 3–9.
6. S. T. C. Coleridge, 'Lay Sermons', in *On the Constitution of the Church and State According to the Idea of Each* (3rd edn), *and Lay Sermons* (2nd edn) (London: William Pickering, 1839) 228.

The charge of mechanism reflected not only specific epistemic, psychological, and, especially in the cases when it was motivated by religious criticism, metaphysical concerns, it also gave voice to a general uneasiness about the impact of industrialism on feeling and about Enlightenment attitudes towards humanity (including the attempt to create a 'science of man'). * * *

* * *

This latter position, which tended to align the forces of interiority (i.e. art, imagination and religion) against industrial society and the philosophy of mechanism, can be found in numerous places, including Carlyle's essays, 'Signs of the Times' and 'Characteristics', where he discusses the 'mechanical' philosophy of utilitarianism, the caricatured Mr Gradgrind of Dickens's *Hard Times*, and Arnold's later *Culture and Anarchy* where he speaks of 'the believer in machinery' as an enemy of culture and where he situates Bentham in the vanguard of the Philistines (in other words, the vanguard of the bourgeois middle classes).[7]

* * *

Mill's advocacy for internal culture and for a re-evaluation of the goals of character education (especially the goals for the cultivation of dispositions of feeling) was conditioned by a sympathetic attention to these criticisms of utilitarianism. As we proceed to outline themes relevant to internal culture, we will come to comprehend how these themes need to be seen in relation to these criticisms.

* * *

INTERIORITY AND ETHICS

In his different surveys of Bentham's ethical views, Mill is particularly keen to demand two revisions. First, he argues that Bentham fails to determine properly the consequences of actions owing to his impoverished understanding of human psychology. For the calculation of consequences to be adequate one requires the science of ethology, i.e. the science of the formation of character.[8] The impact

---

7. Matthew Arnold, *Culture and Anarchy and Other Writings* (Cambridge: Cambridge University Press, 1993) 13.
8. See Mill's *A System of Logic* (New York: Harper & Brothers, 1874), Vol. VI, p. 5. Ethology is part of a far more complex conception of the moral sciences:

    And since it is by these laws [the universal laws of the formation of character] combined with the facts of each particular case, that the whole of the phenomena of human action and feeling are produced, it is on these that every rational attempt to construct the science of human nature in the concrete, and for practical purposes, must proceed.   (VI: 5, 2)

of actions on the human mind and on character must be understood in order to evaluate properly the actions' morality.[9]

A result of this lacuna in Bentham's theory—his 'ignorance of the deeper springs of human character' leading to a miscalculation of the consequences of action—is that it prevented him from appreciating the power of aesthetic activity to shape the moral nature of human beings.[1] To Bentham, the consequences of experiencing art are limited to the pleasures it produces. * * *

Mill's second revision of Bentham is related to the first and stems from his contention that the kinds of ethical evaluation demanded by Bentham's theory are insufficient. He criticizes Bentham in his essay 'Bentham' and in *Utilitarianism* for ignoring the 'sympathetic' and 'aesthetic' features of actions in favour of an exclusive focus on the 'moral' features of actions, and suggests that this gave 'to his philosophy that cold, mechanical and ungenial air which characterizes the popular idea of a Benthamite'.[2] The moral aspect, to which Bentham attends, provokes our reason and conscience to judge an action's rightness or wrongness (through its consequences), and results in moral approval and disapproval. The aesthetic aspect grounds judgements of beauty and ugliness, according to which we admire or despise. Our imagination plays the decisive role here. Lastly, judgements of love, pity or dislike, which are determined by 'human fellow-feeling', depend upon the sympathetic aspect of the act.[3]

Bentham, then, not only miscalculates the consequences of actions, he fails to notice that the specific consequences of an act are not sufficient to explain the evaluations that arise, and that ought to arise, in the face of it. What Bentham and other utilitarians ignore are those ethical judgements that have as their objects something other than the consequences of an act.[4] 'The morality of an action depends on its forseeable consequences; its beauty, and its loveableness, or the reverse, depend on the qualities which it is

9. Mill attests to this in the following:

> Morality consists of two parts. One of these is self-education; the training, by the human being himself, of his affections and will. That department is a blank in Bentham's system. The other and co-equal part, the regulation of outward actions, must be altogether halting and imperfect without the first; for how can we judge in what manner many an action will affect even the worldly interests of ourselves or others, unless we take in, as part of the question, its influence on the regulation of our, or their, affections and desires?   (Mill, *Collected Works*, Vol. X. p. 98)

1. Ibid, p. 113.
2. Ibid, p. 112.
3. Ibid. See also p. 221.
4. For the legitimacy of this as an interpretation of Bentham's ethical views, see Harrison's analysis of Bentham's 'deontology': Ross Harrison, *Bentham* (London: Routledge & Kegan Paul, 1983) 274.

evidence of'.[5] Judgements of admiration or dislike or pity cover the dispositional causes of an action rather than the action's results. They are, in other words, 'backward-looking' rather than 'forward-looking' evaluations.

In the early essay 'Remarks on Bentham's Philosophy' (1833), which is a very good source for understanding Mill's ethical views, he expands on this point:

> A certain kind of action, as for example, theft, or lying, would, if commonly practised, occasion certain evil consequences to society: but those evil consequences are far from constituting the entire moral bearings of the vices of theft or lying. We shall have a very imperfect view of the relation of those practices to the general happiness, if we suppose them to exist singly, and insulated. All acts suppose certain dispositions, and habits of mind and heart, which may be in themselves states of enjoyment or of wretchedness, and which must be fruitful in other consequences, besides those particular acts. No person can be a thief or a liar without being much else: and if our moral judgments and feelings with respect to a person convicted of either vice, were grounded solely upon the pernicious tendency of thieving and of lying, they would be partial and incomplete; many considerations would be omitted, which are at least equally 'germane to the matter'; many which, by leaving them out of our general views, we may indeed teach ourselves a habit of overlooking, but which it is impossible for any of us not to be influenced by, in particular cases, in proportion as they are forced upon our attention.[6]

Beyond noticing from this passage that the Benthamites had developed a 'habit of overlooking' the aesthetic and sympathetic aspects of actions, we can uncover a Millian interest in establishing a sharp division between legislation and ethics. In legislation, the focus on the specific consequences of an action rather than on 'its general bearings upon the entire moral being of the agent' is appropriate.[7]

> The legislator enjoins or prohibits an action, with very little regard to the general moral excellence or turpitude which it implies; he looks to the consequences to society of the particular kind of action; his object is not to render people incapable of desiring a crime, but to deter them from actually committing it.[8]

5. Mill, *Collected Works*, Vol. X, p. 112.
6. Ibid., p. 7.
7. Ibid., p. 8.
8. Ibid., p. 9.

Legislators, in other words, should concern themselves primarily with external behaviour, and, in determining which acts to prohibit, they properly limit their attention to the consequences of the act alone.

In ethics, on the other hand, this kind of attention is insufficient. Mill then, three years after Mackintosh's *Encyclopedia* entry, also interprets Bentham's ethical position as being too juridical. Ethical evaluation demands more than legislative evaluation does; it requires a careful consideration of character, of the interiority of which action is an expression. Exclusive attention on right and wrong means, for a utilitarian, exclusive attention on the consequences of a class of action. When we take into consideration the whole of ethical life, this attention leads us to ignore the importance of the claim that 'no person can be a thief or a liar without being much else'. * * *

* * *

Mill wants the reader to recognize the undesirability of atomizing action and habit for the purposes of evaluation and to see how interconnected aspects of character can be. We cannot be habitual liars without being many other things besides (e.g. inconstant). The propensities to lie or to enjoy pushpin to poetry, he suggests, cluster with other character traits, which may also properly influence our judgement of the action and of the dispositions that produce it. So, though Bentham never ignores habits as potential sources of desirable and pernicious action (thus making them appropriate as objects of evaluation), he fails, according to Mill, to appreciate how habits relate to one's character as a whole.

* * *

SOURCES OF HAPPINESS

Carlyle's proclamation of the 'great truth that our happiness depends on the mind which is within us, and not on the circumstances which are without us' resonates in Mill's treatment of aesthetic experience. Throughout his writings, Mill presents aesthetic experience as yielding a particularly valuable pleasure (i.e. a 'higher pleasure'), which is less dependent on 'external' sources than those pleasures emphasized by Bentham. The defence of 'internal' sources of happiness naturally leads to the problem of what internal states or dispositions produce this happiness; and as we shall see, one's capacity to experience aesthetic pleasures has a non-contingent relation to one's character.

In his *Autobiography*, Mill broaches these themes in his account of how the arts yielded a solution to the problem at the heart of his youthful depression. In one well-noted discussion, he tells how he found a solution in Wordsworth's poetry, which presented 'not mere outward beauty, but states of feeling, and of thought coloured by feeling'. * * *

* * *

The key to comprehending Mill's appeals to art in the *Autobiography* and the implied contrast between the impact of Wordsworth and Weber is to attend carefully to the qualification given for the pleasure of Weber's music, namely, that it is the pleasure of 'mere tune'. This is the fundamental problem. For the pleasure of mere tune, as we find out in the editorial notes for his father's *Analysis*, are pleasures of sensation (i.e. pleasures caused by the sound itself), not pleasures of expression (i.e. the associations connected to the sound).[9] Only the music that excels in expression can be considered truly poetic, that is, artistic. The other music, even if it is highly pleasurable, lacks depth. It is also, importantly, much more likely to be exhausted as a source of pleasure, needing to be 'revived by intermittance, or fed by continual novelty'.

Not all the things that produce pleasures of expression, however, are capable of being an 'inward source of joy'. Pleasures of expression that are merely pleasures of agreeableness, namely pleasures that result from association of an object to ideas of an everyday sort (e.g. children playing or a hot toddy in winter), remain insufficient. They are not aesthetic pleasures such as those provided by Wordsworth's poetry. The feelings evoked by truly 'artistic' music and poetry have a phenomenological character—a certain kind of heft— that other feelings lack.[1]

Mill's explanation of this difference between the types of feeling rests on a theory of the imagination (a theory partially influenced by Ruskin). In aesthetic experience, as opposed to the mere experience of the agreeable, we are carried by a work of art into a 'more majestic world'.[2] This means that we are confronted by or interact with various idealizations (of objects, virtues, etc.) or with the infinite. This confrontation with what Ruskin calls in the second volume of *Modern Painters* 'ideas of Beauty', accounts for the felt distinctness of experiences of the beautiful.[3]

9. John Stuart Mill in James Mill, *An Analysis of the Phenomena of the Human Mind*, 2 vols., edited by John Stuart Mill (London: Longmans, Green & Dyer, 1869), Vol. II, pp. 241–2.
1. The distinction between the agreeable and the beautiful was a commonplace in the period. Mill accepts Coleridge's formulation of the issue, though he rejects his explanation of the differences between the feelings in favour of an associationist account. See John Stuart Mill in James Mill, *Analysis*, Vol. II, p. 252.
2. John Stuart Mill in James Mill, *Analysis*, Vol. II, p. 255.
3. John Ruskin, *Modern Painters*, Vol. II (New York: D. D. Merrill Co., 1893). ° * °

If we ask why the pleasures of poetry or expressive music that go beyond mere agreeableness are different from the pleasures of 'mere tune', the answer is that art engages us with the ideal or infinite, that is, it brings us through webs of association into some kind of contact (e.g. conceptual, affective) with something apparently limitless or ideal. Music or poetry that depends on the 'physical' can do nothing of the kind.

This explains the inexhaustibility of the aesthetic pleasures. Whereas physical pleasures quickly reach a saturation point, at which time we often lose interest in them, imaginative pleasures of the sort we find in art can engage us in more sustainable ways. Contemplation of, or affective reaction to, the ideal or the infinite provides us with a permanent source of profound pleasure, which helped to assuage Mill's fears about the sources of pleasure available to humans. He had discovered a 'source of inward joy' distinct from those that produce pleasures of agreeableness or of sense.

* * *

Mill gives clues as to how aesthetic pleasure depends upon character in his essay 'Thoughts on Poetry and Its Varieties', where he differentiates between the poetic and the narrative.[4] There is a 'radical distinction between the interest felt in a story as such, and the interest excited by poetry; for the one is derived from incident, the other from the representation of feeling'.[5] Stories excite our emotions through showing 'states of mere outward circumstances', while the poetic excites through the 'exhibition of a state or states of human sensibility'.[6] Mill argues that these two sources of affective response—outward circumstance and human sensibility—'correspond to two distinct, and (as respects their greatest development) mutually exclusive, characters of mind'.[7] Thus, a proneness to interest in stories reflects a lack of attention to interiority. Or, put another way, the person consistently attracted to story over poetry is one for whom 'inward joy' will be absent.

* * *

Ordinary life interests us, provokes us, forces us to respond, but does nothing to connect itself to the ideal or the infinite. It is obvious. It is transparent. Events are interpreted using the ready-made categories of a language community, and these categories condition the

---

4. It should be noted that Mill does not mean the narrative form here, as much as the narrative spirit, that is, an emphasis on incident. Thus, a poem can be a narrative, and be completely unpoetic, while a novel can be truly poetic, and be a narrative only secondarily. This is not, then, at least explicitly, an argument for a hierarchy of genres.
5. Mill, *Collected Works*, Vol. I, p. 344.
6. Ibid., pp. 344–5. * * *
7. [Ibid.], p. 345, italics added.

response of children to the stories. In fact, storytelling involves one of the first introductions of these social norms and categories to children.

What we find then, is that the two sources of interest—poetry and narrative—depend for the pleasures they produce on two contrasting dispositions of imagination and feeling. Narrative draws on those imaginations and feelings grabbed by action and by 'outward things'. The narrative mind is the mind of industrial society. It is quickly aroused and absorbed in the excitement of stories, but these stories leave little behind them to engage it. The 'joys and griefs' which 'outward events' excite satisfy the narrative mind, and it lacks the capacity of the imagination needed to rise to a 'more majestic world', which might provide it with other, higher pleasures. The poetic mind, on the other hand, owing to its powers of imagination, finds pleasure in the discovery of the ideal and the infinite. It rejects the speed and exhilaration of industry in order to tarry with the aesthetic (and frequently pastoral) object. The 'internal' character of the feelings associated with poetry such as Wordsworth's derives from its relation to self-reflection and from its connection, through imagination, to ideal and infinite aspects of the world and the self hidden by the 'external' goings-on of social existence in industrial society.

THE PLEASURES OF SYMPATHY

The last revision of Bentham triggered by criticism and embodied in Mill's highlighting of internal culture involves the rejection of a central feature of Bentham's moral psychology—its reduction of almost all motivation to some form of self-interest. This moral psychology reflected an ambition found in the radical French Enlightenment and in the developing field of Political Economy (Bentham was a great admirer of Smith's *Wealth of Nations* and was also closely linked to Ricardo through the mediation of James Mill), namely, the ambition to explain human behaviour as a class of natural phenomena subject to laws. In other words, he was attracted to the idea of establishing a 'science of man', and the premise that human action is driven by self-interest seemed justified and useful in creating such a science.[8]

To Bentham's opponents, the emphasis on self-interest showed how impoverished the utilitarian understanding of the 'internal' was. The utilitarian inner life is not a site of deep conflict or wonder, nor is it, because of that, a site of genuine ethical interest for another; it is comprehensible and consistently directed. The form

---

8. * * * Though Bentham mentions sympathy as a possible motivation for action, he rarely emphasizes it or makes the notion do much work.

that a utilitarian life takes depends more on dealing with external obstacles to satisfaction and less on struggling with the complexities of one's psyche, including, in the view of the critics, the multiplicity of human motivations.

For Mill, Bentham's account of human motivation was not only incorrect, it also had pernicious effects in the realm of moral education, because it (a) blinded the utilitarians to the importance of sympathy both for social life and for the well-being of the individual, and (b) exacerbated a sharpening decline in sympathetic relations with others by ignoring those features of others (e.g. the complexity of motivations) that might engage us and make us more prone to sympathize. The marginalization of sympathy and the pleasures associated with it was a problem that went beyond the secular utilitarians, however. Mill thought it endemic to English life as a whole. This problem—the absence of warmth and sympathetic feelings—served to fuel the literature on the evils of the mechanical and industrial spirit and on the way in which modern societal relations were founded on cash and contract, rather than on intimacy and emotional connection. Driven by these criticisms, Mill diagnosed the causes of this lack of pleasure in sympathy and suggested some ways to remedy it.

* * *

As opposed to those in other countries, particularly in France, for whom the sympathies are of paramount importance for individual happiness, many Englishmen 'almost seem to regard them as necessary evils, required for keeping men's actions benevolent and compassionate'.[9] That is, the English (and here Mill sees Bentham as the paradigmatic Englishman), might think the sympathies are important in so far as they support the performance of duty. Beyond that, they are often more trouble than they are worth.

The English inability to experience pleasure through sympathetic connection with others depends on three different sources. The first, which comes to light particularly in Mill's discussion of his father's aversion to the expression of feeling, is what might be loosely called English stoicism. James Mill 'resembled most Englishmen in being ashamed of the signs of feeling, and by the absence of demonstration, starving the feelings themselves'.[1] The dominant ethos is a form of self-command. As such, expressions of feeling can be seen as extravagant, and, to gender it, as womanly. To sympathize or feel with others and to express it would be more an occasion of pain than of pleasure, because the feelings are taken by both parties to be

9. Mill, *Collected Works*, Vol. I, p. 157.
1. [Ibid.], p. 153.

embarrassments. They are signs of a lack of seriousness and of an unseemly susceptibility to changes in environment.

In the 'Inaugural Address Delivered to the University of St. Andrews', Mill identifies the other two sources. While speaking of why the British take art less seriously than those on the Continent (particularly those in France and Germany), he argues that the British failure to count the arts among the 'great social powers' and the 'agents of civilization' 'may be traced to the two influences which have chiefly shaped the British character since the days of the Stuarts; commercial money-getting business, and religious Puritanism'.[2]

Puritanism 'looked coldly, if not disapprovingly, on the cultivation of the sentiments'. This Puritanism, which Mill in other places identifies as a form of Calvinism, interprets emotion as generally tied to corporeality and to sin. Matthew Arnold was among those Victorians who joined Mill in accusing Puritanism of stunting human development.

The most important cause, for our purposes, of the English inability to experience pleasure in the sympathies is commercial society. Here, there is not a general attack on the affections, as there is in English stoicism and Puritanism. Rather, money-getting tends to incorporate all other pursuits, making them instrumental to the end of increasing wealth. This commercialism has the dual effect of promoting the English sensitivity to violations of duty (i.e. conscience: 'the kind of advantage which we have had over many other countries in point of morals'),[3] while leaving nothing to oppose self-interested behaviour. We find in the 'Inaugural Address' the negative impact this can have on character:

> One of the commonest types of character among us is that of a man all whose ambition is self-regarding; who has no higher purpose in life than to enrich or raise in the world himself and his family; who never dreams of making the good of his fellow-creatures or of his country an habitual object, further than giving away, annually or from time to time, certain sums in charity; but who has a conscience sincerely alive to whatever is generally considered wrong, and would scruple to use any very illegitimate means for attaining his self-interested objects.[4]

This character type emphasizes the Englishman as commercial man, as pursuing self-interested objects (including those of family) but in ways that do not disturb social stability. He is a respecter of rules,

2. Mill, *Collected Works*, Vol. XXI, p. 253.
3. Mill, *Collected Works*, Vol. XXI, p. 253.
4. Ibid.

and since robust feelings often lead to the transgression of those rules and the disruption of expectation, feelings are devalued.

How, then, does one address that impoverishment of the 'internal' indicated by a lack of sympathetic feelings and pleasures? How does one generate enough interest in or concern for the other to promote pleasure in sympathy? In other words, what would this part of internal culture look like? Mill turns primarily to the cultivated imagination as embodied in art and history. * * *

* * *

The pleasures of sympathy require an activity of the imagination that is different from that responsible for aesthetic pleasures, but one which Mill still consistently describes as 'aesthetic' or 'poetic'. It might best be called 'concretization' or the taking up of various aspects of a thing not present and tying them together into an image of a convincing, real unity, which can more thoroughly act upon our feelings and motivations. This is one of the main functions of the imagination, 'which Bentham had not'.[5] The imagination

> enables us, by a voluntary effort, to conceive the absent as if it were present, the imaginary as if it were real, and to clothe it in the feelings which, if it were indeed real, it would bring along with it. This is the power by which one human being enters into the mind and circumstances of another.[6]

It is what constitutes the poet, dramatist and historian: through successful employment of the force of their imaginations, they are able to make something or someone real or particular enough to engage the sympathies.

We can better understand how one cultivates the 'concretizing' imagination necessary for promoting sympathy in an industrializing world by looking at Mill's discussion of history, drama and poetry. His review 'Carlyle's French Revolution' (1837), begins by proclaiming about Carlyle's work that 'This is not so much a history, as an epic poem; and notwithstanding, or even in consequence of this, the truest of histories. It is the history of the French Revolution, and the poetry of it, both in one'.[7] * * *

* * *

For the historian, then, enabling the reader to 'picture to himself what human life was' in any particular historical period is the most basic requirement for engaging the reader's sympathies. By giving

5. Mill, *Collected Works*, Vol. X, p. 92.
6. Ibid.
7. Mill, *Collected Works*, Vol. XX, p. 133.

a sense for the joys, sorrows, hopes, fears, ideas and opinions of a people (including not merely the nobility, but the commoners), one comes to understand the reasons why individuals or groups acted as they did. In so doing, we are better situated to sympathize potentially with the actors and 'to erect ourselves into judges' of conduct.[8] A more 'objective,' fact-based historical approach, including political and military histories, becomes, under this view, less fundamental than various forms of cultural history.

Thus, we see that sympathetic pleasures, and the feeling of unity with others that depends upon these pleasures, itself depends on a particular kind of imaginative capability—a capability that turns people from mere types into concrete individuals with whom we may more readily share affective bonds. This is an imaginative disposition that history and art, which are among the 'great social powers' and 'agents of civilization', serve to cultivate. It is also a disposition that industrialism, according to Mill and other thinkers of the period, deadens. People become means for realizing ends, or cogs in institutional machines, rather than beings in themselves worthy of attention. The conflict of the internal versus the external has one of its decisive engagements in the realm of the sympathies. Whether the internal succumbs or emerges victorious depends in part on how the skirmish between the poetic and the industrial turns out. Mill took the deadening of sympathies in England to be a sign of the undesirable dominance of the latter over the former.

* * *

DAVID DYZENHAUS

John Stuart Mill and the Harm of Pornography[†]

* * *

The Subjection of Women

Mill's opening statement in *The Subjection of Women* was radical by the standards of his day. He will argue, he says, that the legal regime of his day which subordinates women to men is "wrong in itself, . . . one of the chief hindrances to human improvement," and that it "ought to be replaced by a principle of perfect equality,

8. Ibid., p. 136.
† From *Ethics* 102.3 (April 1992): 537–43, 546–51. © 1992 by The University of Chicago Press. All rights reserved. Some of the author's notes have been omitted.

admitting no power or privilege on the one side, nor disability on the other" (*SW*, p. 261).[1]

His statement might seem mild in contemporary liberal democracies, which, however much they might disagree about what equality requires, are committed to attaining it formally for all. Thus they have eradicated by and large the legal disabilities which subordinated women in Mill's time. What remains radical today is Mill's analysis of the nature of women's subordination, one which explains why, despite a legal order characterized by formal commitments to equality, feminists still find that substantive equality of women with men remains a dim prospect.

Mill's stated aim is to argue against the legal subordination of women and for what he calls "perfect equality." But he clearly does not equate absence of legally prescribed inequality with presence of substantive equality. For one thing, Mill does not see legally prescribed inequalities between men and women as much more than the de jure recognition of de facto social relationships based ultimately on what he regards as the root cause of subordination—the superior physical power of males (*SW*, p. 264). Thus the more pressing need is to deal with the social relationships. In addition, while Mill sees the legal victories that would be won were women admitted to the suffrage and were the laws of marriage and divorce radically reformed as essential steps toward the goal of perfect equality, the victories are, given his understanding of the marks of women's inequality, far from sufficient.

The first mark of women's inequality is that it cuts across class boundaries. Power over women is "common to the whole male sex" and jealously guarded since, Mill claims, power over those closest to us seems particularly valuable given that it is those closest to us who are in a position to interfere most with our preferences (*SW*, p. 268). The second mark, which explains the persistence of this power and the certainty of its outlasting "all other forms of unjust authority" is that the power is generally exercised in the privacy and intimacy of the home. This private nature of the power prevents women from combining to articulate their common experience of their subjection. Indeed, says Mill, it is surprising that the "protests and testimony against it have been so numerous and weighty as they are" (*SW*, pp. 268–69).

The third mark is the apparent naturalness of the relationship of inequality. Mill notes that every relationship of domination appears natural to the dominators (*SW*, pp. 269–70). He also notes that subjected classes often appear to accept their subjection as the natural

---

1. J. S. Mill, *The Subjection of Women*, in *Collected Works*, vol. 21, ed. J. M. Robson (Toronto: University of Toronto Press, 1984); cited as *SW* with page numbers parenthetically in the text. * * *

order of things, since even in their initial struggle against domination they complain not "of the power itself but only of its oppressive exercise." And he points out in this regard that women who do complain of the abuse by men of their power suffer uniquely (with children) in being "replaced under the physical power of the culprit" (SW, p. 271).[2]

Mill wants to draw attention to the especially insidious quality of this mark of power. That quality is one which men want and one which they succeed in exacting—having women as their "willing slaves." It is important to spend some time on Mill's analysis of this idea. Men, he says, desire of women more than the obedience which, say, fear of coercion or religious fear might exact from a subject class. This is because the women over whom they most want to exercise power are "most nearly connected with them." What they require, and what they have contrived to acquire, is a morality combined with a sentimentality which will make it the feminine ideal to be placed in a relationship of subjection to a man. To this end, women are educated to believe that their character is the "very opposite to that of men; not self-will, and government by self-control, but submission, and yielding to the control of others." The morality tells them that this is their duty and the sentimentality that it is their nature "to live for others; make complete abnegations of themselves, and to have not life but in their affections," that is, their affections for their husbands and children. If we take together the fact of what Mill calls the "natural attraction between opposite sexes," the "woman's entire dependence on the husband," and that all her social ambition has to be realized through him, "it would be a miracle if the object of being attractive to men had not become the polar star of feminine education and formation of character" (SW, pp. 271–72).[3]

So for Mill the fact that women, or at least many of them, willingly accept their social condition does not detract from the coercive nature of their relationship with men. Indeed, the coercion involved is in a way worse than slavery since what is in fact a relationship of forced inequality is made to appear consensual.[4]

2. See SW, pp. 287–88, for further discussion. As Annas points out, Mill's point does not lose its force because battered wives are no longer legally compelled to return to their husbands so long as de facto social pressures bring about the same result (J. Annas, "Mill and the Subjection of Women," Philosophy, 52 [1977]: 170). In fact, in line with Mill's argument below, we should see that the persistence of de facto social pressures in the absence of legal constraints will make things worse; for it will appear that women consent to return to the abusive situation about which they complained.
3. Compare On Liberty, pp. 229–301, where, in a passage which has caused some difficulty to commentators, he says that one cannot consent to slavery. J. S. Mill, On Liberty, in Collected Works, ed. J. M. Robson (Toronto: University of Toronto Press, 1977), vol. 18; hereafter cited as OL with pages numbers parenthetically in the text.
4. It is worth noting Mill's remark in this regard, which anticipates Virginia Woolf's plea for a "Room of One's Own." Mill says that Uncle Tom, under his first master, "had his own life in his 'cabin' . . . but it cannot be so with the wife" (SW, pp. 284–85).

In sum, for Mill the subjection of women comes about because of a status quo of inequality, which is made most manifest in the private realm and which is made to look natural by a false appearance of consent. And what is pernicious about this regime of inequality is that it prevents women from acting as autonomous individuals, from articulating and exploring their own conceptions of the good life. For it is the promise of autonomy that Mill takes to be distinctive of what he calls "the peculiar character of the modern world": that "human beings are no longer born to their place in life, and chained down by an inexorable bond to the place they are born to, but are free to employ their faculties, and such favourable chances as offer, to achieve the lot which may appear to them most desirable" (SW, pp. 272–73).

If pornography does eroticize inequality, the very circumstances which Mill identifies as the subjection of women are what makes pornography a harm. Pornography is consumed in a private realm. It makes an inequality which is ultimately rooted in superior physical power and thus in physical coercion appear sexually desirable. And, at the same time, it attempts to legitimize itself by claiming the consent of women to their subordination. That is, by eroticizing inequality, pornography plays a special role in sustaining the regime of inequality—the regime which prevents women from articulating and living out conceptions of the good life which rival those that patriarchy rules appropriate.

The crucial move for Mill, the one which brings his understanding of the subjection of women into line with the procensorship feminist understanding of the harm of pornography, is his willingness to deem coercive what has the appearance of consent. In effect, he invokes an idea of false consciousness.

So it seems that if procensorship feminists are right about pornography, Mill would not be sympathetic to an appeal to the consensual nature of either the production or the consumption of pornography. Liberals can make that appeal as part of their justification for opposing censorship of pornography, because the appearance of consent seems to show that pornography satisfies certain harmless male sexual preferences. That women participate in the production of pornography and in the fantasies of men who consume pornography is taken as evidence of the absence of harm. But on Mill's account of subjection, the consent of women to be featured in pornography, and the consent of women to live out the ideas about women's nature which pornography supplies for its consumers, might be entirely manufactured. If so, pornography is especially pernicious because the appearance of consent is given to a deeply coercive relationship.

This conclusion will seem problematic to liberals, especially to those in the Millian tradition. The hallmark of Millian liberalism is taken by both liberals and their critics to be its utilitarian, "want-regarding character"—that is, its respect for people's actual preferences—what appears to them to be good.[5] Whatever liberals think people would desire if they had an understanding of what is really in their interests, liberalism is supposed to be legitimately concerned only with what people take their interests and wants to be. For example, Steven Lukes, in his illuminating monograph on power, argues that liberals, because of their reliance on actual wants, are barred from adopting a radical conception of power which maintains that people's "wants may themselves be a product of a system which works against their interests, and, in such cases, relates the latter to what they would want and prefer, were they able to make the choice."[6]

The puzzle for Mill is then to provide a reconciliation of his concern for what in fact appears to the willing slaves as most desirable—as their "polar star"—with what he thinks they would desire, had they an understanding of what is really in their interests.

Nature and Experience

Mill's solution to the puzzle is found in his complex account of experience as the testing ground for valid observations about human nature. At the very outset of *The Subjection of Women* he says that the authority of men over women would have some claim as a justifiable regime only if it were thought to be so "on the testimony of experience." But for this to be so, women and men must have experienced social life under conditions of perfect equality. Only then could the system of subordination be said to be "conducive to the happiness and well-being of both [sexes]" (*SW*, p. 263). As he puts it, "Experience cannot possibly have decided between two courses, so long as there has only been experience of one" (*SW*, p. 276).

To a large extent, then, Mill's appeal to experience is not to actual but to potential experience. An appeal to actual experience is illicit in this case because actual experience is not merely incomplete, it is also contaminated. Women and men have been denied the benefit of experience which they would have had were women not the passive victims of a regime which reproduces them with a nature suited to the selfish and exploitative interests of men. Indeed, Mill denies that we can have knowledge of the nature of either sex,

---

5. For the term "want-regarding character," see B. Barry, *Political Argument* (London: Routledge & Kegan Paul, 1965), pp. 41–42.
6. Steven Lukes, *Power: A Radical View* (London: Macmillan, 1977), p. 34.

because of the one-sided nature of previous experience. In particular, he says of women's nature that it is "an eminently artificial thing—the result of forced repression in some directions, unnatural stimulation in others." Women have experienced a "hot-house and stove cultivation . . . carried on of some of the capabilities of their nature, for the benefit and pleasure of their masters" (*SW*, p. 276). Even men who do achieve truly affectionate relationships with their spouses cannot know them, for even the best of relationships will be contaminated by the overarching context of subjection (*SW*, pp. 278–79).[7]

How then is knowledge of women's nature to be revealed? It can be revealed, Mill thinks, only when women are liberated from the regime of inequality which silences them. "We can safely assert that the knowledge which men can acquire of women, even as they have been and are, without reference to what they might be, is wretchedly imperfect and superficial, and always will be so, until women themselves have told all that they have to tell" (*SW*, pp. 278–79).[8]

Mill could be understood as supposing here that women need to discover their true nature under conditions of perfect equality, because such knowledge is a prerequisite for women successfully to articulate and to explore a conception of the good life. Alternatively, in line with his remarks about the self-serving aspects of claims about naturalness, Mill could be understood as saying that claims about an inherent human nature should at any time be regarded with some suspicion.

However, Mill is barred by his radicalism from himself deciding between these alternatives. As he tells us, knowledge of women's nature is not "necessary for any practical purpose," since, in accordance with the principle which he claims as the guiding ideal of modern society, "that question rests with women themselves—to be decided by their own experience, and by the use of their own faculties" (*SW*, p. 280).

---

7. Mill's claim here is in line with some of the most radical feminist thought which says that all heterosexual relations are on a continuum, one pole of which is constituted by relations involving overt violence. For example, when he describes the marriage relationship of his day, he does not assert more than that there are extreme cases which reach what he calls the "lowest abysses." But he says that there is a "sad succession of depth after depth before reaching them" (*SW*, p. 288).

8. Because of Mill's emphasis on the importance of the articulation of experience, he would, I think, have been more receptive than many contemporary liberals to the kind of evidence presented by feminists to show the harm of pornography. For liberals have tended to require unattainable hard statistical correlations between sexual assaults and pornography, while feminists rely mainly on the stories women have to tell about men who see them as interchangeable with the women portrayed in pornography (see, e.g., the evidence presented at the Minneapolis hearings, collected in Everywoman, *Pornography and Sexual Violence: Evidence of the Links* [London: Everywoman Ltd., 1988]).

In addition, in the context of his discussion of the subjection of women Mill does not have to opt for either option. For him our present views of women's nature have no standing because what we take as natural is in fact the construct of a regime of inequality. His direct concern is not with the issue of whether women have or could be said to have a nature, but with the suspect use of a claim about their nature to legitimize a regime of inequality. Since any such claim cannot be tested except under conditions of equality, he can focus on the fact that women are prevented from articulating and exploring conceptions of the good life by a regime of inequality.

If Mill has any bias on the issue of nature, it is that men and women will discover, under the right conditions, that they share an interest in leading autonomous lives.[9] He supposes that, insofar as the modern world has experienced autonomy and the progress toward equality which is its condition, that experience has proved beneficial (*SW*, p. 276). His project has been well-described as an "empirical wager."[1] He predicts that his opinion will be vindicated if it is given the opportunity provided by adopting an agnostic position on the topic of women's nature.

In sum, Mill's solution to the puzzle about real and perceived interests and wants is the following. If one's concern is individual autonomy, and if there is reason to suppose that a group's wants were formed under a regime hostile to autonomy, one cannot appeal to those wants to justify the regime. On Mill's construal of utilitarianism, there is not merely a contingent connection between individuality and welfare. His basic utilitarian message is that something cannot count as in my interest unless my assessment of it is achieved under conditions of autonomy, or real control over my life choices. And this conclusion supports a procensorship case, which claims that eradicating pornography is in the real interests of men as well as women.

However, while this solution to the puzzle about real interests is Mill's, it might still be rejected as one repugnant to Millian liberals who take their cues from *On Liberty*. As I have pointed out, the arguments of *On Liberty* are taken to support a principled liberal opposition to censorship. These are the arguments for a narrow harm principle which permits governments to use coercion only to protect individuals from assaults on physical integrity, for a right of autonomy against state intrusions into the area of private morality, and for a right to complete freedom of expression. So there appears to be a fundamental tension in Mill's political theory. The tension

---

9. See [Gail Tulloch, *Mill and Sexual Equality* (Hemel Hempstead: Harvester Wheatsheaf, 1989)], pp. 121–61, for a careful discussion of this issue.
1. Ibid., p. 147.

is dissolved, I shall argue, if *The Subjection of Women* is read as the authoritative text with which *On Liberty* should cohere.

*   *   *

* * * I want to suggest that the right interpretation of Mill's harm principle is the following: governments must not coerce individuals unless their conduct is harmful in the broad sense that includes prejudice to fundamental interests. And all the arguments of *On Liberty* are directed toward supporting the conclusion that among the fundamental interests of individuals, of "man as a progressive being," is the interest in autonomy.

A Right of Privacy

Given this, it would be remarkable had Mill thought that his category of "self-regarding" action committed him to the claim that we can establish a priori the boundaries of a realm of private action into which there can be no state intrusion. Indeed, his argument in this regard in *On Liberty* is as strong as that found in his discussion of the despotism of the patriarchal family in *The Subjection of Women*:

> The State, while it respects the liberty of each in what especially regards himself, is bound to maintain a vigilant control over his exercise of any power which it allows him to possess over others.

As Gail Tulloch has pointed out, to take this idea seriously requires "interferences in family life which go beyond what has been done in most liberal states, including taking strong action against violence in families and rape in marriage."[2]

So, since for Mill the area of self-regarding activity is that which one has on condition that one does not in public or in private harm the essential interests of others, the question of whether pornography should be regarded as falling into this area cannot be answered in advance by a public/private distinction.

The Right to Freedom of Expression

This leaves the issue of Mill's defense in chapter 2 of *On Liberty* of a right to an apparently complete freedom of expression. I want to suggest that Mill's understanding of the right to freedom of expression is not as absolutist as is commonly thought. It is sufficiently complex to permit what we might think of as a liberal censorship policy.

---

2. [Tulloch], pp. 159–60.

In *On Liberty*, Mill does express a general aversion to "forcing improvements on an unwilling people" in the cause of a "spirit of improvement." So we might suppose that persuasion through speech is the only means he would countenance for getting rid of pornography (*OL*, p. 272). Is it that Mill should believe that the "real solvent of public morality" is debate so that his hope is that truth will emerge merely from "free critical discussion"?[3]

The answer to this last question must surely be "no," if we take seriously Mill's account of the subjection of women. For we have seen in Mill's link between women's silence and their lack of autonomy that the very space of discussion is crimped and distorted by an oppressive regime. I think that *On Liberty* can support this answer if we notice a distinction between two methods by which a public debate might be said to control a "spirit of improvement" which aims to control the coercive power of pornographic speech.

On the first method, one hopes debate has this control merely because one hopes that indefinite and uncontrolled conversation will eventually reveal the truth. But any coercive restraints on complete freedom of expression are ruled out. The hope is thus that individuals whose conceptions of the good life contain elements collectively constitutive of oppression will come to recognize that they should reform.

On the second method, debate controls a spirit of improvement in part by establishing what coercive action should be taken in order to eradicate oppressive conceptions of the good life; thus permitting, for example, the censorship of pornography.

It might seem that Mill's defense of freedom of thought and expression in chapter 2 of *On Liberty* can only support the first method. There, on the basis of our recognition of our own fallibility, he presents the following arguments. We should never suppress an opinion since it might be right. Even if we "know" an opinion is wrong, the presence of wrong opinions serves to sharpen our perception and appreciation of the truth. Since the testing ground for truth is experience, we should not constrain expression since that is to limit the experience which is our only ground of determining truth. Thus we cannot impose an opinion on others even if we think that we have sufficient warrant for thinking it true. These arguments are linked to Mill's doctrine that individuals should be left alone to conduct their own experiments in living, since it is through public expression that individuals will learn of the variety of experiments undertaken by others. He says that the "peculiar evil of silencing the expression of an opinion is, that it is robbing the human race; . . . those who dissent from the opinion, still more than those who hold it" (*OL*, p. 229).

3. H. L. A. Hart, *Law, Liberty and Morality* (Oxford: Oxford University Press, 1962), p. 68.

However, this first method seems to presuppose that expression, by contrast with conduct, cannot harm. And there is no evidence in *On Liberty* of Mill holding to a distinction between expression and conduct such that expression is by stipulation incapable of amounting to conduct harmful to others and thus incapable of justifying coercive action. Consider his much discussed distinction between (legitimately) publishing a newspaper article which says that corn dealers are "starvers of the poor" and (illegitimately) saying the same to an angry mob (*OL*, p. 259). That distinction entails that an opinion becomes harmful conduct in a context where its expression threatens interests which require coercive protection. And the procensorship, feminist claim about pornography is that once pornography is understood in the overarching context of women's subordination and inequality, it will be seen as a mode of conduct which plays a special role in maintaining inequality.

Moreover, in chapter 2 of *On Liberty* Mill often speaks of conduct as a form of expression. It would be odd for him to talk otherwise, since his discussion of freedom of expression, when read in the context of *On Liberty* as a whole, is mainly about the importance of individuals being exposed to different experiments in living to give them the resources to engage in experiments of their own. And given the weight Mill attaches in that chapter to learning from actual experience, it is important for him that individual exposure is not merely to beliefs about how to live, but to conduct that amounts to living that way.

And if pornography eroticizes inequality, a question about whether coercive intervention by the state is raised which cannot be settled by a conduct/expression distinction. For in the light of Mill's understanding of experience in *The Subjection of Women*, we need take into account the thought that certain kinds of expression produce experience which is not an adequate testing ground for truth, since that experience is of a regime of inequality which is in fact experience-constraining.

The constraint has two aspects: it constrains the experience of inquiry itself—it silences the articulation of possible experiences—and it prevents from coming into existence actual experience of what it would be like to live those possibilities. To allow this kind of experience to be one's testing ground is to permit an ongoing process of self-validation of an oppressive ideology. One cannot appeal to Mill's dictum that silencing an opinion is an evil when the issue is how to deal with an exercise of male freedom of expression which perpetuates the inequality of women.

Finally, Mill argues in *On Liberty* that his fallibilist position does not commit one to inaction on the basis that, because one's beliefs about what is right can never be assumed to be infallible, they should never be enforced. Mill does not oppose acting on the basis of opinions that have passed the tribunal of experience. He opposes assuming the truth of an opinion "for the purpose of not permitting its refutation." All that he supposes fallibilism to require is to keep the "lists" of debate open so that the action taken remains open to the scrutiny of public debate, and thus to revision (OL, pp. 231–32).

I suggest that this requirement indicates that Mill would have been averse to the first interpretation of the harm principle, that powerful groups can coerce individuals in order to prevent harm. Recall that Mill thinks that social or moral coercion is worse than political coercion because the coercion of the state is at least transparent. The obvious virtue of transparency is that it attracts attention and thus public scrutiny. In addition, if coercive action is going to be undertaken, it must, for Mill, be undertaken after full discussion. And giving a monopoly of legitimate force to the state will, if the state is a liberal one, ensure that state action has been subjected to full public scrutiny.

Moreover, if the legislative policy and mechanisms involved in the state action are carefully crafted so as to make it clear what is at stake—the eroticization of inequality—that policy can plausibly be said to be liberal, one which a Millian might support. The harm in eroticizing inequality is the harm to the fundamental interest we all have in autonomy. Mill's defense of freedom of expression in *On Liberty* is mainly in the service of that same interest. So liberals should squarely face the question whether limiting freedom of expression might not sometimes be justified when the limitation is in the service of, and controlled by, the value of autonomy.

Conclusion

I have tried to show that Mill must be open to the legitimacy of coercive action to eradicate pornography. This does not mean that he would have opted for censorship. Like many feminists today, he might have thought that we need to know a great deal more about pornography than we do at present, or that public education is likely to be more effective and beneficial than coercion which would drive pornography underground. But then there is little or no difference in principle between him and procensorship feminists.

This conclusion follows from an interpretation of Mill which shifts his concerns about substantive equality and individual autonomy to center stage. The argument for it rests on a rich conception of harm, one which embraces harm to fundamental interests, such as the interest in an autonomous life of the kind that is achievable only under conditions of equality. The harm principle still determines which conceptions of the good life we can legitimately condemn, but the domain traditionally accorded by liberals to official neutrality must shrink. For example, the patriarchal conception of the good life is not one about which a liberal state should be neutral because its price is the inequality of women.

This conclusion should matter to liberals not only because it follows from the arguments of the thinker who is rightly regarded as the founder of contemporary liberal political theory. The conclusion also allows liberals to start to take seriously claims about social injustice which would otherwise, as a matter of principle, seem off limits to them.

The conclusion should, I think, also matter to feminists. The dominant ideologies which today vie for political power are liberalism and conservatism. While conservatives are willing to use state coercion to enforce morality, and have in fact sometimes joined with feminists in attempts to use the law to eradicate pornography, their willingness is premised on what for feminists have to be wrong reasons.

Conservatives think that the use of state coercion is justified when there is a threat to what they hold to be the core values of a legitimate status quo. Thus they want to censor pornography because it offends norms which figure among standards of public decency. But similarly they want to preserve the patriarchal character of the status quo. So for feminists who regard eradicating pornography as an essential step in their struggle for women's equality, liberals, who do not have any a priori commitment to the value of the status quo, would seem better allies. And the fact that the most eminent modern liberal was able to foresee some of the main themes of a feminist account of women's inequality should be a useful resource in persuading liberal males to reevaluate their principled opposition to censorship.

*   *   *

MARTHA NUSSBAUM

Mill's Feminism: Liberal, Radical and Queer[†]

Mill's feminism is usually called 'liberal feminism.' Such a designation is in one sense obviously correct, since Mill was a liberal, and his feminism is part of his philosophical thought. 'Liberal feminism,'

[†]   From *John Stuart Mill: Thoughts and Influence*, ed. Georgios Varouxakis and Paul Kelly (Oxford: Routledge, 2010), pp. 130–45. Copyright © 2010 by Taylor & Francis Ltd. All rights reserved.

however, is usually taken to be a bland doctrine focused on same-ness of treatment, with little potential for the radical critique of hierarchies of power or the social deformation of desire. In partic-ular, it is often understood as a kind of formalism that mandates sameness of treatment no matter what the underlying realities are like and no matter where people are socially placed at the start. It is also taken to be a doctrine that focuses on public legal remedies, eschewing all interference with the so-called 'private sphere,' where desire and emotion are pervasively shaped. Feminists who read Mill as holding such a doctrine justly feel that his views are open to a number of strong objections; typically they hold that today's insights render liberal feminism inadequate as a guide to contemporary thought and practice.

Calling this characterization into question, I shall hold up the arguments of *The Subjection of Women*[1] (and of related texts in *On Liberty* and the *Autobiography*) against the major claims of four vari-eties of philosophical feminism that are influential today: liberal feminism, radical feminism, 'difference' feminism and 'queer' femi-nism. I shall argue that *Subjection*, while recognizably in the liberal tradition in its focus on human autonomy, liberty and self-expression, nonetheless anticipates the best insights of radical feminism, with its shrewd analysis of power structures in the family and in sexual relationships and its insightful account of the ways in which power deforms desire. Mill cannot be called a proponent of 'difference' feminism: indeed, he gives us some strong reasons not to buy into Carol Gilligan's programme of naturalizing gender differences. Nonetheless, by according great importance to the cultivation of emotion and imagination in all people, he affirms the most worth-while insight of that deeply defective brand of feminism. Most sur-prisingly, Mill, who writes like a proper Victorian and in many ways was one, turns out to have significant affinities with the 'queer' fem-inism of followers of Michel Foucault. In his assault on the tyranny of convention and the ways in which social notions of normalcy inhibit the development of unusual ways of life, Mill anticipates some of Foucault's most valuable insights. Once again, as with Gil-ligan, he has the best insight without the worst excesses: he attacks deforming social customs without buying into Foucault's dismissal of all norms—including liberal norms—as inherently tyrannical.

I shall conclude, however, that Mill's 'queer' instincts should have been pushed much further. In particular, these aspects of *On Lib-erty* should have informed *The Subjection of Women* far more than

---

1. All page references to *Subjection* (given in the text in parentheses) are to the edition: J.S. Mill, *The Subjection of Women*, edited and introduced by Susan Moller Okin, Indianapolis: Hackett, 1988.

they did. Because *Subjection* stops short of imagining radical alternatives to dominant social norms in the areas of social division of
labour, sexuality and the shape of the family, it remains an excessively
cautious work. It fails to call for 'experiments in living' precisely where
the tyranny of convention is especially deforming. Nonetheless, it is
a work that still offers a great deal to feminist thought. It can provide answers to some of the most powerful charges that feminists
have made against liberalism.

1. *Liberal feminism*

Both friends and foes of Mill often impute to him a view, which they
call 'liberal feminism,' or 'equity feminism,' that focuses on sameness of treatment under law. Typical is the friendly characterization
offered by self-styled follower of Mill, Christina Hoff Sommers, in
her book *Who Stole Feminism?*[2] For Sommers, the follower of Mill, the
'equity feminist' holds that women should have full legal equality
with men, but that once this battle is won, nothing further should be
demanded. Sommers summarizes this view with a quote from
Elizabeth Cady Stanton, who said in 1854, 'We ask no better laws
than those you have made for yourselves. We need no other protection than that which your present laws secure to you.' This equity
agenda, she says is by now 'a great American success story.'[3] Moreover, once women can record their preferences by voting, there
should be an end to all critical scrutiny of women's preferences.
Sommers explicitly imputes to Mill the view that 'any other attitude
to . . . women is unacceptably patronizing and profoundly illiberal.'[4]

Such a view is open to some obvious objections, influentially
developed by Catharine MacKinnon and other radical feminists, and
by now widely accepted within feminist thought generally, and even
within legal thought that is not particularly feminist. Sameness of
treatment, the objection goes, is all very well when people begin in
equal positions, but not when they begin from entrenched hierarchies of domination and subordination. Changing such hierarchies
may, and usually does, require more than simply adopting race-
neutral, class-neutral or gender-neutral laws. Typically, it requires
specific attention to the dismantling of the hierarchy in question,
often through affirmative measures. Even when laws treat people the
same, one should not conclude that there is no injustice: for there

---

2. C. H. Sommers, *Who Stole Feminism?: How Women Have Betrayed Women*, New York:
Simon and Schuster, 1994.
3. Sommers, *Who Stole Feminism?*, p. 22. I examine Sommers's book in detail in: 'American
Women: Preferences, Feminism, Democracy,' in: M. Nussbaum, *Sex and Social Justice*,
Oxford and New York: Oxford University Press, 1999, pp. 130–53.
4. Sommers, *Who Stole Feminism?*, p. 260.

may be a hierarchy in place, and sameness of treatment may perpetuate it.

To give one example of this point from recent American legal history, laws against interracial marriage treated blacks and whites the same: they said, whites can't marry blacks, and blacks can't marry whites. On this basis, when they were challenged for violating citizens' rights to the equal protection of the laws, some courts upheld them. The US Supreme Court, however, did not. In a landmark 1967 case called, remarkably, *Loving v. Virginia* (since the interracial couple in question really were named Mildred and Richard Loving), the Supreme Court said that the laws are obviously a way of upholding 'white supremacy,' and declared them unconstitutional on equal protection grounds. Earlier, in 1954, they handed down a similar judgment concerning the policy of 'separate but equal' schooling. The idea is, sameness is not sufficient for true equality, when it protects an invidious hierarchy. So that is a key objection to the sort of liberal feminism that Christina Sommers defends, which does insist that sameness of treatment is sufficient.

* * *

So far as I can see, however, Mill never endorses, or even comes close to endorsing, the key contentions of the legal-formalist view. Neither in *Subjection* nor anywhere else does he say that once laws are the same for both women and men, then all will be well. He does indeed think that women's suffrage is very important, and that in other ways the 'legal subordination of one sex to the other' (2) ought to be undone. As a Member of Parliament he made good on that view, introducing the first bill for women's suffrage. He also, however, attaches great importance to laws that will redress women's asymmetrical vulnerability in marriage, where he sees that sameness of treatment would not remove an underlying power imbalance. He argues vehemently, for example, for the criminalization of rape within marriage, which surely is not a crime that can be correctly characterized without acknowledging women's asymmetrical physical and economic vulnerability (32).

Moreover, as we shall see, Mill prominently recognizes the social deformation of desire and preference and wishes to change it: so his programme is not confined to the approved Sommers 'liberal' preference-based programme.

In my view, this entire line of critique goes wrong at the start by thinking of liberalism as a view that is in its nature and fundamental motivation insensitive to hierarchies of power. Both historically and in today's most influential versions, liberalism is all about undoing hierarchies of power founded on wealth, class, honour, race, and, by now, sex. It is, at its heart, anti-feudal and anti-monarchical.[5] The problem is not that liberalism itself is unable to acknowledge hierarchies, and to make proposals that will help us to undo them. The problem, instead, is the problem that Mill identifies right at the outset of *Subjection*: men who think they are liberals, and in some ways are so, refuse to carry their insights into the domain of gender. They are quick to see hierarchy in relationships based on class, caste, inherited wealth, even race, and to propose remedies for these traditional asymmetries. Gender, however, seems to them profoundly 'natural,' and they are often unable to see conventional male–female relationships as characterized by unreasonable hierarchies.

One part of traditional liberalism does indeed militate against serious or deep critique of women's inequality: this is the distinction between a 'public realm,' which is the realm of law and justice, and a 'private realm,' which the law must leave alone, and which is putatively run in accordance with different principles, love rather than justice, sentiment rather than law. The public/private distinction was not created by liberalism: we can find it in Aristotle, and we can also find it in traditional Indian thought.[6] Traditional liberalism, however, does indeed recognize such a distinction of realms, and even some contemporary liberals have upheld it.[7] John Rawls, while officially rejecting the public/private distinction and while stating that the family forms part of the 'basic structure' of society that is regulated by principles of justice, in some ways moves uncomfortably close to the older liberal view when he ultimately concludes that the family is a 'voluntary association' like a church or a university.[8]

If the family is off-limits to liberal justice, then it seems right to conclude that many of the most serious inequalities of women cannot be redressed. The education people receive in the family is crucial to their formation as citizens. Even as adults, women's persistent vulnerability to abuse, both physical and mental, surely undermines their attempts to achieve full equality in work and in the political realm. So here is an apt criticism that radical feminists have to make against many traditional liberals. One could hardly

---

5. See my 'The Feminist Critique of Liberalism,' in: Nussbaum, *Sex and Social Justice*.

6. See my 'Sex Equality, Liberty, and Privacy: A Comparative Approach to the Feminist Critique,' in E. Sridharan, Z. Hasan and R. Sudarshan (eds), *India's Living Constitution: Ideas, Practices, Controversies*, New Delhi: Permanent Black, 2002, pp. 242–83 (from conference on 50th anniversary of the Indian Constitution). A shortened version was published under the title 'What's Privacy Got to Do With It? A Comparative Approach to the Feminist Critique,' in: S. A. Schwarzenbach and P. Smith (eds), *Women and the United States Constitution: History, Interpretation, Practice*, New York: Columbia University Press, 2003, pp. 153–75.

7. See the excellent treatment in Susan Moller Okin, *Justice, Gender, and the Family*, New York: Basic Books, 1989.

8. See details in Chapter 4 of: Nussbaum, *Women and Human Development: The Capabilities Approach*, Cambridge: Cambridge University Press, 2000, pp. 241–97.

make this critique of Mill, however. Mill insists that it is both wrong and profoundly inconsistent to talk the language of liberty but to condemn women, in the family, to a lot that is 'worse than that of slaves in the law of many countries' (32). His critique of marital rape and domestic violence, in *Subjection*, is radical: it insists that what happens behind the doors of the family is political, is a matter of law, justice and equality. If there are realms of intimacy that law, for Mill, cannot or should not regulate—and I believe there clearly are, though this is not a topic that occupies his attention in *Subjection*—these are not the realms of concern to radical feminists, who themselves typically defend at least some protections for intimacy, as MacKinnon explicitly does.[9] Once one removes the public-private distinction, one still needs to protect freedom of association, especially intimate association; Mill and radical feminists have no deep disagreement here.

What does it mean, then, to call Mill's feminist thought liberal at all, if it does not simply mean to misread him? It means, I think, in the first instance that Mill carries the traditional liberal critique of feudal and monarchical hierarchies into the sphere of gender relations, asking for the full recognition of human rights and human dignity in these relations. He asks liberal thought to be thoroughgoing and consistent, where it has been half-hearted and inconsistent.

In connection with this demand, Mill places characteristic liberal emphasis on each individual person's right to self-expression and self-development, with education playing a key role in a decent society's attempt to promote these goods for its citizens. Above all, it means that Mill sees each person as an end in him or herself, not simply as a support for the ends of others, or as a continuer of a tradition or a family line. The idea that the individual, not the group, is the locus of moral worth, and that all individuals are of equal and independent worth, not simply deriving their worth from relationships to others, can be said to be liberalism's core normative insight. Mill's point is that traditional liberals have made good points against feudalism by emphasizing the entitlements of the individual and the equal worth of all individuals. In the bosom of the family, however, feudalism has continued to reign, since it is convenient to men to hold that women are not ends in themselves, but means to male comfort and reproduction. By asking the radical question, 'What would it be to treat *all* individuals as ends in themselves?', Mill reveals the radical potential inherent in liberalism.

---

9. Catharine MacKinnon, Law-Philosophy Seminar, University of Chicago, 2003.

2. *Radical feminism*

I turn now to the views of radical feminists Catharine MacKinnon and Andrea Dworkin, which are paradigmatic of what is standardly called 'radical feminism.' I've already indicated that this movement makes criticisms of standard liberalism that do not go through against Mill. I now want to argue that Mill's feminist thought, in its most central aspects, has close affinities with the central positive claims of radical feminist thought.

The central insight in radical feminism is an insight about power. Relations between men and women, as we now find them, are characterized by a systematic hierarchy of domination and subordination. Although this hierarchy is often rationalized by claiming that it has its roots in 'nature,' there is no basis for these claims. The appeal to 'nature' is just an illicit way to rationalize a hierarchy that is deeply habitual and conventional. Radical feminists typically lack interest in how this hierarchy arose. What concerns them is that it is there, it is perceived as natural, unchangeable and right, and it deforms everything. Power differences give rise to women's inequality in law, in society, and in personal relationships themselves.

* * *

Radical feminists are sometimes taken to hold that sexual intercourse itself is always, and inevitably, a form of domination. Some of Dworkin's more hyperbolic statements conduce to this reading, but I think that it is, in the end, a deep misreading.[1] What Dworkin really holds, I would argue, is that we cannot wave away the problem of male sexual violence by simply saying that it is the work of a few 'perverts', or people who are not sexually 'normal.' The problem is in the norms themselves, in the way in which they define male initiative and female compliance, the way in which a husband's 'rights' are understood to include intercourse on demand, and so forth. So it's the whole structure of conventional norms that needs to be reconceived, if sex is ever to express equality on a reliable basis.

In one way Mill makes an odd companion for the forthright sexual talk of MacKinnon and Dworkin, since he was a very reticent writer, in keeping with the manners of his time. Nonetheless, he anticipates their key insights in most respects. In the first chapter of *Subjection*, he makes it clear that he believes male–female relations to be hierarchical, a form of domination akin to feudalism. Both are 'forms of unjust power' and are 'arbitrary' (12). Like the

---

1. See my chapter on Dworkin in: Nussbaum, *Sex and Social Justice*.

radicals, he also targets the notion of 'nature,' saying, '[W]as there ever any domination which did not appear natural to those who possessed it? . . . It hardly seemed less so to the class held in subjection . . . The subjection of women to men being a universal custom, any departure from it quite naturally appears unnatural' (12–13). (Mill supports this contention with an account of how forms of feudal and racial domination have been taken to be 'natural.') More generally, Mill is one of the great critics of the normative appeal to 'nature' in philosophy. Not only in *Subjection*, but also in the wonderful essay 'Nature,' he shows exactly what MacKinnon and Dworkin more briefly show, how nature serves as a screen behind which traditional power interests protect themselves.

Because domination over women is useful to men, it isn't surprising that they cling to it. 'Did not the slaveowners of the Southern United States maintain the same doctrine, with all the fanaticism with which men cling to the theories that justify their passions and legitimate their personal interests?' (12) Precisely because self-interest is so obviously present, however, we should not trust what these people say: we should scrutinize every claim about 'natural' sex differences with a relentless determination to follow the evidence and to weed out bias.

As for the passions and sentiments that shape the relationship between men and women, here Mill makes one of his boldest and most creative contributions. The domination of men over women, similar though it is to other forms of domination in many respects, has, he argues, one important difference. In other areas, what the master needs is that the slave does his assigned job and doesn't rebel. The master doesn't care whether the slave likes the work. All that matters is that the work gets done, and the slave doesn't kill him or run away. The domination of men over women, however, concerns much more daily and intimate matters, connected in a very basic way with a man's self-esteem and self-conception. * * *

*   *   *

Mill's language is reticent, but he is talking about the same thing that MacKinnon and Dworkin are talking about: the eroticization of domination and subordination, the way in which images of the powerful dominating male and the yielding submissive woman structure not just social behavior but the inner life of fantasy and desire themselves. The enslavement of women's minds may begin with ideas of proper meekness and obedience; it goes yet deeper, however, by affecting what women sexually desire and what men find sexually pleasing.

Now of course Mill lacks a detailed psychology of the emotions and desires to back up these claims. What he does have, the associationism he appropriated from his father, is probably not adequate to the task.[2] The same critique can be made of the radical feminists: they have too little interest in developmental psychology and in the nature of emotion and desire. What both Mill and the feminists see clearly, however, is that sexual desire is not an altogether 'natural' immutable phenomenon. Mill does think that there is something that can be called the 'natural attraction between opposite sexes' (16); radical feminists are agnostic here. Nonetheless, they both agree that this attraction is strongly shaped by social norms and power interests, and that this shape serves the interests of men and disserves those of women.

Radical feminists carry this theme further than Mill did, into a detailed critique of pornography and other social institutions that are involved in the reproduction of this deformed sexuality. Andrea Dworkin's fiction powerfully shows, in very frank sexual terms, how fantasies of domination and subordination, deep in the mental lives of both men and women, conduce to the abuse of women. All this is beyond Mill's reach. Nonetheless, he has the key insight—an extraordinary fact in his time, although not without precedent in English literature. * * * We don't know what kinds of conversations about women Mill had with his male friends, but it is easy to imagine that Mill would have been revolted by some common ways of talking about women and would have noticed in himself a reluctance to join in. Whatever the origin of the insight may be, it is an astonishing one, and sufficient to make Mill the first great radical feminist in the Western philosophical tradition. (Plato has a claim, but he didn't see hierarchy in sexual desire itself.)

3. 'Difference' feminism

According to the influential 'difference' feminism of Carol Gilligan and Nel Noddings, women's thinking displays a focus on care, relationship and connection, whereas male thinking typically focuses on autonomy and tends to rely on universal moral rules. Gilligan never quite says that these differences are natural, but she suggests it; Noddings does seem to think that they are natural. Gilligan believes that a good person needs both forms of thinking, both the 'perspective of care' and the 'perspective of justice.' Noddings appears to think that caring is far more important than justice, and that we can dispense with the latter if we sufficiently cultivate the former.

* * *

2. See C. Vogler, *John Stuart Mill's Deliberative Landscape: An Essay in Moral Psychology*, London and New York: Routledge, 2001.

We can say right away that Mill, prudently and rightly, would have resisted a central contention of this tradition: that women's actual ethical reasoning gives reliable information about how women are. Most of the argument of *Subjection* is devoted to a devastating critique of all such claims, establishing that we know next to nothing about how women and men 'are,' so early do power interests enter the picture. To my students, who read Gilligan after reading both Rousseau and Mill, Gilligan looks like a naïve and starry-eyed reinvention of Book V of *Emile*, in ignorance of Mill's trenchant critique of all such naturalizing claims.

Empirical psychology today gives strong support to Mill: experiments done with babies who are first labeled male and then labeled female show that the very same infant will be talked to differently, played with differently and talked *about* differently, depending on whether the experimental subject thinks the baby is male or female. A 'male' baby is typically tossed in the air and played with robustly. The 'girl' is sheltered and held close. The 'boy' is called 'angry' when he cries; the very same cries coming from the little 'girl' are called fear. It is difficult to believe that such differential treatment does not influence development profoundly. That being the case, we ought to say that we are just where Mill believed we were in 1869: there may indeed be innate gender differences, but we know nothing reliable about them. Mill, then, would be correct in his agreement with the radical feminist critique of Gilligan. MacKinnon, speaking of Gilligan's notion of the 'different voice' of women, says, 'Take your foot off our throats, and then we will hear in what voice women speak.' Mill is more polite, but no less damning.

Concerning women's so-called instincts of love and care, Gilligan's central theme, Mill has an additional point to make: given women's powerlessness, they need to ingratiate themselves with men by paying attention to how they feel and by taking care of them. What else can they do? So, what Gilligan thinks of as admirable might just be a sign of subordination.

Here we can observe that the problem has only grown larger with time. Today, given the general aging of populations, there is much more care work to be done in most families: not just children, but also aging parents, and anyone who happens to have a temporary or lifelong disability. Our society still maintains the fiction that this care work will be done for free, by women, out of their instincts of love, and women are often forced to buy into that fiction. The alternative is to be stigmatized as a bad mother or a bad daughter. Even if women know clearly that they do not *want* to care for their aging parents—and so are not 'enslaved' in their minds—they may have no choice but to do this caring with a cheerful face, because it is socially impossible to do otherwise, and society has offered them no decent alternatives.

If emotions of love and caring are to be defended as morally valuable, they must, then, be scrutinized first for signs that they are simply the result of a traditional gendered division of emotional life, and also for signs that they are ways of exploiting women. They, or some forms of them, must be defended as valuable with an independent argument that shows what, and when, they contribute to human flourishing. In *Subjection*, Mill focuses on the critical, suggesting that it is only when men and women live on a basis of true social and legal equality that we can even begin to trust the sentiments they express as possibly non-deformed expressions of their personal choice. In the *Autobiography*, he makes headway on the constructive account. * * *

So, Mill not only shows us how and why we might reject some of the weaker claims of the 'difference' feminists, he also picks out the pearl of insight in the mire, and really gets to work making the kind of argument that would go somewhere as a normative argument. It is because many people, male and female, feel intuitively that male development is lacking in something that women more often cultivate, and that this something is pivotal to human flourishing, that Gilligan's thought has attained the widespread influence it does not deserve. Mill is not a 'difference feminist.' He is something much better, a philosopher who knows how to think evaluatively about the contribution of emotions to life.

4. *Queer feminism*

The final group of thinkers I shall consider are more known for their thinking about sexual orientation than for feminist thought, but the same insights carry over, and there are many feminists who make use of them today. Michel Foucault, and thinkers about sexuality who develop his ideas further (for example Michael Warner and David Halperin), notice that in the sexual domain ideas of what is 'normal' typically have a repressive role. Just like the notion of 'nature,' the notion of the 'normal,' though it parades as a descriptive notion, involves an un-argued slide from the descriptive to the normative: because things usually are a certain way, therefore it's fitting and proper that they be that way. Of course no such conclusion follows. Bad knees, bad backs and bad judgment are all 'normal' in the statistical sense, and nobody would conclude that they are therefore the way things ought to be. In areas where power interests are at stake, however, people make such illicit conclusions all the time. Foucault shows how, time and time again, notions of the normal and the proper tyrannize over people, creating orthodoxies and banishing people who live and think differently. In the sexual domain, the tyranny of the normal has been particularly harsh toward gays and lesbians, and that is a theme of a lot of this writing. But Foucault's thought extends much more widely, calling into question normative ideas of crime and innocence, of madness and sanity.

In the end, Foucault is so suspicious of all norms that he typically advocates only acts of resistance to break their grip. In the works for which he is most known, he refuses to offer any principled account of what should be resisted, or on what grounds. In his last works, however, most unpublished at the time of his death, he seemed to move in a more Millian direction, praising ancient Greek notions of self-cultivation and self-fashioning and condemning as repressive norms that prevent this sort of autonomous activity from taking place.

Mill is the last person whom one would associate with the street theater of Act Up or any other public manifestation of 'queer' radicalism. So far as I know, he never even followed in the footsteps of Bentham, who made fun of the legal and moral judgments against pederasty and the notions of the 'natural' and 'normal' that went with them. (In an essay on pederasty, Bentham commented, '[I]t is wonderful that nobody has ever yet fancied it to be sinful to scratch where it itches, and that it has never been determined that the only natural way of scratching is with such or such a finger and that it is unnatural to scratch with any other.') In *On Liberty*, where reference to same-sex relationships would have been apropos, Mill certainly does not talk about sexual experimentation, or different forms of sexual life. Nor does he call for the repeal of sodomy laws. I would conjecture that he probably found homosexual relations shocking and off-putting, and simply did not wish to talk about them, much though his argument tells in favour of their decriminalization.

Nonetheless, we may contemplate the general nature of Mill's argument and its implications. In *On Liberty*, he strongly condemns the tyranny of social norms over unusual individuals who wish to undertake 'experiments in living.' His hatred of the tyranny of the normal in England, and his preference for France, are all part of his very Foucauldian rejection of the tyranny of ideas of normality, and his support for spaces within which people may flourish in their own way. His 'harm' principle clearly entails that consensual sex acts between adults be legal, a fact that was not lost on Lord Devlin, when he took Mill as his arch-adversary in *The Enforcement of Morals*.

Mill does not articulate his critique of the 'normal' in its rather extreme Foucauldian form, in which all norms whatsoever are to be eschewed, even ethical norms, such as fairness, justice, friendship and love. Like Foucault, he recognizes that such words can often prove the masks of a desire for domination, but he nonetheless clings to some definite norms as good guideposts: ideas such as liberty, self-development and flourishing. So he is like Foucault in his more complex late period, with a dose of liberal autonomy thrown in. As with difference feminism, so here: Mill has the valuable insight without the regrettable excess.

What is deeply to be regretted, however, is that, close though Mill's affinities with 'queer' thought are in *On Liberty*, *The Subjection of Women* is far from being a 'queer' text, or even a text that uses the best insights of *On Liberty*. Despite the radicalism of the text in some domains, Mill never considers any alternatives to the current form of the family organization, monogamous and heterosexual. In *On Liberty* he mentions the unfair treatment of the Mormons, but, while he objects to that treatment, he also makes it clear that he finds polygamy personally abhorrent. Certainly *Subjection* nowhere gives it a second thought. Nor, as I have said, do homosexual relations come in for any rethinking, as they do for Bentham. Even the idea, fairly common at the time, that marriage might be informal, or communal, not contractual, does not surface. In short, none of the sexual 'experiments in living' that were going on at the time, and that cherished classical texts prominently described, get a hearing at all: the text takes its aim to be simply the reform of monogamous heterosexual marriage in the direction of greater emotional and legal equality.

Notoriously, moreover, Mill's conservatism goes well beyond a focus on heterosexual marriage. It includes an unexamined assumption that in such marriages the division of household and childcare labour will remain the conventional one. Women will be able to move outside the home only if they are lucky enough to have servants to share some of these duties. Harriet's own more radical ideas about women's work opportunities, not uncommon in radical circles at this time, are neglected. Once again: such obvious 'experiments in living' as asking men to do some of the washing up and to change a baby's diaper are not even mentioned.

So: why is Mill, so 'queer' in some ways, not 'queer' enough? One could try to say that *Subjection* is already such a shocking work, and Mill is already so aware that he might not get a hearing (see pp. 1–3), that he avoids making it yet more shocking by tying his critique to radical changes in the family. This may be a sufficient explanation for the text's silences, and in that case they would be merely pragmatic and superficial silences. I believe, however, that they may well lie deeper. Despite his radicalism, Mill was in many ways a rather conservative man. If he wanted something as radical as genuine emotional, spiritual and intellectual equality—and I think he sincerely did—he still liked the orderly forms of Victorian life to be observed. So far as anyone knows, he did not sleep with Harriet until after her husband's death. When the pair married, furthermore, and his radical brother George protested this capitulation to convention, Harriet wrote—presumably with her husband's knowledge—a letter so angry and so defensive that it suggests that the couple were clinging, at some deep emotional level, to an institution they had many reasons to reject:

> I do not answer your letter because you deserve it—that you certainly do not—but because tho' quite inexperienced in the best way of receiving or replying to an affront I think that in this as in all things, frankness and plain speaking are the best rule, as to me they are the most natural—also it is best that every one should speak for themselves. Your letters to me and Haji must be regarded as one, being on the same subject and sent together to us. In my opinion they show want of truth modesty and justice to say little of good breeding or good nature which you appear to regard as very unnecessary qualities.
>
> Want of justice is shown in suggesting that a person has probably acted without regard to their principles which principles you say you never [understood?] Want of modesty in passing judgement on a person thus far unknown to you—want of everything like truth in professing as you do a liking [?] for a person who in the same note you avoid calling by their name using an unfriendly designation after having for years addressed them in to say the least a more friendly way. In fact want of truth is apparent in the whole, as your letters overflow with anger and animosity about a circumstance which in no way concerns you so far as anything you say shows and which if there was any truth in your profession of regard should be a subject of satisfaction to you. As to want of the good breeding which is the result of good feeling that appears to be a family failing.
>
> The only small satisfaction your letter can give is the observation that when people desert good feeling they are also deserted by good sense—your wish to make a quarrel [?] with your brother and myself because we have used a right which the whole world, of whatever shade of opinion, accords to us, is as absurd as unjust and wrong.[3]

To get this angry over the suggestion that perhaps they ought to have lived experimentally rather than conventionally betrays, I suggest, a

3. Quoted in: F. A. Hayek, *John Stuart Mill and Harriet Taylor: Their Correspondence and Subsequent Marriage*, London: Routledge & Keegan Paul, 1951, pp. 176–77.

deep attachment to conventional respectability. If the couple had the courage to prefer love over public opinion, it was not because they were deaf to its voice.

What *Subjection* should have had, its modern feminist reader feels, is an institutional chapter asking what sorts of new rules for marriage, and what alternative lifestyles, what 'experiments in living,' this argument concerning the hierarchy of the sexes might suggest. Once we recognize that sexual domination is artificial rather than 'natural,' and once we recognize that it has, on the whole, not worked out so very well, depriving society of women's talents, depriving children of paradigms of equality, and depriving men and women of a type of happiness that requires equality,—it seems that the next step would be to ask, 'What different ways of doing things might we try out?' Mill, sadly, fails to take this next step.

Modern feminists can justly feel, however, that the text itself leads up to that next step. Its feminist readers have understood the way in which it points beyond itself. Modern Millians, lacking Mill's particular rhetorical problems and/or his particular personal hang-ups, have built upon his insights to ask the questions he fails to ask, imagining different ways of dividing household labour, of arranging for the care of children and the elderly, of supporting the demands of same-sex couples for legal and emotional equality. And they have done so in part because of the ideas of *On Liberty*, ideas of individual self-expression and freedom that are deeply woven into the 'radical' and 'queer' feminist movements, much though they would hesitate to call themselves liberals.

Mill's feminist thought, then, is not that dreary pablum popularly known as 'liberal feminism.' It is radical thought, both then and now, and it has deep affinities with the best in contemporary radical feminist thought. At the same time, it cultivates well an insight about the value of emotions that difference feminism cultivates poorly. And it hunts down pernicious social notions of the 'natural' and 'normal' with much greater philosophical depth and consistency than the often polemical works of queer theory. It does all this, moreover, while being recognizably liberal, that is, built around ideas of personal autonomy, self-expression and individual worth.

Indeed, Mill's thought gives us ways of answering the most common charges made by feminists against liberal thought today. To the charge that liberalism is 'too individualistic,' Mill can reply that the most valuable insight in liberalism is that of the equal and separate worth of each and every person. Far from being 'too individualistic' in that normative sense, conventional liberalism has not been individualistic enough, since it has allowed men to treat women as reproducers and caregivers, rather than persons of equal worth in their own separate right. Such a liberalism can value care and community, but it will not value these ideas uncritically, since they have often been used to exploit women.

To the charge that liberalism accepts all preferences as given and hard-wired, offering no criticism of the social deformation of emotion and desire, Mill can reply that this may be true of many liberals, but it is not in the least true of him. Moreover, his critique of desire, far from being an 'illiberal' element in his thought (as Sommers suggests, though not about Mill), is actually essential to his liberal programme: for it's only when we see how people are enslaved that we can think how to set them free.

Finally, to the imagined Foucauldian charge that liberalism proposes definite norms to guide choice and is therefore bound to be tyrannical, Mill can reply that the defense of liberty requires some definite norms. If the only advice is 'resist authority,' we could as well use this to resist norms of equal respect and equal liberty as to resist norms of gender discrimination. So the protection of people from tyranny requires normative commitment, commitment embodied in a good legal regime—particularly when convention gives little protection. What else could possibly protect the weak against the powerful?

On balance, then, Mill's feminist thought, while incomplete in many ways, is still alive philosophically, and still provides valuable guidance. When we consider how much women's position in the world has changed in the 200 years since Mill's birth, we can see that many of these changes were directly urged by Mill's thought. Still other and very significant changes, which he does not directly recommend, are nonetheless strongly suggested by the underlying ideas that inhere in his arguments. These facts should show us how insightful, and how radical, a feminist Mill was.

GEORGIOS VAROUXAKIS

John Stuart Mill on Race[†]

John Stuart Mill paid a great deal of attention to the significance for politics of differences of what was called at his time 'national characters'. It is arguable that the category of national character was not as marginal in the younger Mill's thought as the cursory nature of references to it by subsequent students and the absence of its detailed consideration in existing scholarship would have one believe

[†] From *Utilitas* 10.1 (March 1998): 19–32. © Edinburgh University Press 1998. Reprinted with permission of Cambridge University Press. Unless otherwise indicated, notes are by the author. Some of the author's notes have been abridged.

(to say nothing of statements implying that it amounted to little more than an argumentative weapon).

Discussions about national and—what would be called today—cultural characteristics were, in Victorian Britain, inextricably associated with discussions about 'race', and the term was often substituted for 'nation', 'nationhood', or 'national character'.[1] Even more attention was attached to the role of race in France at the same time.[2] It was certainly not accidental that Tocqueville came to examine seriously the possible significance of racial origin during his first stay in America.[3] Mill was thus bound to address the question of the extent to which national character was formed or influenced by race or other physical factors such as climate.[4] His attitude towards the theories concerning these issues that were abroad at his time is illustrated in the following pages and the extent to which he followed the relevant scientific disciplines is assessed. For all his concessions to some of the stereotypes of the century Mill is shown to have been on the whole in the forefront of attempts to discredit the deterministic implications of racial theories and assert the ascendancy of 'mind over matter', a view corroborated by the responses of his contemporaries. Criticisms by later scholars sometimes fail to place him in the context of his time and inevitably find his references to race unacceptable. For instance, E. D. Steele did less than justice to Mill when he wrote that '[h]is writings furnish examples of judgements on the basis of race or national character'.[5] Though it is very much the case that he often made pronouncements on the basis of national character, Mill was far from equating or confusing the latter with race and denounced—and did a lot to discredit—the usual association of the two during the nineteenth century.[6] In a

---

1. See George Watson, *The English Ideology: Studies in the Language of Victorian Politics*, London, 1973, pp. 198–212; Paul B. Rich, 'Social Darwinism, Anthropology and English Perspectives of the Irish, 1867–1900', *History of European Ideas*, xix (1994), 779; Christine Bolt, *Victorian Attitudes to Race*, London, 1971, *passim*. * * *

2. See Jacques Barzun, *Race: A Study in Superstition*, New York, 1965, p. 6, and *passim*; M. Seliger, 'Race-thinking during the Restoration', *Journal of the History of Ideas*, xix (1958), 273–82. * * *

3. See James Schleifer, *The Making of Tocqueville's 'Democracy in America'*, Chapel Hill, 1980, pp. 62–72; also Seymour Drescher, *Dilemmas of Democracy: Tocqueville and Modernization*, Pittsburgh, 1968, pp. 274–6.

4. Bentham had mentioned '*race* or *lineage*' as one of the many 'circumstances influencing sensibility': see Jeremy Bentham, *An Introduction to the Principles of Morals and Legislation*, ed. J. H. Burns and H. L. A. Hart, with a new introduction by F. Rosen, Oxford, 1996 (*The Collected Works of Jeremy Bentham*), p. 67. Another of these circumstances was climate: ibid.

5. E. D. Steele, 'IV. J. S. Mill and the Irish Question: Reform, and the Integrity of the Empire, 1865–1870', *Historical Journal*, xiii (1970), 435.

6. Steele's statement quoted above was preceded by the remark that 'Mill was sometimes critical of the doctrine, common in his day, that certain races or peoples were inferior to others in their aptitude for free and progressive institutions: but only when he thought it was being strained, and used in too deterministic a fashion.': ibid. It will be shown in the following pages that, both with regard to Mill's reaction to racial theories

similar vein, Bruce Mazlish wrote that 'Mill even flirted with a kind
of racial theory of character.' Mazlish proceeded to substantiate
this assertion by citing what Mill wrote to his French friend, Gustave d'Eichthal, on 14 September 1839, after having received the
former Saint-Simonist's latest work which dealt with the relations
between the black and the white races:

> I have long been convinced that not only the East as compared
> with the West, but the black race as compared with the Euro-
> pean, is distinguished by characteristics something like those
> which you assign to them; that the improvement which may be
> looked for, from a more intimate and sympathetic familiarity
> between the two, will not be solely on their side, but greatly
> also on ours; that if our intelligence is more developed and our
> activity more intense, *they* possess exactly what is most need-
> ful to us as a qualifying counterpoise, in their love of repose
> and in the superior capacity of animal enjoyment and conse-
> quently of sympathetic sensibility, which is characteristic of
> the negro race.
>
> I have even long thought that the same distinction holds,
> though in a less *prononcé* manner, between the nations of the
> north and south of Europe; that the north is destined to be the
> workshop, material and intellectual, of Europe; the south, its
> 'stately pleasure-house'—and that neither will fulfil its desti-
> nation until it has made its peculiar function available for the
> benefit of both—until our *work* is done for their benefit, and
> until we, in the measure of our nature, are made susceptible of
> their luxury and sensuous enjoyment.[7]

The above text is not sufficient proof that Mill 'flirted with a kind
of racial theory of character'. The term 'race' was used quite loosely
at the time this letter was written, and various characteristics were
attributed to 'races' as a matter of course, without regard to whether
they were biologically inherited or simply cultural traits occurring
in these groups.[8] D'Eichthal's short work to which Mill was referring
was based on the assertion that the two races, the white and the
black, were possessed of biologically inherited mental and social

---

in general and to their application to the case of the Irish in particular, Steele's concession
is an understatement.

7. Bruce Mazlish, *James and John Stuart Mill: Father and Son in the Nineteenth Century*,
London, 1975, p. 407; the passage quoted is to be found in *The Earlier Letters of John
Stuart Mill 1812–1848*, ed. Francis E. Mineka, 2 vols., Toronto, 1963 (henceforth
Earlier Letters), *Collected Works of John Stuart Mill* (hereafter *CW*), xiii. 404.

8. The fact that Mill went on to ascribe to the peoples of the south of Europe (as opposed
to those of the north) characteristics similar to those he agreed with d'Eichthal in
attributing to the black race (as opposed to the whole of the white race) goes some way
towards suggesting that he was not speaking in strictly biological terms.

characteristics peculiar to each.[9] Of course, d'Eichthal's work drew implications very different from those characterising the racial theories of the second half of the nineteenth century. Far from exalting racial purity, the whole point d'Eichthal was making was that the two races should associate with each other and produce the 'race mulâtre'. Yet, it remains the case that d'Eichthal's premises were based on theories asserting that the differences between whites and blacks were constitutional differences and that these physical differences resulted in the two races having different geniuses, habits, religious propensities, and so on.[1] What is not clear is how far Mill shared the premises behind d'Eichthal's benign theories.[2] But even if he did not object to them in 1839, his thought on the subject developed considerably during the following decades and the Mill who wrote *The Subjection of Women* had moved a long way from any tacit acceptance of such premises and theories.

During the earlier years, Mill's most direct and explicit public reference to the subject of race—to which he himself drew attention in later instances[3]—was made in his review of the five first volumes of Michelet's *Histoire de France*, written in 1844. After praising Michelet for having endeavoured to assign to the several races that were mixed on French soil 'the share of influence which belongs to them over the subsequent destinies of his country', Mill observed:

> It was natural that a subjective historian, one who looks, above all, to the internal moving forces of human affairs, should attach great historical importance to the consideration of Races. This subject, on British soil, has usually fallen into hands little competent to treat it soberly, or on true principles of induction; but of the great influence of Race in the production of national character, no reasonable inquirer can now doubt. As far as history, and social circumstances generally, are concerned, how little resemblance can be traced between the French and the Irish—in national character, how much! The same ready

---

9. Gustave d'Eichthal and Ismayl Urbain, *Lettres sur la Race Noire et la Race Blanche*, Paris, 1839, pp. 14–19.
1. D'Eichthal had adduced the researches of W.-F. Edwards and E. Geoffroy Saint-Hilaire (ibid., p. 15). Both were well known scientists. Edwards was one of the major exponents of theories asserting the importance of race in history and society: see Banton, pp. xiii, 31.
2. On 25 December 1840, having received one more of d'Eichthal's ethnological works, Mill wrote to him: 'You are very usefully employed in throwing light on these dark subjects—the whole subject of the races of man, their characteristics and the laws of their fusion is more important than it was ever considered till late and it is now quite *a* [sic] *l'ordre du jour* and labour bestowed upon it is therefore not lost even for immediate practical ends.' *Earlier Letters*, CW, xiii. 456. By this time d'Eichthal had become a leading member of the *Société ethnologique* which was presided over by W.-F. Edwards: see Barrie M. Ratcliffe, 'Gustave d'Eichthal (1802–1886): An Intellectual Portrait', *A French Sociologist Looks at Britain: Gustave d'Eichthal and British Society in 1828*, ed. Barrie M. Ratcliffe and W. H. Chaloner, Manchester, 1977, p. 151.
3. See [Mill], CW, xv. 691.

excitability; the same impetuosity when excited, yet the same readiness under excitement to submit to the severest discipline—a quality which at first might seem to contradict impetuosity, but which arises from that very vehemence of character with which it appears to conflict, and is equally conspicuous in Revolutions of Three Days, temperance movements, and meetings on the Hill of Tara. The same sociability and demonstrativeness—the same natural refinement of manners, down to the lowest rank—in both, the characteristic weakness an inordinate vanity, their more serious moral deficiency the absence of a sensitive regard for truth. Their ready susceptibility to influences, while it makes them less steady in right, makes them also less pertinacious in wrong, and renders them, under favourable circumstances of culture, reclaimable and improvable (especially through their more generous feelings) in a degree to which the more obstinate races are strangers. To what, except their Gaelic blood, can we ascribe all this similarity between populations, the whole course of whose national history has been so different?[4]

A little further on Mill disagreed with a specific instance of Michelet's application of the racial model of explanation. The French historian had attributed to race (the Germanic race in this case) what he called 'that voluntary loyalty of man to man, that free adherence, founded on confiding attachment, which was characteristic of the German tribes, and of which, in his opinion, the feudal relation was the natural result'. Michelet had asserted that this 'personal devotedness and faith in one another' of the Germans was missing in the case of the Gauls, who were already possessed by 'that passion for equality which distinguishes modern France'.[5] Mill's comment follows: 'We think that M. Michelet has here carried the influence of Race too far, and that the difference is better explained by diversity of position, than by diversity of character in the Races.' Mill accounted for the difference by the circumstance of the conquerors being a small body scattered over a large territory, which prevented them from relaxing the bonds which held them together.[6] 'Similar circumstances would have produced similar results among the Gauls themselves' was his retort to Michelet.[7]

4. J. S. Mill, 'Michelet's History of France', *Essays on French History and Historians*, ed. John M. Robson, Toronto, 1985, *CW*, xx. 235.
5. Cf. Ceri Crossley, *French Historians and Romanticism: Thierry, Guizot, the Saint-Simonians, Quinet, Michelet*, London and New York, 1993, pp. 205–6.
6. Cf. Guizot's explanation of the peculiarities of English history in terms of the circumstances of the Norman conquest, translated and endorsed by Mill in J. S. Mill, 'Guizot's Essays and Lectures on History', *Essays on French History and Historians*, *CW*, xx. 291–2. * * *
7. J. S. Mill, 'Michelet's History of France', *CW*, xx. 237.

The above qualification notwithstanding, Mill's adherence to some of the views that were abroad at his time, concerning the significance or race in the formation of national character, was part of his approach to the subject. And when, sixteen years later, he was criticized by Charles Dupon-White on the ground that he had denied the influence of races, Mill replied that he had 'pleinement' admitted this influence in his article on Michelet. This having been said, however, and as far as theoretical discussion is concerned, it is the limit of his adherence to the commonplace views on the significance of race that is more remarkable than the fact of the adherence itself. In that same letter Mill proceeded to explain to Dupon-White that, though he did not deny the significance of the racial factor, what he disagreed with was the tendency, which was most conspicuous in the nineteenth century (as a result of that century's reaction against the eighteenth century), 'celle d'attribuer toutes les variétés dans le caractère des peuples et des individus à des différences indélébiles de la nature, sans se demander si les influences de l'éducation et du milieu social et politique n'en donnet pas une explication suffisante.'[8] * * *

Thus, while accepting vaguely that racial origin is one of the factors influencing the formation of national character, Mill went further to establish that racial predisposition in itself could prove nothing and was liable to be modified out of any recognition through the agency of circumstances such as institutions, historical accidents, and human effort. An instance of Mill's careful depreciation of the role of both race and, more generally, physical causes occurs in the very article on Michelet, closely following the theoretical discussion of the significance of race. There, having admitted the importance of the influence of 'geographical peculiarities' in the formation of national character,[9] he proceeded to praise Michelet for not being unaware of the tendency of provincial and local peculiarities to disappear. * * *

Many other instances occur—in Mill's correspondence in particular—where he protested against the inordinate importance that he thought most of his contemporaries accorded to race.[1]

8. "that of attributing all the varieties in the character of peoples and of individuals to the incredible differences of nature, without wondering if the influences of education and of the social and political environment do not give a sufficient explanation" [Editor's note].
9. J. S. Mill, 'Michelet's History of France', CW, xx. 237.
1. In a letter to Charles Wentworth Dilke, referring to the latter's book Greater Britain: a Record of Travel in English-speaking countries during 1866 and 1867 (1868), Mill's only criticism 'of a somewhat broader character' was 'that (in speaking of the physical and moral characteristics of the populations descended from the English) you sometimes express yourself almost as if there were no sources of national character but race and climate', while Mill himself believed 'the good and bad influences of education, legislation, and social circumstances . . . to be of prodigiously greater efficacy than either race or climate or the two combined': J. S. Mill, Later Letters, CW, xvii. 1563 (Dilke's book was

In 1850 he attacked his erstwhile friend Carlyle for having asserted
that negroes were born servants to the whites who were 'born *wiser*'.
Mill criticized Carlyle for his disrespect of 'the analytical examination of human nature'; his failure to apply the mode of analytical
examination 'to the laws of the formation of character' had led Carlyle to 'the vulgar error of imputing every difference which he finds
among human beings to an original difference of nature.'[2] * * *

Mill concluded: 'It is curious withal, that the earliest known civilization was . . . a negro civilization. The original Egyptians are inferred,
from the evidence of their sculptures, to have been a negro race: it
was from negroes, therefore, that the Greeks learnt their first lessons in civilization'.[3]

In his writings on Ireland, it was one of Mill's main aims to show
that the alleged failings of the Irish were not 'natural' to them, but
were due to misgovernment. In his *Principles of Political Economy*,
he wrote, concerning the Irish, that it was a 'bitter satire on the
mode in which opinions are formed on the most important problems
of human nature and life', to find people 'imputing the backwardness of Irish industry, and the want of energy of the Irish people in
improving their condition, to a peculiar indolence and *insouciance*
in the Celtic race'. He commented that: 'Of all vulgar modes of
escaping from the consideration of the effect of social and moral
influences on the human mind, the most vulgar is that of attributing the diversities of conduct and character to inherent natural differences.' Any race would be indolent and idle, he stressed, if the
arrangements under which they lived and worked resulted in their
deriving no advantage from forethought or exertion. * * *

Another important instance of Mill's pronouncing on race occurs
in *The Subjection of Women*. In his attempt to discard theories of
women's inferiority founded on alleged physical differences between
men and women and inferences thereof, he enlisted the example of
national characters and their alleged racial determination. His mode
of arguing in this respect was by admitting the existence of some
primordial physical differences between different human groups
(races, sexes), and subsequently trying to prove that social circumstances, human will-power and self-discipline ('mind over matter'

'very successful': see Bolt, p. 38; cf. ibid., p. 103). Also, in a letter to John Boyd Kinnear
(referring to Kinnear's *Principles of Reform: Political and Legal*, London, 1865), Mill
stated as one of the chief points on which he differed from the author that the latter
ascribed 'too great influence to differences of race and too little to historical differences
and to accidents as causes of the diversities of character and usage existing among mankind': J. S. Mill, *Later Letters*, CW, xvi. 1093.

2. J. S. Mill, 'The Negro Question', * * * CW, xxi. 93; first published in *Fraser's Magazine*,
xli (January 1850), 25–31.

3. J. S. Mill, 'The Negro Question', CW, xxi. 93.

as he had said apropos of Michelet) could lead such physical predispositions to directions opposite to those they were supposed to
be destined to take. Among his examples were, of course, the French,
as well as other groups such as the Irish, the Greeks, the Romans,
and the English. Mill protested against 'the unspeakable ignorance
and inattention of mankind in respect to the influences which form
human character', which was, he asserted, the greatest of the difficulties which impeded 'the progress of thought, and the formation of
well-grounded opinions on life and social arrangements'. * * *

But History taught another lesson, by showing 'the extraordinary
susceptibility of human nature to external influences, and the
extreme variableness of those of its manifestations which are supposed to be most universal and uniform,'[4] And in an attempt to
refute arguments to the effect that the alleged 'greater nervous
susceptibility of women is a disqualification for practice',[5] Mill
employed the example of races to assert that experience of races did
not show those of excitable temperament 'to be less fit, on the average, either for speculation or practice, than the more unexcitable'.
His examples were the French and the Italians, compared with the
Teutonic races, and especially with the English, and the Greeks and
Romans compared with the northern races, and so on.[6] Statements
such as these made in The Subjection, written in Mill's maturity,
not only offer a theoretical rejection of biological determinism, but
also would suggest an unequivocal belief in the malleability of
human nature and therefore in the improvability of the character
of the various nations. But, while declaring his rejection of physical determinism, Mill spoke in a way that betrays his use of many
of the stereotypes of his contemporaries based on race, climate or
geography. Where he differed is in his assertion that the alleged
natural predispositions in question could lead to results very different from those they seemed to lead to at present, if they were appropriately guided by institutions and human will.[7]

4. J. S. Mill, The Subjection of Women, Essays on Equality, Law, and Education, CW, xxi.
277.
5. Ibid., p. 307.
6. 'The French, and the Italians, are undoubtedly by nature more nervously excitable than
the Teutonic races, and, compared at least with the English, they have a much greater
habitual and daily emotional life: but have they been less great in science, in public
business, in legal and judicial eminence, or in war? There is abundant evidence that the
Greeks were of old, as their descendants and successors still are, one of the most excitable of the races of mankind. It is superfluous to ask, what among the achievements
of men they did not excel in. The Romans, probably, as an equally southern people,
had the same original temperament: but the stern character of their national discipline, like that of the Spartans, made them an example of the opposite type of national
character; the greater strength of their national feelings being chiefly apparent in the
intensity which the same original temperament made it possible to give to the artificial.'
Ibid., pp. 309–10.
7. Cf. J. S. Mill, A System of Logic: Ratiocinative and Inductive, * * * CW, viii. 856–60
(book VI, ch. iv, sect. 4: 'Relation of mental facts to physical conditions').

If one compares Mill's letters to d'Eichthal (1839, 1840) and his review of Michelet (1844) with all his later pronouncements on race, there seems to be a shift of emphasis in his statements around the middle of the nineteenth century. In the early 1840s he asserted that race was one of the factors that influenced national character and should therefore be studied and taken into account. From the end of that decade onwards, and with increasing intensity, he went out of his way to stress how little importance race had. This shift was probably due to his growing realisation of the uses to which racial theories were being put. Historians of anthropological or racial theories have stressed the increasing occurrence during the second half of the century of overtly racist theories which—unlike d'Eichthal's orientalist ethnological ventures of Saint-Simonist[8] inspiration—led to conclusions disturbing to Mill with regard to issues such as slavery, international relations, the government of dependencies as well as women's rights.[9] The worst consequence of the growing popularity of racial theories was the determinism (or, as Mill would put it, the fatalism) that followed as the main implication of the acceptance of such theories. Another factor that, during the 1840s, must have brought home to Mill the full implications of the attribution of mental and moral characteristics to physiological differences was Comte's insistence on the inferiority of women, on the grounds afforded by Gall's phrenological studies.[1]

Apparently it was not accidental that Mill was singled out as the target of more than one article written by one of the major exponents of racial determinism in Britain. James Hunt was the founder (1863) and President of the Anthropological Society of London. He was 'an ardent racialist' and strongly in favour of slavery.[2] He was a follower of the Edinburgh anatomist Robert Knox. Knox has been called Gobineau's British counterpart,[3] 'an almost hysterical

8. Cf. *Les Saint-Simoniens et l'Orient: vers la modernité*, ed. Magali Morsy, Aix-en-Provence, 1990.
9. See [Michael Banton, *Racial Theories* (Cambridge: Cambridge U Press, 1987)], pp. 54–60, and *passim*; [George W. Stocking, Jr., *Victorian Anthropology* (New York: Free Press, 1987)], pp. 102–9, and *passim*. Cf. Zeev Sternhell, 'Racism', *The Blackwell Encyclopaedia of Political Thought*, ed. David Miller, Janet Coleman, William Connolly, Alan Ryan, Oxford, 1991, p. 413: 'As a political theory and as the basis for a theory of history, racism became a factor in European history in the second half of the nineteenth century.'
1. See, in particular, Mill's letter to Comte of 30 October 1843: *Earlier Letters, CW*, xiii. 604–11. On Mill's disagreement with Comte, cf. Maurice Mandelbaum, *History, Man, and Reason: A Study in Nineteenth-Century Thought*, Baltimore, 1971, pp. 168–9. * * * On Tocqueville's attitude to race see [James Schleifer, *The Making of Tocqueville's 'Democracy in America'* (Chapel Hill, 1980)], pp. 62–72; Melvin Richter, 'Debate on Race. Tocqueville's-Gobineau Correspondence', *Commentary*, xxv (1958), 151–60. * * *
2. John W. Burrow, *Evolution and Society: A Study in Victorian Social Theory*, Cambridge, 1968, pp. 118–36 (especially pp. 121, 130). See also Ronald Rainger, 'Race, Politics, and Science: The Anthropological Society of London in the 1860s', *Victorian Studies*, xxii (1978), 51–70; [Christine Bolt, *Victorian Attitudes to Race* (London: Routledge, 1971)], pp. 4, 6–7, 15, 18–19; Banton, pp. 59–60.
3. Sternhell, p. 414. See ibid. on Hunt's racism.

racialist', who had asserted, in *The Races of Man* (1850), that 'race is everything; literature, science, art—in a word, civilization, depends on it'.[4] Hunt dedicated an entire article to an attack on Mill's explicit rejection of racial explanations in the *Principles of Political Economy* and his failure to take any account of the racial factor in his other major works, *Considerations on Representative Government* and *On Liberty*.[5] Hunt did not fail to pay ample lip-service to Mill's qualities as a thinker and logician, and maintained that he wrote the article on 'Race in Legislation and Political Economy' in order to induce Mill and his followers to cease neglecting what Hunt regarded as the scientifically proven all-importance of the racial factor. Hunt had earlier written an article entitled 'Race in History' in which he had attacked directly the historian H. T. Buckle (who professed to be influenced by Mill's *Logic*) and also extended his criticisms to J. S. Mill and Bentham.[6] Hunt's 1867 presidential address to the Anthropological Society was 'another attack on Mill'.[7] There is no evidence of Mill's having read Hunt's articles referring to himself or the rest of the anthropologist's writings.[8] But, if he did, they do not seem to have convinced him at all, if one is to judge from Mill's even more outspoken denunciation of racial determinism in *The Subjection of Women*.[9]

For all his exhortations for the scientific study of differences among societies Mill does not seem to have followed closely developments in the new disciplines of ethnology and anthropology. Besides his failure to refer to most of the main figures in the field and their work, there is also his own admission to the same effect. When, in 1863, the Anthropological Society was founded by Hunt and his followers who had broken away from the Ethnological Society,[1] Mill wrote to Max Kyllmann (who had apparently referred to that Society in his previous letter to Mill):

> The Anthropological Society I hear of for the first time from your letter. I should suppose from the publications it announces that its objects must be very much the same as those of the

4. Burrow, p. 130.
5. [James Hunt], 'Race in Legislation and Political Economy', *Anthropological Review*, iv (1866), 113–35. Hunt began his article by quoting Mill's forceful statement (in the *Principles of Political Economy*) about the vulgarity of 'attributing the diversities of conduct and character to inherent natural differences': ibid., 113 (J. S. Mill, *Principles of Political Economy*, *CW*, ii. 319).
6. See Rainger, 63–4.
7. Ibid., 64.
8. Hunt is not mentioned anywhere in Mill's works or extant correspondence; nor is Knox.
9. See *supra*. In fact, Mill's almost tedious invocation of a great number of historical examples that seemed to serve his argument in *The Subjection of Women* may have something to do with the intensification of debates about racial and physical determinism after around 1850.
1. See Rainger, 51–70.

> Ethnological Society which already existed. The names men-
> tioned are all new to me except two: Capt. Burton . . . and Mr
> Luke Burke. . . . It is possible that some of the others may be
> distinguished names, for I am very little acquainted with the
> present state of this class of studies.[2]

Though Mill was acquainted and even corresponded with a number
of scientists whose work was related to the issues involved in the
study of races, he did not regard studies in the field of natural sciences as relevant to his interest in character. He found more congenial the approach of scientists such as his acquaintance, Thomas
Henry Huxley, who 'considered a subject such as human heredity
to be a scientific matter from which he personally would draw no
political or nonscientific conclusions.'[3] Referring to an article written by Huxley in 1865 Mill wrote to J. E. Cairnes that it was particularly good, 'notwithstanding what I venture to think heretical
physiology, which, however, he clearly sees, and as clearly shews,
not to affect in the smallest degree the moral, political, or educational questions, either as regards negroes or women.'[4]

    What has been argued so far is not meant to obscure the fact
that Mill's failure to develop his projected science of 'ethology',
in combination with his pre-Darwinian approach to the natural sciences[5] must be held to account for the fact that he did find himself
obliged to accord race a certain—unclear—role (simply because he
had not gone as far as he had hoped in developing the science that
would demonstrate beyond doubt the way in which character was
formed by circumstances). Though he made strenuous efforts during
the last three decades of his life to depreciate the importance of
physical factors in the formation of national character, it has
already been seen that he stopped short of denying them any significance whatsoever. This was less obvious in his theoretical statements on these subjects than in his tacit assumptions and his use of
language. The extent to which these tacit assumptions concerning
the relation of physical factors to national character could compromise some of his theoretical arguments can be tested in a reference
to French national characteristics, which appears in Chapter III of
his *Considerations on Representative Government* ('That the Ideally
Best Form of Government is Representative Government'). Mill
asserted that, when it came to 'the influence of the form of

2. J. S. Mill, *Later Letters*, CW, xv. 840–1.
3. Rainger, 65. * * *
4. J. S. Mill, *Later Letters*, CW, xvi. 1057–8. Mill was referring to: T. H. H.[uxley],
   'Emancipation—Black and White', *Reader*, v (20 May 1865), 561–2. * * *
5. On the state of Mill's knowledge about Darwin see John M. Robson, *The Improvement
   of Mankind: The Social and Political Thought of John Stuart Mill*, Toronto and London,
   1968, pp. 273–5; Mazlish, pp. 423–4.

government upon character', the superiority of popular government over every other would be found to be 'still more decided
and indisputable'. This question depended upon 'a still more fundamental one—viz. which of two common types of character, for
the general good of humanity, is it most desirable should
predominate—the active, or the passive type'.[6] In this context Mill
came to the subject of the passive character's envy:

> In proportion as success in life is seen or believed to be the fruit
> of fatality or accident and not of exertion, in that same ratio
> does envy develop itself as a point of national character. The
> most envious of all mankind are the Orientals. In Oriental
> moralists, in Oriental tales, the envious man is markedly
> prominent. . . . Next to Orientals in envy . . . are some of the
> Southern Europeans. The Spaniards pursued all their great
> men with it. . . . With the French, who are essentially a south-
> ern people, the double education of despotism and Catholicism
> has, in spite of their impulsive temperament, made submission
> and endurance the common character of the people, and their
> most received notion of wisdom and excellence: . . .[7]

It is not entirely clear what Mill held to account for the character
traits attributed to the French. Is it the fact that they are 'essentially
a southern people'? Or is it 'the double education of despotism and
Catholicism' that 'in spite of their impulsive temperament, made
submission and endurance the common character of the people . . .'?
It would indeed make sense, given Mill's aim to convince his
readers that 'the passive type of character is favoured by the government of one or a few, and the active self-helping type by that of the
Many',[8] to assert that it was despotism that made the French passive
and envious. But then, what does their being 'essentially a southern
people' have to do with this argument?

Of course, the confounding of different sets of causes is no contradiction in Mill's own terms, given his assertion that race and other
physical factors do have some small part in the formation of national
character. What generates considerable difficulty is that, by allowing race the part he did, Mill was unable to define clearly and
unequivocally the exact nature of the concept of national character
and its legitimate unit. In other words, for all his talk of national
character, he did not define what groups had a 'character', what
exactly constituted a nation. Most times he spoke of it as a political
unit, referring to the inhabitants of what is called today a nation

6. J. S. Mill, *Considerations on Representative Government, Essays on Politics and Society,*
   CW, xix. 406.
7. Ibid., p. 408.
8. Ibid., p. 410.

state, but he also often spoke of ethnic, cultural, or 'racial' groups as possessing a national character. Thus, while he spoke some times of the Scottish and the Welsh characters as fairly distinct from the English, it seems that he often included the Scottish and Welsh in what he called the English character. These difficulties are due to the imprecision surrounding the concept of a nation, and Mill was not more imprecise about it than others during his time and since.

Thus, some of Mill's arguments concerning national character are rendered ambiguous due to his having indulged in discussions involving assumptions related to race or climate and geography more often than he would consciously—or theoretically—have admitted and condoned. At the same time, in order to do justice to him, it should not be lost sight of that, in doing so, he was in good company. Compared with most of his well-known contemporaries Mill can be said to have indulged in the temptation of racial explanation remarkably less than them (except probably Tocqueville, whose position was similar to Mill's). Though he lacked the scientific buttressing he needed, he made strenuous efforts to use what materials he had (mainly consisting of carefully selected historical examples) in order to substantiate his claims concerning man's progressive nature.

The study of Mill's views with regard to race leads to a broader conclusion concerning his political thought and activity, namely to a corroboration of recent interpretations of Mill stressing the over-whelming significance of his commitment to rationality as a unifying and fundamental constituent of his conception of virtue and the good life.[9] Part and parcel with this view comes the recognition of the extent to which 'Mill was always a child of the enlightenment'[1] in his overall outlook and the underlying purposes of his intellectual and political activity. The analysis of Mill's views on race attempted in the preceding pages comes to support the view that sees Mill as in essence attempting to adapt and translate to the intellectual climate of the nineteenth century a world-view and aspirations rooted in the Enlightenment of the eighteenth century while purging the latter of what he saw as its historical immaturity and naiveté.[2] Mill often presented himself as somehow standing above the dispute between the two centuries and effecting a mature synthesis of what was good in each. Yet, all the concessions he was prepared to make to opposite viewpoints notwithstanding, when it came to a test he opted for what he would call the eighteenth-century position. This attachment to an eighteenth-century viewpoint is exemplified in Mill's treatment of differences of national character

9. See H. S. Jones, 'John Stuart Mill as Moralist', *Journal of the History of Ideas*, liii (1992), 287–308; also John Skorupski, *John Stuart Mill*, London, 1989.
1. Ibid., p. 5. Cf. Mandelbaum, pp. 198–9, and *passim*.
2. For a recent version of such a view of Mill see Skorupski, pp. 1–47 and *passim*.

between various 'portions of mankind'. For all his assertions of originality and distance from what he called 'the eminent thinkers of fifty years ago',[3] in dealing with differences of national character he consciously declined to follow the directions contemporary discussions were taking, especially from the moment he came to realize the decidedly non-enlightenment implications these directions were bound to have. (He explicitly referred to the emphasis placed on race and physical factors in the formation of national character as a result of the reaction of the nineteenth century to the philosophy of the eighteenth.[4]) Thus, although his discussions of national character strike one as incomparably more sophisticated than those of thinkers such as Hume or Montesquieu, it remains the case that the framework within which he conducted such discussions was far closer to Hume and Montesquieu than it was to Gobineau, Robert Knox, Carlyle, Comte, or the spokesmen of the London Anthropological Society in the 1860s. His deliberate effort to concede as little importance as possible to race and other physical factors, even at the risk of being—as he actually was—exposed to the criticism that he was not sufficiently scientific, was the result of a strong determination to stand by certain assumptions about rationality and potential for improvement that were dear to him.

3. See Stefan Collini, Donald Winch, and John W. Burrow, *That Noble Science of Politics: A Study in Nineteenth-Century Intellectual History*, Cambridge, 1983, p. 133.
4. See J. S. Mill, *Later Letters*, CW, xv. 691. Cf. *Earlier Letters*, CW, xiii. 605; *The Subjection of Women*, CW, xxi. 263.

John Stuart Mill: A Chronology

1806   Mill is born on May 20; in October, Napoleon defeats the Prussians in Jena (where Hegel is teaching and completing his *Phenomenology of Spirit*) and becomes the master of Europe.

1809   Home education begins with learning ancient Greek.

1812   Composes a history of Rome and an ode to Diana; massive invasion of Russia by Napoleon's troops.

1815   Defeat and exile of Napoleon; end of the Congress of Vienna, which redrew the borders of Europe (an agreement that lasted almost forty years) and brought back old monarchs, almost entirely ignoring nationality.

1820   Spends a year of residence in France with the family of Jeremy Bentham's brother.

1821   War of national independence of Greece against the Ottoman Empire begins; ends successfully in 1832.

1822   First publication, "Two Letters on the Measure of Value," in the *Traveller*.

1823   Forms Utilitarian Society; begins his career with East India Company as a clerk.

1824   Founding of the *Westminster Review*.

1825   Contributes to founding the London Debating Society.

1826   His "mental crisis"; starts connection with Coleridge's followers Frederick Dennison Maurice and John Sterling.

1829   Withdraws from attendance at the London Debating Society; passage of Catholic Emancipation Act.

1830   Visits Paris during the July Revolution and writes reports for the *Examiner*; meets Thomas Carlyle and Harriet Taylor; reads writings from "those of the St. Simonian school."

1831   Publishes "The Spirit of the Age."

1832   The First Reform Act passed; death of Bentham.

1834   Publishes "Notes on Some of the More Popular Dialogues of Plato."

1835   Founds and edits the *London Review*.

1835   Publishes review of the first volume of Tocqueville's *Democracy in America*.

1836   Publishes "Civilization"; his father dies.

1838   Publishes "Bentham."

1840   Publishes "Coleridge" and reviews the second volume of Tocqueville's *Democracy in America*.

1843   Publishes *The System of Logic*.

1844   Publishes "Essays on Some Unsettled Questions of Political Economy."

1848   Publishes *Principles of Political Economy*; revolution in France and establishment of a republican government; Friedrich Engels and Karl Marx publish *The Communist Manifesto*.

1849   Publishes "Vindication of the French Revolution of February 1848"; John Taylor dies.

1851   Marries Harriet Taylor; coup d'état by Louis Bonaparte, who is then proclaimed Emperor Napoleon III in a plebiscite.

1852   Publishes "Whewell on Moral Philosophy."

1853   Crimean War (alliance of Britain, France, and Turkey against Russia) begins; ends in 1856.

1858   Retires from the East India Company upon its dissolution; publishes *A Constitutional View of the India Question*, the first of a series of pamphlets in the *Examiner*; death of his wife in Avignon, France, while they are traveling in southern Europe; thereafter he will spend part of each year in Avignon.

1859   Publishes *On Liberty*, "Thoughts on Parliamentary Reforms," the first two volumes of *Dissertations and Discussions*, and "A Few Words on Non-Intervention."

1861   Publishes *Considerations on Representative Government*; U.S. Civil War starts; national unification of Italy.

1862   Publishes "Centralization" and a review of John Elliot Cairnes's *The Slave Power*.

1863   Publishes *Utilitarianism*.

1865   Publishes *An Examination of Sir William Hamilton's Philosophy* and *Auguste Comte and Positivism*; U.S. Civil War ends; elected Liberal MP for Westminster.

1867   Second Reform Act passed; Parliament rejects his proposed law on the extension of suffrage to women; publishes "Inaugural Address Delivered to the University of St. Andrews" and the third volume of *Dissertations and Discussions*.

1868   Loses seat in Parliament at the general election; publishes *England and Ireland*.

1869   Publishes *The Subjection of Women*.

1870   Franco-Prussian War begins; publishes *Chapters and Speeches on the Irish Land Question*.

1871   Paris Commune takes place; national unification of Germany.

1873   Dies on May 7 in Avignon; posthumous publication of *Autobiography*, *Chapters on Socialism*, and *Three Essays on Religion*.

Selected Bibliography

• indicates texts included or excerpted in this Norton Critical Edition.

This small selection of Mill's works, as well as commentaries on them and on Mill's political and philosophical thought more generally, is intended essentially for undergraduate students. The thirty-three volumes of *The Collected Works of John Stuart Mill* (CW), published by the University of Toronto Press (1963–91) under the general editorship of John M. Robson, is an indispensable source. Each volume contains a very informative introduction, with bibliographical and critical annotations to Mill's texts. In relation to the three essays included in this Norton Critical Edition, volume 1 (*Autobiography*), volume 10 (*Utilitarianism*), volume 18 (*On Liberty*), and volume 21 (*The Subjection of Women*) are of importance. The best bibliographic resource for commentaries is the *Mill Newsletter*, established in 1963 and incorporated in the journal *Utilitas* in 1988. The bicentennial of Mill's birth in 2006 generated a number of conferences (primarily the Bicentennial Conference organized by University College London and the British Academy) and publications, to which I can only partially do justice.

I have divided this Bibliography as follows: first, I have selected those among Mill's works that complement the reading of *On Liberty*, *Utilitarianism*, and *The Subjection of Women*; I have then included titles that help understand the historical and intellectual context within which Mill was born and educated, and in which he developed his ideas; finally, I have made a small selection of the most recent commentaries on each of these three essays (a few were included in the previous Norton Critical Edition of Mill's work).

Essays, Short Writings, and Books by Mill Relating to *On Liberty*, *Utilitarianism*, and *The Subjection of Women*

"Law of Libel and Liberty of the Press" (*Westminster Review*, 1825), reprinted in CW, vol. 21, pp. 1–34. Written at the age of eighteen, the article is an interesting example of Mill's style of reasoning and writing when he was still a radical utilitarian.

"On Marriage" (1832–33?), unpublished and inspired by Harriet Taylor ("She to whom my life is devoted has wished for a written exposition of my opinions on the subject"), printed in CW, vol. 21, pp. 35–49.

"Tocqueville on Democracy [vol. 1]" (*London Review*, 1835), reprinted in CW, vol. 18, pp. 47–90. The review of the first of Tocqueville's two volumes, wherein the idea of the tyranny of the majority is reiterated as the negative force that dominates individual character.

"Civilization" (*London and Westminster Review*, 1836), reprinted in *CW*, vol. 18, pp. 117–47. On the cultural and material circumstances of civilization and cooperation as its main expression, which requires the development of individual faculties and the moral disposition to partnership, a threshold too high to be met by numerous countries in Europe and elsewhere.

"Bentham" (*London and Westminster Review*, 1838), reprinted in *CW*, vol. 10, pp. 75–115. A severe critique of the man he described as a "one-eyed" thinker, the emblem of abstract rationalism.

"Coleridge" (*London and Westminster Review*, 1840), reprinted in *CW*, vol. 10, pp. 117–63. A companion to "Bentham" with the proposal of an ethical foundation to sustain any project of social reform.

"Tocqueville on Democracy [vol. 2]" (*Edinburgh Review*, 1840), reprinted in *CW*, vol. 18, pp. 153–204. This is less warm than the review of vol. 1 and guards the reader "against attaching to [Tocqueville's] conclusions . . . a character of scientific certainty. . . . Democracy is too recent a phenomenon, and of too great magnitude, for any one who now lives to comprehend its consequences."

A System of Logic (London: John W. Parker, 1843), reprinted in *CW*, vols. 7–8. This is Mill's most important philosophical endeavor, with chapters on induction, demonstrations, the limits of the explanation of the laws of nature, and fallacies, Book VI is entirely devoted to the logic and method of moral sciences, discussion of liberty and necessity, the prospect of ethology (the science studying the formation of character), and the art of living, which is a theoretical introduction to *On Liberty* and *Utilitarianism*.

"Vindication of the French Revolution of February 1848" (*London and Westminster Review*, 1849, under the title, "The French Revolution of 1848 and Its Assailants"), reprinted in *CW*, vol. 20, pp. 317–63. A passionate defense of the democratic and republican character of the Revolution of 1848 against its conservative detractors.

Principles of Political Economy (London: John W. Parker, 1848), reprinted in *CW*, vols. 2–3. His economic theory, but also essential to understanding the relationship between "means" and "ends" in the formation of individuality. Variations to the chapters "On Property" and "On the Probable Futurity of the Labouring Classes" (in Book II) were added in the third edition (1852), which marked a relevant change in his conception of a just society and the quality of life, with reflections on government's responsibility in education and the preservation of nature from industrial contamination.

"Statement on Marriage" (1851), a private and unpublished personal agreement between him and his wife on the occasion of their marriage, printed in *CW*, vol. 21, pp. 97–98. A document on his conception of marriage as a mutual partnership, which he reiterates in *The Subjection of Women*.

"Enfranchisement of Women" (unsigned), by Harriet Taylor (*Westminster and Foreign Quarterly Review*, 1851), reprinted in *CW*, vol. 21, pp. 393–415. Mill included it under his name in the second volume of *Dissertations and Discussions*. A radical pamphlet on women's civil and political equality, the right to divorce, and full open access to professions.

"Papers on Women's Rights" (1847–50?), unpublished, printed in *CW*, vol. 21, pp. 378–92. Attributed to both of them or solely to his wife; a blueprint of women's rights, civil, social and political.

"Wife Murder" (*Morning Chronicle*, Aug. 28, 1851), *CW*, vol. 21, pp. 1183–86.

"Whewell on Moral Philosophy" (*Westminster Review*, 1852), *CW*, vol. 10, pp. 167–200.

"Remarks on Mr. Fitzroy's Bill for the More Effectual Prevention of Assaults on Women and Children" (1853), a few copies only printed for distribution, *CW*, vol. 21, pp. 101–08.

Considerations on Representative Government (London: Parker, Son, and Bourn, 1861), reprinted in *CW*, vol. 19. A companion to *On Liberty* and the most important nineteenth-century treatise on the theory of representative government as a modern form of democracy. Mill discusses participation in local government and advocacy movements, his conception of representation as a form of participation and control, and the attempt to combine competence in administration with parliamentary accountability.

Auguste Comte and Positivism (London: N. Trubner & Co., 1865), reprinted in *CW*, vol. 10, pp. 261–368. Mill's reckoning with French social thought and his criticism of Comte's "liberticide" theory of society and progress.

"Inaugural Address Delivered to the University of St. Andrews" (1867), reprinted in *CW*, vol. 21, pp. 215–57. A statement on the value of higher education with curricula that should include both classics and science.

"The Contagious Disease Acts" (1871), reprinted from the minutes of the Royal Commission of 1870 in *CW*, vol. 21, pp. 349–71. Evidence presented to the commission on the policies of compulsory inspection, control and treatment of women suspected of prostitution, and the attempt to contain venereal diseases among soldiers. Important for his arguments in *On Liberty* on the harm principle, on the duty of government to provide security without interfering in adults' moral behavior, and on equal treatment.

"Chapters on Socialism" (1879, posthumous), reprinted in *CW*, vol. 5, pp. 703–53. A reflection written at the end of his life on the antiproperty doctrines developed among workers in several European countries, in which he criticizes centralized or state-based socialism and advances an idea of democratic socialism as cooperative, based on decentralization, equality of opportunity, responsibility, and self-government.

General Works on Mill's Times, Life, and Thought

Ashcraft, Richard. "John Stuart Mill and the Theoretical Foundations of Democratic Socialism," In *Mill and the Moral Character of Liberalism*, ed. Eldon J. Eisenach. University Park: Pennsylvania State UP, 1998. Starting from Mill's autobiographical statements, proposes an interpretation of his political thought as based on commitments to the principle of democracy and a cooperative socialism.

Bain, Alexander. *James Mill: A Biography*. London: Longmans, Green, 1882. The most complete biography of Mill's father written by a disciple of John Stuart Mill.

———. *John Stuart Mill: A Criticism; with Personal Recollections*. London: Longmans, Green, 1882. Bain expresses a negative judgment on the influence played on Mill by Harriet Taylor.

Berger, Fred R. *Happiness, Justice, and Freedom: The Moral and Political Philosophy of John Stuart Mill*. Berkeley: U of California P, 1984. An excellent reconstruction of the relationship between the three works by Mill included in this Norton Critical Edition.

Burrow, J. W. *The Crisis of Reason: European Thought, 1848–1918*. New Haven: Yale UP, 2000. A useful guide to intellectual history in the age of Mill.

Capaldi, Nicholas. *John Stuart Mill: A Biography*. Cambridge: Cambridge UP, 2004. The most complete biographical study, arguing that Mill's philosophy attempts to combine the traditions of the Enlightenment and Romanticism.

Carlisle, Janice. *John Stuart Mill and the Writings on Character*. Athens: U of Georgia P, 1991. Nicely reconstructs Mill's education, sources and works, and personal life as a literary text of his philosophy.

Collini, Stefan. *Public Moralists: Political Thought and Intellectual Life in Britain, 1850–1930*. Oxford: Oxford UP, 1991. A brilliant reconstruction of the ideas and main protagonists of the Victorian age, with chapters on Mill as "public moralist" and the reception of his political ideas until the 1930s.

Compton, John W. "The Emancipation of the American Mind: J. S. Mill on the Civil War." *Review of Politics* 70.2 (2008): 221–44. Argues that Mill thought that the struggle against slavery would restore the meaning or vitality of the founding principles of liberty and equality in the United States.

Devigne, Robert. *Reforming Liberalism: J. S. Mill's Use of Ancient, Religious, Liberal, and Romantic Moralities*. New Haven: Yale UP, 2006. Challenges prevailing interpretations of Mill as an icon of liberalism through a comprehensive reconstruction of his rich background, ancient and Romantic philosophy, and secular and religious sources.

Eggletston, Ben, Dale E. Miller, and David Weinstein, eds. *John Stuart Mill and the Art of Life*. Oxford: Oxford UP, 2011. Commentaries on central themes in Mill's life and philosophy: "rule"/"act" utilitarianism, qualitative and quantitative pleasures, and conception of happiness (Jonathan Riley, Wendy Donner); education and moral character starting from his "mental crisis" (Elijah Millgram, Philip Kitcher); his alternative conception of modernity and the role of art and virtue in the industrial age (Robert H. Haraldsson, Nadia Urbinati, Colin Heydt).

Eisenberg, Jay M. *John Stuart Mill on History: Human Nature, Progress, and the Stationary State*. Lanham, MD: Lexington Books, 2018. Interprets Mill's theory of society and progress in the light of his emendation of abstract rationalism and the recovery of history.

Halévy, Elie. *The Growth of Philosophical Radicalism*. Trans. Mary Morris, with a preface by John Plamenatz. London: Faber and Faber, 1972. An old and still unsurpassed reconstruction of the philosophical and intellectual ideas associated with Bentham's circle.

Hamburger, Joseph. *Intellectuals in Politics: John Stuart Mill and the Philosophical Radicals*. New Haven: Yale UP, 1965. Proposes a rich historical account of the years 1830–1840, in which Mill broke with the Benthamites.

———. Review of *James and John Stuart Mill: Father and Son in the Nineteenth Century* by Bruce Mazlish. *History and Theory* 15 (1976): 328–41. An overview of the genre of psychohistory applied to Mill's mental crisis and his relationships with his father and his wife.

Hayek, Friedrich August von. *John Stuart Mill and Harriet Taylor*. London: Routledge and Kegan Paul, 1951. A fundamental document concerning the influence of Taylor on Mill's ideas and work.

Heydt, Colin. *Rethinking Mill's Ethics: Character and Aesthetic Education*. London and New York: Continuum, 2006. A stimulating study of the social and political role of education, starting with Mill's idea of an "inner culture."

Kahan, Alan S. *Aristocratic Liberalism: The Social and Political Thought of Jacob Burckhardt, John Stuart Mill, and Alexis de Tocqueville*. New York: Oxford UP, 1992. An attempt to make sense of the complexity of historical liberalism through an analysis of the similarities among these three nineteenth-century authors around the idea of "aristocratic liberalism."

Kinzer, Bruce. *J. S. Mill Revisited*. New York: Palgrave Macmillan, 2007. Explores the intertwining vicissitudes of Mill's later political philosophy and activism with Victorian politics, resisting the temptation of playing the young against the mature Mill.

Larsen, Timothy. *John Stuart Mill: A Secular Life*. Oxford: Oxford UP, 2018. A compelling short book on Mill's relation to religion in an age in which self-defined secularists were fervent believers in secularism and the search for spirituality.

Loizides, Antis. *John Stuart Mill's Platonic Heritage: Happiness through Character*. Lanham, MD: Lexington Books, 2013. Situates Mill's theory of individuality and character formation in his appreciation of ancient culture, particularly Greek.

López, Rosario. *Contexts of John Stuart Mill's Liberalism*. Baden-Baden: Nomos, 2016. Relates Mill's advanced liberal views to his philosophy and methodology of knowledge.

Mazlish, Bruce. *James and John Stuart Mill: Father and Son in the Nineteenth Century*. London: Hutchinson, 1975. Dramatizes the story of James and John Stuart Mill as protagonists of an intense yet loving struggle at the source of the evolution of liberal ideas—about love, sex, and women, wealth and work, authority and rebellion—which ushered in the modern age.

Mill, James. *Political Writings*. Ed. Terence Ball. Cambridge: Cambridge UP, 1992. Contains two essays relevant to J. S. Mill, "Education" and "Government." Also includes Thomas Babington Macaulay's "Mill on Government," published in the *Edinburgh Review* in 1829, which was a strong criticism of Mill's father's dogmatism and had an impact on J. S. Mill's criticism of the eighteenth-century model of "dogmatic rationalism."

Packe, Michael St. John. *The Life of John Stuart Mill*. London: Secker & Warburg, 1954. A classical biographical text that reconstructs Mill's life and works from a precocious childhood through a legendary career.

Philips, Menaka. "The 'Beloved and Deplored' Memory of Harriet Taylor Mill: Rethinking Gender and Intellectual Labor in the Canon." *Hypatia* 33.4 (2018): 626–42. Examines Taylor's writings to illuminate and challenge interpretations of her relationship to Mill.

Reeve, Richard V. *John Stuart Mill: Victorian Firebrand*. London: Atlantic Books, 2007. An account of Mill's extraordinary and unique education in the making of the most significant English thinker of the nineteenth century, an advocate of the most advanced reforms of his age, excellent theorist and also journalist.

Robson, John A. *The Improvement of Mankind: The Social and Political Thought of John Stuart Mill.* London: Routledge & Kegan Paul, 1968. A comprehensive reconstruction of his life, political engagement, and philosophical thought.

Rosen, Frederick. *Mill.* Oxford: Oxford UP, 2013. An original study of Mill's moral and political philosophy; explores the main themes of his writings and illustrates his influence on subsequent philosophers, logicians, and economists.

Ruggiero, Guido de. *The History of European Liberalism.* New York: Oxford UP, 1927. An old yet useful reconstruction of the main political ideas concerning liberty, justice, and society in Mill's times.

Ryan, Alan. *The Philosophy of John Stuart Mill.* Atlantic Highlands, NJ: Humanities Press International, 1990. A clear and sympathetic analysis of Mill's theory of liberty and its coherence with utilitarianism.

Skorupski, John. *John Stuart Mill.* New York: Routledge, 1989. An intellectual biography with an excellent account of Mill's logic of social sciences, utilitarianism, and liberalism.

———. *Why Read Mill Today?* London and New York: Routledge, 2006. A small and compelling book on good reasons to read Mill.

• Skorupski, John, ed. *The Cambridge Companion to Mill.* (Cambridge: Cambridge UP, 1998). An essential collection of commentaries on the entire spectrum of Mill's thought (essays by Alan Ryan and Wendy Donner are included in this Norton Critical Edition).

Urbinati, Nadia. *Mill on Democracy: From the Athenian Politics to Representative Government.* Chicago and London: U of Chicago P, 2002. Studies the classical sources for Mill's theory of government and political liberty.

Urbinati, Nadia, and Alex Zakaras, eds. *J. S. Mill's Political Thought: A Bicentennial Reassessment.* Cambridge: Cambridge UP, 2007. Collects commentaries exploring key elements of his political philosophy in various domains: liberty, equality, and despotism (Jeremy Waldron, Mario Morales, Nadia Urbinati); socialism and the theory of utility (Baum Bruce, Fredrick Rosen); democracy, representation, and individuality (Alan Ryan, Dennis F. Thompson, Alex Zakaras); the inspiration of the ancients and education (Jonathan Riley, Wendy Donner); nationalism, the government of "backward" peoples, theories of intervention and the problem of colonization (Georgios Varouxakis, Karuna Mantena, Stephen Holmes, Michael Walzer).

Varouxakis, Georgios. *Mill on Nationality.* London: Routledge, 2002. A fine study of Mill's ideas on national self-determination, which marked state building in his time.

• Varouxakis, Georgios, and Paul Kelly, eds. *John Stuart Mill—Thought and Influence: The Saint of Rationalism.* London and New York: Routledge, 2010. A collection of essays in which autobiographical and theoretical elements combine in an attempt to show the legacy of Mill's moral and political thought in several domains: the formation of human character and his own program of inner culture (Bruce Kinser, Terence Ball, Donald Winch); his contribution to the development of logic (Frederick Rosen); his theory of duty and virtue and the hierarchy of different kinds of pleasures (Wendy Donner, Jonathan Riley); and his conception of liberty in relation to both German idealism and his revised theory of utility (John Skorupski, Peter Singer). The essay by Martha Nussbaum on Mill's feminism is included in this Norton Critical Edition.

Wright, T. R. *The Religion of Humanity: The Impact of Comtean Positivism in Victorian Britain*. Cambridge: Cambridge UP, 1986. A useful reconstruction of the impact of the religion of humanity (first expounded by Comte) on a wide range of prominent Victorians, among them Mill, who cultivated the ambition of replacing Christianity with an alternative religion based on scientific principles and humanist values.

Yuichiro, Kawana. *Logic and Society: The Political Thought of John Stuart Mill, 1827–1848*. New York: Palgrave, 2018. Reconstructs his intellectual production from the recovery of his "mental crisis" to the publication of his *System of Logic* and *Principles of Political Economy*, the building blocks of Mill's three essays published in this Norton Critical Edition.

Zakaras, Alex. *Individuality and Mass Democracy: Mill, Emerson, and the Burdens of Citizenship*. Oxford and New York: Oxford UP, 2009. A study of the role of individuality and human excellence as central to democratic politics.

On Liberty

• Anderson, Elizabeth. "John Stuart Mill and Experiments in Living." *Ethics* 102 (October 1991): 4–26.

Arneson, Richard. "Mill versus Paternalism." *Ethics* 90 (January 1981): 470–89. A very compelling argument in defense of his theory of liberty.

Berlin, Isaiah. *Four Essays on Liberty*. Oxford: Oxford UP, 1969. A pillar of post–World War II liberalism and conception of liberty. Berlin's essay "John Stuart Mill and the Ends of Life" complements his classic "Two Concepts of Liberty."

Boire, Richard Glen. "John Stuart Mill and the Liberty of Inebriation." *Independent Review* 7.2 (2002): 253–58. A short and polemical piece with references to several passages from *On Liberty* concerning Mill's engagement in debates about alcohol prohibition, relevant to the modern-day regulation of drugs.

Bromwich, David, and George Kateb, eds. John Stuart Mill, *On Liberty*. New Haven and London: Yale UP, 2003. With influential essays by George Kateb (on the uniqueness of this text), Jean Bethise Elshtain (on the issue of authority), Owen Fiss (on personal and political freedom), Richard A. Posner (on liberty of thought and conduct), and Jeremy Waldron (on the vulnerability of individual freedom of choice in relation to opinion).

Bruce, Baum. *Reading Power and Freedom in J. S. Mill* (Toronto: U of Toronto P, 2000). A comprehensive study of Mill's social and political thought that engages his theory of liberty with feminism, utilitarianism, and conditions of workers.

———. "J. S. Mill and Liberal Socialism." In Urbinati and Zakaras, eds., *J. S. Mill's Political Thought* (see above). An interesting interpretation of the legacy of Mill's social thought in the non-Marxist socialist tradition.

Cowen, Nick. "Millian Liberalism and Extreme Pornography." *American Journal of Political Science* 60.2 (2016): 509–20. An application of Mill's theory of liberty to internet-driven phenomena; argues against considering Mill as justifying restrictions on the viewing of some pornographic material, with reference to the harm principle and his feminist commitments.

• Dworkin, Gerald, ed. *Mill's "On Liberty": Critical Essays*. Lanham, MD, and New York: Rowman & Littlefield, 1997. Reprint of some classical commentaries on his theory of liberty in relation to toleration (Lewis), paternalism (G. Dworkin, Arneson), harm to others (Skipper; Lyons), the principle of offense vs. the harm principle (Feinberg), and the issue of pornography (David Dyzenhaus, included in this Norton Critical Edition).

Dworkin, Ronald. *Taking Rights Seriously*. Cambridge, MA.: Harvard UP, 1977. Chap. 11, "Liberty and Liberalism," is a defense of Mill's liberty against conservative interpretations (see Himmelfarb below).

Feinberg, Joel. "The Child's Right to an Open Future." In *Ethical Principles for Social Policy*, ed. John Howie. Carbondale: Southern Illinois UP, 1983. Argues that autonomy rightly held by autonomous adults exists as a right-in-trust held by children, who are not yet autonomous but are expected to become so; interesting in relation to Mill's distinction between liberty as "security" and as "autonomy."

Gordon, Jill. "John Stuart Mill and the 'Marketplace of Ideas.'" *Social Theory and Practice* 23.2 (1997): 235–49. Examines the metaphor of the "marketplace of ideas" commonly associated with Mill (though he never used this term).

Gray, John. *Mill on Liberty: A Defense*. London: Routledge, 1983. A compelling analysis of Mill's conception, arguing that a dualism exists in it between liberty as "security" and as "autonomy."

Habibi, Don A. *John Stuart Mill and the Ethics of Human Growth*. Dordrecht, Boston, and London: Kluwer Academic Publishers, 2001. Proposes a useful reconstruction of the place of Mill's political and moral philosophy in the context of the debates on freedom in the post–World War II era.

Hansson, Sven Ove. "Mill's Circle(s) of Liberty." *Social Theory and Practice* 41.4 (2015): 734–49. A short account of Mill's *On Liberty*, with arguments about the harm principle as a doctrine of antipaternalism.

Himmelfarb, Gertrude. *On Liberty and Liberalism: The Case of John Stuart Mill*. New York: Alfred A. Knopf, 1974. Critically discusses Mill's theory of liberty from a conservative perspective (see Ronald Dworkin's response above).

Jacobson, Daniel. "Mill on Liberty, Speech, and the Free Society." *Philosophy & Public Affairs* 29.3 (2000): 276–309. Proposes a clear analysis of the harm principle and the tensions it produces in *On Liberty*.

Marwah, Inder S. *Liberalism, Diversity and Domination: Kant, Mill and the Government of Difference*. Cambridge: Cambridge UP, 2019. A challenging parallel analysis of Kant's and Mill's treatments of racial, cultural, gender-based, and class-based difference and how they reacted to pluralism.

Morgan, Glyn. "The Mode and Limits of John Stuart Mill's Toleration." *Nomos* 48 (2008): 139–67. A thorough account of Mill's views of toleration and liberty more broadly; argues against Berlin's critique of Mill's liberty principle and explores many important strands of Mill scholarship, in addition to closely considering both *On Liberty* and *Utilitarianism*.

Turner, Piers Norris. "The Absolutism Problem in 'On Liberty'." *Canadian Journal of Philosophy* 43.3 (2013): 322–40. Discusses the specific question of how Mill's absolute formulation of the liberty principle can be reconciled with his utilitarian commitment.

Tunick, Mark. "Tolerant Imperialism: John Stuart Mill's Defense of British Rule in India." *Review of Politics* 68.4 (2006): 586–611. Argues that Mill's

justification of British imperialism is not the result of racism, but the outcome of a historical view he shared with eighteenth-century scholars that a
certain type of despotism is necessary to make a people ready for self-rule (as
had already occurred in Europe).

Riley, Jonathan. "Is Mill an Illiberal Utilitarian?" *Ethics* 125 (2015): 781–96.
Disagrees with Turner's interpretation of Mill's liberty principle (see above),
as it makes Mill into an illiberal, standard utilitarian.

Semmel, Bernard. "John Stuart Mill's Coleridgian Neoradicalism." In *Mill and
the Moral Character of Liberals*, ed. Eldon J. Eisenach. University Park: Pennsylvania State UP, 1998. Proposes a reading of Mill's philosophy sympathetic
to social obligation and spiritual perfection, somehow closer to conservatives
than radicals.

Stephen, James Fitzjames. *Liberty, Equality, Fraternity*. Dublin: Liberty Press,
1993. Originally published in 1873 and still the sharpest criticism of the Mill
essays included in this Norton Critical Edition.

Ten, C. L., ed. *Mill's "On Liberty": A Critical Guide*. Cambridge: Cambridge UP,
2009. A set of excellent commentaries on seminal Millian themes by C. L. Ten
(a reconstruction of Mill's theory of liberty against liberticide positivism),
Henry R. West (a case for *On Liberty*), David O. Brink (on the principle of freedom of expression), Jonathan Riley (on racism, blasphemy, and free speech),
Gerald F. Gaus (on the controversial principle of neutrality), Robert Amdur
(on Rawls's critique of *On Liberty*), Frank Lovett (on the possibility of consensual domination), Wendy Donner (on moral autonomy), Jeremy Waldron
(on Mill and multiculturalism), Justine Burley (on liberty as an experiment of
living), and Robert Young (Mill and Dworkin on paternalism).

Utilitarianism

Clayes, Gregory. *Mill and Paternalism*. Cambridge: Cambridge UP, 2013. Rein-
terprets Mill's theory of justice and liberty as aspiring to a "utilitarian republican" philosophy that enhances equality through democratic paternalism.

Donner, Wendy. *The Liberal Self: John Stuart Mill's Moral and Political Philosophy*. Ithaca and London: Cornell UP, 1991. Compares Bentham and Mill on
their conception of hedonism and concludes with the consistency of Mill's
On Liberty and *Utilitarianism*.

Fuchs, Alan E. "Mill's Theory of Morally Correct Action." In *The Blackwell
Guide to Mill's Utilitarianism*, ed. Henry R. West. Oxford: Blackwell, 2006.
Argues that Mill holds some moral and legal rules as indefensible, regardless
of the circumstances.

Jacobson, Daniel. "Utilitarianism without Consequentialism: The Case of John
Stuart Mill." *Philosophical Review* 117.2 (2008): 159–91. Proposes a challenging
interpretation of Mill's faithfulness to utilitarianism but not consequentialism.

Lyon, David. *Rights, Welfare, and Mill's Moral Theory*. Oxford: Oxford UP,
1994. A compelling analysis of challenging themes in Mill's theory concerning the limits of rights and liberty in relation to the general welfare.

Lyons, David, ed. *Mill's Utilitarianism: Critical Essays*. Lanham, MD, and Boulder,
CO: Rowman & Littlefield, 1997. A reappraisal of Mill's utilitarianism in the light
of his political and moral philosophy through a collection of reprinted essays by

J. O. Urmson, D. G. Brown, D. Lyons, F. R. Berger, A. Gutmann, H. R. West, P. Railton, E. Anderson, and D. Brink.

Medearis, John. "Labor, Democracy, Utility, and Mill's Critique of Private Property." *American Journal of Political Science* 49.1 (2005): 135–49. Examines the development of Mill's views on socialism, with particular attention to his changing mind on the "labor justification" of private property and the recognition of the antidemocratic and unfair consequences of the capitalist economic system.

Miller, Dale E. *J. S. Mill: Moral, Social and Political Thought.* Cambridge: Polity P, 2010. A basic reconstruction of Mill's moral philosophy.

Nussbaum, Martha. "Mill between Aristotle & Bentham." *Daedalus* 133.2 (2004): 60–68. Argues that the main value of Mill's *Utilitarianism* lies not so much in his theory of utility but in the "subtle awareness of human complexity" that put Mill closer to Aristotle than Bentham, although his notion of happiness gives central place, unlike in Aristotle, to the "emotional elements of the personality," as Nussbaum's reading of the "Marmontel passage" in Mill's *Autobiography* shows.

Riley, Jonathan. *Liberal Utilitarianism: Second Choice Theory and J. S. Mill's Philosophy.* Cambridge: Cambridge UP, 1988. Proposes a defense of utilitarianism as social and political philosophy.

Ryan, Alan. Introduction to John Stuart Mill and Jeremy Bentham, *Utilitarianism and Other Essays.* London: Penguin, 1987. Very informative and incisive, rendering complex moral arguments in plain and clear language; the collection includes excerpts from Bentham's *An Introduction to the Principles of Morals and Legislations* and from Mill's *System of Logic*, along with Mill's "Bentham," "Coleridge," and "Whewell on Moral Philosophy."

Sen, Amartya, and Bernard Williams, eds. *Utilitarianism and Beyond.* Cambridge: Cambridge UP, 1982. A quasi-dialogue between Mill and an anti-utilitarian critic.

Stephen, Leslie. *The English Utilitarians.* New York: Putnam's Sons; London, Duckworth & Co, 1900. A classic reconstruction of the moral philosophy of Bentham and the two Mills.

Sumner, L. Wayne. *Welfare, Happiness, and Ethics.* New York: Oxford UP, 1996. Helps situate Mill's conception of general utility and liberty, and proposes a theory of welfare in relation to his theories of liberty, happiness, and satisfaction.

West, Henry R. *An Introduction to Mill's Utilitarian Ethics.* Cambridge: Cambridge UP, 2004. A useful guide to Mill's moral and social philosophy.

Williams, Bernard. *Ethics and the Limits of Philosophy.* London: Routledge, 1985. Although not directly devoted to Mill, develops an important criticism of utilitarianism's ethical rationalism that challenges Mill's moral philosophy.

The Subjection of Women

Adams, Jad. *Women and the Vote: A World History.* Oxford: Oxford UP, 2016. A global history of women's right to vote from earliest times to the present day.

Aiken, Susan Hardy. "Scripture and Poetic Discourse in *The Subjection of Women*." *Publications of the Modern Language Association* 98.3 (1983):

353–73. An interesting analysis of the poetic and mythos as subtext models Mill used to persuade an unsympathetic audience of a radically subversive thesis.

Annas, Julia. "Mill and *The Subjection of Women*." *Philosophy* 52 (1977): 179–94. Invites us to pay more attention to Mill's essay, but criticizes his traditional portrait of women.

Ball, Jennifer. "J. S. Mill on Wages and Women: A Feminist Critique." *Review of Social Economy* 59 (2001): 509–27. Argues that his defense of the sexual division of labor was primarily a result of his attachment to the "sentimental family," not his political economic concern with efficiency; his conception of care made him privilege women's traditional role.

Bhandary, Asha. "A Millian Concept of Care: What Mill's Defense of the Common Arrangement Can Teach Us About Care." *Social Theory and Practice* 42.1 (2016): 155–82. Defends Mill's attention to care and ties it to contemporary feminist care ethics and the critique of liberal feminism.

Boralevi, Lea Campos. "Utilitarianism and Feminism." In *Jeremy Bentham*, ed. Tom Campbell, and Frederick Rosen. London: Routledge, 2017. Argues that utilitarianism is not compatible with feminism, and that historical feminism was produced by classical utilitarianism.

Botting, Eileen Hunt. *Wollstonecraft, Mill, and Women's Human Rights*. New Haven: Yale UP, 2016. Proposes a comparison between these two authors and argues that their ideas, "stripped of their Eurocentric biases," are an important contribution to thinking about human rights in universal terms.

Burgess-Jackson, Keith. "John Stuart Mill, Radical Feminism." *Social Theory and Practice* 21.3 (1995): 369–96. Confutes the liberal reading of Mill's feminism.

Caine, Barbara. "Elizabeth Cady Stanton, John Stuart Mill, and the Nature of Feminist Thought." In *Elizabeth Cady Stanton, Feminist as Thinker: A Reader in Documents and Essays*, ed. Ellen Carol DuBois and Richard Candida Smith. New York and London: NYU P, 2007. Examines Stanton's engagement with Mill's work and her agreement with his view of ideal marriage, although she had more affinity with Wollstonecraft's radicalism.

Guillin, Vincent. *Auguste Comte and John Stuart Mill on Sexual Equality: Historical, Methodological and Philosophical Issues*. Leiden and Boston: Brill, 2009. A reconstruction of the philosophical differences between Mill and Comte through the issue of women's equality.

Hirschmann, Nancy J. "Mill, Political Economy, and Women's Work." *American Political Science Review* 102.2 (2008): 199–213. Discusses the fact that he did not extend his notion of productive labor to include household as "reproductive" labor, yet this conclusion would be consistent with his theoretical commitments; a "blind-spot" in political economy, which has persisted to our times.

Jacobs, Jo Ellen. *The Voice of Harriet Taylor Mill*. Bloomington: Indiana UP, 2002. Counters a role given to Taylor by her critics, beginning with Bain (see above).

Jacobs, Jo Ellen, ed. *The Complete Works of Harriet Taylor Mill*. Bloomington: Indiana UP, 1998. This useful collection shows that Taylor was not simply Mill's wife.

Jacobs, Lesley A., and Richard Vandewetering, eds. *John Stuart Mill's "The Subjection of Women": His Contemporary and Modern Critics*. Delmar, NY: Caravan Books, 1999). A useful collection of the main essays on Mill's book from his time to ours.

Mann, Hollie, and Jeff Spinner-Halev. "John Stuart Mill's Feminism: On Progress, the State, and the Path to Justice." *Polity* 42 (2010): 244–70. Argues that feminism marked his political conception entirely, demanding a radical transformation of power relations in the social and political domains.

Mendus, Susan. "John Stuart Mill and Harriet Taylor on Women and Marriage." *Utilitas* 6 (1994): 287–89. Argues that their texts on women are more radical than usually thought as they anticipated central themes within twentieth-century radical feminism.

Okin, Susan Moller. *Women in Western Political Thought*. Princeton, NJ: Princeton UP, 1979. A historical overview from the ancients to the moderns, depicting Mill as a theorist who defended political equality but not an egalitarian conception of the family.

Qizilbash, Mozaffar. "Capabilities, Happiness and Adaptation in Sen and J. S. Mill." *Utilitas* 18 (2006): 20–32. On the similarities between the two philosophers whose feminist ideas influenced their views on liberty, social justice, and happiness.

Rossi, Alice S., ed. *The Feminist Papers: From Adams to de Beauvoir.* 2nd ed. Boston: Northeastern UP, 1988. A basic anthology with documents on the historical context, biographies, and bibliographies of the most important feminist authors, among them Mill and Harriet Taylor.

Saunders-Hastings, Emma. "No Better to Give than to Receive: Charity and Women's Subjection in J. S. Mill." *Polity* 46 (2014): 233–54. Analyzes Mill's views on private charity and their relation to his feminism and argues that he viewed the practice of private charity as symptomatic of an ethos of dependence on private benevolence, emblematic of an imbalance in the social structure of power that reinforces women's subjection.

Smith, Elizabeth S. "John Stuart Mill's 'The Subjection of Women': A Re-Examination." *Polity* 34.2 (2001): 181–203. Relies on his letters and political activities to show that he was willing to temper his public statements in order to win support for what he thought to be the most pressing women's issue: suffrage. This explains his avoidance of "hot-button" issues like divorce and the extrafamilial role of women.

Smith, G. W. "J. S. Mill on What We Don't Know About Women." *Utilitas* 12 (2000): 41–61. Places his feminism in the context of his broader theory of liberal empiricism.

Urbinati, Nadia. "J. S. Mill on Androgyny and Ideal Marriage." *Political Theory* 19 (1991): 627–49. Argues that, influenced by the Saint-Simonians, Mill tried to go beyond "masculine" and "feminine" conceptions of character to delineate the autonomous individual as comprehending traits of both.

Waldron, Jeremy. "Mill on Liberty and on the Contagious Diseases Acts." In *John Stuart Mill's Political Thought: A Bicentennial Reassessment*, ed. Nadia Urbinati and Alex Zakaras. Cambridge: Cambridge UP. 2007. A thorough examination of Mill's position in the Royal Commission on the Contagious Diseases Acts in relation to his conception of the harm principle and equality.

Index